HERESY IN THE
LATER MIDDLE AGES

TO

A. S. NEILL

Heresy in the Later Middle Ages

THE RELATION OF HETERODOXY
TO DISSENT c. 1250–c. 1450

by

GORDON LEFF

VOL. I

'Di oggimai che la chiesa di Roma,
per confondere in sé due reggimenti,
cade nel fango e sé brutta e la soma'

Dante, *Purgatorio*, XVI, 127–9

MANCHESTER UNIVERSITY PRESS
BARNES & NOBLE, INC., NEW YORK

Printed in Great Britain by Butler & Tanner Ltd, Frome and London

Contents

Preface

This book is an attempt at synthesis. It is not, however, a comprehensive study of all later medieval heresy in the manner of Lea's *History of the Inquisition*. I have included as much about Joachim of Fiore, St Francis, and Eckhart as the inquisition, and many of the central figures were not heretics at all. The reason is that my concern has been with the place of heresy in the outlook of the later middle ages. I have sought to treat the main heretical beliefs of the epoch in the context of its intellectual and spiritual climate. The convergence between the heretical and non-heretical is the theme of this book. It is pre-eminently a study of heterodoxy passing into dissent and ultimately heresy. Its major premise is that heresy, far from being alien to Christian society, had its source in the tensions between Christian precept and religious practice; it differed from orthodoxy in the means which it sought to overcome them. Accordingly attention has been directed principally to the making of heresy. This has entailed giving prominence to many seemingly abstract notions; for this I can only ask the indulgence of those whose interest lies in action, and suggest that they turn to those sections which contain it.

The dates within which this study falls are not rigid. While it rarely goes beyond 1450 it includes much that happened before 1250. That it does not extend to the Albigensians, beyond the summary in the Prologue, is intentional. The Cathar heresy played only a subsidiary role in the later middle ages; it differs from the other heresies treated here in not only containing important non-Christian elements but in being in decline by 1300. I have omitted all references to sorcery and to what appear to me to have been only transient groups or individuals such as the Gugliemites. The bibliography does not include works for those aspects not considered in the text.

I have made no attempt to achieve consistency over the spelling or usage of names. The temptation was to render all names in their native form; but it has seemed to me better to appear arbitrary in writing Basel but Constance, John Gerson but Pierre d'Ailly, rather than reduce them to a somewhat unnatural conformity. Again, the degree of quotation, as well as Latin spelling, varies. Sources which are accessible or well-known, such as the political writings of the thinkers discussed in chapter five, have been only occasionally cited *in extenso*. Where this is not the case, or, as with Eckhart, the argument demands close textual support, quotations are fuller.

My obligation to others appears at every stage. The first and most universal is to all those pioneers, Denifle, Ehrle, Haupt, Lea, Oliger and others, whose work forms the basis of so much of our knowledge in this and allied fields. We who utilize it are indeed ants sitting on the shoulders of giants, although we do not always see farther. More personally, I must thank Mrs. Margaret Aston, Miss Marjorie Reeves, Miss Beryl Smalley and Dom David Knowles for reading the text and for advice and criticism. Without the help of Miss Reeves the sections on Joachim of Fiore would have been more inadequate. To the Colloquium on heresy, held by the 6th section of the École Pratique des Hautes Études, at Royaumont in 1962, and particularly its secretary, M. Jacques Le Goff, I owe invaluable stimulus as well as knowledge. I have been helped by many libraries including the Vatican and Angelica, Rome, the Bodleian, British Museum, Bibliothèque Nationale, Paris, Staatsbibliothek, Munich, School of Slavonic Studies, British School at Rome, Pierpont Morgan, New York, and of course Manchester University. The John Rylands Library made the writing of this book possible. No-one who has experienced its hospitality is likely to forget it. For me it went far beyond what any reader has the right to expect. The greater part of my work was done there from books which were ever gladly put at my disposal. I wish to express my deepest gratitude to the librarian and staff. I do so also to Manchester University for unfailing financial help which enabled me to work for periods abroad. The Secretary and members of the Manchester University Press have once again made the routine of publication an enjoyable partnership. The typing has been done by many hands, and to all those concerned I offer my appreciation. Finally I must acknowledge Norman Cohn's *The Pursuit of the Millennium* for bringing me to the study of heresy. Profoundly though I disagree with his interpretation it was through reading his book and following his bibliographical trail that I came upon much that has gone into this book. I dedicate it to a man, my headmaster for nine years, who has shown the perennial need for dissent even when we no longer punish heresy.

York.   G. L.
1 July 1966

Abbreviations

ABAW
Abhandlungen der königlichen bayerischen Akademie der Wissenschaften (Historische Klasse) Munich.

AFH
Archivum Franciscanum Historicum (Quaracchi).

AFP
Archivum Fratrum Praedicatorum (Rome).

AKG
Archiv für Kulturgeschichte.

ALKG
Archiv für Literatur und Kirchengeschichte des Mittelalters vols. I–VII (Berlin 1885–92) ed. H. Denifle and F. Ehrle.

Angelo of Clareno, *Historia*
Angelo of Clareno, 'Historia septem tribulationum' in ALKG II (1886) 106–55, 249–327.

Archives
Archives d'Histoire doctrinale et littéraire (Paris).

BF
Bullarium Franciscanum (ed. J. H. Sbaralea and F. Eubel). 5 vols.

Bib. Max. Pat. Vet.
Biblioteca Maxima Patrum Veterum (Lyon 1677).

BSFS
British Society for Franciscan Studies.

BSSV
Bolletino di società di studi Valdesi (Torre Pellice).

CMH
Cambridge Medieval History.

Collecta
Magistri Johannes Hus, *Sermones de tempore qui collecta dicuntur* (ed. A. Schmidtová, Prague 1959).

Corpus
P. Fredericq, *Corpus documentorum Inquisitionis haereticae pravitatis Neerlandicae*, 4 vols. (Ghent 1889–1900).

Denifle and Chatelain
H. Denifle and E. Chatelain, *Chartularium Universitatis Parisiensis*, 4 vols. (Paris 1889–96).

De Vooght, *L'Hérésie*
Paul de Vooght, *L'Hérésie de Jean Huss* (Louvain 1960).

Döllinger, *Beiträge*
I. I. von Döllinger, *Beiträge zur Sektengeschichte* vol. II (Munich 1890).

Douie, *Fraticelli*
D. L. Douie *The Nature and the Effect of the Heresy of the Fraticelli* (Manchester 1932).

DTC
Dictionnaire de Théologie Catholique (Paris).

Duplessis d'Argentré, *Collectio*
C. Duplessis d'Argentré, *Collectio judiciorum de novis erroribus* 3 vols. (Paris 1775).

D.W.
Meister Eckhart, *Die Deutschen Werke* (Stuttgart).

EHR
English Historical Review (London).

Fasciculus
Fasciculus Rerum Expetendarum et Fugiendarum 2 vols. (ed. E. Browne, London 1690).

Friedberg
E. Friedberg, *Corpus iuris canonici* 2 vols. (Leipzig 1879–81).

FZ
Fasciculi Zizaniorum, ed. W. W. Shirley (Rolls Series 1858).

Gonnet, *Enchiridion*
Enchiridion Fontium Valdensium (Torre Pellice 1958).

Gratien, *Frères Mineurs*
P. Gratien, *L'histoire de la fondation et de l'évolution de l'ordre des Frères Mineurs au 13e siècle* (Paris and Gembloux 1928).

Lea, *Inquisition*
H. C. Lea, *A History of the Inquisition in the Middle Ages*, 3 vols. (London and New York 1888).

L.W.
Meister Eckhart, *Die Lateinischen Werke* (Stuttgart).

McDonnell, *Beguines*	E. W. McDonnell, *The Beguines and Beghards in medieval culture* (New Jersey 1954).
McFarlane	K. B. McFarlane, *John Wycliffe and the Beginnings of English Nonconformity* (London 1952).
Mansi	J. D. Mansi, *Sacra conciliorum collectio* (Venice 1779–82).
Manuel	B. Gui, *Manuel de l'Inquisiteur* (éd. et traduit par G. Mollat) 2 vols. (Paris 1926–7).
Martène and Durand	E. Martène and V. Durand, *Thesaurus novus anecdotorum* 5 vols. (Paris 1717).
MGH	*Monumenta Germaniae Historica* (Hanover).
Misc	S. Baluze and J. D. Mansi, *Miscellanea* 4 vols. (Lucca 1761–4).
Mon	*Historia et Monumenta Johannis Hus et Hieronymi Pragensis* 2 vols. (Nuremberg 1558).
Mosheim	J. L. Mosheim, *De Beghardis et de Beguinabus* (Leipzig 1790).
Muratori	L. A. Muratori, *Rerum Italicarum Scriptores.*
Neues Archiv	*Neues Archiv der Gesellschaft für ältere deutsche Geschichtskunde.*
Palacký, *Documenta*	F. Palacký, *Documenta Mag. Joannis Hus* (Prague 1869).
P.L.	J. P. Migne, *Patrologia Latina.*
PRS	*Johannes Hus, Magister Universitatis Carolinea Universitatis Posiciones, recommendationes sermones* ed. A. Schmidtová (Prague 1958).
Quint	J. Quint, *Meister Eckehart: Deutsche Predigten und Traktate* (Munich 1955).
Raynaldus	O. Raynaldus *Annales Ecclesiastici* (Lucca 1738–59).
RHE	*Revue d'histoire ecclésiastique* (Louvain).
Rot. Parl.	*Rotuli Parliamentorum* (London 1832).
RPT	*Realencyklopädie für protestantische Theologie und Kirche* (Leipzig).
SPAW	*Sitzungsberichte der Königlichen preussischen Akademie der Wissenschaften* (Berlin).
Théry *Edition Critique*	G. Théry, 'Edition critique des pièces relatives au procès d'Eckhart' *Archives* I (1926) 129–268.
TRHS	*Transactions of the Royal Historical Society.*
Trithemius, *Annales*	Johannes Trithemius, *Annales Hirsaugiensis* 2 vols. (St. Gall 1690).
Wilkins	D. Wilkins, *Concilia Magnae Britanniae et Hiberniae* 4 vols. (London 1737).
Workman	H. B. Workman, *John Wyclif,* 2 vols. (Oxford 1926).
WS	Wyclif Society (London).
ZKG	*Zeitschrift für Kirchengeschichte* (Gotha).

Prologue

The nature of medieval heresy

Heresy is defined by reference to orthodoxy. It does not exist alone. A doctrine or a sect or an individual becomes heretical when condemned as such by the church. For this, there has to be a body of accepted beliefs to violate and a recognized authority to enforce it. In their absence, to profess even the most outrageous opinions is to operate in a doctrinal—as opposed to a moral or a legal—vacuum; the community may be scandalized; the law may be broken; but there will be no officially constituted outlook against which they offend.

Now it was precisely the existence of such a prevailing orthodoxy, defined by the church and jointly enforced with the lay power, that distinguished medieval society. In this sense it was a closed society. Every member belonged to the church, and his or her salvation depended upon living and dying within it. To be outside it, for whatever reason, was to be anathema, whether as an infidel—pagan, Jew, or Moslem—or as a heretic. But whereas the first category was a matter for lamentation, opprobrium or crusade, according to circumstances, a heretic was the church's immediate concern: either to be restored or punished. There could be no intermediate position. The church was God's communion; to reject it, or be rejected by it, was to reject God. It was to be excluded from society, which was by definition Christian, in its civil no less than its spiritual aspect.

In these conditions heresy was endemic, since to step outside the accepted framework was to be opposed to authority. But heresy was far from an automatic process in which error was inseparable from excommunication and burning. In the first place, as we shall have ample occasion to see, error was of various degrees, and far from uniformly heretical. Moreover, it often took generations to define, as in the disputes over the poverty of Christ within the Franciscan order.[1] In the second place, heresy was not just a matter of doctrine but also one of discipline—pertinacious error. The heretic was one who persisted in his mistake, refusing correction after his fault had been shown to him. It was for obduracy that he was finally punished after all efforts to make him abjure had failed. Consequently the test of heresy was a

[1] See ch. I and II below.

I

moral and practical one—willingness to submit; and conviction for it was an admission of defeat. It meant failure to save a soul from certain damnation: in consigning a man to the flames he was being consigned to the devil. Hence the great—often tireless—efforts to gain a recantation; what was at stake was a man's eternal life and obedience to God's saving will on earth. The church, as the medium for both, was, in asserting its authority, affirming God's law. Only if this is grasped can the zeal with which heresy was combated be understood: the misconception that belief can be enforced, and the undoubted injustices and cruelties which accompanied efforts to do so, must not blind us to the very genuine concern to save souls and the conviction that it was done in the service of God. Even Hus's judges, certain though they were of his guilt, tried to the end to persuade him to abjure.[1]

From this it follows that, initially at least, heresy was a deviation from accepted beliefs rather than something alien to them: it sprang from believing differently about the same things as opposed to holding a different belief. With the egregious exception of the Cathars —whose non-Christian origins exclude them from this discussion, even though their evolution followed parallel lines—heresy during the middle ages was an indigenous growth; its impulse was invariably the search for a fuller spiritual life, and it drew upon the common stock of religious concepts to implement it. Whatever its forms, medieval heresy differed from orthodoxy and mere heterodoxy less in assumptions than emphasis and conclusions. It became heresy from pressing these too far. From the eleventh to the fifteenth centuries, its aspirations were common to all religious reform: namely, the desire to emulate the life and teachings of Christ and his Apostles; and more particularly to seek a return to the precepts of the gospel through a life of poverty—or one of complete simplicity—and preaching. That it frequently became debased, or a subterfuge, as with the Free Spirit,[2] and was rarely found in its pure form, should not blind us to the power of this desire. What ultimately turned it into heresy was the failure to gain ecclesiastical sanction. It was usually then, in a group's subsequent development as a proscribed sect, that its original impulse took on a directly anti-sacerdotal character. In doing so it inevitably changed. What—except for the heresy of the Free Spirit, which was not a sect but an outlook, the origins of which are not clearly known[3]—began as

[1] See pp. 650 ff. below.　　　　[2] See ch. IV below.
[3] For this reason much that follows hardly applies to the Free Spirit.

an accentuation of a particular aspect of belief, or life, became a rival outlook; its adherents came to regard themselves as Christ's true apostles and their struggle against the church as part of the wider struggle between the forces of Christ and Antichrist. As such, even if it did not lead to the formation of an independent church, it meant the sect's transformation into an autonomous body with its own tenets. These, as we shall mention shortly, despite their diversity, had a number of features in common. Central to them all was the fact that they were under the ban of the church; hence in continuing to practise and propagate their beliefs they were acting in opposition to its authority. Inevitably, therefore, to be heretical was also to be anti-sacerdotal; for ultimately, whatever the circumstances, a heresy received its final stamp, as heresy, from the church. In that sense, heresy was born when heterodoxy became, or was branded, dissent; and more specifically when the appeal—common to the Waldensians, Franciscan sects, English Lollards and the Hussites—to the bible and to the evangelical virtues of poverty and humility, became, or were treated as, a challenge to the church. It was then that protest became uppermost, conceived henceforth in directly anti-sacerdotal terms. This point was the culmination in the conflict between a group and authority. There was, as we shall see, a regular progression from initially non-heretical belief to open heresy; all the main sects began by embracing the commonly accepted tenets; only subsequently, in the course of growing hostility between them and the church, did they take on a more extreme, and often debased, form. Excepting the Free Spirit—and, of course, the Cathars—their sources were the accepted sources, and often objects of universal veneration: the bible, the Apostles' church, St. Francis, and even Joachim of Fiore. Those who sought to follow them, in their own way, believed that they were the true Christians and the hierarchy, which persecuted them, the heretics. Even Wyclif—with Peter Valdes, the one really influential medieval heresiarch in the strict sense—would have rebutted his posthumous condemnation and recoiled from the actual consequences of his teaching.

We must therefore see medieval heresy as internal to medieval society, and seek its evolution within the circumstances and attitudes of the time rather than as something ready-made. Our starting point must be that none of the main sects from the twelfth century onwards (excepting the Cathars and periodic revolts) was initially heretical; nor did they owe their distinctiveness to the imprint of an original heresiarch, with the exception of Wyclif. It was not from the condemned doctrines of Roscelin's tritheism, or the Latin Averroists, or even Joachim of Fiore's teachings on the Trinity, that the important movements sprang; but from St. Francis's image, and Joachim's vision—never itself proscribed—of a new era. Even the claims of the adepts of the Free Spirit had affinities with the more extravagant mystical strivings of the thirteenth and fourteenth centuries. These, together with the great moral questions over simony, worldliness, and wealth in general, belonged to the issues exercising society at large; they arose over the recurrent need to find new modes of living and to remedy existing ones. Hence there was a convergence between heresy and orthodoxy; it it not too much to say that from the later twelfth century onwards all the most prominent heretical movements—centred on poverty, prophecy, the mystical search for God, the nature of the church—bore directly upon the major contemporary intellectual and doctrinal themes; the preoccupations among the learned found a resonance, albeit often distorted, in popular religious life.

In the transition from one to the other the operative term is heterodoxy: either by giving a new, unorthodox, significance to existing concepts, such as in the Franciscan Spirituals' treatment of poverty, or the Ockhamists' use of God's absolute power; or by framing new conceptions, which deviated from the accepted norms, such as Joachim of Fiore's division of the world's history into three ages instead of the existing two,[1] or Eckhart's teaching on the birth of the word in the soul.[2] In every case, these notions were censured without being anathematized, except for the doctrine of the poverty of Christ. But in more extreme, debased versions—such as the various kinds of Franciscan, and other, Joachism of the fourteenth and fifteenth centuries, and the pantheistic mysticism of the Free Spirit—they became open heresy and were condemned as such.

Now to seek for any direct causal relation between such heterodoxy and the heresies with which it became associated would be misconceived as well as impossible. Heresy, as a phenomenon rather than a transitory event, was neither exclusively doctrinal nor exclusively social: there can be no heresy without belief, and no sect without adherents. The first gives it identity, the second significance. Accordingly the formation of a heresy must be sought in the coalescence of doctrinal and historical factors. We have to explain how a doctrine like that of the poverty of Christ can so change its import that while its apostle, St. Francis, was canonized, its more extreme followers were,

[1] See pp. 70 ff. below.   [2] See pp. 282 ff. below.

less than a century later, persecuted and finally condemned: why what for Innocent III was spiritual reform became for John XXII doctrinal error.[1] These are questions which focus upon Christian society; they can only be answered by considering heresy as part of it.

As this study will show, medieval heresy from the thirteenth to the fifteenth centuries was an extreme—and sometimes violent—expression of the problems confronting medieval society. Its source was the tension between Christian precept and practice, which the church was decreasingly able to overcome; and it was actuated by a similar desire to reconcile them—in this case by taking the law of Christ into its own hands. Doctrinally, it was fed by the growing heterodoxy which marked later medieval life spiritually, intellectually and politically: some of these concepts, like poverty, were common to all religious reform; others, like Rhineland mysticism,[2] the political doctrines of Marsilius of Padua[3] and Conciliar theory, as well as the growing gap between revealed truth and natural experience, following the condemnation of Averroism and Aristotelianism in 1277,[4] were new developments which reflected the breakdown of the older outlook. At the same time, the older heresies, especially the evangelical claims of the Waldensians, were a potent factor in generating anti-sacerdotalism as can be seen in most of the popular heresies of the fourteenth and fifteenth centuries. Perhaps most pervasive of all was the growing sense of apocalypticism. It centred upon Joachim of Fiore's prophecies of the opening of the seventh and final age of the church in 1260; that year was marked by the first outbreaks of bands of Flagellants, who, beginning at Perugia, spread over most of Christendom—the first of succeeding waves over the next 150 years. But Joachism did not end there. As we shall see it entered into the very lore of the Franciscan order and indeed went far beyond it.[5] From the second half of the thirteenth century there was a stream of vaticinations foretelling the imminent coming of Antichrist and the destruction of the world. The sense of impending doom was not confined to persecuted sects, but permeated much of the outlook of the later middle ages, affecting some of its most prominent figures, like the line of Czech reformers,[6] Waldhausen, Milíč of Kroměříž, Matthew Janov, and later the Hussites, as well as ecclesiastics like Pierre d'Ailly, John Gerson and of course

---

[1] See pp. 157 ff. below.   [2] See pp. 31 ff. below.   [3] See pp. 413 ff. below.
[4] See pp. 32 ff. below and G. Leff, *Medieval Thought* (London 1958, 1959, 1963) 229 ff.
[5] See pp. 79 ff. below.   [6] See pp. 610 ff. below.

Wyclif. It not only made for an attitude of uncertainty, liable to erupt in times of crisis, but for condemnation of the present state, above all of the church: there was, as we shall see, a growing tendency to identify the pope with Antichrist and to make the sins of the hierarchy the cause of the disasters which would befall the world. These feelings were intensified by the periodic upheavals which occurred during the later middle ages: the Black Death of 1348–50 was the signal for a renewed outburst of mass flagellation greater than anything which had gone before;[1] the devastation of the 100 Years' War led to endemic disorders over a considerable part of France, with bands of soldiers—the free companies—taking the law in their own hands, and to the rising of the Peasants (the *Jacquerie*) in 1351. In England, the cumulative strains of war and plague issued in the Peasants' Revolt of 1381, which, while certainly not inspired by Wyclif, for a brief time challenged the existing order. At Rome there was the short-lived revolutionary commune of Cola di Rienzo in 1347,[2] whose mingled aspirations of a return to the grandeurs of the past and the apocalyptic visions (derived from the Franciscan Spirituals) of a new era of purity and poverty, ended in his condemnation as a heretic. Italy itself was the scene of endemic wars between the papal and imperial armies and the different Italian states. The Great Schism from 1378–1415 seemed to confirm the sense of impending dissolution; and its healing was more than offset by the Hussite reformation which withstood twenty years of war, inflaming religious unrest in Germany and the rest of Central Europe as well as for a time releasing one of the most powerful waves of chiliasm—among the Taborites.[3]

These developments are reflected in the heresy of the later middle

---

[1] See pp. 475 ff. below.

[2] Cola di Rienzo is one of the best documented figures of this later period due to his letters, which have been published in four volumes by P. Puir, *Briefwechsel des Cola di Rienzo* in *Vom Mittelalter zur Reformation II* (Berlin 1912–29, 5 vols.). See also P. Puir, *Cola di Rienzo, Darstellung seines Lebens und seines Geistes* (Vienna 1931).

Under the influence of the Spirituals and Fraticelli, Cola believed in the coming age of the Holy Spirit. But once in power after his *coup* in May 1357 he lived surrounded by pomp and luxury. His success went to his head; he had coins struck in his image, and he proclaimed a new era in which Rome had world jurisdiction. He was forced to flee after being deposed by a noble counter-revolution in December 1347, taking refuge with the Fraticelli in the Apennines. He later crossed the Alps to Prague, where he sought the aid of Charles IV, the emperor. In 1354 Cola marched on Rome with 500 troops, and enjoyed two more months of frenetic power before the populace rose against him and he was beheaded. For a good brief account see G. Mollat, *Les papes d' Avignon (1305–78)* 241–8.   [3] See pp. 688 ff. below.

ages. From the later thirteenth to the fifteenth centuries its main themes
—poverty, prophecy, union with God, a return to the true apostolic
church—crystallized the main preoccupations of the epoch among both
laymen and religious. This is not to say that to each of these topics there
corresponded a specific heretical sect, or that indeed each was always
to be found separately. Rather these were the *foci* around which the
main movements gathered, frequently resulting in an amalgam of
several different doctrines. But more important, as we have already
suggested, this gave rise to what we might call an outlook of protest.
The fact that it was engendered by the common experience of opposition and persecution led inevitably to certain attitudes which seem
superficially to have affinities with subsequent Protestantism. But in
recognizing these, we should also remember the distance dividing
them; none of the heretical movements thought in terms of a different
kind of church, but rather the renewal of the existing one: even when
this took the form of claiming to be the true church, with Waldensians,
or belief in a new spiritual church, among the Franciscan Spirituals, its
role was conceived in apostolic terms. Nor did demoting the sacraments mean justification by faith, or repudiation of papal authority the
denial of a catholic church. That one ultimately led to the other must
not make us anticipate the event.

First among these traits, we may mention the sense of election
common to most sects. If they were social outcasts, they were also
God's chosen, the true defenders of Christ's law. Their sufferings in
this world were merely the continuance of Christ's in the same cause
of evangelical truth. With him, they would be on God's right hand at
the day of judgement; and for those who, like the Franciscan Spirituals,
believed that this would be preceded by a third and final era of peace
on earth, triumph over their adversaries was near. In either case, theirs
were the tribulations which Christ's disciples had to endure in the
struggle against Antichrist. The form it took varied: the Franciscan
Spirituals, the English Lollards and the Hussites (though not all for the
same reasons), came in their different ways to open insurrection; the
Waldensians and the Free Spirit remained largely clandestine, the latter
also quietist. The Waldensians and Taborites constituted themselves
into separate churches, where the others were content to affirm their
version of the truth. In general, however, the belief in final victory
bred a sense of righteous acceptance of present suffering, which was
broken only in extreme circumstances.

Secondly, the taking of Christ's law into their own hands entailed a

B

rejection of that of the church. In particular it led to investing all sovereignty in the bible, as the repository of God's word, to be translated, interpreted and preached by themselves. It was to stress individual judgement and experience at the expense of ecclesiastical authority in all its ramifications—decretals, enactments of synods, and the sheer weight of post-apostolic tradition. It was also to reject its sacramental life, and, with it, outward forms and ceremonies as well as the role of the hierarchy: the majority of feasts and fasts, saints' days, veneration of images, prayers, the saying of offices, and, for the Cathars, Waldensians and Taborites, and to some extent the heresy of the Free Spirit and Wyclif, the sacraments themselves together with the distinctive place of the priesthood. In their stead was put the direct rapport between the individual believer and God's word. The turning away from the church's mediation thus made for the almost universal tendency in all the main heresies towards simplicity of belief and personal piety: it was actuated by the desire to strip away the accretions with which the church had overlaid Christ's life and teaching. The return to Christ could therefore only be made through renouncing the ways of the present church, which were generally identified with Antichrist. It is to be found at its most extreme in the debased mysticism of the Free Spirit, where the discovery of God in the soul released the individual from all earthly laws, including those of the church. But in general it was nearer to a puritanical insistence upon godly living; quality of life was the test of individual probity and the condition of all priestly power. For the Waldensians, Wyclif and the Taborites, a sinful priest could not administer the sacraments; nor did the latter reconcile a sinner with God: this came only from God's acceptance of the inner contrition worked by his will.

This emphasis upon the quality of life explains the central importance of poverty—or at least austerity—as the most universal and venerable of all the impulses to religious reform. As we have said, it was shared by all the religious reforming movements, ecclesiastical and lay alike: the hermits, the Cistercians, the mendicant orders, as well as the *Pauperes Christi*, Arnoldists, the Humiliati, the Beguines, and the Waldensians. It was the driving force behind the Franciscan Spirituals and later the Fraticelli, and it led to the conflict between the Michaelists and John XXII. It was also advocated in a different, though no less extreme sense, by Wyclif and the Czech reformers. In all these cases—except for the Franciscan conventuals—it was less a legal concept of owning nothing than a practical state of living without superfluity. As such it was also a moral criterion, at once the test of true apostlehood and the measure of the church's departure from Christ's teaching. Its observance went together with the right to preach God's word, a right reserved not for those who had been ordained, but for the just man whose spiritual fittedness was proclaimed by his way of life. It was therefore open to any man who practised what he preached.

Now the veneration of poverty, in addition to being one of the hallmarks of most heretical movements, provided them with what may be called an historicism: an historical justification of their opposition to the church. This entailed once again reaching back to the bible and to the practices of the early apostolic church. These showed that not only had Christ and his disciples lived without property or wealth, but that they had renounced all secular jurisdiction and temporal power. Their subsequent possession had come from Constantine's endowment of the church which had been wrongfully accepted by the then pope, Sylvester I. He had thus violated Christ's teaching and disqualified himself and his successors from being Christ's true successors. Accordingly the power and the wealth of the present-day hierarchy were a usurpation: the true disciples of Christ, in dissociating themselves from it, and returning to the apostolic path, were also combating Christ's enemies and Antichrist. Such was the outlook which, originating with the Waldensians, is to be found in one form or another amongst most sects—the Free Spirit and the Cathars here, as elsewhere, excepted. Whatever the variations, the central theme, that decline set in with Constantine's donation, was a recurrent one. With the Spiritual Franciscans it was harnessed to a Joachist scheme of the coming end of the sixth age of the church[1] and the beginning of the seventh which, after a fierce struggle, would usher in a new era where the apostles of poverty would triumph.[2] For Wyclif, as for the Waldensians and Marsilius of Padua, the path of return to Christ was through forcible disendowment and expropriation of the church and the loss of its temporal jurisdiction. For Hus and the Czech reformers, lack of possessions and something like the poor usage (*usus pauper*) of the Franciscan Spirituals,[3] were the necessary condition of a truly Christian priesthood. For all of them, and many untainted by heresy, wealth and worldliness were the source of the church's—and the world's—ills.

---

[1] This did not come from Joachim himself, who saw the age of Constantine as the great age of peace. I am indebted to Miss Marjorie Reeves for drawing my attention to this point.

[2] See pp. 79 ff. below.

[3] See pp. 100 ff. below.

For the Free Spirit, the most enigmatic of all the heresies, poverty was a variable factor; some of its adherents seem not to have considered it at all, but in general it was regarded by them as an essential element in initiation to spiritual perfection and complete freedom of the spirit. Only when this state had been reached could all restraints be cast off and one's desires indulged in every direction. For those members of the heresy who lived as Beghards and Beguines, poverty, or at least simplicity and austerity, was a regular part of their outward life, often accompanied by mendicancy. Nor did poverty have the same historical role for the heretics of the Free Spirit, since their mystical aspirations were, by definition, timeless, concerned with transcending all earthly laws, not returning to those of Christ. The dubious nature of the heresy makes it—with Catharism, but for quite different reasons—almost an invariable exception.

Later medieval heresy was thus more than mere protest or revolt, whether from moral or political motives. While it could be any or all of these, in its totality it constituted an alternative to the prevailing outlook. Far from being the work of a lay spirit or of unbelief, it was drawn from the very elements which made up the body of Christian belief. The challenge to the church lay in contraposing these to the existing order. Poverty, the renunciation of all possessions on the model of Christ and his disciples, was physically incompatible with the continuance of the church as a corporation; its entire structure rested upon its endowments, taxation, tithes and jurisdiction. Without them, it would have had no visible identity or continuity. The winning of its own privileges and immunities, and the unfettered power of its own hierarchy, had been the basis of its reform in the eleventh century. Similarly to have permitted unauthorized interpretation and preaching of the bible, to say nothing of discounting the sacraments in favour of individual experience, would have been to deny the church's very *raison d'être* as the mediator between man and God.

Now in seeking the causes of this revulsion against the church there are two distinct considerations. The first is that heresy was endemic in medieval society, as the form which all sustained dissent must ultimately take. It was therefore a spectrum which extended from the petty heresiarch to the very foundations of Christian theory and practice. For that reason it cannot be identified with a specific group or class.[1]

[1] The attempt to depict heresy in terms of class struggle begins from three basic misconceptions: first that heresy can be identified with a single class or a single programme. This is sufficiently refuted by the contents of this or any other book on the

The revolt of the Franciscan Spirituals was motivated by an almost fanatical fervour which at its outset was directed not to the church at large but within their own order; it changed its character only as the result of persecution, its members eventually becoming the subversive bands of the Fraticelli. The Waldensians, on the other hand, were from the first pious laymen who preached a doctrine of poverty hardly distinguishable from that of St. Francis; yet within a mere eight years (1176–84) they were banned by the church. By the beginning of the thirteenth century they were directly attacking it. Throughout the middle ages, which they survived, their support was drawn mainly from the lower orders—peasants, weavers, shoemakers, smiths. Here, then, in the Spirituals and the Waldensians, we have initially two very similar doctrines, which for long had a different import and were upheld by different groups with a different place in society—one religious living within the bosom of the church; the other lay and excommunicate. A parallel contrast can be found between the Beguines and their male counterpart, the Beghards. The Beguines were drawn predominantly from aristocratic women during the first century of their existence; and even in the fourteenth century, the statutes of many houses demanded some kind of financial or property contribution towards their maintenance.[1] The Beghards, from what is known of them, seem to have always come from the poorer social strata. This may well account for the apparently greater incidence of the heresy of

---

subject: Wyclif and Hus cannot simply be grouped with Peter of Valdes or Peter John Olivi's followers, nor did their teaching carry the same import. Wyclif, for example, wanted expropriation of the church in a way quite foreign to Olivi. Secondly, it assumes that heretics uniformly wished to overthrow present society and take over political and economic control. In fact they usually sought to withdraw from it; even when they did attack the present order, the church was invariably their target, not secular rulers. Thirdly, medieval heresy did not represent an alternative base of social or economic power: it was drawn not from the predominantly 'rising bourgeoisie', but either ecclesiastics or poor and simple men. The latter might be oppressed but they were not the representatives of a new economic order which was fettered by the existing feudal mode of production; the former objected to economic wealth and wanted not its transference but its abolition. Hence, even had they succeeded in overthrowing their rulers, heretical sects would not have been the 'midwives of social change' but mere 'utopians' seeking to put the clock back. It seems more feasible, as well as more historical, to treat heresy as genuine dissent, rather than purely as a manifestation of the class struggle. This is to deny not its social nature but the attempt to relegate everything else to it.

[1] E. G. Neumann, *Reinisches Beginen und Begardenwesen* (Meisenheim am Glan 1960) 93 ff.

the Free Spirit among them than the Beguines; but the fact remains that similar groups attracted disparate sections of society. It is borne out by both the English Lollards and the Hussites, who received their initial impetus from theologians and ecclesiastical reformers; in the case of the Hussites they continued to direct it through the twenty years of the Hussite Wars.

Above all, this diversity is shown in the universality of its themes, which were those of Christian belief as a whole, not the preserve of sects. In the middle ages the road to heresy was paved with piety; only when breaking point was reached did it take a new direction and become open dissent and sometimes revolt. In the cycle from heterodoxy to dissent a sect inevitably underwent a change. Once proscribed, its members became social outcasts, at war with authority, whether waged clandestinely or openly. This in turn coloured its outlook which became more extreme and directly anti-ecclesiastical. It developed its own lore with its own *dramatis personae*. Thus for the Fraticelli, John XXII continued, long after his death, to be the villain of the piece, and poverty the great truth around which their history and that of the world revolved. In such circumstances the appeal was to a different type of adherent from when the struggle was still within the Franciscan order—one more radical and less intellectual, concerned with action rather than doctrinal nuances, and above all nursing a sense of injustice. It is no accident, therefore, that a sect in decline—or driven underground—tended to be drawn from the lower social groups, by definition more militant. The Fraticelli of the later fourteenth century were of quite a different composition from the days of Angelo of Clareno; the mystical fervour of the Spirituals had given way to the bitterness characteristic of any group of outlaws. As so often, the descendants bore little relation to their forbears. The same is true of both the Cathars and the English Lollards. The Cathars had until the time of the Albigensian Crusade (c. 1209–26) enjoyed the support of a large and influential part of Provençal society; many of the nobility, including Raymond, Count of Toulouse, were their sympathizers. After the virtual destruction of the sect, as well as Provençal life, by the Northern French nobles, it gradually sank to the bottom of society. By the end of the thirteenth century its adherents were almost exclusively artisans and peasants. For English Lollardy the decline was much swifter; after a brief period of vitality among Wyclif's supporters at Oxford, who were made innocuous by the early 1380s, it became a movement without a head, confined to unbeneficed priests and pious laymen. Any aristocratic support which it might have initially enjoyed, was dissipated by Oldcastle's abortive rising of 1414. Its subsequent survivals were among draymen, weavers and other artisans with the usual sprinkling of lower clergy.

In heresy, as in most things else, like bred like: both the Waldensians and the Hussites in their different ways exercised an appeal which was strong enough to withstand all the attacks directed against them. Each retained its original character to marked degree; and there was little degeneration into being a mere anti-group. The Hussites continued to be akin to a national reforming movement, whilst the Waldensians from the outset had always been the sect of the pious poor, who by entering it became members of a new church. The cohesion of both movements accounts for their survival not just as groups but as distinctive outlooks.

It is therefore misconceived to treat heresy or a sect as something constant; heresies differed from one another and underwent change in the course of their evolution: a movement in decline often showed marked divergences from when it had been in the ascendant. To take one phase to the exclusion of the other is to make nonsense of it. Accordingly social composition is as much a matter for enquiry as outlook. It is no more amenable to a prior identification with one class than it is with one tenet. Beyond calling it dissent or protest, who made it, when and how, and with what results, are variable factors which cannot be decided in advance.

Finally, heresy is to be distinguished from mere disaffection, even if it becomes anti-ecclesiastical. Risings like Cola di Rienzo's or the Jacquerie or even the Peasants' Revolt, in which the archbishop of Canterbury, Sudbury, was decapitated, were not primarily the work of doctrinal or religious dissent, nor did they leave behind any distinctive outlook. On the other hand, this is not to deny that religious outbreaks could not become social risings—as with the Taborites and Flagellants —or that they did not have political or social repercussions. Indeed heresy always had social and political implications; and it is these which, as we have said, gave it importance.

The growth of popular piety

This brings us to the second consideration of the cause of heresy: its social context. There are two distinct aspects. The first concerns society in general and especially the church; the second, the local factors— geography, social structure and so on—of the different areas in which heresy developed. The first was an institutional no less than a spiritual matter.[1] While worldliness and wealth played a central part in the revulsion against the church and the search for new religious forms, these shortcomings were not peculiar to the later middle ages. On the contrary the desire for spiritual renewal by a return to first evangelical principles had underlain the monastic reforms of the tenth, eleventh and twelfth centuries. Rather, what distinguished the period from c. 1250 to 1450 was the fact that these impulses no longer found an outlet in the foundation of new religious orders under the aegis of the church. Instead these centuries witnessed a series of extra-regular movements outside it. In this sense the difference between the earlier and the later middle ages was less one of spirituality than of ecumenicality: between the church's ability to canalize the main religious currents and alienation from them. Ultimately it was the difference between ecclesiastically approved reform and ecclesiastical repression; and it is this shift in emphasis that signalizes the changed context of heresy in the later middle ages.

This change arose from the very nature of the church, as the spiritual and intellectual arbiter of Christendom. As the communion of all believers, it was confronted increasingly with the problem of how to remain spiritually comprehensive and yet institutionally effective: to meet intellectual and spiritual developments without impairing its authority. In the earlier middle ages it had itself been at the heart of the successive monastic and ecclesiastical movements, which from the tenth to the twelfth centuries had transformed its position. But its very success in achieving independence of all lay interference sowed the seeds of its subsequent loss of position. It grew in wealth and privilege; and as with any corporation, safeguarding its rights and enforcing its dues became a major preoccupation. Their definition in canon law marked it off as a body from the rest of society and made it increasingly rigid. Inevitably, therefore, it appeared as one more privileged body— a collector of taxes as well as the keeper of men's souls. It was this duality which made it so vulnerable to opposition, for one tended to undermine the other. To demand tithes, a comprehensive tariff of fees extending from birth to death, taxes for crusades, and to enforce customary dues upon tenants of ecclesiastical lands, to say nothing of pursuing temporal policies often indistinguishable from kings' and princes', was to appear much as any other lay lord. At the same time the church

---

[1] What follows largely supersedes the writer's 'Heresy and the decline of the medieval church' in *Past and Present*, 20 (November 1961) 36-51.

claimed to speak for every sort and condition of men. In one sense it did; socially, it was a mirror of society, comprehending extremes of wealth, rank, way of life and intellectual attainment; spiritually it ministered to all men and it controlled education. Materially it dispensed charity and tended the sick and needy. But in order to make its voice effective it resorted to those very attributes of wealth and exclusiveness which removed it further and further from the gospel on which it was founded. As a consequence by the end of the twelfth century it was less and less able to compete with the claims of the Cathars, Arnoldists, Humiliati, and Waldensians, that they were the true Christians in their pursuit of poverty and simplicity. The parallel evolution of both the Cluniac and Cistercian monastic orders to positions of wealth and privilege removed from the church what had been the main vehicles of religious fervour during the two preceding centuries: a fact eloquently testified by the failure of the Cistercian missionaries to make any impression upon the Cathars in Languedoc.[1] Only the coming of the Friars, dedicated to poverty and preaching, gave a new focus to fervour which otherwise would have had no orthodox outlet. But they were to be the last. The Fourth Lateran Council in 1215 decreed that there should henceforth be no new religious orders;[2] even the Dominicans had for a time to choose the rule of one of the existing orders—that of the Augustinian canons. In retrospect this decision must be regarded as a turning point in the development of both the medieval church and heresy. Behind the plausible explanations against permitting a proliferation of unauthorized orders, lay the hostility of the secular church to these new groups of poor preachers; Innocent III who had done more than anyone else to foster them[3] bowed to it. Nevertheless his foresight had ensured the existence of St. Francis's and St. Dominic's bands; and in recognizing them he had presided over the birth of what was to be the dominant religious and intellectual force of the thirteenth century. He had also shown himself sympathetic to similar groups of pious laymen among the Waldensians and Humiliati, although not to Peter Valdes. But he had become increasingly alarmed at the spread of heresy, which led him, after all other efforts had failed, to the other equally momentous decision of preaching a crusade against the Cathar heretics in Languedoc in 1209.[4]

In the end the final balance had come down in favour of repression. It marked the parting of the ways for religious reform. The mendicant

[1] See pp. 36 ff. below.   [2] Mansi, *Concilia*, vol. 22, ch. 13, 1002.
[3] See pp. 40 ff. below.   [4] See pp. 39 ff. below.

orders soon became involved in the work of the church and the universities. In 1227 cardinal Ugolino, protector of the Franciscan order, became pope Gregory IX and within five years he had entrusted the Dominicans and Franciscans with the working of the papal inquisition. These responsibilities, and sheer numbers, transformed the mendicants from wandering bands of preachers into highly organized orders extending over Christendom: mendicant poverty gave way to property and buildings, libraries, study, and the paraphernalia of government. It was their revulsion at the change which led the Franciscan Spirituals to demand a return to the simple apostolic precepts of their founder; but, as we shall see, in vain. To have done so would have been to dismantle what had become an indispensable part of the church. Here we come upon one of the constant factors in the tension between the demands of Christian first principles and institutional responsibility. It was not that the Franciscans and Dominicans, any more than the church as a whole, became morally degenerate in abandoning their early rigours. They had taken on a new role. They had now to fulfil an office and no longer merely observe their own practice. The majority continued to preach and when necessary to beg; but they did so by the second half of the thirteenth century as some activities among many rather than as a way of life. Nevertheless the effect of the mendicant orders upon the religious and intellectual life of the thirteenth century is incalculable. Without them—or similar groups—the position of the church must have been very different. Yet there was a limit to what they could do, even in combating heresy as inquisitors, or acting as confessors and spiritual advisers to the groups of religious women springing up. In the sense that they were not succeeded, the Fourth Lateran Council's ban on new orders was the watershed in the expansion of the church; although the impetus of the mendicant orders carried the church along for the next seventy or so years, by the end of the thirteenth century there were no further ecclesiastically sponsored groups to maintain it. Instead there was a growing number of unofficial groupings such as the Beguines and Beghards of the Low Countries and the Rhineland; the Beguins in Provence, followers of the Provençal Spirituals; the Tuscan Spirituals fleetingly constituted as the Poor Order of Celestinian hermits before Boniface VIII forced them to disband. These were all in varying ways seeking to realize a life of simple piety; if not withdrawal in the monastic sense, it expressed a quietist desire to an independent existence outside the recognized orders.

One of its most remarkable aspects was the great number of religious women involved. The female question (*Frauenfrage*) became a new and important element in religious and social life from the later twelfth century.[1] Their numbers grew rapidly during the thirteenth century, and by the fourteenth century their regulation was a continuing problem for the ecclesiastical authorities. Despite attempts to prove otherwise,[2] these groups were of aristocratic and patrician origin; only in the later thirteenth century did they become increasingly plebeian, with many beguinages becoming poor houses in the fourteenth century.[3] In the earlier stages economic motives can have been of little or no account: the desire to live a religious life was common to large sections of society; in the case of women it was also the only way to some kind of independent existence which had its own significance. As such it was an outlet from the confines of a man's world, as well as a vocation; but it could hardly be said to have offered economic security, let alone an inducement to material improvement. On the contrary, the problem of religious women arose precisely because there were too many for the existing communities. This was particularly true of the North, where in contrast to Italy, only a part of them was able to enter one of the established orders—especially the Cistercians.[4] The latter from the time of St. Bernard had been strongly opposed to unofficial religious groups outside the cloister.[5] At first the Premonstratensians had established convents for them in Northern France and Germany, thereby keeping them within the purview of orthodoxy. But by the beginning of the thirteenth century the Premonstratensians had followed the example of the Cistercians in wanting to follow a purely claustral life freed from the responsibilities of female oversight. This led women for a time to look to the Cistercians; but they, too, soon refused to continue to admit them, since it entailed too much effort and organization.[6] In 1212 their chapter general laid down the maximum number of nuns for each convent; in 1220 the incorporation of further women into existing ones was stopped; and finally in 1228 the ban was extended to the founding of new houses. Thus within the first few years of the

[1] For this see above all H. Grundmann, *Religiöse Bewegungen im Mittelalter* (Hildesheim 1961). See also E. W. McDonnell, *The Beguines and the Beghards* (Rutgers 1954), who deals mainly with Belgium. The orthodox Marxist view is put by J. Koch, *Frauenfrage und Ketzertum* (Berlin 1962).

[2] J. Koch, *Frauenfrage und Ketzertum.*

[3] McDonnell, *Beguines* 82.

[4] Grundmann, op. cit., 174 ff., who treats the question in detail.

[5] Ibid., 175.   [6] Ibid., 203 ff.

thirteenth century, the traditional monastic outlets open to women had virtually dried up. Already their paucity had led to the formation of unofficial groups—the Beguines—and these were now systematically extended. They were essentially a North European phenomenon: south of the Alps the earlier tendency to live in convents later extended to the mendicant orders, particularly the Franciscans. In 1316 there were 198 women's convents in their Italian province compared with 40 in Germany, although the number of inmates in the Italian convents was probably smaller. The Dominicans, on the other hand, were always more numerous north of the Alps; and the much lower total of women's houses in 1277—only 40 compared with 18 elsewhere— was to some extent offset by the greater number of inmates to a house: 300 for example at Strasbourg.[1] It was only in the later fourteenth century that the German Beguines came more and more to adopt the rule of the Franciscan and Dominican third orders. But that was after nearly 200 years of largely independent development.[2]

The term Beguine first appears at the end of the twelfth century. Its etymology probably derived from the word Albigenses, to denote a heretic;[3] they were regarded as such in the bishopric of Liège during the second part of the twelfth century, for wishing to follow a life of poverty and chastity. Because they were compelled to do so independently of a recognized religious order, they were frequently condemned and burned.[4] The hostility towards them was not mitigated when they were taken in hand by individual priests. One of the first to do so was Lambert le Bègue, whose surname was almost certainly the result of his association with the Beguines rather than the origin of their name; he was accused of heresy.[5] Whether Lambert was their founder or not, he helped to orientate them towards a life of poverty and chastity, translating parts of the bible and writing a history of St. Agnes for the group to whom he ministered.[6]

An equally formative influence was Marie of Oignies (d. 1213) under whom, at Nivelle, groups of unattached women were brought together in houses near a hospital or a river. It was her confessor Jacques of Vitry who obtained from Honorius III, Innocent III's successor, per-

---

[1] These figures are from Grundmann, ibid., 313 ff.
[2] Neumann, *Reinisches Beginen* 163 ff.
[3] Grundmann, op. cit., 178, 181. See also *Dictionnaire de Spiritualité* (art. Beguines, etc.) I, cols. 1341–52.
[4] Grundmann, ibid.
[5] Grundmann, ibid., 181.   [6] McDonnell, *Beguines* 71 ff.

mission to direct religious women to a common life not only in Liège but France and Germany.[1] Communities soon spread rapidly over these lands, established in all the main towns. Whereas in Belgium they tended to be self-contained communities—or *curtes*—in Germany, especially the Rhineland cities, they lived in houses, their numbers running into hundreds: in Cologne, for example, in 1300, there were about 575 Beguines in 12 houses; by 1351, the total had risen to 1170, declining to 1150 in 1400, and 976 in 1450.[2] Cologne and Strasbourg were the two largest centres; elsewhere, as in Mainz for example, the maximum never went beyond about 90 women in 1300.[3] Gradually by the middle of the thirteenth century, the earlier hostility towards them had disappeared. In 1233 Gregory IX in the bull *Gloriam virginalem* allowed them to live a cloistered life; this was not to recognize them as an order; but it in effect enabled women, who were unable to enter a monastery, to join them; and a rule was also drawn up for them.[4] The claustrated Beguines, living mainly in Belgium, were generally accepted as leading a virtuous life; hostility was reserved for those who wandered and begged. By about 1245 Beguine no longer meant heretic.[5]

Yet this relative tranquillity did not last. To begin with the Beguines were not a constituted order; and although the Fourth Lateran Council's ban on new ones did not specifically apply to women, they were never officially acknowledged. This made them vulnerable to attacks both from other orders jealous of their own privileges, especially of mendicancy and preaching, and from the secular church, for acting independently of it. William of St. Amour, for example, berated them for cutting their hair and taking a habit, when they had not been approved by the curia, and demanded their excommunication.[6] In the province of Mainz, as early as 1233, a synod accused them of laziness for living on alms, and lack of chastity, charges repeated in 1244, together with measures to make them work and live in stability instead of wandering from place to place.[7] The second General Council of Lyons in 1274 reiterated the ban on new orders;[8] and from this time onwards the Beguines, and their male counterparts, the Beghards, increasingly came under fire, first from local clergy and then, from 1312, as we shall see, the papacy. In the second place, the Beguines, in not being a

---

[1] Grundmann, op. cit., 170 f.
[2] Neumann, op. cit., 76.
[3] Ibid., 79.
[4] McDonnell, *Beguines* 6.
[5] Grundmann, op. cit., 186.
[6] Quoted in Grundmann, ibid., 323.
[7] Ibid., 326.
[8] Mansi, *Concilia* 24, ch. 23, 96–7.

constituted order with a rule and a system of government, were vulnerable to heterodoxy and infiltration from dubious elements. Theirs
was a state which demanded no binding vows as such, but rather
obedience to the statutes of the house or community concerned, and a
promise to live in chastity for the duration of membership. There was no
pledge to poverty, though simplicity of life was of its essence: they were
to live on the product of their manual labour—mainly spinning and
weaving—as St. Paul had enjoined. Theirs was therefore an intermediary status, under ecclesiastical supervision, but open to anyone
accepting these conditions. Not surprisingly it was susceptible to heresy
both in the accessibility of Beguine (or Beghard) houses and in the
lack of theological preparedness of the inmates, for the most part simple
women or unlettered men. The life especially lent itself to the Free
Spirit who, disguised in the habit of grey, went from house to house
along the Rhine and other arteries.[1] Finally, as the thirteenth century
progressed, the mendicant orders, it is true with growing reluctance,
had, as we have mentioned, come to be responsible for women.[2] A
succession of papal decrees led to their incorporation into the two
orders, despite the latter's resistance to unlimited extensions of their responsibility. During Gregory IX's pontificate three rules for women's
convents evolved: that by the pope, when he had been the Franciscans'
cardinal protector, which all new Italian foundations had to take;
that of the Cistercians, and that for the convent of S. Sisto at Rome,
drawn up by the Dominicans in 1221.[3] But these underwent frequent
change during the next thirty years. It was not until the 1260s that a
degree of uniformity among the two women's orders was achieved and
their relations with their male counterparts regularized. In 1263, the
Franciscan convents were renamed the order of St. Clare in the new
constitutions of that year. Neither order had voluntarily accepted the
responsibilities for visitation and spiritual care of women, and it was
mainly under pressure, as much from the women themselves as from
the papacy, that they finally yielded. Thus it is not hard to see why,
when even the mendicants were so reluctant to take them, so many

[1] See ch. III below.

[2] Grundmann, op. cit., 206 ff. Both orders had early been associated with women's
convents: St. Dominic from 1206, when, engaged in preaching against the Cathars,
had founded the convent at St. Prouille, in Languedoc. St. Francis while warning the
brothers off against involvement with women, made an exception for Clara of
Assisi who in 1212 dedicated herself to a life of poverty; he drew up a simple rule
for her and her companions, known as the Poor Clares, at St. Damien Assisi.

[3] Grundmann, op. cit., 236 ff.

women remained outside any order. No amount of unofficial oversight and protection which the Beguines received both from the local clergy and the Friars[1] could ultimately save them from the recurrent charges that they were an illicit movement which should be suppressed. Under repeated attacks, and actual suppressions during the fourteenth century, they gradually regularized their position by taking the rule of the Franciscan third order for pious laymen and women, who in their own houses followed a simple code of conduct under the oversight of superiors.[2] By then, however, they had become a focus for a variety of conflicting forces.

The growth of the Beguines and Beghards is the clearest indication of the inability of piety to find an accepted institutionalized outlet in the high and later middle ages. Whilst the mendicants just squeezed through the door before it was closed by the Fourth Lateran Council, these two groups were caught in it, and remained wedged there. Their ambivalent position evoked correspondingly ambivalent feelings towards them; those who lived a cloistered life in the Flemish towns succeeded on the whole in becoming an established part of the community and the diocesan system.[3] In France similarly St. Louis took them under his protection. But there continued to be individual groups, scattered over Northern Europe, while in Germany they never adopted a claustral life. Hence, as we have said, the fluctuations in membership and opportunity for heresy. Institutionally, they were conceived to be self-supporting; hence they never adopted a philosophy of poverty on Franciscan lines;[4] the regulations of most of the German houses demanded some kind of property as condition of entry, the performance of manual labour within the house, and banned begging.[5] This reflects the higher social stratum from which they originated, a fact substantiated by the records of numerous houses.[6] The flight from unnecessary possessions does not suggest entrepreneurial inclinations, nor do the Beghards, who seem to have been composed of the poorer sort, appear to have harboured revolutionary designs: on the contrary, the charges against them were that they begged and believed in the immoral pantheism of the Free Spirit, which was individual libertinism—the solvent of any social or self-discipline. That both the Beguines and the Beghards came in time to be drawn from the lower social strata reflects the social function of

---

[1] See Neumann, *Reinisches Beginen* 124, in this connexion.
[2] Ibid., 164–5.   [3] McDonnell, *Beguines* 6.
[4] Grundmann, op. cit., 351.
[5] Neumann, *Reinisches Beginen* 92 ff.   [6] Ibid.

their houses and communities as poor houses. It accounts for the repeated failures to suppress them in the fourteenth century as centres of heresy. For over and above the subversive elements they attracted, they fulfilled a necessary function in the life of a town from whose officers they usually received protection.[1] Ultimately, then, unofficial piety was the result of the church's failure, or refusal, to make it official. In consequence it took on a life of its own, which despite its dangers was never extinguished. As so often in the later middle ages, it was as a source of piety that the Beguines and Beghards were also a focus of heresy.

The centralization of the Church

Meanwhile throughout the thirteenth and fourteenth centuries, the church was becoming more and more centralized. With Innocent III (1198–1216)[2] its administrative, political and financial unity under the curia at Rome, had been finally established. It was the culmination of the policy begun by the Gregorian reformers in the eleventh century: papal jurisdiction in all important disputes, elections to bishoprics, the despatch of legates, the hearing of appeals, had all become enshrined in canon law. In 1199, Innocent had levied a general tax on the clergy to finance his projected crusade, and again in 1215. It was repeated at intervals during the thirteenth century until Boniface VIII finally came to grief in attempting to prevent Philip IV (the Fair) of France and Edward I of England doing the same to their own clergy. Innocent III's pontificate unquestionably marked the apogee of the medieval papacy. No pope ever again wielded his authority over high and low alike, nor combined his deep spiritual insight with the gifts of statesmanship. To that extent the decline in his thirteenth-century successors was one of personality. But it was also more: Innocent in helping to bring papal government to a new pitch, despite his tendencies to allow more freedom to the local authorities,[3] set the tone for the lawyer statesmen who succeeded him; the days of the theologian popes were over: Benedict XII was the exception. The majority of thirteenth- and fourteenth-century popes were organizers and administrators, men of action rather than thinkers or idealists. The complete unfittedness of Celestine V was largely, though not entirely, due to his own character; but the fact

[1] Neumann, *Reinisches Beginen*, 125, 141.
[2] A. Fliche, C. Thouzellier, Y. Azais, *La Chrétienté romaine (1198–1274)* 11 ff.
[3] Ibid., 148 ff.

remains that the office of pope in the later thirteenth century was far more appropriate to worldlings like his successor Boniface VIII, who used it to plan campaigns and form alliances, to say nothing of aggrandizing their families, than it was to a pious and unworldly hermit, the one pope who might have healed the Franciscan schism. The truth was that the pope had to run an empire, which however it might differ in ultimate *raison d'être* from secular kingdoms, was greater in scale and ramifications than any of them. The papacy as the one supranational authority had evolved an international government to give it effect. Had it been confined to merely spiritual affairs, its spiritual standing might have matched its political power. That it did not was above all due to Sicily, the climax in the two hundred year-long struggle between empire and papacy: if Sicily finally shattered the pretensions of the one, it debased the ideals of the other. The thirteenth-century popes' desire to drive Frederick II and his successors from that kingdom and from Italy embroiled the papacy in a succession of wars. From the pontificate of Innocent IV (1243–54) Sicily dominated its policies, inevitably accentuating its political attributes at the expense of its spiritual ones. The inherent papal dependence upon a lay coadjutor brought it into alliance first with Edmund, younger son of Henry III of England, and then, when that had failed, with Charles of Anjou, brother of St. Louis, king of France. Initiated by Innocent IV and continued by Alexander IV and Clement IV, the aim was the reconquest of Sicily from the Hohenstaufen successors of Frederick II: the reward for doing so was possession of the kingdom by the conqueror; the price, in addition to the cost of the operation, the promise never to unite Sicily with the German empire and tribute to the pope as final suzerain: in the case of Charles of Anjou, 50,000 marks deposit and a yearly payment of 8000 ounces of gold.[1]

The cost of these plans, finally achieved with Charles of Anjou's defeat of Manfred, the reigning king of Sicily, at Benevento in 1266, cannot be measured in purely material terms: it forced the popes to turn to every available resource, financial, political and ecclesiastical, to realize them: the exploiting of dispensations and provisions to benefices, which, under Innocent IV, became a major—and not over-scrupulous—industry; the levying of taxes upon the clergy, such as the 'crusading' tenth in 1255; the raising of loans from Tuscan bankers at usurious rates (a practice banned by the church); and above all the levying of wars. The constant need to scheme and organize inevitably

[1] CMH VI, 183 f.

directed spiritual means into temporal ends. Crusade and excommunication became mere declarations of war; and relied for their efficacy not, as with Gregory VII or even Innocent III, upon spiritual, but physical force.

Boniface VIII's defeat at the hands of Philip the Fair in 1303 was the dénouement, not for the church as a whole, but for the papacy as a secular power; it marked the end of political pretensions which had dominated the policies of most of the thirteenth-century popes. Henceforth, at Avignon, it turned its attention to its one sphere where it could still exercise international authority—the governing of the church. In that sense Boniface VIII's humiliation acted as a catharsis: it purged the papacy of its grosser secular aspects and set it upon a less grandiose, more genuinely ecclesiastical, path. Not that the Avignonese papacy[1] ceased to have a 'foreign policy'. But it now directed itself to the more limited aim of recovering Rome and the papal states. Although this involved most of its popes—except for Benedict XII—in Italy, and led John XXII into renewed struggle with the emperor, Louis of Bavaria, this was now on a less all-consuming scale. In particular, except at the height of the conflict with Louis of Bavaria, which was mainly a war of words—from the emperor's side—it did not involve the papacy with other powers: the air was not full with the proclamation of crusades and bans against opponents but reserved more for infidels and heretics.[2] To this end, the Avignon popes sought to mediate between Christian kingdoms, especially England and France, at war from 1337. Above all, there was no attempt to tax the clergy without royal assent. The papacy was now on the defensive; and had to suffer the hostility of secular legislation, such as the statutes of Provisors and Praemunire in England in 1351, and 1353 and 1365,[3] as well as the unprecedented assault upon a religious order in Philip the Fair's suppression of the Templars and the confiscation of their wealth in 1311—which Clement V confirmed at the Council of Vienne in 1312.[4] Moreover, where Boniface VIII had claimed to tax the clergy for papal purposes, the Avignon popes re-

[1] For the papacy at Avignon see especially G. Mollat, Les papes d'Avignon (1305–1378) 9th edn., (Paris 1949); and B. Guillemain, La cour pontificale d'Avignon (Paris 1962).

[2] With the outbreak of the Great Schism in 1378, however, the practice returned. The turning point in Hus's career was his opposition to one such crusade by John XXIII against Ladislas of Naples in 1408. See ch. IX, pp. 635 ff. below.

[3] M. McKisack, The Fourteenth Century (Oxford 1949) 280–1.

[4] See Mollat, Les papes d'Avignon 367 ff.; also E. Müller, Das Konzil von Vienne (Münster i. W. 1934).

versed the position by advancing money to secular rulers.[1] This was true especially of the French kings: it was here that the real benefits from having the popes as neighbours—Avignon was not itself on French soil—derived. Besides making them loans, the popes granted them certain imposts from benefices, such as tenths, annates, and subsidies; the proceeds from the clerical tenths raised for a crusade in 1312 and 1333 seem both to have gone to the king of France.[2] The kings of England, Anjou, Castille, Majorca and Naples, all at some time received similar benefits[3] but not to the same degree as France.[4] The latter was also aided politically, especially in the time of John XXII and Philip the Tall who were on close personal terms.[5] Although it is undoubtedly true that the Avignon popes were pro-French, this was less from servility than self-interest. The popes had two great concerns: to regain control of Rome and the papal states and to renew the crusade in the East. The first demanded French co-operation in Italy; the second their acquiescence in ending the Hundred Years' War with England. Accordingly papal policy was as much concerned with mediating between France and England as to advance French interests. The attempts of Clement VI, Innocent VI and Urban V to bring about peace failed and only increased English suspicions.

Indeed perhaps the most significant change in the position of the church, at least its hierarchy centred on the curia, was the growing hostility towards it. Wyclif's violent attacks upon it in the last part of the fourteenth century were, for all their special brand of vitriol, but a more violent expression of the widespread attitude of distaste and criticism. Its object was not just the personal failings of the clergy, but the malfunctioning of the church as an institution: its very constitution as system and a hierarchy were, as we shall have occasion to see, being called into question well before the Great Schism. The latter's duration for nearly forty years brought it to a head in the series of general councils of which Constance (1414–18) was the high point: there, not only were the rival popes deposed, but plans put forward for the reform of the church. That they were abortive meant that eventual reform had to come from outside and in a more violent form as it did with Luther and the Reformation.

Now these changes in the position of the papacy and the church were at once due to its own internal developments and those in medieval society. On the one hand, the impulse to the centralization continued,

[1] Mollat, op. cit., 394.   [2] Ibid.
[3] Ibid.   [4] Ibid., 395.   [5] Ibid., 398 ff.

and increased, after the removal of the papacy to French soil in 1305. Nothing could be more facile than to see this new epoch as one of decline either morally or institutionally. To do so would be firstly to confuse the policies of a few individuals with the church as a whole, as well as to interpret political—and for the most part sincerely held views on the danger of Hohenstaufen control in Sicily and Italy—as signs of moral degeneration. On the contrary perhaps the most remarkable fact about the pope's position was that it was intensely personal. Once elected, the pope was a sovereign more absolute—as well as far-reaching —than any lay ruler. He could make and unmake policies, promulgate new laws and revoke old ones, institute councils, initiate crusades, as well as exercise his jurisdiction in all financial and legal matters. In doing so, his actions naturally affected the church and largely determined the character of the college of cardinals and the curia. But, even when pursued with the vigour and continuity of Innocent IV and his immediate successors, it could still be brought to a sudden halt by the advent of a new pope. Gregory X and later Celestine V are both clear examples of the way in which the bellicose policies of the thirteenth-century papacy were momentarily interrupted and a new direction taken. Had the former, in particular, lived longer the events of Boniface VIII's pontificate may never have happened. Again, it was largely due to the personal conduct of Urban VI in 1378 that the Great Schism broke out. It is therefore necessary to distinguish between popes no less than it is between kings; a line of autocratic and warlike monarchs in neither case necessarily entailed institutional or moral decline, even though authority and prestige waned.

This was very much the position of the Avignon popes. They no longer enjoyed the universal standing of their predecessors of a century earlier, but they were at least their equals as individuals, and in the cases of John XXII, Benedict XII, Clement VI and Urban V, for different reasons, more than ordinary. John XXII, in particular, as an organizer and as a presence, was in the mould of a world ruler; and the central place of the curia in the affairs of Christendom during his pontificate was the closest that the later medieval papacy came to emulating the universality of an earlier epoch.

Secondly, the popes were not synonymous with the church. Indeed one of the difficulties of discussing the church as an entity is that to do so is to falsify it. It was, as we have said, as diverse as society itself. An archbishop or a bishop had as much in common with a parish priest as a lord with a villein, and often little with his fellow bishops. They were appointed for a variety of reasons—for political services, for being papal officials or successfully petitioning the papal curia; for spiritual or scholastic or administrative reasons. It is true that a man could be more than one of these; but in general the distinction was reasonably clear cut. In England, for example, during the thirteenth century, of 78 bishops between 1215 and 1272, forty-two fell within the category of administrators and magnates, and twenty-two were officials and civil servants.[1] During the fourteenth century[2] the civil servant element grew with the growth of government. Consequently there was a growing dependence upon the king and pope; the bishops were caught between the upper and nether millstones of papal authority and royal control. On the whole, apart from the reigns of Philip the Fair and Edward I, there was surprisingly little real friction between their masters. The provision to offices and benefices by the pope was usually in accord with royal desires, and in fourteenth-century England appointment of aliens to English bishoprics was virtually unknown.[3] Indeed one of the arguments of Clement VI in favour of retaining it in papal hands was that it was the king's surest means to getting the best choice.[4] There was much truth in this: for the system of papal provisions, in centralizing appointments, took them out of the hands of local pressure groups. There is strong reason to believe that it originated not with the papacy, but from below, as a method of arbitrating between rival claimants.[5] On theoretical grounds it could be upheld as favouring the best candidate; in practice it favoured the king; and the French kings of the fourteenth century positively enjoined the extension of papal reservations.[6] As to England, Clement VI is reputed to have said that if the king of England asked him to appoint an ass as bishop, he would have obliged.[7] Only in the cathedral chapters was there a strong alien element of absentees. Similarly in any clashes between king and pope, as in France over secular and ecclesiastical jurisdiction,[8] the clergy were the sufferers and

[1] W. A. Pantin, *The English Church in the fourteenth century* (Cambridge 1955) 10 ff. See also M. Gibbs and J. Lang, *Bishops and Reform, 1215-72* (Oxford 1934) on which these calculations are based.

[2] See, however, J. R. L. Highfield, 'The English hierarchy in the reign of Edward III', *Transactions of the Royal Historical Society* 6 (1956) 115–38, who rightly warns against treating such categories as self-contained.

[3] Ibid., 56.   [4] Ibid.

[5] G. Barraclough, *Papal Provisions* (Oxford 1935), especially 153 ff.

[6] Mollat, *Les papes* 400.

[7] Quoted in Pantin, op. cit., 13, 56.

[8] Examples in Mollat, *Les papes* 400 ff.

the kings usually the gainers. At the same time the standard of education among the higher clergy rose steadily. Of the 78 aforementioned thirteenth-century English bishops, forty were university graduates;[1] and the proportion was still higher for Edward II's reign, with twenty-nine out of forty-five.[2] In 1302, Winchelsey, as archbishop of Canterbury, quashed the election of the prior of Ely because he had 'insufficient literature';[3] and in 1360 Robert Stretton, a clerk of the Black Prince, was examined and failed three times before finally being consecrated in 1360.[4] There were many ecclesiastics who were neither learned nor good, but there are no grounds to suppose that the clergy of the later middle ages were as a whole worse than those of the preceding age: quite the contrary. We have only to think of such names as Winchelsey, Luttrell, Grandisson, Bradwardine, FitzRalph, Stratford, Courtenay in England to recognize their high calibre. Among the lower clergy, on the other hand, improvement is less certain; and there can be no denying that much of the ammunition directed against the church was supplied by the endemic abuses to be found there, both among individuals and the system. To begin with, pluralism, non-residence and simony were inseparable from preferment at the hands of a donor whether king, monastery or lay lord. There was a constant pressure upon appointments, which was aggravated by the imbalance between demand and supply, leaving a large number of priests permanently without livings. It was no accident that unbeneficed priests were one of the mainstays of the Lollard movement in England and that there was frequent mention of priests in all the main heretical sects. Moreover, many of those installed as vicars received the meagrest stipends. Not surprisingly then, standards among the lower clergy were low, and they remained largely untouched by education as well as the other reforms of the church. Illiteracy was high and preaching largely non-existent; concubinage was frequent, and there was an incitement to exploit spiritual offices for money—one of the main charges of Wyclif and the Hussites as it had been in the twelfth century. For a time the friars undoubtedly filled the void, both as preachers and as confessors. But during the fourteenth century they became an even greater object of reprobation than the secular clergy, the target of Wyclif's later years as also of Chaucer's satire.

[1] Pantin, op. cit., 10. In Edward III's reign 57, or perhaps 60, were; but, on the other hand, the number of theologians had not increased from the 13 or 14 of Henry III's reign. Highfield, art. cit., 126.

[2] Pantin, ibid., 14.   [3] Ibid., 17.   [4] Ibid., 13.

The main gravamen of the attack upon the church and the religious orders in the later middle ages was financial and moral. In part this was the result of the papacy's increased centralization at Avignon, which led it enormously to extend the collation of benefices:[1] under John XXII's bull *Execrabilis* they came to cover all those where there was no title holder, so that there was no effective limit to papal nomination. Elective jurisdiction was virtually extinguished; those appointed had to render payment of their first year's income to the papal curia, which also received the revenues during vacancies. The demand for money was insatiable; it was needed to finance the papacy's Italian wars, which under John XXII took over 63 per cent of total expenditure,[2] and also, with Clement VI, the building of the new palace at Avignon. Even then, the popes had to resort to loans and other financial means. Not surprisingly papal demands caused a continuing outcry, and sometimes open opposition from ecclesiastics.[3] At the same time the mendicant orders had lost their dynamism; they were now just additional bodies of religious, enjoying similar privileges and endowments. Whether they were more lax, or whether it was from a sense of betrayal, they were more reviled than other groups by the later fourteenth-century critics —a far cry from a century before.

Now it was precisely this sense of betrayal which underlay most of the criticism of the later medieval church. It was directed at the contrast between the life of the present hierarchy and that of Christ and his apostles; and it came, as it had always come, principally from ecclesiastics, often those in the highest positions, like Nicholas of Clamanges, Dietrich of Niem, Pierre d'Ailly and John Gerson, who had seen at first hand the effects of the preoccupation with wealth. In an epoch when the church had ceased to be revivified spiritually, the demand was increasingly for its reform as an institution. It was focused upon the papacy in particular, whose financial exactions and, later, schisms, were seen as the source of its ills. It was here, in its failure to retain its authority and to satisfy the demands which confronted it as an institution, that its decline lay. The moral failings with which it was charged—simony, pluralism, immorality, greed, injustice—were common to the whole middle ages and indeed to all ages. The failure of the later medieval

[1] See Mollat, *Les papes* 527 ff.

[2] Ibid., 489.

[3] E.g. the ecclesiastics of the dioceses of Cologne, Bonn, Zanten, Soest and Mainz signed a pact of mutual assistance in 1372 not to pay the tenth demanded by Gregory XI. Mollat, *Les papes* 520-1.

church lay not in these but in the absence of a countervailing spirituality. Law, finance and government, all at a higher pitch than ever before, were the only alternatives it could offer.[1] But they were not a substitute for the fervour which had passed from its control with the waning of the mendicant orders.

The religious temper

These social and institutional developments in religious life were accompanied by correspondingly far-reaching changes in outlook. They were in large part due to renewed contact with the East and above all with the Moslem world.[2] From the first third of the twelfth century there had been an influx of new ideas: an amalgam of Aristotle's works, previously known only in certain books of his logic, some Greek science and medicine, and the main Arabian and Jewish systems of thinkers such as Alfarabi, Avicenna, Averroes, Avicebrol and Maimonides. The translations of these diverse works into Latin were, initially, overlaid by Neoplatonism, from which much of the true Aristotle was only gradually separated when the authentic Neoplatonic texts were translated later in the thirteenth century. At the same time, there were the Manichaean doctrines which underlay Catharism, and which came through the Bogomils in Bulgaria. Both kinds of ideas, in their different ways, were a challenge to Christian teaching; and to both the church offered resistance. But whereas much of the Aristotelian-Arabian corpus was adapted and incorporated into the Christian systems of the thirteenth century, Catharism was rejected outright and later combated by the inquisition. Nevertheless the more subversive notions of both permeated other sects. The dualist tendencies of Catharism were to be found among the Waldensians until the end of the fourteenth century, and the impact of Arabian and Greek concepts led to the spread of pantheism, determinism and mysticism. Whilst the first two, associated with the Amaurians (from Amaury of Bène, condemned with David of Dinant and John Scotus Erigena in 1210) and the Latin Averroists, were directly non-Christian, it was mysticism fed by thirteenth-century translations of Proclus, Plotinus and the psuedo-Dionysius which came to be one of the main streams of unorthodoxy. The search for God in the soul, with its emphasis upon inner experience, tended towards depreciating the sacraments and the mediation of the priesthood, even

---

[1] For an account of their development, see Mollat, op. cit., 441 ff.
[2] For what follows see Leff, *Medieval Thought*, 171 ff.

where it did not lead to identification of the soul with God, as it did with the Free Spirit. Mysticism became the complement to a life of withdrawal and quietism which was so strong an impulse among the Beguines and other extra-regular groups; but it also provided the justification for rejecting the authority of the church in favour of the authority found within. Hence in the search for new spiritual forms mysticism played an increasingly important part in the later middle ages.[1] In northern Europe it was centred upon the Rhineland and the Low Countries. To the so-called nuptial mysticism of St. Gertrude, Gertrude of Hackeborn and Mechtild of Magdeburg, was added a new speculative mysticism derived from Neoplatonism. Under the influence of Albert the Great it came to be associated with German Dominican houses, centred on the Rhine, especially Strasbourg and Cologne. Its greatest exponents were Dietrich of Freiburg and above all Meister Eckhart. Eckhart created a new school of Rhineland mysticism which, under his pupils Tauler and Suso, helped to give rise to the Friends of God, groups of spiritual men who practised austerity and detachment[2]—the orthodox counterpart to the clandestine groups of the Free Spirit. It also inspired Ruysbroeck (1293–1381) the greatest of the Flemish mystics. On the whole, however, speculative mysticism was as remarkable for the affinities which are to be found with it, in the pantheism of the Free Spirit, as for its influence upon mysticism as a whole. The phantasies of the Free Spirit were essentially a deformation of the same Neoplatonic source; and it is the one heresy to be ascribed to a doctrine rather than to an organized sect. For the most part, mysticism, especially from the second half of the fourteenth century, was subjective, often to the point of being indistinguishable from histrionics. Most of its exponents, with the marked exception of St. Catherine of Siena, who belonged to the Dominican third order, were laymen, either hermits or recluses as the English mystics, or lay groups, as with the *Devotio Moderna* founded by Gerard Groot at

[1] The best general account of medieval mysticism is by J. Leclercq, F. Vandenbroucke and L. Bouyer, *La spiritualité du moyen âge* (Paris 1961).

[2] The precise nature of the Friends of God is still far from clear, in particular the so-called Friends of God from Oberland, and Rulman Merswin, for whom see J. M. Clark, *The Great German Mystics* (Oxford 1949) ch. v. and P. Strauch, *Schriften aus Gottenfreundliteratur* (Halle) (1927–9). These are ramifications which lie beyond the scope of the present book, as indeed mysticism as a whole does. I have deliberately resisted the strong temptation to enter into an account of its development after Eckhart (for whom see ch. III below) since it would have taken us into another field and impaired the attempt to give unity to the present one.

Deventer in the Netherlands. St. Catherine was in the spiritual tradition of intense fervour and visionary denunciation of ecclesiastical abuses associated with Conrad of Offida (1237–1306), John of Parma (1209–88), Jacopone of Todi (1228–1306) Angelo of Clareno (1247–1337) and Angelo of Foligno (1248–1309). Similarly, of the fourteenth-century English mystics, only the anonymous author of the *Cloud of Unknowing* drew upon speculative concepts in his use of the pseudo-Dionysius's negative theology. The ramifications of these developments lie outside our scope; it is enough to stress the all-pervasiveness of mysticism as the dominant spiritual outlook of the fourteenth and fifteenth centuries. It was associated with almost every movement, orthodox as well as heterodox; it embraced the Dominicans and the Franciscans, the Brethren of the Common Life as well as the Free Spirit and the Fraticelli; and it extended to every land.

It was accompanied by parallel changes in the intellectual climate.[1] The later thirteenth and fourteenth centuries were punctuated by a series of condemnations, first of the determinism—and up to a point pantheism—associated with Aristotelianism and Averroism, and then later the reaction to these in Ockhamism. In their own way, universities represented a challenge to the comprehensiveness of the church no less than unregulated mysticism did; for the arts course had by the middle of the thirteenth century become based almost exclusively upon Aristotle's works. It meant that there was a body of non-Christian texts taught by professional philosophers as sufficient in their own right; they could be without reference to and untutored by theology—which belonged to a distinct and higher faculty and which might or might not be studied after graduation from the arts course. Accordingly profane non-Christian knowledge, especially at Paris, grew up side by side with Christian teaching. Their different conclusions, when taken by themselves, could conflict. The clash between them led to the Paris and Oxford condemnations of 1277 when altogether nearly 250 propositions inimical to Christian doctrine were proscribed.[2] This was a turning point; henceforth there was a gradual withdrawal from the attempt to apply reasons taken from natural knowledge to the tenets of faith. Faith and natural knowledge were increasingly treated as separate

[1] See Leff, *Medieval Thought* 176 ff., 224 ff.

[2] Of these 219 were condemned at Paris by the bishop Stephen Tempier, and 30 at Oxford by Robert Kildwardby, archbishop of Canterbury, eleven days later (18 March 1299). They are to be found in Denifle and Chatelain, I, no. 473, pp. 543–55, and no. 474, pp. 558–9.

domains. In emphasizing their independence Ockham and his followers stressed the complete freedom of God's will to the point where, logically, he could do anything save contradict himself.[1] In particular, this led to minimizing the importance of intermediaries between God and his creatures. God could dispense with supernatural virtues like grace, as well as natural causes. The uncertainty which flowed from such speculations caused growing concern to the authorities; and a first condemnation of 51 articles taken from Ockham's writings was followed by a series against his followers at Paris in the 1340s. Superficially, as we shall see, there was a correspondence between some of these propositions and those for which Eckhart and the Free Spirit were condemned: in each case it arose from a similar tendency—though from quite distinct premises—to by-pass intermediaries. It was one which, above all, struck at the authority of the church.

If these constituted the general conditions for the growth of heresy in the later middle ages, they invariably coalesced in a town or urban area or along important routes. Heresy, if not an urban phenomenon, had its *foci* in towns and comparatively populous regions, like Lombardy, Languedoc, the Rhineland, Flanders, Northern France, the Passau diocese—the meeting point between Bohemia, Austria and Bavaria, through which the Danube flowed. These were the main and continuing centres of heresy. In such regions, fostered partly by tradition and partly by physical factors, the necessary conditions for heresy were present: easy movement enabling the foundation of sects; congregations of populations from which they were drawn; concentration of wealth to support them either by mendicancy or manual labour; the existence of towns in which they could live either clandestinely or out of the reach of the church.[2] In this connexion it is noteworthy how much less

---

[1] See pp. 294 ff. below.

[2] It was the absence of such a combination of factors in England which largely accounts for the absence of heresy there until the time of Wyclif. Geography, in the shape of the English channel, acted as a barrier to the movement of heretics in significant numbers. (That they occasionally passed across it is to be seen from Henry II's prohibition against the heretics in the Constitutions of Clarendon. W. Stubbs, *Select English Charters*, 9th edn., pp. 172. But even here there is no clear evidence that they were heretics. See J. B. Russell, *Dissent and Reform in the Early Middle Ages*, 224 ff.) Strong government, through royal control of the English cities, prevented the kind of urban autonomy enjoyed in other parts of Europe. Consequently there was neither the scope for direct heretical inspiration nor the foci to sustain it, nor, as a result, a tradition to foster it. Each of these elements had to exist in varying degrees if a sect

frequent the denunciations of heretics were in the Italian towns—with their much greater autonomy from local bishops—than in those north of the Alps. But whether they enjoyed this autonomy or not, towns came nearest to being independent units with a distinctive life, which was either hostile, or indifferent, or less subject, to the behests of the church. It was there that both heretics and the mendicants went to spread their doctrines.

Towns were likewise the intellectual centres of society; they were the home of the schools and friaries, the sources of so much of the intellectual and spiritual ferment of the high and later middle ages. Not surprisingly, therefore, heresy was inseparable from urban life. To say this is not to deny that there were rural movements: a large part of the Waldensians lived clandestinely in the localities of central Europe and among the Alps, as did the English Lollards along the Welsh marches. But for them to be of more than local significance, indeed to be identified, they had also to be based on towns, as all the main sects were. Even the Hussites, who came closest to a national movement, had their nerve centre in Prague and a number of important cities. Towns were the yeast in the leaven; only by their ferment could ideas be set in motion and new sects emerge.

The inquisition[1]

Finally, there was the repression of heresy and the growth of the inquisition. It was a halting development; not until the pontificate of

---

was to come into being and survive. Franciscan poverty and prophecy in Provence and Italy, Rhineland mysticism, the universality of Waldensianism had no chance of happening in England where none of these factors was present. It is not without significance that Lollardy, when it came, was soon driven not only underground but to the borderlands of Wales and the West Country.

[1] There are many books on the inquisition. The most comprehensive is still H. C. Lea's *A History of the Inquisition in the Middle Ages* (3 vols., London and New York 1888); many of its facts have been superseded or supplemented, but it provides a conspectus which is all the more remarkable for being a pioneer work. No one involved in the study of medieval heresy can afford to ignore Lea, or fail to marvel at his achievement. Nevertheless, for all its mastery of the scene, Lea's volumes are almost entirely devoid of insight into its significance. He failed to appreciate that heresy was about life and death *issues* as well as life and death: for all his enumeration of the different heretical doctrines, he seems rarely to have grasped their meaning for either their adherents or their persecutors, or if he had it is certainly not communicated to the reader.

Among the more recent histories may be mentioned: M. Vacandard, *L'Inquisition*

Gregory IX was the machinery finally established. By then heresy had
been a problem for over a century. There had been cases of dualists
being banned as early as 1022 (at Orleans) by Robert II of France;[1] but
it was with Tanchelm at the beginning of the twelfth century that the
attention of the church was increasingly given to combating heresy. In
1119 a council at Toulouse denounced those who denied the sacraments.[2] At about this time there appeared two prominent heretics, in
Henry of Lausanne and Peter of Bruys, whose sects, the Henricians and
the Petrobrusians, infested parts of Southern France and Germany.[3]
First Peter the Venerable, abbot of Cluny, and later St. Bernard
preached against them. In the second half of the twelfth century France
and Lombardy were the two main areas of heresy. Already by 1147,
St. Bernard painted an alarming picture of religious decay in the county
of Toulouse:[4] churches without congregations; congregations without
priests; priests without ministries. Feasts were left unobserved and
births and deaths were unaccompanied by the sacraments. He attributed Henry of Lausanne's success to his pretence to piety in the
absence of priestly piety. But even St. Bernard's eloquence could not
revivify the church there. Catharism took increasing hold in Languedoc,
and in 1167 its adherents were able to hold a great council at Felix de
Caraman.[5] To it assembled delegates from all parts of the region as well
as from Saxony, France and Lombardy. Presided over by Niquinta,
pope of the Cathars, bishops were consecrated and other enactments
made for what had become an independent church.

Meanwhile, heresy was on the increase elsewhere. In Brittany, Eudes
of Stella was condemned in 1148 at the Council of Rheims as a Mani-
chee; he claimed that he had come to judge the world, and gained a

---

(Paris 1912); and article in *D.T.C.*, vol. 7, cols. 2016–68; J. Guiraud, *Histoire de
l'Inquisition au moyen âge* (2 vols., Paris 1935–8). This was to have been completed by
a third volume; as it stands it covers France, Italy and Spain, to the end of the thirteenth century. It contains the fullest account of events for these areas, but its un-
satisfactory arrangement is further marred by the lack of an index, making it difficult
to use. There is the same lack without the same excuse in Fliche etc., *La Chrétienté romaine*, which covers most of the thirteenth century. See also H. Maisonneuve, *Études
sur les origines de l'Inquisition* (Paris 1942); J. M. Vidal, *Bullaire de l'Inquisition française
au XIVe siècle* (Paris 1913); and A. S. Turberville, *Mediaeval Heresy and the Inquisition*
(London 1920). For other titles see bibliography at the end.

[1] Guiraud, *Inquisition* 1, 2. But see J. B. Russell, op. cit., for the view, often convincing, that many so-called dualists in the eleventh century were not dualist.
[2] Ibid., 3.   [3] Ibid., 3 ff.   [4] Ibid., 6.
[5] Ibid., 25.

following.[1] Others were discovered at Le Mans; there were groups of self-styled apostles[2] at Vézelay, and above all at Rome, under Arnold of Brescia, who preached the need for evangelical poverty and attacked the church for not following it: he was finally burned by Frederick Barbarossa in 1155.[3] But, excluding the Cathars, the most important new sect was that of the Poor Men of Lyons, founded by Peter Valdes, a merchant of that city, in about 1170. In his doctrine of poverty, and his life as a wandering preacher, Valdes closely resembled St. Francis a generation or so later; the difference was that whereas St. Francis was recognized by Innocent III, Valdes, after initially seeking approval from Alexander III, was prohibited from preaching by the bishop of Lyons and formally condemned by Lucius III, together with the Arnoldists, Cathars and other sects, at the Council of Verona in 1184.[4]

It was at this council that the foundations of the inquisition were laid. Not that reference to heretics had been absent from earlier legislation. The Council of Toulouse in 1119,[5] the Second Lateran Council in 1139,[6] the Council of Sens in 1140,[7] the Council of Rheims in 1148[8] and the Council of Tours in 1163[9] had all been in some degree concerned with heresy. The last named council under Alexander III had been the first to lay down the clergy's duty to enquire into any sects and to imprison their members and confiscate their goods. This did not amount to a new activity, but rather drew attention to an existing responsibility to act against heretics. By the time of the Third Lateran Council in 1179 this injunction had become a call to a crusade.[10] The intervening years since the Council of Tours had seen a progressive increase in heresy, above all in Languedoc and Lombardy. In Languedoc the strong anti-ecclesiastical tradition of Provençal society favoured the Cathars; in the face of widespread support for the heretics among the aristocracy, the clergy were unable to make any impact upon them. In Lombardy the autonomy of the towns correspondingly hampered the ecclesiastical authorities. To overcome the heretics, Christian lords in Gascony, Languedoc, Spain and Brabant were enjoined by the Council to take up arms against them and confiscate their goods. Here for the first time heresy was being treated as a universal malaise which concerned society as a whole and which must be warred against as the infidel was. Five years later at the Council of Verona general exhortation gave place to

---

[1] Guiraud, *Inquisition*, 14–15.   [2] Ibid., 13.   [3] Ibid., 28–9.
[4] Mansi, *Concilia* 22, 488.
[5] Ibid., 21, 226.   [6] Ibid., 532.   [7] Ibid., 559 ff.
[8] Ibid., 843.   [9] Ibid., 1177.   [10] Ibid., 231–2.

the first series of specific measures to extirpate heresy. The term now came to include groups of poor men—the Waldensians, the Arnoldists, the Passagini and the Josephini—as well as the Cathars, also called unwarrantedly Publicani and Patarines. In the Council's celebrated decree *Ad abolendum*,[1] which was the outcome of Alexander III's reconciliation with the emperor, Frederick Barbarossa, there were to be regular yearly or twice-yearly enquiries by archbishops, bishops, or their representatives, in their provinces and dioceses. They were to demand on oath from two or three reliable witnesses whether they knew of any heretics or conventicles; those refusing to swear were to be treated as heretics, and those accused of heresy were to appear before the archbishop's tribunal. The guilty were to be excommunicated and handed over to the secular authorities; cities which refused to co-operate were to be put under ban. None of these measures was in itself new; they were now regularized. Nor did they institute any new machinery; trial and judgement remained within the purview of the spiritual courts; only when they had passed sentence of excommunication, did the lay powers inflict condign punishment. The decree's importance lay in transforming these different elements into an active procedure; henceforth the clergy were systematically to act as inquisitors.

The next step came with Innocent III's practice of appointing special papal legates for specified areas. Although Innocent did not add to the existing laws on heresy, here, as in so much else, he gave the question a new significance. Heresy was no longer an isolated problem eliciting spasmodic attempts to treat it. It was now at the centre of his policy to reform the life of the church, intimately joined with his policy of fostering genuine evangelical piety of which St. Dominic's and St. Francis's bands were to be the most important expressions. Events were partly responsible for this change. Heresy was on the increase everywhere, and in Languedoc it threatened completely to overwhelm the ineffectual opposition of the church. This above all was the arena of Innocent's efforts against heresy, first by preaching and missions and then by war. The failure of one led to the other. It was due less to any inconsistency on Innocent's part than the ambivalence inherent in the problem: the primary aim was to win back men from error; but if this failed, then the church, in renouncing the attempt, renounced the culprit by handing him over to the secular arm for punishment. In theory the two phases were distinct; in practice they were interdependent. Coercion—whether by imprisonment or confiscation

[1] Ibid., 477.

(Innocent never envisaged burning) or arms—took over where conversion stopped, or, more accurately, failed.

The history of the suppression of the Provençal Cathars, or, as it is
generally known, the Albigensian Crusade, and of the events leading
up to it, is not directly our concern, since it lies outside the scope of this
book.[1] The main points may be briefly recounted. In 1199, soon after
his accession to the papal throne, Innocent III confirmed the constitution *Ad abolendum* in the decree *Vergentis in senium*.[2] He also began
sending Cistercians as missionaries to Languedoc, first simple monks,
then Peter of Castelnau and a little later, in 1203, the abbot of Cîteaux,
Arnold-Almaric. Their efforts as preachers and in public disputation
met with no success, while in mode of life their pomp and wealth put
them at a disadvantage compared with the evangelical simplicity of the
Cathar *perfecti*: a contrast that seemed to embody the Cathar belief in
the conflict between the material and the spiritual. It was not lost on
Innocent in his repeated disparagement of ecclesiastical decadence. Even
the band of dedicated missionaries under Dominic of Guzman, the
future founder of the Dominicans, who practised the same austerities
of poverty as the heretics, had no effect. The significance of both lots of
missionaries lay in the future: the full papal powers with which Innocent
invested the Cistercians foreshadowed those of the permanent inquisitors, although Innocent never considered them in that light; and
St. Dominic's missionary zeal was the germ of the Order of Preachers
who, *inter alia*, were to be the mainstay of the inquisition. In addition to
these spiritual disadvantages Innocent's representatives were handi-
capped by the support which the Albigensians had from the Provençal
nobility, with Count Raymond VI of Toulouse at their head: despite
his intermittent professions of orthodoxy, his sympathies seemed to lie
with the heretics. Innocent early turned to the French king for help:
between 1204 and 1209 he applied to him for support seven times.[3]
But Philip II had his hands full with John of England and was not
prepared to risk his gains of English territories in Normandy and
adjacent areas. Innocent for his part was concerned to enforce orthodoxy,
not to dismember Raymond's lands; and he only reluctantly accepted

[1] Among the numerous books mention may be made of Guiraud, *Inquisition* I and
P. Belperron, *La croisade contre les Albigeois* (Paris 1959).
[2] A. Fliche, C. Thouzellier and Y. Azais, *La Chrétienté romaine* 294; *Patrologia
Latina*, vol. 214, 537, and vol. 216, 1214.
[3] C. Petit-Dutaillis and P. Guinard, *L'Essor des Etats d'Occident* (*Histoire Génerale*,
ed G. Glotz, vol. 4, pt. 2; 2nd ed., Paris 1944) 64.

this unforeseen consequence in 1215. The catalyst which brought it about was the assassination of Peter of Castelnau in January 1208 by one of Raymond's followers. Innocent demanded Raymond's expulsion of the heretics, and, when it was not forthcoming, excommunicated him and absolved his vassals from fealty to him.[1] Raymond took fright and submitted to the pope's demands in June 1209. But too late. Innocent had already appealed to the northern French nobles for a crusade against Toulouse. Nominally under the conduct of Arnold-Almaric, it was soon in the hands of Simon de Montfort, a pious but brutal baron; neither Philip II nor his more important feudatories were involved. Like most such expeditions holy war soon became indistinguishable from mere war: towns were sacked, like Béziers; defenders were murdered; and inhabitants massacred. Within two years (1209–11) Languedoc submitted, Raymond being left with Toulouse and Montauban; the rest was carved up among the crusaders and the church, Arnold-Almaric receiving the archbishopric of Narbonne.

Raymond now obtained the intervention of his son-in-law in 1215, Peter of Aragon, after the latter had failed to gain assent to his becoming protector of Languedoc. But at the battle of Muret, in September of that year, his army was routed by Simon de Montfort and Peter was killed. Raymond took refuge in England. With the help of Philip II's son, the future Louis VIII, Simon now became count of Toulouse, a position which Innocent III finally recognized at the Fourth Lateran Council in December 1215. But Toulouse revolted and Simon was killed besieging the city. With his death the revolt spread: and Raymond's son, who succeeded his father as Raymond VII in 1222, regained most of his father's lands, despite a further intervention from the northern nobles in 1219. By 1223, most of the crusaders had fled leaving the surviving heretics to resume occupation. Such a state of affairs could not last indefinitely; and in 1225 Louis VIII, now king of France, having gained Simon de Montfort's rights to Toulouse, led a new crusade: Raymond VII had offered to submit to him but he was excommunicated. Louis rapidly overran the whole area, only Avignon offering resistance; when it was overcome, in September 1226, there was general submission, which not even the French king's premature death could undo. Raymond VII was forced to make his peace with the French regent at the Treaty of Paris in 1229. He retained his lands in Toulouse, Agenais and elsewhere. Four years later, in 1233, he promulgated the statutes for the hunting of heretics which introduced the

[1] Ibid., 65 ff. for a succinct résumé of the main events.

D

inquisition into France. Catharism lingered on until the first decades of the fourteenth century, but it had been effectively destroyed together with Provençal society. Like the Fourth Crusade, the Albigensian Crusade ended among the ruins of what it had sought to save.

But there was also a more positive side to Innocent's dealings with heresy and unofficial piety.[1] Although the Waldensians proper had gone too far from the church to be reclaimed, the pope was able to take similar groups under the church's aegis. Here Innocent displayed a consistency and insight which his predecessors lacked. His actions show how narrow the borderline between piety and heresy could be and how closely it depended upon the local factors. The banning by the bishop of Lyons of Peter Valdes and his followers from preaching was a decision which could as well have gone the other way, had there been the distinction between dogmatic and moral preaching which Innocent made for the Humiliati of Lombardy in 1201.[2] The latter differed from the Waldensians by continuing to live in their homes as opposed to being wanderers. Alexander III had forbidden them, together with the Waldensians, from preaching openly, and they too suffered excommunication.[3] But in 1201 Innocent, after a commission had sat for two years, constituted a group of them into a new brotherhood, made up of both a claustral order and a lay (or second) order of pious men and women living and working in houses, as well as a third order, the forerunners of the Franciscan and Dominican tertiaries: its members were not a community but lived simple, pious lives under supervision.[4] Innocent thus saved the Humiliati for the church, where the Waldensians had already become a counter-church. But he only proceeded against the Waldensians after having despatched three Cistercian abbots to Metz in 1199 to enquire into them.[5] Not even then did he take the step of indiscriminately proscribing all Waldensians, but formed a group under Durandus of Huesca (a converted Waldensian) in southern France, into the Catholic Poor in 1207.[6] They had to fight for survival against the hostility of the local clergy, and especially the bishops of Narbonne and Tarragona. Innocent III, in upholding them against the latter, repeated to them Durandus's warning against the perils of the church's failing to distinguish good from bad.[7] But despite the pope's support, the Catholic Poor did not long survive: an example of the pressures from within the church making for heterodoxy. Like

---

[1] These have been treated by Grundmann, *Religiöse Bewegungen*, ch. 1–3.
[2] Ibid., 61.   [3] Ibid., 65–6.   [4] Ibid., 71 ff.
[5] Ibid., 97 ff.   [6] Ibid., 100 ff.   [7] Ibid., 114.

the Beguines, Durandus and his company, in living on alms and preaching, were taken for heretics.¹ They were finally banned by Innocent IV in 1247 for unauthorized preaching; their remnant entered the Augustinian Hermits in 1256.² Another group under Bernard Primus,³ pledged to a similar life of vagrant poverty, was recognized by Innocent III in 1210. It suffered similar hostility from the authorities, and vanished after 1212.⁴ It was with the recognition of St. Francis's band that Innocent finally succeeded in harnessing evangelical fervour to the church. By that act, and in the support he gave to St. Dominic, he came nearest to fulfilling the aims of spiritual renewal which elsewhere had eluded him.

The regularization of the inquisition by Gregory IX was only a logical extension of what Innocent III had done. The Fourth Lateran Council had reaffirmed the two decrees of *Ad abolendum* and *Vergentis in senium*;⁵ and in order to make them more efficacious, the Councils of Narbonne (1227) and Toulouse (1229) ordered bishops to institute 'synodal witnesses' to make enquiries in the localities.⁶ Meanwhile there had been a series of enactments by secular rulers who had been urged on since the Third Lateran Council. The Council of Verona in 1184 had itself been set up through the joint efforts of Lucius III and Frederick Barbarossa. The kings of Aragon, Alphonse II in 1194 and Peter II in 1197, had both decreed the expulsion of heretics;⁷ but Peter II went further in including the death penalty among the punishments,⁸ although the practice of burning itself went back to the Roman Empire. In 1220 the emperor Frederick II decreed that all guilty of heresy were to be outlawed and their goods confiscated; if they remained unreconciled for more than a year they were to be treated as declared heretics.⁹ Frederick proceeded to enforce these measures aided by the papal legate, Ugolino, who, as Gregory IX, incorporated the decree into his register¹⁰ and made Innocent III's letter to the bishops of Viterbo and Orvieto in 1201 part of canon law by including it in his

¹ Ibid., 115. ² Ibid., 116–17. ³ Ibid., 118 ff.
⁴ Ibid., 124–5.
⁵ Maisonneuve, *Études* 114 ff., who points out that Innocent said nothing about punishment of heretics but only that their goods should be confiscated.
⁶ Ibid., 205; Mansi, 23, 19 ff.
⁷ Maisonneuve, ibid.
⁸ Mansi, 22, 673 ff.
⁹ Fliche, Thouzellier, Azais, *La Chrétienté romaine* 301; MGH. *Leges* IV, vol. II, 108–9.
¹⁰ Fliche, etc., loc. cit.; *Registers* (ed. L. Auvray) I, 539.

decretals.[1] In 1224 Frederick II went further. In a letter to the archbishop of Magdeburg, he directed the burning of convicted heretics,
or alternatively the cutting out of their tongues. Two years later, James
II of Aragon renewed Peter II's edict.[2]

Gregory IX took the final step in regularizing these different
measures in his constitution *Excommunicamus et anathematisamus*.[3] The
heretic condemned by the church was to be handed over (relaxed) to
the secular judge to suffer the due desert of burning. Sentences of excommunication were renewed against the main sects, including the
Cathars, Patarines and Poor Men of Lyons, as well as their accomplices
(*fautores*) and supporters, and whoever communicated with them or
failed to denounce them. All those so convicted were to be deprived of
their civil rights and excluded from public office. Preaching on matters
of faith was forbidden to laymen. All convicted of heresy were denied
Christian burial. The descendants of heretics down to the second generation were excluded from ecclesiastical office. Another decree provided
for perpetual imprisonment—the so-called wall (*murus*).[4]

During the next few years, these procedures became generalized into
a system: with burning, loss of rights, confiscation, and perpetual imprisonment, demolition of houses and financial penalties, went the
secrecy of trials, indictment on the evidence of undisclosed witnesses,
and above all the creation of a permanent body of inquisitors to give
them effect. Technically these differed from the secular clergy only
in having legatine authority from the pope to act within a specified
area. There was nothing new in this, as we have seen from Innocent
III's use of Cistercians and St. Dominic in Languedoc. Only now, their
jurisdiction was clarified and harnessed to a regular procedure. As
developed by Gregory IX, inquisitors were judges acting on papal
authority; they were delegated for a region over which they were
empowered to condemn and excommunicate heretics and their followers, and, as in the case of Conrad Marburg—appointed to oversee
south Germany in 1227—to put whole areas under interdict.[5] They
therefore had their power independently of the local bishop. Not that
one displaced the other. In May 1231, for instance, Gregory IX (at the
very time he was completing these developments) entrusted the arch-

---

[1] E. Friedberg, *Corpus iuris canonici*, II, Bk. V. tit. VII, 782. Fliche, etc., op. cit., 309.
Guiraud, *Inquisition* II, 404–5.
[2] Fliche, etc., ibid.
[3] *Registers*, I, 539. Friedberg, op. cit., II, Bk. V, tit. VII, c. 13, 787–9.
[4] *Registers*, ibid.   [5] Fliche, etc., ibid. 312.

bishop of Bourges with investigating heresy in the region of Rheims and Charité.[1] The episcopal inquisition was also active in Toulouse at the same period, where it worked in conjunction with Dominican preachers.[2] It was the gradual constitution of the two mendicant orders into regular full-time inquisitors which marked the full-fledged emergence of the papal inquisition.

In April 1233, the pope empowered the Dominicans to conduct a general inquisition into the provinces of Bordeaux, Bourges, Narbonne and Auch and ordered the Dominican general of Southern France to designate inquisitors for this task. At the same time Robert le Bourgre (an apostate Cathar) was made inquisitor for Northern France.[3] Already by the edict of Ravenna in 1232 Frederick II had extended his earlier anti-heretical legislation to the whole of the German empire;[4] and under Conrad of Marburg it was carried into Hungary and Bohemia. During the next twenty years the inquisition expanded. The Franciscans joined their Dominican confrères in 1238; further legislation was passed, notably by Frederick II in 1238 and 1239, and under Innocent IV, at the Councils of Narbonne (1244), Béziers (1246), Valence (1248) and Albi (1254).[5] It is noteworthy that both Gregory IX and Innocent IV, the implacable enemies of Frederick II, drew upon the emperor's anti-heretical legislation. This was one area where they united. Innocent IV in his bull *Extirpanda* also went further in authorizing torture, and formally incorporated Frederick's decree that condemned heretics should be burned as well as their houses destroyed.[6]

By the second part of the thirteenth century, the inquisition had become regularized. It was essentially a joint machinery operated by the mendicants, papacy and episcopacy in conjunction. Despite conflicts over jurisdiction among the friars and the local clergy, it is false to see them as mutually exclusive. Any drive to extirpate heretics demanded mutual co-operation. Even the forms of trial and condemnation presupposed a degree of assent between the inquisitors and representatives of the clergy and locality. A bishop had the same power of judging and sentencing as an inquisitor, and he continued to use it. Moreover much of the legislation was promulgated by archiepiscopal and episcopal synods, especially the councils held in Southern France during the pontificate of Gregory IX and Innocent IV. The council of

[1] Ibid., 314.
[2] Ibid., 316; Guiraud, *Inquisition* II, 35.   [3] Ibid.
[4] Fliche, etc., ibid., 313; and MGH. *Leges* IV, vol. II, 194 ff.
[5] Maisonneuve, *Études* 210 f.   [6] Ibid., 212.

Albi in 1254, to stimulate the zeal of laymen, offered a reward of one mark for every heretic taken.[1] Similarly the inquisition's activities in France were greatly aided by the support of St. Louis, the king, who in 1228 promised two marks for the capture of a heretic: the ordinances of that year have been described, with perhaps pardonable exaggeration, as making every Frenchman an inquisitor.[2] They were incorporated into the Treaty of Paris with Raymond of Toulouse in 1229. It led to the king and the count in 1242 jointly putting down a further revolt there, culminating in 1244 with the capture of Montségur and the burning of 200 heretics.[3] The weapon which had been largely forged against the Albigensians now virtually completed their destruction.

By the middle of the thirteenth century, then, a new permanent arm had been created to combat heresy. It covered most parts of western Christendom with the exception of England; and although it was never formally established there, the hunting of the Lollards at the end of the fourteenth century led to the introduction of much the same features— if not legal procedures—as those already in being on the Continent; the difference is that in England the operations remained in the hands of the ordinaries.

The procedures of the inquisition have often been described.[4] Here we may briefly mention the most important ones, since our concern with the inquisition will be in its operations rather than its formal aspects as an institution. Technically it constituted a court with plenary powers to try and condemn those suspected of heresy. The inquisitors were at once judges and prosecutors, who arrived at the verdict and passed sentence. This power—in effect absolute, despite qualifications— was exercised by inquisitors delegated by both the pope and ordinaries. In order to limit its abuses Clement V in the decree *Multorum querela*, passed at the Council of Vienne in 1312, laid it down that papal and episcopal inquisitors should act in conjunction.[5] The most singular feature of inquisitorial procedure[6] was that it could act on denunciations by anonymous witnesses and all cases were heard in secret. These led to a citation to appear before the inquisitor on a suspicion of heresy;

---

[1] Maisonneuve, *Études*, 219.   [2] Ibid., 222 ff.   [3] Ibid., 222–5.

[4] See particularly Vacandard article 'Inquisition' in DTC, vol. 7, 2016–68. Also Turberville, *Mediaeval Heresy*, pt. II.

[5] Clementines v, tit. III, ch. I., Friedberg, II, 1181 ff.

[6] What follows is based mainly upon Bernard Gui, *Practica Inquisitionis heretice pravitatis* (ed. C. Douais, Paris 1886). Summarized by G. Mollat, *Manuel de l'inquisiteur* I, XLIV ff.

it could be repeated on three successive Sundays or feast days.[1] Failure to appear rendered the accused contumacious and provisionally excommunicated, a sentence which became final at the end of a year. For known heretics an order of arrest was issued; it applied to the civil authorities who, together with any others involved in the capture, were reimbursed from the confiscated goods of heretics. Once before the tribunal, the accused was interrogated either by the inquisitor or his deputy in the presence of two ecclesiastics of standing,[2] with a notary to take down the deposition.[3] Since these were not recorded verbatim,[4] the notary was one of the central figures in an inquisitorial process. The interrogation was conducted without any of the ordinary accompaniments of civil law; guilt was established either by confession or on the testimony of witnesses, which, contrary to civil law, could be from perjurers, criminals and excommunicates.[5] Their validity rested with the judge,[6] who had recourse to the evidence of witnesses if he was unable to gain a confession. This was his primary aim; and coercion could be used to achieve it: imprisonment, fasts and torture, which while theoretically not to endanger life or limb,[7] led to numerous abuses, which Clement V sought to check in *Multorum querela* and *Nolentes.* How important coercion had come to be may be gauged from Bernard Gui's reaction against the safeguards which these decrees provided:[8] in fact, however, the need to get the assent of the bishop to the inquisitor's judgements was overcome by the inquisitors becoming the bishops' delegates.[9] In cases where the verdict was heresy, sentence was delivered through an assembly composed of local notables, ecclesiastical and lay; this was a safeguard against the miscarriage of justice, although it was mainly a formal one. Sentences were sometimes pronounced in a general sermon (*sermo generalis*) or *auto da fé*[10] where a number of cases were dealt with together; but they could as well be done individually. The penalties imposed by the court were restricted to those who abjured: hence they were regarded not as punishments but as penances, of spiritual benefit to those who had seen their error. For the obdurate, who refused to retract, the court could do nothing: they were excommunicated (if ecclesiastics, degraded)[11] and abandoned

---

[1] Douais, 4 ff. [2] Ibid., 188, 191.
[3] Ibid., 188, and 214. [4] Ibid., 243.
[5] Ibid., 214-15. [6] Ibid., 215. [7] Ibid., 284.
[8] Ibid., 174 and 188. [9] Ibid., 30.
[10] Mollat, *Manuel* II, 122 ff. for Bernard Gui's full description of it.
[11] Ibid., 144 ff. for an account of the procedure.

(or relaxed) to the secular power with the dishonest prayer to spare them from mutilation and death.[1] Even then, a last-minute supplication could be granted if followed by repentance and denunciation of any accomplices:[2] the prisoner would then be returned to the inquisitor for appropriate action.

There was a wide range of punishments: perpetual imprisonment, either solitary and in irons and on diet of bread and water (*murus strictus*), or a less restricted confinement (*murus largus*);[3] the wearing of crosses as a sign of infamy;[4] the performance of major or minor pilgrimages, lasting up to three or four months;[5] fines, which were supposed to defray the expense of the tribunal and be used for good works;[6] confiscation of goods, total for those abandoned to the lay power, even if they afterwards repented and were imprisoned:[7] in the case of France, the proceeds went to the king; elsewhere, in Italy and in Germany, they were shared, usually between the locality, the inquisition and the papal court. Finally houses in which heretics had sheltered were to be destroyed[8] and the inquisitor could employ their materials on building new edifices such as hospitals.[9] Heretics were deprived of all civil rights.[10]

The extraordinary jurisdiction exercised by inquisitors also extended to remission and commutation; by their right of grace they could exempt anyone from the worst penalties if he should come forward and confess his own errors or reveal those of others within a pre-scribed period, usually a month.[11] This so-called 'time of grace' was fre-quently used; nor, as Bernard Gui pointed out, was it unprofitable since it usually led to the capture of more heretics.[12]

The arbitrary nature of these procedures need hardly be stressed. Inevitably they led to cruelties and abuses; but they should not be exaggerated. It has been calculated that of a total of 930 condemnations by Bernard Gui, the inquisitor for Toulouse from 1307 to 1324,[13] 307 were imprisoned, and 139 relaxed to the secular arm[14]—a compara-tively small number for nearly a generation of one of the most intensive phases of inquisitorial activity in the middle ages. No total estimate for

---

[1] Douais, *Practica*, 127.   [2] *Manuel* II, 140 ff.
[3] Douais, 101, 102, 105, 152, 154, 159.
[4] Ibid., 37, 42, 89, 98.
[5] Ibid., 60 and 100.   [6] Ibid., 36–44, 50.   [7] Ibid., 19–25, 120–3.
[8] Ibid., 59, 160.   [9] Ibid., 60.   [10] Ibid., 60 ff.
[12] Ibid., 182–4.   [11] Ibid., 185.
[13] See *Manuel* I, VI ff.
[14] Ibid., LIII; figures taken from Vacandard, *Inquisition* 322.

the whole period is possible; but it is unlikely to have exceeded thousands. It is not however quantitatively that the importance of medieval heresy can be properly assessed. For this we must look to its significance for contemporaries. The fact that a whole elaborate machinery was created and extended to most parts of western Christendom is the best proof of it. From the time of Innocent III onwards heresy became one of the central preoccupations of church and secular power alike. It grew with the middle ages, just as heresy increasingly merged with criticism of the church and spiritual life.

Ultimately, medieval heresy must be measured by its impact upon society. From the later twelfth century until the sixteenth century, it was continually combated by an increasing array of forces. But it was never overcome: and in the heresy of the Hussites, and to a lesser degree the English Lollards and the Waldensians, passed into the Reformation. Such a progression in one form or another was inherent in medieval society: on the one hand, heresy was an inevitable accompaniment of dissent in a world of orthodoxy; yet the very process of defining one in relation to the other narrowed the area in which heterodoxy could remain uncondemned. In that sense heresy was the outlet of a society with no outlets. Their absence made tensions into explosions, and common aspirations the programme of sects. Only when the latter became independent churches did heresy lose its impact. Instrumental in the crisis of the later medieval church, it waned with the waning of the church's ecumenicality. That was the paradox. Medieval heresy arose from within medieval society and declined with its supersession. It was a catholic phenomenon concerned with the universal issues confronting a catholic society. As such it must be treated.

PART ONE

Poverty and Prophecy

I

The Disputes within the Franciscan Order

The coalescence of the doctrines of poverty and Joachism within the
Franciscan order during the later thirteenth century and the struggles
to which they gave rise in the fourteenth century are sufficiently well
known. Their consideration here is not another attempt to recount
them, nor is it even principally concerned with Franciscan history as
such. It is rather treated as the clearest—indeed the classic—instance of
heresy as the outcome of conflicting interpretations of common beliefs:
its evolution took place not only within the church among believers,
but among practising religious. It owed nothing to subversion or non-
Christian sources or the inspiration of heresiarchs. It was *par excellence*
heresy bred exclusively from Christian tenets. But its interest is more
than as a case history: Franciscan poverty and prophecy went far
beyond the confines of the Franciscan order; they became one of the
major preoccupations of Christendom during the first half of the fourteenth century, at once dividing the church and giving rise to a number
of heretical groupings outside it. There was thus something like a chain
reaction from doctrinal division to open heresy, from discord within
the hierarchy of the church to popular opposition towards it, or at
least, the papacy. While the process was neither direct nor simple, the
development from orthodoxy to heterodoxy, and eventually heresy,
can be clearly followed, the more so, as throughout, the issue was one
of Christian practice: the emulation of the poverty of Christ and the
Apostles as a way of life. To this end all theory was subordinated, or
rather it was theory conceived in terms of practice—that of poverty.

It was the central place of poverty which distinguished the Franciscan
disputes from the other main areas of heresy; for, while it may be conceded that they all turned on matters of belief and so ultimately of
religious practice, and that in all of them austerity of life or lack of
possessions played an important role, for the Franciscan order the
nature of poverty was *the* issue: the problem from the outset was, and
remained, one of observing its rigour; questions of definition arose as
a result of giving effect to it in daily life. Theory was called in to define
practice rather than the other way round. In this case in the beginning

was the deed—of St. Francis's mendicancy; the word came to clarify it, but stayed, as words so often do, to sow discord. As word succeeded upon word, theory became joined with practice, but never to the latter's exclusion or in independence of it; poverty remained about wealth and goods and the possession or lack of them. Similarly with the theories of Joachim of Fiore, they, too, came to be adjuncts of poverty, invoked to give it the sanction of history as much as to explain history. The greater the tribulations of the adherents to poverty therefore, the more they looked to Joachism to confirm them. Joachism of itself, without the sufferings of the zealots to nurture it, would hardly have attained the importance it took on; it largely revolved round poverty.

Nothing in the history of the struggle within the Franciscan order is more striking than this transformation of Joachism from an independent propheticism to a justification of Franciscan poverty. Joachim's conception of the third age, which formed the framework of his outlook, came to centre upon the struggle over poverty. As we shall see with Peter John Olivi and his followers like Ubertino of Casale the transition to the new order was seen in terms of a struggle against the present one, in which St. Francis would be the saviour. The apocalyptic element was focused upon the coming dénouement between the spiritual church, true to the principles of St. Francis, and the carnal church, the seat of worldliness and corruption. That the emphasis came to be put increasingly upon the iniquities of the popes, especially Boniface VIII and John XXII, did not alter the essential perspective of redemption through evangelical poverty or diminish the belief in a third dispensation. It likewise remained the focus of the Spirituals' followers, the Provençal Beguins and the different groups of Fraticelli in Italy; while in another predominantly legalistic form poverty became the source of the renewed conflict between John XXII and Michael of Cesena and his followers, the erstwhile opponent of the Spirituals. Even when the original participants in these disputes had passed from the scene their echoes were still to be heard, albeit indistinctly, until the fifteenth century among the heretical sects to which they had given rise.

Thus the struggle over poverty had widespread ramifications, embracing a diversity of groups and lasting for the greater part of a century. In particular it operated at two main levels. Firstly, in the Franciscan order itself between the rigorist minority, usually known as the Zealots or Spirituals, and the Conventuals or Community representing the majority as the official wing of the order. Secondly, there was the more popular level outside the order, made up of those who, like the Provençal Beguins, were simple lay followers of the Spirituals drawn from the populace of Provence, or who, like the Fraticelli and Michaelists, originated as Franciscan dissidents. In each case they gave a more popular and extreme expression to the same issues as those which divided the Franciscan order, the Fraticelli and the Michaelists ultimately becoming openly heretical. In view of this division, therefore, we shall consider each of these two aspects separately, devoting the present chapter to the dissensions among the Franciscans themselves and the next to their wider effects.

Within the Franciscan order the struggle over poverty was in two distinct phases, each separated from the other in kind as well as in time: that between the Spirituals and the Community which lasted effectively for over forty years from the 1280s until towards the end of the second decade of the fourteenth century; and that which broke out in 1321 over the doctrine of Christ's absolute poverty and involved the erstwhile leaders of the community under Michael of Cesena, the order's general, in conflict against Pope John XXII. Although the issue for both was poverty, the principles raised were so different that they bore only the most formal resemblance to one another. The struggle of the Spirituals involved the entire conception of poverty as a way of life and the path to redemption; it raised the question of the nature of the Franciscan order, in which the Spirituals' strong sense of evangelical mission fostered their Joachist leanings; these traits were intensified under persecution at the hands of the Community and John XXII. By 1320 the Spirituals as a movement within the order had been effectively crushed, leaving only a legend of martyrdom among the Beguins of Provence and excommunicated groups of Fraticelli in central and southern Italy and Sicily.

The controversy over the poverty of Christ, on the other hand, was from the outset predominantly theoretical and legal: it concerned poverty as it affected the order's standing rather than as an end in itself; it was directed less to some divinely ordained goal than to the status of Christ's mendicant life as justification for the order's existing way of life. That this, too, led ultimately to the banning of the pope's opponents and the growth of a new heretical sect—that of the Michaelists or Fraticelli de opinione—should not obscure these fundamental differences. The discord over the doctrine of the poverty of Christ bore little affinity to the evangelical poverty preached by the Spirituals. It was more in the nature of a coda to the Community's position that poverty consisted in the renunciation of proprietorship rather than in a life of rigorous austerity. Each represented a different—even contradictory—element in the Franciscan order, the juxtaposition of which goes far to explain the dissensions within it. We must now examine each in turn.

The legacy of St. Francis

The struggle over poverty between the Spirituals and the Community arose out of the very evolution of the order. What began as a personal quest by St. Francis and a handful of followers was gradually transformed into an organized way of life, embodied in an institution which, to remain in being, demanded the possessions and organization St. Francis had shunned. It was from this contradiction that conflict sprang. Ultimately, St. Francis's conception was too immediate and too individual to bear the weight of a hierarchy; it was more suited to an eremetical than a conventual life. St. Francis had been the first to see this, in his withdrawal from the leadership of the order probably before 1219[1] as the need for authority grew. Nakedness in all its forms, of the body as well as the mind, was for him the only state appropriate to a true vision of the naked Christ on the cross. The difference between St. Francis and the Conventuals was the difference between thinking in terms of the primitive life of Christ, and the apostles, and the corporate life of the church; it was a difference in images—or to employ current terminology—models. Neither was necessarily more authentic than the other; they were from divergent starting points and followed divergent paths. As such they were from the outset incompatible; and the attempt to merge the two in the end made them irreconcilable. St. Francis was distinguished above all by his identification with the life of Christ. This went beyond taking Christ and the apostles as examples merely to be followed externally, to an intensely personal recreation of Christ's own experiences. The parallels are plain and have been noted in the past.[2] They include the use of phrases like 'peace be to this house';[3] fasting for the same period of forty days as after Christ's baptism, from Epiphany to Easter;[4] sending out his followers in pairs to preach;[5] and so on. It was stated verbally in the opening words of the first extant

[1] The case for 1217 or 1218 has been argued by Mrs. R. B. Brooke in *Early Franciscan Government* (Cambridge 1959), 76 ff.

[2] For a recent description see M. D. Lambert, *Franciscan Poverty* (London, 1961), 53 ff.   [3] Ibid., 54.   [4] Ibid., 55.   [5] Ibid.

rule of 1220: 'This is the life of Jesus Christ's gospel, which brother Francis sought from the lord pope';[1] it was reiterated in a modified form in the second rule of 1223 confirmed in a bull from Honorius III: 'This is the rule and life of the brothers minor, namely to observe the holy gospel of our lord Jesus Christ by living in obedience, poverty and chastity.'[2] It finds its supreme expression three years later in his stigmatization with the wounds of Christ, a happening which his followers subsequently took as giving a divine imprint to his life and work. Accordingly, both they and St. Francis took their authority directly from Christ.

This intimate dependence of one upon the other made St. Francis's conception at once more personal and inflexible than that of other religious orders. He saw his rule as the direct outcome of a divine revelation that he was to live according to the gospel. No one else had pointed his path for him. He had simply put into a few simple words what God had ordained, and the pope, Innocent III, had subsequently confirmed.[3] They therefore allowed of no modification; for it was from God not from man. St. Francis's vehemence here may not unjustly be seen as one of the sources of future division. 'The lord called me by the way of simplicity and showed me the way of simplicity. I do not want you to mention to me any rule, either of St. Augustine, or St. Benedict or St. Bernard.'[4] Such was his reply to the friars who looked to a more settled dispensation. For St. Francis the pattern of the order had been established in heaven, once and for all time. Accordingly its sanctity was inviolable; and from this it was but a short step to treating its amendment as betrayal. St. Francis did not; but the Spirituals as his self-appointed descendants did. Conflict was endemic from the first.

The most heightened form in which St. Francis expressed this attitude is undoubtedly his Testament.[5] For long regarded as the

---

[1] H. Boehmer, *Analekten zur Geschichte des Franciscus von Assisi* (Leipzig 1904), *Regula non bullata quae dicitur prima*, 1. In the 3rd ed., Tübingen, 1961, the pagination has been changed.

[2] 'Regula et vita minorum fratrum haec est, scilicet domini nostri Jesu Christi sanctum Evangelium observare vivendo in obedientia, sine proprio et in castitate', *Regula confirmata* (ibid., 29).

[3] Et postquam Dominus dedit michi de fratribus, nemo ostendebat michi quid deberem facere, sed ipse Altissimus revelavit michi quod deberem vivere secundum formam sancti evangelii. Et ego paucis verbis et simpliciter feci scribi et dominus papa confirmavit michi (ibid., *Testamentum* c. 4, 37).

[4] Ibid., 86.   [5] Ibid., 36–40.

E

pinnacle of St. Francis's thinking, written at the very end of his life, it has recently come in for demotion as just another of his numerous declarations of faith which in its partiality has no special claim to pre-eminence.[1] We may grant the premises without accepting this con-clusion. None of St. Francis's writings is the work of ratiocination; all are intensely personal statements of intense religious feeling, expressing the mood of the hour; but they were nevertheless part of a unified outlook and like the colours of the spectrum they all reflected the same source. The recent tendency to exaggerate the inconsistencies in St. Francis is as psychologically jejune[2] as the older view of undeviating persistence. Like most men his consistency was that of ultimate equili-brium between different pulls, not a tightrope; but while this might entail periodic contradictions between one position and another there was an underlying unity, a fulcrum to which they returned. If St. Francis's Testament emphasized certain things to the exclusion of others this was because it was a final statement of his fears and wishes; while these might be matters of the moment which differed from those in his previous pre-Testament at Siena,[3] and might have been different again had he lived to make another, their import is in keeping with what he had always held. Little in it is new; and in view of the significance which it was to have for the Spirituals in the future its contents are worth considering. In the first place its emphasis was upon the divine nature of his conversion from a life of sin to that of a Friar Minor.[4] Secondly, he stressed his faith in and obedience to the church, whose priesthood he wished 'to fear, love and honour as his lords'[5] and whose sacraments were the corporeal expression in this world of Christ's body and blood.[6] Thirdly, he restated the primitive ideal of the order: the

[1] See K. Esser, *Das Testament des heiligen Franziskus von Assisi* (Münster-i-W 1949) whose conclusions are discussed in Lambert, op. cit., 22 ff.

[2] Lambert, op. cit., 29 treats Esser's evaluation of the Testament as 'having done away with its special position among the writings of St. Francis'. But this is to beg two vital questions: First, by what criterion is one work to be judged more authori-tative than another? Because a man writes a work in a period of great emotion this does not disqualify it; indeed it may reveal more of his inner thoughts than a more considered statement. Second, to what or to whom does its 'special position' refer? From the point of view of the subsequent history of the order it was for the Spirituals just that special position which made it so important. For posterity St Francis's insistence that it was to be inseparable from the rule allows of no honest choice other than to accept its authority, especially when its difference from his past declara-tions was one of emphasis.

[3] Esser, op. cit., quoted in Lambert, 25 n.1.

[4] Boehmer, op. cit., nos. 1, 2, 3, 4, 36–7.   [5] Ibid., no. 3, 36.   [6] Ibid.

requirement of every postulant to give all that he had to the poor and to be content instead with one patched tunic and no more;[1] the injunction to voluntary manual labour for work's sake and not for gain;[2] and when their labour had been unrewarded to beg from door to door.[3] Fourthly, there was a warning against possessions and privileges. They were to treat their churches and habitations not as their own, but, in keeping with holy poverty, merely as the dwelling places of wanderers and pilgrims.[4] Nor were they to seek from the pope any special favours.[5] Fifthly, the firm obligation upon all brothers to obey their superiors was reinforced by St. Francis's own declaration that he wished 'to be a captive in their hands'.[6] Finally, there were the injunctions on how to treat the Testament and the rule. The Testament was not to be taken as another rule but as St. Francis's exhortation for best observing the existing rule. They were to be kept together for ever and both read at chapters. Neither was to be glossed but to stand in the words which God had given to St. Francis *simpliciter et pure*.[7]

These were the main provisions of the Testament. Their consonance with St. Francis's outlook as a whole is indisputable. All the main elements were there: the divine inspiration of the rule coupled with the equally divine authority of the church, to which unfailing loyalty and obedience were due; the love of Christ as expressed corporally in the eucharist no less than in devotion to his earthly life; the sanctification of poverty and simplicity and the abhorrence of privilege, together with the need for almost blind obedience to superiors. Apart from the explicit disavowal of papal concessions the one new feature of the Testament was its own addition to the rule and the binding nature of both. It was St. Francis's gloss to end all glosses; and its significance lay in its irrevocability, not its contents. With all its omission of detail— such as the ban on money or horse-riding—it was in essence a restatement of St. Francis's deepest beliefs. No one could call it a document of revolt or even an unreasoning *cri de cœur*; it preserved the balance between the demands of evangelical mission and ecclesiastical obedience; and as always in St. Francis's legal declarations there was more about discipline than poverty. He envisaged his own role within the framework of the church's authority. From the same Lord came both his devotion to the church and the knowledge of 'what ought to be

[1] Boehmer, op. cit., no. 4, 37.
[2] Ibid., no. 5.
[3] Ibid., no. 5, 38.
[4] Ibid., no. 7.
[5] Ibid., no. 8.
[6] Ibid., nos. 9 and 10, 38–9.
[7] Ibid., no. 11, 39.

done', which was inscribed in his rule. Emulation of Christ's life was the foundation of St. Francis's ideal; but its pursuit was set firmly within the sacramental life of the church. Faithfulness to the rule went with obedience to superiors, within the order and outside it. Francis had practised both, but it was a balance which could soon be upset, as it was within a few short years. With Gregory IX's bull *Quo elongati* of 1229 the testament was set aside.[1] Henceforth what had hitherto been a statement for the whole order increasingly became the manifesto of a minority. Loyalty to St. Francis was contraposed to submission to authority; the Testament was put against papal decrees.

These were the issues which were to divide the Spirituals and the Community; they arose out of the very circumstances which followed St. Francis's own departure from the scene. Where for him there had been but one voice—of God speaking to him through the church—for his successors his own voice came to have an authority of its own. This was where the Spirituals diverged; it renders any attempt to make St. Francis one of them unreal. The Spirituals arose as a reaction against modifying St. Francis's ideal. However much they both shared the same devotion to evangelical poverty, for the Spirituals it was also a doctrine of revolt through which they set up the authority of St. Francis against that of their superiors and ultimately the papacy. Poverty thus became transformed from an adjunct to the life of the church into a challenge against it: from an end in itself into the signal for the end of the existing dispensation.

The extent of the divergence between St. Francis and the Spirituals is the best testimony to the changes in interpretation which the same ideas can undergo. The most discrepant conclusions may issue from common premises, as we shall repeatedly have occasion to observe. When it occurs, the cause seems invariably to be less from any initial difference in conception than subsequent interpretation. This is usually to be sought in circumstances; and in the case of the Franciscan order in the early—and indeed inevitable—contradiction between the primitive ideal of St. Francis and the growing demands for regulation and government.

That the issue was over evangelical poverty was of the essence of the conflict. It is this which distinguished the Franciscans from the Dominicans and accounts for their vicissitudes. Had it been anything else, even learning—against the vanity of which Francis was ever on guard—it is hard to imagine a struggle of comparable magnitude. For

[1] See pp. 65 ff. below.

poverty is the one ideal which, if followed literally, militates against growth and ultimately coherence; in its full rigour it entails vagrancy, or at the very least, impermanence, and the absence of all possessions, including books; it thus denies the means by which any but the most immediate contact between its adherents can be maintained. The limitations which it demands are appropriate only to small groups; for a body numbering hundreds, let alone thousands, scattered over a continent, it becomes a contradiction in terms. It was a contradiction which St. Francis never resolved, although his own retirement from the leadership, to become simply a brother in the order, suggests perhaps an awareness of it. It was accentuated by St. Francis's devotion to the example of Christ, which he took as a complete lack of possessions save what was needed to maintain life by begging or manual labour. St. Francis was so imbued with this ideal that at no time did he attempt to amplify it in any detail. He merely took it as the pattern for his own life and that of his followers. How central it was can be seen from the nature of his allusions to it; it was the support upon which everything else rested rather than a specific adornment. Almost invariably poverty was coupled with references to Christ's life, the two, inseparable in themselves, forming the basis of Franciscan life. Thus, as we have already mentioned, each of the rules of 1221 and 1223 (as well as the references to the first unrecorded rule of 1201[1]) begins with a declaration of allegiance to the evangelical life of Christ: in the words of the rule of 1221, 'to live in obedience, chastity and poverty and to follow the doctrine and footsteps of our lord Jesus Christ, who said (Matt. 19: 21) "If you would be perfect go and sell all that you have and give it to the poor, and you shall have treasure in heaven . . ." '.[2]

This conviction that the example of the life of Christ entailed complete poverty was reiterated throughout St. Francis's different pronouncements. The same rule speaks of the need for all brothers to emulate the 'humility and poverty of our lord Jesus Christ' who should have nothing in the world beyond the food and clothing mentioned in I Timothy, 6: 8.[3] They should, moreover, rejoice in the company of 'pauperes, et debiles, infirmos et leprosos', while begging.[4] The latter should cause them no shame; but should be remembered the better from the example of Christ 'who for us became poor and a wanderer (hospes) and lived on alms, and also the blessed Virgin and his disciples'.[5]

---

[1] Boehmer, op. cit., 88–9.
[2] Matthew 19: 21, Regula non bullata I; Boehmer, op. cit., I.
[3] Boehmer, ibid., 9, 9–10.   [4] Ibid., 10.   [5] Ibid.

Alms were the 'inheritance and the justice which Jesus Christ our lord gained for us', and those who earned them by their labour deserved them most. Only that which was from charity and alms would survive this world and be rewarded by God.[1] Poverty was therefore the highest honour as well as a bounden duty for those who wished to follow Christ: renunciation of the goods of this world was the condition of entry to Christ's brotherhood.[2] As he quoted Luke (14: 33), in his Admonition on Perfect Obedience: 'He who does not forsake all that he possesses cannot be my disciple.'[3]

Now this conception went beyond merely material considerations; it represented an attitude of self-abnegation, of disavowal of man's earthly nature. St. Francis's sublime sense of wonder at the marvels of the world, his capacity to rejoice in the birds and flowers and sun, had its counterpart in his deep aversion from sin. His love of Christ went with his loathing of human infirmities and anything that ministered to them. 'Let us hate our body with its vices and sins, for by living carnally it wants to take from us our love of Christ and eternal life, and lose itself and all things in hell.'[4] Sin has made us impure; from 'out of the heart of men proceed evil thoughts, adulteries, fornications, murders, thefts, covetousness, wickedness, deceit, lasciviousness, an evil eye, blasphemy, pride, foolishness' (Mark 7, 21: 22).[5] Purity of heart consisted in despising the things of this world and seeking those in heaven.[6] We could not therefore seek wisdom or prudence in our natural state, but rather strive to be simple, humble and clean. We should hold our bodies in contempt since, through sin, we were all wretched and impure. Rather than desire to rise above others, we should subordinate ourselves to all human kind on account of God.[7] Accordingly, we may see St. Francis's ideal as the liberation of the spirit from its earthly toils: at once a rejection of worldliness and of submission to the world. On the one hand it was a refusal to pander to carnal desires and to seek relief from sin by indulging its cravings; on the other, it demanded open confrontation with man's wretchedness and a turning to God for salvation. This meant following the path of Christ in a life of humility,

---

[1] Boehmer, ibid. These are paralleled by similar passages in the rule of 1223 (e.g. 6, Boehmer, ibid., 32–3, which do not seem to lessen their previous force).

[2] Boehmer, op. cit., *Regula prima* 22, 19.

[3] Boehmer, ibid., *Verba admonitionis* 3, 42.

[4] Ibid., *Regula prima*.   [5] Ibid., 20.

[6] Ibid., 20. *Verba admonitionis* 16, De munditia cordis.

[7] Ibid., 53 *Epistola ad fideles* 9.

poverty and obedience to God; each was inseparable from the other: humility meant poverty of spirit[1] just as perfect obedience meant renunciation of all possessions.[2] Remove one and the others fell away. Thus unmitigated and all-embracing poverty was integral to such a conception; it was not a separate vow which could be detached or modified, but the tangible expression of the spirit of humility and obedience to Christ: the only state appropriate to his emulation: the way of apostolic life.

It is hardly surprising, then, that St. Francis never sought to give precision to this idea; it sufficed that Christ and the Virgin and the apostles were the examples. For that reason in neither of the two extant rules nor in his other writings did St. Francis go beyond a general admonition against possessions. Each of the rules has one sentence expressly devoted to the subject of property: that of 1221 stated that 'they were not to appropriate any place to themselves or retain it';[3] that of 1223 somewhat more comprehensively extended the ban to 'homes, places or things'.[4] Nothing was said of public possessions for the order as a whole, nor should it be expected. The whole tenor of St. Francis's injunctions was utter renunciation for Christ just as Christ had given his life for his Father.[5] It is therefore idle to look for conceptions like dominion or property or formulated distinctions between proprietorship and use. Everything written by St. Francis or about him points unerringly to his abhorrence of all possessions. To give all that one had was, as we have seen, the condition of true apostleship; and the converse seems to have been equally true: namely that nothing should be held in proprietorship. Perhaps the clearest indication of this was the incident at Rivo Torto, Assisi, where St. Francis and his companions left the shed in which they had lived at the coming of a peasant with his ass.[6] Here the provision that the brothers should not exclude others by appropriating a place to themselves can only be taken to apply to them as an order, not just as individuals. A similar disavowal of property is also to be seen in the initial refusal of St. Francis to accept a new building

[1] Ibid., 46 . . . qui vere pauper est spiritu, se ipsum odit et eos diliget *Verba admonitionis* 14.
[2] Ibid., 42. Dicit dominus in evangelio (Luke 14, 33): 'Qui non renuntiaverit omnibus que possidet, non potest meus esse discipulus . . .' *De perfecta obedientia*.
[3] Ibid., *Regula non bullata* 7, 8.
[4] Ibid., *Regula bullata* 6, 32.
[5] Ibid., *Epistola ad capitulum generale* 6, 61.
[6] I. Celano, *Legenda S. Francisci* (*Analecta Franciscana* x, 44), quoted in Lambert, *Franciscan Poverty*, 44.

for the brothers from the municipality of Assisi—and his attempt to pull it down—until it was explained that it belonged to the commune and not to him.[1] If this contains the germs of the later arrangement between papal dominion and Franciscan use, there seems little doubt that for St. Francis its application was restricted to the barest necessities and that he would have regarded its extension to cover gifts and endowments as a betrayal of his ideal. It seems inconceivable that one who showed such a revulsion against all superfluity could have countenanced for the order what he prohibited for the individual brothers. Money he regarded with especial repugnance; the prohibition upon it was absolute. It was, he said, the work of the devil to blind those who received it.[2] If found it was to be treated as the dust beneath their feet and anyone touching it as an apostate and thief.[3] It was also the one payment which was never to be received for labour or taken as alms.[4]

The temper of St. Francis's outlook towards poverty here and elsewhere was far closer to the Spirituals than to the Community. The austerity of a life reduced to the barest minimum for bodily needs, which he prescribed, set the standard for the Spirituals. Their ideal of the *usus pauper* was of the same order as St. Francis's practice; 'his habit was sordid, his person contemptible and his face unkempt (*indecora*)' wrote an eyewitness of St. Francis's appearance.[5] It expressed his belief that 'we should hate our bodies with its vices and sins'.[6]

The legacy left by St. Francis to his followers, then, was a state of mind as much as—if not more than—a code of conduct. It sprang from a mystic sense of communion with God which sought expression in active emulation of Christ's life rather than inner withdrawal. This was its distinctiveness; its medium was that of men living evangelically and preaching the gospel. Herein lay the difficulty of attempting to codify it into a rule: it was to generalize an experience, of its nature essentially personal; to put into words what were primarily images; to invest symbols with a precision which they could never adequately bear. What for St. Francis was an inseparable unity could too easily be pulled apart into conflicting strands where obedience vied with poverty, and righteousness with humility. To this extent both parties deviated from St. Francis's own example and precepts. Yet it could be argued that, had he been under the same duress as those who shared his ideal of

---

[1] Lambert, ibid., 45.   [2] Boehmer, *Regula non bullata* 8, 8.
[3] Ibid., 9.   [4] Ibid.
[5] Ibid., *Ex Thomae historia pontificum Salonitariam et Spolatensium* 106.
[6] Ibid., *Epistola ad fideles* 52-3.

poverty, he would have been driven into self-imposed exile, even though not revolt. His Testament bears witness to his adamantine insistence upon the order's *status quo*. However one regards the circumstances which made for the mitigation of poverty, its occurrence cut at the root of St. Francis's belief; it not only opened up a schism within the order, but the strife which it engendered took both parties away from their founder's behests. St. Francis would no more have identified himself with the recalcitrant apocalypticism of the Spirituals than the evasive legalism of the Community. But this must not be allowed to blur the difference between them. The Spirituals, for all their excesses, were St. Francis's true heirs; their very extremism was an extension of his. In essence they asked for no more than he: the right to follow the same path of self-abnegation. It was refusal which made them rebel, where St. Francis would have retired. But they shared the same source; and when given the opportunity—as with Liberato's and Angelo's band—it took a similar form in a life of poverty and simplicity.

The ambiguities, then, which the Franciscan order inherited came from the very unambiguousness of St. Francis's vision. Its simplicity transcended the complexities of words. On the one hand, the prohibitions on poverty, money, and horse-riding, the limitations on the number of tunics, the regulation of discipline, were perfunctory just because they were completely assumed. On the other, the problem of buildings and organization were virtually ignored because they had no place in the ideal of evangelical poverty; above all, poverty itself was more implied than stated. Trouble arose, as it was bound to, when the direction of the order passed into other hands, and its pattern changed from that of a band living according to the model of Christ and the apostles to a mass movement. Organization challenged ideal, and conflict could only have been averted had one ceded to the other. In fact they did not. It became an issue between one firmly constituted order, in which its demands as a body came before the precepts of its founder, or small groups pledged to poverty. It was along these lines that the order divided, until the cumulative effect of the Community's denial of poverty, in practice, led to its abrogation in theory by John XXII. By then, however, the Spirituals, as the true disciples of poverty, had been vanquished; and it only remained for their victors to suffer for a form of words whose substance they had never honoured.

From an early stage in the order's history the question of poverty was never far from the forefront. The extreme form in which St. Francis had conceived it was incompatible with great numbers and responsibility: preaching, learning and participation in the life of the church, entailed the stability, organization and buildings against which St. Francis had enjoined. The conflict had already been apparent in St. Francis's lifetime; and his awareness of it can be discerned in his Testament. The need to overcome it formed one of the guiding threads in the order's development over the next eighty years; it engaged the attention not only of its leading members but of successive popes. The intervention of the latter, although intended as arbitration, became itself one of the main sources of discord, since in the eyes of the Spirituals it represented the very glossing of the rule, against which St. Francis warned in his Testament. It was, therefore, a derogation of its sacrosanctity and an added cause of their own intransigence against authority. Ultimately the Spirituals came to be associated with opposition to papal intervention while the Community upheld it.

We may, for convenience, distinguish three main phases in the dispute over poverty. First, from the death of St. Francis to 1279 and the bull *Exiit qui seminat*, during which the two rival doctrines of poverty gradually became defined. Second, the nearly forty years of open struggle from c. 1280 until c. 1318 between the Spirituals and the Community, where the Spirituals' belief in absolute poverty became joined to a Joachist conviction that the sufferings of its adherents marked the end of the present era and the coming of a new age. Third, the aftermath with the final condemnation of the doctrine of evangelical poverty by John XXII in 1323: the subsequent history of its defenders forms part of the next chapter.

The modification of poverty

The first period is from our point of view more in the way of a prologue to the main struggle between the Spirituals and the Community. It saw the gradual crystallizing of their different viewpoints. On the one hand, the official regulation of the order's affairs in three papal bulls legalized its poverty. On the other, its essentially formal nature, adapted to the needs of large-scale organization with far-reaching apostolic responsibilities, only served to emphasize its distance from St. Francis. Increasingly the issue became one of practical observance rather than theoretical acceptance of poverty itself. It is not too much to say that it was official adhesion to the ideal of absolute poverty, both within the order and the papal curia, which lay at the root of the trouble; for it posited a universal criterion which, from the nature of the order's standing as one of the two new major religious movements, invited deviation. The pledge to absolute poverty at a time when buildings, schools, books and the wherewithal to provide them were ever more in demand, could be little but a legal fiction; even more, it inevitably affected standards of behaviour as well: the friars became accustomed to their own churches, to being involved—if only indirectly—in commercial transactions, in having libraries, in living at a degree of comfort far removed from that of St. Francis and his first disciples. In these circumstances the concept of absolute poverty became a standing reproach —a source of discord rather than a common bond.

The process began within three years of St. Francis's death in 1226. In 1229 Gregory IX, who as Ugolino,[1] had been cardinal protector to the order, issued the bull *Quo elongati*.[2] This took the form of a series of replies to the queries of the brothers over important matters in the rule. Its two most momentous provisions concerned the St. Francis's Testament and possessions. The first was declared invalid because it had not received the assent of the ministers of the order; it was not therefore binding upon St. Francis's successors.[3] This seeming technicality was to be of the greatest consequence. In effect it freed not only the order but also the papacy from any obligation to treat the rule as inviolate, since one of the main points of the Testament had been its solemn prohibition on glossing the rule or receiving papal letters.

This was recognized in the bull; and in stating it first, it cleared the ground for that very papal intervention against which the Testament had warned. Thus *Quo elongati* introduced a new principle: in permitting the rule to be glossed, it, by implication, contraposed papal authority to the authority of St. Francis. However faithfully Gregory IX and his successors believed themselves to be acting in the true interests of the order and according to the true wishes of its founder, they were in effect arrogating legislative power to themselves. The rule, whatever they might say, was not, as it stood, sacrosanct. Hence from the outset the question of authority became inseparable from the question of poverty, with the result that St. Francis, the personification of a loyal son of the church, became the rallying point of disaffection to its

[1] For Ugolino's role as cardinal protector see R. B. Brooke, *Early Franciscan Government* (Cambridge 1959) 62 ff.

[2] BF I (ed. Sbaralea, Rome 1759), no. 56, 68a–70b.

[3] Ibid., 68b.

pontiffs by the end of the thirteenth century. As if to set the seal upon the connexion, *Quo elongati* then went on to legislate over the order's goods in two respects. The first dealt with money. It will be recalled that in the 1223 rule—the official one, in the formulation of which Gregory IX had himself played a leading part—money had been banned. But in certain extremities, such as procuring necessities for sick brothers or special clothing to meet the rigours of climate, ministers and superiors alone might accept such gifts from *amici spirituales*—provided they were never in the form of money.[1] Gregory IX now permitted this to include all immediate necessities which the brothers desired. Their procurement was to be by an agent (*nuncius*), who would represent not the brothers but the alms giver or the person from whom the goods were obtained. The brothers were not to be involved in any money transaction; the agent was to make payment for what was needed immediately and ensure that no money remained.[2]

Nevertheless this arrangement extended the range of necessities indefinitely; and, although it dissociated the *nuncius* from any connexion with the brothers, it in effect established the machinery for purchasing goods. The way was opened for an ever wider interpretation of needs, and it was widened further by the subsequent legislation of Innocent IV. The other changes made by *Quo elongati* gave legal definition to Franciscan poverty. In doing so it virtually determined the nature of the Franciscan order until John XXII's revocation in *Cum inter nonnullos*. *Quo elongati* attempted to reconcile absolute poverty with the satisfaction of material needs by distinguishing between use of goods and possession of them. Beginning from the rule's renunciation of houses and belongings of any kind, the bull affirmed that this applied to property held both privately and in common.[3] For utensils, books and movable goods, however, the brothers were allowed their use, although they could not sell them or alienate them without the permission of their cardinal protector.[4] Thus the lines of future development were laid, in which absolute poverty was preserved by what was in effect a legal fiction. From this flowed almost all the troubles of the order. It allowed the ideal of St. Francis, which in the context of the order's development was incapable of realization, to act as a rallying point for

[1] Boehmer, op. cit., *Regula bullata*, no. 4, 31–2.
[2] BF I, no. 69a.
[3] Nec in communi nec in speciali debeant proprietatem habere (ibid.).
[4] Sed utensilium ac librorum, et eorum mobilium, quae licet habere eorum usum habeant . . . (ibid.). This was to be with the cardinal protector's permission.

those who remained true to it. When in all but name the founder's decrees had been passed by, the name was preserved, thereby undermining the reality which belied it. In *Quo elongati* two divergent paths were opened; they were not to meet save to cross one another.

Gregory IX, then, inaugurated a new pattern. In the first place, he undermined St. Francis's authority in favour of that of the pope, above all in setting aside the validity of the Testament. In the second place, he made it possible for goods to be held and acquired without infringing the claim to evangelical poverty. These ensured that the order would develop along conventual lines blurring the differences between it and the Dominicans, who had only for a time renounced property in common. Over the next decade the pressure against absolute poverty increased as the need for new buildings, entailing money and resources, was met by a mounting flow of alms. This was reflected in the next act of papal legislation, by Innocent IV in the bull *Ordinem vestrum*, of 1245.[1] It marked the further amelioration of poverty already suggested in *Quo elongati*: in particular money previously reserved for necessities could now be used also for commodities, and the taking of money as alms, previously debarred, was permitted via the *nuncius* as agent.[2] Although these provisions transgressed limits which Gregory IX had expressly enjoined—including that which forbade the agent to keep any money for himself—it would be hard to deny that Gregory had himself set the tone. Having dismantled St. Francis's safeguards against papal interference, and modified the application of poverty, it is not to be wondered at that his successors should go further.

Already the effects of this relaxation had led to reaction among the rigorists who wished to follow St. Francis's example. Angelo of Clareno in his *Historia septem tribulationum* recorded that during the generalate of Crescenzio of Jesu, (1244–1247), sixty-two brothers in Italy were persecuted for protesting against it.[3] Their opposition centred on precisely the concessions which had come from the papacy: namely, the acceptance of money, 'the enormous acquisitions', the exchange of habitats, the buildings in cities and—one of the continuous themes of the more extreme disciples of St. Francis—the desertion of divine wisdom for the 'curiosam et sterilem' knowledge of Aristotle and masters of dialectic.[4]

These were the accompaniment of—or, in the eyes of the rigorists,

[1] BF I, no. 114, 400–2. [2] Ibid., 400–1.
[3] ALKG III, *Item tercia persecutio sive tribulatio* 256–8.
[4] Ibid., 257–8.

the penalties for—being a learned order engaged in official work. They became ever more prominent as its activities increased. Indeed two years after *Ordinem vestrum* Innocent IV in 1247 issued another bull *Quanto studiosus*, in which he allowed the order to alienate commodities through procurators appointed by the papacy and acting as papal representatives; they were to administer all goods and to buy as directed by the order's superiors.[1] At about the same time manual labour also ceased to be part of the brother's regime. It is true that under the generalate of John of Parma, from 1247 to 1257, there was for a time a return to something like Franciscan first principles. The emphasis was upon the pursuit of poverty. John himself set the tone, as 'clad in one tunic and a habit of poor cloth'[2] he went on foot from one province to another visiting the order. In addition to his own personal example and the correction of abuses, he gained the suspension of the papal concessions in *Ordinem vestrum* and *Quanto studiosus* probably sometime between 1249 and 1251.[3] It is also true that his successor, St. Bonaventure, who was general for the next 18 years, succeeded in maintaining equilibrium within the order, but he did so on a basis of steadily growing papal concessions in the interests of learning and preaching.

The appearance of Joachism

In retrospect John of Parma's generalate can be seen to have been an interlude in the progress towards material well-being and institutional regularity, even though St. Bonaventure continued to keep in abeyance the provisions of *Ordinem vestrum* and *Quanto studiosus*.[4] Within a generation of St. Francis's death the brothers' way of life became indistinguishable from that of their confrères among the other mendicant orders. Whatever the justifications, poverty had little part in the practical life of the order.

It was this discrepancy between theory and practice which rendered the Franciscans so vulnerable. More than anything else it marked their difference from the Dominicans. The latter were subjected to the same

---

[1] BF I, no. 235, 487–8.

[2] Angelo of Clareno, *Historia septem tribulationum*, ALKG II, 267–8.

[3] Lambert, op. cit., 106.

[4] At the chapter general of Narbonne, 1260, where the constitution of the order was drawn up. F. M. Delorme, 'Diffinitiones capituli generalis Narbonensis (1260)', in AFH III (1910), 491–504.

attacks from the secular masters at Paris University in the early 1250s[1] and later had to face the condemnation of many of Aristotle's doctrines in the 1270s, with which their own doctors, Albert the Great and St. Thomas Aquinas, were particularly identified. But they underwent none of the same internal dissensions.[2] Their members were not discredited from association with Joachist ideas or suspected of subversion. There was no cause for papal intervention in their affairs. Yet each of these occurred in the Franciscan order during the same period, and were to become accentuated subsequently.

They may all be traced to the issue of poverty. To begin with, the controversy between the mendicants and the secular masters at Paris University, led by William of St. Amour, came to have, for the Franciscan order, wider ramifications than the initial question of their rights to teach and to beg.[3] It led not only to the attacks of Gerard of Abbeville and Robert Kilwardby, among others, a decade later upon their doctrine of absolute poverty, as we shall mention shortly, but it also introduced a new element with the appearance in 1254 of the *Introductorius in Evangelium Eternum* by Gerard of Borgo San Donnino. In it Gerard, a young Franciscan at the order's Paris house of studies, identified three of Joachim of Fiore's major works with the Eternal Gospel of the third age.[4] This was the first public confrontation with Joachim's prophetic writings;[5] and in the debased form in which Gerard presented them they were from the first under a handicap from which they never recovered. Nor did the Spirituals. The ensuing scandal caused John of Parma to resign, despite pleas for him to continue in office,[6] and led to his subsequent investigation at the hands of

[1] See D. Douie, *The Conflict between the Seculars and the Mendicants at the University of Paris in the thirteenth century* (Aquinas Society Paper No. 23, London 1954), and F. X. Seppelt, *Der Kampf der Bettelorden an der Universität Paris in der Mitte des 13 Jahrhunderts* (Breslau 1907); and M. Bierbaum, *Bettelordern und Weltgeistlichkeit an der Universität Paris* (Münster 1920).

[2] For the condemnations, see the author's *Medieval Thought* (London 1958 and 1963) 228 ff.

[3] William of St. Amour's main work was his *De periculis novissimorum temporum*.

[4] The standard account is H. Denifle's 'Das Evangelium aeternum und die Commission zu Anagni', ALKG I, 1885, 49–142.

[5] His doctrine of the Trinity was condemned at the Fourth Lateran Council in 1215. See E. Jordan's article on Joachim of Fiore in DTC, vol. VIII (cols. 1425–58), col. 1431. This is still one of the best general introductions to Joachim's outlook and to Joachism. See also works of H. Grundmann, M. Bloomfield, M. Reeves and B. Töpfer in Bibliography.

[6] See Lambert, op. cit., 106 ff.

St. Bonaventure, his own nominated successor,[1] Even though John was cleared of heretical associations, he retired to a hermitage.

John of Parma's vicissitudes became part of the Spirituals' lore; his fall, probably more than anything else, accounts for the hostility of the zealots towards St. Bonaventure.[2] It is not too much to see it as the catalyst in the growth of their intransigence to authority.

Doctrinally, the long-term effects of Gerard's work were no less far-reaching; for it changed the meaning of Joachim's outlook. As interpreted by Gerard it now came to inspire heterodoxy, and in years to come, among the Fraticelli, heresy. Joachim's division of the history of the world into three ages, though essentially prophetic, was not heretical; if it invited apocalypticism it gave no grounds for anti-sacerdotalism. His speculations never departed from the sacramental framework of the church in which contemplation was joined to action. His own life was one of sanctity, as abbot of the Cistercian monastery of Curazzo, in Calabria, and then as founder of the new monastic order of Fiore.

The latter, recognized by Celestine III in 1196, came to number 32 houses, and these were undoubtedly an important factor in the spread of his influence.[3] Although Joachim was keenly responsive to the issues of his own day, his thinking was predominantly symbolic. His view of history was a counterpart to that on the Trinity, and conceived in trinitarian terms. It was for his theological teachings that he was condemned at the Fourth Lateran Council in 1215, having opposed Peter Lombard's definition of the Trinity with one which appeared to deny the divine essence.[4] Apart from this his orthodoxy was not impugned, as it had not been during his own lifetime. Nevertheless his historical writings made a heady draught; and it is little wonder that the nuances and symbolism were set aside by those who saw in them the annunciation of a new age. This was accentuated by Joachim's own penchant to numerical calculations[5] and the precision with which he

---

[1] See Lambert, op. cit., 109.

[2] E.g. Angelo of Clareno.

[3] Jordan, art. cit., and M. Reeves, 'The Liber Figurarum of Joachim of Fiore' in *Mediaeval and Renaissance Studies* II (1950) 57-81.

[4] Jordan, art. cit., 1431.

[5] For a discussion of Joachim's numerical symbolism, see M. Reeves, 'The Liber Figurarum of Joachim of Fiore' in *Mediaeval and Renaissance Studies* II, (1950) 78, where it is shown how for Joachim the number 7 represents 'the inner spiritual, contemplative reality' (e.g. Expositio in Apoc 16vb). This article is one of the most perceptive and illuminating pieces of writing on Joachim known to me.

specified the duration and character of the different periods (*tempora*).[1] Of the three ages spanning the whole of creation, the first, of the Father, covering the period of the Old Testament, had passed, and the second, of the Son, beginning with king Osias, had almost run its course. It would then be succeeded by the third and final age, that of the Holy Spirit, which would lead to the final end of the world and the Last Judgement. Each age had certain formal resemblances to the other; they were divided into seven periods, alternating between calm and turbulence and associated with a particular group of men: the first age was that of married men; the second of clerics; the third of spiritual monks of whom the Benedictines were the precursors. Each had or would have three great men. Both the second and the third age would at their end witness the coming of Antichrist, as well as the appearance of Christ. At the same time, for the second and third ages at least, there was something like a dialectical interplay between their different elements. Whereas the first age had been the age of the flesh, the second comprised both flesh and spirit, leading in the third age to the triumph of the spirit. Thus the spiritual monks, who were to be its harbingers, originated in the second age with St. Benedict's order; they were the agents by which the dualism between flesh and spirit would be finally resolved in the third age. This could only happen by struggle, after which calm and peace would reign. Accordingly the picture which Joachim presented was at once a continuity by means of discontinuity: the unfolding of the pre-ordained pattern through alternating struggle and peace.

Now it was precisely in the transition from the second to the third age that Joachim's outlook had such relevance for the generation succeeding his. In the first place he computed the duration of the second era at 42 generations, each of thirty years, from the birth of Christ. This led to 1260 as the year when it was due to end and be replaced by the third and final era. But whereas Joachim was not entirely definite, since the last two generations might not last for thirty years each,[2] Gerard of Borgo specifically took it for the

---

[1] Ibid., 103–4. It went back another twenty-one generations to the time of Osias; but these constituted its period of dormancy (*initiatio*) still within the first age. Only in the lifetime of Zachariah, the father of John the Baptist, did it come to fruition (*fructificatio*) with the replacement of the Old Testament by the New (Denifle *Das Evangelium aeternum*, ibid., 103); *Concordia Novi ac Veteris Testamenti* (Venice 1519) Bk. II, tract I, ch. 4, 8rb.

[2] E.g. *Concordia*, Bk. V, ch. 6, 63va, ch. 14, 67vb, ch. 89, 118ra.

F

time when Antichrist would appear.[1] Joachim seems mainly to have confined himself to its multiples.[2] Either way the effect was to put a definite term to the present; and men as diverse as Robert Grosseteste, Adam Marsh, Hugh of Digne, William of St. Amour, St. Bonaventure, John of Pecham, not to mention Olivi and the Spirituals generally, shared, in their different ways, an apprehension of change.[3] There was a common tendency to denounce the evils of the time. William of St. Amour went so far as to identify the mendicant orders themselves with Antichrist.[4] Moreover the outbreak of the Flagellant movement in 1260 seems to have been directly due to a belief in the coming end of things.[5]

In the second place, for Joachim the years from 1200 to 1260 were to be the culmination of the change from the second to the third age. On the one hand they would be ones of 'great tribulation',[6] reaching a final crescendo with the advent of the first Antichrist to mark the end of the second era. While in a general sense, of course, the seventh age would inaugurate a new era of peace, the tribulations leading up to its consummation would become progressively more intense. In Joachim's words: 'One thing we can say with certainty: the sixth age will be worse than the previous five ages, and the seventh age will be worse than the sixth, and both will be filled with the evil doings of the dragon of the Apocalypse.'[7] The sixth age, especially, would witness great persecutions culminating, in the seventh, with the appearance of the first

[1] ALKG I, 123.

[2] Although he does on occasion finally translate his analogies of days into years: 'Sunt etenim menses 42 siue dies 1260. Nichilque aliud designant quam annos 1260 in quibus novi testamenti sacramenta consistunt' (*Concordia* 118r; ALKG I, 136). Normally, however, Joachim's practice was to infer the number of years from the analogy of days, e.g. the sixth age from the sixth day of the week.

[3] For a general summary see Jordan, art. cit., 1436 ff. Also M. W. Bloomfield, 'Joachim of Flora', *Traditio* 13 (1957) 249-311.

[4] Jordan, ibid. See Douie, *Fraticelli* 22.

[5] See, for example, R. Manselli, 'L'Anno 1260 fu anno Giochinitico?' in *Il movimento dei disciplinati nel settimo centenario dal suo inizio (Perugia 1260)* (Convegno Internazionale, Perugia, 1960), 99-108.

[6] Denifle, art. cit., 113.

[7] Unum dicimus secure, quod deterior erit sextus precedentibus quinque, et septimus deterior sexto, et uterque repletus erit felli [text: felle] draconis. Et ipsi sunt duo ultima capita ipsius draconis in quibus maxime pugnaturus est in hoc tempore sexto (ibid., 124. *Expositio in Apocalypsim* 207rb). The reference is to the beast with the seven heads in the Apocalypse (Revelation 12, 3; 13, 1) who, as Satan, was driven from heaven and came down to earth. His heads traditionally represented the great empires of the world. According to Joachim the sixth of them would be the first Antichrist; the seventh the second Antichrist.

Antichrist. On the other hand, the sixth age would also bring the first heralding of the spiritual understanding of the Old and New Testaments which Gerard of Borgo San Donnino took for the everlasting gospel. This would come with the opening of the sixth of the seven seals of the holy book foretold by St. John of the Apocalypse.[1] Joachim usually placed its occurrence during the fortieth generation of the second era, i.e. after 1200;[2] but as the Anagni commission, which examined his works, justly complained, his words also implied the end of the forty-second generation.[3] In the beginning of the forty-second generation the Jews would be converted and the schism between the Greek and Latin churches healed.[4] Joachim also envisaged their union under a final great Roman pontiff, the leader of the New Jerusalem in its struggle with Babylon.[5] But he never developed the notion, as the later Joachists would, of an angelic pope. With the opening of the seventh seal God's mystery would be finished.[6] Henceforth, after the vanquishing of Antichrist by the rider on the white horse,[7] who Joachim surmised would be the reincarnated Christ,[8] the rest of time would belong to the third age. A period of sabbatical peace would then reign, the era of those who would love God in 'joy and solemnity'. The peace of the seventh age would be finally broken by the coming of the second Antichrist—Gog—followed by Christ's second advent, the ending of the world, and the Last Judgement.[9]

In the third place, however, the highly schematic nature of Joachim's thinking, far from engendering a world of abstractions, was fertile in allusions to the contemporary one. Here we must distinguish between their significance for Joachim and for the Joachists of subsequent generations. There can be no doubt that the focus of Joachim's attention was upon the transition from the second to the third state, namely the sixth and seventh epochs of the second state. Their symbolization in the sixth and seventh seals of the book of the Apocalypse formed the

---

[1] 'Erit autem hoc in apertione sexti sigilli . . . qui est sextus in ebdomada sexta' (Denifle, ibid., 113; *Concordia* v, ch. 84, 112va).

[2] 'Nimirum quia in tempore isto, in quo agitur 40a generatio, opportet auferri velamen littere a cordibus multorum . . .' (ibid.).

[3] ALKG I, 112.

[4] Ibid., 120; *Concordia*, Bk. v, tract. I, ch. 7, 9rb.

[5] ALKG I 120; *Concordia*, Bk. IV, ch. 31, 56rb.

[6] Rev. 10, 7, ibid., 114.   [7] Rev. 19, 11.

[8] 'Cum autem aperte liqueat eum qui sedet in equo albo Christum esse Jhesum. . . .' ALKG I, 124; *Expositio in Apocalypsim* 207rb.

[9] ALKG I, 132–3; *Concordia*, Bk. v, ch. 84.

key to his outlook. It was only with their opening that the book could be read; and this could only be done by the lamb, i.e. through the coming of Christ. Once achieved, the barrier between true spiritual illumination and knowledge of the letter would be down; the third age would begin. Here Joachim effectively stopped. The third age was conceived less in itself than as the consummation of the second age; all the elements were already in existence: they merely had to reach full fructification. In this sense it can be truly said that Joachim conceived history 'not in a single pattern of "threes" but in two co-existing patterns, one of "twos" and the other of "threes" ';[1] and more specifically as a series of parallels between the transitions from one status to the next.

It was in inspiring others to seek the vehicles for these changes that Joachim was to have such an impact; for this endowed his own predominantly symbolic—even poetic conception—of spiritual revelation with the seeds of an historicism. When these began to ripen in the later thirteenth century, Joachism germinated into perhaps the most challenging alternative to the existing dispensation which the later middle ages was to know.

The reasons are not far to seek. To begin with, there was the analogy between the ending of the first and second ages.[2] Just as the first was transformed into the second by Christ, and personified in the order of clerics,[3] so the second would culminate in the third with triumph of the new order of monks, who would personify it, over the forces of Antichrist. As Christ represented a qualitative change from his predecessors, so would the spiritual monks over theirs. This would consist above all in the supersession of action by contemplation, and would distinguish the seventh age of the second era from the sixth.[4]

In a series of eloquent antitheses Joachim pointed to the differences between the three great eras of the world: the first was under the law, the second under grace, the third would have still greater grace; the first was one of knowledge, the second of partial wisdom, the third would be of full understanding; the first was in servile servitude, the second in filial servitude, the third would be in liberty; the first was in

---

[1] Reeves, 'Liber Figurarum,' 74.

[2] Credendum est, ut ea concordia inter secundum statum et tertium habeatur, que habita est inter primum et secundum, (Denifle, ibid. 105).

[3] 'In secundo statu fructificavit ordo clericorum inchoatus a Christo et sanctis apostolis per actionem predicationis . . .' (Denifle, 116; Concordia, Bk. IV, ch. 33, 57ra.)

[4] 'Nimirum quia ut ad sextam etatem labor, ita ad septimum pertinet contemplatio', ibid.

suffering, the second in action, the third would be in contemplation; the first was in fear, the second in faith, the third would be in charity; and so on.[1] Through the new order of contemplation 'which until our own time remained in sterility' the eternal gospel (*evangelium eternum*) would be revealed,[2] expressing the living spirit of which St. John of the Apocalypse spoke: 'And I saw another angel fly in the midst of heaven, having the everlasting gospel to preach unto them that dwell on the earth, and to every nation, and kindred, and tongue and people.'[3] As coming from Christ the contemplatives would make eternal what had previously been transitory and temporal; as the successors of the clergy, where there had been activity there would now be contemplation and wisdom; as the harbingers of the new era they would suffer joyfully and patiently the torments of Antichrist.[4] They would follow in Christ's footsteps fulfilling the words of the prophets.[5] But, although they would be a new order, they would not embrace a new faith or a new church; they would rather be a higher expression of the same religion.[6] Should anyone, then, lament that what had been partial should now become universal? Of course not, replied Joachim.[7] For him the new spiritual order and the new age would simply signalize the fulfilment of Christ's teaching. 'My Father worked hitherto, and I work';[8] and now the Holy Spirit works, whose work would be greater than either.[9] The spirit would have triumphed over the letter.[10]

Now it was precisely here that Joachim's thinking was most betrayed by followers like Gerard of Borgo San Donnino; they substituted an entirely new order for the existing one. Where Joachim had spoken

[1] ALKG I, 131–2, *Concordia*, Bk. v, ch. 84.

[2] 'contemplativa interim perfectione usque scilicet ad hec tempora nostra in sterilitate manente', ALKG I, 116, *Concordia*, bk. iv. ch. 33, 57ra.

[3] Rev. 14, 6, (ALKG I, 111). This is the commission's summary of Joachim's view expressed in his *Super quatuor evangelia*.

[4] Ibid.

[5] videntes illum ordinem, qui imitatur vestigia Christi, in virtute spirituali sustentabit eum munimine auctoritatis sue, et confirmabit verbis testimonii sui, annuncians complenda esse in eo vaticinia prophetarum (ibid.).

[6] Neque enim super dissolutionem suam poterit dolere, cum se in meliore successione permanere cognoscet. Scimus enim quod, ut alius ordo designetur in precessore, et alius in successore, non facit diversitas fidei sed proprietas religionis (ibid.).

[7] Ibid., 112.

[8] John, 5, 17.

[9] . . . ita spiritus sanctus opere magis quam voce de filio et de se loquatur . . . (ibid, 105). *Expositio in Apocalypsim*; Introduction, ch. 5.

[10] Ibid., 136. *Expositio in Apocalypsim*; Introduction, ch. 6, 6 rb.

figuratively they spoke literally. That Joachim himself, judged by strictly orthodox canons, went beyond the permissible limits can hardly be doubted; as the Protocol of the Agnani commission frequently stressed, by dividing the eras of creation into three, instead of the accepted two of the Old and New Testaments, he was in effect implying the displacement of the church and the sacraments by another dispensation in the third era; an additional general judgement was interposed between the final coming of the second Antichrist and the Last Judgement.[1] Before the whole of humanity was finally called to account, the church appeared to be making its own special tribute. Such an impression of anti-sacerdotalism was accentuated by the impalpability of Joachim's own symbolism: terms like 'ecclesia spiritualis', 'spirituales viri' and references to the 'figures' of the sacrament hiding the true reality all tended towards such an effect.

Nevertheless, despite these deviations from orthodoxy, Joachim's import is plain. He was concerned with spiritual renewal; the changes between one era and the next constituted the progressive unfolding of the gospel, not its supersession; the coming of the spiritual monks was to revivify the church not to replace it. The discontinuity only accentuated the underlying continuity. The eternal gospel was not a new gospel but full spiritual understanding 'sent to us by Christ and the apostles according to the faith of the sacraments';[2] it was 'that which is in spirit, for that which is in the letter is temporal not eternal'.[3] The spiritual understanding to which the spiritual monks would attain, was itself the 'image of the Spirit' which came from the 'image of the Father' of the Old Testament and the 'image of the Son' of the New Testament;[4] it therefore derived from the bible and did not exist independently of it.[5] In the same way the new contemplatives of the third era were, as we have seen, the realization of the monks of the second order. Like the angel of the Apocalypse they would 'ascend from the face of the sun having the sign of the living God'; they would come in full freedom

---

[1] E.g. ibid., 106, 108, 115, 116, 120, 122, 123, 125, etc.

[2] 'Sed quare vel a domino evangelium regni, vel a Johanne evangelium eternum, nisi quia illud quod mandatum est nobis a Christo vel apostolis secundum fidem sacramentorum . . .' (ibid., 111).

[3] Ibid., 128; Expositio in Apocalypsim 95vb.

[4] Quoted by Denifle (ALKG I, 54) from Concordia, Bk. II, tract I, ch. 29, 186.

[5] Quid est evangelium eius? Illud quod procedit de evangelio Christi . . . Sciendum quod littera veteris testamenti commissa fuit populo Judeorum, littera novi testamenti populo romano, spiritualibus autem viris spiritualis intelligentia, que ex utraque procedit (ALKG I, 127; Concordia, Bk. II, tract I, ch. 7, 9rb.)

'to renovate the Christian religion and to preach the word of God'.[1] The Commission interpreted their role of purgation as meaning that it would occur within five years—by 1260 with the advent of the third era.[2] The spiritual church would result from this purification; in an age when the spirit had triumphed and the veil had been stripped from the gospel, the Jews would be rapidly converted to Christianity[3] and the churches of the East and West reunited.[4] Joachim was criticized by the commission for making this the work of the Holy Spirit and not the church, just as he was for implying that the church in the second age was Babylon;[5] but this was again to take the image for the reality.

It is not easy to unravel much of Joachim's meaning over the order of events or the possible identity of his scriptural symbols in the transition to the third age and beyond. Whereas the three great figures of the first and second eras were drawn from the Old and New Testaments—Abraham, Isaac and Jacob, for the first, and Zachariah, John the Baptist and Christ for the second[6]—those for the third were the man clothed in linen[7] and two angels of the Apocalypse, one with the sickle,[8] the other having the seal of the living God.[9] This last would be the renovator of the church, who would rebuild God's temple, as the head of the new Jerusalem. Like the angel of the Apocalypse, he would ascend from the East.[10] Joachim neither suggested that he would be a pope nor identified him with St. Francis, nor indeed said, as the commission implied, that he would rule the world.[11] Of the two Antichrists, Joachim tentatively suggested that the first would be a king and the second a pseudo-prophet,[12] which Gerard of Borgo San Donnino interpreted as an anti-pope. Beyond these vague allusions Joachim

[1] ALKG I, 105; *Concordia*, Bk. IV, ch. 31, 56rb.

[2] This is how the commission summarized him here (ALKG I, 106).

[3] quatinus et rebellis hactenus Judeorum populus ablato velamine cordis sui convertatur ad deum (ibid., 113; *Concordia*, Bk. V, ch. 84, 112va.)

[4] The interpretation of the commission (ALKG I, 120), *Concordia*, Bk. II, tract. I, ch. 7, 9rb.

[5] Ibid., 118–19, 120.   [6] Ibid., 101.

[7] 'And I heard a man clothed in linen, . . . and when he shall have accomplished to scatter the power of the holy people, all these things shall be finished' (Daniel 12, 7, ibid.).

[8] 'And I looked, and behold a white cloud, and upon the cloud one sat like unto the Son of Man, having on his head a golden crown, and in his hand a sharp sickle' (Rev. 14, 14, ibid.).

[9] Rev. 7, 2 (ibid.).   [10] *Concordia*, Bk. IV, ch. 31, 56r.

[11] Denifle, ALKG I, 105.

[12] ALKG I, 109. *Concordia*, Bk. V, ch. 65, 95r–v, ch. 104, 124r–v.

offered little firm guidance. But he had suggested enough to incite others to fill in the blanks. Within a generation an accepted pattern had grown up of an angel, or saviour, pope as the initiator of the third age and an anti-pope as the final Antichrist, who would herald its destruction.

As for the sacraments in the third age, they would take on the same spiritual meaning and cease to be merely external signs. The water of baptism was but the visible symbol of grace divinely infused. 'God alone infuses grace and does works and virtues.'[1] Just as in the second era remission of sins by penitence was made in the 'clarification of the Son', so in the third era it would be done in the 'clarification of the Holy Spirit'.[2] So long as these actions appeared as figures, the truths they expressed would not be realized. Accordingly, they must be set aside.[3] They represented Christ's condescension to men's infirmity, providing a means by which they might reach him;[4] they were necessary so long as they saw but through a glass darkly, when the truth could not be truly known. They belonged therefore to the state of carnal understanding. With the clarification of the Holy Spirit they would not disappear but, rather, the spirit would pass beyond the symbol.[5] As with so much else in Joachim, how this affected the sacraments was far from clear. Joachim repeatedly spoke of these earthly symbols being consumed in God's fire, for which he was reproved by the commission.[6] The same figurative meaning is to be seen in his use of Peter and John. They stand for types of religious life—Peter that of the second age, John for the third, rather than for different churches.[7]

Joachim, then, saw the eternal evangel and the third age as essentially the spiritualizing of Christian faith; they constituted the full intelligence of what already existed. There was no suggestion of an alternative either to the church or the bible; each was merely to reach its

---

[1] ALKG I, 134. *Concordia*, Bk. II, tract. I, ch. 2, 7v.

[2] ALKG I, ibid. *Concordia*, Bk. v, ch. 77, 105vb.

[3] Tamdiu erim ostenduntur figure, quamdiu veritas figurarum consummata non est . . . oportet ex toto evacuari figuras (ALKG I, 134; *Concordia*, Bk. IV, ch. 37, 58vb).

[4] 'Quare sic? Quia infirmatus est Christus in nobis, ut nos essemus fortes in ipso; condescendit infirmitati nostre, ut nos ascenderemus ad firmitatem suam' (ALKG I, 134; *Concordia*, Bk. v, ch. 74, 102vb).

[5] Ibid.

[6] Ibid., 136.

[7] ALKG I, 116 ff.; *Concordia*, Bk. II, tract. 2, ch. 5; Bk. III, pt. I, ch. 14; Bk. IV, ch. 33; Bk. v, chs. 68, 81, 117. *Expositio in Apocalypsim*, Introduction, chs. 19, 20, 24.

fullest and most universal expression in the third age: the heathen would be converted and the believers would understand; the spirit would enlighten where the letter had veiled. Yet by framing this metamorphosis as an apocalyptic vision Joachim invited the interpretations which he himself eschewed. For the accepted two eras and one final judgement he substituted three and two, and thereby translated to his own age the happenings normally reserved for the end of the world. There were to be two upheavals instead of one; and the fact that the first was set in the near future, a mere two generations away, could hardly in the context of his prophecies fail to arouse apocalyptic visions. Moreover, he had provided a ready-made cast: the forces of evil as Antichrist; the good represented by a new spiritual order. It needed only an extension of these antitheses to reach two churches and two gospels, angelic popes and anti-popes. These additions had all been made by the end of the thirteenth century, by which time Joachism had become a force in its own right, and one which bore only a remote resemblance to its progenitor.

The first indication of these developments came with Gerard of Borgo San Donnino's Introduction to the Eternal Gospel. As we have already said, the extreme form in which he presented the eternal evangel made it from the outset subversive and heretical. What for Joachim had been a spiritual interpretation became for Gerard a book— or rather books. The new gospel instead of being, as with Joachim, the consummation of the bible, superseded it. In place of the Old and New Testaments he put Joachim's own writings, namely his *Concordia*, *Expositio in Apocalypsim* and *Psalterium decem chordarum*. The year 1200 now became the time when 'the spirit of life had departed from the two testaments to become the eternal gospel', composed of Joachim's three books.[1] Their author became the angel of the Apocalypse, who, after the sounding of the sixth trumpet, appeared from heaven 'clothed with a cloud', and 'a rainbow was upon his head'; 'his face was like the sun' and he bore in his hand 'a little book open'.[2] The book was Joachim's

[1] Quod circa Mcc annum incarnationis dominice exivit spiritus vite de duobus testamentis, ut fieret evangelium eternum. Hoc probatur XV capitulo d, et XXIII b. Quod liber Concordiarum vel Concordie veritatis appellaretur primus liber evangeli eterni, probatur XVII capitulo g, et quod iste Concordie sit Joachim, habetur per totum istud (ms istum) capitulum. Quod liber iste, qui dicitur Apocalipsis nova, apellaretur secundus liber probatur . . . Similiter quod liber, qui dicitur Psalterium decem cordarum, sit tertius liber eiusdem evangelii, probatur (ibid., pp. 99–100).

[2] Revelation 10, 1, 2. Iste doctor sive angelus apparuit circa MCC annum incarnationis dominice. Hoc est ille liber de quo loquitur hic . . . (ibid., 133).

book; and when he had spoken 'the seven thunders uttered their voices, which were the mysteries of the seven seals'.[1] This image was to have a lasting effect, and was later to be applied to Peter John Olivi by the Beguin followers of the Spirituals in Provence. But Gerard did not stop there. To the identification of the eternal gospel and its author he added that of the new spiritual monks who were to preach it and usher in the third era. These were to be his own order of the Franciscans; and St. Francis their founder was the angel of the sixth seal 'who had the seal of the living God upon him'.[2] Elsewhere he spoke of them as being an order of bare-footed monks,[3] which had clearly an analogy with the Franciscan devotion to poverty. Finally Gerard, as we mentioned earlier, gave 1260 as the date for the coming of Antichrist. He thus provided the *dramatis personae* for Joachim's epic;[4] he made tangible what Joachim had left symbolical. In doing so he entirely altered its import. It now became not simply apocalyptic but revolutionary; the church was to be challenged from without rather than renewed from within; it was to be superseded rather than transformed.

How much of this was from Gerard himself is not clear. His Introduction, together with his own gloss upon Joachim's writings,[5] has not survived. All that remains are seven articles among the thirty-one which were drawn up by the Paris masters and sent to the pope for condemnation;[6] the remainder were taken from Joachim's *Concordia*. What does seem indisputable is that Gerard's conclusions were not the only ones being drawn from Joachim's writings;[7] nor did his condemnation put an end to Joachist tendencies among reputable thinkers. On the contrary, Gerard's Introduction seemed to crystallize certain notions within the Franciscan order for a generation to come. Thus St. Bonaventure in his *Legenda S. Francisci* made the same identification of St. Francis with the angel of the sixth seal, 'ascending from

---

[1] Rev. 10, 4. (ibid., 132).

[2] 'Usque ad illum angelum, qui habuit signum dei vivi, qui apparuit circa MCC incarnationis dominice' quem angelum frater Gerardus vocat et confitetur sanctum Franciscum (ibid., 101).

[3] This is included in the list of errors given in Matthew Paris, *Chronica Majora* (ed. Luard) Rolls Series VI, London, 1882, 335-9.

[4] Ibid., p. 123.

[5] Ibid., pp. 99-100.

[6] Apart from that given by Matthew Paris as mentioned above n. 3, the list is printed in Denifle and Chatelain, *Chartularium universitatis Parisiensis*, vol. I (Paris 1889) no. 243, 272.

[7] Jordan, art. cit., 1443.

the East having the seal of the living God';[1] and it became standard among the Spirituals, especially Olivi and Ubertino of Casale. This in turn helped to put the mendicant orders, and the Franciscans in particular, in the role of the new order of spiritual monks. St. Francis and St. Dominic were likened to the two prophets of the new era, Enoch and Elias, and their followers its agents.[2] Above all it engendered a growing apocalyptic sense which manifested itself not only in treatises prophesying the coming of Antichrist,[3] but, certainly from the end of the century, his identification with popes hostile to the Spirituals. We shall have cause to discuss these developments more fully later. For the present it is enough to observe that they were to be found principally among the Spirituals, as the accompaniment of their growing conflict with the Community. Joachism ministered both to their sense of mission and to their sufferings. They were a new spiritual order; they opposed possessions and learning; they were persecuted for their devotion to the teaching of St. Francis, the herald of the new dawn.

Events bore out their prophecies. They also provided them with martyrs. Both John of Parma and Gerard of Borgo San Donnino suffered for the cause of Joachism, however differently they may have conceived it. John's views are not known. He was for long regarded as the real author of the Introduction, and he was known as a Joachist.[4] Even though the work was not his, he suffered for it, and so, with his fall, did the whole Spiritual cause. Gerard himself was imprisoned, and his book burned; he was forbidden to teach, and died in captivity. He too became one of the zealots' heroes, as can be seen in Angelo of Clareno's *Historia septem tribulationum.*[5] Thus from an early stage in Franciscan history, rigorism and Joachism, in one form or another, went together. Even before Gerard of Borgo San Donnino and John of Parma, Hugh of Digne, who seems to have been the prototype of the Spirituals, was a Joachist, as well as an upholder of the most rigorous poverty. In his *De finibus pauperum* he called poverty 'a way of life'.[6] It

---

[1] Sub apertione namque sexti sigilli 'vidi', ait Johannes in Apocalypsi, 'alterum angelum ascendentem ab ortu solis habentem signum dei vivi'. Hunc dei nuntium amabilem Christo . . . fuisse Franciscum, indubitabili fide colligimus. (St. Bonaventure, *Legenda de Sancti Francisci* Prologue, *Opera omnia*, vol. VIII (Quaracchi 1898), 504b.)

[2] Ubertino of Casale, *Arbor vitae* (John Rylands, MS. 200) 409va. For Olivi and Ubertino see below pp. 144 ff.

[3] Jordan, art. cit., 1441 ff.   [4] Ibid., 1442.

[5] *Historia* (ALKG II, 276 ff.).

[6] *De finibus pauperum* in AFH V (1912) 282.

was this sense of mission which Joachism fed, until the two became eventually fused by tribulation.

Although this did not occur for another generation, the necessary elements were thus already in being by 1250; and the affair of the Eternal Evangel had an important part in their development. More than anything else it heightened the insurgent side of Joachim's doctrine. It thereby brought it down into the political—or at least ecclesiastical—arena: to be judged as much by what it implied as what it was. Accordingly Joachism became a practical issue, its partisans being early identified with extremists such as Gerard of Borgo. This did not disqualify it from serious consideration, nor did it at first exclude moderates like St. Bonaventure and Pecham from drawing upon it and interpreting it. Indeed, at this stage, it would have been meaningless to talk of Joachism as a single outlook. Salimbene's reaction to Gerard of Borgo San Donnino was simply to dismiss his 'fatuities and falsities against abbot Joachim's doctrines';[1] this must have been the view of many.[2] Even as late as the pontificate of Clement V (1305–14), the pope consented to listen to Arnold of Villanova[3] expound Joachim's doctrine without offence, and he stifled his boredom by thinking of other things.[4] John XXI, on the other hand, was among Joachim's sympathizers.[5] Moreover, although the bishop of Arles, who had been a member of the Anagni commission,[6] condemned his doctrines at a provincial council in 1263,[7] Joachim was not proscribed as heretical, or censured, beyond the ban on his view of the Trinity imposed by the Fourth Lateran Council in 1215.

Gerard's condemnation did, however, point to the perils inherent in embracing Joachim's doctrines too closely. Perhaps even his example, despite its association with zealots like Hugh of Digne and John of Parma, would not have of itself prevented the absorption of Joachim. But the outbreak of the Flagellant movement in 1260, the year of Joachist prophecy, together with the growth of the heretical Apostles, condemned in 1274 at the Council of Lyons,[8] set the seal upon its heretical

---

[1] Jordan, art. cit., 1443.

[2] See H. Grundmann, *Studien über Joachim von Flore* (Munich 1927) 157–92.

[3] For Arnold of Villanova see ch. II below.

[4] Menendez Pelayo, *Historia de los Heterodoxos Españolas* I, 603.

[5] Jordan, art. cit., 1447.

[6] He was then Florentinus, bishop of Acre. It was he who actually made the examination of Joachim's doctrines in the Protocol (Denifle, art. cit., ALKG I, 88–90, 102).   [7] Jordan, art. cit., 1444; Mansi *Concilia*, vol. 23, 1001.

[8] For the False Apostles see pp. 176 ff. below.

tendencies. This was inevitable. Its apocalyptic nature made it the vehicle of those who wished to change the existing order; like any doctrine of change it was congenitally on the side of the reformers. It only needed resistance and persecution from its opponents to make them revolutionaries. This happened to the Spirituals, as we shall see. Before we can do so, however, we must first trace the events which precipitated such a development.

St. Bonaventure's doctrine of poverty and 'Exiit qui seminat'

On his resignation as general John of Parma appointed as his successor St. Bonaventure (John of Fidanza),[1] one of the greatest scholastics of the thirteenth century, who, in the comparatively short time allowed to him before he was plunged into the world of affairs, had come near to fashioning a distinctive system. Bonaventure's generalate marks the watershed in Franciscan history. For eighteen years from 1257 to 1274 he rode out the conflicting currents within the order. His resignation and death put an end to any lasting equilibrium; and the next seventy years were a period of prolonged struggle. This is not the place to attempt to assess St. Bonaventure's role in the order's history. Eighteen years of comparatively untroubled rule are themselves an achievement, the more so when seen in the light of the subsequent strife. At the same time they must in some degree be held accountable for what ensued. Even if we only say that Bonaventure as a man did all that he could in the interests of the order, but that the problems were too deep-seated for a lasting settlement, he is implicated in the failure—be it the failure of the order to contain its divergent pulls. In fact, however, St. Bonaventure was more than a passive agent. It is not too much to say that his very moderation helped to accentuate the opposition between the extremes by fostering both. On the one hand, he was in himself and his outlook a conventual rather than an extremist: a scholar and an organizer rather than a hermit or a wayfarer like John of Parma. While the latter favoured learning he was not prepared to mitigate poverty in its interests; Bonaventure was. Unlike John of Parma, he also sought to the full papal privileges, as the papal bulls of the time illustrate.[2] During his period of office the Franciscan order reached new

---

[1] For John of Parma's resignation see Salimbene, *Chronica* (Ed. O. Holder-Egger) MGH, Scriptores, XXXII (Hanover-Leipzig 1905-12) 309-10; and Angelo of Clareno *Historia*, ALKG II, 271.

[2] BF, vols. II and III passim.

degrees of organization; buildings and endowments increased. In form it followed much the same evolution as the Dominicans, and this in itself took it farther from St. Francis's simple conception. An institution had replaced a band. On the other hand, St. Bonaventure held just as firmly to the theory of absolute poverty for the order as a whole, and for moderation in the lives of the brothers individually. The life and ideals of St. Francis remained those of the order. Bonaventure thus also kept alive the belief in poverty; indeed, its enunciation in his *Apologia* gave the discussion a new direction. It became the starting point for Pecham and above all for Olivi and Ubertino of Casale. In consequence, leaving aside the more urgently apocalyptic attitudes of the Spirituals towards St. Francis and his Testament, the doctrine of poverty came to revolve around St. Bonaventure's own formulations. In a different tone and a more extreme form, what the Spirituals demanded was substantially what St. Bonaventure had affirmed. The difference between them was that he conceived poverty within a conventual framework, harnessed to learning, buildings, papal privileges and stability, where they saw it as an end in itself; hence their opposition to *Exiit qui seminat*,[1] which enshrined St. Bonaventure's outlook. It was this difference which ultimately put them on opposite sides. Yet Bonaventure, as we shall now consider, was instrumental in creating it, and so indirectly the conflict which resulted.

The first, and perhaps most notable, feature of the *Apologia pauperum* is the changed basis of poverty compared with St. Francis: or, rather, whereas St. Francis had never attempted to give it a *raison d'être* beyond taking it as the badge of Christ and the true evangelical life, Bonaventure did. In doing so poverty was relegated from being an end in itself, and its own justification, to one among a number of ways in which Christ's perfection could be manifested. The root of all goodness was charity; and Christ had reduced all that concerned God's law to it.[2] While it was absolute (*secundum se*) in Christ, it could be present in varying degrees among his creatures, either generically (*in genere*), when it denoted the accomplishment of some particularly difficult act of excellence, such as giving all, or according to circumstances (*ex circumstantia*), such as giving to one's neighbour.[3] Imperfection could be

---

[1] See below pp. 97 ff.

[2] Sciendum est igitur quod radix, forma, finis complementum et vinculum perfectionis caritas est, ad quam magister omnium Christus legem, prophetas et per consequens universa dei documenta reducit (*Opera omnia*, vol. VIII, Quaracchi 1898 (233–330), ch. III, 2, 244b).   [3] Ibid., ch. I, 8, 238a.

distinguished correspondingly.[1] Accordingly, although both absolute goodness and absolute evil were immutable, relative perfection and imperfection could be modified to become their opposites.

Thus generic perfection could in certain circumstances become imperfection, if, say, the act of giving all was motivated by vainglory; and conversely, the generically imperfect act of, say, fleeing death could become circumstantially perfect if it entailed suffering more gloriously for God, as happened with both Christ and St. Paul.[2] From this two consequences followed. The first was that, within, Christ acted from the most perfect charity and all that he did was informed by absolute goodness. Externally, however, his actions could vary in degree of perfection or indeed imperfection.[3] The reason was that, in the external world, Christ, from his own perfection, was condescending to man's imperfection. This did not diminish Christ's own absolute goodness; but it meant that the external form which it took could be imperfect.[4] As St. Augustine said, when St. Paul acted more nobly than Christ, this did not exalt him above Christ; Christ remained higher than Paul because he was more merciful.[5]

This in turn led to the second consequence: namely, that there could be no direct comparison between the actions of Christ and other men. They flowed from different sources: one from perfect charity, the other from imperfection. In this sense Christ was inimitable. The distinction between Christ's internal and external works meant that what was perfect for Christ was not perfect for men. In purely circumstantial

[1] Ibid.   [2] Ibid., 9, 238a–b.
[3] Ex his patenter liquet, quid de Christi operibus veraciter sentiendum est. Nam cum loquimur de Christi operibus, potest fieri sermo de eius opere interiori aut exteriori. Interius dicimus opus operans, exterius opus operatum. Omne autem opus Christi operans sive interius est perfectissimum, quia ex perfectissima caritate processit . . . Opus vero eius exterius in se consideratum aliquando fuit perfectum de genere actus . . . aliquando imperfectum . . . (ibid., 10, 238b).

To make the distinction between internal and external correspond to subjective and objective, as Lambert does (op. cit., 135) is a travesty of Bonaventure's meaning. Absolute charity is just as 'objective' as its external manifestations; temporally the latter appear distorted as a stick in water appears bent. In fact both refer to something whole and complete.

[4] quia ipsa condescensio Christi, qua Christus membris condescendebat infirmis et imperfectis ex sublimitate procedebat perfectissimae caritatis. . . . Ac per hoc verum est quod Christi perfecta sunt omnia opera ad ipsum relata; verum etiam est quod Christus aliqua fecit opera, infirmorum in se suscipiendo personam et ad nostra condescendo infirma et imperfecta (ibid., 10 and 11, 238–9).

[5] immo Christus sublimius, quia misericordius (ibid., 10, 238b).

terms many of his external works were imperfect and mediocre;[1] there-fore it was untenable to identify perfection with conformity to Christ's works, and imperfection with deviation from them,[2] as comparison between the actions of Christ and St. Paul, or John the Baptist, showed.[3] So far as men were concerned, perfection and imperfection differed not as opposites, but as more and less good.[4] While this could not be absolute, it could have degrees. Of the two which St. Bonaventure distinguished, the first was necessary and, like a precept, universal and binding; the second was supererogatory and, like a counsel, a matter of individual inclination. Together they were said to be perfect; but, separately, only what was necessary was qualifiedly perfect, while what was supererogatory, taken alone, was imperfect.[5]

Now it was from the latter that evangelical perfection derived; as the product of the habit of charity[6] it enabled a man to conform to Christ, and so supererogatorily avoid evil, do good and suffer adversity—the three components of evangelical perfection. Without following St. Bon-aventure further in his distinctions, enough has been said to see how far removed from absolute perfection evangelical perfection was. Not that he denied it a supernatural source in charity: it was rather that his own conception of true goodness was so completely supernatural that only the remotest participation in it was possible to man in his natural state. It is important to emphasize the unqualified theocentricity of St. Bona-venture's outlook, in order to appreciate the difference from St. Francis's. For St. Francis, also, as we have seen, charity was one of the cardinal virtues; but so was poverty. Virtue resided in the emulation of the life of Christ; and that was as far as he went. For St. Bonaventure, beside

---

[1] Actus autem Christi sunt multiformes et varii, et quamvis in comparatione ad Christi personam omnes sint perfecti, tamen secundum naturam proprii generis quidam sunt excellentes, quidam mediocres, quidam condescensivi, sicut in praece-dentibus aliqualiter patuit et subsequenter magis patebit. (ibid., ch. II, 10, 242a).

[2] Sane si verum est, sicut concludit, quod perfectio dicat universalem conformitatem ad opera Christi et imperfectio dissonantiam, multa per omnem modum sequuntur absurda (ibid, 11).　　　　　　　　　　[3] Ibid., 242a–b.

[4] Propter quod diligens lector advertat quod perfectio et imperfectio non differunt sicut duo contraria, sed sicut maius bonum et minus bonum . . . (ibid., 14, 243b).

[5] Ibid., 245a–b.

[6] A habit is a moral state—either for good or bad—which engenders actions of a corresponding kind. It can arise either naturally through the repetition of like actions, or it can be supernaturally infused, as in the case of grace and charity, when it will inspire a desire to do good: its accomplishment will be limited by the will's resources. For that reason evangelical perfection, as coming from the will in a state of grace, cannot pass beyond a certain degree of imperfection.

the sublimity and inaccessibility of absolute charity, everything else paled: all that was not absolute charity was by definition imperfect. This included poverty. Accordingly, from the outset, poverty for him was on another plane as compared with St. Francis: true, it was the badge of Christ, but one which referred to his humanity rather than his divinity. It had none of the aura which had led St. Francis to revere it as a virtue in its own right. It is not therefore surprising that St. Bonaventure was not regarded by the Spirituals as one of themselves; in attitude, if not in outlook, he was at the opposite pole from St. Francis. St. Francis sought God from the world; St. Bonaventure turned away from the world to God.

This must not be taken to mean that St. Bonaventure did not embrace the ideal of poverty; he did, as we shall see. But he did not venerate it for itself. The whole of his treatise was designed to show why absolute poverty was justified, where for St. Francis it had been its own justification. Admittedly, this was partly due to the vagaries of time. What St. Francis had taken for granted now had to be defended against detractors and defined for the brothers. Even so, in the process, the evangelical life was demoted from perfection to imperfection, and poverty displaced by charity.

The change can be plainly seen in St. Bonaventure's discussion of poverty. He was concerned with two main problems: one was to uphold the doctrine of absolute poverty; the other, to reconcile it with the use of goods.

The first followed from the virtues of evangelical perfection already enumerated; each of these entailed its own cognate precepts. Thus in order to shun evil, in its three manifestations of visual and carnal desire and pride, Christ enjoined the abandonment of all possessions (poverty), abnegation of the will (obedience), and self-castration (chastity).[1] To pursue the good, he followed, on the one hand, the active life of condescending to his neighbour, such as by loving his enemies, and on the other, the way of contemplation in directing the mind towards God in ecstatic love of him.[2] To suffer adversity he accepted whatever came,

---

[1] magister Christus ad perfecte declinandum concupiscentiam oculorum consulit quod haec omnia temporalia relinquantur. . . . Ad perfecte declinandum superbiam vitae suadet quod voluntas propria abnegetur. . . . Ad perfecte declinandum concupiscentiam carnis edocet quod omnis experientia secundam actum generativae potentiae abscindatur . . . (ibid., 5, 245b.)

[2] . . . quae secundum duplicem viam, scilicet activam et contemplativam, in duobus consistit, videlicet in condescensione ad proximum et in sursusmactione mentis in deum (ibid., 6, 245b–246a).

G

with joy and patience.[1] As Bonaventure showed, all of these virtues had been embodied in the rule.[2] It was not, however, enough merely to respect them; they also needed to be practised. Hence the vow to observe them.[3]

Now there were varying degrees of evangelical perfection, according to the degrees of charity[4] and how faithfully its obligations were observed.[5] Bonaventure here studiously avoided invidious comparisons between the different religious states. Nor did he condemn those who were not sworn to poverty: on the contrary, allowing for his fair-mindedness and moderation, the whole of his case ultimately rested upon the permissibility—both legal and moral—of ecclesiastical possessions. Only if the church were the rightful owner of what the Franciscans consumed could the order be said to be in absolute poverty. Thus, when it came to poverty, Bonaventure had to defend what was virtually indefensible. He had on the one hand to acknowledge the compatibility of property with a true religious life; on the other he had to exalt poverty as the justification for the Franciscan way of life. It is hard to envisage how anyone could have succeeded; and despite the power that Bonaventure brought to the task one cannot but feel that he was happier in exalting charity. He makes many telling points, but even he could hardly use moral arguments to buttress legal arguments which conflicted with their morality.

What, then, were the properties of poverty which gave it a special place among the evangelical perfections? Bonaventure's answer was founded upon the contrast between charity and cupidity. Just as charity was the source of all goodness, cupidity was the root of all evil.[6] While as a sin it was an affliction of the spirit, it was occasioned by material possessions. Only their renunciation, spiritually and physically, could overcome it.[7] This double abdication, both of the world and the desire

---

[1] Quae quidem attenditur non solum in hoc, ut quis patienter adversa perferat . . . verum etiam ut ex fervore divini amoris magno desiderio illa praeoptet et cum gaudio magno sustineat . . . (ibid., 7, 246a).

[2] Ibid., 10, 246b–247a.

[3] Ibid., 11, 247a. Ex his omnibus aperte clarescit quod religionis votum in statu perfectionis collocat (ibid., 14, 248a).

[4] Quamquam enim totius huius perfectionis origo sit caritas, multum tamen facit ad eius complementum ipsa operatio . . . (ibid., 19, 249b).

[5] Ibid.

[6] Huic autem fundamento sive radici directe adversatur cupiditas, de qua scribitur ad Timotheum: 'Radix omnium malorum est cupiditas' (Tim. 1, 6: 10) (ibid., ch. vii, 1, 272a).   [7] Ibid., 2.

for it, which constituted poverty of the spirit, was in turn the source of evangelical perfection and the emulation of Christ.[1] It therefore consisted in the total absence of temporal goods, so that he who practised it lived by that which was not his.[2] This was of its essence, as St. Bonaventure recognized, and from it flowed all his other arguments: for once granted that a man had to live from what was not his own, he could not be called the proprietor of what he was enjoying.[3] Now this state could be either individual or communal;[4] and since each could be without the other,[5] there could be two forms of poverty. The first was that in which there were no personal possessions, but where everything belonged to the community; the second consisted in total abdication both of private and communal possessions, subsistence depending upon other sources.[6] To the first corresponded monasticism, with its prototype in the multitude of believers described in Acts (4,32): 'neither said any of them that aught of the things which he possessed was his own; but they had all things in common'.[7] The second form had its exemplar in the life of the apostles instituted by Christ, when he sent them out to preach with the injunction: 'Provide neither gold, nor silver, nor brass in your purses, nor scrip for your journey, neither shoes, nor yet staves.'[8] St. Bonaventure unhesitatingly took the doctrine of Christ's and the Apostles'

[1] Si igitur gemina haec abdicatio, mundi scilicet et concupiscentiae eius, quae etiam paupertas spiritus dicitur, ipsa est qua radix omnium malorum perfecte amputatur . . . certa potest ratione concludi quod perfectionis evangelicae, per quam Christo configuramur . . . radix est et fundamentum (ibid., 3, 272b).

[2] Ex his potest colligi paupertatis evangelicae ratio, videlicet, quod ipsa sit virtus temporalium abdicativa bonorum, qua quis, nil proprium habens, sustentatur de non suo (ibid., 4, 273a).

[3] Et quoniam dupliciter contingit rerum temporalium abdicare dominium, dupliciter etiam sustentari de non suo (ibid.).

[4] ideo paupertatis evangelicae duplex est modus duplexque perfectio. Cum enim duplex sit rerum dominium, privatum scilicet et commune, unum quidem spectans ad determinatam personam, alterum vero ad determinatum collegium (ibid.).

[5] et primum abdicari possit, retento secundo, possit etiam abdicari secundum cum primo (ibid.).

[6] duplex erit secundum hunc duplicem modum paupertatis perfecta professio, una videlicet qua quis, temporalium omnium privato seu personali abdicato dominio, sustentatur de non suo, id est non sibi proprio, communi tamen iure cum aliis participato et simul possesso; alia vero qua quis, omni rerum abdicato dominio tam in proprio quam in communi, sustentatur de non suo, id est non sibi proprio, sed alieno . . . (ibid.).   [7] Ibid.

[8] Matthew 10: 9. Secundae autem paupertatis exemplar et forma in vita praecessit apostolorum, quam perfectionis magister Christus eisdem instituit, quando ipsos ad praedicandum misit, sicut legitur in Matthaeo . . . (ibid., 5, 273b).

absolute poverty as the basis of Franciscan poverty: it entailed an 'extreme and penurious' form of renunciation which extended not only to possessions, but also to money.[1] It was for those who wished to emulate Christ.[2]

Having asserted the perfection of Christ's standard of poverty,[3] supported by a mass of patristic citation,[4] St. Bonaventure devoted the greater part of the remainder of his book to treating three vital qualifications to it: first, examples taken from the bible which showed Christ as having had possessions; second, the existence of property within the church; and third, Franciscan practices, such as the retention of buildings and the use of money. Bonaventure met the assertion that Christ had infringed his own rule, by pointing to the distinction between Christ's internal and external actions. In particular he applied it to the central problem of Judas's bag of money carried for the apostles. Far from impairing Christ's perfection it served the threefold aim of consoling the poor, confuting heretics, and setting an example to believers. These corresponded to the monastic orders in the communal form in which the money was held; to the prelates in dispensing it to support the priesthood and relieve the poor; and to the apostles in the use to which its contents were put when a purse was carried.[5] Thus actions, in themselves imperfect, became in Christ's hands perfect. The bag, far from being an incitement to cupidity, became an object of piety.[6] St. Bonaventure added point to the distinction by observing that Christ gave the bag to the disciple he foresaw would betray him.[7]

[1] In his igitur verbis dominus apostolis et praedicatoribus veritatis extremae ac penuriosae paupertatis formam servandam imponit quantum ad carentiam non solum possessionum, sed etiam pecuniarum et aliorum mobilium . . . (ibid.).

[2] Hanc paupertatis normam tanquam speciali prerogativa perfectam et Christus in se ipso servavit et apostolis servandam instituit (ibid.).

[3] Ibid., 273b–277b.   [4] John 13, 28–9.

[5] Habuit enim Christus loculos ad consolandum infirmos, ad refellendum improbos et ad informandum perfectos (ibid., VII, 35, 284a) . . . Respectu autem impiorum fuit actus commonitorius, primo quidem ad refellendum haereticos (ibid., 36).
. . . Respectu vero perfectorum fuit actus informativus. Siquidem quantum ad modum habendi forma fuit perfectionis in ecclesiasticis personis . . . (ibid., 37, 284b).
. . . Quantum autem ad modum dispensandi forma fuit perfectionis in ecclesiae prelatis, ut exemplo Christi ecclesastica bona dispensent . . . (ibid., 38).
. . . Quantum vero ad modum utendi forma fuit perfectionis ipsis apostolis, ac ceteris huiusmodi paupertatem professis, ut, cum ex amore paupertatis semper carere loculis cupiant, solum quando apertae necessitatis urget articulus, loculos ferant (ibid., 39, 285a).   [6] Ibid., 40, 285b.

[7] quia nullus de Christi discipulis periit nisi qui loculos portavit (ibid., 36, 284a).

From here it was but a short step to the solution of the second problem, of the church's dominion of temporalia; for if one of the justifications of Judas's bag was that it set an example to the church in disposing of its wealth, it must be permissible for the church to have property. Bonaventure's arguments in favour of this conclusion derived from what he had earlier said about degrees of perfection. Just as there were diverse modes of chastity, so also of poverty: hence to possess goods in common did not imply imperfection.[1] In the first place the clergy, as St. Jerome said, could live from tithes and oblations and 'naked follow the naked cross', because they enjoyed the nakedness of heart and body which spurns all superfluity.[2] If it was not so great as the nakedness of the monks, who renounced all right to private possessions or to their own will, or the greatest nakedness of all, of the apostles and their followers, it was great enough for perfection.[3] Although, therefore, the greatest perfection lay with those who aspired to imitate Christ's nakedness and the nakedness of the cross most completely, the church also participated in it.[4] St. Bonaventure here characteristically tried to strike a balance. It was true that the church's possessions did not impair its perfection, but it was equally absurd to pretend that its state was the height of perfection; this would be to place the present dispensation above the way of Christ and the apostles.[5] So far, St. Bonaventure had not said more than one could envisage St. Francis having said. It was with the second reason in favour of ecclesiastical possessions that he went beyond

[1] Non tamen ex hoc debet vel potest inferri, quod abdicatis rerum proprietatibus, possidere aliquid in communi sit imperfectum, quia sicut perfectae castitatis diversi sunt modi . . . sic et in modis perfectae paupertatis intelligendum est (ibid., 16, 277b).

[2] Ibid., 21, 279b.

[3] Nuditas autem cordis et corporis triplicem habet gradum. Nam quaedam est magna, quae attenditur in abiectione omnis superfluitatis et proprietarie possessionis. Et haec, quanquam non sit de necessitate, est tamen de congruentia status et ordinis clericalis. . . . Est et alia nuditas maior, quae non solum consistit in his, verum etiam in abdicatione potestatis possidendi proprium et abnegatio propriae voluntatis; et haec competit regularibus et coenobitis. . . . Est et tertia nuditas, quae consistit in praedicta sunt et insuper in abdicatione omnis transitoriae facultatis . . . et haec his competit apostolis et apostolicis viris (ibid., 22, 279b–280a).

[4] Verum est quidem quod ecclesiastica praedia sine detrimento perfectionis haberi possunt; quod autem sint ad perfectionis cumulum, sentire vel dicere adeo absurdum est ut ex hoc status modusque vivendi praesentium temporum vitae Christi praeferatur et apostolorum; quod est apertissime falsum (ibid., ch. VIII, 9, 289a–b).

[5] Si quis enim hoc sentiat quod census in culpa sit causaliter vel formaliter, cum Manichaeo errat. . . . Si quis autem intelligat censum esse culpae occasionem, a sententia veritatis non deviat (ibid., ch. VII, 24, 280b).

such a hypothetical boundary. He did so by distinguishing between what was of itself sinful, and that which was the occasion for sin. Now property fell into the second category; money, for example, was only an impediment to entering the kingdom of heaven if it was the occasion for an inclination to evil or a distraction from the good.[1] Since the priesthood belonged to the perfect, the church was not implicated in these evils; they only concerned the imperfect.[2] Even allowing for the customary qualification to this position, in the example of Christ's absolute poverty, it is hard to reconcile Bonaventure's defence of tribute with St. Francis's abhorrence of money.

The third ground for upholding church property was that it helped the church to serve God; in so far as it ministered to this end, and belonged to the church as a whole, it was to be praised; but not for itself.[3] It was the appeal to its higher end which justified ecclesiastical possessions and marked them off from mere private wealth which had no such purpose; it permitted a religious to be dispensed from poverty by a prelate.[4] This was doubtless a reference to the practice of friars who on becoming bishops no longer followed the rigour of the rule: it was to become one of the issues between the Spirituals, who opposed it, and the Community, who defended it; and it again points to another of St. Bonaventure's affinities with the latter. Ultimately, however, Bonaventure's defence of church property rested upon a parallel notion of condescension to that used to explain Christ's occasional resort to money and possessions: the church's involvement in this world implicated it in its imperfections for the support of the poor and its own priesthood.[5] This

---

[1] Nullo enim modo pecunia impedimentum difficultatis dei regnum intrare volentibus praestat, nisi quia vel est occasio inclinationis ad malum, vel distractionis a bono (ibid.).

[2] Verum est quidem quod census perfectis non tam vehemens nec tantorum est peccatorum occasio, . . . hinc est quod perfecta temporalium rerum abdicatio perfectis consulitur, non imperfectis (ibid., 28, 281b).

[3] Quodsi dixerit non se laudare possessiones quascumque, sed tantum communes et ecclesiasticas et domino dedicatas (ibid., ch. viii, 17, 291b).

[4] quod aliud competit perfectioni praelati, qui est persona communis, aliud perfectioni personae privatae. Et ideo, quamquam ratione praelationis quivis religiosus a statu paupertatis ad dispensationem temporalium possit assumi, impium tamen est hoc ad consequentiam trahere (ibid., 22, 293b).

[5] Licet igitur summi sacerdotes sive pontifices, quia curam habent non solum quantum ad perfectos et validos verum etiam infirmos et imperfectos, quos pascere debent exemplo et verbo et pro loco et tempore corporali subsidio, salva perfectione possessiones susceperint ad sustentationem pauperum et ecclesiae ministrorum (ibid., 22, 294a).

at once preserved its perfection and explained its limitations. Just as imperfection was not *ipso facto* sin, so perfection did not reside exclusively
in justice (i.e. grace and charity) but also in mission.[1] Thus St. Bonaventure sought to vindicate both absolute poverty and church property.
To what extent he succeeded must ultimately be a matter of opinion;
he certainly vindicated his order against the grosser arguments of
Gerard of Abbeville. But the inherent contradiction in making Franciscan poverty the highest state of attainable perfection, while not
diminishing the apostolic nature of the church, inevitably diminished
both: poverty, however exalted, was compromised by the qualifications made in favour of property; the church, however much the repository of perfection, was not so perfect as those who followed Christ's
example of absolute poverty. The appeal was to two—contradictory—
notions, where St. Francis's had been to one.

The third problem, the justification of Franciscan poverty as apostolic,
was in effect the corollary to the second. Once it was accepted that the
church could licitly exercise dominion over goods, why could it not
also own those enjoyed by the Franciscan order? And conversely, if
absolute poverty consisted in the total renunciation of all possessions,
as St. Bonaventure had already said, ownership must reside elsewhere.
These were the two propositions that he sought to establish. He began
by affirming the church's legal right—having already asserted its moral
right—to hold property; this was sanctioned in both divine and human
law, as his copious citations from canon law showed. It entitled the
church not only to tithes and offerings, but also to territorial possessions
—fields, towns, castles, counties[2]—without undermining its perfection.[3]
Next he had to show that this right also extended to Franciscan property.
This at once raised the distinction between use and possession, which
St. Bonaventure had earlier touched upon when discussing the two
different forms of poverty.[4] It was here that he reached the heart of the
case against Franciscan poverty, particularly as it had been developed
by Gerard of Abbeville in his *Contra adversarium perfectionis Christianae.*
According to Gerard, in the consumption of goods it was impossible to
separate use from possession; food eaten and clothes worn belonged to
those who received them. Accordingly the Franciscans were their
rightful owners. This in turn nullified the claim for papal dominion,
since dominion implied some benefit from what was possessed. But

[1] Ibid., ch. IX, 4, 295b.
[2] Ibid., ch. X, 11, 308a.
[3] Ibid., 309 a–b.   [4] Ibid., ch. VII, 3, 273a.

where use entailed consumption there could be none.[1] The arguments
were essentially legal, but in replying to them St. Bonaventure characteristically broadened the basis of discussion. He began by enumerating
the four categories of dominion: ownership (*proprietas*), possession,
usufruct and simple use (*simplex usus*). Of these only the last was
necessary to sustain mortal life: it marked the limit to which temporal
renunciation could go.[2] It was for those who followed Christ in his
extreme poverty; in return for the abdication of all worldly possessions,
they were content to live strictly by the use of goods which were not
theirs.[3] It was here, in specifying the quality of their poverty, that St.
Bonaventure went beyond Gregory IX's legislation in *Quo elongati* in
two respects. The first was in the more precise legal definition of use,
which identified it with bare subsistence; the second was in stressing
its penurious nature: for St. Bonaventure the words 'strict' (*arcto*)
and 'use' were almost inseparable from Franciscan poverty. It accompanied all his definitions of it, where it was invariably conceived as the
rigid restriction of use to bare necessities, in the way commended by
St. Paul: 'And having food and raiment let us be content.'[4] Dominion
was distinguished from use, then, not merely in law but in fact: legal
poverty meant practical penury, and absence of possessions austerity of
life. The pledge to one entailed the other. Nowhere did St. Bonaventure come closer to St. Francis than here; if over the theoretical foundations of both poverty in general and Franciscan poverty in particular
there was a radical difference, they were fundamentally in accord over
its practice. Poverty for each meant living in poverty.[5] It went with

---

[1] Gerard of Abbeville, *Contra adversarium perfectionis Christianae*, ed. S. Clasen in
AFH 31 (1938), 277–83, 32 (1939) 133.

[2] intelligendum est quod cum circa res temporales quatuor sit considerare, scilicet
proprietatem, possessionem, usumfructum et simplicem usum; et primis quidem tribus
vita mortalium possit carere, ultimo vero tanquam necessario egeat: nulla prorsus
potest esse professio omnino temporalium abdicans usum (ibid., ch. XI, no. 5, 312a).

[3] Verum ei professioni quae sponte devovit Christum in extrema paupertate
sectari, condecens fuit universaliter rerum abdicare dominium arctoque rerum alien-
arum et sibi concessarum usu esse contentam (ibid.).

[4] Timothy I, 6: 8. E.g., Cum autem circa temporalium bonorum possessionem duo
considerare contingat, dominium videlicet et usum, sitque usus necessario annexus
vitae presenti; evangelicae paupertatis est possessiones terrenas quantum ad dominium
et proprietatem relinquere, usum vero non omnino reiicere, sed arctare, iuxta illud
quod dicit Apostolus ad Timotheum: 'Habentes alimenta et quibus tegamur, his
contenti sumus' (ibid., ch. VII, 3, 272b–273a).

[5] Evangelica paupertas . . . perfecte ipsam profitenti suadet omnibus temporalibus
debet nudari quoad affectum atque dominium, et arcta sustentatione necessitatis esse

mendancy, humility, modesty[1] and a host of other virtues which Bonaventure enumerated in extolling it.[2] St. Bonaventure was to be a powerful influence upon the conception of poverty of Olivi and Ubertino of Casale, as we shall mention. Certainly he gave, for the first time, official formulation to the rigorist belief in poverty as a way of life. For that reason it marked a turning point in the doctrine.

On the two legal issues raised by Gerard of Abbeville, St. Bonaventure denied both. To the charge that the pope gained nothing from over-lordship of the order's goods, St. Bonaventure replied that the gain was a spiritual one in helping Christ's servants. On the count that the friars owned what they consumed St. Bonaventure cited the example of the son of a household who consumed his father's goods without being proprietor of them:[3] the order's case was parallel. But he also once again went beyond these purely legal points when he asserted that no one could be compelled to acquire possessions if he did not wish to do so.[4] This, one feels, was for him the real issue. Poverty was ultimately an attitude; it sprang from a supererogatory impulse to perfection; it was essentially a desire to emulate Christ. In itself it could never constitute complete perfection: that lay with absolute charity; but the greater the aspiration to poverty, the more perfect. Ultimately, then, poverty was a spiritual quality, which reflected a greater good.

This was the essence of St. Bonaventure's doctrine of poverty; and it

---

quantum ad usum . . . sic arctitudinem usus servet quod sustentationem naturae necessarium non devitet; sic necessitati subveniat quod ab arctitudine non recedat (ibid., ch. XII, 20, 322b–323a).

[1] . . . in quibus simul iunctis integra consistit ipsius perfectio, non solum in abdicatione proprietatum verum etiam in acceptatione necessariorum, cum videlicet quis mendicat et accipit, ut acceptione penuriosa purgetur, verecunda humilietur . . . (ibid., 33, 327b).

[2] St. Bonaventure devotes five pages to enumerating the virtues engendered by external poverty (ibid., ch. IX, 298a–302a).

[3] respondebimus quod lex illa civilis non habet hic locum. . . . Nam retentio domini huiusmodi rerum cum concessione usus facta pauperibus non est infructuosa, cum sit patri pauperum meritoria et professioni filiorum Christo famulantium opportuna. Nec obstat quod adversarius obiicit de rebus, quae usu consumuntur, quod in eis proprietas non separatur ab usu. Hoc enim fallit in peculio profectitio filiifamilias, ubi filiusfamilias usum habet, et tamen proprietas nec ad momentum residet penes ipsum. Sic et de ordine huiusmodi pauperum respectu Romanae ecclesiae intelligi debet (ibid., ch. XI, 7, 312b).

[4] Patet igitur per haec verba legis expressa, neminem posse proprietatem sive dominium, immo nec possessionem acquirere nisi vere vel interpretative animum acquirendi habeat (ibid., 9, 313a–b).

accounts for its ambivalence. On the one hand, it sought to define it in terms of a greater good—charity. On the other, it sought to exalt it over all other ways of life. At one and the same time it was both less than perfect, and the summit of humanly attainable perfection. It was both relative and absolute. There could be perfection which was not absolute—as with the church—and yet absolute poverty was the greatest perfection, as with the Franciscan order. Throughout his treatise St. Bonaventure was preoccupied by the need to balance the two, with the added complication of having to make the second depend upon the first. Thus he was faced with the paradox that Franciscan poverty, which was itself the summit of perfection, depended upon the lesser perfection of the church for its achievement; for it was only by virtue of the latter's dominion that Franciscan poverty was absolute. It is true that St. Bonaventure at one point went so far as to declare that it was not the concern of the Franciscans to whom belonged what was not theirs;[1] but the tenor of his whole work was to show precisely why the owner was the church. He was therefore led to qualifying what St. Francis had taken as self-evident. This was ultimately the difference between their doctrines of poverty. Bonaventure was always torn between adhering to St. Francis's belief in its absolute worth and his own awareness of its relative value. It was more perfect, and yet not more perfect.[2] Beside this, his problem of answering Gerard of Abbeville's legal arguments paled; and it is not without interest that Gerard made no attempt at a counter-reply.[3]

We can say, then, that St. Bonaventure's *Apologia pauperum* marked a new stage in the doctrine of absolute poverty for two reasons. In the first place it changed its moral basis away from the predominantly devotional attitude of the Spirituals, who regarded it as an end in itself, while giving moral substance to the predominantly legalistic formulations of *Quo elongati*. Long before John XXII's attack on the doctrine of absolute poverty, charity had become, with St. Bonaventure, its

[1] *Epistola de tribus quaestionibus*, 6, ibid., 333a. Cui igitur horum proprietas assignabitur? Respondeo ego quod cuiuscumque sit, non est mea nec ordinis, et hoc mihi sufficit ad meae conscientiae puritatem.

[2] E.g. ch. XI, 3, 311b.

[3] In this connexion I cannot agree with Lambert, op. cit., 139, that this was the weakest part of Bonaventure's work; his reason seems to be that Bonaventure was a theologian and not a lawyer. But this is not convincing. Bonaventure's reply to Gerard meets him on his own legalistic ground. Moreover, it is the same as that which Bonagratia of Bergamo, a litigious controversialist if ever there was one, was to give to John XXII in 1322. See below pp. 239 ff.

foundation. In the process, poverty could not but lose some of its force, if only because it was not its own justification. At the same time, however, Bonaventure also restored the substance of poverty; in addition to giving a greater precision to its legal status, in his definition of Franciscan use, he reaffirmed it as a way of life which must be observed in the deed as well as in the letter. This was his second great contribution: for the first time the obligation to austerity was enshrined in the order's vow to absolute poverty. Here, as we have earlier said, St. Bonaventure spoke with the authentic voice of St. Francis. But he was also doing more; he was enunciating what with Olivi and the Spirituals was to become the doctrine of the *usus pauper*, poor living. The phrase already occurs in the *Apologia*, in a citation from the *Glossa ordinaria*;[1] more important than its verbal form, however, St. Bonaventure made it the criterion of true poverty. It was here precisely that the disputes between the Community and the Spirituals were to centre.

St. Bonaventure's generalate was a watershed in Franciscan history both in practice and in doctrine. In each he has a claim to be regarded as a second founder of the order; in each he tried to adjust St. Francis's ideals to different circumstances; and in each this entailed reformulating them: if the voice was that of St. Francis it spoke in the language of the administrator and the scholastic, and its sound was modified accordingly. Herein lay the change. Hence it is not enough to try to assess St. Bonaventure solely in terms of whether he was true to, or betrayed, St. Francis. *Au fond* the difference between them was the difference between the Franciscan order in 1215 and 1269.[2]

St. Bonaventure's outlook was officially embodied a decade later in the papal bull *Exiit qui seminat*, which was in almost every respect inspired by the *Apologia*. The bull was designed to be a definitive statement of Franciscan poverty, and expressly prohibited any future reopening of the question.[3] *Exiit* was at once an exposition of Franciscan poverty along the lines laid down by St. Bonaventure, and a recapitulation of the provisions of the rule as modified by Gregory IX

---

[1] 'Memor illius praecepti: Nolite possidere aurum neque argentum, pecuniam quae ad pedes apostolorum ponebatur, non sibi recondebat, sed ad usus pauperum, quia sua patrimonia reliquerant' (*Apologia*, ibid., ch. VII, 32, 283a–b).

[2] Ibid., 233 n. 4 as the earliest date of composition.

[3] BF III (Ed. Sbaralea), Rome 1765, 415b–416a. Itaque sub poena excommunicationis, et privationis officii, ac beneficii, districte praecipimus ut praesens constitutio, cum ipsam legi contigerit, sic prolata est, sic fideliter exponatur ad litteram; concordantiae, contrarietates, seu diversae, et adversae opiniones a lectoribus seu expositoribus nullatenus inducantur.

and his predecessors: the first served as the justification for the second. Compared with Bonaventure's *Apologia* it lacks, understandably, depth and symmetry of construction: it simply takes some of his more salient arguments to defend the order's practice. As with Gregory IX in *Quo elongati*, Nicholas III assumed the role of the order's mentor, having been its cardinal protector. But unlike Gregory IX he did not attempt to set aside what had already been laid down; he confirmed all that had been said in *Quo elongati*, including the reasons for the invalidating of St. Francis's Testament.[1]

While, in underwriting the concessions which the order had received during the past half century, *Exiit* merely confirmed what had long been accepted, it also sought to invest it with a more explicit legal and moral basis and to give it finality. In that sense it was a new stage in the order's evolution; that it changed nothing in practice—even the abuses —explains why it did not succeed. But it provided those in search of change with an official justification.

Its point of departure was the absolute nature of Franciscan poverty, which consisted in total renunciation of both private and communal possessions, as formulated by Gregory IX and his successors.[2] Thus at the outset *Exiit* leaned upon previous papal declarations for its definition of poverty; although it began by quoting the words of the rule that 'the brothers shall appropriate nothing, neither home nor place nor anything', this was of itself too imprecise a foundation. In this lay the twin causes of its unviability: namely the initial vagueness of the rule; and subsequently Gregory IX's distinction between use and possession which could only be upheld by modifying poverty out of recognition. Hence the paradox that Franciscan poverty owed to papal interpretations both its absoluteness and its progressive relaxation. The Community accepted each as inherent in the other; the Spirituals denounced the second and distrusted the first. Where both sides agreed was in seeing papal declarations as the foundation of Franciscan poverty. *Exiit* in that respect, gave the process its final stamp. In particular it sought to justify absolute poverty by the example of Christ's life, which he had shown by word and deed to be the path of perfection. Here *Exiit* drew upon St. Bonaventure. Firstly, it employed his argument of Christ's condescension to the imperfect, to rebut the argument of Judas's bag.[3]

---

[1] BF III, 415a.

[2] sitque declaratum per eumdem praedecessorem Gregorium nonum, et nonnullos alios, hoc servari debere tam in speciali quam etiam in communi (ibid., 407a–b).

[3] Ibid., 407b.

Secondly, it invoked the same distinction between necessity and legal right to distinguish between use and possession. Extreme necessity knew no law, and its fulfilment required no other justification than that.[1] St. Bonaventure had invoked a fourfold distinction in temporal possession to show that the renunciation of dominion did not entail the denial of use. *Exiit* increased the number to five: adding the right of use (*ius utendi*) to the first three, of proprietorship, possession and usufruct, and making simple use, the last one, simple use of fact (*simplex usus facti*) to emphasize its purely natural standing freed from any legal connotation.[2] It was over the relation of the *ius utendi* to *simplex usus facti* that dissension was to rage between John XXII and the order, over the poverty of Christ. For *Exiit*, like St. Bonaventure, simple use amounted to purely natural demands for sustaining life, and bore no relation to the possession or abdication of the other four rights. The only thing outside its purview was money, which the brothers were precluded from using.[3] This led thirdly to its considering the claim (of Gerard of Abbeville) that there could be no dominion without benefit from what was owned; it met this by St. Bonaventure's argument that, for the papacy as the owner of Franciscan goods, the gain was spiritual.[4] Examples were taken from the rule—such as the performance of the divine office —to show that they implied the use of books and other articles.[5] Both the papacy and the order participated in an enterprise which was not only 'observable, possible and permissible, but meritorious and perfect'.[6] Everything was held by the Roman church, the friars having nothing but simple use, for the greater glory of God.[7]

Previous bulls had not combined the sense of moral mission with precise legal definition as *Exiit* did; in doing so it came nearest to stressing poverty as a way of life in the manner of Bonaventure and Hugh of Digne. This can be seen especially in the fourth and last of its Bonaventuran traits: its injunction to moderation. If it was less a plea for the *usus pauper* than *usus moderatus*, it nevertheless sought to associate absolute poverty with a life of poverty. Superfluity, in any form, was condemned as derogating from poverty; and in no circumstances was

---

[1] sic nec ipsis fratribus iure poli in extremae necessitatis articulo ad providendum sustentationi naturae via omnibus extrema necessitate detentis concessa praecluditur; cum ab omni lege extrema necessitas sit excepta (ibid., 408a).

[2] Ibid.   [3] Ibid.

[4] Retentio namque dominii talium rerum cum concessione usus facta pauperibus non est infructuosa domino cum sit meritoria ad aeterna (ibid., 408b).

[5] Ibid., 408b–409a.   [6] Ibid., 409a.   [7] Ibid.

provision to be made for the future.[1] The abdication of all possessions meant the restriction of use to necessities. In this respect *Exiit* was a departure from past declarations; in echoing Bonaventure's injunctions to austerity it established a precedent to which appeal could be, and was, made by the Spirituals in their struggle against laxity. The bull also contained other provisions, such as those against the holding of lands, granaries and vineyards,[2] which were again to be important issues in the succeeding decades. It omitted much that Bonaventure had said, not least his argument justifying the consumption of goods in use; but this was to be taken up again in the struggle with John XXII. It nevertheless contained enough to become one of the main sources of appeal for both the Spirituals and the Community. As officially embodying St. Bonaventure's amalgam of qualified poverty with strictness of life, it did something to mitigate the long-established departure from absolute poverty in all but name. In doing so, it helped to shift the grounds of dispute away from theory to practice; or more exactly, absolute poverty being generally assumed, the question turned on its observance: did the vow to poverty entail an obligation to strictness in the use of goods (*usus pauper*) or was it enough in itself? This henceforth became the central issue dividing the Spirituals from the Community.

Olivi: the 'usus pauper' and prophecy

It was with Peter John Olivi that the problem of poverty first resolved itself into a dispute over the *usus pauper*. The reasons lay in growing laxity. Olivi was not, as we know, the first to call attention to it; nor in doing so was he being at all revolutionary. St. Bonaventure, in his official letters, had inveighed vehemently against the abuse of poverty within the order on a number of occasions. His first letter, to the ministers and guardians of the order, on being elected general, sought the causes 'why the splendour of our order is to some extent tarnished'. Among them he put the 'multiplicity of transactions for which money, which above all things is inimical to our order's poverty, is avidly sought, incautiously received, and more incautiously dispensed'.[3] He also spoke of cases of idleness, evagation, importuning for possessions,

---

[1] Insuper nec utensilia, nec alia quorum usum ad necessitatem, et officiorum sui status executionem licet habere . . . ad ullam superfluitatem habere divitias, seu copiam, quae deroget paupertati . . . (ibid., 409b).

[2] Ibid., 412a.   [3] *Epistolae officiales*, Epist. I, *Opera Omnia* VIII, 468–9.

elaborate buildings, over-familiarity with those not of the order, the search for wills and burials, frequent and costly changes of places, and extravagance. A second letter written to the provincial ministers after the Paris chapter of 1266[1] again exhorted them to act against sumptuousness in buildings, clothes and books, and greed for wills and burial in Franciscan cemeteries; such excesses were bringing the order into disrepute. It was 'a profane lie to profess the highest poverty and yet to refuse to submit to penuriousness (in the use) of things'.[2]

These statements could well be taken as the text for Olivi's doctrine of the *usus pauper*. It was not in essentials a departure from St. Bonaventure. As Olivi frequently reiterated, most of what he said could be found in Bonaventure's *Apologia* and his letters to the order on poverty, as well as in Pecham's treatises. Olivi even acknowledged charity as the source of true perfection.[3] Indeed, despite their contrary roles in the order, St. Bonaventure and Olivi showed marked affinities in outlook. Both were moderate, traditionalists by preference, and innovators only by circumstances; they were among the few in the order who were both prominent in its affairs and original thinkers in a wider theological and philosophical context, men for whom poverty was only one of many problems—in marked contrast to the majority of the Spirituals; they both stressed obedience as much as poverty—again unlike most Spirituals. Yet their careers were at opposite poles: the greater part of St. Bonaventure's was spent at the top, first at Paris, as one of the outstanding thinkers of the day and holder of the Franciscan chair in the university there, and then as general of the Franciscan order for eighteen years—the longest period of office of any. Olivi, on the other hand, was dogged by condemnation and suspicion in both walks, as scholastic and as friar. Where Bonaventure went down to posterity as the order's second founder and his writing exalted, Olivi became the uncanonized saint of a new sect, the Provençal Beguins, and his works condemned.

How are we to account for the difference? Why should Bonaventure's teaching on the need for a life of austerity have become suspect when formulated by Olivi as the doctrine of the *usus pauper*? Why were his philosophical and theological opinions, novel but not heretical, repeatedly subjected to censure? Why did Olivi, the advocate

---

[1] Ibid., 470–1.   [2] Ibid., 471a.

[3] E.g., Septimum autem, scilicet quod paupertas non est perfectio sed instrumentum perfectionis, si intendit dicere quod non est illa finalis perfectio, que soli competit charitate, verum dicit (F. Ehrle 'Olivis Leben und Schriften', ALKG III, 409–552, at 522. Olivi's reply to St. Thomas Aquinas on poverty).

of obedience to papal and ecclesiastical authority, become the rallying point for disaffection towards them? The answers lie in a complex of considerations. To begin with, there was the worsening of the internal climate in the decade after St. Bonaventure's death; the unity which he had managed to preserve had by 1280 been openly breached by the Community's persecution of the Spirituals in the March of Ancona as we shall consider in the next chapter.[1] The question of poverty had passed from being mainly one of interpretation to a *casus belli*, dividing the order irreconcilably. In such circumstances the *usus pauper* became the badge of insurrection; insistence upon it, however moderate as with Olivi, ceased to be the predominantly moral exhortation which it had been with St. Bonaventure, and became an open challenge. It thereby lost any of its earlier neutrality. For better or for worse Olivi, as its advocate, entered the arena, and had to suffer the consequences of being treated by the Community as a subverter of the order.

There was also Olivi's vulnerable personal position due to a series of censures of his doctrines, beginning in 1279 and continuing at intervals throughout the rest of his lifetime and beyond. These formed one of the central threads in the dispute between the Spirituals and the Community; and we shall encounter them repeatedly in the forty years from 1279. For the moment, however, it suffices to stress the inevitably compromising effect that they had both upon Olivi personally and the Spirituals as a party; they presented the Community with one of its most powerful weapons, and one which was used with no small lack of scruple after Olivi's death, in the climax to the debate between the two sides at Vienne from 1309 to 1312. What caused Olivi to be suspect in the first place is a matter of conjecture. It may well have been the somewhat novel way in which some of his opinions were framed; it can hardly, on the face of it, be ascribed to his views on poverty,[2] since

---

[1] For details see pp. 168 ff. below.

[2] This is the opinion of J. Koch in 'Die Verurteilung Olivis auf dem Konzil von Vienne und ihre Vorgeschichte' *Scholastik*, v (1930), 489–522. This is an attempt to establish three theses: that Olivi's theological condemnations were only resorted to after the failure to gain the condemnation of his doctrine of poverty; that the form they took—as excerpts with graded censures, such as 'false' and 'heretical', instead of merely as theses stating the error—was of momentous importance for the future; and that Olivi was forerunner of the Nominalists. Of the first two points, that on the cause of the censures is mere conjecture; moreover, on Professor Koch's own showing, if Olivi's philosophical and theological opinions portended the errors of the four-teenth-century Nominalists, they would have justified censure in their own right. On the second point, it is hard to see why Professor Koch makes such a fuss: the

they had little place in the earlier condemnations; and by the time Olivi was called to account for them at the Paris chapter of 1292 they had long been known. As so often happens, once a man has been censured his reputation is likely to be permanently damaged. Olivi himself attributed his failure to become a master to this very cause;[1] and there can be little doubt that if it helped to make a martyr of him to the Spirituals, it made him suspect to the more extreme members of the Community. It must also be remembered that the first attacks on Olivi followed in the direct wake of the massive Paris condemnations of 1277, when the authorities would have been particularly sensitive to any doctrinal aberrations. Finally, there can be no doubt that Olivi's own leanings contributed to his difficulties; we may grant that he was a moderate, and fundamentally orthodox, but one cannot escape the impression of a certain deviousness in his make-up. Moderate in tone, his influence was upon the extremists; a lucid scholastic, he was also a fervent Joachist. Even the qualifications which he was compelled to add to his teachings were again qualified. He seems to have been a man who lived on two planes; or perhaps he simply lacked the indiscretion of an Ubertino of Casale, in not being able to throw prudence to the winds when the occasion seemed to demand it.

Whatever the cause may be—and we shall probably never know it—the moderation of Olivi's doctrine was singularly at variance with the hostility it provoked. His first encounter with authority was before 1279 when Jerome of Ascoli, then general of the Franciscans (1274–79) and later Pope Nicholas IV (1288–92), declared some questions by him on the Virgin to be erroneous and ordered them to be burned.[2]

---

change is one of *pro forma*, not of substance. That the censure of Eckhart, Ockham and his followers was by 'extract' instead of 'thesis' made them neither more nor less culpable or vulnerable than their predecessors. We shall consider the third point, on the nature of Olivi's doctrines, below.

[1] Veritatem dico in Christo Jesu et non mentior, testimonium mihi perhibente conscientia in spiritu sancto, quod quadam grandi erubescentia quodamque conscientiae stimulo Parisienses ambitiones perhorrescens vobis et sociis vestris scribere non curavi. . . . Putasne innuisset deus in cor praelati mei, ut me tanquam suspectum de veritate aut forte tanquam falsarium veritatis abiceret, diffamaret, reprobaret, ac condemnaret, ut sic tandem abiectum et humiliatum ille qui humilia respicit et qui ignobilia et contemptibilia mundi elegit, ad suum familiare consortium et colloquium me indignissimum sola sua gratia traheret et elevaret (*Quodlibeta*, quoted in Koch, art. cit., 496 n. 27).

[2] *Historia*, ALKG II, 288, and 'Series condemnationum et processuum contra doctrinam et sequaces P. I. Olivi' (ed. L. Amoros) in AFH 24 (1931) 502.

H

According to Angelo of Clareno, who reported the incident, it in no way prejudiced Jerome against Olivi; and later, as pope, he countered those who sought Olivi's persecution by praising his virtues.[1] This is very likely; for it did not prevent Olivi from having his opinion asked during Nicholas III's enquiry into poverty which issued in *Exiit qui seminat*.[2] It may well have been that he was actually present at its publication.[3] But such honour was short-lived. Three years later, in 1282 at the Strasbourg chapter-general, Olivi was attacked for sowing errors among his followers;[4] and an examination of his doctrines was entrusted to a commission of seven theologians, four masters and three bachelors at Paris.[5] The reasons for the attack are uncertain. If they were because of Olivi's doctrine of the *usus pauper*, then it was more than a little ironical that Jerome of Ascoli's successor, Bonagratia of St. John in Persiceto, was at the same chapter urging the observance of the *usus pauper*.[6] It has been conjectured that the polemic against a certain 'Brother 'Ar' '[7] in which Olivi was at this time engaged led to his victimization for his views on poverty.[8] Yet the censures themselves were of much wider import; and since Olivi had already been admonished for theological error it would be more plausible to regard the

[1] ALKG II, 288.

[2] ALKG III, 415.

[3] This took place at Soriano. Olivi was certainly in Rome at the time: quas Rome . . . conscripsi (ibid.).

[4] Amoros, art. cit., 503; ALKG III, 416, quoting from the *Chronicle of 24 Generals*.

[5] These were Droco of Provence, John of Valence, Simon of Lans, Arlotto of Prato, masters, and Richard of Middleton, Giles of Bensa, or Baysi, and John of Murro, bachelors. (ALKG, ibid., 416–17).

[6] This is reported by Ubertino of Casale in his defence of Olivi's doctrines, written nearly thirty years later. 'Nec obstat quod procurator produxit litteram fratris Bonagratie, in qua determinat nos tenere ex perfectione nostra ad usum pauperem.' ALKG II, 385. See also 387. There is no trace of the letter itself.

[7] See ALKG III, 477–9. Douie, *Fraticelli* 85, and Koch, art. cit., 498. Ehrle's suggestion that it stood for Arnold of Roccafolio rather than (as Sbaralea had believed) Arlotto of Prato, one of his Paris censors, seems the most likely. Arlotto was too senior (he became general in 1285) to be attacked with impunity—nor was it in Olivi's nature to disparage authority. Arnold, on the other hand, was at that time a bachelor and from Olivi's own province, where he was a staunch upholder of the Community; it was he who at the Milan chapter of 1285, together with thirty-five brothers, accused Olivi of being the head of a 'superstitious sect in Provence', ALKG III, 14. See below p. 106.

[8] This is Koch's view, 'Die Verurteilung', to justify which Bonagratia of St. John in Persiceto is transformed into Olivi's protector (ibid., 496 ff).

list drawn up by the Paris theologians as *bona fide*, rather than a pretext. Where there can be little doubt is that they were the turning point for Olivi. From this time on he was a marked man. Although he was at length rehabilitated by Matthew of Aquasparta and Raymond Gaufridi, he never rose to be above lector in the order; and he had to face further investigations in the early 1290s.

The 1283 proceedings were, to say the least, summary.[1] Olivi was not allowed to leave his province to defend himself. Two documents were drawn up. The first was a series of excerpts from his writings, known as the *Rotulus*, in which each statement was condemned as heretical, or false, or presumptuous, as the case may be.[2] The second was in the form of a letter containing twenty-two counter-theses by Olivi's judges, affirming what they conceived to be the true position; signed by them, it is known as the Letter of the Seven Seals.[3] Olivi was next confronted by the theses at Avignon and compelled to endorse them. They were then ordered to be read in every convent in the province,[4] and Olivi's writings were withdrawn.[5] A brief summary of Olivi's subsequent vicissitudes must suffice here.[6] For two years Olivi was deprived of his writings and was without a copy of the *Rotulus*; on gaining one, in 1285, he made his reply to the charges against him in three separate documents.[7] Meanwhile Bonagratia of St. John in Persiceto had died at

---

[1] Described by Olivi in his letter of justification to the Paris censors, printed in ALKG III, 418–21; see also ibid., 416–18.

[2] The original is not extant; but its contents are known through Olivi's reply to it, published as the second of three apologetic writings by D. Laberge, 'Fr. Petri Ioannis Olivi, tria scripta sui apologetica', in AFH 28 (1935), 130–55, 374–407. In it Olivi treated the accusations against him under twenty-two heads, the same number as the counter-statements in the Letter of the Seven Seals. Ehrle, however, without giving references, stated that the *Rotulus* contained 'about 34' theses, ALKG III, 421. He is followed in this vague statement by Douie, *Fraticelli*, 86, and Lambert, op. cit., 155, neither of whom gives evidence to support it.

[3] Published by G. Fussenegger, *Littera septem sigillorum*, AFH 47 (1954) 45–53.

[4] et quod rotulus predictus cum quadam solemni littera ei, ut videtur, e directo opposita per omnes conventus nostre provincie coram fratribus omnibus publice legeretur quasi in signum reprobationis evidentioris et horribilioris (ALKG III, 418). See also ibid., ch. xxx, 14 and 417.

[5] Ibid., 417.

[6] For fuller accounts see Ehrle 'Olivis Leben und Schriften' ALKG III 409–552. Also Douie and Lambert, op. cit., and DTC vol. xi art Olieu (Olivi) by Callaey cols. 982–99.

[7] Laberge, op. cit., where Olivi recounts his deprivations, 132 ff. See also his letter of justification ALKG III, 420–1.

Avignon shortly after Olivi's abjuration;[1] the vacancy was not filled until the election of Arlotto of Prato, at the chapter-general of Milan in 1285. It was there left to him to decide the future of Olivi's works which, until he did so, were to remain unread.[2] At the same chapter Olivi was publicly accused by Arnold of Rochafolio, provincial of Provence, and thirty-five others, of being the 'head of a superstitious sect', and the cause of dissension and error there.[3] The charge stuck, and Olivi, in life and death, was never freed from its stigma. For him personally, however, the worst was now past. Arlotto, after summoning Olivi before him at Paris, died in the following year without lifting the ban.[4] In 1287 Olivi, having satisfactorily expounded his doctrine of the *usus pauper* at the chapter of Montpellier, was appointed lector at the convent of St. Croce, Florence, by the new general, Matthew of Aquasparta.[5] He remained there until Matthew of Aquasparta's successor, Raymond Gaufridi, made him lector at Montpellier.[6] He thus returned to Provence, where he continued until his death in 1298. Olivi's rehabilitation, though precarious, held. Although he had to defend his doctrine of the *usus pauper* before the Paris chapter of 1292, and his followers and his doctrines seem to have been under attack during the last decade of the century,[7] he was never again subjected to the indignities of 1282-5.

[1] Bonagratia had been unable to conduct the proceedings against Olivi at Avignon, and had deputed the task to Arlotto of Prato, who succeeded him as General in 1285. Bonagratia died soon afterwards. Quoted from the *Chronicle of the 24 Generals*, ALKG III, 417.

[2] . . . quod diligenter inquirant in suis provinciis si quis frater habeat questiones aut aliquid de scriptis fratris Petri Ioannis de provincia Provincie, et omnia inventa auferant, nec aliquem eis uti permittant quousque per generalem ministrum aliud fuerit ordinatum. A. Callebaut, 'Acta Capituli Generalis Mediolani celebrati anno 1285', AFH 22 (1929) (273-91) 289.

[3] ALKG III, ch. XXXII 14: consilium fratris Ar[naldi] de Rochafolio tunc ministri provincie Provincie et XXXV fratrum minorum de provincia eadem in quo concorditer asserunt illi fratres, et fratrem P[etrum] Jo[hannis] esse caput superstitiose secte et divisionis et plurium errorum in eadem provincia Provincie.

[4] ALKG III, 430; also Angelo Clareno *Historia*, ibid., II, 295-6, which gives a much more colourful account, showing both Olivi and Arlotto in a favourable light. Arlotto, despite having twice been in the role of Olivi's judge, was warmly regarded by both Angelo and Ubertino of Casale, who bracketed him with Matthew of Aquasparta and Gaufridi as 'preclaros scientie theologie doctores' (ibid., II, 387).

[5] ALKG II, 389, and III, 431.

[6] Ibid.

[7] Ibid., III, 191, where Ubertino of Casale reported that his exposition satisfied the chapter: 'remansit capitulum paccatum et contentum'. Ubertino also denied (ibid., II, 389) that Nicholas IV condemned Olivi's doctrines, as Raymond Fronsac implied

But within a year of his death his works had been banned in Provence by the chapter-general at Lyons in 1299, and his adherents persecuted.[1] His name was to remain in the forefront of the order's history for the next twenty-five years, as we shall have occasion to see.

Olivi's doctrines fall into three divisions: his philosophical/theological teachings; the *usus pauper*; and his Joachism. Although the last two are primarily our concern, something must also be said of the first group, since it played an important part in the disputes between the two sides from 1309 to 1312, culminating in the decrees of the Council of Vienne. Moreover, they should help in assessing the nature and degree of Olivi's heterodoxy. We must accordingly turn to Olivi's three apologias with which, as we have mentioned, he sought to justify himself against the accusations made in the *Rotulus* and the Letter of the Seven Seals. The *Rotulus*, in particular, became the centre of the controversy over Olivi's orthodoxy; although it has been lost, Olivi's replies, especially the second[2] and fullest, form a comprehensive statement of his own outlook. It was framed under twenty heads which, excluding those concerned with the *usus pauper* and cognate matters, comprised the following topics: universals and created being; free will; God's nature; and marriage. In his reply to the Letter of the Seven Seals he dissociated himself from the last seven articles (16–22) on the grounds that he had never taught anything else; these included the statement that grace constituted an absolute quality in the soul, and that it was increased independently of any change in the soul.[3] The majority of Olivi's arguments show a tendency to distinguish categories from entities: he thereby sought to reduce the number of independent elements of which being was comprised as well as simplifying the attributes of God. Thus he explained the statement excerpted from him in the *Rotulus*, 'that the credible does not represent real credible things, but derives only from the disposition of the believer', by defining

---

—ibid., III, ch. XXXIII 14: 'continetur lictera felicis recordationis domini Nicholai pape IIII, in qua reprobat doctrinam fratris P[etri] Jo[hannis] generalibus verbis'; see also ibid., 15.

[1] Ibid., 15–16. This took place under the General John Minio of Murrovalle. See Amoros, art. cit., 504.

[2] i.e. following Laberge, 'Tria Scripta', AFH 28, 130 ff.

[3] Ibid., 130, Responsio I ad litteram magistrorum. Koch, art. cit., 515–21, adduces a series of statements by Olivi, from his *Quodlibeta* on grace and God's will, to prove that he was a forerunner of the fourteenth-century Nominalists. Within the terms of our discussion, however, we shall confine ourselves to Olivi's explanations of his condemned articles.

credibility as a disposition to believe; it was therefore general to all belief, whether the object was an actual thing or a matter of faith, such as God or the Trinity, which could not be located in *rerum natura*.[1] Similarly, he held that a universal could not actually exist outside the mind; otherwise it would both inhere in individuals and be present everywhere else.[2] Again, he denied that matter contained its own formal tendencies (elsewhere known as 'seminal reasons'), but in this case, as he said, he was in good company among ancient philosophers like Aristotle and also many contemporaries.[3] Undoubtedly the most potentially far-reaching of Olivi's propositions was the one implying that terms such as movement, relation and so on did not stand for distinct essences or forms, but were mental categories, referring to one and the same being.[4] Olivi equivocated here, in a way reminiscent of fourteenth-century thinkers like Buckingham and Holcot; it was, he said, a philosophical rather than a theological matter, and he was only reciting what other philosophers had said.[5] But if taken together with his other positions it unquestionably looked along the path to Ockham and his followers, in treating general terms as descriptive rather than as substantive.

At the same time there was much in Olivi's replies which conformed to the Augustinian tradition associated with the Franciscan order. In the first place, he was very much in accord with the post-1277 hostility towards Aristotle, an attitude he shared with his confrère John Pecham who, as archbishop of Canterbury, instituted a second condemnation of Aristotelian, and especially Thomist, propositions at Oxford in

---

[1] Laberge, ibid., p. 135: reply ad primum dictum. Olivi also complained, as he did with most of the articles, that his words had been torn from their context.

[2] Reply ad octavum: . . . in tota questione illa intendo astruere quod universale quantum ad suam universalitatem nihil ponat in actu nisi solum in intellectu, et . . . intendo probare quod, si universale secundum suam universalitatem esset actu in rebus, sequeretur quod non solum esset in suis individuis, sed etiam esset per praesentialem existentiam in omnibus aliis rebus . . . (ibid., 154). Once again Olivi had good cause to resent the construction put upon his meaning.

[3] Ad nonum, ibid., 154-5. Although his attempt to include St. Augustine among them was going too far.

[4] Ad vigesimum: Haec sunt illa quae directius fidem catholicam tangunt. Inter praedicta autem interponuntur quaedam alia quae potius sunt de materia philosophica quam theologica utpote: an distinctio omnium praedicamentorum ponat semper necessario diversitatem essentialem inter ipsa, aut solum aliquando ponat differentiam rationum realium tantum . . . (ibid., 404).

[5] Ibid., 405-6. Koch, art. cit., 515 ff. uses this quite unwarrantably as evidence of Olivi's Nominalism.

1284.[1] Secondly, what he said on the relation of the soul to the body was clearly prompted by an Augustinian desire to safeguard the soul's spiritual identity: of its different parts only its sensitive faculty was in direct contact with the body. The intellective or rational soul, on the other hand, was not: in that sense it was not directly united to the body as its form, save through the sensitive soul. Here, too, Olivi successfully vindicated himself from misrepresentation by his censors through showing that this in no way implied the separation of man's body and intellect into two distinct beings.[2] The same Augustinian trait can be seen when he affirmed man's dependence upon God's special illumination for adequate understanding of anything, since his natural powers did not suffice. Indeed he here closely approached Bonaventure in emphasizing the special nature of such divine irradiation.[3]

There were yet again other propositions to which one can attribute no wider significance beyond Olivi's interest in them. Among these was a number devoted to what we might call questions of cosmology or physics. Here his judges were far behind Olivi in grasp and originality; they appeared to have no comprehension of such problems as whether, and if so how, God could create an actual infinity[4]—a problem which was to become prominent in the earlier fourteenth century, and was pregnant with possibilities.[5] They even went so far as to censure him for adopting St. Thomas Aquinas's and Aristotle's distinction between creation and conservation,[6] which was later also to command general assent. By no stretch of the imagination could these have been taken to be subversive; and in showing an interest in them Olivi was anticipating subsequent developments.

[1] See the writer's *Medieval Thought*, 228 ff.

[2] Ad decimum. Ibi enim dico quod pars animae intellectiva non unitur corpori ut forma, quamvis uniatur ei substantialiter; ibi etiam dico quod anima rationalis sic est forma corporis quod tamen non est hoc per omnes partes suae essentiae, utpote non per materiam seu per partem materialem, nec per partem intellectivam sed solum per partem eius sensitivam.... Ego autem illic ostendi ... quod haec duo stare possunt absque hoc quod pars intellectiva sit forma corporis. (Laberge, art. cit., 155). Cf. also 'Tertium' where he affirms that the soul is both simple in itself and able to unite with the body (ibid., 140).

[3] quod sic nullus homo ex potentiis et habitibus ac proprietatibus naturalibus sibi datis posset aliquid intelligere vel cogitare, etiam mala vel indifferentia vel connaturalia, sine aliquo speciali influxu alicuius irradiationis gratuitae ... (Secundum, ibid., 140). This immediate dependence is in addition to the general dependence of all creatures upon God, ibid.　　　　[4] E.g. ibid., 19, 400.

[5] See the author's *Gregory of Rimini*, ch. IV, 'The New Cosmology'.

[6] Laberge, ibid., 7, 153.

Finally, there were the questions concerning God. Some, as we have just mentioned, dealt with what he could do in the natural world; others concerned his will and knowledge.[1] Particularly in what he had to say on God's future knowledge Olivi anticipated Duns Scotus; for he distinguished the way in which God knew what was yet to come from what was already in being or had been.[2] His views were evidence of a probing—if not profound—mind several moves ahead of his accusers. In this connexion, the charge which Olivi appeared to feel most keenly was that against his Trinitarian doctrine. Having replied to it in the two earlier documents he then wrote a further and third apology devoted entirely to substantiating his position. It forms a treatise in its own right;[3] and offers no grounds for censure. In it, as in the second apology,[4] Olivi was concerned to argue first that the divine essence, as common to all three divine persons, when taken in its most absolute sense referred only to its essence, and when taken less strictly included the concepts of the three persons of the Trinity; and secondly, that the divine persons as all sharing in the divine essence could each be conceived as one aspect of it.[5] There is no question in what Olivi wrote of his having posited either a separate divine essence—distinct from the essences of the divine persons—or separate essences for each of the divine persons, the implications attributed by the commission of

---

[1] E.g., 17, 18, 20, ibid., 395 ff., 399 f., 403 ff.

[2] Ibid., 18, 399.

[3] The articles on the Trinity in the reply to the Rotulus (document no. 2) were 4, 5, 6. For the third apology see Laberge, AFH, 29 (1936) 98–141 and 365–95.

[4] Quintum. Inter praedicta autem ponitur unum aliud dictum meum ex eadem quaestione sumptum sic: 'per hoc igitur, quod essentia producens et essentia producta sunt idem cum essentia divina absolutissime accepta, per hoc convenit divinae essentiae absolutissime acceptae, quod sit plura supposita' (ibid., 28, 147).

[5] loquendo de divina essentia, prout est communis tribus personibus et tres simul et singillatim comprehendens et prout ipsa est absolutissime et abstractissime sumpta, absque videlicet omnia determinatione aut cointelligentia alicuius relationis aut proprietatis personalis, sic non est generans, nec genita, nec procedens; et sic loquitur decretalis [Innocentii papae III]. Loquendo de ea prout est propria huius vel illius personae, et prout est per aliquam proprietatem personalem determinata et ad determinatum modum existendi appropriata, sic in patre est generans, in filio genita, in spiritu sancto procedens; et sic loquuntur sancti . . . (ibid, 29, 99).

Item in quibusdam earum dicitur quod filius est de substantia patris genitus, et spiritus sanctus de substantia utriusque. Et in quibusdam illarum dicitur quod filius non est genitus de paternitate aut de aliqua relatione personali ipsius patris, sed potius de substantia vel essentia eius, et simile dicitur de spiritu sancto respectu patris et filii (ibid., 131).

seven.[1] In the third apology Olivi, in addition to his own arguments, quoted chapter and verse from nearly every possible source of authority to show his consonance with tradition; he undoubtedly made his case. Perhaps the best evidence for Olivi's fundamental soundness is that even when his doctrines were examined by a commission of the Council of Vienne none was condemned; and only three, on Christ's spear wound, the soul as the form of the body, and on baptism, were considered dubious.[2] Of these only one—on the soul—was included in the *Rotulus* of 1283. If doctrinally Olivi was sometimes the victim of his own formulations, he was far more the victim of circumstances: both the general intellectual climate of uncertainty and the suspicion of his ideas within his own order. None of the opinions for which he was arraigned in 1283 in fact ever became heresy or was prohibited, and much, especially his philosophical speculations, became accepted currency in the next century.[3]

On poverty and the affairs of his order Olivi was, if anything, even more restrained; in addition to his unfailing deference to authority, so marked in his three replies, he allowed himself no room for speculation or innovation. All that he said on the subject had been already said, in substance, by St. Bonaventure and Pecham,[4] to whose authority, in

[1] Letter of Seven Seals, arts. 1 and 2, quoted by Olivi in his first reply (ibid., 28, 126).

Koch, art cit., 515 attributes Olivi's error to his identifying individuation with personality, and consequently tending to attribute a separate idea or reason to each. It is true that Olivi speaks of *ratio communis* and *ratio singularis* (AFH, 29, 132 ff.) but not in order to juxtapose God's essence to the divine persons: on the contrary, the terms are employed to show that the divine persons cannot be subsumed under them, since a *ratio singularis* does not entail the notion of being produced—which is in what the relation between the divine essence and the divine persons consists. Nor is there anything that I have seen in Olivi's treatise to suggest the identification of personality and individuation: Olivi, indeed, treats the persons as merely another, and less absolute, aspect of the divine essence, as the quotations above show.

[2] *Fidei catholicae fundamento*, BF v, no. 196, 86. The one reference to the sacraments in the *Rotulus*—on marriage—was not mentioned in the bull.

[3] From Koch's attribution of Nominalist tendencies to Olivi, Lambert, op. cit., draws the unwarranted conclusion that 'it is becoming increasingly clear that the basic charges brought against Olivi in 1283 were the same as those alleged against the Nominalists in the fourteenth century' (p. 156). They were not, as the censures against Ockham, John of Mirecourt, Nicholas of Autrecourt and others show. See pp. 294 ff. below.

[4] Fratris Johannis Pecham: *Tractatus tres de paupertate* (ed. C. L. Kingsford, A. G. Little, F. Tocco, Aberdeen 1910).

Pecham adopted a similar position to St. Bonaventure. On the one hand he stressed

his writings after 1279, he added *Exiit qui seminat*. The kernel of Olivi's teaching was, as we have said, the obligation to observe the *usus pauper* by those vowed to evangelical poverty. In this sense, he made formal and explicit what St. Bonaventure and Pecham had only implied; but it was this very attempt to establish the *usus pauper* as both a concept in its own right and as inseparable from the vow of poverty which made it the bone of contention; for it became a legal as well as moral commitment. What had previously been a general exhortation now carried a series of specific requirements, all of which were to be found in the rule. To have accepted it would have meant dispensing with a multitude of concessions and ameliorations. No wonder it caused so much opposition. From this point of view the *Rotulus* is instructive; for in addition to enabling us to grasp the essentials of Olivi's position, it also shows how it was regarded by the representatives of the Community. As we have mentioned earlier, Olivi devoted four articles to poverty in his reply to the *Rotulus*.[1] The first of these put the question whether the *usus pauper* was included in the vow of poverty as integral to it.[2] Olivi's affirmations were called by the commission 'commonly false and dangerous to our state'. The Letter of the Seven Seals had framed this objection as the statement that the *usus pauper* 'was in no way included in the vow of evangelical poverty; and to say the contrary is erroneous'.[3] They also defined the *usus pauper* as 'extreme necessity'.[4] Olivi, in reply, was able to fall back upon the authority of Bonaventure, Pecham and Hugh of Digne, as well as *Exiit qui seminat*. The choice is instructive. Together they constituted the principal—if

the permissibility of living on alms gained other than from begging or manual labour (ibid., 23–6); upheld the obligation to obey the pope; and endorsed the compatibility of the provisions of *Quo elongati* with St. Francis's ideals (ibid., 30–2). On the other, he insisted strongly upon restrictions of use to a rigour in keeping with the vow to absolute poverty. He attacked, in particular, excessive building, and the holding of granaries and cellars (ibid., 33–8); he also reiterated the prohibition on the use of money (ibid., 33 and 40 ff.). More than Bonaventure he elaborated upon the conditions conforming to penury, as for example, 'vile food' (49–50). Most interesting of all is the evidence of his Joachism (67–76): he enumerated the seven heads of the dragon in terms not dissimilar from Olivi—duplicity, secular knowledge, oppression of the poor, cupidity, carnality, desire for earthly glory, hypocrisy—and foretold that the righteous poor would be persecuted by Antichrist.

[1] 13, 14, 15, 16, Laberge, art. cit., AFH 28, 381 ff.

[2] Tertium decimum. Post hoc ponitur aliud dictum meum sumptum ex quaestione: 'an usus pauper includatur in consilio seu voto paupertatis evangelicae, ita quod sit de eius substantia et integritate' (ibid., 381).

[3] Ibid., 382.   [4] Ibid.

not the only—sources of the doctrine. Of these *Exiit* was posterior to Olivi's first treatise on the question,[1] while both Bonaventure and Pecham represented the moderate standpoint among the Community. Hugh of Digne alone belonged both to the Spirituals and an earlier generation;[2] and there seems every reason to believe, on the existing evidence, that his treatise on poverty, *De finibus paupertatis*,[3] was the starting point of the doctrine of the *usus pauper*. If, as seems very probable, St. Bonaventure's *Epistola de tribus questionibus* was beholden to Hugh's exposition of the rule,[4] he could well have been influenced also by what Hugh had to say on poverty. Even if he was not, there seems little doubt that Olivi was.

There was a greater radicalism in Olivi's attitude to the *usus pauper* which corresponded to Hugh's. This consisted less in any difference of conception than in the degree of obligation it imposed. For Olivi, as for Hugh of Digne, extreme penury was so inseparable from the vow of poverty that there could never be any dispensation from it. For Bonaventure, on the other hand, there were mitigating circumstances. It was here that Olivi, for all his moderation, parted company from Bonaventure, and took over the essentials of Hugh of Digne's position. Hugh had written his *De finibus paupertatis* with the aim of defending the rule and its injunction to absolute poverty, which he regarded as the distinguishing feature of the Franciscan order.[5] He accepted the distinction between use and possession; and on the basis of it enunciated the three main characteristics of the *usus pauper*, which the Spirituals were to uphold. The first was its specific nature. Hugh gave ten requirements for fulfilling the vow of poverty, which began with initiation into the *usus pauper* and included tattered habits, bare feet, a ban on riding and money, a life of wandering, mendicancy and self-denigration.[6] The second feature was that it was obligatory: it was the expression of poverty. From this followed the third, that no one—popes included—could dispense a brother from its obligation.[7] In short, austerity of life

---

[1] ALKG III, 531, where he wrote: 'sufficiat michi ad presens ad confutationem predicti erroris adducere verba expressissima Nicholai pape [III] in declaratione super regulam fratrum minorum edita, que idcirco in questione de usu paupere non posui, quia nondum erat facta'.

[2] See Salimbene's reference to his influence upon John of Parma and others who formed his disciples at Hyères in Provence, *Chronica* 231 ff.

[3] Ed. C. Florovsky, AFH 5 (1912) 277–90.

[4] Lambert, op. cit., 117.   [5] Florovsky, art. cit. 283.   [6] Ibid.

[7] Item nullus hominum quantecunque auctoritatis potest ex quacunque causa dispensare in sollempni voto vel continencie, vel paupertatis (ibid., 284).

was built into the vow of poverty; it was not merely a general desideratum but its embodiment. For Hugh, then, the *usus pauper* was both tangible and indispensable. That was his particular legacy to Olivi and the Spirituals. In their hands it became a formal obligation to be observed in its own right; their insistence upon recognizing it for such was, as we have said, the main issue between the two sides.

Olivi substantially followed Hugh of Digne; and in the sense that he posed the question of the inclusion of the *usus pauper* in the vow of poverty he may be said to have initiated the disputes over it. Significantly, when replying to the strictures in the *Rotulus*, it was in the 'most famed and holy' Hugh's *De finibus paupertatis* that he found his greatest support; he quoted there verbatim Hugh's arguments in favour of strict poverty, and his ten conditions for its observance.[1] At the same time Olivi was careful to point out that the *usus pauper* was not to be taken as some fixed measure from which there could be no departure; it rather consisted in applying its principles in the light of circumstances.[2] In this respect Olivi was less uncompromising than Hugh, and there was, on occasion, more than a hint of the accommodation which could too easily engender laxity. Thus extreme poverty must not lead to danger or imperfection; it must not be too strict in confining what was necessary to the immediate present, nor too broad in extending to the present what was needed for the whole of life.[3] Olivi here came close to *Exiit's* conception, which he invokes.[4] Extreme poverty was for him essentially a relative term; but nevertheless a determinate one.[5] While its application could vary, its obligation was constant.

Elsewhere Olivi had elaborated the conditions of observance of the

[1] Laberge, art. cit. 28, 383–4.

[2] Ibid., 385.

[3] quod solum illo modo sub voto cadere potest, secundum quem ipsum votum nihil implicet in se periculi aut imperfectionis . . . sciendum tamen quod praesens necessitas discrete est intelligenda, quia non nimis stricte nec nimis large. Nimis enim stricte sumeretur, si nihil aliud de presente reputetur esse necessarium nisi illud quo necessario indigeo pro usu praesentis momenti; nimis autem large, si totum illud quod ad totam vitam nostram posset esse necessarium, pro praesenti necessitate accipiatur (ibid., 384–5).

[4] Ibid.

[5] Si vero dicatur quod in eo quod dixi pauperem usum seu extremam necessitatem, sub modo et sensu praedicto sumptam cadere sub voto indeterminate, dixi falsum et periculosum, pro eo quod votum debet cadere super materiam certam et determinatam. . . . Non enim accipitur hic indeterminate secundum omnem modum aut quoad omnia sua, sed solum eo modo quo medium virtutis moralis (ibid., 386).

usus pauper.¹ Having affirmed that without the *usus pauper* the highest poverty was devoid of perfection,² he likened it to form in relation to matter: just as matter alone was a shapeless flux, so was the abdication of all dominion unaccompanied by practical poverty.³ It brought contempt upon those who professed it.⁴ Since the vow was designed to achieve perfection, its implementation must be flexible: certain of its precepts were to some degree indefinite, so that a modest deviation from them was a venial rather than mortal sin—as, for example, in the case of infringing the requirements of temperance or humility.⁵ Since human nature was prone to such failings, to make them all mortal sins would be inimical to the order's life.⁶ Other transgressions (such as adultery) were, however, too serious to permit their infraction.⁷ The same applied to the *usus pauper*, violation of which, because it was indeterminate, was not automatically a mortal sin; it only became so through repetition, making what should be poor usage, rich.⁸ Local adjustments there might be, but no dispensation. Once the vow of poverty had been taken it was immutable. Here the rigorist side of Olivi came to the top: he was willing to compromise on details but not principles. He denied emphatically that friars who became bishops could be released from obligation to the *usus pauper*.⁹ For this he was

¹ Olivi's writings on poverty are scattered among his works: see M-Th. d'Alverny 'Les écrits théoriques concernant la pauvreté évangélique', *Positions des Thèses de l'École Nationale des Chartes*, Paris 1928, 5–8. Printed extracts from a question on the *usus pauper*, written before *Exiit qui seminat*, and from a subsequent polemic defending it, are to be found in ALKG III, 507–14.

² Respondeo et dico quod usum pauperem discrete tamen et rationabiliter acceptum esse de integritate et substantia perfectionis evangelice . . . Non enim invenies aliquam paupertatem altissimo modo valere ad altissimam virtutum perfectionem nisi ei adiungatur pauper usus (ALGK III, 507–8).

³ Circa primum autem sciendum quod sicut forma se habet ad materiam, sic usus pauper se habet ad abdicationem omnis iuris. Unde sicut materia sine forma est informis et confusa, instabilis, fluxibilis et vacua seu vana et infructuosa, sic abdicatio omnis iuris sine paupere usu se habet (ibid., 508).

⁴ Ibid.

⁵ Modicus enim defectus temperantie non est mortale, nisi quando est tantus quod magis homo debet censeri intemperatus quam temperatus (ibid., 509).

⁶ Ibid.   ⁷ Ibid.

⁸ Unde non omnis deviatio a paupere usu in professoribus suis mortale inducit, sed quando est talis et tanta, quod pensatis hinc inde circumstantiis potius debet censeri dives usus quam pauper (ibid., 510).

⁹ Ad quartam questionem, qua de usu episcoporum de statu evangelico assumptorum queritur, dicendum quod indubitanter est tenendum eos ad usus pauperis observantiam teneri et aliquo modo amplius quam antea tenerentur (ibid., 511).

censured by the commission of seven.[1] If, Olivi argued, the way to perfection was through the precept and practice of poverty, it could never be dispensed with; indeed, so far as bishops were concerned, the sublimity of their office correspondingly demanded the highest perfection, which could only be attained through poverty.[2] The discrepancy between this ideal and current practice was made by Olivi the occasion of a diatribe against the pomp and splendours of prelates, regulars as well as seculars; they travelled on horses; they were surrounded by hosts of servants and companions; they were richly adorned; they kept luxurious tables.[3] The tone was reminiscent of his *Postilla* on the Apocalypse. Were one friar to live in such self-indulgence and worldliness he would be judged to be in mortal sin.[4] Olivi modified his position in his reply to the *Rotulus* by allowing that in cases where the cure of souls demanded it, bishops could enjoy greater abundance.[5] On the question of procurators, for which he was again censured in the *Rotulus*,[6] Olivi made a clear distinction between what was done as condescension from a state of perfection and what was indulgence to imperfection; the latter was a concession to weakness designed as a safeguard against worse happening.[7] Procurators belonged to this second category.[8] In his defence against the verdict of the *Rotulus*, Olivi cited both Gregory IX and Nicholas III to show that the order had no power to appoint procurators;[9] but his main argument rested on the pledge to absolute poverty, which precluded any litigation over property.[10] He also appealed to the example of Christ and the Apostles.[11]

---

[1] Laberge, art. cit., vol. 28, no. 14, 387.   [2] ALKG III, 511.   [3] Ibid.

[4] Quia unus frater vivens ita laute et otiose et pompose . . . qui tamen hodie iudicabitur communiter esse in statu salutis, credo communi omnium iudicio iudicaretur esse in statu dampnationis (ibid., 512).

[5] Item, per observantiam voti de pauperi usu, nunquam intendi excludere, quin in casu in quo esset necesse vel utile multis et pretiosis uti, secure possent talibus uti, et praecipue ubi hoc esset necesse vel utile regimini animarum . . . (Laberge, art. cit., vol. 28, 14, 390).

[6] Ibid., 15, 390 ff.   [7] ALKG III, 513.

[8] Primo modo clarum est quod instituere non possunt, cum ipsi nullam habeant iurisdictionem in rebus legatis vel datis. Secundo autem modo non bene ad presens intelligo quod hoc possit fieri secundum perfectionem et condecentiam status nostri . . . etsi forte possit hoc fieri secundum indulgentiam et imperfectionem infirmis concessam (ibid.).   [9] Laberge, art. cit., 28, 391.

[10] quomodo ergo perfectis nihil habentibus in proprio vel communi licebit non solum secundum veniam sed etiam secundum perfectionem alios incitare, instruere, et movere ad causarum litigia seu iudicia pro se ipsis? (ibid., 392).

[11] Ibid., 392–3.

Here, once more, it was the principle that Olivi was attempting to establish; modifications to it must be recognized for such, even if justified by circumstances. The same applied to what he said about debt: as an obligation to repayment it was not permissible, except perhaps in extreme necessity where money was not involved. If, on the other hand, it was based simply on good faith, and did not infringe the state of the order, it could be allowed for small amounts to maintain their way of life. In that case it came nearer to being alms.[1]

Olivi's doctrine of poverty was not a mere continuation of St. Bonaventure's, as we have seen. Although the germs of it can be found in the *Apologia pauperum*, and Olivi himself regularly invoked Bonaventure, their emphases were different. Bonaventure saw poverty in terms of the greater perfection of charity; it remained conditional and dependent upon a higher virtue for its *raison d'être*. Olivi, on the other hand, saw poverty as the condition of interior perfection. With Bonaventure he acknowledged that charity alone was the source of perfection while poverty was merely an external act which bore no comparison with the theological virtues.[2] Unlike Bonaventure, however, Olivi related poverty directly to charity; the greater the contempt of *temporalia* the greater the charity from which it derived.[3] Poverty was the means of withdrawing man from this world, extinguishing his love of things and curiosity about them. Only the poverty which achieved this was well-founded; so long as love of worldly things remained there could be no true charity.[4] Accordingly poverty for Olivi was not just a doctrine of a particular religious order or just one way among others—even if the best—of emulating Christ; it was the material prerequisite of attaining formal perfection within. He who sought it must first relinquish exterior interests (*negotia*) and with them the worldliness and cupidity which they bred.[5] This was thus a call to a life of renunciation, not only of ownership of goods but of the world; it meant living in humility and abnegation in order to attain charity

[1] ALKG III, 513–14.

[2] MS. Vatican Borghese 357 *Questiones de perfectione evangelica*, f. 66rb-va.

[3] ex eo quod maior contemptus temporalium est signum et actus maioris caritatis (ibid., 81ra).

[4] sola enim paupertas sic accepta funditur, extinguit cupiditatem et amorem rerum temporalium. Quamdiu enim homo amat opulentum usum vix sine cupiditatis initio esse potest que caritas est venenum (ibid., 80vb).

[5] quia enim qui vult interiori perfici, primo oportet exteriora negotia et sensibilia obiecta relinquere, quod est principium paupertatis accipiendum . . . (*Postilla super Mattheum* MS. Vat. Lat. 1001, f. 40rb).

and freedom of the will.[1] Conceived thus poverty was a moral state which must inform the whole of a man's life. As such it militated against learning equally with possessions; against the pomp of official life within the Franciscan order as much as against the granaries and buildings which sustained it.[2] It included among the enemies of Christ the disciples of Aristotle and Alexander the Great as well as the Saracens, Jews and heretics;[3] the opponents of the *usus pauper* within the order as well as the enemies of poverty outside it. Olivi's Questions on Evangelical Perfection abound in the same kind of apocalyptic veneration of poverty, and Joachist certainty in its final triumph, as are to be found in his *Postilla* on the Apocalypse.[4] The appeal to Christ's life was for him, as for St. Francis and Hugh of Digne, the final confirmation of its sanctity. This gave to Olivi's enquiry a different orientation: it was directed towards the conditions necessary for the fulfilment of the vow to absolute poverty: namely obligation to the *usus pauper*. Hence if Bonaventure can be called the theoretician of poverty as a doctrine, Olivi can be called the theoretician of its practice; where the first touched lightly on its observance, the second made it the centre of his teaching, which by building it around the *usus pauper*, changed the context of the discussion. After *Exiit* the theory of absolute poverty remained dormant until John XXII challenged it forty years later; controversy shifted to what it entailed in everyday life. The cause lay largely with Olivi.

The impact of Olivi's introduction of the *usus pauper* is testified by the fierceness of the reaction to it during his own lifetime as well as in the later disputes between the two parties. Something of the heat which it generated can also be seen from Olivi's second treatise on the question, written some years after the first.[5] Here, in contrast to the earlier one, it was sharply polemical; it had something of the same tone as Ubertino of Casale's writings, as well as a hint of Joachism in its castigation of the new pseudo-religious and pseudo-apostles for their attacks upon the followers of St. Francis, the renewer of Christ's gospel.[6] Yet, at the same time, Olivi also took pains to associate the official outlook of the order with him; in addition to the customary references to Bonagratia of St. John in Persiceto, Bonaventure, Pecham, and the statutes of Narbonne, he also recounted how at the Paris chapter he had

[1] MS. Borghese 357, 81ra.
[2] MS. Borghese 357, 81va, 83va.   [3] Ibid., 81vb, 64vb.
[4] E.g. MS. Borghese 357, 59rb, 61r-v.
[5] ALKG III, 514-17.   [6] Ibid , 514-15.

seen St. Bonaventure openly lament the unchecked abuses against poverty.[1]

If Olivi's rigorism over the principles of poverty marked him off from the Community and was the main cause of his veneration by the Spirituals, there were divergencies from the zealots—in their way no less fundamental, even if of far less practical moment. These were his attitude towards authority and learning. To take the second first: although, as we have seen, Olivi was outspoken in his hostility against Aristotle and Averroes and the profane learning for which they stood, he was himself a thinker of a high order. Temperamentally he was one of the few, on the Spirituals' side, who put reason before emotion in arguing his cause; he was essentially a scholastic, bringing the same method and approach of the schools—for all his invective against them[2]—to the problems of the order as he did to theological and philosophical matters. He displayed none of the flights of imagination or mysticism to be found in Ubertino of Casale's or Angelo of Clareno's treatment of the same topics. But where they both distrusted learning, he respected it; and in his treatise on evangelical perfection he put learning before manual work for those able to benefit from it.[3] He also regarded a life which was both active and contemplative as superior to one which was merely contemplative.[4] Thus in some respects he was closer to Bonaventure than to his own followers.

This was even more true of the way in which he regarded authority. At all times he advocated unconditional obedience to the pope, the church and his superiors. So far as the first was concerned it can be seen most clearly in his treatise on pope Celestine V's abdication.[5] This was written probably in 1297 to refute the Spirituals' assertions that because

---

[1] Nichilominus tamen in tantum dolebat de communibus laxationibus huius temporis, quod Parisius in pleno capitulo me astante dixit quod ex quo fuit generalis, nunquam fuit quin vellet esse pulverizatus, ut ordo ad puritatem beati Francisci et sociorum eius et ad illud, quod ipse de ordine suo intenderat, penveniret (ibid., 517).

[2] Ibid., 514–15.

[3] Ex hiis ergo iam patere potest quod simpliciter et absolute melius est vacare studio quam corporalibus operibus active; predictis in casibus tamen predictis melius est vacare quam studio. . . . Ex quo patet quod erronee locuti sunt qui dixerunt quod pauperes religiosi melius facerent si vacarent labori manuum pro sui sustentatione quam quia studio vacant (ibid., 504).

[4] Perfectior est et magis meritoria illa vita que est ex utraque (activa et contemplativa) permixta . . . (ibid., 503).

[5] L. Oliger (ed.) 'Petri Iohannis Olivi, De renuntiatione papae Coelestini V' in AFH 11(1918) 309–73.

I

Celestine had abdicated as pope in 1295, the election of his successor Boniface VIII was invalid. The hostility of the Spirituals to Boniface VIII sprang from his revocation of the concessions which Celestine V had made to the Tuscan Spirituals. We shall discuss the consequences in the next chapter. For the present we may simply observe that under the influence of Joachism they came to identify Boniface VIII with the first Antichrist, and to regard his overthrow as the beginning of the seventh age. Opposition to Boniface came also from the cardinals Jacob and Peter Colonna, later protectors of the Spirituals.[1] Thus Celestine's abdication entered into the Spiritual's lore and was to play an important part in their Joachist speculations. Olivi's attitude could not have been further removed from theirs. In his treatise he set himself to establish along strictly scholastic lines the legitimacy of Celestine V's abdication; he did so by taking twelve current arguments for the opposite view[2] and confuting them. His main contention was that the pope had absolute power, which was binding in all that he decreed, provided it was not against the true faith. This extended to his right to abdicate,[3] which far from being contrary to either divine or human law, derived from the need for each pope to name a successor.[4] Just as the College of Cardinals participated in a pope's appointment, so it could in accepting his abdication. There was nothing which made his office irrevocable.[5] To renounce it required the assent of no superior authority, but only the free choice of the individual concerned.[6] Elsewhere[7] Olivi affirmed that the pope should be obeyed in all matters concerning faith and morals[8] because he was the head of the church and possessed universal authority over the whole world. Even the emperor was subject to him.[9] A true pope could not err just as the church could

---

[1] H. Denifle, 'Die Denkschriften der Colonna gegen Bonifaz VIII und der Cardinäle gegen die Colonna', ALKG v (1889) 514.

[2] *De renuntiatione* 336–8.

[3] Constat enim ex omnibus predictis quod papa potest novam legem condere de quocunque quod non est contra Christi fidem et legem. . . . Sed papam posse renuntiare papatui, non est contra articulum fidei nec contra aliquod preceptum Christi . . . (ibid., 351).

[4] Ibid., 353.

[5] Ibid., 358.

[6] Ad secundum dicendum quod renuntiare non est actus exigens superioritatem super persona renuntiante, sed solum libertatem . . . (ibid.).

[7] M. Maccarrone, 'Una questione inedita dell'Olivi sull'infallibilità del papa', *Rivista di Storia della Chiesa in Italia*, 3 (1949), 309–43. Taken from MS. Vat. Lat. 4986.

[8] Ibid., 331.   [9] Ibid., 336.

not. He could make new laws so long as they did not contravene Christ's laws.[1]

Olivi's most outspoken dissent from the Spirituals was in his letter to Conrad of Offida, leader of the Italian Spirituals, written two years earlier in September 1295.[2] He attacked them for the three errors of calumniating Boniface VIII, disavowing papal interpretations of the rule and attempting to secede from the order. Olivi's attitude here showed that there was the unbridgeable gulf of authority between him and the Spirituals. Ultimately, Olivi, for all his equivocation, deferred to it, whereas the Spirituals, by 1295, were challenging it. For Olivi, as for St. Francis, the pledge to poverty and obedience, no matter how great the tension between them, was inseparable, with each equally indispensable. It was for that reason that Olivi was less their leader in life, than a legend after his death.

The letter to Conrad of Offida makes this startlingly plain. It could have been written by a pope. In it Olivi went so far as to speak of the extremists as being 'implicated in errors and heresies';[3] he defended both *Quo elongati* and *Exiit*, in the first justifying Gregory IX's supersession of St. Francis's Testament, and in the second exculpating Nicholas III from responsibility for the abuses against poverty.[4] He was even more outspoken against what he regarded as the extremists' subversion of the rule, the observance of which he had always regarded as sacrosanct;[5] he solemnly warned them that they would be implacably opposed;[6] and replied to their text from the Apocalypse, which they gave as the grounds for their secession, with the example of St. Francis's early companions, Giles, Leo and Massio, who had remained loyal to the order.[7] Olivi was at once too orthodox and too sophisticated to accept the simplified priorities of the Spirituals; his rigorism towards poverty was at least counterbalanced by his reverence for authority. His outlook remained within the frame of the order, as his Exposition of the

---

[1] MS. Vat. Lat. 4986, f. 87r.

[2] Ad secundum dicendum quod renuntiare non est actus exigens superioritatem super persona renuntiante, sed solum libertatem . . . (*De renuntiatione* 358).

[3] Tertium est quod i[i]dem ex hoc reputantur instar illorum erroribus et heresibus com[m]isceri (ibid., 372).

[4] Iterum papa vere dicit quod si sanctus Petrus ibidem intendisset ultra precepta regule imponere nova et regularia precepta ordini et successoribus suis, quod hoc facere non poterit 'cum non habet imperium par in parem' (ibid., 371).

[5] E.g. ALKG III, 523: quod vovere predictam obedientiam est de substantia perfectionis evangelice tanquam unum de principalibus consiliis Christi; also ibid., 533.

[6] Oliger, *De renuntiatione*, ibid., 372.   [7] Ibid., 372–3.

Rule, written shortly before his death, amply demonstrates.[1] In the last analysis he accepted it, with all its shortcomings and divergences from St. Francis's behests, whereas the Spirituals did not.

There remains finally to consider Olivi's Joachism. Like the other facets of his thinking it was distinctly individual. To call it balanced would be a contradiction in terms, since it was essentially apocalyptic; but it had about it an impersonality that contrasted markedly with, say, Ubertino of Casale's personal vituperation of Boniface VIII. The main source for it is Olivi's *Postilla* on the Apocalypse, which remains unprinted.[2] A papal enquiry into the work was instituted by John XXII in 1318, because of its widespread influence among the Provençal Beguins;[3] it was not, however, finally condemned until 1326.[4]

An assessment of Olivi's *Postilla* has to come to terms with the question, almost unanswerable at this distance of time, of its compatibility or otherwise with his other writings. Does it denote that Olivi was a split personality, or at least led a double life: law-abiding on the surface and subversive beneath it? Or is it of a piece with his outlook as a whole? Opinion has recently come to favour the second hypothesis.[5] As a reaction against the quite unwarranted interpretations put upon Olivi's views by the 1319 commission this is understandable. He was there made out to be a Joachist of the wildest sort, insurrectionary and antisacerdotal, preaching the overthrow of the present dispensation. He was nothing of the kind, as we shall see. Nevertheless he was talking another

---

[1] This is to be found in the *Firmamentum trium ordinum* (Venice 1513) 106–24, under the title: 'Tractatus sive expositio super regulam S. Francisci secundum divinum doctorem fratrem Petrum Johannis'. The Paris edition for 1512, entitled *Firmamenta* etc., has no corresponding section by Olivi. In his exposition Olivi reaffirms the validity of the papal interpretations of the rule and pledges total obedience to the holy see. He also discusses the order's organisation, an aspect totally absent among the other Spirituals.

[2] The known manuscripts are: Rome, Biblioteca Angelica 382 (D.2.14), used here; Vatican Borghese 38; and Florence, Biblioteca Laurenziana, conv. sopp. 382 and 397. See V. Doucet: 'De operibus mss. P. J. Olivi', AFH 28 (1935) 156–97, 408–42. There are printed extracts from the papal enquiry of 1319 in Baluze, *Misc.* II, 258–70, and a longer series of propositions (taken from Florence and Paris mss) in Döllinger *Beiträge* II, 526–85, which have been taken here in conjunction with MS. Angelica 382.

[3] Bernard Gui, *Manuel* I, 108–14: see below 159 ff.

[4] See especially Edith Paztor: 'Le polemiche sulla "Lectura super Apocalypsim", di Pietro di Giovanni Olivi' in *Bull dell' Ist. Stor. Ital. per il medio evo*, no. 70 (1958) 365–424.

[5] See especially R. Manselli, *La 'Lectura super Apocalipsim' di Pietro di Giovanni Olivi* (Rome 1955). For the contrary view, see E. Benz, *Ecclesia Spiritualis* (Stuttgart 1934), which seems to me untenable and distorting.

language and living in a different world from his everyday one; and it would be idle to minimize the discrepancy. However impersonally, he was nevertheless in his *Postilla* on the Apocalypse foretelling the imminent and cataclysmic end of the existing order; he was invoking the renewal of Christ's teaching; he was opposing the coming state to the present; contrasting the evil and worldliness of the majority of clerics and believers with the purity and spirituality of the few who would succeed them. This in general terms was his message; and because it was a message it was inevitably prophetic and hortatory, and in another key from Olivi's non-apocalyptic works.[1] The difference between them is the difference between the intoxication of a vision and the hard light of reason; they can both be known by the same man; they can both share common traits; but they are not the same. Nor do they necessarily mean inconsistency. The time is long past for historians still to aspire to that will-o'-the-wisp; consistency is the exception for the majority of mankind; and where it is found it is as likely to be the result of lack of personality as exceptional personality. For most men there is a subterranean side which, at the very least, contrasts with that which is uppermost. There is every reason to suppose its existence in Olivi; as expressed in his *Postilla* it forms a pendant to the balance and sobriety of his daytime personality. Here at the end of his life[2] he gave vent to the indignities and failures which he and his ideas had suffered for more than twenty years. His theme was the conflict between the false and the true faith, and the coming triumph of the latter at the hands of St. Francis's disciples. Lamentation and bitterness at the abuses of the present were offset by exaltation at their imminent downfall. The setting of the struggle was largely taken from the events of his own lifetime; and its successful outcome was entrusted to St. Francis and his followers.

It is here that Olivi was both true to his other self and in opposition to it. Much of what he says is so close to his own experience that it is, as we shall observe, almost autobiographical. Yet in order to see his own beliefs vindicated he was prepared to invoke the very agency of violent struggle between the forces of Antichrist and Christ which he so

---

[1] On the other hand, the distinction between them must not be made too absolute. As we mentioned earlier, there are distinctly Joachist elements in Olivi's Questions on evangelical perfection. They are united on the sanctity of poverty and hostility towards the profane learning of Aristotle.

[2] In 1297. This date is mentioned in his assessment of the ending of the sixth age. Döllinger, *Beiträge* II, 48, 570–1. Angelica 382, 81rb.

strongly denounced in his letter to Conrad of Offido. It is true that he conceived it differently from the extremists, in that he put the emphasis upon the agency of Christ not men; throughout his *Postilla* he remained strictly impersonal towards the *personae* involved: he made no attempt to translate the successive Antichrists or kings into real persons or to give events precise dates. But this was merely to stop before reaching the final extreme; he was still following the same path of apocalyptic reckoning, however soberly he negotiated it. We must therefore recognize that the *Postilla* on the Apocalypse showed Olivi in another light, one where his evangelical beliefs became harnessed to an historicism. The difference was less in the sudden casting off of reason than in directing it to ends that too easily became irrational; less in any loss of restraint—Olivi throughout showed his characteristic restraint—than in plausibility. His outlook remained the same; it was in the hopes of its realization that his *Postilla* stood apart from his other works. Prophecy and wish-fulfilment took over, short-circuiting the accepted limitations.

We should not expect, then, to see another Olivi in the *Postilla*, but rather the same man dealing in a different medium, or more exactly in another role—that of social critic and prophet. He is easily identifiable; the central issues are those of poverty and the *usus pauper*; there are no wild extravagances or personal vituperation, or anything that could be taken as an attack upon the church's authority. Above all, Olivi's treatment is highly individualistic. In the sense that it was conceived in terms of Joachim's periodization it is Joachist, and it is meaningless to deny it; on the other hand, the way in which he adapted it was very much his own, and constituted a new development in what might be called Franciscan Joachism. How much he owed to Hugh of Digne and John of Parma we shall probably never know; but that he was only following an already well-established line of succession within the order is beyond dispute. Moreover, in his identification of St. Francis with the angel of the sixth seal, we know that St. Bonaventure had already preceded him.[1] Nevertheless, what emerges from his *Postilla* is a distinctive interpretation of Franciscan history; the central role which he allotted to his order makes the work more than simply another biblical commentary or Joachist tract.

A comparison with Joachim of Fiore best illustrates this. In particular it emphasizes the divergences in their time-scale. The tendency, already strong in Joachim, to focus upon the transition from the second to the

[1] St. Bonaventure, *Legenda Maiora*, prologue, 1 (*Analecta Franciscana* x, 558).

third state, and more specifically the sixth and seventh ages, becomes even stronger with Olivi. The consequence was that Olivi translated Joachim's primarily impersonal and symbolic prognosis of the end of the second state into historical terms; in doing so he gave it a new import. To begin with, Olivi shifted the turning point from the transition between the sixth and the seventh ages to that between the fifth and the sixth. Moreover, he made them run currently for all but the first six years of the thirteenth century, dating them from St. Francis's conversion to the evangelical life.[1] Secondly, as a result, Olivi depicted the struggle of the carnal and the spiritual churches as that between the forces of the fifth age and the sixth age; he thereby shifted its focus one age back although the outcome would lead on to the seventh age. Thirdly, he invested each of the two sides—or ages—with the characteristics drawn from his own time. The carnal church was made up of those who followed Antichrist, denying poverty and defending the pagan learning of Aristotle and Averroes. The new order of contemplatives now became the Franciscan order, or, more accurately, St. Francis's true disciples. The conflict between them formed the theme of the transition from the fifth to the sixth age. There was none of Gerard of Borgo San Donnino's attempt to substitute a new gospel for the existing one; rather Olivi directly transferred Christ's mantle to St. Francis; he was the herald, and his poverty the badge, of Christ's second coming. The role of the Holy Spirit, so important to Joachim, was not mentioned.

These changes were of the greatest significance; they meant the harnessing of Joachim's world schema to the history of one particular epoch. As Manselli rightly says, Olivi substituted a dynamic concept of history,[2] while remaining true to Joachim's trinitarian conception and especially what was perhaps its central feature: the prolonged overlap—or, more accurately, interaction—between the fifth and sixth ages. For this reason it is unreal to contrast Olivi's dynamics with Joachim's statics;[3] it is rather that Olivi's dynamism was far more pronounced, and played a key role in his interpretation.

---

[1] Döllinger, ibid., 40, 559–60; Angelica 382, 73ra. Also Borghese 38, 14va: sic etiam sextus status a beato Francisco est inchoatus durante adhuc quinto et concurrent cum ipso fere per 100 annos.

[2] *La Lectura* 189. He also preceded the commentary proper with a conspectus consisting of thirteen 'notabilia' in which he presented his scheme of history. Although he owed most to Joachim of Fiore he was also strongly influenced by Richard of St. Victor. [3] Ibid.

This becomes clearer from an examination of Olivi's system, which can for the purposes of discussion be considered under three heads: the nature of the fifth age; the nature of the sixth age; and their convergence. The fifth age, though originating with Charlemagne, corresponded to its closing phase in the thirteenth century; this was the period when its evils reached their height[1] and the church had become the seat of the forces of Antichrist,[2] which Olivi identified with the carnal church.[3] Like Joachim, and unlike Spirituals such as Ubertino of Casale and Angelo of Clareno, Olivi was always careful to separate the carnal church from the existing church; the commission of 1319 accused him of making them the same,[4] but this is untrue. On the contrary, Olivi on more than one occasion explicitly distinguished the different elements of the church, among which he included the new spiritual men of his own order.[5]

Olivi enumerated the main signs, or tribulations, of evil in the decline of the fifth age. The first was the laxity of the church and the self-indulgence of its members, clerics, monks, and the mass of believers alike; the second was the appearance of the heresy of the Manicheans and Waldensians which the abuses in the church had engendered; the third was the multiplication of 'religious hypocrites', drawn from the first group, who warred against the spirit and example of Christ by spreading error and confusion.[6] Olivi squarely put the blame for the

---

[1] In fine quinti status erat spiritus et vita Christi seu Christus in spiritu quasi crucifigendus (Döllinger, II, 35, 555; Angelica 382, 67vb).

[2] Döllinger, II, 52, 575; Angelica 382, 100va.

[3] Per hanc sedem principaliter designatur carnalis clerus in hoc vero tempore et toti ecclesie presidens, in quo quidem bestialis vita transcendens singulariter regnat et sedet (Angelica 382, 100va).

[4] See pp. 159 ff. below.

[5] ita quod boni sunt in ea [ecclesia carnalis] sicut pauca grana auri inter immensos acervos arene, et sicut pauca grana tritici sub immenso cumulo palearum (Angelica 382, ibid.).

[6] Ad cuius evidentiam nota quod communia malia omnibus temporibus ecclesie et humano genere communia . . . erant tria gravissima circa finem quinte temporis ventura quoruma prima fuit effrenata laxatio clericorum, monachorum et laicorum seu vulgarium plebium fraudibus; secunda sumens a predicta occasionem hereticorum Manicheorum et Valdensium eis in multis consimilium et multa et pestifera inundatio. Tertium aliorum ypocritalium religiosorum cum primis multiplicatio et spiritus Christi, et vite eius ab omnibus impugnatio, quamvis sub diversis modis et prandibus, ut fiat perplexior[a] temptatio fere inducens in errorem electos (Döllinger, ibid., 34, 553; Angelica 382, 64va).

[a] Döllinger, prolixior.

church's decay upon the 'enormous cupidity and ambitions' of its prelates and abbots.[1] In a scathing passage he designated all those implicated in it as 'locusts' because of their personal insignificance and their
collective greed.[2] The second group—of heretics—spoke for itself;
Olivi, like Joachim, invoked them on a number of occasions as a
clear indication of the church's rotten state; although the Manicheans
were no longer a serious threat when Olivi was writing, the Waldensians were;[3] and Olivi shared with Joachim and Ubertino of Casale a
horror of heresy. Olivi was perhaps most bitter towards the third
group. This is not surprising, since he had suffered repeatedly throughout his career from misrepresentation and censure by theologians and
scholastics, not least at Paris, which he made the target for some of his
most piercing shafts. At Paris, even more than at Rome, Olivi seemed
to see the presence of Antichrist in the twin evils of veneration of
Aristotle's and Averroes's pagan philosophy and the assaults of the Paris
masters upon his order's doctrine of evangelical poverty.[4] His denunciations of profane learning were as strong as anything in Ubertino of
Casale's *Arbor vitae*, and read much more strangely from one who was
himself a speculative thinker; here indeed there was something of a
split in Olivi between the scholastic and the prophet. He especially
attacked the anti-Christian conclusions to which the study of Aristotle
and Averroes led: the denial of creation, free will, or an individual
immortal soul, and the acceptance of the natural world as self-sufficient
in itself.[5] The question of poverty, as before, turned on the place of the
usus pauper;[6] and it is interesting that he coupled those who disputed it

[1] Döllinger, ibid.; Angelica 382, 64va–vb.

[2] Döllinger, ibid., 554; Angelica 65ra–va.

[3] Manselli, *La Lectura* 204–5, seems to underestimate their danger.

[4] acceperunt enim ingenium et clavem ad aperiendam et exponendam doctrinam
Aristotelis et Averrois, commentatoris eius, et ad excogitandum profunda et voragin-
osa dogmata obscurantia solem christiane sapientie et evangelice vite et purum aerem
religiosi status ipsius . . . (Döllinger, ibid., 554–5; Angelica 382, 67rb).

[5] Quidam etiam talia dogmata philosophica sine paganica suis theologicis tractanti-
bus inseruerunt ut ex eis[a] multi clerici Parisius philosophantes omnes articulos fidei
rejecerint praeter virtutem[b] dei et solam philosophiam mundanam dixerint esse
veram et humano regimini sufficientem. Dixeruntque mundum ab eterno fuisse . . .
ponuntque unum solum intellectum in omnibus hominibus, et fere negant arbitrii
libertatem (Döllinger, ibid., 555; Angelica 382, 67 rb–va).
   [a] Döllinger, ipsi; [b] Döllinger, unitatem.

[6] quidam eorum dicunt paupertatem altissimam non esse de substantia perfectionis
eius, et quod eius est habere sufficientia aut saltem necessaria in communi; quidam vero,

with those who embraced pagan philosophy, as both being apostates from the true faith of Christ. These different groups of the locusts would all suffer the same fate in the end; with the coming of Christ and Jerusalem they would be consumed with fire and burned.[1] Laxity, heresy, and errors against Christ's teaching—in the form of a denial of the *usus pauper* and the embracing of pagan philosophy—these were the features of the church in the decline of the fifth age. They were the work of Antichrist and, as we shall see, his main weapons in his struggle against the spiritual harbingers of the sixth age whose advent would ultimately bring about his downfall.

Olivi likened these tribulations to the sufferings of Christ on the cross: each meant a corresponding laceration of his spirit. Thus in the first tribulation, clerical oppression represented the wounds in Christ's feet; clerical rapaciousness and fraudulence those in his hands; while clerical luxury pierced his side and heart.[2] They signalized the presence of Antichrist within the church; just as each of the previous four epochs was represented by an appropriate animal, so the fifth was described by the beast or dragon. It was in this epoch that it transferred its seat to the Roman church. This was the cause of the church's ills.[3] By the beast Olivi meant the followers of Antichrist, whom he described in the first tribulation; although they were part of the church they were not synonymous with it. Olivi was beyond all doubt explicit in confining the carnal church to them; they were, however, but one element in the church of the faithful.[4] We have here one of the most important aspects

---

quod usus pauper[a], id est altissimae paupertatis secundum debitas circumstantias proportionatus non est de substantia eius (Döllinger, ibid; Angelica 382, 67rb).

[a] Döllinger, paupertatis.

[1] Ibid.

[2] In prima autem tribulatione clericales conculcant plebeios quasi pedes per fastum[a] arrogantie et per contemptum contumelie seu parvificentie, seu per rapine molestiam et per calumnie fraudulentiam sunt eorum manus rapientes bona de manibus aliorum. Per lateralem autem sive visceralem aperturam luxurie cruciant eorum corda et viscera (Döllinger, ibid., 555–6; Angelica 382, 68ra).

[a] Angelica 382, faustum.

[3] Nota, quod sicut post quatuor animalia quatuor primos status sanctorum designantia sublimata est generalis sedes Romane ecclesie . . . sic in eodem quinto tempore post quatuor bestias a Daniele visas quatuor primis sanctorum ordinibus contrarias sublimata est sedes bestie, i.e. bestialis caterve, ita ut numero et potestate prevaleat et fere absorbeat sedem Christi, cui localiter et nominaliter est commixta, unde et sic vocatur ecclesia fidelium sicut et illa que vere est per gratiam sedes et ecclesia Christi (Döllinger, ibid., 52, 575; Angelica 382, 100rb).

[4] Döllinger, ibid., no. 54; Angelica 382, 100va.

of his *Postilla*: as in St. Augustine's *City of God* the church was conceived as containing all believers, the reprobate as well as the elect;
their final separation would come only after the Last Judgement. For
Olivi, the carnal church constituted the carnal or unspiritual religious,
within the church, not *a* church—still less *the* church—in its own right.[1]
The importance of the distinction need hardly be stressed: Olivi was not
attacking the church, but its abuses; not its existence, but its personnel.
This marks him off from many of his Provençal followers who did just
that: making the church of Rome the carnal church, and thereby
turning criticism of temporal shortcomings into an attack upon its
divine institution.

Against this combined assault upon the true faith by the carnal
religious, the heretics they engendered, and the false doctors who
dominated the later fifth age, stood the spiritual men who presaged the
sixth age. St. Francis was their herald, and his followers were those of
his order who held fast through thick and thin to his teachings on
poverty. Thus Olivi counterposed his own order to the carnal church;
and virtually all that he said about their struggle, which would issue in
the overthrow of the first Antichrist, was drawn from the history of his
own time. Like St. Bonaventure before him, Olivi saw St. Francis as
the angel of the sixth seal; his stigmata was the sign of the living God
upon him, the testimony of his divine mission.[2] Just as Christ had replaced Judaism with the new law, so St. Francis in the sixth age of the
carnal church would renew the life and teaching of Christ.[3] The appearance of St. Francis marked the opening of the sixth age; his rule was the
authentic gospel of Christ given to his order, as Christ gave the gospel

---

[1] Super huius modi vero malitiam non cessant zelatores sancti huius quinti temporis
effundere fialam detestationis in celebris increpationis, ita quod regnum eius velit
nolit evidenter appareat omnibus et etiam ipsismet tenebrosam (Döllinger, ibid.,
no. 53; Angelica 382, 100rb–va).

[2] constat etiam per indubitabile testimonium S. Francisci et ineffabili sanctitate et
innumeris dei miraculis confirmatum et precipue gloriosissimis stigmatibus a Christo
impressis patet,[a] ipsum angelum apertionis fore sexti signaculi, habentem signum dei
vivi, signum scilicet plagarum Christi crucifixi . . . et hoc ipsum per claram et fide
dignam revelationem est habitum, prout a fratre Bonaventura . . . (Döllinger, ibid.,
20, 540; Angelica 382, 52va).

[a] Döllinger, vere esse.

[3] Sicut in sexta etate reiecto carnali iudaismo et vetustate prioris seculi venit novus
homo Christus . . . sic in sexto statu reiecta carnali ecclesia et vetustate prioris seculi
renovabitur Christi et vita et crux, propter quod in primo eius initio Franciscus
apparuit (Döllinger, ibid., 8, 532; Angelica 382, 13rb).

to his Apostles.[1] After Christ, St. Francis was the principal founder of the sixth age, a second Elias, in the image of Christ. 'His face was like the sun',[2] because it was entirely devoted to contemplating God.[3]

In what, then, did the sixth age consist? As with Joachim of Fiore it represented for Olivi the appearance of the true evangel of Christ and the renewal of the church, leading finally to the overthrow of Babylon or the carnal church—for having deserted Christ—and the establishment of Jerusalem.[4] The ensuing period until the end of the world would last as long as the preceding Christian era.[5] In the new spiritual revelation which would be open to the sixth age, Olivi followed Joachim closely;[6] it would excel all the previous ages in grace and understanding, love of Christ and humility, preferring contemplation and passivity to action.[7] Above all, the mantle of Christ would be transferred to the new elect, the disciples of St. Francis.[8] Their appearance at the nadir of the fifth age 'when the sun of faith and ecclesiastical order was black'[9] was accompanied by tremors in many parts of the earth, including Olivi's home town of Béziers.[10] As the first five ages of the first era of the Old Testament were denied knowledge of Christ's secrets in the New Testament, so only after the final opening of the sixth age by St. Francis's disciples would there be full spiritual illumination.[11] At the height of the struggle with Antichrist the spirit of Christ and St. Francis would descend, and the gospel of his disciples would shine triumphant and impervious against all calumnies and lies; it would represent celestial truth against the false terrestial writings of the pseudo-prophets, and its coming would lead to universal understanding.[12] As the apostle of poverty and humility St. Francis would put the sea

---

[1] Döllinger, ibid., 20, 539; Angelica 382, 52va.   [2] Rev. 7; 2.

[3] Döllinger, ibid., 40, 559; Angelica 382, 73ra.

[4] Döllinger, ibid., 1 and 2, 528–9; Angelica 382, 11vb–12ra and 31va–34vb.

[5] Döllinger, ibid., 6, 531; Angelica 382, 13vb–14rb and 52rb–vb.

[6] E.g. Döllinger, ibid., 10, 11, 12, 532–4; Angelica 382, 32rb–34vb.

[7] Döllinger, ibid., 535: also 13 and 14, 536; Angelica 382, ibid.

[8] sic etiam gloria parata finali ecclesiae quinti status, transferetur propter eius adulteria ad electos sexti status (Döllinger, ibid., 17, 537; Angelica 382, 33vb).

[9] Döllinger, ibid., 19, 538, and 24, 542; Angelica 382, 52va–53ra.

[10] Döllinger, ibid., 24, 543; Angelica 382, 53rb.

[11] Nam in prioribus quinque ecclesiae statibus non fuit concessum sanctis quantumcunque illuminatis aperire illa secreta huius libri, que in solo sexto et septimo statu erant apertius reseranda, sicut nec in primis quinque etatibus veteris testamenti fuit concessum prophetis clare aperire secreta Christi et novi testamenti in sexta etate reserandis secreta et reserata (Döllinger, ibid., 41, 561; Angelica 382, 73rb).

[12] Döllinger, ibid., 560–1; Angelica 382, 72va–vb.

and land under his feet, rather than above him, like the angel of the Apocalypse,[1] in order to destroy all wealth and carnal luxury.[2] Olivi suggested that the Franciscans would not be alone in crushing the carnal church; for at one point he spoke of Elias and Enoch as the two prophets of the two preaching orders—i.e., the Dominicans and the Franciscans, an attribution followed by Ubertino of Casale.[3] The first was more devoted to external order and discipline; the other inclined more to contemplation; but both professed the same evangelical faith. To these must also be added the numerous other orders which had existed concurrently with them for a hundred years.[4] Yet effectively it was upon the Franciscans and their founder that Olivi's interest was focused; it was with him the sixth age began; it was in his hand that the book of Christ was first fully opened;[5] it was he who would convert the heathen to Christ,[6] and would himself reappear, it was said, for a second time on earth to comfort his order at the height of their struggle with Antichrist.[7]

This was the setting to what we may call the third facet of Olivi's analysis: namely, the clash between the forces of the fifth and sixth ages. As we have already suggested, perhaps the most distinctive feature of Olivi's *Postilla* was the long period of overlap between the fifth and the sixth ages; here he moved away from Joachim in treating the sixth age as something entirely new, not as already in gestation during the previous epoch; if the monks of St. Benedict were the precursors of the

---

[1] Rev. 10: 2.

[2] Et nota quod hic angelus (S. Franciscus) non posuit supra se mare et terram, sed potius sub pedibus suis, quia per altissimam paupertatem, austeritatem et humilitatem omnes mundanos divitias et honores[a] et delicias sub suis pedibus conculcabit nullique adulatorie aut pro mundano questu se carnaliter seu viliter subdet (Döllinger, ibid., 41, 562; Angelica 382, 73va).

[a] Döllinger, homines.

[3] *Arbor vitae*, Bk. v, ch. 3, f. 409va. See pp. 153 ff. below.

[4] Döllinger, ibid., 44, 564; Angelica 382, 76ra–rb.

[5] Döllinger, ibid., 40, 559–60. Angelica 382, 72vb–73ra.

[6] Döllinger, ibid., 560; Angelica 382, ibid.

[7] Olivi attributes the story to Leo, one of St. Francis's companions: he is characteristically cautious about it: Audivi etiam a viro spirituali valde fide digno et fratri Leone confessori et socio beati Francisci valde familiari quoddam huic scripture consonum quod nec assero nec scio, nec censeo[a] asserendum, scilicet quod tam per verba fratris Leonis quam per propriam revelationem sibi factam perceperat quod Franciscus in illa pressura[b] temptationis Babylonice . . . resurget gloriosus (Döllinger, ibid., 29, 549; Angelica 382, 55va).

[a] Döllinger adds esse. [b] Angelica 382 pressum.

friars, they no longer had any spiritual affinities for Olivi, who tended to put all the existing religious on the other side of the fence from the new Spirituals. But, more important, Olivi saw the whole of the thirteenth century as the unfolding of the conflict between the forces of the two ages; all its main religious developments were the outcome of it. Here he went beyond Joachim and enumerated his own scheme. This consisted of four different 'openings' of the sixth age; only when they had all been achieved would the sixth age finally come into being, and the fifth age, and with it the reign of Antichrist, be superseded.

Of these four openings, the first had come with the initiation of the Franciscan order and the drawing up of its Rule; the second with Joachim of Fiore's prophecies; the third would be with the destruction of Babylon by the beast with the ten horns—that is, the ten kings of the Apocalypse;[1] the fourth was with the revival of the spirit of Christ and St. Francis then under attack by the carnal church (Olivi was referring to the condemnation of the rule and evangelical poverty, especially by the Paris masters).[2] Whereas each of these events had been put forward separately as the starting point for the sixth age[3] Olivi bracketed them together as being complementary, in the manner of the four evangelists of Christ's advent.[4]

Only when Babylon had been temporally annihilated would the inception of the sixth age be complete.[5] The preliminaries to this centred on the clash between the carnal church and St. Francis and his followers; and more particularly in the persecution of the latter for reviving Christ's teaching and following his example of evangelical poverty and mendicancy.[6] During this phase black was made to appear white; many religious and masters asserted that to have possessions was

---

[1] Rev. 17: 12.

[2] As can be seen from the context in which he discusses the events connected with it. See below.

[3] Döllinger, ibid., 21, 540–1; Angelica 382, 52va.

[4] Sciendum autem quatuor predictas sententias predictas, sane assumptas, non esse sibi contrarias sed concordes . . . sic hec sexta apertio sumpsit quoddam prophetiale initium a revelatione Abbatis[a] et consimilium, a renovatione vero regule evangelice per servum eius Franciscum . . . a predicatione vero spiritualium suscitandorum et a nova Babylone reprobandorum . . . a destructione vero Babylonis (Döllinger, ibid., 22, 541; Angelica 382, 52va–vb).

   [a] Döllinger adds Joachim, which of course it is.

[5] Döllinger, ibid., 23; Angelica 382, 52vb.

[6] Döllinger, ibid., 24, 542; Angelica 382, ibid.

more perfect than to be without them.[1] Hostility towards the chosen
would grow, and the entire world would be affected. 'The sun would
become darker and the moon like blood' as the struggle against them
became more intense: there would be schism and subversion among the
religious and many pledged to evangelical poverty would fall by the
wayside before the church was revivified.[2] It would happen after the
death of St. Francis, among his disciples, just as Christ's law was
assimilated by his apostles after he had been crucified.[3] Olivi was at
pains to demonstrate the parallel, and to show especially that it required
a lapse of several generations before, on the one hand, the truths for
which both Christ and St. Francis stood could be assimilated by the
populace, and, on the other, for the errors and wrongs committed
against the upholders of the evangelical life to be exposed.[4] Thus if
St. Francis was heir to Jesus, the doctors and religious who persecuted
the Spirituals were the direct descendants of Herod in their attempts
to destroy those who were loyal to Christ's poverty.[5] For Olivi the
struggle between the two sides was not only the indispensable prerequisite to the destruction of Babylon, but the centrepiece of his structure: to show its importance he gave ten reasons why conflict between
them would be inevitable.[6] This perhaps more than anything else in-
dicates how far he had come to despair of a peaceful reform of the
church by the last years of his life; it must weigh strongly against any
claim to reconcile his views here with what he said elsewhere. The
reasons themselves would seem to confirm this: the first was from
the very nature of the carnal church: its assaults upon evangelical life
would increase until it was justly condemned by God;[7] the second lay in
the concordance with the destruction of the synagogue following the

[1] ita quod multi, qui magisteriis et prelatione videbantur quasi sol, sic facti sunt
nigri, ut usque hodie sentiant et doceant statum evangelicum mendicitatis non esse
statum perfectionis, vel esse statum evangelice mendicitatis esse statum dampnationis,
aut saltem minime perfectionis, et quod habere aliquid in communi est perfectius
et magis evangelicum quam non habere (Döllinger, ibid.; Angelica 382, 53ra).

[2] Döllinger, ibid., 25, 543–4; Angelica 382, 53rb.

[3] Döllinger, ibid., 26, 544; Angelica 382, ibid.

[4] Döllinger, ibid., 27, 546–6; Angelica 382, 53va–54ra.

[5] unde et sicut primus Herodes necavit infantes ut occideret Christum infantem,
sic circa primordialem infantiam huius ordinis, regibus mundi devote adorantibus
Christi paupertatem in ipso, novus Herodes doctorum carnalium dampnavit statum
evangelicum evangelice mendicitatis (Döllinger, ibid., 546; Angelica 382, 54ra–rb).

[6] Döllinger, ibid., 31, 550–1; Angelica 382, 56ra–vb.

[7] Döllinger, ibid., 550; Angelica 382, 56rb.

crucifixion of Christ at the end of the first age;[1] the third and fourth were that the persecutions revived evangelical truth;[2] the fifth, sixth, seventh and eighth were all concerned with the retribution to which the conduct of Babylon would lead;[3] the ninth reason lay in its denial of poverty and its laxity;[4] and the tenth in the apostasy to Antichrist and the pagan philosophy which it thereby engendered.[5]

How closely this seeming inevitability of the holocaust sprang from Olivi's own experience can be seen in his account of the final dénoue-ment. It would, he said, be precipitated by the abandonment (discessio) of the true pope for a pseudo-pope, as foretold by St. Paul in II Thes-salonians 2: 3: 'there will be a falling away first, and that a man of sin shall be revealed, the son of perdition.' This would in turn be followed by the pseudo-pope's repudiation of evangelical poverty;[6] thus supported by the mass of the people, the church would become its chief obstacle.[7] Olivi did not specifically identify this pseudo-pope with Antichrist, but since it was the latter who would condemn the Franciscan rule[8] they were probably one and the same, as we shall shortly discuss. The battle would now be joined,[9] but not, so far as the elect were concerned, in the violent manner suggested literally by the scriptures; rather than waste and ravage, the Spirituals would conduct themselves with the mildness appropriate to evangelical life:[10] a characteristic Olivi touch. Nor would the devil or the beast, his symbol on earth, be permitted to kill them.[11]

Olivi enlisted the figures and events of the book of the Apocalypse to describe the struggle, translating them into the history of his own era,

---

[1] Döllinger, ibid., 550; Angelica 382, 56rb.   [2] Ibid.

[3] Döllinger, ibid., 550-1; Angelica, 382, 56rb-va.

[4] Döllinger, ibid., 551; Angelica 382, 56va.

[5] Döllinger, ibid., 551; Angelica 382, 56va-vb.

[6] Döllinger, ibid., 39, 559; Angelica 382, 70ra.

[7] Olivi compared them to the river Euphrates impeding the journey of those wishing to follow the path of evangelical poverty: potestas enim papae et multitudo plebium sibi obediens et favor eius est quasi magnus fluvius Euphrates impediens transitum et insultum emulorum evangelici status in ipsum (Döllinger, ibid., 39, 559; Angelica 382, 73rb).   [8] Döllinger, ibid., 41, 560; Angelica 382, 73rb.

[9] The spirit of Christ and St. Francis would descend among their disciples: Idcirco sciendum quod a tempore solemnis impugnationis et condempnationis evangelice vite et regule sub mystico Antichristo fiende et sub magno amplius consummande, spiritualiter descendet Christus et eius servus Franciscus et evangelicus discipulorum eius cetus contra omnes errores et malicias mundi et contra totum exercitum demonum et pravorum hominum (ibid.).

[10] Döllinger, ibid., 45, 565-7; Angelica 382, 77rb-va.

[11] Döllinger, ibid., 46, 568; Angelica 382, 77va.

while at the same time rigorously excluding personalities. The beast ascending from the earth stood for the multitude of bestial peoples sunk in error and infidelity; its sixth or seventh head killed by the *sancti* was that of the pseudo-pope and his pseudo-prophets who had sown confusion in the church.[1] The principal demons leading the faithful into temptation were the seven heads of the dragon. Of these the last two were the mystic—or first—Antichrist, who would appear at the end of the second age, and the great Antichrist whose coming would presage the end of the world.[2] Olivi had some difficulty in deciding whether Gog was to be the seventh head or the tail of the dragon. But all persecutions of the elect were from Antichrist.[3] Moreover, all that concerned the great Antichrist included the mystic Antichrist as his forerunner.[4] The beast ascending from the sea[5] represented the carnal and secular Christian peoples, and its many heads the carnal princes and prelates; one of them was killed by St. Francis's coming, for the stronger the impact of evangelical poverty and perfection, the greater the blow to laxity; but this only caused it to revive again even more strongly.[6]

When the first beast, representing the apostate church, ascended from the earth it bore two horns—the pseudo-religious and the pseudo-prophets—feigned in likeness to those of the lamb (!), Christ; they were Antichrist's most powerful temptations, since they were in the guise of Christ's teachings.[7] They would reveal themselves by their condemnation of all those who opposed their worship of cupidity and carnality, and what appeared to be the universal teaching of the doctors of the church; they would make the pseudo-pope, himself set up by the king of the first beast, adored and believed more than Christ and his gospel, consigning to the secular arm all those zealots who opposed him. His name would be from the number 666, which Olivi arrived at by treating it as a product of the three orders of lay, clerics and religious who adored him;[8] Olivi also surmised that it could be from the period from Pipin until six years hence, which would be 666 years.[9]

---

[1] Döllinger, ibid.; Angelica 382, 77va–vb.

[2] Döllinger, ibid., 47, 568–9; Angelica 382, 81rb.   [3] Ibid.

[4] Döllinger, ibid., 48, 569; Angelica 382, 92v.

[5] Rev. 13; 1.   [6] Döllinger, 48, 569; Angelica 382, 92vb.

[7] Cum autem apostatrix bestia de terra religiosorum ascendet in altum, cum duobus cornibus pseudo-religiosorum et pseudo-prophetarum falso similibus veris cornibus agni, tunc erit validissima tentatio mistici Antichristi (Döllinger, ibid., 570; Angelica 382, 92vb).

[8] Döllinger, ibid.; Angelica 382, 92vb–93ra.

[9] Döllinger, ibid.; Angelica 382, 93ra.

K

This was to lead Angelo and Ubertino to identify him with Boniface VIII.[1] Even more noteworthy, Olivi located the scene of their nefarious activities in the Paris condemnation of evangelical poverty in the forty-second generation—that is, in the 1250s under William of St. Amour; he also implicated the Emperor Frederick II (d. 1250) who was condemned by the Council of Lyons in 1245.[2] From then began the notoriety of the doctrine of evangelical poverty. This in turn led to further attacks in the same generation which Nicholas III's decretal (*Exiit qui seminat*) was designed to answer.[3] In another passage, where Olivi treated the third tribulation of the church at this time, he mentioned the attempts by the Paris masters to justify possessions by taking the example of Christ's bag.[4] All these arguments against poverty, together with the pursuit of profane knowledge, were to be judged as the work of Antichrist.[5] It was hardly surprising that, although Olivi named no names, he inspired his followers to regard their opponents both in the curia and the Community as the agents of the beast, and to believe that their imminent overthrow would institute a new evangelical life true to the rule.

The election of Celestine V and his successor only three years from the end of the forty-second generation was associated by Olivi with 'certain other worsening matters'.[6] What they refer to is uncertain; but, on the surface, it is hardly complimentary to Boniface VIII.[7] Moreover, Olivi recounted the view that Frederick II or his seed was the severed head of the beast which would reappear in the time of the mystic Antichrist (i.e. at the end of the forty-second generation);

---

[1] See below pp. 153, 172.

[2] Ex tunc [sexto anno conversionis Francisci] omnis persecutio sui evangelici status spectat ad persecutiones Antichristi. Et secundum hoc in sequenti 42a generatione cepit Parisius persecutio quorundam magistrorum condemnantium evangelicam mendicitatem. In ipsa etiam fuit Fridericus secundus cum suis complicibus persequens ecclesiam propter quod et in ipsa ab imperio depositus fuit in concilio generali per Innocentium IV facto Lugduni (Döllinger, ibid., 571; Angelica 382, 83vb).

[3] Tertia vero tribulatio transfigit manus per apparentiam celebris auctoritatis ecclesie generalis . . . nam Christus habuit loculos et recepit magna convivia . . . (Döllinger, ibid., 36, 557; Angelica 382, 68rb).

[4] Written Nicholas IV, but quite clearly referring to *Exiit qui seminat*, (Döllinger, ibid., 48, 571; Angelica 382, 83vb).

[5] Ibid.

[6] In fine autem huius 42e generationis contigit novitas electionis Celestini pape et successoris eius et quorundam aliorum nunc ingravescentium (ibid., 572).

[7] i.e. the abdication of Celestine V, regarded by many as having been contrived by Boniface. See T. S. R. Boase, *Boniface VIII*.

having conquered France he would occupy it and the Roman empire, supported by five other kings. He would then appoint a false religious as pseudo-pope, who would pronounce against the rule, making those who were apostates to it bishops, and persecuting and expelling those ecclesiastics who remained true to it and opposed Frederick in its support.[1] Olivi refused to commit himself on the veracity of this prophecy;[2] but he added that those who held to it regarded it as the fulfilment of what St. Paul had predicted in II Thessalonians 3.[3] This appearance of the mystic Antichrist would unleash from God the attacks of the angels of the Apocalypse.[4] As the corruption of the carnal church of Babylon increased under the instigation of Antichrist, it would be attacked by ten kings and their armies;[5] it would then fall into its three divisions, of the elect who had suffered every tribulation in their loyalty to Christ, and the followers of the Antichrist, some adhering to him, some to the ten kings.[6] The judgement of God upon it would then follow, and it would be no more.[7] Once again Olivi did not specify how its end would be brought about, merely citing a number of possible interpretations.[8] What is certain is that its downfall would be the exaltation of the spiritual church, as the destruction of the synagogue had meant the emergence of the Christian church.[9] Such was the change due at the end of the thirteenth century, leading to the reunion of the Greek and Latin churches, and the extension of the faith

[1] quod Fridericus prefatus cum suo semine sit respectu huius temporis quasi caput occisum, et quod tempore mistici Antichristi ita reviviscat in aliquo de semine eius, ut non solum Romanum imperium sed etiam Francis an ipso devictis obtineat regnum Francorum, quinque ceteris regibus Christianorum sibi coherentibus. Statuet in pseudo-papam quemdam falsum religiosum qui contra regulam evangelicam excogitabit . . . promovens in episcopos professores regule prefate sibi consentientes, et exinde expellens clericos et priores episcopos et faciet dispensationem dolosam promovens in episcopos qui semini Frederici et specialiter illi imperatori et sibi et suo statui fuerint adversati . . . fuerant adversati, ac persequens omnes qui regulam predictam ad purum et plene voluerint observare et defensare (Döllinger, ibid., 49, 572-3; Angelica 382, 93ra).
[2] Quid autem horum erit vel non erit, dispositioni divine censeo relinquendum (Döllinger, ibid.; Angelica 382, 93ra-rb).
[3] Döllinger, ibid.; Angelica 382, 93rb. See p. 134 above.
[4] Döllinger, ibid., 52-8, 573-6; Angelica 382, 102rb.
[5] Döllinger, ibid., 65, 578; Angelica 382, 102va.
[6] Döllinger, ibid., 67; Angelica 382, ibid.
[7] Döllinger, ibid., 70, 579; Angelica 382, 102vb.
[8] Döllinger, ibid., 77, 581; Angelica 382, 102vb-103ra.
[9] Döllinger, ibid., 78, 582; Angelica 382, 109ra-rb.

to all peoples.[1] For Olivi its coming was not an occasion for bombast or militant certainty; reason could not establish or refute it, although deductions could be made from scripture as to the imminent judgement which would follow the opening of the sixth and seventh seals—a course that Olivi followed to compute its probable date at around 1300.[2]

Olivi's *Postilla*, then, was not a call to action, still less an attack upon the church; it was rather a sustained defence of Franciscan poverty against its detractors and an affirmation of its ultimate triumph. It sought to give the struggles over it a cosmic significance, and loyalty to it an eschatological justification. It was therefore from the outset conceived on a supra-human plane, as a battle between God and Satan. For this reason its unfolding was beyond human agency; far from inciting men to take their fate into their own hands it pointed the lesson of obedience to Christ's commandments: quietism and humility, suffering and patience in the name of Christ and in the hope of the future: these were the keynote. The message was too restrained and subtle for Olivi's followers; it stood in stark contrast to the impatience and presumption which he took to task in his letter to Conrad of Offida, where he said: 'The revivification of the spirit of Christ and the reformation of the evangelical state is not a human matter; nor can it or should it be done by man; but only by Christ, at whose divine call and action the spirit of the truly humble will rise up against the false pride and arrogance of Babylon.'[3]

Here Olivi summed up his own brand of Joachism; it was prophetic; it was a condemnation of the carnal church; it was an invocation to radical change. But it was for God, not for man, to achieve; man's duty was obedience to his superiors and loyalty to Christ's example. The very imminence of change made it an incentive to patience, not action. A believer's place was within the church, not as a schismatic outside it.[4]

---

[1] Döllinger, ibid., 80; Angelica 382, 113vb.

[2] Döllinger, ibid., 582–3; Angelica 113vb. Thirteen was the product of 6 and 7. But Olivi was characteristically cautious.

[3] Oliger, AFH 11, (1918) 370.

[4] Cf. Olivi's own interpretation of the passage in Revelation: 'Come ye out of her, my people, that ye not be partakers of her sin' (Rev. 18: 4) with the passage in his letter to Conrad of Offida upbraiding the Spirituals for theirs: for Olivi it referred principally to dissociation from the sins of Babylon and withdrawal from friendship with their perpetrators: Et nota quod hic principaliter loquitur de exitu ab imitatione et participatione scelerum eius . . . (Döllinger, II, 76, 581; Angelica 382, 107ra).

Two conclusions follow from this examination. The first is that if, for Olivi himself, we can reconcile theory with practice, this was hardly to be expected of his followers. The whole tenor of his *Postilla* was of condemnation; divine judgement would punish transgressions against the true faith; the luxury and persecutions of the carnal clergy would bring about their downfall. What for Olivi were historical categories drawn from the events of his age could be, and were, easily hypostasized. The conventional images with which he clothed his ideas became for less subtle minds entities. In that sense, there was nothing in the *Postilla* which could be justly construed as an attack upon the existing institutions, still less upon the faith.

But there is a second consideration—namely, Olivi's own consistency; and here it can hardly be doubted that, while fully exculpating Olivi from all subversive intent or insurrectionary inclinations, his *Postilla* was the expression of a profound hostility towards the church hierarchy of his time. He regarded its abuses as the work of Antichrist, and looked forward to their divine punishment, which he saw as imminent. There can be no denying the apocalyptic element which, however moderately expressed, pinned Olivi's hopes upon the sudden supersession of the present state by a new era. Although he was conscious of the uncertainties inherent in such speculations, he indulged in them and expectantly awaited their outcome. In doing so he abandoned, however circumspectly, the orthodox position of one final judgement in favour of a second and immediate redress. We can sympathize and understand—and indeed hope—with Olivi; but we have also to recognize that he had altered the accepted order of events, and in doing so encouraged others to take them into their own hands. It was for this reason, together with his tenacious adherence to the *usus pauper*, that his name became the rallying point for the Spirituals and the downtrodden both within his order and outside it. Olivi was perhaps the supreme example of heterodoxy becoming heresy in others.

The Vienne disputes and the condemnation of Franciscan poverty and prophecy

The decisive importance of Olivi's doctrines for the order was fully shown in the twenty-five years following his death; both within it and outside it his name and teachings became at once the rallying point for the zealots and the dividing line from their opponents. All the main issues in dispute before, during, and after the Council of Vienne derived from him.

So far as the Franciscan order itself was concerned the struggle centred primarily around the persecution of the Spirituals, especially in Provence, crystallizing in open confrontation between the representatives of the two parties at the papal court in the years immediately preceding the Council of Vienne (1311-12). The details of the events have often been recounted.[1] Here we are confining ourselves to the issues involved. These, as we have said, were a direct legacy from Olivi: the observance of poverty in the order, and especially the status of the *usus pauper*; and the probity of Olivi's own doctrines. In 1309 following, it appears, the intercession of Arnold of Villanova with the pope, Clement V, on the Provençal Spirituals' behalf, the Spiritual leaders were summoned to the papal curia. There the pope issued the bull *Dudum ad apostolatas*,[2] exempting them from the jurisdiction of their superiors while their case was examined by a three-man papal commission. This was a setback for the leaders of the Community; but after a year had elapsed they summoned up courage to protest in full consistory against the Spiritual's continuing immunity. Their grounds for doing so were that the Spiritual leaders were *fautores* and abettors of heresy, as the supporters of Olivi's errors, which they recounted from the *Rotulus* of the 1283 Paris censure.[3] They failed to make their case; but five months later they repeated their charges, concentrating their attack upon Olivi into eight articles:[4] these included the three to be reproved at the Council of Vienne.[5] The Community's accusation had the effect of diverting attention, to some degree, away from the question of poverty (upon which, as we shall see, the Community was utterly on the defensive) to Olivi. The change was reflected in alterations to the commission investigating the Spirituals' complaints; it was now increased to include members of the Community. Four questions had been put to the parties: on the influence of the Free Spirit within the order; the observance of the rule; Olivi's teachings; and the sufferings

---

[1] The clearest and most authoritative account is by L. Oliger—doyen of Franciscan historians in the generation succeeding Ehrle (who was himself a Jesuit)—in DTC 14 (ii) Spirituals, coll. 2522-9. The main events are also contained in Gratien, *L'Évolution* 419 ff.; Douie, *Fraticelli* 143 ff.; Lambert, *Franciscan Poverty* 149 ff. The sources are almost entirely to be found in Ehrle, ALKG, vol. II, 355-416 and vol. III, 1-195.

[2] BF v, 65. For what follows see Oliger art. cit., cols. 2534-7.

[3] ALKG, II, 365-74.

[4] Ibid.: the first appeal was included in the second one, delivered in private before John cardinal Murrovalle, the cardinal protector of the order.

[5] *Fidei catholicae fundamento*, BF v no. 196, 86. See below pp. 155 ff.

of the Spirituals in Provence.[1] These now gave rise to a series of replies and counter replies, bringing to a climax the exchanges which had been going on between the two sides over the previous year. No decision was reached, however; and in due course two more commissions were established—one on poverty, the other on Olivi's writings—under the auspices of the Council of Vienne.[2] Their decisions were issued in the two bulls of *Exivi de paradiso* and *Fidei catholicae fundamento*. Altogether some forty treatises were written, of which about half have been found and edited.[3] For sheer intensity of output this pamphlet war rivals anything which had gone before. It was the high watermark of the doctrinal struggle between the two parties, culminating in these two decrees of the Council of Vienne in 1312. Henceforth, after a hiatus, the two topics were reopened in a different form and between different antagonists—as the question of the poverty of Christ and the culpability of Olivi's *Postilla* on the Apocalypse. Neither had been more than mentioned during the preceding controversies, but both sprang from the issues which had then been raised.

The main antagonists in the battle were Ubertino of Casale, for the Spirituals, and Raymond Fronsac, procurator of the order, and Bonagratia of Bergamo for the Community. Raymond Gaufridi, formerly general of the order until deposed by Boniface VIII in 1295, also contributed a reply to the four questions of the first papal commission; he may also have collaborated with Ubertino in other writings, until his death in 1310.[4] There were also treatises by Richard of Conington, Peter Aureole and Alexander of Alexandria on behalf of the Community, and Nicholas of Lyre for the Spirituals;[5] but, apart from Ubertino's reply to Alexander,[6] the day-to-day fighting was between Ubertino and his two opponents. From the point of view of the

[1] Oliger DTC 2534; Ehrle, loc. cit. [2] ALKG III, 39.

[3] See A. Heysse 'Responsio "Beatus Vir"' in AFH 42 (1949) 213-14, where the full list is given. The main source is Raymond of Fronsac's catalogue, Ehrle, ALKG III, 5-32.

[4] Angelo of Clareno suspected poison by the Community as the cause, since it coincided with the deaths of two other Spirituals (*Historia*, ALKG II, 133).

[5] Published by F. Pelster, 'Nikolaus von Lyre und seine Quaestio de usu paupere', AFH 46 (1953) 211-50. Nicholas supported the Spirituals' contention that Christ's poverty consisted not only in the renunciation of jurisdiction but 'in parce utendo rebus necessario vite' (ibid., 236); and that 'ex voto paupertatis fratres obligantur ad usum pauperem rerum' (ibid., 247).

[6] *Circa materiam de usu paupere*, edited by A. Heysse in AFH 10 (1917) together with Ubertino of Casale's *Super tribus sceleribus* 116-22.

Community this was unfortunate; for there can be little doubt that Bonagratia of Bergamo and Raymond of Fronsac were no match for Ubertino; not only did they lack his fire and power of expression, but they were singularly incapable of making the best of an inherently weak case. They relied increasingly upon personal innuendo, which while it occasionally throws a personal detail into relief, as in their accusation that Ubertino rode into Avignon on horseback, nearly knocking down Richard of Conington who was on foot,[1] did little to enhance their side's claims. Each of the other three defenders of the Community did better.

As we have already remarked, the differences between the two parties were over poverty and Olivi's teachings; to the second of these nothing of substance was added, and Ubertino counter-attacked Bonagratia and Raymond of Fronsac in *Sanctitati apostolice*[2] by turning the accusation of heresy back upon them. If, he said, the Spirituals were culpable for supporting Olivi, so were the Community for appointing him lector at Florence and Montpellier.[3] Moreover, by demanding the lifting of the Spirituals' exemption, they were guilty of implying that the pope had erred.[4] Finally Ubertino rejected the charges against Olivi as a diversion from the real object of their hostility towards him— namely, his insistence upon the *usus pauper*;[5] and he quoted Olivi's own submission of loyalty to the pope both in the ending to his *Postilla* on the Apocalypse and on his death-bed.[6]

It was to the issue of poverty that Ubertino devoted most of his eloquence. Although not primarily a thinker in Olivi's detached cast, Ubertino was more than a mere amplifier of his master's voice.[7] To begin with, he shared something of St. Francis's mystical devotion to poverty; he gave it the same primacy, and hardly touched on other questions connected with the order, like obedience or permissible

---

[1] ALKG III, 104, in *Sapientia edificavit.*

[2] ALKG II, 377–416.   [3] Ibid., 382–3.   [4] Ibid., 383.

[5] Principalis etiam causa iracundie in libros fratris P[etri] est quia in eis efficacissimis rationibus ostenditur modus presentis relaxationis regule et sancto evangelio et nostre perfectionis voto formaliter (?) contrarius et multiplicibus transgressionibus involutus; et maxime invehitur contra ipsorum doctrinam erroneam quam devulgant et predicant . . . quod paupertas Christi et Apostolorum in evangelio imposita et paupertas nostre regule in voti substantia nullum moderamen vel artationem in usu rerum includit, sed solam expropriationem (ibid., 384–5).

[6] Ibid., 407–8.

[7] For Ubertino see F. Callaey, *L'Idéalisme franciscain spirituel au XIVe siècle* (Louvain 1911); also article by P. Godefroy, in *DTC* 15 (ii), 2020–34.

degrees of borrowing, as Olivi had done. Secondly, Ubertino was both more specific and more comprehensive in his defence of poverty, extending it to books, granaries, vineyards and buildings, as well as to the use of money and to litigation. Thirdly, he came near to regarding the distinction—or perhaps more strictly, its interpretation as—between use and possession as one of the prime sources of the order's ills.

His most sustained treatment of the meaning of poverty was in *Super tribus sceleribus*, written probably in 1311, in answer to Alexander of Alexandria's *Circa materiam de usu paupere*, which it incorporated.[1] The latter work was in many ways the most telling one from the Community. It argued that the vow to absolute poverty consisted solely in the abdication of all possession; nothing was pledged about restricted use. The *usus pauper* could not therefore be considered obligatory; it was rather a moral obligation arising from the state of poverty (*ex condecentia status*.)[2] This led on to an examination of the differences between the two concepts of poverty. As renunciation, it was definite and constant, and inseparably associated with certain actions.[3] As *usus pauper* it was not: to begin with, possession could be renounced and yet usage not be poor; conversely, there could be poor usage and possession, as with hermits.[4] Next, the concept of the *usus pauper* was a negative one expressing a defect, and to this there was no pledge.[5] Then, and the most effective thrust of all, it did not allow uniformity: what was poor for one was not for another: the gently nurtured had different needs from the peasant.[6] Hence instead of uniformity of observance there would be diversity. It was an argument which cut both ways; for if it vindicated the Community's concept, it did so at the expense of St. Francis's: gentle nurture would have had no claim with him in the face of Lady Poverty's imperatives. The argument of the treatise was, then, essentially legalistic and *ex silentio*: it pointed to the absence of the written word in anything referring to the *usus pauper*; it showed that there was nothing in the rule prohibiting the eating of 'good bread' or the drinking of 'good wine';[7] it claimed that without a firm criterion of what could and could not be done, enforcement, and so obedience,

---

[1] Heysse, AFH 10 (1917) 116 ff.

[2] Ibid., 117.

[3] Ibid., 116.

[4] nec sonat usum pauperem, quia posset quis abdicasse dominium rerum et tamen uti rebus non penuriose . . . sicut econtrario habens proprietatem potest stricte vivere sicut heremite proprium habent et paupertatem non vovent (ibid., 116-17).

[5] Ibid.   [6] Ibid.   [7] Ibid., 118.

were not possible, and the novice would be confused.[1] To the argument that every vow must be accompanied by its appropriate action—i.e. obedience was to obey, chastity to be chaste—it rejoined that the act of poverty was to renounce possession of what was used.[2] Finally, we may note the theological argument of the superiority of inner poverty over the outward form of the *usus pauper*, and compare it with St. Bonaventure's, where they had been treated as complementary.[3]

Effective as the Community's reply might be on one level, it ignored the vital matter of the relation of the order's poverty to the practice and precept of St. Francis and his mentor Christ. It was to this that Ubertino turned in his reply in *Super tribus sceleribus*. He began by denying that abdication and poor usage could be contraposed to each other as two distinct definitions of poverty,[4] an assumption by the Community which was entirely gratuitous. In response he was content to base himself upon the words in *Exiit*, which, throughout all these exchanges, remained one of the Spirituals' prime sources together with the words of St. Francis, Bonaventure and Pecham. The *usus pauper*, he said, was merely the practice of living and using things in simple *usus facti*—as necessities—as Christ and Mary had lived.[5] It consisted not in any one act but in a mode of life, which was poor as opposed to rich.[6] He sought in the rule's injunction the equivalents to precepts and prohibitions which had

[1] . . . quia ea que cadunt sub voto semper obligant et ubique, non enim sunt localia . . . difficile etiam erit discernere quis erit usus pauper et quantum se extendit et quantum non . . . Et ideo sanam doctrinam reputamus dicere quod votum regule nostre fertur super certo et determinato, puta super abdicatione dominii et proprietatis; super incerto autem et indeterminato, sicut est usus pauper, non cadit votum: votum enim quod cadit super certo et determinato, sicut super abdicatione dominii, omnes obligat equaliter; si autem caderet super usum pauperem, non posset obligare equaliter, propter diversitatem personarum in ordinem degentium, quibus non potest indici equalis usus. . . . Et ideo, quia non cadit sub voto, non tenemur ad usum pauperem ratione voti, sed ex condecentia status (ibid., 118–19).

[2] Quidam est usus ad quem tenentur fratres voti, sicut velle non habere proprium, quantum ad actum interiorem, et uti re ut non sua, quantum ad actum exteriorem (ibid., 120).

[3] cum actus interior paupertatis est velle non habere proprium vel dominium in aliqua re, quod est magis meritorium quam usus pauper, quia dare voluntatem deo est magis meritorium quam dare actum (ibid., 119).

[4] Ibid., 123

[5] debes scire quod usus pauper accipitur a nobis pro illa consuetudine vivendi et utendi rebus simplici facti usu, quam Christus et eius mater sanctissima secundum dicta sancti evangelii et sanctorum in sue vite decursu communiter tenuerunt (ibid., 124).

[6] Ibid.

to be observed: such as those against the use of money, shoes, excess clothes and so on.[1] These together formed the substance of the *usus pauper*;[2] they were thus more than a mere moral obligation *ex bono et equo*, but inherent in the vow of poverty.[3] Moderation in use was a constant theme both in the writings of the founder and his successors, as well as in the order's constitutions, all of which Ubertino cited liberally. To deny it was blasphemy,[4] and failure to observe it the source of all abuses in the order.[5] He scorned the Community's identification of the act of poverty with using what was not theirs: only someone not vowed to chastity would have a right to the use of a spouse, and the same applied to poverty and poor use;[6] like the vows to chastity and obedience, the vow to poverty must be totally observed. To exclude moderation would be to exempt the Friars Minor alone from an obligation incumbent upon all other religious.[7] Ubertino also dealt effectively with the Community's claim that the *usus pauper* lacked the determinateness to be generally enforceable. The question was not one of quantity, but proportion; renunciation was not a fixed amount, but in relation to needs: those of a sick man were clearly greater than of one in health.[8] He particularly followed Olivi in taking the *usus pauper* as a norm to be observed according to discretion rather than a fixed point from which any deviation was a mortal sin; not every sin was mortal, otherwise there would be no small sins. The *usus pauper* was an obligation binding upon all, but one which must be interpreted in the light of reason and according to circumstances.[9] The vow must be tempered by man's incapacity. But, like Olivi, he condemned the vow of poverty without the practice of the *usus pauper* as a mockery from which all perfection was drained. Instead of penury, which starved the carnal appetites, there would be opulence which fed them.[10]

---

[1] Ibid., 130–4.

[2] omnia enim consilia que ad virtualem perfectionem supererogationis vite apostolice et ad pauperem usum spectant perfectionem in regula . . . (ibid., 133).

[3] Ibid., 136.   [4] Ibid., 143.   [5] Ibid.

[6] Ibid.   [7] Ibid.

[8] Usus enim pauper obligat omnes ad vitandam equaliter superfluitatem et opulentiam, non equalitate quantitatis sed proportionis; si enim infirmus indiget pluribus tunicis et cibis delicatis, sanus autem non, nulla est singularitas, ymo vera communitas si quilibet habet quod est necessarium sibi (ibid., 154).

[9] Non igitur oportet quod quantitas usus pauperis determinetur in puncto cuius medium non est punctabile, nec secundum uniformitatem rationalem, sed potius secundum quod recta ratio dicat, pensatis debitis circumstantiis, secundum diversitatem personarum, negotiorum, temporum et locorum (ibid., 163).   [10] Ibid., 167.

Ubertino, here as elsewhere, made poverty inseparable from use; its perfection lay in conforming to Christ's example: patched habits, no fixed abode, pilgrims wandering bare-footed, receiving what they were given but holding nothing for the morrow; such was his ideal. It informed all that he wrote; loyalty to it was the basis of his attack and the plea for his defence. If it was a practical conception it was given a theoretical, or at least a doctrinal, justification: and there can be little doubt that it had the sources on its side. Ubertino could and did quote endlessly from the order's authorities as well as from *Exiit*: he had the confidence that came from conviction: his very exaggerations were part of it. He was a man both exultant in his loyalty to an ideal and outraged by its abuse. He could invoke unbroken passages from his witnesses, where his opponents could only gloss fragments. Their lameness is as patent as his buoyancy.

This can be seen in the other exchanges between them. The two most important writings on poverty known to us were *Sanctitas vestra* and the *Rotulus iste*;[1] they were strongly contrasting. *Sanctitas vestra* was the most comprehensive of Ubertino's writings of this period. It sought to expound the principles of the rule under the seven main headings of poverty, simplicity, purity, humility, prayer, charity and concord; with each he pointed to the divergence between the original intention and present practice. For Ubertino they stood or fell together; and it was his belief in their unity which made his conception of evangelical poverty so much richer than that of his opponents—and, it is fair to add, so much more in the authentic spirit of St. Francis. Poverty, to be evangelical, must also be simple, pure, humble, lived in prayer, charity and peace; ultimately the *usus pauper* was the totality of this ideal. It was by its consonance with the latter and not in any mere legal act of abdication that true poverty lay. In *Sanctitas vestra* Ubertino took poverty in this wider setting to show how the failure to observe the *usus pauper* meant the violation of virtues indispensable to evangelical perfection. St. Francis's poverty, he said, had come from Christ; not only did a possessionless state not allow possessions either in common or in private, but by the the same token it was also pacific, permitting of no litigation.[2] The

---

[1] Edited by Ehrle in ALKG III, 51–89 and 93–137. There was also his *Declaratio*, ibid., 162–95, written in August 1311 in reply to the Community's reply to *Sanctitas vestra*, ibid., 141–60, which is almost exclusively polemical and added little new to the discussion.

[2] est expropriativa, ita quod nichil nec in communi nec in speciali possint sibi appropriare, nec aliquis frater nec toto ordo . . . Ac per hoc est eorum paupertas

infringement of this ideal had led to relaxation, and compelled those zealous for it to intercede with the pope for judgement. St. Francis in his Testament had prohibited all papal letters and the granting of privileges.[1] Ubertino, while not disputing Gregory IX's invalidation of the Testament's power to bind St. Francis's successors, was yet inclined to regard St. Francis's intentions as a precept, which certainly expressed God's will.[2] Thus in common with the rest of his party Ubertino looked to the Testament as a source of authority, although here, unlike in his *Arbor vitae*, he did not say so with the same immoderation.[3] He began by putting the blame upon the order's abuse of the popes' good intentions.[4] To this he added the standard Franciscan authorities to prove the violation of the rule by current practices over clothing, buildings, granaries, vineyards, and so on. Often he sounded the authentic note of St. Francis's disciple, as when recounting the founder's refusal to enter large buildings and insistence upon dwelling in modest ones. He contrasted St. Francis's injunction to regard themselves as pilgrims always ready to abandon wherever they were, with the litigation of the present day:[5] this had gone so far that the recent constitutions (probably those of Toulouse in 1307)[6] demanded complete freedom of possession before building. Undoubtedly the greatest novelty in Ubertino's position was towards the time-honoured distinction between possession and use. After ridiculing the pretence, that the papal procurators alone handled money for the order, as an enormous fallacy and the deadly poison of evangelical poverty,[7] he went on to deny the legality of the current practice. He thereby attacked the foundation of the order's existence.

---

pacifica, quia ex status sui condicione cum nulla creatura habent unde possint litigare, quia hoc solum est eis proprium inter omnia mundana, nichil habere proprium (ALKG III, 52).

[1] Ibid.

[2] Non tamen dissencio a sententia domini pape qui fratres dicit ad illius mandati observanciam non teneri, quia non obligavit successorem suum, cum non habeat imperium par in parem. Quia iure humano non est dubium quod nichil poterat precipere . . . sed per modum precepti voluit nobis explicare intentionem suam, quam habuit in regula a spiritu sancto, et quam asserebat pro certo esse domini voluntatem . . . (ibid., 54).

[3] See pp. 152 ff. below.

[4] Et sancti pontifices nostris verbis inducti, bona intentione dederunt nobis privilegia ignorantes quod nostro statui repugnent et quod nos abutamur eisdem (ALKG III, 54).

[5] Ibid., 65.

[6] Ibid.

[7] Ibid., 66.

His grounds for doing so were firstly that St. Francis had never sought
such an arrangement, as both his life and his Testament bore witness;[1]
and secondly that, since superfluities were not allowed, they could not
come under the pope's dominion. Accordingly, the brothers were the
proprietors of all that was not absolutely necessary.[2] This included
vineyards, granaries, books, produce that they sold, and so on: none
of these passed through the pope's hands, and for that reason they
could not be attributed to the procurators, who could only have authority over what the pope received.[3] Besides being usurpers, then, the
brothers were also avid questors after wealth who more resembled
misers and merchants than Minors.[4] The force of the argument, impressive though it is, depended upon the withdrawal of papal privileges
to be effective; for it was precisely in papal sanction of the various
practices, which Ubertino had condemned as superfluities, that the justification of the Community's position ultimately lay. Morally, and in
terms of St. Francis's authority, its adherents had not a leg to stand on;
the only thing in common between their conception of poverty and
St. Francis's was the legal definition. As ways of life their affinities were
unrecognizable: the Community could point to all manner of precise
reasons for the path that it followed; what it could not legitimately
do was to pretend that it was the same as St. Francis's. Ubertino accordingly not only attacked what he regarded as superfluities, but also the
basis upon which they rested—namely, papal privileges. Once more he
invoked St. Francis's rejection of all papal glosses on the rule to make
his own plea that those who wished should be allowed to follow the
rule as St. Francis had enjoined—purely and simply in its original form

---

[1] Certe nec beatus Franciscus voluit hoc a papa petere quod possessio esset sua et
usus nostri; immo voluit quod proprietas esset vel prelatorum vel condecentium
vel communitatum, ut per hoc nulla fixio daretur fratribus quin possent, quando
dominis placeret, expelli. Quod ostendit in testamento suo et in legenda, cum dicit
quod domos locorum pauperculas non inhabitarent ut proprias, sed ut peregrini et
advene alienas (ibid., 71).

[2] Ex premissa ergo recepcione domini pape patet quod non transit in suum
dominium nisi illud quod recipit; sed non recipit nisi dominium illarum rerum
quarum usum facti fratribus licet habere . . . omnium ergo superfluorum talium
dominium non transit in papam, cum expresse asserat hoc fratribus non licere; nec
est verisimile quod velit patrocinium prestare delictis; ergo talium convincuntur
fratres esse proprietarii, cum illarum rerum non possint dominium aliud demonstrare
(ibid., 83).

[3] Ibid., 83–4.

[4] Ibid., 85.

as pope Honorius had confirmed it.[1] He ended with the solemn warning, which he had already given five or more years earlier in the *Arbor vitae*,[2] that there would be no peace in the order until those true to St. Francis's primitive ideal should be allowed to be so.[3] Secession, therefore, was the only solution.

The other prominent aspect in Ubertino's standpoint was his strong distaste for profane learning; here he was not perhaps so different from Olivi as might at first appear, since he was largely echoing what the latter had said in his *Postilla* on the Apocalypse. In particular Ubertino attacked the organisation of studies at Paris and the ambition, rather than a love of study for its own sake, which fired brothers to keep books.[4] He contraposed this preoccupation with what was falsely called knowledge to the innocence and contempt for the world and devotion to prayer which should be part of the brothers' true vocation. He recalled that St. Francis had said that learning should be directed to divine wisdom and informed above all by the spirit of God.[5]

As an exposition of the Franciscan ideal *Sanctitas vestra* was perhaps Ubertino's most mature and considered work. It possessed a balance and restraint—if not order—lacking in many of his writings, while it supported its moral fervour with shrewd technical arguments and the usual abounding examples. The *Rotulus*[6] written later in the same year (1310) was a very different work. Here Ubertino in twenty-five articles unleashed a broadside of cases showing how the vow of poverty had been abused. These covered most of the by now standard charges: wearing of shoes, sumptuous buildings, collecting money, the particular scandal of using *bursarii* to carry money for brothers on journeys,[7] excess food and drink, possession of granaries and vineyards, the selling of candles, litigation over property, idleness, learning at Paris, and the

---

[1] Et ista regula, sicut est a patre nostro beato Francisco instituta, daretur illis qui eam servare pure et sine glosa cupiunt et se reputant dei adiutorio posse adimplere. Et de hoc credo vos multum deo servire et beato Francisco et ecclesie sancte dei et magnum ex hoc premium inpetrare. Hoc solum et nichil aliud pro me peto et pro multis bonis fratribus . . . quia sic continet nostra pura professio qua vovemus regulam observare, non dicendo 'secundum declaracionem', nisi simpliciter regulam fratrum minorum per dominum Honorium confirmatam (ibid., 87).

[2] Bk. v, ch. III.

[3] Et secure audeo dicere quod in ordine pax non erit usquequo vicarius dei eam licteraliter tradat volentibus eam servare . . . et sic nunquam pax erit (ALKG III, 87).

[4] Ibid., 73–4.   [5] Ibid., 72.
[6] Ibid., 93–137.   [7] Ibid., 104.

persecution of those who attempted to reassert evangelical poverty by following the *usus pauper*. Ubertino again reiterated the obligation to observe it, not as a formula precisely stated in the rule, with every infraction a mortal sin, but as a prohibition against anything which would impair the highest poverty.[1] He also appealed to the pope for freedom to return to the literal observance of the rule.[2] As an indictment, the *Rotulus* probably carried more weight than any of Ubertino's other writings; there can be little doubt that the failure to make an effective reply to it in *Sapientia edificavit*, by Bonagratia of Bergamo and Raymond Fronsac,[3] led them to try the diversion of Olivi's teachings and personal calumny. Even more significant, the *Rotulus* became the basis of the papal commission's report on the state of observance within the order, which in turn gave rise to *Exivi de paradiso*.[4] Indeed, Ehrle long ago pointed out[5] their striking affinity. Great, then, as the impact of the *Rotulus* was, it was not enough to gain the reversal of the system or their separation from it which the Spirituals sought.

Ultimately, as we have said, the Community's position rested on a series of legal definitions and privileges. As long as they remained in force the order would continue fundamentally as it was. Nor did any of its defenders look far beyond this legal framework of dominion and use. Here they found ample support in St. Bonaventure's *Apologia* and papal decrees. Peter Aureole,[6] for example, adopted Bonaventure's argument of Christ's greater perfection than St. Paul, through condescension, to show that Christ's poverty was more perfect than John the Baptist's, even though the latter had lived in greater austerity. The reason was that Christ was entirely without dominion, and poverty was the absence of dominion.[7] He also held that necessary use was not synonymous with restricted use, but merely with simple *usus facti*, i.e.

---

[1] ALKG III, 134–5.

[2] Ibid., 137.

[3] Included in the text of the *Rotulus iste*.

[4] See G. Fussenegger: 'Relatio commissionis in concilio Viennensi institutae ad decretalem "Exivi de paradiso" praeparandam' AFH 50 (1957) 145–77.

[5] ALKG III, 90.

[6] In the question from his Quodlibet, edited by E. Longpré in AFH 23 (1930) 42–56 under the title 'Le quolibet de Nicolas de Lyre', to whom he mistakenly attributed it. See F. Pelster, 'Nikolaus von Lyre und seine Quaestio de usu paupere', AFH 46 (1953) 211–50. It is also to be found in *Firmamenta tria ordinum* (Paris 1512), 86, 87, 88.

[7] AFH 23, 54.

that which entailed no legal right, but derived from the need for self-preservation.[1] Another prominent legal point invoked by the Community was that, whereas there could be no dispensation from the vow of poverty, there could be from poor use; otherwise no brothers could have become bishops.[2] This supported their view that the question of the *usus pauper* was merely a verbal quibble.[3] But this was hardly an answer to Gaufridi's claim, to which it was directed, that if chastity and obedience entailed use so did poverty.[4]

The divergences, then, between the two sides were more than those of interpretation. They rather represented the collision of two different outlooks which could not co-exist within the same body. For the Spirituals poverty was a way of life; for the Community, an arrangement. For the Spirituals it went together with humility, simplicity, a contempt for the world and a desire to emulate Christ; for the Community it was the badge of an order prominent in the service of the church. If for both it was to the greater glory of God, their ideas of glory differed: for the Spirituals it lay in abnegation, for the Community in organization. Two such differing conceptions within the same order were bound to clash; and in the context of the founder's intention the Spirituals had every right to feel aggrieved and betrayed. Their plea for release to pursue their own interpretation would in the circumstances have been the fairest course.

The persecutions which the Spirituals underwent belong to the next chapter. Here it needs once more to be recalled how deeply rooted their belief in the evangelical meaning of poverty was. It constituted a faith in its own right, or, more strictly, it became the criterion of fidelity to Christ. Nowhere is this more vividly seen than in Ubertino of Casale's

---

[1] Ibid., 56.

[2] ALKG III, 155 in the response of Bonagratia of Bergamo and Raymond Fronsac to Gaufridi's reply to the papal commission's four questions. It was a point made by Richard of Conington, provincial of England and a supporter of the Community, in his treatise on poverty edited by A. Heysse, AFH 23 (1930) 105.

[3] ALKG III, loc. cit.

[4] Ibid., 143. Gaufridi's treatise is to be found at the beginning of the reply to it by Bonagratia and Raymond Fronsac, ibid., 142-4. It is a measured and balanced piece of work and not without cogency, as this particular point testifies: e.g., Nescimus enim ad quid prosit vovere virtutem et non tenere ad aliquem eius usum, ut vovere castitatem et non teneri ad usum castitatis, vel vovere obedientiam et non teneri ad usum obedientie; sic non videmus magnum meritum vovere paupertatem et non teneri ex voto ad aliquem usum eius.
The strong similarity between this argument and Ubertino's in *Super tribus sceleribus* suggests that the latter may have drawn upon it.

L

Arbor vitae,[1] which was a sustained peon in praise of Christ and the Virgin. For us its devotional fervour is of less immediate concern than the apocalyptic vision of the fifth book. This is noteworthy for its almost complete Franciscanizing of the Apocalypse, so that it became an almost direct transposition of the Spirituals' philosophy. In this Ubertino went beyond Olivi and Joachim, although he was indebted to them for virtually all his symbolism, and the sequence of events: for example, the three tribulations of the Antichrist—of religious laxity, heresy, and the Paris persecutions, with pagan learning in the guise of theology;[2] the identification of the locusts with the religious;[3] the coming of St. Francis to convert the infidels.[4] In most of these Olivi was followed verbatim. But, on the other hand, while Ubertino remained true to the Joachist schema, the different ages of the church are treated more perfunctorily, and there is not the vital sense of interaction between the fifth and the sixth ages which is to be found in Olivi's *Postilla*. Instead we are treated to a far more vivid account of Christ's renewal in the person of St. Francis, for both of whom Ubertino felt a kinship which shines out in all his writings. The question of periods was secondary to the significance of St. Francis's divine mission to restore evangelical perfection to the church. As with all Franciscan Joachism, St. Francis was for Ubertino the angel of the sixth seal, bearing the 'five pearls' of the stigmata in the sign of the living God.[5] It was upon St. Francis, in his devotion to poverty, humility and charity, that Ubertino's Apocalypse centred. He contrasted St. Francis's purity of faith with the laxity and corruption in the church, which he subjected to unbridled attack.[6] In this he went far beyond anything he subsequently wrote; and there seem good grounds for believing that the *Arbor vitae*, originally written in response to requests[7] by his confrères at the monastery of Alverna, was not known to the world at large during his lifetime.[8] His many reprobations included Celestine V's abdication and what he regarded as the usurpation

---

[1] The text cited here is from Rylands MS. 200.   [2] Ibid., ff., 427ra–429va.

[3] Ibid., f. 426vb.   [4] Ibid., 429va–vb.

[5] E.g. Idcirco ad perpetuum rei memoriam sue passionis impressit in carne Francisci (ibid., f. 412va). See also Bk. v, chs. 3 and 4.

[6] Especially chs. 7 and 8 of Bk. v.

[7] The prologue tells how he had been variously importuned to explain parts of the bible, to write on the Apocalypse, and to describe Jesus's life and passion (f. 3).

[8] This seems clear from the absence of all reference to the work throughout the main controversies and tribulations of Ubertino's career. It is inconceivable that Bonagratia of Bergamo would not have used it in his indictment of Ubertino of 1317, or that it would not have been alluded to at his trial in 1325 had it been known.

of the papal throne by Boniface VIII; he characterized the latter as the precursor of the great Antichrist, and Benedict XI as the beast ascending from the earth; he also abused Clement V.[1] All this went, it is true, much further than Olivi, but it does not warrant us in saying that Ubertino condemned the church as a whole or identified it in its entirety with the whore of Babylon, let alone that he was preaching its subversion. It was much more a personal vilification of those he felt had betrayed the order. Indeed, the dominant impression of Ubertino's *Arbor vitae* is its essentially personal character; it lacked the intellectual structure of Olivi's work. It was the repository for all Ubertino's main beliefs, albeit expressed with less restraint than subsequently. As such it was essentially a spiritual manifesto sanctifying poverty and the teachings of St. Francis, and decrying his betrayers. The struggle between the two sides was projected in supernatural terms, as that between Christ and Antichrist. The change from Joachim of Fiore hardly needs stressing: while remaining true to his scheme of history, the impersonal forces of divine destiny became translated into the *dramatis personae* of Franciscan history; the future and the past were read almost exclusively in Franciscan terms; the symbols were invested with a new meaning. But the apocalyptic sense of impending change still remained. For all the variations the theme remained Joachim's. If St. Francis and St. Dominic were the twin prophets, the Elias and Enoch[2] of the new age, it was with the new age that Ubertino was concerned; and if it was upon St. Francis that Ubertino devoted his greatest fervour this was because of his special role in its attainment. Ubertino recounted Francis's example of poverty and humility and charity; his special position after Christ;[3] and the sanctity of his Testament which forbade all papal glosses.[4] He attacked pagan learning, the Paris theologians and the corrupt clergy.[5]

---

[1] Ibid., Bk. v, chs. vii and viii. In the Venice edition of 1485 these references are to be found ff. 447a–448b. I have been unable to locate them in MS. Rylands 200.

[2] Inter quos in tempore Helie et Enoch, Franciscus et Dominicus singulariter claruerunt, quorum primus seraphico calculo purgatus et ardore celico inflammatus totum mundum incendere videbatur. Secundus vero ut cherub extentus et protegens lumine sapientie clarius et verbo predicationis facundus supere mundi tenebras clarius radiavit (ibid., 409va).

[3] Unde fuit Franciscus similis Christo non solum in profunda humilitate sed etiam in viscera pietate et in vite simplicitate et in fervente charitate et desiderio salutis summe (ibid., 411ra).

[4] Et istis pensatis scio quod regula valde bene servari potest. Et ideo sicut scripta est sic volo quod servetur ad literam sine aliqua glosa (ibid., 421va).

[5] Ibid., chs. 7 and 8, and especially ff. 428 and 429.

He invoked the authority of St. Francis's companions, like brother Leo,[1] and the definitions of poverty by Spirituals, like Hugh of Digne, to show that the *usus pauper* was an inseparable part of evangelical poverty.[2] It was all there as it was to be found in the pamphlets of 1309–12; even the warning on the need to allow the Spirituals to secede.[3] Franciscan Joachism had thus become the vehicle of the Spirituals' aspirations; it brought them the faith of having God on their side. In that belief they were prepared to suffer all persecution until their cause should be rewarded and their enemies overwhelmed.[4]

This state of mind, common to so many of the Spirituals, was exemplified in the writings of Ubertino and of Angelo of Clareno;[5] in defending evangelical poverty they were fighting for God; in remaining true to St. Francis they were being loyal to Christ. Poverty thus had for them a cosmic significance which their opponents did not share. It was part of an almost mystic union with God, which had to be lived, not legislated for. It was this difference in conception which ultimately separated Ubertino and Angelo from, say, Raymond of Fronsac and Bonagratia of Bergamo. Whether one was superior to the other is not to the point; it is rather that they were at variance with each other as visions of perfection. They represented different experiences. It was hardly surprising that they could not agree.

---

[1] *Arbor Vitae*, 419ra.

[2] Ibid., 421vb–422ra.   [3] Ibid., ch. III.

[4] Ubertino's subsequent career after the decisions of the Council of Vienne concern us only indirectly. He remained at Avignon in the household of cardinal Orsini until 1325, refusing to re-enter the Franciscan order, with the revocation of the Spirituals' exemption. He escaped punishment in 1316 when the Provençal Spirituals were summoned to Avignon by John XXII. The latter, after unavailing attempts to persuade him to rejoin the Franciscans, transferred him to the Benedictine monastery at Gembloux, near Liège, in 1317. But he continued, in fact, to reside at Avignon. The attack upon him for heresy by his old adversary, Bonagratia of Bergamo, cut no ice with the pope, who continued to favour him. In 1322 he contributed a solution to the pope's question on the poverty of Christ, *De altissima paupertate Christi* (part of which is published in Baluze *Miscellanea* II, 279–80) which conceded them a natural, but not a legal, right to what they had. This was substantially the position of the Perugia encyclical (see below pp. 163 ff.); not surprisingly it found no acceptance with John XXII, who refused to separate natural and legal rights. In 1325 Ubertino was accused of heresy and put on trial before a papal court; but he fled into oblivion. He may have joined the Franciscan dissidents at Louis of Bavaria's court; he may have been captured and burned by the inquisition. See Douie *Fraticelli* 128–32 and DTC 15, 2023–4.

[5] For an account of Angelo's apocalyptism, see below, pp. 172 ff.

The culmination of their war of words came in the two bulls *Exivi de paradiso*[1] and *Fidei catholicae fundamento* issued by Clement V in the Council of Vienne on 6 May 1312. The first, as we have said, dealt with poverty, the second with Olivi. Of the two the latter came nearer to vindicating the Spirituals, since it condemned only two propositions and gave a third as less probable than its alternative. Moreover, none of these mentioned Olivi by name, and it is arguable that the second of the two condemned—the denial that the substance of the soul was body's form—was not Olivi's view. The first, that Christ was still alive when he received the spear wound on the cross, was; and so was the third, that baptism only remitted sin but did not confer grace.[2] Nevertheless, they represented a very meagre harvest from years of calumniating Olivi as a heretic and his adherents as fautors of heresy; and they must be regarded as clearing, rather than blackening, the names of both Olivi and his Spiritual supporters.

Exivi, on the other hand, while *prima facie* seeming to justify the Spirituals, in fact denied them their main demands: neither the *usus pauper* nor, in the event of its rejection, freedom to secede, was recognized, thereby leaving the main causes of contention unresolved. It was one more compromise between legalized unrestraint and moral exhortation to restraint. It followed *Exiit* in being but another gloss on the rule, a tradition against which the Spirituals were in revolt. Accordingly, however favourable to them it might be in detail it was against them in substance.

It began by reaffirming, as *Exiit* had done, the three vows of the rule without qualification,[3] at the same time distinguishing between particular obligations which had the force of precept and those which were counsels. While transgression of some was a mortal sin, for others it was not.[4] Within the first category of precept came all the main injunctions of the rule over clothing, shoes, riding, preaching, fasting, and so on.[5] The brothers were also cautioned not to accept more than they needed in alms.[6] The handling of money or its receipt in churches through offerings was prohibited.[7] They were to have recourse to the 'spiritual friends' only in case of illness, or need for clothing, or pressing necessity.[8] On the sixth chapter of the rule, that 'the brothers may appropriate nothing', the bull recited, in terms almost identical with Ubertino's *Rotulus*, the list of abuses over rents, wills, granaries, vineyards,

---

[1] BF v, 81.　　　　　　[2] Ibid., 86.
[3] Ibid.　　　　　　　　[4] Ibid., 81b.　　　　　[5] Ibid.
[6] Ibid., 82a.　　　　　[7] Ibid., 82b.　　　　[8] Ibid., 83a.

buildings, and rich furnishings, which it condemned.[1] At the same time it left the decision over granaries and vineyards to the discretion of superiors, just as it did the number of tunics required.[2]

On the question of the *usus pauper*, mentioned for the first time in an official papal pronouncement, the bull came down decisively on the side of the Community in confining it to the conditions prescribed in the rule. If this was a moral recognition of the Spirituals' case that such an obligation existed, it favoured the Community in denying it any force in its own right. It only strengthened such an impression when it went on to prohibit either side from calling the other heretical on account of supporting it or attacking it, since the onus of proof had always been with the Spirituals.[3]

Exivi and *Fidei catholicae* virtually marked the end of the debates between the Spirituals and Community as two relatively free and equal parties. A last plea to the pope from Ubertino of Casale gained nothing. Among the Tuscan Spirituals there was secession, rebellion and flight to Sicily.[4] Nevertheless the prospect of settlement for a brief interlude appeared brighter than at any time since Gaufridi's generalate (1289–92); for in 1313 Gonsalvo of Valboa, general of the order since 1304 and one of the fiercest opponents of the Spirituals, died and was succeeded by the accommodating Alexander of Alexandria. This change followed measures by Clement V in the previous year against members of the Community in Provence, where he had deposed the provincial and deprived fifteen others of office;[5] he also exiled Bonagratia of Bergamo to the convent at Valcabrère, where he remained until after Clement's death in 1314.[6] Alexander of Alexandria seemed about to open an era of pacification; he appointed superiors favourable to the Spirituals in the Provençal convents of Narbonne, Béziers and Carcassonne, and the Spirituals obeyed him by returning to them.[7] Only Tuscany remained

---

[1] BF v, 83a. [2] Ibid., 84b.

[3] Ex praemissis autem succrevit non parum scrupulosa quaestio inter fratres, videlicet utrum ex suae professione regulae obligentur ad arctum et tenuem sive *pauperem usum* rerum ... dicimus quod fratres minores ex professione suae regulae specialiter obligantur ad arctos usus seu pauperes, qui in ipsorum regula continentur, et eo obligationis modo, sub quo continet seu ponit regula dictos usus. Dicere autem, sicut alique asserere perhibentur, quod haereticum sit tenere usum pauperem includi vel non includi sub voto evangelicae paupertatis praesumptuosum et temerarium iudicamus (ibid., 85a).

[4] Angelo of Clarena, *Historia*, ALKG II, 140.

[5] Oliger, DTC 14, art. cit., 2537.

[6] Ibid. [7] Ibid.

in ferment, and with concord reigning elsewhere it might have been re-stored there. But the new dispensation was not to be; both Alexander and Clement died in 1314; and the old strife was resumed in Provence, where the deposed superiors of the Community regained control and renewed their persecutions.[1] This led the Spirituals to revolt, in turn, and with the help of the local populace they took over the convents of Narbonne and Béziers. They became the rallying points for Spirituals far and wide as centres of poor use. They were now excommunicated by one of the Spirituals' most bitter enemies, Bertrand de la Tour, provincial of Aquitaine.[2] Charges and counter-charges followed, while both the post of general and the papal throne remained vacant. Finally in 1316 each was filled, John XXII becoming pope and Michael of Cesena general of the order at the chapter-general of Naples.[3] The two chief players in what was to be the final dénouement over the poverty of Christ were now in their places.

The stages leading to it have been told often enough;[4] we shall have something to say about them, as they affected the Spirituals, in the next chapter. What concerns us now is the effective divergence between the paths of the Spirituals and the Community. After the issue of John XXII's bull *Quorumdam exigit* in 1317,[5] which was virtually an ultimatum to the Spirituals to obedience and surrender, the latter became a hunted group no longer of independent standing. Individuals like Angelo and Uber-tino remained, but they no longer spoke as leaders of a recognized group. By 1319 the dissentients in Provence had been effectively crushed, and those in Sicily and Italy had become fugitive groups. Moreover, and this is the point which must be emphasized, this achieve-ment was the combined effort of John XXII and Michael of Cesena, both of whom insisted upon the Spirituals' return to obedience.

As an adjunct to this desire to restore order and to crush subversion John XXII in 1319 instituted an enquiry into Olivi's *Postilla* on the Apocalypse. The reason is not far to seek. It had for long, together with the veneration of Olivi, entered into the lore of the Spirituals and their Beguin supporters, as we shall see in the next chapter. Bernard Gui, the inquisitor for Provence, saw it as one of the main sources of heresy among the Beguins.[6] That it was known in a debased form there can be no doubt. In particular, Olivi's teaching on the carnal church had come to mean the entire church of Rome, to which was contraposed

---

[1] Ibid. [2] Ibid., 2538. [3] Ibid.
[4] E.g., Oliger, Gratien, Douie, Lambert, op. cit.
[5] See below, pp. 231 ff. [6] *Manuel* I, 110.

the spiritual church of the true believers. It was the nearest thing to a direct attack upon the church and the pope's position; it threatened their authority in a way that the doctrine of poverty did not: but at the same time both had their roots in disobedience, and both therefore must be crushed. John XXII had not been slow to react to this situation. At the end of 1317 and the beginning of 1318 he issued two bulls against these tendencies. The first, *Sancta Romana*,[1] was directed against the rebel Tuscan Spirituals, who had migrated to Sicily; it referred to their claim to have been authorized by Celestine V as a separate order, even though this had been quashed by Boniface VIII. The second, *Gloriosam ecclesiam*,[2] openly accused them of propagating the notion of a carnal and a spiritual church, all authority having passed to the latter. Nor was John XXII the first to have turned his attention to Olivi's *Postilla*.[3] Ubertino in his defence of Olivi in *Sanctitati apostolice* had had to meet that very charge, namely, that Olivi's *Postilla* had described the Roman church as the great whore of Babylon.[4] Ubertino's defence of the *Postilla* was indeed one of the charges brought against him by Bonagratia of Bergamo in 1318, and it was resurrected as one of the seven articles at his trial for heresy in 1325.[5] As might be expected of Ubertino's long-standing opponent, a series of extreme and entirely unfounded opinions were attributed to Olivi, making him appear an implacable enemy of the church, which he of course was not.[6] The Community's hostility to Olivi was, as we have amply seen, of long standing: and the frequent references to him in the polemics at the time of the Council of Vienne, as the leader of a subversive sect, although themselves a repetition of accusations made intermittently since the Milan chapter of 1285, may well, in the light of what has been said, have referred to the dissemination of Olivi's apocalyptic views among the Beguins of Provence. Moreover, the Marseilles chapter-general of 1319 had once again condemned Olivi's writings[7] which, it has been suggested, was an attempt

---

[1] BF V, 134–5.

[2] Ibid., 137.

[3] For the sequence of events leading up to the condemnation see Pasztor, *Le polemiche*.

[4] ALKG III, 370: Pasztor, art. cit., 372.

[5] Pasztor, ibid., 374. L. Oliger, *Tractatus de Christi et Apostolorum paupertate*, AFH 22 (1929) 306, has argued convincingly that Bonagratia's attack was made in 1318 and incorporated into the charges at his trial in 1325, under which they appear in Baluze, *Misc.* II, 276–9.

[6] Baluze, ibid., 276.

[7] Reported in *Series condemnationum et processuum contra doctrinam Petri Johannis Olivi*, ed. L. Amoros, AFH 24 (1931) 509–10. Pasztor, art. cit., 377.

to anticipate John XXII's own condemnation of the *Postilla*, although in fact it did not take place then.[1]

Papal proceedings against the work, therefore, were a logical outcome of these circumstances, and above all the prevalence of its influence among the Spirituals and Beguins whom John XXII determined to put down. He first initiated an investigation into the *Postilla* in 1317 under the cardinal bishop of Ostia, Nicholas of Prato.[2] The following year a commission of eight theologians was appointed; they drew up a list of sixty censured propositions,[3] published in 1319; but it was not until 1326 that the *Postilla* was finally condemned by the pope.[4] The reason for the delay is not certain; a lost papal bull of 1322 spoke of the pope's 'reserving judgement' on the matter.[5] Nor is there any actual documentary record of the 1326 condemnation. What seems clear is that John XXII took a very personal interest in the issues raised by the *Postilla*; a sermon of his attacked its conception of the sixth age on much the same grounds as the commission of Anagni had criticized Joachim's conception of a new era. It would transfer to men in this world the faculties reserved for the elect in the next: they would then in their wisdom no longer be voyagers (*viatores*) but *comprehensores* in full possession of understanding without need of a mediator,[6] i.e. the church. Here, then, was ample cause for John's rejection of it. But even more, it helps to point the connexion with the pope's attack upon the doctrine of absolute poverty.

The 1319 examination of Olivi's *Postilla* is revealing in two aspects. The first is the degree of prejudice with which Olivi's statements were interpreted. Time and again conclusions were drawn and meanings attributed to Olivi which were quite unwarranted from the context. This applied especially to Olivi's references to Babylon and the carnal church, which were repeatedly taken by the commission to mean the Roman church.[7] Similarly Olivi's descriptions of the two Antichrists, the pseudo-popes, pseudo-prophets, and tribulations, were all censured. The masters equated them all with symbols for the church without making the least attempt to establish their assumption. From this they had little difficulty in finding their import heretical.

In the second place, however, and undoubtedly of greater significance, the commission rejected the entire apocalyptic foundation of

---

[1] Pasztor, ibid.   [2] ALKG III, 545; Pasztor, ibid., 373.
[3] Baluze, *Misc.* II, 258-70.   [4] Pasztor, art. cit., 369.
[5] Ibid., 382.   [6] Ibid., 412.
[7] E.g., articles 3, 7, 10, 12, 19, 20, 21, 27, 48, 49, 50, 53, 54, 55, 56, 57.

Olivi's outlook. Like the Anagni commission before it, its members vehemently denied the conception of the church's seven ages, and especially the superiority of the sixth and the seventh over the preceding five.[1] It was to posit two primacies of the church instead of one: for that which originated with St. Peter would be superseded by a second renewal in the sixth age.[2] At the same time they rejected the description of the fifth age as a period of growing darkness,[3] and interpreted the reform, renovation and new insight which were to come with the sixth and seventh ages as the replacement of Christ's evangel by a new gospel:[4] an interpretation on a par with that given to Olivi's views on the carnal church. Accordingly, when they came to the role assigned to St. Francis as the angel of the sixth seal, and his doctrine of poverty as the return of the true teaching of Christ, they dismissed it as far-fetched and sometimes heretical.[5] In particular they took exception to Olivi's charges of persecution against the upholders of poverty and the *usus pauper*, as implying that the church had been subverted like the synagogue in the time of Judaea.[6] They also protested at his saying that, after Christ and Mary, St. Francis was the greatest observer of evangelical life;[7] the comparison between St. Francis and his disciples with Christ and the Apostles;[8] and the struggle between the forces of

[1] *Misc.* II, arts. 1, 2, 8, 11, 16, 17, 18, 19.

[2] Art. 18 p. 261a: Haereticus, sive ponat in ecclesia duos primatus ecclesiae, quorum primus in quinto tempore ecclesiae deficiat, et secundus in sexto tempore incipiat, quod haereticum reputamus. Confitemur tamen unum esse primatum in tota ecclesia dei penes Romanam ecclesiam residentem, quia Petro incipiens, sine interruptione et translatione usque nunc continuatus est. . . .

[3] E.g. articles 4, 21, 24, 40, 56.

[4] Art. 5 p. 259b: Haereticus quoad tria. Primo quantum ad hoc quod dicit revelandum esse in hoc vita singularem perfectionem vitae et sapientiae Christi, quasi nondum aut non ita ad plenum ipsa fuerit hactenus revelata . . . Secundo . . . quod vetustas prioris temporis est sic universaliter repellanda ut videatur nova ecclesia tunc formari, veteribus iam rejectis. . . . Tertio . . . quod adventus Christi in spiritum evangelicae vitae reformans et perficiens ecclesiam primitus iam fundatum recte et proprie per quandam autonomasiam appropriatur tempori sexto.

[5] E.g. articles 21, 22, 23.

[6] Articles 25, 30, 51.

[7] Haereticus quantum ad hoc quod dicit quod beatus Franciscus post Christum fuit primus et principalis fundator sexti status quem supra descripsit, intelligendo per comparationem ad Apostolos (ibid., 38, 266a).

[8] Ubi videtur de regula beati Francisci, quam vere et proprie illam evangelicam . . . quod si haec verba capit secundum intellectum et declarationem decretalis *Exiit qui seminat*, verum dicit. Si autem intelligit . . . quod regula beati Francisci sit vere et proprie idem et idipsum quod Christi evangelium et e converso, et quod dominus

the fifth and sixth ages, represented by the carnal church, Babylon, on the one side, and the new Spirituals, the followers of St. Francis, on the other.[1]

The commission of 1319 was a landmark. For the first time it showed the unmistakable interconnexion between poverty and prophecy. The glory of evangelical renewal belonged to those who followed Christ through St. Francis; the teachings and life of the one were re-enacted in those of the other. Poverty was their badge; full understanding their goal. Those who were alone true to the one would gain the other. Everything thus depended upon the acceptance—or disavowal—of the twin beliefs, in a new age and the sanctity of poverty. Each buttressed the other; and conversely to destroy one was to destroy the other.

In the context of the sixty articles nothing could be plainer than the apocalyptic nature of Franciscan poverty, and *vice versa* of the Franciscan, or rather Spiritual, nature of apocalypticism. As we have emphasized on previous occasions, the convergence between the two underlay the beliefs of the majority of the Spirituals; it had also, as we shall describe in more detail, become the source of Beguin ideals. The connexion was no theoretical one; it had long been given practical expression in the resistance to the Community and to the inquisition in Provence. With the publication of the commission's censures, the full extent of their interdependence was revealed. We are not warranted in speculating what effect they had on the mind of John XXII; but it hardly requires the elaborate theory of Joseph Koch[2] to suggest that it

---

papa non habet potestatem super eam sicut super evangelium . . . hoc totum simpliciter reputamus haereticum et ridiculum et insanum (ibid., 22, 261b). See also no 31, 264.

[1] Articles 50–60.

[2] J. Koch, 'Der Prozess gegen die Postille Olivis zur Apokalypse', *Recherches* 5 (1933) 302–15. The thesis of the article is that *Exiit*, as embodying the doctrine of Christ's absolute poverty, was an obstacle to the condemnation of the *Postilla* on the Apocalypse, in turn one of the main sources of inspiration to the Spirituals. Accordingly, the pope in his determination to destroy the latter, and thereby the *Postilla*, had also to destroy the doctrine of absolute poverty in *Exiit*. Koch implies, without any support, that the question of the doctrine of Christ's absolute poverty was abstracted from the 1319 condemnation of the *Postilla* on the Apocalypse. Nothing is gained from such speculation—for that is what it is. It may readily be granted that the pope was struck by the obvious in Olivi's *Postilla*, namely, the central role of poverty in Franciscan Joachism, but it does not follow that the exact thesis for subsequent attack on the doctrine came from there, or that it was formulated in the pope's mind as the need to destroy *Exiit*. The assault on the doctrine when it came hit at the entire

brought him to realize that the Franciscan doctrine of poverty had to be discredited. As long as it could be invested with a divine origin in Christ, it would remain a rallying point to those who opposed—or were opposed by—the authority of the church. If it could be shown that Christ had not lived in poverty, then poverty could hardly be made the standard of his disciples. There can be little doubt, then, that by 1319 the full subversive nature of the doctrine of absolute poverty had become clear; and that, especially in view of the daily struggle of the inquisition against its adherents in Provence, its dangers were fully apparent to John XXII. In the measures he was taking both against Olivi's teachings and the Spirituals and the Beguins, it could only be a matter of time and place and circumstance before the reckoning came.

When it did, in 1321, it arose precisely from the pope's measures against its adherents. Far from being a bolt from the blue, as has so often been implied, it could hardly have failed to come to the fore when the papal inquisitors were investigating without remission the very beliefs censured in 1319 by the commission on the *Postilla*. The occasion has been better known than the causes. A Beguin summoned before the Dominican inquisitor, John of Belna, at Narbonne, asserted in his confession, amongst other things, that Christ and the apostles had possessed nothing in common or in private. When the inquisitor came to read out the indictment before the local council of notables, preparatory to passing sentence, he was challenged on this point by a Franciscan, Berengarius of Talon.[1] To Berengarius, as a Franciscan, the belief in the absolute poverty of Christ and the apostles was the basis and justification of Franciscan poverty. Far from being heretical it was sound doctrine, as laid down in *Exiit qui seminat*. When ordered by John of Belna to recant, Berengarius stood firm.[2] Both appealed to the pope, who summoned Berengarius to Avignon. The pope then publicly posed the question, whether it was heretical to affirm that Christ and the apostles had possessed nothing. The debate was opened; all theologians were asked for an opinion.[3]

---

tradition of papal legislation from *Quo elongati* onwards. Indeed, the reference to *Exiit* in Article 22 of the 1319 condemnation, taken as crucial by Koch (ibid., p. 308) could be interpreted as a safeguard against the extremist interpretation of *Exiit*.

[1] The main account of the struggle between John XXII and the supporters of Michael of Cesena is to be found in the so-called chronicle of Nicholas the Minorite, himself a Michaelist, in Baluze, *Miscellanea* II, 206–358. Many of the relevant documents, such as John XXII's bulls, have now been edited.

[2] Baluze, *Misc.* II, 207.   [3] Ibid.

The controversy which followed was of a very different nature from the previous disputes on poverty. In the first place it was no longer an internal dispute within the order. The antagonists were now the order —or its leaders—versus the pope. In the second place, the parties were not the same. The Spirituals as a group had been crushed by the joint action of John XXII and Michael of Cesena from 1317 onwards; the incident which led to the reopening of the question was part of this operation—the mopping up of the stragglers. Now, however, the challenge which John XXII sent out was to the order itself: it threatened the very basis of its existence, in the time-honoured distinction between use and possession. In the third place, the issue was therefore a different one: it was one of theory, indeed of *raison d'être*, where earlier it had been one of observance. In a sense the Community, or more strictly the order, was now suffering from the literalness with which the Spirituals had interpreted their vow of poverty; the former, in their daily lives, were probably no more distinguishable by poverty than their confrères among the other orders. But they were pledged to it as a concept, and their organization had been built upon it. That they fully believed in it can hardly be in question, as the intensity of their struggle against John XXII, its detractor, testifies; it is rather that belief and practice had—as we have amply seen—already diverged so far that what the order was now fighting for was a form of words rather than a way of life. Nevertheless, the outcome of the struggle was heresy; heresy, moreover, where there had previously been orthodoxy; schism where unity had reigned; disobedience from those who in other days had made the voice of authority the supreme law.

The struggle opened with John XXII's decree *Quia nonnunquam* of 26 March 1322, which was designed to lift the ban imposed by *Exiit* upon any further discussion of the question of poverty.[1] This evoked an almost immediate response from the order at the chapter-general at Perugia: a letter was sent to the pope, and two encyclicals were issued defending the doctrine of absolute poverty.[2] Both said much the same thing: that the order's form of poverty had been determined in *Exiit*, which had in turn been commended by the pope. It was therefore part of canon law and could not be reversed.[3] The longer version[4] drew upon Bonaventure's *Apologia* as well as a wide range of authorities in its defence. Like St. Bonaventure it stressed the spiritual benefits of poverty in freeing the mind from earthly cares.[5] It also defended the

[1] BF v, 224b–225b.   [2] Baluze, *Misc.* II, 208b–211b.
[3] Ibid., 208a–b.   [4] Ibid., 208b–211b.   [5] Ibid., 209a.

bag carried by the Apostles as being for the use of others, not for themselves; they, like the order, had held goods only by simple *usus facti*.[1] This was merely to apply their own legal standing to the Apostles; it hardly introduced a new concept into what, since Bonaventure at least, had been recognized as the state common to both the order and to Christ and the Apostles.[2]

The order's reply only provoked John to further action. In *Ad conditorem canonum* he effectively destroyed the order's doctrine; for he not only reasserted his right to abrogate previous legislation, but cut the ground from under the Minors by renouncing papal dominion. The bull was in two versions;[3] the second, following a reply by Bonagratia of Bergamo,[4] elaborated the legal arguments in the first. The pope's position was essentially a restatement of previous arguments drawn from all sides. After having recited the origin of the existing arrangement of the order's goods, he went on to use Bonaventure's argument, that charity was the source of perfection, to rebut the encyclical's that poverty removed concern for temporal goods: it was quite the contrary so far as the division between use and possession was concerned.[5] Next, he reverted to Gerard of Abbeville's claim that goods consumed in use could not be owned by someone else; it was not the order which had naked use, but the papacy which was naked of any possession,[6] a point which he pressed by taking examples from usury. Moreover, and here he introduced a new element, use, whether of fact or of right, must legally entail the right of dominion, for who could truly claim that it was the intention of Nicholas III in *Exiit* to retain possession of every egg and loaf of bread in the order? And was such control not in fact verbal rather than real? Far from enhancing their life, this system had harmed it, encouraging schism and persecution. It also harmed the reputation of the papacy, particularly in the use of procurators.[7]

The second version was both an elaboration and a modification of the first. It exempted churches and goods dedicated to divine use from the previous papal renunciation of dominion.[8] But it reiterated more firmly the obligation to ownership in any other forms of use; there must

---

[1] Baluze, *Misc.* II, 210a.

[2] This was the gist of the encyclical's arguments; they were answered in due course by John XXII in *Ad conditorem canonum*. Lambert, op. cit., 229, tends to overstress the encyclical's importance.

[3] The first version is in BF v, footnote 235b–7a; the second ibid., text 233b–46b.

[4] Ibid., 237n.–46n.   [5] Ibid., 236n.

[6] Ibid.   [7] Ibid.   [8] Ibid., 238a–240b.

always be a right of use (*ius utendi*) in anything used, and this, according to law, meant dominion over things which were consumed in use.[1] Thus John finally struck at the root of Franciscan poverty by refusing to separate use in fact from the right of use; consumption also meant dominion; the usufruct of anything consumed went with the right to consume it: ownership must be with him who exercised the right. What in effect John had done was to reject the non-legal, purely natural status of simple *usus facti*, and with it the distinction between use by necessity and use by right: use of anything, whatever the purpose, carried the right to exercise it. It was a summary decision, and one which went against the division between natural and civil law which had underlain *Exiit*. Michael of Cesena and his followers were not prepared to relinquish it.

With *Ad conditorem canonum*, John XXII effectively destroyed Franciscan poverty; for whether or not his moral and legal arguments were accepted he had withdrawn his ownership from all but the order's immediate religious possessions. The final blow came with *Cum inter nonnullos* in November 1323.[2] It was a short document, devoted exclusively to the question of whether Christ and the Apostles had held anything either privately or in common. The answer was to condemn as heretical the assertion that they had not. Its grounds were that there were many references in scripture to Christ and the Apostles having had some possessions, and that to say otherwise would be to deny them the right of using what they had. This was impiety: accordingly it was condemned.[3] The seeming simplicity of this statement after the legal complexities of *Ad conditorem canonum* must not mask the fundamental community of assumption between them. *Ad conditorem* expressed what *Cum inter* implied. John XXII equated use with the right of use, thereby excluding use of simple fact as an independent category: this was to rebut the proposition put forward by the order in the Perugia encyclical, that Christ and the Apostles had had only *simplex usus facti*, as a natural as opposed to a legal right. Accordingly, both as a statement of fact and of law the bull condemned the notion of Christ's absolute poverty. It has sometimes been remarked that nothing was said in the bull of dominion or ownership.[4] But where was the need? John had achieved his aim of denying (*a*) that Christ and the Apostles

---

[1] Ibid., 240b–241a.   [2] Ibid., 256–9.   [3] Ibid., 258–9.

[4] Lambert op. cit., 237. It seems misleading to describe *Ad conditorem* as a bull 'dealing with essentially administrative matters'. On the contrary its elaborate distinctions formed the very core of John's legal position.

had always lived without possessions; and (*b*) that what they had used had been of necessity and not of right. Dominion or ownership were implied in both; or, more exactly, propertylessness was excluded, and with it absolute poverty. The blow to the Franciscan ideal was correspondingly twofold: it made a myth of evangelical poverty, and it made their own claim to emulate it hollow. If total renunciation was true neither in fact nor in law, it was otiose and unnecessarily hazardous to go to the other extreme and assert that Christ had held dominion. It was enough for the pope's purposes to show, as he had done, that the converse—absolute and undeviating poverty—was untrue.

The effect of John's legislation was the practical and legal undermining of Franciscan poverty. It marked the end of a hundred years of papal legislation. The wheel had turned full circle from the defence of absolute poverty to its condemnation. What had begun as a concept of evangelical perfection ended as heresy. Those who had looked to the papacy to uphold it now had to submit to its rejection, or fight. Within the order both courses were followed. The erstwhile leaders of the Community under Michael of Cesena and Bonagratia of Bergamo led the opposition. A new war of words broke out, but this time between the pope and his former allies, and no longer over the practice of poverty but the letter; nor in the setting of the Apocalypse. Nevertheless, the effect was not so far different from the previous struggles: as before, authority and obedience became the real issues; and what had originated as a matter of doctrine developed into a struggle of allegiance. Before long support for absolute poverty became joined to denial of John XXII as rightful pope. Heterodoxy once again passed into heresy. The ways in which it did so, not only in 1323 but in the preceding fifty years, will be the subject of our next chapter.

II

Spirituals, Beguins and Fraticelli

To turn from the predominantly doctrinal aspects of poverty and prophecy to their practical manifestations is not to enter another world. It is rather to see the same one in another dimension. Virtually every phase in the disputes we have examined, from the setting aside of St. Francis's Testament in *Quo elongati* onwards, arose from the actual life of the Minors as a whole: the condemnation of Gerard of Borgo San Donnino, the resignation of John of Parma, the writings on poverty of St. Bonaventure, *Exiit qui seminat*, the discordant career of Olivi, the disputes between the Spirituals and Community in the first decade of the fourteenth century, the decrees of the Council of Vienne, the final repression of the Spirituals under John XXII and Michael of Cesena, were not isolated incidents confined to a small section of the order. They were the central events in its evolution. We have now to consider the circumstances in which these questions of poverty and apocalyptic belief gradually culminated during the earlier fourteenth century into open dissent; and more specifically how from heterodoxy within the Franciscan order heresy against the church was born.

Undoubtedly the most significant fact in this progression was that it extended beyond the Franciscan order. This was not simply a matter of the various groups of Fraticelli ending outside it; it was rather that, in the course of their alienation from authority, the Spirituals, especially in Provence, embraced other sections—namely the Beguins and sympathetic citizens in cities like Narbonne and Béziers—who together confronted society with the issues of poverty and Joachism in a heightened form. The dissensions within the order therefore had a universality which impinged upon Christendom itself. Or, perhaps more strictly, they came to crystallize problems affecting Christendom as a whole. This can be seen at both the macrocosmic and the microcosmic levels. On the one hand, the main arena was the papal curia, culminating first in the Council of Vienne, in 1311–12, and then in the successive condemnations by John XXII of the Spirituals, Beguins, Fraticelli, and the followers of Michael of Cesena; it was in the intensified struggle of this second phase that these various groups, which often had nothing in common, gradually became the different sects of the Fraticelli. On the other hand, the struggle marked the fusion of the doctrines of poverty and Joachism; while frequently merely a debased amalgam of the original elements, this combination nevertheless formed the ideological driving force behind the various groups of Spirituals. It became more and more openly heretical the further it became removed in time from its authors—mainly Olivi—and the greater the persecution suffered by its adherents. Thus in both cases, sources which had initially been non-heretical became, under pressure, heretical. Extremity of circumstances bred extremism of outlook.

The Tuscan Spirituals: Angelo of Clareno[1]

The lineage of the Spirituals goes back a long way—in one sense to the immediate companions of St. Francis (like brothers Giles and Leo) who formed their inspiration. From the outset they represented an alternative, primitive ideal to the official one. Certainly a zealot group existed in the 1240s, since Angelo of Clarena referred to the persecution of 62 or 72 *zelani* by Crescenzio of Jesi, general of the order from 1244 to 1247;[2] this would suggest that some sort of party was already in being. The nearest the Spirituals ever came to having an authoritative voice in the order's councils was under John of Parma (general 1247–57) and to a lesser extent under Raymond Gaufridi (general 1289–95). But in each case their generalates ended badly: for John in resignation,[3] for Gaufridi deposition by Boniface VIII.[4] Essentially the Spirituals' role was that of dissentients, and by the end of Bonaventure's long generalate in 1274 they could no longer be contained within the framework of the order. From that time onwards their history becomes increasingly a record of protest and persecution. 1274 marked not only the departure of Bonaventure to the cardinalate, followed shortly by death; it was also the year of the Second Council of Lyons, under the impact of which the first of the three groups of Spirituals emerged: those of the March of Ancona. They came into prominence because of their protest against rumours circulating from the Council that all the orders were to be allowed property.[5] The story was false; but it brought the

[1] This account is taken mainly from L. Oliger's authoritative article in DTC 14, 2522–50, which is based upon the findings of some fifty years of research, including his own pioneering contributions. The main sources for the following events are Angelo of Clarena's *Historia* and *Epistola Excusatoria*.

[2] *Historia* in ALKG II, 258–9.   [3] Ibid., 270.

[4] Ibid., 305; Oliger, ibid., 2530.   [5] Oliger, art. cit., col. 2528.

Ancona Spirituals, under their leader Liberato (Peter Macerato), into collision with their provincial superiors.[1] The following year, having been imprisoned in distant hermitages, four of them were cited to appear before the provincial chapter: although agreement was reached after three days of argument, it was transitory. The support which the Spirituals attracted caused their superiors, including four other provincial ministers, to prosecute them. At the next provincial chapter in 1278, Liberato, Angelo and a number of other zealots were sentenced to perpetual imprisonment and deprived of books and the sacraments. They continued thus, in unspeakable conditions, for eleven years, until 1289 when Raymond Gaufridi, recently elected general, took up their case and had them released.[2] He despatched them on a mission to Armenia, in response to the request of king Hayton II. It was so successful that Hayton sent a message of thanks to the 1292 chapter at Paris. But further trouble awaited the Ancona zealots: their enemies in the Community led the Syrian provincial of the order, jealous of their success, to write to the king of Armenia to beware of the Spirituals. Although Hayton cleared them of the accusations of heresy and schism, their position became more difficult and they decided to return to Italy.[3] The hostility with which they were met by the provincial of the March of Ancona determined them, with the backing of Gaufridi and other prominent Italian Spirituals such as Conrad of Offida and Jacopone of Todi, to appeal direct to the newly elected pope, Celestine V. The latter, as the hermit Peter of Murro, was already known to them.[4] He granted their request to be allowed to follow St. Francis's rule independently of their superiors, and, in effect, constituted them into a new order—that of the 'Poor hermits of Celestine', with Liberato as their leader and under the protection of cardinal Napoleon Orsini.[5]

What followed was one of the decisive moments in the history of the Spirituals; instead of opening a new path, which, if followed, could have averted the future *impasse* between the two parties, it made conflict virtually inevitable. For within a year of Celestine's decision he had abdicated, to be succeeded by Boniface VIII who revoked all his predecessor's concessions. The effect was felt far beyond Liberato's group:

---

[1] The events which followed are described by Angelo of Clarena in his *Epistola excusatoria*, ALKG I, 521–33. See also his *Apologia pro vita sua*, addressed to Alvarus Pelagius, ed. V. Doucet, AFH. 39 (1946) 63–200.

[2] Oliger, art. cit., 2529; Angelo, *Historia*, ALKG II, 305.

[3] Oliger, ibid.; *Historia*, ALKG II, 307–8.

[4] *Historia*, ibid., 308.   [5] Oliger, ibid.; *Historia*, ibid.

it signalized a blow against Spirituals everywhere, turning their frustrated hopes of reform within the existing framework into renewed apocalyptic visions of cataclysmic change. The impetus which it gave to this sense of impending destruction of the present order was perhaps the most important consequence of Boniface VIII's actions. The already strong Joachist belief that the end of the century would see the end of the sixth age was powerfully reinforced. The event entered into the Spirituals' lore; Celestine V became the precursor of the new era, and the last of the line of legitimate popes; Boniface VIII was treated almost universally as a usurper, and variously as the precursor of Antichrist and the mystic Antichrist himself. Whatever the differences in detail, the central fact remained that—for the Spirituals—Celestine V's abdication was the work of Antichrist and succeeding popes his agents. The struggle between evil and righteousness had begun: between the corrupt hierarchy and docile believers of the carnal church on the one hand, and the Spirituals, as the true heirs of St. Francis, the renewer of Christ's teaching, on the other. This was Ubertino of Casale's message in his *Arbor vitae*:[1] it was the attitude which Olivi combated in his letter to Conrad of Offida defending the legality of Celestine V's abdication;[2] it is to be found, as we shall see, in numerous forms among the Beguins and Spirituals of Provence. It was hope in the immediate future born of hopelessness in the immediate present. Boniface's refusal of liberty to the Spirituals seemed to have sealed the outlets which could now only be made by the angels of the seven seals. As so often failure to reform helped to create the conditions for revolt. It became one more source of conflict between the Community and the Spirituals.

So far as Liberato and his companions were concerned, Boniface's annulment meant renewed persecution, though not at first from the pope. During 1395–6 they took refuge on the island of Trixonia, in the gulf of Corinth, ruled by Thomas Sole. Their enemies then discovered their whereabouts and denounced them to the local nobles as Manichees. They were able to disprove the charge; but Boniface VIII, having been persuaded of the Spirituals' hostility towards himself by the new general of the order, John of Murrovalle, now intervened. In the bull *Saepe sacrum* (since lost) he asked for their expulsion.[3] As a result the Spirituals settled in Thessaly, where they remained until 1304–5. Their stay was far from tranquil; there was the usual reconnoitring of their position by members of the Community, who caused

[1] See above, pp. 152 ff.   [2] See above, pp. 121 ff.
[3] Mentioned in Raymond of Fronsac's Catalogue ALKG III, 12.

the patriarch of Constantinople to excommunicate Liberato and his companions in 1301.[1] After fruitless negotiations for them to go on another mission to the East—through the refusal of John of Murrovalle—and the failure of their messages to reach the pope, the group decided to return to Italy.[2] Benedict XI had succeeded Boniface VIII; but by the time Liberato reached him at Perugia the pope was dying. The Spirituals decided to settle in the kingdom of Naples until the election of a new pope;[3] but once again the leaders of the Community, under the new general, Gonsalvo of Valboa, who succeeded John of Murrovalle in 1302, had taken action against them. Charles II, king of Naples, ordered their persecution; and Thomas of Aversa the inquisitor proceeded against them. At first—perhaps because of his hostility towards the Franciscan order[4]—he was helpful to Liberato, advising him to seek out the new pope, Clement V: Liberato, however, fell ill at Viterbo, and spent the remaining two years of his life at the nearby hermitage of St. Angelo di Vena.[5] Thomas of Aversa's attitude then underwent a complete change; he arrested and tortured the remainder of the group, together with members of the pseudo-Apostles, before they were finally expelled from the kingdom.[6]

Henceforth with the removal of their chronicler—Angelo of Clareno—first to Perugia in 1305, where he joined cardinal Napoleon Orsini, and then, after a period in the Romagna, to Vienne in 1311 to plead the cause of his followers, the Ancona Spirituals fade from sight. They were certainly in being in the area around Rome, and Angelo kept in contact with them during his fateful sojourn at Avignon from 1311 to 1318.[7] But the centre of the stage becomes occupied by the Spirituals and their supporters in Provence. Not only were they the direct heirs to Olivi's teachings, but they represented a region in a way in which the Ancona Spirituals never did. The latter remained a small band of wanderers, important mainly for their fame as sufferers in the

---

[1] Oliger, art. cit., 2531; *Historia*, ALKG II, 317. The Patriarch's death shortly afterwards was regarded by the Spirituals as an act of divine retribution. *Historia*, ibid.

[2] *Epistola excusatoria*, ALKG I, 530; *Historia*, ALKG II, 319.

[3] In the diocese of Trevento, 1304–5, Oliger, art. cit., DTC 14, 2529.

[4] This is Douie's suggestion on the grounds that he was suspended from teaching for seven years for doubting St. Francis's stigmata (*Fraticelli*, 59 and note 6).

[5] *Epistola excusatoria*, 531; *Historia*, ALKG II, 320–1; Oliger, art. cit., 2532.

[6] *Historia*, ALKG II, 321–7. Angelo says that Thomas of Averso repented of his cruelty on his deathbed, ibid.

[7] In his *Epistola excusatoria* he described it as worse than any of his other hardships (ALKG I, 532).

name of poverty and evangelical perfection. Beyond their spokesman, Angelo, there is little point of contact with them.[1] That they were Joachist can hardly be doubted. Angelo's *Historia*, as well as his letters to his followers, written during his years at the papal court and in Provence, give abundant evidence of it. The very number of the Spirituals' tribulations—seven, of which the last remained unwritten— show his awareness of the sequence to be followed before final triumph; moreover, of these the fifth and the sixth tribulations bring the group's sufferings to a climax, just as the fifth and sixth ages, in Joachist prophesy, were the culmination of evil before the coming of the seventh age of tranquillity. There is the same tone of censure and horror at the prevalent evils of heresy and laxity, as in Olivi and Ubertino;[2] the common references to the beast killing the spirit of Christ;[3] and a similar play on numbers and their Greek alphabetical equivalents.[4] Above all there is the sense of impending change: Angelo was not an historicist like Olivi or a polemicist like Ubertino, but he shared their belief that the present age was the sixth age, and in the coming conflict between the adherents of Christ—the followers of St. Francis and poverty—and Antichrist.[5] His outlook was prophetic, less by the drawing upon Joachim himself than in invoking members of his own order

---

[1] They continued to live in Central Italy and the March of Ancona; and in 1317 the bull *Sancta Romana* was directed against them. Angelo himself returned to organize them in 1318 on a Franciscan model; he remained moderate as he had been throughout his life, although not regarding John XXII as canonically elected. For his subsequent career including his relations with John XXII, see Douie, *Fraticelli*, 62–9.

[2] E.g. ALKG II, 130–1 and 294.

[3] Ibid., 137.

[4] E.g., Fi dicamus est ex duobus gamis figuratum F, que senarium numerum important et est in alfabeto Grecorum XXI et precedit X grecum, quod quidem X apud Latinos XX est in alfabeto. Et post ipsum X sequitur Y, quod apud Grecos est fy. Fy Franciscum dicit, cuius paupertas, humilitas et obediencia a serpente, qui de celo ruit infra sextum ecclesie tempus multipharie multisque modis a propriis et extraneis expugnatur (ibid.).

[5] . . . in fy precedentes eam quasi in feria sexta in qua inundat iniquitas presertim in hiis qui signa iusticie ferunt, et fidei et caritatis evacuacio apparet fere in omnibus et vane sciencie multiplicatio subintravit pro cultu pietatis in lugentibus et appetitus nominis sciencie ardenter et sine rubore assumitur ab hiis qui promiserunt se solum Christum et hunc crucifixum semper querere et amare . . . ex hiis apparet amplior solito solucio, errorum et heresum multiplicacio, ordinis minorum a S. Francisco previsa et prenunciata divisio, quam divisionem post non longa tempora sequitur antichristiana vexacio iuxta prefati sancti predicacionem propheticam et per Helyam omnium restitucio et in fy X sequente seraphici status et in Hebreis, Grecis et Latinis plena et perfecta multiplicacio (ibid., 137–8).

like St. Francis and John of Parma.[1] It was essentially Franciscan, inspired by the belief in St. Francis's unique role as Christ's successor[2] and the ultimate fulfilment of his ideal among those loyal to the rule, which, as for all the Spirituals, was inviolate and not to be modified by papal privileges.[3] Celestine V occupied a very special place.[4]

Angelo's outlook is strikingly revealed in a letter written to Philip of Marjorca after 1329, in the aftermath of the condemnation of the doctrine of Christ's absolute poverty.[5] In it Angelo foresaw the end of the present era as the result of God's wrath at the abuses within the church. This alone (*sola vexatio*) rather than the customary Joachist *schema* would bring about the appointment of a false pope, whose errors the majority of believers would take up, deserting the teachings of Christ for the temptations of wealth and pride.[6] Only a few martyrs would remain true to evangelical poverty; and they would have to practise it away from the erring multitude. Many would perish and the confusion which would follow could only be surmounted by a return to the literal observance of the rule of St. Francis. God would then finally relent and renew the life of the church.[7]

There are several interesting features about Angelo's predictions. The first is his claim that they were based upon what St. Francis had foretold.[8] It coalesced with the influence of Joachim and the Joachist authorities and the usual figures of Franciscan Joachism. Secondly, faith in Christ's coming was combined with unqualified quietism. The injunction of Olivi to Conrad of Offida to let God judge and not to anticipate his future actions was reiterated by Angelo. In Angelo's case it is the more noteworthy for coming after John XXII's condemnation of Franciscan poverty, an action which Angelo regarded as heretical.[9]

---

[1] E.g., ibid., 282–3.

[2] E.g., Vobis enim, Christi spiritus ad Franciscum ait, datum est nosse misterium regni dei, ceteris autem in parabolis . . . (ibid., 267). See also his letters, ibid., I, 558–9, 60.

[3] Ibid., II, 297–9.

[4] He describes his renunciation as 'seduction' (ibid., 289).

[5] ALKG I, 566–9. The margin of the manuscript, according to Ehrle (ibid., 566) has the name 'Phillipus de Maioricis' written in another hand. Ehrle also pointed out that since the letter mentions the capture and recantation of Peter of Corbara (the imperial anti-pope) it must have been written after 25 August 1329 (ibid., 567).

[6] Ibid., 566.   [7] Ibid., 567.

[8] Ista et alia multa S. Franciscus predixit, que adhuc suo tempore mundo clarebunt (ibid., 567).

[9] Qui enim excommunicat et hereticat altissimam evangelii paupertatem, excommunicatus est a deo et hereticus coram Christo (ibid., 569).

Angelo was here clearly referring to John XXII; and in the letter he sought to dissuade the brothers against censuring a pope who was himself culpable of false decrees: he already stood self-condemned without the need for others to do so. In due course Christ would sit in judgement upon him.[1] Instead of intervening in such affairs Angelo counselled them to be concerned with their own personal lives.[2] Angelo's faith in the evangelical truth of the rule buttressed his quiet-ism; his prophetic conviction went with acceptance of his tribulations meekly and in full obedience. For him, as for Olivi, the onset of the future was best met by submission to the present.

Nevertheless, if Angelo's convictions were conceived in predomi-nantly Franciscan terms his inspiration owed much to Joachism, as we have already mentioned. In particular he drew upon two important pseudo-Joachist sources, the Angelic Revelations of Cyril (*Oraculum Angelicum Cyrilli*) and the Prophecies of the Erithrean Sibyl (*Vaticinium Sibillae Erithreae*). The first, originally written in Greek, were probably from Southern Italy.[3] Preceded by a purported exchange of letters between Cyril, a hermit of Mount Carmel, and Joachim of Fiore, the work comprised eleven chapters. The text is usually found with a pseudo-Joachist commentary not originally part of it.[4] The prophecies themselves were said to have been given to Cyril by an angel. They range through many of the main Joachist topics, including the custom-ary Italian identification of Frederick II and his descendants with the last world emperor, the sixth or seventh head of the dragon, who would usher in the last violent phase of the sixth age,[5] and the line of reforming —angelic—popes who would help to achieve the sabbatical peace of the seventh age.[6] The Erithrean Sibyl's prophecies,[7] written after Frederick II's death by an Italian Joachist,[8] likewise dealt with the

---

[1] ALKG I, 567.   [2] Ibid.

[3] Edited by P. Puir in *Das Briefwechsel des Cola di Rienzo: Vom Mittelalter zur Reformation* (general editor, K. Burdach), vol. II pt. 4 (Berlin 1912) 223–327.

[4] Ibid., 224, 250, 309.

[5] Ibid., 308–9.

[6] Ibid., 305. The interpretation of the Commentary.

[7] Edited by O. Holder-Egger in *Neues Archiv.* vol. 15 (1889) 155–73, and vol. 30 (1904) 328–35. These prophecies had a long Byzantine tradition, going back to the Tiburtine Sibyl in the fourth century and embodying the writings of the Pseudo-Methodius in the seventh century and Adso, *De ortu et tempore Antichristi*, in the tenth century. F. Kampers, *Die Deutsche Kaiseridee* (Munich 1896) and M. E. Reeves 'Joachimist Influences on the idea of a Last World Emperor' *Traditio* 17 (1961) 324.

[8] Holder-Egger, vol. 15, 149.

perfidy of the Hohenstaufen and the desertion of evangelical poverty.[1] In both works, Frederick II and his progeny were treated as the precursors of Antichrist; and from this rooted belief in their evil role arose the widespread conviction that Antichrist's coming would be presaged by a final emperor—Frederick III—descended from Frederick II who would establish him as a pseudo-pope.[2] Angelo shared this expectation. As we shall see, it was also prevalent among the Provençal Beguins. Angelo invoked both sets of prophecies, attributing to Cyril the foretelling of Olivi's ordeal and to the Erithrean Sibyl the deception practised upon Celestine V.[3]

Thus, within an essentially practical and non-speculative outlook, Angelo evinced the main symptoms of Franciscan Joachism: a belief in the imminent triumph of evangelical poverty and the true teaching of Christ as given by St. Francis to his disciples. Beyond the destiny of the Franciscan order there was virtually no interest in the cycle of history as such: the future of the world was subsumed under the future of the Franciscans.

How prevalent this conception had become by the early fourteenth century can be seen from a number of other examples of Franciscan Joachism; and it will be as well to discuss them now as an essential preliminary to our examination of events in Provence where the Spirituals' outlook was most widely diffused.

---

[1] Ibid., vol. 15, 144-5. vol. 30, 331.

[2] For a résumé of this topic, see the article by Marjorie Reeves, 'Joachimist influences on the idea of a Last World Emperor' op. cit. As she says 'the essence of the Joachist view lies in the belief that the greatest persecution of the church—the *Antichristus pessimus*—must precede the third age . . .' (ibid., 324). That is to say, the new era of peace and happiness comes after the first advent of Antichrist—'within history'; and the second coming—of Gog and Magog—is but the epilogue to this world, 'the final flick of the dragon's tail' (ibid.). Besides Antichrist, thirteenth-century Joachism gradually came to associate two other figures with this violent change from the sixth to the seventh age: a World Emperor, who was usually responsible for establishing the first Antichrist in the guise of a pope, and a series of Angelic Popes. Although the emperor was usually regarded as an evil tyrant, especially by Italian Joachists, who identified him with the line of Frederick II, he could also be a force for good (Reeves, art. cit., 326-8). From our point of view, however, the main emphasis was upon a future emperor, usually Frederick III, who would be the instrument of Antichrist's advent. Miss Reeves (art. cit., 326) attributes the reference to a future Frederick to the Erithrean Sibyl (Holder-Egger, art. cit., 15, 168).

[3] ALKG II, 289-90. He does not seem to have used the *Liber de oneribus*, the pseudo-Joachist tract so influential upon Hugh of Digne and John of Parma. Edited by Holder-Egger, *Neues Archiv* 33 (1907) 139-87.

Arnold of Villanova and Franciscan Joachism

The phenomenon of Franciscan Joachism was but one of a number of forms which the Calabrian abbot's doctrines took in the hands of his pseudo-disciples. It was for that reason often closely mingled with non-Franciscan elements such as a belief in Frederick II as the forerunner of Antichrist (e.g. in Olivi, Ubertino and Angelo), or Arnold of Villanova's exaltation of Frederick II as the final world Emperor,[1] or the glorification of Venice in the *Prophecies of Merlin*. Yet in essence its message concerned the regeneration of the world through the defeat of Antichrist by the followers of St. Francis. As such it was coloured by three main elements: the sense of imminent change; the sufferings of those true to Christ and St. Francis (the Spirituals themselves); and the renewal of the church by Christ's representatives. As with Joachim the discontinuity of the first was counterbalanced by the continuity of the second and third: cataclysm there would be but as the result of the steadfastness of those who had adhered to Christ. As the representatives of evangelical perfection their triumph would see not the displacement of the church but its renovation. All the main works of Franciscan Joachism eschewed institutional change. The church would remain as it had always been, a divine institution; its personnel had betrayed it and it would be they who would perish. In consequence the dominant tendency of the Spirituals was to conceive salvation in personal terms, and increasingly through the coming of a line of angelic popes charged directly by God with the reform of the church. In that sense, of seeking an alternative not to the church but only to its pastors, high and low, who had proved unworthy of it, the Spirituals were neither revolutionary nor anti-ecclesiastical. Both their desire for its reform and hostility to its abuses sprang from their same zeal for the church: their attack was not upon the bride of Christ but the whore of Babylon. This is the context in which their belief in an *ecclesia spiritualis* contraposed to an *ecclesia carnalis* must be seen; they were not two different churches but the same one in different roles; or, more precisely, in different hands—those of the followers of Antichrist and of Christ. The task of the coming dénouement would be to restore it to the latter.

We may best begin with Arnold of Villanova for two reasons. First, although not a Franciscan and only later in his life—in its last decade—

---

[1] He was condemned posthumously for, among other things, putting more value upon the revelations of Cyril than the scriptures (M. Menendez Pelayo, *Historia de los Heterodoxos Españoles*, III (Buenos Aires 1945) 608.

drawn to the cause of the Provençal Spirituals, he had an important influence upon them and figured in one of the main works of popular Franciscan Joachism of this period, the *Liber de Flore*. Second, he shows in his own writings the progression from non-Franciscan apocalypticism to one which came to embrace much of the Spirituals' outlook: from this point of view he represented a non-Franciscan source.

Arnold of Villanova was that rare species, a man of genuine independence in both belief and action.[1] He was essentially a traditionalist who through the intensity of his fervour became heterodox; his loyalty to the simple theological virtues of charity and humility made him the advocate of evangelical poverty; and he used his high connexions at the papal court to champion its critics amongst the lowly of Provence. Arnold owed his unique position principally to his skill as a doctor. As physician at the court of Aragon he was sent on a mission to the French king sometime after 1297, when he had already written the first version of his *De tempore Antichristi*.[2] Its appearance at Paris caused his arrest there; and he was only released after a written recantation, which he promptly disavowed. He then appealed to Boniface VIII to have the verdict of the Paris masters, who had condemned it as dangerous, reversed. During 1301 and 1302 Arnold became the pope's physician, curing him of a stone; although the pope refused Arnold's request he treated the matter in private consistory. It was then that Arnold went to Provence where he began his association with the Spirituals and Beguins, to whom he became mentor.[3] After Boniface VIII's death Arnold again tried to have the case of his condemned work re-heard by Benedict XI, but he was once more imprisoned, probably for his outspokenness.[4] He was released soon after the pope's death. He

---

[1] For Arnold of Villanova, see J. M. Pou y Marti, *Visionarios, beguinos y fraticellos catalones* (Vichy 1930). M. Menendez Pelayo, op. cit., vol. III, ch. III. H. Finke, *Aus den Tagen Bonifaz VIII* (Münster 1902) CXXVI. R. Manselli, 'La religiosità di Arnaldo da Villanova' in *Bulletino dell' Istituto Storico Italiano per il Medio Evo*, 63 (1951) 1–100.

Both Finke and Manselli contain editions of Arnold's own treatises. Finke has a series of his apocalyptic and political writings (CXXVII–CCXI) and Manselli's appendix includes the Introduction to the *De semine scripturarum*. The main sources for Arnold's doctrines discussed here are Vatican MSS. Vat. Lat. 3824 and Vat. Lat. 5740 for his *Expositio super Apocalypsim*.

[2] The account of the events which follow can be found in Arnold's *Protestatio facta Perusii coram dominio camarario summi pontificis*. Finke, op. cit., CXCII–CXCIII.

[3] He wrote for them the two treatises, the *Informatio Beguinorum* and the *Lectio Narbone* (Manselli, art. cit., 77–91); see pp. 182 ff. below.

[4] *Protestatio*, Finke, op. cit., CXCIV–V.

repeated the attempt with Clement V, in an address to him at Bordeaux in 1305.[1] The new pope, however, does not appear to have taken Arnold's writings very seriously,[2] while valuing him for his medical skill. Until his death in 1311, Arnold campaigned continuously for the Spirituals persecuted in Provence; Angelo of Clarena credited him with gaining the pope's intervention which led to the enquiry into their sufferings and culminated in the decrees of the Council of Vienne.[3] In 1316, three of Arnold's works were condemned at the Council of Saragossa, but by then his influence had been established.[4]

Arnold's thinking is distinguished from that of the majority of the Franciscans in two respects. In the first place it was fundamentally biblical. Nearly all his speculations on the future were drawn from scriptural prophecies, especially Daniel; so, too, were his criteria of evangelical perfection. Thus he differed from the other main authorities of Franciscan Joachism—Olivi, Ubertino and Angelo—as well as from Joachim himself, in not transposing the bible into history. This affected his whole outlook. To begin with it was essentially static and non-historical.[5] To read Arnold's *De tempore Antichristi* is to remain within the limits of biblical exegesis; there is little conception of history as a series of ages, each with its own characteristic. Even the references to the sixth and seventh seals, although showing an awareness of Joachist periods, had no formative part in Arnold's doctrine. Indeed it can be said that Arnold had no system; merely the conviction, compounded of current portents and scriptural authority, that the end of an epoch was at hand. To the extent that this would be signalized by the coming of Antichrist, whose defeat would introduce a new era of peace, we may concede his Joachism; but it was only the vehicle for beliefs which were of non-Joachist inspiration. The effect is that Arnold's apocalyptic views became merely a series of citations rather than the unfolding of an historicism. Hence they lack the element of excitement which is to be found in true Joachism.

The second feature of Arnold's thought was that it was avowedly

---

[1] *Presentatio Burdegalensis*, ibid., CCII–CCXI.

[2] It was during his *Interpretatio de visionibus* in 1309—the *Rahonament*, now preserved only in a Catalan text (Menendez Pelayo, op. cit., vol. III, 564–94)—that Clement V thought of other things, ibid., 603 (Letter of Clement V to James II of Aragon).

[3] ALKG II, 129. He had previously done the same with Benedict XI: Finke, op. cit., CLXXXVI–VII.

[4] Manselli, art. cit., 35–7; Menendez Pelayo, op. cit., 604–11.

[5] This has also been pointed out by Manselli, art. cit., 23.

proselytizing; he sought to broadcast the truths of scripture to the widest possible audience. Arnold conceived himself as the agent of a higher purpose, devoid of personal glorification: time and again he affirmed the need for modesty and condemned those with pride as being for ever excluded from an understanding of God's wisdom. There can be no doubt of his genuine disinterestedness; it gave him that lack of fear or favour which was his most conspicuous quality. This is shown in Arnold's writings. They are narrow in range, direct, and edificatory; there is none of Olivi's brooding speculation or the flights of Ubertino's poetic mysticism, nor the sense of destiny which all the Franciscan thinkers had. But they were also more down to earth, and for that reason their impact—or at least their import—was more immediate; there was no chance of misinterpreting Arnold as Olivi was misunderstood, and correspondingly there was more that could be followed in practice. In that sense, Arnold acted as a foil to Olivi: if Olivi provided the historical framework Arnold helped to fill it with references to specific events and persons. These increasingly concerned the struggle between the Spirituals and their opponents; in the process, poverty came to the fore, where, at the outset, as in the *De tempore adventus Antichristi*, it had not been mentioned. But always the context remained biblical and moral rather than historical.

Although Arnold published a Commentary on the Apocalypse, which remains unprinted,[1] its conventionality gave it no influence upon the Spirituals in Provence or Franciscan thinking in general. His first treatise of note was *De tempore adventus Antichristi* for which, as we have seen, he was imprisoned in Paris. He then rewrote it,[2] defending it on the grounds that it was incumbent upon him to make known the

---

[1] Vat. Lat. 5740. This contains nothing strictly Joachist, but follows the accepted lines of biblical exegesis. Pou y Marti *Visionarios* 46 ff. considers that Arnold was a Joachist both in his Introduction to *De semine scripturarum* and his *Expositio in Apocalypsim*, where (ff. 8–9) he does employ a trinitarian division. But, if as Miss Reeves rightly says, the test of Joachism is belief in a third age *in this world*, Arnold fails to pass it. For Arnold the seventh age will lead not to a thousand year reign of peace on earth, but directly to the Last Judgement. E.g. Per sex enim tribulationes intelliguntur omnes tribulationes vite presentis, que per sex decurrit etates. *Septima vero tribulatio est illa que suscitabitur in generali iudicio* (my italics, G.L.) (Pou y Marti, ibid., 51). It is of interest that Arnold of Villanova was attacked by Henry of Harclay not for upholding a third age but for his efforts to prophesy the date of Christ's second coming from the Book of Daniel. F. Pelster, 'Die Quaestio Heinrichs von Harclay über die zweite Ankunft Christi', *Archivio italiano per la storia della pietà* I (1951) 60 ff.

[2] This is the version published in Finke, op. cit., CXXIX–CLX.

coming end of the world and to turn men's minds away from trivial to momentous matters.[1] Basing himself upon texts from scripture he argued that the references to more than one end of the world meant that several epochs were contained within the final phase of the world's duration, in which they were now living. It had begun with Christ.[2] The present age would finish by the end of the fourteenth century.[3] He then went on to foretell that Antichrist would appear in a holy place, probably in 1378, although he disclaimed any certainty for the date.[4] The important point for him was that it accorded with scripture, which he called 'the mirror of God'.[5] Already there had occurred the loss of the holy places to the Moslems and the struggle between the forces of Antichrist and the forces of Christ represented by the Franciscans and the Dominicans. They would be followed by the final advent of Christ, the lamb, and the Last Judgement.[6] So far all that had been predicted had been fulfilled up to the expulsion of Charles of Anjou from Sicily.[7] There only remained the reunion of the Latin and Greek churches, the disappearance of the barbarian nations, and the advent of Antichrist, to be followed by that of Christ.[8] The seventh age would then begin, a time of tranquillity and universal peace, in which Christ would be adored and there would be 'one pastor and one shepherd' (John 10: 16):[9] this suggests Arnold's belief in an angelic pope so common in fourteenth-century Franciscan thinking. Here Arnold emphasized that such truths

[1] Finke, ibid., cxxix.

[2] . . . quia non dixit finem sed fines aperte significans quod plura tempora continentur sub una finali mensura durationis mundi sub qua plura centenaria continentur. Est ultima etas, que a Christo incepit . . . usque ad finem mundi (ibid., cxxxi).

[3] Arnold's exact words are: Que ideo ultima revera dicuntur, quia priusquam duo centenaria compleantur status presentis seculi finietur (ibid., cxxxi). They followed his date of 1297 as the present time of writing, and, taken in the context of what follows are to be understood in the sense of 'before two more centuries are out' rather than 'within another two hundred years'. For he shortly adds: 'quod erit circa septuagesimum octavum annum centenarii sequentis, videlicet quarti decimi a salvatoris adventu' (ibid., cxxxi).

[4] Ibid., cxxxii.

[5] Specula vero domini est sacra scriptura, ibid., cxxx.

[6] Ibid., cxxxii.

[7] Ibid.

[8] Post que non restant nisi quattuor de hiis que predixit: quorum primum est quod ecclesia Grecorum coacta reunietur ecclesie Latinorum; secundum est dissipatio barbare nationis, et illi iam regnant in parte per quos hec implebuntur; tertium est adventus Antichristi; quartum vero est adventus domini ad iudicium (ibid., cxxxii–iii).

[9] Ibid.

were essentially supernatural and not susceptible to natural knowledge independently pursued.[1] At the same time, because of the certainty of God's disposition of the future, it was permissible to investigate its likely outcome by computation: indeed God had revealed many future events to the faithful, such as Daniel's prophecy of Christ's advent on earth and his passion, or of the coming of Antichrist.[2] Thus, with the bible as the means, the future could be foretold; and it was a duty to foretell it: one of Arnold's guiding principles. By this means, again with reference to Daniel, Antichrist's appearance could be calculated, as Arnold had done: to deny this would be to imply that Daniel had spoken in vain.[3] Arnold was here upholding not philosophical but Catholic reasoning; the proofs lay with scripture,[4] although there could never be absolute certainty in anything which depended upon human actions.[5] Arnold's fondness for prediction is also to be seen in his references to the Erythrean Sibyl for whose prophecy, that the time of Antichrist would be the fourteenth century, he claimed the authority of St. Augustine in *De civitate Dei*.[6] Arnold ended the treatise with a nine-point résumé which served to reinforce the primarily biblical and hortatory nature of his message.

The same combination is to be found in nearly all Arnold's works. He stated his subject in the Introduction to his *De semine scripturarum* as 'de prophetis dormientibus', i.e. their dreams and revelations. But an understanding of them was reserved only for the truly humble who loved God.[7] In this work he was concerned to apply what may be called semantics to the letters of the alphabet, examples of which are already to be found in his *De tempore adventus Antichristi*. Thus the letter X which is in the form of a cross stood for the advent of Christ, and in the twentieth century of the city of Rome and the thirteenth since the Incarnation, it signified that, by their term, Babylon would have expired and Christ's cross have been renewed. Arnold with characteristic integrity did not pretend that it was certain; only that it showed the

---

[1] Ibid.

[2] Set cum certitudo sit omnium futurorum in deo, tunc, si ab ipso fuerint aliquorum futurorum tempora revelata, non erit inordinatum aut inconveniens illorum noticiam querere vel investigare computatione. . . . Constat autem quod a deo sunt revelata populo fideli tempora plurium eventuum, sicut tempus primi adventus Christi et tempus passionis ipsius, ut patet Danielis IX, et etiam tempus adventus Antichristi, sicut patet XII eiusdem (ibid., CXXXVI).

[3] Ibid., CXXXVIII.

[4] Ibid., CXXXX. [5] Ibid., CXLIII. [6] Ibid., CXLVII.

[7] Published in Manselli, 'Arnoldo da Villanova', 47–59.

use of scripture in helping to designate the sixth and seventh ages.[1] God's mysteries were revealed to man in the visions of prophets like Daniel and John of the Apocalypse;[2] and every letter of the alphabet, no matter how great or small its importance, had its part in making known God's law.[3] The course of all creation was thus unfolded in the pages of scripture.[4] Its elucidation provided Arnold with the basis of his apocalypticism. In due course, however, through his disillusionment with the course of events and his contact with the Provençal Spirituals and Beguins, it took on an increasingly Franciscan form of Joachism. Not that it ever became truly historicist: rather it incorporated a growing belief in the significance of poverty and the sanctity of those pledged to observe it in all its rigour. He was particularly concerned with the falling away from Christian principles to be seen in the desire for profane knowledge and the things of this world.[5] Evangelical poverty and the *usus pauper* now became the criterion of loyalty to Christ; and conversely the persecution of its adherents the work of Antichrist.[6] Arnold was especially incensed at the Spirituals' oppression in Provence for the very reason of their devotion to poverty:[7] he regarded it as a blow against the foundation of the church itself. In his two works written for the Beguins, the *Informatio Beginorum*[8] and the *Lectio Narbone*,[9] Arnold came to define evangelical perfection as the

---

[1] Nos autem summus in XXo centenario urbis Romae et in XIIIo Christi centenario . . . unde et secundum eum designat quod in fine huius centenarii carnalis ecclesie, seu Babilon, expirabit ut in sequenti centenario designato per *x* literam, que habit formam crucis et fuit per Cesarem Augustum circa Christi adventum inventa, renovetur et exaltetur crux Christi. . . . Hec breviter recitavi nihil habens certam nec etiam aliquam rationem ad hoc vel ad oppositum, magno nomine dignam, nisi quod scriptura, more suo nobis utili designat a tempore sexti et septimi status extremum iudicium imminere et quasi iam in ianuis esse (quoted in Manselli, 'Arnoldo da Villanova', 14).

[2] Ibid., 47.   [3] Ibid.   [4] Ibid., 57.

[5] See, for example, his address to Benedict XI (1304) in Finke, *Aus den Tagen*, CLXXXIII, in which he treats these as signs of the coming of Antichrist, to take place during the fourteenth century. . . . Et adeo iam laycis innotescit quod feratur communiter non esse apostolicam predicationem ipsorum, cum illa loquantur in suis sermonibus, que Christus per eos non efficit, sed potius Antichristus (ibid., CLXXXV).

[6] Ibid., CLXXXIII–VII.

[7] Et quotquot inveniebant fateri quod imitatio vite Christi et apostolice quantum ad pauperem usum temporalium rerum pertinebat eorum observantie regulari, diris carceribus impie mancipabant. Nam iam palam erubescunt sui status destruere fundamentum ab ecclesia Romana limitatum et consignatum (ibid., CLXXXVI–VII).

[8] Published in Finke, *Aus den Tagen*, CCI–CCII.

[9] Published by Manselli, 'Arnaldo da Villanova' 77–91, in an Italian version.

observance of the four virtues of the highest poverty, complete humility, charity and unswerving chastity,[1] together with the avoidance of the prevalent vices of curiosity, vanity and superfluity.[2] The highest poverty consisted in two things: to have only that which was necessary for sustaining physical life; and the pursuit of the spiritual life with no care for the future by laying up goods.[3] This entailed the avoidance of all litigation, and the cultivation of Christ's virtues of patience, meekness and modesty.[4] It also meant a devotion to Christ's, and his mother's, example of poverty, by wearing patched habits, eating frugal fare and the entire absence of dwellings or other possessions, with not even, on death, a tomb of one's own.[5] He who aspired to perfection must not only reject all excess, but avoid all unnecessary curiosity, whether of having, knowing or seeing. It was precisely such vanity and cupidity which had infected the majority of men, clerical and lay, and led to the multitude of sins like simony.[6] Arnold, because he took the bible as the exclusive repository of all truth, was particularly antipathetic to profane learning: only knowledge founded upon scripture rendered man God's friend; philosophy only divided them, making man disputatious and hypocritical.[7] As St. John of the Apocalypse had said, understanding lay with Christ who could alone open and close the book of the seven seals.[8] Increasingly then, Arnold came to set his unceasing predictions of the coming of Antichrist within the context of the struggle between the Spirituals and their persecutors; devotion to poverty came to have something of the same significance for him as for the Franciscan Joachists; but it was a moral rather than an historical one. It was important because, together with humility, charity and chastity, it constituted the virtues of the true Christian; it

---

[1] Finke, CCI.   [2] Manselli, ibid., 78.

[3] . . . quod nichil habeant vel habere velint nisi quod est precise necessarium ve ad cultum vite spiritualis . . . vel ad sustentationem cotidianam vite corporalis ut operimenta et alimenta, que tali sustentationi solum sufficiat. Secundum quod sollicitudinem hec necessaria procurandi pro futura tempore totaliter a se pellant (Finke, CCI).   [4] Ibid.   [5] Manselli, ibid., 78.

[6] per la quale vanitade et superfluitade è caduto il populo delli Christiani, et magiormente li layci e li cleri secolari, in fuocho di cupidità di quadagniare et di multiplicare richezze in tutti modi disordinati, come s'è usura, barateria, ingano, simonia . . . (ibid., 87).

[7] Ma propria scientia delli Christiani è quella per la quale l'uhomo è puì gratiosa e puì piacie a Dio e per la quale gli crescie l'amore suo. Et è cosa certa, che per sapere di phylosofia, non è l'uhomo maggiore amielo di Dio, ma maggiore disputatore . . . e puì ypocrita (ibid., 89).   [8] Ibid., 90.

N

was a sign of the spirit of Christ and indispensable to a true understanding of his truths. In that sense it may be said that it remained
subordinated to prophecy; an essential prerequisite rather than an end
in itself.

Arnold returned to his favourite theme in his address to Clement V
at Bordeaux.[1] Pride was the sin of Satan: it made pseudo-prophets of
those who were governed by it, speaking not with the words of Christ,
but those which issued from the mouth of the dragon.[2] The prophecies
in the bible, and of Cyril and the Sibyl, gave to his outlook a practical
cast, more marked than that of Olivi or Ubertino; he became the
champion of a specific geographical group as well as an idea. He was a
man of action where they were primarily men of letters. Their messages
converged but they differed in origin and emphasis. Arnold's advocacy
of the Spirituals and Beguins of Provence complemented Olivi's and
Ubertino's enunciation of the Franciscans' historical mission: his deeds
no less than Olivi's writings entered into their lore. The one gave historical reality to the other's historical speculations. This is to be seen
most vividly in the anonymous Spiritual tract, the *Liber de Flore*,
written after 1305.[3] There both Arnold and Olivi figure prominently.
Arnold was treated as a real historical figure, whereas Olivi was a
personification: he was described as a new Hector foretelling the downfall of a new Troy, namely, the destruction of the Franciscan order.[4]
Arnold's actions, from the condemnation of his *Tractatus de tempore
adventus Antichristi* to his appeal to the papal chamberlain at Perugia,
after Benedict XI's death, were described as actual events,[5] as were also
the tribulations of Liberato's group[6] and the sufferings of the Provençal

---

[1] *Presentatio Burdegallensis* (1305) in Finke, *Aus den Tagen* (CCII–VII).

[2] Ibid., CCVIII.

[3] Known in only three manuscripts: the fourteenth Arras MS. 138 (fol. 85v–106v),
and the two seventeenth-century MSS. in the Biblioteca Valliceli, Rome, nos. 32
and 33. A full description of the book, with a ten-page extract, is given by H. Grundmann, 'Liber de Flore', *Historisches Jahrbuch*, 49 (1929) 33–91, on which the present
account is based.

[4] Ita et novus Hector, scilicet frater P[etris] J[ohannis] militans in ecclesia nove
Troye, i.e. ordinis fratrum minorum novam destructionem annunciabit. . . . (Grundmann, op. cit., 55, n.50; Arras, fol. 103v).

[5] E.g., Consequenter dicit quod in prima resticencia modus scilicet predicantis,
reprobaretur, sicut factum fuit Parisius et in curia Romana. . . . Et in secunda (scilicet
resistentia) consignaretur quod factum est Perusiis post mortem Benedicti per cardinales. Quam consignationem et resistenciam fieri deus ordinauit ad hoc . . . scilicet
amplexum seu cultum sue virtutis (ibid., 88).

[6] Ibid., 53, n.46.

Spirituals and their followers.[1] There was even the attack upon the two Franciscan cardinals John of Murrovalle, general from 1296–1302, and Gentile of Montefiore, which Arnold of Villanova had also made in his address before Clement V and renewed in 1309,[2] in his *Interpretatio de visionibus et somniis*.[3]

More significant, however, is the influence of Arnold's method of biblical prediction; the prophetic element in the *Liber de Flore* owed as much to Arnold's culling from the bible and the Cyrillan and Sibylline prophecies as to Joachist historicism: even if it also went beyond him in introducing a series of angelic pastors which we shall mention shortly.

There was a sense of the succession of ages, which is *par excellence* of the essence of true Joachism. But the *Liber* followed Arnold in seeking the figures of Christ and Antichrist in the bible[4] and in his use of the alphabet;[5] it also drew the same conclusions over evangelical perfection.[6] Finally, there was a corresponding hostility towards all forms of natural and profane knowledge, the predilection for which was regarded as the tempting of Antichrist, leading men away from the teachings of Christ and the true doctrines of the church.[7]

In addition to the strong partisanship of the *Liber de Flore* for Arnold of Villanova, it also represented another tradition. This originally derived from the Greek church, with the belief in a line of so-called angel popes, or angelic pastors. The prototype for this were the Leo oracles, prophecies over the future of the Byzantine empire dating from

---

[1] It mentions, for example, John of Picquigny, a champion of reform in Provence and protector of Bernard Délicieux in his fight against the inquisition—for which he died excommunicate: See M. Dmitrewski, 'Fr. Bernard Délicieux, sa lutte contre l'Inquisition' in AFH 17 (1924) 183–218, 313–37, 457–88; 18 (1925) 3–32.

[2] Grundmann, ibid., 62 and 64, n.76, i.e. the *Rahonament*.

[3] Menendez Pelayo, op. cit., III, 512–36.

[4] Et proprie dicit 'opinio', quia id quod predicabat, dato quod habuisset per revelationem, tamen ipse proponebat per modum scholastice discussionis vel considerationis, sicut apparet adhuc in primis edicionibus eius (Grundmann, ibid., 87–8).

[5] And: *immediate viderent suas figuras*, id est immediate cognoscerent utrum in studiis suis procederent ad ymaginem Christi vel Antichristi (ibid., 85).

[6] Hanc autem noticiam, ut dicit, habebunt ex conclusione omnium rationum eius, que est conclusio evangelice perfectionis (ibid.).

[7] Duo tamen omittere non intendo. Primum quod quidam draconis inter electos astucia diabolica communitus vexabit et concassabit plurimos a tramite veritatis. . . . Secundum quod literali sciencia mathematica, non divina, quidam ipsa nimium insignitus inter ipsos repugnare conabitur. . . . Et propter hoc necesse est ut universa scandala veniant, quia si cecus cecum ducit, ambo in foveam cadunt (ibid., 89–90).

the ninth and tenth centuries and ascribed to the emperor Leo the Wise.[1] They entered the Joachist canon, although they had, in fact, nothing to do with Joachim; and by the later thirteenth century had become one of the Spirituals' main vehicles for expressing their aspirations. The most noteworthy composition upon which the *Liber de Flore* drew was the *Vaticinia Anselmi*: it described fifteen popes, some historical, some prophetic, the first of whom was Nicholas III and the last eight were future popes. The work was falsely attributed to Anselm, an apocryphal bishop of Marsico. From the later fourteenth century it became joined to another series of fifteen studies which were—equally wrongly—made the work of Joachim of Fiore. It was in the form of thirty revelations, the combined effort of Joachim—whose fifteen came first—and Anselm, that they were known from the later fourteenth to the sixteenth centuries.[2] They served to inspire many similar compilations in the sixteenth century, the various *Libri de summis pontificibus*, doing for the humanists what the earlier versions had done for the Spirituals and the Fraticelli.[3] While the Prophecies of Joachim sprang from the milieu of the Fraticelli, and were written before 1356,[4] the *Vaticinia Anselmi* belonged to the last part of the thirteenth century; some manuscripts give the date of composition as 1278, but add that it was not published until after the death of Boniface VIII.[5] Except for

---

[1] H. Grundmann, 'Die Papstprophetien des Mittelalters' in *Archiv für Kulturgeschichte*, 19 (1929) 77–138. These derived from the Sibylline and Methodian texts mentioned p. 174 note 7 above together with the book of Daniel which was the source of these Byzantine prophecies (Grundmann, ibid., 82–3). The *Liber de Flore* also drew upon the *Horoscopus*, an astrological paraphrase of papal prophecies, translated from the Hebrew probably before 1305 (Grundmann, 'Liber de Flore', 41).

[2] Thus the edition of Venice 1589, is entitled *Vaticinia sive Prophetiae Abbatis Joachimi et Anselmi Episcopi Marsicani* (unpaginated). I have used this one together with Pierpont Morgan Library (NY) MSS. 272 and 402. MS. 272 is in a fifteenth-century hand of Italian provenance. It runs from Honorius IV to Eugenius IV of the historical popes. MS. 402 is from the fourteenth century, also Italian, and runs from Nicholas III to Urban VI. Both give the names of the popes. But MS. 272, besides containing the better text, also includes four angel popes.

[3] The Venice edition also contains a series of sixteenth-century popes.

[4] Grundmann, 'Die Papstprophetien', 114–16 wrongly dated it to the years immediately before the Great Schism by identifying the fifteenth pope with Gregory XI for his betrayal of Urban V. In fact, however, John of Ruspescissa had already cited both series, the second (beginning with the words to the first caption—to Nicholas III—'Ascende calve') in *Vade mecum in tribulatione* (*Fasciculus* II 501) and in his *Vaticinia*, J. Bignami-Odier, *Etudes sur Jean de Roquetaillade* (Paris 1952) 151 ff. I owe this knowledge to the kindness of Miss Marjorie Reeves.

[5] Ibid., 93.

the first portrait (no. 16) which represents Nicholas III,[1] they were a prose rendering into Latin from the Greek of the Leo oracles. Their real interest lies in the captions accompanying the portraits of each pope who, following custom, were depicted by animals—as, for example, a bear for Nicholas III to denote nepotism. These, usually of only one sentence, summed up the character of the different pontificates. Thus the caption to Celestine V runs: 'The elevation of poverty, obedience, chastity, and the destruction of the hypocrites.'[2] Apart from this one, all the other judgements on the first six popes (nos. 16–22) are uncomplimentary or condemnatory. With no. 23, however, we begin the line of angelic popes, and with them the prophetic part of the *Vaticinia*. Each of the subsequent eight popes furthers the establishment of a new age: the first (no. 23) sees the power of the clergy and the monks restored, and simony ended;[3] the second (24), depicts the prevalence of goodness and grace;[4] the third (25) the establishment of unity;[5] and so on. It is the apocalyptic vision at its most direct and Franciscan; and it almost certainly originated from a Spiritual milieu.[6] Undoubtedly, the most significant aspect of the *Vaticinia* was the reliance upon existing institutions to effect a spiritual reformation: the popes themselves would be its agents, not a new spiritual church. The call was for a return to first principles within the existing framework, which was the foundation of the Spirituals' outlook.

The third element in the *Liber de Flore* was common to the majority of popular Joachist writing, namely, the various prophecies of Cyril and the Sibyl, which we have already met in Arnold of Villanova. To these, however, must be added firstly the Book of Merlin,[7] which, unlike the previous two, was also an account of true events. Written

---

[1] Caption: 'Genus nequam ursa catulos pascens'. Grundmann (ibid., 92) pointed to the parallel with Dante's description of Nicholas III:

e veramente fui figliuol dell' orsa,
cupido si per avanzar gli orsatti (*Inferno* XIX, 70–1).

In most MSS., including Pierpont Morgan Library MSS. 272, 402, the names of the historical popes are stated in the caption.

[2] Elatio paupertatis, obedientia, castitas castrimazia, et hypocritarum destructio.

[3] Potestas, coenobia ad locum pastorum rebibunt, simonia cessabit.

[4] Bona gratia.   [5] Potestas unitas erit.

[6] Grundmann (ibid., 100 ff.) surmises that they were transmitted to the west in their Latin form by Liberato or his followers who brought it to Perugia in 1304. If so, Angelo of Clareno was not affected by these prophecies.

[7] For both an edition of a French version and a series of studies on its different aspects, see L. A. Paton, *The Prophecies of Merlin*, 2 vols. (New York 1926–7) upon which the present account is based.

probably during the 1270s,[1] the predictions were largely related to Italian history of the twelfth and thirteenth centuries. Two of its main themes were the excellence of Venice and the widespread corruption of the church; the author, although of papalist sympathies, repeatedly refers to the prevalence of cupidity and simony, whose source he saw in the desire for wealth.[2] He took as his example the simony of 'three of the wisest prelates in the papal court', one German, one Milanese and one Roman. Each of them carried a prediction: of war between the Imperialists and the Papalists (Gibelline and Guelf); of disasters to Milan as punishment for its sins; and of the coming of an angelic pope. Together with these went the theme of the 'Dragon of Babilone' (Antichrist), to recount whose doings was one of Merlin's missions on earth. Although not confined to these topics, the apocalyptic element in *Merlin* was important, and helped to stimulate what, by the beginning of the fourteenth century, had become an established genre of popular prophecy.

The *Liber de Flore* was itself in the form of a text, with a commentary upon it by an 'annointed one' who provided historical testimony for the more sibylline utterances. As we have already mentioned, it was concerned primarily with the Spiritual Franciscans and their sufferings at the hands of their persecutors. On the pattern of the *Vaticinia Anselmi*, it was divided into history and prophecy. The first part traced the fortunes of the order through successive thirteenth-century popes, from Gregory IX to Boniface VIII; the second then described the advent of four angelic popes who would usher in a new era. As Spiritual polemic it has all the life and immediacy that the jejune stereotypes of the *Vaticinia Anselmi* lack. But it is also more; it comes nearest to giving permanent voice to popular Spiritual lore; what Olivi was too sophisticated and restrained to believe, and Ubertino, in his consuming preoccupation with Christ and St. Francis, did not say, the *Liber de Flore* expressed. Sharply, but usually without loss of proportion, the writer arraigned the main succession of thirteenth-century popes for betraying Christ's teachings and persecuting those who upheld them. Within a Joachist setting of struggle between the forces of Antichrist and the elect, it described the vicissitudes of the Franciscan order. Papal interference in its affairs had from its onset been an unmitigated evil. The germ of iniquity had begun with Gregory IX;[3] he,

---

[1] Paton, ibid., vol. II, 33.   [2] Ibid., 157–60.

[3] non amicus fidei sed temporalium rerum maximus amplexator (Grundmann, 'Liber de Flore' 43).

far from being a friend of the true faith, was the chief covetor of temporal possessions. The writer was equally harsh towards Nicholas III, whom it held responsible for the order's subsequent corruption:[1] a sign of his extremism, since even uncompromising radicals like Ubertino of Casale made *Exiit qui seminat* one of their main supports. Gregory X, as in the *Prophecies of Merlin*, was considered a good pope;[2] but, as one would expect, Celestine V was the hero of this first historical period: the forerunner of the angelic popes, and as yet too good for this world.[3] His abdication was illegal. Among other uncomplimentary remarks about Boniface VIII, he was called the great dragon.[4] There were also, as we earlier mentioned, criticisms of other near contemporaries, including the two Franciscan cardinals, John of Murrovalle and Gentile of Montefiore, the latter being described as a little dragon, the creature of Boniface VIII, the great dragon.[5]

But this anatomy of the popes was more than merely a recital of their failings or, occasionally, their virtues. The main issues were not lost from sight. Evangelical perfection was pitted against the growing wealth, laxity and worldliness of the majority of ecclesiastics. The Franciscan order was the repository of virtue; in it were to be found those who remained true to the fullest humility, meekness, and poverty.[6] In particular they remained loyal to the *usus pauper* in the face of the calumnies of the pseudo-religious who, under the pretext of defending the true faith, attacked them.[7] Thus the Franciscan order was itself divided into the elect, who followed St. Francis's ideal, and those who had deserted the path of truth. The turning point would come in 1298, as predicted by Merlin. It would herald the gradual waning of the forces of evil, accompanied by new tribulations on a scale hitherto undreamed

---

[1] Tempus enim medium pontificem iniquum, ut dixit, et inter pastorem angelicum dicitur tempus vestigiorum illius iniqui, quia non solum successores eiusdem fuerunt de plantario suo, sed insuper in ceteris ecclesiis regnaverunt et exuberanter semina viciorum eius, sicut in revelatione Horoscopi plenissime declaratur (ibid., 65 n.78).

[2] Of his death it says: et deficiet in ecclesia bonus pastor (ibid., 50 n.38).

[3] Ibid., 57; quo seduxerat Celestinum, et forma conversacionis inordinate (ibid., 83).

[4] Ibid.

[5] Sed ideo vocat eum draconium diminutive, ut innuat, quod magni draconis illius temporis proles erat (ibid., 90). [6] Ibid., 81.

[7] talis autem confusio regnavit in illis filiis predicti status . . . scilicet audacter et constanter et intemperate sunt persecuti confratres suos volentes et suadentes observantiam evangelice perfectionis ... persecuti sunt eos qui usum pauperem asserebant pertinere ad status eorum perfectionem et regulam fundatoris. Quos pseudoreligiosi pretendentes zelum custodiendi sinceritatem in statu persecuti sunt imponentes calumpniam superstitionis (ibid., 80, n. 2).

of; these were necessary to punish the evildoers.[1] Although not put into Joachist terminology, this change was equivalent to the ending of the sixth age. It would be followed by the overcoming of the separation within the church of those who truly sought the way of Christ from those who were blinded by their own pride. The reunification of all the faithful in Christ would be the work of the angelic popes.[2] At this point in the treatise, speculation, pure and simple, takes over, as the future deeds of the four angel pastors are recounted. The first, appropriately a poor devout monk from heaven, would, to the sounds of music and rejoicing, rectify the world, supported by a king descended from heaven; the schism between east and west would be ended; the emperor would himself become a Franciscan; the use of arms would be abandoned.[3] The second angel pope, a Frenchman, would heal the division between France and Germany.[4] The third, an Italian Spiritual, would reform his own order and distribute the goods of the church to the poor, their rightful owners;[5] the fourth, a Gascon, would receive the homage of Gog and Magog and unify the entire world.[6] After him would come the great Antichrist and the end of the world, at which point the treatise also ended.

The affinities of this vision with the outlook of the Spirituals scarcely need stressing. In the first place, the Franciscan order is very largely the instrument of regeneration personified by the angel popes both in their virtues and their religious habit. In the second place, their deeds together constituted the Spirituals' programme as found, in essentials, in Olivi and Ubertino of Casale: namely, the unification of the world, the reform of the church, the triumph of poverty. Finally, there was that same almost messianic sense, which was *par excellence* one of the features of the more extreme Spirituals: not simply of the impending end of all things temporal, but the conviction that they were themselves the instruments by which it would be brought about.

The *Liber de Flore* was the final product of Franciscan Joachism in a recognizable form. It had shed much of Joachim's original grand vision; the scheme of history had been superseded by the events of the order's history; the framework of change had shifted from a cosmic to a local scale; personalities had displaced personifications; and the future had become a matter of immediate Spiritual aspirations. Franciscan content had usurped Joachist form. Yet enough remained to give them continuity, above all the belief in impending regeneration which could only

---

[1] Grundmann, 82.   [2] Ibid., 85.   [3] Ibid., 71–2 and n.97, n.98, n.100.
[4] Ibid., 72–3, n.102.   [5] Ibid.   [6] Ibid., 74.

be realized through the tribulations of those who remained true to Christ (and St. Francis). Joachim's legacy of apocalypticism remained the ultimate source of the Spirituals' messianism.

These, then, were the works—of Arnold Villanova, the *Vaticinia* and the *Liber de Flore*, and the prophecies upon which they drew—which helped to form the climate of the Spirituals' world in the first few decades of the fourteenth century. Together with the influence of Olivi and Ubertino of Casale, the exploits of Liberato and Angelo of Clareno, the struggle of Bernard Délicieux and his lay supporters against the Inquisition in Provence, they came to constitute the Spiritual's ideological justification. It cannot be overstated that it was founded upon a desire to regenerate the church, not to destroy it or replace it. Failure to appreciate this must in the end mean failure to understand the Spirituals and Beguins as well as the Fraticelli. To the end their struggle was against individuals, not an institution; even when, as we shall see, they came to regard John XXII as a false pastor, they did not thereby deny the authority of the papacy: they sought his replacement by a true pope. At the beginning of the fourteenth century, well before the persecutions had reached their height, this adhesion to the church is equally pronounced. Olivi, as we know, protested his loyalty and submission repeatedly: Ubertino, even when near to blasphemy in what he said about Boniface VIII and Benedict XI, still put his faith in the advent of a righteous pope;[1] while Arnold of Villanova's traditionalism has already been remarked. Both the *Vaticinia Anselmi* and the *Liber de Flore*, in their very design of foretelling the regeneration of the church by a new line of popes, were testimonies of loyalty to it; indeed, the latter specifically distinguished between the church as divinely ordained and those who abused it.[2] Accordingly, we now have to examine how, despite such genuine protestations, condemnation for heresy was the final outcome.

The Apostles: Gerard Segarelli and Dolcino[3]

The most extreme example of the combination of poverty and prophecy, at this time, was to be found outside the Franciscan order among

[1] *Arbor vitae*, Bk. v, ch. VIII.

[2] . . . decor et decus matris ecclesie ille summus noscitur Jesus Christus; sed eius vicarius non Christi doctrinam sequetur ut convenit (ibid., 68).

[3] What follows is based upon the accounts by Bernard Gui, *Manuel* I, 84 ff. and II, 66 ff., together with the anonymous treatise on Dolcino and other documents to

the so-called Apostles or *pseudo-Apostolici*. Themselves of no lasting importance, they gave a foretaste of the explosive consequences which could flow from harnessing a belief in apostolic poverty to Joachism unconstrained by any authority. The sect, according to Bernard Gui[1] and Salimbene, the Franciscan chronicler,[2] originated with Gerard Segarelli, at Parma, in 1260—the Joachite year of change. Its beginnings were not markedly different from those of other such groups, i.e. the Waldensians or the Franciscans, which sought a return to apostolic purity; and Segarelli soon attracted followers. They lived like wanderers, begging and preaching. Segarelli was himself illiterate.[3] He seems to have sought neither to found a new order nor to proclaim a new doctrine, but was content to live as one among other apostles, with beard and long hair, white tunic and sandals, in imitation of Christ and his disciples. They were probably one of many such unofficial groups against which the reaffirmation of the Fourth Lateran Council's ban on new orders was directed by the Second Council of Lyons in 1274.[4] It had no effect upon Segarelli.

In 1284, after an existence of twenty years, Honorious IV condemned the Apostles in the bull *Olim felicis*.[5] The authorities were ordered to proceed against them and their supporters, imprisoning them or, if necessary, handing them over to the secular arm. It was repeated by Nicholas IV in 1290. In 1294 four Apostles, two men and two women, were captured at Parma.[6] Segarelli was finally taken and imprisoned by the bishop of Parma, who for a time allowed him the freedom of his palace.[7] He was burned in 1301,[8] only to be replaced by the much more formidable Dolcino.

The sect was by now widely diffused throughout Lombardy, and Dolcino, aided by his two close companions, Margaret and Longinus, proceeded to propagate a species of militant Joachism. In two letters[9] addressed to all the faithful Segarelli claimed God's direct authority for himself and his followers. Their obligation to poverty dispensed them

---

be found in Muratori, *Historia Fratris Dulcini* vol. 9, pt. v (ed. Arnoldo Segarizzi) Città di Castello, 1907. See also F. Tocco, 'Gli Apostolici e Fra Dolcino' *Archivio Storico Italiano*, 5th series, vol. 19 (1897) 241–75, and E. Dupré Théseider, 'Fra Dolcino: storia e mito' BSSV 104 (1958) 5–25, which adds little new. Neither does E. Anagnine, *Dolcino e il movimento ereticale all'inizio del Trecento* (Florence 1964) which also contains disconcerting inaccuracies.

[1] Muratori, ibid., 17. [2] Tocco, art. cit., 243. [3] Ibid.
[4] Mansi, 24, ch. 23, 96 f. [5] Text in Muratori, ibid., 18. [6] Tocco, art. cit., 247.
[7] Ibid. [8] Muratori, 19. [9] Ibid., 19 ff.

from all external obligation; those who opposed them, lay and secular, Friars Preachers and Friars Minor, were the devil's ministers; in persecuting the Apostles they were attacking the true spiritual and apostolic church and would be killed: any survivors would become members of their sect. Dolcino claimed a special revelation from God which enabled him to foretell events to come. Drawing upon a debased Joachism he divided the world's history into four ages, each distinguished by its mode of life. The first had been that of the fathers, patriarchs and prophets of the Old Testament, where marriage had been a good and praiseworthy institution. The second, with the coming of Christ, had been that of the saints who had shown the true faith by living in humility, patience, poverty and chastity which had displaced marriage and abundance. This age had endured until Sylvester and the donation of Constantine when possessions had been reinstated in order to safeguard the great numbers of new converts to the Christian faith. Later, however, as ardour cooled, St. Benedict had inaugurated a new spiritual order to rekindle it, away from the temptations of the world. When in due course the monks had themselves lost their zeal, St. Francis and St. Dominic had appeared to found their congregations. It was now, in their aftermath, when they too had gone the way of their predecessors, that Dolcino and before him Segarelli had been sent by God to lead the faithful back to the true apostolic life. The time for new orders was past; the fourth age would be marked by the return to Christ.

Thus for Dolcino not only were there four rather than three ages, but there were no subdivisions within them. St. Francis had lost his Franciscan prerogative as angel of the sixth seal. He and his followers were not the new spirituals of the future but the last of the old orders. The future lay with no orders; and Dolcino stressed the difference between his Apostles and the mendicants as lying in the absence from his sect of any kind of possessions or organization.[1] The donation of Constantine had not been the turning point that it was for the Waldensians or even the Spirituals, but merely the pattern for a church which had become officially established. As outside the Franciscan order, Dolcino could afford to take a detached view and regard St. Francis as but the continuator of St. Benedict and the confrère of St. Dominic.

Dolcino went on to predict the events of the next three years. A new emperor, Frederick II of Sicily (1296–1337), would arise. He would establish new kings in Italy and put Boniface VIII to death. There

[1] Ibid., 21.

would be a holy pope, appointed by God, not the cardinals; he would be joined by the Apostles (Dolcino's sect) and the true remnants of the priesthood, all infused with the Holy Spirit. Together with Frederick of Sicily and the new kings they would rule until the advent of Antichrist.

In the second letter, written in 1303,[1] Dolcino claimed that he had a following of 4000 Apostles. He elaborated upon his previous prophecies in which the next three years would see the desolation of the church and the religious orders by Frederick of Sicily as emperor.

The complete list of twenty errors ascribed to the Apostles by Bernard Gui[2] displays a similar range of anti-sacerdotalism to that of the Waldensians: the Roman church was not the true church (art. 1); its power had been transferred to the Apostles (Dolcino's sect) (art. 2); those who belonged to it were free of all outside authority (5 and 6); they were absolved from sins and alone could be saved (7–10); a pope had no power unless he lived like St. Peter, in poverty and humility and without coercive authority (11); the whole priesthood from the time of Sylvester, except for Celestine V, were prevaricators and seducers (12); there was no need for religious orders or payments of tithes (13 and 14); carnal relations were not sinful (15 and 16); it was better to live without vows than with vows (17); oaths were prohibited (20); churches were no more worthy of prayer to God than stables or piggeries, and Christ could as well be adored in the mind as in church (18 and 19).

In 1307 after a series of complaints by the ecclesiastical authorities in Lombardy, the pope, Clement V, ordered a crusade against Dolcino in bulls addressed to the archbishop of Milan and his suffragans.[3] Under the bishop of Vercelli an army was raised. Dolcino and a number of supporters had withdrawn to a mountain in Novara. He and about forty followers were finally captured on 23 March 1307. After being held captive and tortured for three months, Dolcino, Margaret and Longinus were finally handed over to the secular arm and burned.[4]

---

[1] 22 ff.

[2] *Manuel* II, 100 ff. and Muratori, 24–5. The account given of Dolcino's teaching by the anonymous Italian writer (ibid., 7 ff.) elaborates upon Dolcino's prophecies and practices: according to this source Dolcino claimed the power of life and death over his followers. But this may well have been due to the exigencies of war, in being under siege by the bishop of Vercelli. More interesting are the undertones of Catharism (the writer repeatedly refers to them as *Garzaari*): thus Dolcino would go to heaven, whence, first Enoch and Elias, and then he, would return to earth to combat Antichrist (ibid., 8).   [3] Ibid., 26 ff.   [4] Ibid.

This was not the end of the sect; it continued to linger on in both Italy and Spain, where a letter attacking it was written by Bernard Gui to the archbishop of Compostella in 1316.[1] Its adherents were still to be found in south France in 1321 and 1322[2] and in Trentino ten years later,[3] as well as in Padua around 1350, Sicily in 1372, Narbonne in 1374, and Lübeck in 1402.[4] But compared with the Spirituals and Provençal Beguins, the pseudo-Apostles were merely a ripple on the surface. Their greatest claim to immortality remains in Dante's *Inferno*[5] rather than the world of men.

Spirituals and Beguins in Provence

So far we have been concerned with the preliminaries to the main question: namely, the struggle first of the Spirituals and Beguins with the papacy, and then that of the Fraticelli. The tendencies we have just discussed found fullest expression in Provence from about 1300 to 1325. It was there that the different elements which made up the Spirituals' world of poverty and prophecy converged in a veritable popular front between the Franciscans and their lay followers— the Beguins, and the citizens of towns like Narbonne and Béziers. It was there, too, that the doctrines of absolute poverty and Franciscan Joachism came to be identified with open subversion, and were both ultimately condemned by John XXII: poverty in 1323, and Olivi's *Postilla* on the Apocalypse in 1326, as we have seen. Finally, it was in Provence that the fate of the Spirituals was decided. After their resistance was broken, by about 1325, the Spirituals as a force ceased to exist; what had constituted an alternative in its own right to the official wing of the order, with its distinctive practices and principles, disintegrated. All that remained were scattered dissident groups in Central and Southern Italy, and the increasingly unreal remnant of the Community which followed Michael of Cesena into opposition against John XXII. Until 1325 the challenge was of one way of life by another, each

---

[1] *Manuel* I, 84 ff., and II, 108 ff., Muratori, 33 ff.

[2] Ibid., 75 ff.   [3] Ibid., 79 ff.   [4] Ibid., xxxvIII.

[5]   Or di' a fra Dolcin dunque che s'armi,
      Tu che forse vedrai lo sole in breve,
      S'egli non vual qui tosto seguitarmi,
      Si di vivanda, che stretta di neve,
      Non rechi la vittoria al Noarese,
      Ch'altrimenti acquistar non saria lieve.
          (*Inferno*, c. xxvIII, v, 55). Quoted by Segarizzi, ibid., vII.

with its own lore and traditions; the issues were, therefore, about fundamentals. After 1325 they were narrowed down into little more than anti-papalism (mainly against John XXII, long after he was dead) and became trivial. Hence the overwhelming importance of Provence in the history of the movement.

We may best begin with the *Practica inquisitionis* of Bernard Gui, Dominican inquisitor for Toulouse from 1307 until 1324, when he became bishop of Tuy (Galicia) until his death in 1331.[1] His work was designed both to describe the procedures of the inquisition and the different heretical sects, and is a rich source of information. While much of what it says is also to be found elsewhere,[2] it is especially enlightening as the expression of official attitudes, enabling us to see who and what were regarded as dangerous, and why. This is particularly true for Olivi who, as we shall see, was effectively the central figure in the case. The importance that Bernard Gui attached to the Franciscan dissidents can be gauged from the fact that of a total of ninety pages given to discussing the different heretical sects—Cathars, Waldensians, pseudo-Apostles—forty are devoted to them:[3] even allowing for Gui's first-hand knowledge of them, the proportion remains high.

Four salient facts emerge from Gui's description of the Provençal Beguins, all in varying degrees, borne out by the inquisitorial records. The first was the pre-eminent importance of Olivi as an authority. His writings were not only translated into the vernacular, but regarded as sacrosanct. In particular Gui saw his *Postilla* on the Apocalypse as one of the main sources of the Beguins' errors:

Their pestilential errors and opinions derive in part from the works and treatises of Peter John Olivi, born at Sérignan, near Béziers, namely from his Postilla on the Apocalypse, which they possess in Latin and translated into their own language. . . . And they say and believe that the said brother Peter John had his knowledge revealed to him by God, especially his Postilla or Exposition on the Apocalypse. They partly also owe their errors and

---

[1] This can be found in two editions: in full by C. Douais, *Practica inquisitionis heretice pravitatis, auctore Bernardo Guidonis* (Paris 1886); and abridged by G. Mollat, *Manuel de l'inquisiteur* (Paris 1926), with a parallel French translation, which is the one used here. For details of Bernard of Gui's career see Mollat, op. cit., VI–VII.

[2] E.g., Baluze, *Misc.*, especially vols. II and III, and the Collection Doat (Bibliothèque Nationale, Paris, cabinet des manuscrits), especially vols. 27, 28, 35 and 37.

[3] In Mollat's edition. 'De secta Beguinorum', I, 108–91 (allowing two pages for each page of text due to the parallel French translation).

opinions to the tradition of what the same brother Peter John is said to have told his companions and the Beguins in his own lifetime.[1]

Finally, a third source of error was the distortion and misinterpretation of Olivi's teachings by the Beguins themselves.[2] The responsibility of Olivi, particularly his work on the Apocalypse, was a theme to which Gui returned frequently. Elsewhere he described how Olivi was venerated as the greatest of the Apostles, the only one, except for St. Paul, whose doctrines had never been challenged on any point by the church: 'But the entire doctrine of St. Paul and brother Peter John is to be held wholly by the church and not altered in a single letter'[3]—a singular fantasy in view of the series of censures which it had undergone, and even more when among Olivi's tenets that of Christ's lance wound, condemned at the Council of Vienne in *Fidei catholicae fundamento*,[4] was singled out for emphasis.[5] Nevertheless, the fact remains, attested not only by Gui but by the inquisitorial records, that Olivi was regarded by his followers not only as 'true and catholic' but as a saint: 'Also they commonly call the same brother Peter John uncanonized holy father.'[6] Some went even further, and identified him with the angel of the Apocalypse (Rev. 7: 2) 'whose face was like the sun, and he had in his hand an open book', because 'to him alone among all the doctors had been manifested the truth of Christ and the understanding of the Apocalypse'.[7]

Accordingly it was to Olivi that the Beguins turned for authority and guidance. No doubt this devotion was accentuated by the apocalyptic sense which he had himself helped to engender in them. 'They say', wrote Gui, 'that the writings and doctrines of the said Peter John are more necessary to the church of God in this time of the end of the world than the writings of any other doctors or saints, excepting those of the Apostles and the Evangelists; for he (Olivi) affords a greater understanding of the malice of Antichrist and his disciples, that is, the pharisees who are the priests and religious of these times.'[8] At the same time, it seems clear, a tradition had grown up which had made a cult of Olivi:

They say that if God had not provided the church of God with the said brother Peter John, or someone like him, the whole world would have been

---

[1] Ibid., 110-12. [2] Ibid., 112. [3] Ibid., 138.
[4] BF v, no. 196, 86; see pp. 155 ff. above. [5] *Manuel* I, 138.
[6] Ibid. [7] Ibid., 138-40. [8] Ibid., 140.

blind and heretical. Also, that they who do not accept the doctrine or scripture of the same brother Peter John are blind, since they do not feel or see the
truth of Jesus Christ; and those who censure and condemn his doctrine are
heretics. They also say that the said brother Peter John is the light and the
flame which God sent into the world, and those who do not see it walk in the
darkness.[1]

This veneration was largely due to the Beguin practice of meeting
together in conventicles to read Olivi,[2] itself the outcome of the long
Spiritual tradition in Provence, going back to the days of Hugh of
Digne. As we have already remarked, the most notable feature of
Provence was precisely this cohesion among the Spirituals and the local
populace; there can be little doubt that in the first quarter of the fourteenth century it owed much to Olivi as its focus.

With Olivi as the uncanonized saint and authority of the Provençal
Spirituals and Beguins, it is not difficult to infer that most of their
doctrines, however debased, were ultimately from him. This fact under-
lies the other three aspects of the movement in Provence. The first
two concern in greater or lesser degree Olivi's teaching; the third derives from the Beguins' own experiences: as treated by Gui, in the
aftermath of their defeat by the inquisition, they reflect the changes in
outlook wrought by their struggle.

So far as the first two are concerned, they can be treated along the
now familiar lines of poverty and prophecy. Bernard Gui regarded
their belief in Christ's absolute poverty as one of their main errors:
'The Beguins—or those commonly so-called, since they call themselves the poor brothers of penitence of the third order of St. Francis—
believe first that our lord Jesus Christ, as a man, and his Apostles
possessed nothing privately or in common, because in this world they
were perfectly poor. This they call perfect evangelical poverty. . . .'[3]
With this went their devotion to the *usus pauper*, the obligation to
which, following Olivi, they considered remained upon friars who
became bishops.[4] Since they regarded the evangelical poverty of the
Franciscan order as the highest state of perfection within the church,

---

[1] *Manuel* I, 140.
[2] dictosque libros [fratris Petri Johannis] in vulgari legunt sibi ipsis in suis familiaribus et amicis in suis conventiculis et in suis mansiunculis, quas vocant domos paupertatis, tali vocabulo usitato, et informant se et alias quos possunt ex doctrina pestifera
eiusdem (ibid., 142).
[3] Ibid., 118.
[4] Ibid., 126.

they treated its observance as perpetually binding.[1] They took up the Spirituals' outcry against the granting of granaries and vineyards, denying that the pope had the power to do so.[2]

It was in their apocalypticism, however, that the explosiveness of their outlook was most evident; it shows how, for all his personal moderation, Olivi had fashioned a vehicle of almost unlimited anti-ecclesiastical potential which, under the pressure of the inquisition, became realized. To begin with, the Beguins shared the commonly held Spiritual belief that 'the rule of St. Francis is the life of Jesus Christ, which he followed in this world and enjoined his apostles to observe'.[3] St. Francis himself was, after Christ and his mother (some also added the Apostles), the greatest exponent of the evangelical life and the renovator of the church in the present sixth age. Anyone who fought against or contradicted the rule of St. Francis was attacking Christ's evangel; and if he persisted in this, he became a heretic.[4] This applied to the pope[5] with, as we shall see, the widespread consequence that, among the Beguins, John XXII was considered heretical. Accordingly the rule was inviolate.[6] This latent defiance of authority becomes manifest in Gui's account of the Beguins' attitude towards the church and the coming of Antichrist. Here they went far beyond Olivi, even if he is, as with Gui, regarded as their instigator.

Reformed, or rather deformed, by the doctrines taken from the Postilla of brother Peter John they say that the carnal church, by which they understand the Roman church—not confined to the boundaries of Rome itself, but extending over all the territory of the Roman empire—is Babylon, the great whore of which John of the Apocalypse spoke.[7]

To this carnal church, to which the mass of the reprobate belonged, they contraposed the spiritual church, composed of spiritual and evangelical men living according to the life of Christ.[8] Not all the Beguins thought thus; others saw only one church, as Olivi did, to which both the carnal and the spiritual belonged. Where they all agreed was on the destruction of the carnal church, before the preaching of Antichrist, by king Frederick II and his accomplices, whom they called the ten kings to correspond with the ten horns of the beast of the

[1] Item, dicunt quod perfectior status qui sit in ecclesia dei est status ordinis fratrum minorum, qui paupertatem evangelicam voverunt et promiserunt . . . ubi paupertatem evangelicam promiserunt, ad quam servandam sunt perpetuo obligati (ibid., 126).
[2] Ibid., 120.   [3] Ibid.   [4] Ibid.   [5] Ibid.
[6] Ibid., 120-2.   [7] Ibid., 142.   [8] Ibid., 144.

Apocalypse.[1] The end of the sixth age, which had been initiated by St. Francis, would see Christ's rejection of Babylon, as the synagogue had been rejected previously; just as the Jews had crucified Christ, so the carnal church had crucified and persecuted the life of Christ in the persons of the Franciscan poor and Spirituals.[2]

Just as, after rejection of the synagogue, Christ had chosen a small number of elect who founded the primitive church, so after the rejection and destruction of the carnal church in the sixth age, which they say is the present one, there will remain the few elect, Spirituals and evangelical poor, belonging mainly to the two orders of St. Francis, the first and the third.[3] From these they will found the spiritual church, humble and good, in the seventh and last age of the church, which will begin with the death of Antichrist.[4]

As with Olivi, the Franciscans were to be the instrument of divine regeneration. They would be filled with the Holy Spirit.[5] There would be two Antichrists, the spiritual or mystic Antichrist, and the real or greater Antichrist, for whom the first (a pope) would be a preparation.[6] After the defeat of the first Antichrist the Spirituals would convert the Jews; the army which would arise would be of the angel having the sign of the living God—not unexpectedly St. Francis, his stigmata being the imprint of his divinity.[7]

So far, despite the exaggerations and crudities, the picture presented retains recognizable affinities with Olivi, but as such it was far from complete. The addition of elements alien to Olivi, and in many ways the most potent in the Beguin outlook, took three main forms. There was firstly the traumatic experience of the burning of the four Spirituals at Marseilles in 1318, for refusing to submit to the decrees of John XXII in *Quorumdam exigit* and recognize the authority of the Community. We shall mention the occurrence in due course; here its importance lies in its place in Beguin lore. More than any other single incident in the struggle between the ecclesiastical authorities and the Spirituals and Beguins, it became the central event in the Beguin calendar. Its victims were saints and martyrs, on a par with Olivi; and conversely its perpetrators were of Antichrist. The Spirituals' 'crime' was that they wished to preserve and maintain the purity, truth and poverty of the said rule of St. Francis; and because they refused to consent to the relaxation of the

---

[1] *Manuel* I, 144. [2] Ibid., 144–6.

[3] I.e. The full members of the order proper, and the penitents composed of pious laymen. The second order was that of St. Clare—the Poor Clares—for whom St. Francis drew up a rule. See Prologue p. 20 above.

[4] *Manuel* I, 146. [5] Ibid. [6] Ibid., 148. [7] Ibid.

rule or to accept the pope's dispensation from it or give obedience to him or others in respect of this, they were unjustly condemned for defending the truth of the evangelical rule. Therefore they were not heretics but Catholics and glorious martyrs . . .[1]

Some, according to Gui, regarded their execution as the spiritual crucifixion of Christ.

It had led to the making of relics from their burned remains: 'They conserved them, kissed them and venerated them as with the relics of other saints.'[2] In some cases their names and the dates of their condemnations had been inscribed into a calendar and invoked in Beguin litanies.[3] In short, they had given rise to a new martyrology. Secondly, the fate of the four Marseilles Spirituals affected the attitude of the Beguins not only to their own confrères, but inevitably to the pope and the church authorities as well. If men could be wrongly condemned, those who condemned them must themselves be culpable. The event, coming within two years of John XXII's offensive against the Spirituals, more than any other crystallized the hostility of the Beguins towards the pope. Henceforth he was regarded at the very least as a false pope, and, as we shall mention, frequently as Antichrist. The change in attitude towards him is expressed by Bernard Gui as follows:

They also say that if the lord pope ordered or approved this condemnation by the inquisitor, he is himself a heretic and the greatest of all, since he should, as head of the church, defend evangelical perfection. Accordingly, he has lost papal power and is no longer pope; he is not to be obeyed by any of the faithful, and the papal throne has become vacant.[4]

The church itself came under the same condemnation. Not only was it often, as we have seen, identified with the carnal church and Babylon. It was also accused of 'having become drunk with the blood of martyrs, that is of the four friars minor condemned and burned at Marseilles'.[5]

Thirdly the accumulated resentment against pope and church found fullest expression in the apocalyptic vision of the coming dénouement. All the religious orders would be destroyed by Antichrist's persecutions, except for the Franciscan order, which would be divided into three parts, the Community, the Fraticelli in Italy, and the Spirituals and

---

[1] Ibid., 128.   [2] Ibid., 132.   [3] Ibid., 134.
[4] Ibid. The pope was also a heretic for his bull *Quorumdam exigit* in which he dispensed the brothers from parts of the rule—e.g. having granaries and vineyards (ibid., 124–6).
[5] Ibid., 142.

their adherents observing the rule of St. Francis in its purity. Of these only the third would survive[1]—a sign, among other things, of the lack of contact between the Italian and Provençal dissident groups. As to the Antichrists, the first was John XXII whose persecutions they were suffering.[2] The second, and greater, Antichrist was already born, his advent being variously computed for the years 1325, 1330 and 1335.[3] After the destruction of the carnal church a series of great wars would follow causing vast carnage; France would be overrun by the Saracens, and Narbonne occupied; the women there would be raped until, with the death of Antichrist, the world would be converted to peace by the suffering disciples of St. Francis.[4] Bernard Gui ended his account of Beguin beliefs with an almost plaintive protest against their obloquy for John XXII.[5]

Although he was sometimes contradictory,[6] and, like most of his contemporaries, misconceived Olivi's *Postilla* on the Apocalypse, Gui's testimony is on the whole an authoritative summary of the Beguin outlook, which is authenticated from other sources. From our point of view it provides a valuable survey of the religious and ideological con-figuration of Provence during the period c. 1300–25. The actual course of events which formed its background has been frequently described.[7] Here only the salient ones will be recounted as a preliminary to con-sidering the Beguins themselves.

The Beguins were first officially mentioned at the council of Béziers presided over by the archbishop of Narbonne in 1299. Its fourth canon condemned them for violating the ban on new orders, and preaching without authorization. Their excuse that they were not preaching but

---

[1] Item, dogmatizant quod omnes religiones seu ordines destruantur in persecutione Antichristi, excepto ordine sancti Francisci quem distingunt in tres partes, quarum unam dicunt esse communitatem ordinis et secundam dicunt esse illos qui appellati sunt Fratisselli in Ytalia et tertiam dicunt esse tam in fratribus quos vocant spirituales servantibus spiritualem puritatem regule sancti Francisci quam in fratribus de tertio ordine eisdem adherentibus; et prime due partes, ut aiunt, destruentur et tertia remanebit usque ad finem mundi duratura . . . (ibid., 146).

[2] et dicunt esse primum Antichristum illum papam sub quo fiet et sub quo iam fit, ut aiunt, persecutio et condemnatio eorumdem (ibid., 148).

[3] Ibid.   [4] Ibid., 150.   [5] Ibid., 152.

[6] E.g. he early on describes some of them as leading a life of manual labour and others begging from door to door (ibid., 116). Later he implies that they did not want to work (ibid., 136).

[7] Ehrle, ALKG i–iv, Gratien, *Frères Mineurs*, and more recently R. Manselli, *Spirituali e Beghini in Provenza* (Rome 1959) who has utilized unpublished material from the Collection Doat (Bibliothèque Nationale, Paris).

communing with God was rejected, and they were prohibited from meeting.[1] Amongst other things they seemed to have been predicting the imminent ending of the world and the coming of Antichrist.[2] In the same year, also, as we know,[3] Olivi's writings were proscribed at the Franciscan chapter-general at Lyons. The course was set for the persecution of the Spirituals. There began the first phase of their tribulations, lasting until 1309, when Clement V summoned the leaders of the Community and the Spirituals to Avignon.[4] The three years of debate which followed at the papal court, with immunity granted by the pope to the Spirituals, were in the nature of a truce. But irreparable damage had already been done by the earlier repression. Ubertino of Casale, as we have already seen, gave three hundred as the number of Spirituals who had been imprisoned. Many were maltreated. Some died. Among them were Raymond Aureoli and John Primi of Villa-franca, whose names resound to Ubertino's indignation in his Vienne treatises. Accused of being followers of Olivi, they were sent to Aragon and imprisoned, where they died.[5]

These measures all took place under Gonsalvo of Valboa, who had succeeded John Minio of Murrovalle as Franciscan general in 1302. In due course, however, he was forced to modify his position under the impact of the charges being made by Ubertino and Gaufridi at Avignon. In early 1310 (or late 1309), in preparation for the chapter-general to be held at Padua, Gonsalvo issued an encyclical; in it he admitted to widespread relaxations of poverty and 'the monstrous abuse of dues', which were undermining the foundation of the order.[6] The Padua chapter decided to exclude all superfluities and to make them over to the church.[7] But in face of the fundamental division in outlook between the two parties, this could never have been more than a gesture, however sincerely intended. By this time, and indeed for the past generation, the Spirituals were separated from the Community not only by a different conception of poverty, but by an eschatology which

---

[1] Mansi, *Concilia* XXIV, 1215-18; Manselli, op. cit., 39-40.

[2] Manselli, op. cit., 40.   [3] See above p. 107.

[4] Angelo of Clareno (*Historia*, ALKG II, 359). It will be recalled that the initiative came from Arnold of Villanova. Arnold himself, in his interpretation of Frederick II of Sicily's dream, says that he prompted the king to intervene with the pope (Menendez Pelayo, III, 727-70).

[5] ALKG II, 300, and 386-7. Manselli, op. cit., 88 for this and other instances.

[6] Manselli, ibid., 90, quoting from Glassberger: *Chronica* (*Analecta Franciscana* II, 117.)

[7] Manselli, loc. cit.

had itself been moulded by the conflict. Persecution and schism had become accepted as their lot, to be borne with patience as a divine ordinance: it was the sign of election.

Another source of division between the two parties, so far as Provence was concerned, was the support of the citizens for the Spirituals in their strongholds at Narbonne, Béziers, Carcassonne, Lodève and elsewhere. It had grown up in the last years of the thirteenth century in common hostility against the Dominican-staffed inquisition; in the early years of the fourteenth century it crystallized into a movement of protest led by Bernard Délicieux and a group of prominent citizens, including John of Picquigny, honoured in the *Liber de Flore*.[1] Already as far back as 1280 there had been protests from Albi and Carcassonne to the king of France, Philip the Bold; and in 1285 to the pope, then Honorious IV.[2] Bernard Délicieux, himself a Provençal born at Montpellier, in addition to sharing the common Spiritual proclivities to mysticism and Joachism, was also a man of action and an alchemist like Arnold of Villanova. The movement of opposition that he created in 1297 became a force in its own right. At first it had nothing to do with the dissensions within the Franciscan order, though Bernard was himself a Minor. It was directed to gaining royal intervention to rectify the unjust sentences passed by the inquisition upon thirty-six suspects in Narbonne.[3] He and the other leaders like John of Picquigny gained access to Philip the Fair, the king, who, while giving them a certain degree of support, never actively took sides.[4] In 1303 Délicieux's exposure of fraudulence by the inquisition, over an earlier agreement, led to the burning of fifteen of its houses in Carcassonne and the organization of a citizens' militia;[5] they shortly after forced the transfer of the inquisition's detainees to the royal prison there.[6]

---

[1] See p. 185 above. The authoritative account of the movement is by M. Dmitrewski: 'Fr. Bernard Délicieux: sa lutte contre l'inquisition.' AFH 17 (1924) 183–218, 313–37, 457–88. AFH 18 (1925) 3–32.

[2] Dmitrewski, art. cit., 17, 191.

[3] Ibid., 198–204. According to R. W. Emery, *Heresy and Inquisition in Narbonne* (New York 1936) it was only in the fourteenth century that Narbonne became seriously troubled by the inquisition. It is surprising that his explanation for this change takes no account of the dissensions within the Franciscan order, and the ensuing struggle between the inquisition and the Spirituals and Beguins—surely the main reason.

[4] Ibid., 206–8. Philip did, after his first audience with Bernard Délicieux, fine the bishop of Albi 20,000 livres tournois (ibid., 208).

[5] Ibid., 215–17.   [6] Ibid., 314–15.

The ramifications of the movement extended to Spain and Italy. Délicieux was in contact with the house of Aragon and with Arnold of Villanova; he even in 1304 attempted unsuccessfully to transfer Carcassonne's allegiance from the king of France (because of his studious lack of support) to Ferrand, son of James of Marjorca.[1] This marked the movement's zenith. From then onwards it lost momentum. In April 1304 Benedict XI excommunicated John of Picquigny and ordered the arrest of Délicieux;[2] the latter, now increasingly absorbed in Joachist prophecy, was subsequently accused of complicity in Benedict XI's death (July 1304) which, like Arnold of Villanova, he had prophesied.[3] Although cleared, he was subsequently rearrested on a mission to Paris, at the end of 1304.[4] Meanwhile in Carcassonne the inquisition and repression took over: by September 1305 fifteen people had been hanged and the town fined 60,000 livres. Even some of the Dominicans protested against this severity.[5] In 1306 the new pope Clement V ordered an enquiry; Délicieux was once more released.[6] His fate subsequently became merged with the Spirituals of Provence: and in 1317 he was one of the sixty-two who were arrested by John XXII at Avignon, although he was tried separately for his erstwhile offences.[7] Already in a state of decline he never recovered; he was probably already dead by the time his sentence of degradation and perpetual imprisonment was pronounced.[8]

By the end of the first decade of the fourteenth century the different alignments had been formed. On the one hand was repressive authority which might vary in its specific relationship to the pope, but whose constant factors were the inquisition and the more intransigent leaders of the Franciscan Community. On the other there were the forces of dissent, a coalition of Spirituals, Beguins and Provençal citizens. Both sides were already in being, and had been in action, when Clement V imposed his truces of 1306, on the inquisition, and 1309, on the Community. When the second one was broken after the deaths of himself and Alexander of Alexandria, Franciscan general, in 1314, the struggle which ensued spread to all the different elements. The intervention of the new pope John XXII on the side of repression gave it a new character. It became total, ending with the destruction of the Spirituals and Beguins as a movement and the submission of the towns of Provence to the inquisition. The climax was reached in the years from 1317 to 1321.

[1] Ibid., 325–9.   [2] Ibid., 331.   [3] Ibid., 332–3.
[4] Ibid., 335–6.   [5] Ibid., 336–7 and 459.
[6] Ibid., 459–62.   [7] Ibid., 465–8.   [8] Ibid., 18, 3–19.

As has often been recounted, John XXII's election as pope in September 1316, following that of Michael of Cesena as Franciscan general a few months earlier at Naples, inaugurated a new period of activity after the double interregnum. They were faced with a state of open revolt within the order. On Alexander of Alexandria's death in 1314, the superiors favourable to the Spirituals, who had been instituted in Provence, were once more displaced by adherents of the Community. The case of Narbonne was especially grave, for William of St. Amantio, one of the leading Spirituals, was ousted by William of Astre, one of their main enemies.[1] Within a few months the Spirituals there and at Béziers had counter-attacked, and had once more taken over the convents. These became the rallying points for Spirituals far and wide, including five from the province of Aquitaine, who were excommunicated by Bertrand de la Tour, their provincial.[2]

In Italy matters had already gone further and were effectively out of control. At the end of 1312, as a reaction against persecution by the Community, the Spirituals of Florence, Arezzo and Siena had left their convents and taken over adjoining ones. Attempts to regain them by the Community had failed;[3] and in July 1313 Clement V addressed the bull *Ad nostri apostolatus* to the prelates of Genoa, Lucca and Bologna ordering them to make the Spirituals return to their obedience. This led to putting the convents under interdict and the excommunication of their inmates in 1314.[4] The rebels, under their leader, Henry of Ceva, fled to Sicily in the hope of finding asylum with Frederick II, Arnold of Villanova's protector. Despite the failure of James II to drive them out, they were ultimately compelled to migrate to Calabria. In due course they became known as the Fraticelli.[5]

Thus there was schism on two fronts. Different though their manifestations were—that of Tuscany never went beyond isolated migratory groups—their combined effect could only be to heighten tension and put a premium upon extreme measures. John XXII was the man to enforce them.[6] Himself more masterful than extreme, he could rapidly

[1] Oliger, DTC 14, art. cit., col. 2538.
[2] Ibid., See also L. Oliger, 'Fr. Bertrandi de Turre processus contra Spirituales Aquitaniae (1315)' AFH 16 (1923) 323–55.
[3] Oliger, DTC 14, cols. 2538–9; Angelo of Clareno, *Historia*, ALKG II, 139.
[4] Oliger, ibid., 2539.   [5] BF v, no. 297, p. 135a.
[6] For John XXII, see G. Mollat, *Les papes d'Avignon* (Paris 1950) 38–67; Baluze (ed. G. Mollat) *Vitae paparum Avenionensium* (Paris 1914–27) vol. III; N. Valois, 'Jacques Duèse, pape sous nom de Jean XXII', in *Histoire littéraire de France*, vol. 34 (Paris 1914) 391–630.

become so in the face of opposition. He was an authoritarian not a tyrant; but tyrannizing came naturally to him when roused. By training a canonist, he tended to see the theological and moral issues, which divided the order, in legal terms. Evangelical perfection became a question of discipline in which the desire to follow Christ was made to cede to the obligation to obey superiors, and Christ's absolute poverty revolved around the legality of enjoying use while disclaiming possession. Between the upper and the nether millstones there was no room for tender consciences: morality was contraposed to legality; or, to be fair to John, two different moralities, of which only one was legally admissible. A choice had to be made: those who chose to follow Christ *ipso facto* rejected the pope. In such circumstances it is not surprising that John fought not only the Spirituals but also the Community; nor that in each case the struggle became total on both sides. No pope ever utilized his authority more fully to confound his enemies.

In his dealings with the Spirituals John XXII was aided by Michael of Cesena, who from the outset was hostile to the Spirituals. On Michael's election, those in Provence made three requests to him: that he would confirm Clement V's deposition of the sixteen Provençal superiors; that the brothers should be allowed to observe the rule according to the decrees of the Council of Vienne, and not according to the partial judgement of the Community; and that the orthodoxy of the Minors of Narbonne and Béziers should be publicly recognized.[1] Although the only immediate reply was a counter-attack by Bertrand de la Tour and Bonagratia of Bergamo,[2] action was not long in coming from the new pope. First he wrote twice to the king of Aragon, Frederick II, asking for the expulsion of the Tuscan Spirituals in Sicily.[3] Next he charged two cardinals, Berengar Frédol and Arnold of Auch, to write to the Spirituals at Narbonne and Béziers ordering a return to obedience; on their refusing he entrusted the commission to Vital du Four and Napoleon Orsini.[4] Addressed to Michael of Cesena and the provincial of Provence,[5] it revealed the pope's attitude to the dissidents: the insistence upon authority. Since the brothers belonged to a single order they had to abide by its discipline; there could be no place for

[1] Ehrle, 'Die Spiritualen' ALKG IV, 60–61 quoted in Manselli, op. cit., 128.

[2] Manselli, ibid.

[3] BF v, no. 256, 110–11, March 1317; Manselli, op. cit., 130.

[4] Vital du Four was one of the Spirituals' most bitter opponents and Napoleon Orsini one of their main supporters. Manselli, op. cit., 130.

[5] BF v, 119n.–120n.

short and vile habits which differed from the rest, or for separate convents. To overcome these differences the brothers in question were to be distributed among the other convents.[1] This was tantamount to the overthrow of the entire Spiritual position without any concessions or guarantees. Five days later they were summoned to appear before the pope at Avignon within ten days, under pain of excommunication.[2] Angelo of Clareno's recital of how they marched north, a total of sixty-two brothers—forty-six from Narbonne, fifteen from Béziers, and Bernard Délicieux—remains the classic account:[3] of their arrival at the papal curia in the middle of a May night (22nd) and their vigil there until daylight; of their inquisition and arrest one by one as the pope rapidly lost patience with their explanations; of the few, like Ubertino of Casale, who stood up to him. They bear recalling because, although probably not even John XXII could foresee the outcome, it was in these incidents that the Spirituals' end was being enacted. Although most of them survived as individuals, those who entered the papal court that day vanished as a movement.[4]

The Spirituals' summons to Avignon was followed by the return of the convents of Narbonne and Béziers to the Community; then in October 1317 came the bull *Quorumdam exigit*.[5] This was the rod with which John XXII broke the Spirituals. It constituted a definitive interpretation of the points at issue, in terms of discipline. In John's own words: 'Poverty is great, but integrity is greater; and obedience is the greatest good.' Poverty was concerned with goods, obedience with the mind and spirit.[6] It was the argument of one who did not see beyond legal definitions; after the passion of St. Francis and the perception of Bonaventura it remains something of a descent from the heights to see the attributes of poverty handled so jejunely. For those who believed in its spiritual quality, as the Spirituals did, it was an affront to their *raison d'être* as Minors. More specifically, it granted their superiors the power to regulate habits and to hold granaries and vineyards to assure the necessities of life.[7]

---

[1] BF v, 119n.–120n.   [2] Ibid., no. 266, 118–20.

[3] *Historia*, ALKG II, 142–9.

[4] Douie, *Fraticelli*, 18–20, gives a vivid, if somewhat effusive, rendering of the main incidents.

[5] BF v, n.289, 128–30.

[6] Magna quidem paupertas, sed maior integritas; bonum est obedientia maximum . . . Nam prima rebus, secunda carni, tertia vero menti dominatur et animo (ibid., 130b).

[7] Ibid.

After the bull's publication Michael of Cesena sought to gain its acceptance by the Spirituals imprisoned in the curia. In the presence of Bonagratia of Bergamo they were read its contents on 12 October 1317, and over the next two days they were individually required to make their submission to its demands: to wear the normal long habit and to discard their short habits; to accept the general minister's decisions over granaries and vineyards; and to obey his authority and the bull.[1] At the end 25 remained adamant; one group of seven among those who refused, said that the concessions of granaries and vineyards and long habits was 'contrary to Christ's evangelical counsel and the highest poverty which he had observed and imposed on the Apostles'; it therefore contradicted their own promise in the rule to observe Christ's evangel.[2] Others like Arnold Raymondi were prepared to change their habit but not to accept granaries and cellars, for the same reason as the seven—that it derogated from the highest poverty.[3] All the dissentients were united in the belief that evangelical perfection lay in absolute poverty and that the bull would undermine it.

John XXII was not slow to take action. Within a month, on 8 November, he had instructed Michael Lemoine to proceed against the 25 regardless of any special concessions they may have received from Celestine V or Clement V, his predecessors.[4] The Dominican inquisitor, the Spirituals' most implacable persecutor, who was said to have tried to dissuade Clement V from granting them immunity,[5] was entrusted with the task in what seems to have been a special capacity.[6] By the beginning of May 1318, the number of obdurate had been reduced to five.[7] Of these four were condemned as heretics and handed over to the

[1] The document containing Michael of Cesena's declaration and his interrogation of the brothers is printed in Manselli, *Spirituali*, appendix II, 291–6 from MS. Latin 4350, B.N., Paris.

[2] Ibid., 295.

[3] Ibid., 293.

[4] BF V, n.293, 132–3, cited by Manselli, op. cit., 150.

[5] BF V, n.203, 89; Manselli, ibid., makes this inference.

[6] J. M. Vidal, *Bullaire de l'Inquisition*, 38–9: 'ex speciali commissione sanctissimi patris et domini Domini Johannis divina providentia pape XXII inquisitor et iudex contra quosdam pseudo fratres heretica labe respersos eisque adherentes ubilibet per totum ordinem deputatus (ms deputatos), ac etiam reverendi patris fratris Michaelis, generalis ministri prefati ordinis, commissarius in hac parte'; quoted in Manselli, op. cit., 157–8 n. 1, who was the first to draw attention to the fact.

[7] The full account is in Michael Lemoine's deposition of the sentence contained *Misc.* II, 248–51. It gives an elaborate recital of the stages of consultation through which he went—calling in bishops, prelates, masters and bachelors of theology, and

secular arm, and burned at Marseilles on 6 May 1318. The other was
sentenced to perpetual imprisonment.[1] Their crime was that for which
they had already been arraigned: namely the refusal to accept the decree
of *Quorumdam exigit* and obey its provisions over habits, granaries and
cellars. To the ecclesiastical authorities the issue was disobedience; to
the Spirituals it was evangelical perfection.[2] Persecution soon spread to
the Beguins, its harvest ripening from devotion to poverty and Olivi
into full-fledged Joachist anti-sacerdotalism of the kind we encountered
in Bernard Gui's testimony. Before long the questions of habits,
granaries and cellars had become part of the wider struggle of the
righteous against the iniquities of Antichrist and the carnal church. A
letter written by some Spiritual fugitives shortly after the Marseilles
executions already expresses these beliefs; as the death of Antichrist
would be followed by the extermination of those who had betrayed
Christ, so the death of the present pope—John XXII—would see the
triumph of those who had been true to Christ and suffered for him.[3]
Within the next few years they became widespread.

Early on, the authorities saw Olivi's writings, especially his *Postilla*

---

communicating with the papal curia—before finally condemning them as heretics.
He had also called in the bishop of Marseilles, Raymond, in an effort to make the
heretics see the gravity of their fault; and had finally had the errors read in consistory
and confirmed as heretical (ibid., 248–9).

[1] J. M. Vidal, *Bullaire de l'Inquisition*, 249–50.

[2] [quod papa] non habuit nec habet auctoritatem nec potestatem faciendi quasdam
declarationes, commissiones et praecepta contenta in quadam constitutione sive
decretali . . . quae incipit 'Quorundam', et quod ipsi domino papae non tenebantur
obedire, maxime in eo quod ipse in ipsa constitutione virtute obedientiae et sub
excommunicationis poena mandavit quod praenominati . . . eorumque complices
quosdam habitus curtos et strictos a communitate memorati ordinis discrepantes, quos
assumpserant, deponerent, et aliis secundum ipsius generalis ministri arbitrium sive
iudicium induerentur, ipsique generali ministro in habitu et forma sive figura habitus
et quaestu bladi et vini pro vitae necessariis fratrum, etiamsi reponenda essent in
granariis et cellariis conservanda et in omnibus aliis et per omnia secundum beati
Francisci regulam et declarationes editas super eam et constitutionem sive ordina-
tionem ipsius domini papae Iohannis humiliter obedirent, et pertinaciter asseruerunt
illam blasphemiam in sanctam sedem Romanam, videlicet quod ea quae in constitutione sive decretali de habitu et quaestu et similibus mandabantur, erant contra
consilium Christi evangelicum et eorum votum de altissima et evangelica paupertate
quam Christus servavit et Apostolis ac professoribus evangelicis imposuit ad servandum,
et quod nulli mortalium cum secura conscientia in eis poterant obedire (ibid., 248a–b).

[3] Ibid., 272; quoted also in Manselli, op. cit., 159–60. The views were contained
in a letter written by Michael Lemoine to the curia at Avignon.

on the Apocalypse, as the main influence. Doubtless they were correct. At the time of the Marseilles sentences, Michael Lemoine blamed Olivi's *Postilla* and said his works should be burned.[1] In 1318, his tomb at Narbonne, which had long been a centre of devotion, was destroyed and his remains removed.[2] The same year saw a Catalan compendium of the work in circulation: *De statibus ecclesie secundum expositionem Apocalypsis*.[3] While following the structure of Olivi's *Postilla* it went beyond him, just as the Beguins did in their eschatological speculations, by naming names unnamed by Olivi and inserting dates which Olivi had left blank. At the end of the second state Babylon would be destroyed and the spiritual church, composed of the Minors and others true to Christ, would come into being. Olivi would be its master. The mystic Antichrist who would condemn the life and teaching of Christ would be a pope. The Roman church had become the carnal church and the pope John XXII its Herod in his desire to destroy Christ's evangel. The progression is a familiar one, and in the circumstances inevitable. Olivi's *Postilla*, as we saw in the last chapter, became the subject of an official investigation and was finally condemned in 1326.[4]

This offensive against the Spirituals and their Beguin followers continued until about 1325 by when their resistance had been effectively broken. The last great trial was that of Adhémar of Mosset, between 1332 and 1334.[5] A knight of Roussillon, he was accused by James the king of Majorca in whose service he was, of being a Beguin. It seems probable that the motives were personal grievance and had no real foundation; certainly, Adhémar consistently refused to confess to what

---

[1] Et quia constat nobis quod praefati errores, immo haereses, manifeste processerunt sive originem habuerunt a venenato fonte doctrinae, immo verius seductrinae, quam frater Petrus Johannis Olivi Biterensis diocesis super Apocalypsi(m) et in quibusdam eius opusculis contra honorem sanctae Romanae ecclesiae et auctoritatem eiusdem temere scriptitavit, et doctrinam eius et libros dicti fratris Petri tamquam continentes et dogmatisantes errores fidei catholicae et sacramentis ecclesiasticis (*Misc.* II, 249b–250a).

[2] Reported in Bernard Gui: Fuit autem corpus eius inde extractum et alibi portatum et absconditum, sub anno domini MoCCCoXVIIIo; set ubi sit a pluribus dubitatur et diversi diversa circa hoc locuntur et dicunt (*Manuel* I, 192).

[3] J. Pou y Marti, *Visionarios, beguinos y fraticelos*, 483–512, for its refutation by Guy of Terrena general of the Carmelites and Peter of Palud, after having examined it, 483–512. Also Manselli, op. cit., 164–7.

[4] Baluze, *Misc.* II, 258–70 for the sixty censored articles.

[5] J.-M. Vidal, 'Procès d'inquisition contre Adhémar de Mosset, noble roussillonais, inculpé de béguinisme (1332–1334)' in *Revue d'histoire de l'église de France* I (1910) 555–89, 682–99, 711–24; Pou y Marti, op. cit., 171 ff.

had become the stock inquisitorial questions for Franciscan Joachism: whether he believed in the coming age of the Holy Spirit and a new spiritual order, and whether he was devoted to Olivi. Of his conviction or otherwise we do not know. After this case, the Beguins fade from the scene. If the main cause of their disappearance was repression, their own apocalyptic beliefs doubtless contributed: expectations of imminent change cannot be sustained indefinitely; when the tribulations mount and the years pass without relief, hope in the future must wane. It is in the nature of all such beliefs that they are too intense to last and usually burn themselves out.

The testimonies of the Beguins

When we turn to the testimonies of the Beguins themselves, the accusations of Michael Lemoine and Bernard Gui are abundantly confirmed. While they, like the papal commission on the *Postilla* on the Apocalypse, misrepresented Olivi's views they were not over-stating their (for them pernicious) effect upon the Beguins. As we have earlier seen from Bernard Gui, Olivi was the sun in the Beguin firmament;[1] his authority outshone all others', and his prophecies, usually debased into the crudest eschatology, lighted their future. The influence of Olivi, there can be no doubt, was the source of Beguin eschatology precisely because it provided the one ingredient needed for all such belief, namely authority. Moreover it differed from the Apocalypse of St. John in seemingly being addressed to them. Olivi was a Provençal; his *Postilla*, as we have seen, mentioned his own town of Béziers; he had lived much of his life there; and long before his death he had been associated with Provençal followers—called a sect by his enemies. The Beguins' faith in him was therefore well nurtured. Even if it did not become apocalyptic before say 1318, they had been practising an Olivi cult long before then. It is not unreasonable to suppose that the two elements of poverty and prophecy were present from the first, if in differing degrees, and even if prophecy did not come to predominate until after the Marseilles burnings in 1318. If Olivi provided the authority his teachings provided the inspiration which helped to shape the Beguins' eschatology: if it only materialized under inquisitional pressure it was latent from the beginning.

The most heightened form in which Olivi's influence is to be found

---

[1] This is how it is actually described in the *Compendium* on the Apocalypse: 'facies eius erat sicut sol'. Pou y Marti, op. cit., 501–2; Manselli, op. cit., 182–3.

among the Beguins is the confession of Prous Boneta in 1325.[1] It is
exceptional not only in length; but also because it was conceived more
as a vision than as a series of beliefs. Prous Boneta lived in Montpellier
and had as a child made a pilgrimage to Olivi's tomb at Narbonne.
Fifteen years later, as a consequence, she received the three gifts of the
Holy Spirit.[2] Her testimony was in the same revelatory vein. She recounted how once, in the Franciscan church at Montpellier, the service
having ended and the church emptied, she was transported in spirit to
the first heaven by Christ, who, in the form of a man, then spoke to her.
He told her that on the day she had gone to Olivi's tomb she had been
born to God in spirit, after nine months of conception.[3] He then went on
to explain the future apocalyptic course of events. Christ's evangel had
been extinguished with the condemnation of Olivi's writing—almost
certainly the *Postilla* on the Apocalypse, since it is used in the singular
(*scriptura*). This had led to the withdrawal of God's grace; the sacrament of the eucharist had lost its truth, and writings of the Holy Spirit
(which had been transmitted to Olivi) destroyed.[4] This in turn implicated John XXII, who, in condemning Olivi, had like Ciaphas,
crucified Christ; in contrast his predecessor, Clement V, was compared
to the good man who put Christ's body into the tomb.[5] We are left in
no doubt that John XXII was the villain. Like Adam, he had lost God's
grace and could never regain it.[6] As Adam's sin was too great to re-
deem him when he had eaten the apple so was John XXII's after he had
sent the Minors to their death.[7] He had sinned also for declaring that

---

[1] It has been edited by W. H. May, 'The confession of Prous Boneta, heretic and
heresiarch' in *Essays in Medieval Life and Thought, presented in honour of A. P. Evans*
(New York 1955) 3–30. I have used the manuscript text, Collection Doat, vol. 27,
B.N., Paris, ff. 51v–82r. May in his introductory remarks suggested dualist influences
as well as Joachist ones. This seems doubtful.   [2] Doat 27, f. 56.

[3] . . . in tali die ipse dominus deus concepit ipsam Naprous in spiritu, et quod ipsa
die eadem qua ipsa fuit in Narbona supra sepulchrum dicti fratris Petri Johannis,
ipse dominus peperit eam in spiritu et dedit sibi ipse deus tria [dona] . . . (Doat, 27,
f. 56r-v).

[4] quando destructum fuit evangelium Christi tunc incepit deficere in parte gratia
dei, scilicet quando scriptura fratris Petri Johannis fuit condemnata, quia tunc sacramentum altaris suam perdidit veritatem. . . . Item asseruit quod deus dixit sibi quod
Christus duas naturas habuit . . . et quod contra naturam divinam destructa est
scriptura spiritus sancti qui datus erat dicto fratri Petro Johannis (ibid., f. 57v–58r).

[5] Ibid., f. 58r.   [6] Ibid., f. 6or.

[7] Item dixit sibi Christus quod ita magnum fuit peccatum istius pape [Johannes
XXII] quando tradidit morti fratres minores quam magnum fuit peccatum Ade
quando comedit pomum (ibid., f. 59r).

Christ and the Apostles held possessions privately and in common, whereas they had observed the highest poverty; in this they had been followed by St. Francis and his disciples.[1] For these reasons Christ called the pope 'by the most horrible of all names, Antichrist'.[2] Prous then recounted what Christ had told her of St. Francis and Olivi: he likened St. Francis to Elias who had borne witness to the life of evangelical poverty initiated by Christ. Olivi was Enoch in his testimony to the divinity of the scriptures.[3] Antichrist had killed both.[4] It was to Olivi, however, that Prous devoted her main interest. He, not St. Francis, was *par excellence* the herald of the new age and its personification. She frequently referred to him as holy father, and she regarded his writings as the voice of the Holy Spirit. She dated the beginning of the new era of the church (she did not specify whether it was the seventh age or the third state) from his appearance; all that he had said was to be believed as the gospel of the Holy Spirit.[5] In this Prous appears to have gone both farther back and farther beyond any other Joachist in the Franciscan milieu. On the one hand, she was nearer to Joachim than any of them—Olivi included—in actually thinking in terms of a gospel of a third age, differently as she conceived it from the Calabrian abbot. Like Gerard of Borgo San Donnino she was concerned to find literal counterparts to Joachim's figurative expressions. Thus Olivi's was the new gospel of the Holy Spirit; it replaced the sacraments, such as the eucharist and confession; they were no longer necessary: only belief in the Holy Spirit.[6] On the other hand, the substitution of Olivi for St. Francis, and his writings for the bible, was to overstep by far previous limits; it was to turn Franciscan Joachism into an Olivi cult. St. Francis, it is true, did not entirely disappear, as we have already seen: he remained the angel of the sixth seal, 'having the seal of

---

[1] Doat, f. 61r–v.   [2] Ibid., f. 62r–v.

[3] Item dixit sibi Christus, ut asserit, . . . quod ille Elias fuit sanctus Franciscus, et ille Enoch fuit sanctus pater, frater Petrus Johannis. . . . Ita videlicet quod sanctus Franciscus portavit testimonium pauperis vitae quam Christus incepit, et frater Petrus Johannis tulit testimonium divinitatis in sancta scriptura . . . (ibid., f. 64v–65r).

[4] Ibid., f. 64v.

[5] quod credat verbis quae ipsemet dixit, que omnia dixit esse opus spiritus sancti, asserens quod tempus novum dicti spiritus sancti et novus status ecclesiae habuit initium in dicto fratre Petro Johannis, et consequenter in ipsa quae loquitur, sicut dixit, et sic nunc est status ecclesiae novus in quo credere oportet in opere spiritus sancti (ibid., f. 76r).

[6] Ibid., f. 77r, although the sacrament of penance still remained: sed sacramentum poenitentiae adhuc dicit remanere.

the living God'; but he was effectively subordinated to Olivi, who was the angel with a face like the sun, and came directly next to the third angel who was identified as the Holy Spirit.[1] The audacity of Prous's images was of course exceptional; the Holy Spirit, Christ, and Olivi, and indeed herself, as Olivi's spiritual counterpart, were all on the same plane.[2] It was a vision, after all; yet it was made from the common materials of Franciscan Joachism; despite its manifest inconsistencies and blasphemies, it had an underlying coherence. Its framework was trinitarian; Prous, here too, came nearer to Joachim in her awareness of periods: of the three states, the first, of the Father, had run from the beginning of the world until the birth of Christ; the second, of the Son, until God had endowed Olivi with the Holy Spirit.[3] Just as Christ had struggled in single combat with Antichrist, so did the writing (*scriptura*) of the Holy Spirit given to Olivi (and also to Prous).[4] The strangeness of her world is due, besides her own deranged state, to its highly personal nature; her mere half-dozen characters bear little relation to the hordes of pseudo-prophets, at war with the disciples of Christ. Nevertheless Prous in her sanctification of Olivi and her condemnation of John XXII was talking of common experiences. She was also influential because of the revelatory form her views took; and a number of Beguins, particularly women, quoted her.

The majority of testimonies followed Bernard Gui's account, and their recurrent topics, of Olivi, the Marseilles martyrs, granaries and cellars, the Franciscan rule, John XXII, reflected, of course, the inquisitors' questions put to them. Some were more individual, like Bernard di na Jacma,[5] who in addition to holding the full range of Beguin beliefs (in the sanctity of Olivi; the inviolable evangelical nature of the rule, and the powerlessness of the pope to dispense from it; the innocence and orthodoxy of the Marseilles and other Spirituals who

---

[1] Ibid., f. 79r.

[2] With Prous and Olivi, if anything, higher upon it. God, she said, ruled the church by two material bodies, Christ and Mary, and two spiritual bodies, Olivi and Prous: Item dixit quod quemadmodum deus reget ecclesiam per duo corpora carnis, scilicet corpora Christi et Mariae, eodem modo reget ecclesiam per duo corpora spiritus dati fratri Petro Johannis praedicto et etiam spiritus dati ipsi Naprous loquenti (ibid., f. 80r).   [3] Ibid., f. 66r.

[4] Item dixit sibi Christus . . . quod filius dei bellavit cum diabolo solus pro solo, et quod simili modo scriptura sancti spiritus dati dicto fratre Petro Johannis bellavit cum Antichristo sola pro solo et dixit illi deus . . . quod ipsamet Naprous erat illa cui debebat dari spiritus sanctus (ibid., f. 66v–67r).

[5] P. A. Limborch, *Liber Sententiarum*, 307–9.

P

had been burned, and were martyrs; the errors of the pope and the inquisitors in prosecuting them; and the poverty of Christ and the Apostles[1]) also believed in the three ages. The second would end with the coming of Antichrist and the persecution of evangelical poverty, and would be succeeded by a 'time of benignity'.[2] The Roman church, which would be identified with carnal church, the great whore of Babylon, would then be replaced by a new church, as the synagogue of the Jews had been rejected for the church of Christ.[3] There would be a mystic and a great Antichrist; but Bernard was undecided whether John XXII was the former or whether the two Antichrists were not one. He believed, however, that the great Antichrist would have run his course and be dead by 1330,[4] making the end of the second age imminent. It would be brought about through the election of a false pope from among the spiritual fugitives in Sicily—probably Henry of Ceva or Angelo of Clarena—by Frederick II. The pope would then flee, and Frederick, together with nine other kings, would attack and destroy the kingdom of France.[5] The identification of the two Spirituals' leaders with Antichrist could have been due, as Manselli has suggested, to a feeling of desertion through their withdrawal from the immediate struggle.[6] It may also have been due to muddled thinking of which there is abundant evidence among the testimonies. Bernard himself had clearly attempted to work things out for himself, and this probably explains his occasional uncertainties. He also showed signs of some-thing of the same mystic sense as Prous, which, though not sustained,[7] may have made for a certain incoherence.

---

[1] P. A. Limborch, *Liber Sententiarum*, 307–8.

[2] Item dixit quod se credidisse quod tria tempora erant ecclesie. . . . Secundum tempus incepit a Christo, et durabit usque ad Antichristum vel usque ad persecucionem vite evangelice, quod tempus est appropriatum filio. Et tercium tempus erit usque ad finem mundi, quod erit tempus benignitatis, et est appropriatum spiritui sancto (ibid., 308).

[3] Item dixit se credidisse quod sicut synagoga Judeorum fuit reprobata et rejecta adveniente ecclesia primitiva, quia crucifixit Christum, ita adveniente nova ecclesia in tercio statu reprobabitur et rejicietur ecclesia ista nostra, quia persequetur et perse-quitur vitam domini Jesu Christi in viris evangelicis, et succedet tercia ecclesia. Item dixit se credidisse quod ecclesia Romana, quam ipse ecclesiam carnalem apellat, sit illa babilon meretrix magna . . . (ibid.).

[4] Item dixit se credidisse quod infra annum quo computabitur incarnacio domini M° ccc° xxx Antichristus maior fecerit cursum suum et erit mortuus (ibid.).

[5] Ibid., 309.   [6] Manselli, op. cit., 199.

[7] E.g., Item dixit quod ipse existens in quadam passione semel dixit quod adhuc dominus Jesus Christus in sua propia persona crucifigeretur (Limborch, 309).

Another more wide-ranging spirit was William Dominici Verrerrii, a candlemaker from Narbonne, who had long been a fugitive and publicly excommunicated.[1] He believed that Olivi was an uncanonized saint now in paradise, and that his writings and doctrines were likewise good and holy and had been approved by the Council of Vienne.[2] He also believed in Christ's absolute poverty.[3] From a certain Minor he had heard that by the eleventh horn of the beast, of which John of the Apocalypse spoke, was to be understood a certain poor king who would be elected by a false pope, his creature. The false pope would be Angelo of Clareno, who would then desert his order, the most exalted and best in the world: ten kings from the East would then rise against him. They would humiliate the church, especially the eleventh king.[4] Meanwhile a band of twelve Minors would journey to Greece and convert the Greeks and afterwards the Saracens. They would return to the Roman church and say: 'You others have killed the friends of God.'[5] For William Dominici Verrerrii, John XXII was a heretic and the mystic Antichrist, who would precede the great Antichrist as John the Baptist had come before Christ.[6] The reason was that he had been responsible for the burning of the four Spirituals at Marseilles, who had sought to observe in purity their vow of evangelical perfection against the pope's attempt to impose granaries and cellars and long habits upon them.[7]

William was clearly exceptional, with an awareness of the outside world, as his references to Vienne and Greece—which might have been drawn from Liberato's exploits—and Angelo of Clareno show. He was against authority at every point. The majority of those interrogated

---

[1] Published in Manselli, op. cit., 321-4, from Collection Doat vol. 28, ff. 240r-245v.

[2] Item fratrem Petrum Iohannis quondam ordinis minorum credidit esse sanctum in paradiso non canonizatum et eius scripturam seu doctrinam credidit esse bonam et sanctam et approbatam fuisse asserit per concilium Viennense (Manselli, ibid., 321).

[3] It emquod Iesus Christus non habuit aliquid in proprio nec in communi (ibid.).

[4] Ibid., 321-2.

[5] Ibid., 322.

[6] et etiam quod iste dominus Iohannes papa erat misticus Antichristus, quia sicut beatus Iohannes Baptista paravit viam Iesu Christo, ita iste dominus Iohannes parat et paravit vias illi maiori Antichristo futuro (ibid.).

[7] Item habebant dictum dominum Iohannem papam suspectum quod esset hereticus et misticus Antichristus pro eo quod condamnaverat quattuor minores Massilie condemnatos et combustos, vel quia fecit eos condemnari, pro eo quod petebant puram observationem votorum suorum et quia dominus papa fecerat decretalem super granariis et celariis habendis per eos et disposuerat de eorum habitibus (ibid.).

tended to repeat the standard opinions on Olivi, John XXII, granaries and cellars, the four Spirituals of Marseilles, the carnal church, with little variation. This was primarily because these were the questions asked them, as Bernard Gui's description of the form of interrogation shows.[1] In that sense the awareness by the authorities of what they were seeking played a part in what they found; but only formally. These testimonies were the Beguins' beliefs recounted again and again. The part played by the cult of Olivi cannot be over-estimated. By 1320 it had been established for a generation during which his writings had helped to mould the outlook of an entire sect. His identification with the angel of the Apocalypse 'whose face was like the sun', holding in his hand an open book was more than figurative; it expressed the Beguin faith in him as the divinely-inspired source of their illumination, which through his writings had been made known to them. Confession after confession tells not only of his sanctity but of instruction from his works which had been read in the vernacular. Of these by far the most common was his *Postilla* on the Apocalypse. In its popular rendering it had become a handbook of anti-papalism, far removed from the studied non-commitment of the original. Thus Peter Hospitalis, who claimed to have heard it read in the vernacular at more than thirty different places, understood from it that the Roman church was Babylon.[2] So did Peter Dominici and William Ruffi for whom its persecutions—drunk with the blood of martyrs—and wealth had taken it away from Christ.[3] Both treated Olivi as a sacred authority: Dominici went so far as to claim that even should the pope condemn his doctrine in a thousand bulls, or with the assent of an entire general council, it would remain true.[4] William Ruffi was more temperate, merely averring that his teacher was 'good and catholic' and that he was a holy father and a great doctor and the angel described in the Apocalypse

---

[1] *Manuel* I, 156–74.

[2] de qua postilla audivit ipse pluries legi etiam plus quam xxx vicibus in vulgari, et plura se audivisse et retinuisse recognovit, et specialiter quod frater Petrus Johannis exponit in dicta postilla Romanam ecclesiam esse illam babilonem magnam meretricem . . . (Limborch, *Liber Sententiarum*, 388.)

[3] Item asserit se credere et tenere esse vera illa que frater Petrus Johannis scripsit in postilla super apocalipsim de babilone meretrice magna sedente super bestiam, per quam intelligit et exponit esse ecclesiam Romanam (ibid., 385; for Ruffi, ibid., 316).

[4] Item asserit quod si papa condempnaret doctrinam seu scripturam prefati Petri Johannis, ipse non reputaret eam condempnatam quantumcunque poneret dictam condempnacionem sub mille bullis et quantumque condempnaret eam de consilio cardinalium et omnium prelatorum, vel eciam tocius concilii generalis (ibid., 385).

with a face like the sun. God had specially chosen Olivi to tell of the final age of the church and to warn of the coming of Antichrist.[1] William also claimed to have heard Olivi's works read many times in the vulgar tongue.[2] So likewise did Peter Calveti, who believed that they had been approved by Clement V.[3] For Maria de Serra, as for many other Beguins, Olivi was their father and an uncanonized saint, since it had been reserved for God alone to sanctify him in life and death.[4] The same view was held by Matthew Terrenus, who, with William Ruffi, believed that the future had been revealed to Olivi by God;[5] while Raymond Stephan, in addition to taking him as the authority for identifying the Roman church with the carnal church,[6] defended the doctrine of Christ's absolute poverty and the Spirituals' refusal to accept granaries and vineyards in his name.[7] But this was unusual. Although, as we shall mention, evangelical poverty played a central role for the Beguins, they looked to Olivi, at least in their testimonies, for his guidance upon the future. He was not always misinterpreted, even if, as with Raymond de Buxo, conclusions were drawn which were not Olivi's: thus after correctly confining the carnal church to the reprobate within the Roman church, Raymond then went on to deduce, from Olivi's words, the death of Antichrist within fourteen years.[8] The same number was given by Peter Hospitalis,[9]

---

[1] Item quod tota doctrina fratris Petri Johannis Olivi est vera et catholica, et habuit eam per illuminacionem spiritus sancti, per quam cognovit veritatem evangelicam et regule sancti Francisci, quem vocant sanctum patrem et magnum doctorem, et quod est ille angelus de quo scribitur in Apocalipsi, quod facies eius erat ut sol, et habebat librum apertum in manu sua, et quod illi clarius fuit revelatum tempus futurum, et illa que debent contingere pro tempore futuro, quam alicui alii doctori (ibid., 316).

[2] Item ipse frequenter audivit legi sibi et aliis in diversis locis de libris in scriptis predicti fratris P. Johannis in vulgari transpositis (ibid.).

[3] Ibid., 318.

[4] Item dixit se audivisse in sermone publico in Narbona quando fiebat festum de fratre P. Johannis quod dictus frater P. Johannis erat pater eorum et sanctus non canonizatus, et non opportebat quod per hominem canonizaretur, quia deus canonizaverat eum in vita et morte, ut dicebant, et ipsa credidit ista esse vera (ibid., 319).

[5] Ibid., 320–1.   [6] Ibid., 322.   [7] Ibid.

[8] Item credidit informatus per scripturam dicti fratris P. Johannis quod infra XIIII annos computandos a presenti tempore Antichristus maior complevisset cursum suum (ibid., 298).

[9] Item credit et asserit quod Antichristus et eius persecutio erit et fiet infra breve tempus . . . opinatur tamen quod erit infra annos XIIII consumpmata (ibid., 388).

which, since their inquisitions took place in 1321, would have made 1335 the year of the beginning of the third age. Calculation varied, 1330 being, as we have seen, the date for Bernard di na Jacma, and 1325 for Peter Moresii.[1] This, of itself, is of little significance: it was the making of the calculations—and the apocalyptic expectations they expressed—which was. Condemnation of Olivi's writings, even when it was acknowledged as having taken place—many Beguins believed that his doctrine had been approved at the Council of Vienne[2]—made no difference; indeed it only hardened conviction in the pope's culpability.

The Beguins' dissociation from any sense of obedience to the pope is perhaps the most striking feature of their attitude. For them the pope had irredeemably lost his authority; whether he was the mystic Antichrist or just a heretic was an opinion which varied, but that he was not the rightful pope was universally accepted. This was tantamount to open rebellion as we can see from the uncompromising indifference of Peter Moresii to papal enactments: he not only believed that Olivi's teaching had, alone with St. Paul's, remained unrefuted by the church, and was to be held to the very letter, Olivi having received the same revelation as the other holy doctors;[3] but that any condemnation of it was *ipso facto* unjust: besides such censures having no power to bind they rendered those responsible for them—whether pope or general council—heretical.[4] In particular, after defending Olivi's doctrine of Christ's spear wound from the Council of Vienne's admonition, he openly rejected the findings of John XXII's commission of eight theologians who had condemned the sixty articles taken from the *Postilla* on the Apocalypse.[5] Peter Moresii's challenge is all the more remarkable for being made from knowledge rather than ignorance; he was clearly

[1] Limborch, *Liber Sententiarum*, 303.

[2] E.g., Bernard di na Jacma (ibid., 308), William Ruffi (ibid., 316), Peter Tort (ibid., 329).

[3] Item quod non fuit aliquis doctor excepto sancto Paulo et predicto fratre Petro Johannis cuius aliqua dicta non fuerint per ecclesiam refutata, set scriptura et doctrina sancti Pauli et predicti fratris P. Johannis est tenenda totaliter per ecclesiam, nec est una lit[t]era dimittenda. . . . Item quod revelacio sancte scripture facta fuit eidem sicut alicui de sanctis doctoribus (ibid., 306).

[4] Item quod si doctrina predicti fratris P. Johannis per ecclesiam condempnaretur talis condempnatio esset iniusta, et si dominus papa condempnaret cum concilio generali et si dominus papa excommunicaret illos qui tenerent contrarium talis excommunicationis sentencia tenentes contrarium non ligaret. Item quod quicunque scripturam seu doctrinam predicti fratris P. Johannis in toto vel in parte condempnaret esset hereticus ex hoc facto (ibid.).

[5] Ibid.

a man of intelligence and some learning, who knew accurately both the contents of the Vienne decrees and the conclusions of the papal commission of 1319. He must therefore have been aware of the seriousness of contesting their authority, which he did plainly from a conviction in Olivi's sanctity.

Such a juxtaposition of Olivi's probity with John XXII's guilt was not infrequent; Olivi was vindicated in the same act of inculpating the pope for heresy. Raymond Stephan was another who refused to accept his judgement, with or without the cardinals, against Olivi's *Postilla*, and who doubted the validity of the sentence of excommunication to enforce it.[1] Bernard di na Jacma's grounds were somewhat different: he believed that Olivi's doctrine, except for certain articles, had been approved by the pope at the Council of Vienne and, since a general council could not err, they could not be condemned by John XXII.[2] But he did not, as we have already mentioned, confine his approbation of Olivi to legal reasons, regarding him as an uncanonized saint and holy father.[3] For Peter Tort,[4] likewise, Olivi had been vindicated by the Council of Vienne, except for certain doubtful articles.[5] He had also read Olivi in the vernacular and understood that all that he had written had been revealed to him by God. He had also heard it preached that Olivi's doctrine was more necessary to the church in this age than that of any other doctor, except for the writings of the saints and apostles; for it told most about the end of the world, and without it mankind would have been in ignorance and darkness.[6] He had read that Olivi was the angel in the Apocalypse with a face like the sun; of all the doctors he alone had not had one word of his writings condemned—which conflicts, of course, with what he had just said of the condemned articles at Vienne. Whoever tried to condemn them was himself a heretic.[7] Olivi was the one great doctor who had not been canonized.[8] Tort's evidence

---

[1] Ibid., 322–3.   [2] Ibid., 308.   [3] Ibid.
[4] Ibid., 325–30.   [5] Ibid., 329.
[6] et quod tota scriptura eius erat vera et sibi fuerat revelata, et nichil de suo in dicta scriptura posuerat, set solum illud quod ei a deo fuerat revelatum. Dixit etiam se audivisse in sermonibus factis per fratres minores de Narbona tempore quo fiebat festum de dicto fratre P. Joh[annis], quod doctrina et scriptura sua erat magis necessaria ecclesie pro isto tempore finali quam doctrina cuiuscunque sancti doctoris, exceptis apostolis et evangelistis, quia ut dicebant magis fuerant sibi revelata illa que circa finem mundi fieri debebant quam alicui sancto doctori, et quod totus mundus fuisset in tenebris et ignorancia veritatis, nisi dictus frater P. Joh[annis] fuisset et scriptura eius . . . (ibid.).
[7] Ibid.   [8] Ibid.

is the more interesting since he attributed all his statements to what he had heard from others; he himself had qualifications over Olivi's teaching on Christ's spear wound, and accepted the sanctity of the rest because he believed they had been approved by the Vienne Council.[1]

That the cult of Olivi helped to form the Beguins into a distinctive sect cannot be doubted; belief in the sanctity of his person and his teachings gave a focal point to their tribulations. Olivi was *par excellence* their saint, presiding over their lives and guiding their destinies. As a man, he was never less than good, catholic and holy; frequently he was the angel of the Apocalypse, the open book in his hand communicating Christ's truths revealed to him alone.[2] At times his marvels passed the bounds of comparison. William Ademarius, a weaver, believed the *Postilla* on the Apocalypse was 'of such wonder that if all the heads of all the men in the world were one, they could not have written it, unless through [the inspiration of] the Holy Spirit'.[3] But veneration also took a tangible form. There are references to visits to Olivi's tomb, and the celebration of his feast at Narbonne.[4] Sick children were taken there to be healed; for example, Sybil Cazelle brought her daughter,[5] and John Orlach his son.[6] Both attributed their subsequent cure to the intercession of Olivi, whom they regarded as a saint. For that reason the persecutions of John XXII united them more firmly in their defence of Olivi. More than once, as we have seen, the pope owed his own condemnation, as heretic or mystic Antichrist, to his attack upon Olivi's writings: the one represented Christ, the other Antichrist, or at least his forces. Accordingly in condemning Olivi he was crucifying Christ.[7]

---

[1] Limborch, *Liber Sententiarum.*

[2] E.g., ibid., 316; Doat 28, f. 230r.

[3] Item quod frater Petrus Iohannis fecerat unum librum super Apocalipsim qui erat mirabile opus et tale quod si omnia capita hominum omnium de mundo essent in uno capite non potuissent fecisse tale opus, nisi fuisset per opus spiritus sancti (Doat 28, f. 230r.).   [4] E.g. Limborch, op. cit., 327.

[5] Item scripturam fratris Petri Iohannis credidit esse bonam et catholicam et dictum fratrem Petrum Iohannis [MS. Iohannem] esse sanctum et quandam filiam suam, quae patiebatur infirmitatem in gutture . . . ad sepulcrum suum duxit et curata fuit et credidit tunc et adhuc credit quod per orationem dicti fratris Petri curata fuerit (Doat, vol. 27, f. 18r; also Manselli *Spirituali* 37 n.2).

[6] quondam filium suum infirmum dicto fratri Petro sicut sancto devovit et ad eius sepulcrum portavit credens ipsum filium fuisse sanatum per dicti fratris Petri merita, quem reputabat sanctum et credebat (Doat 27, f. 25r; Manselli, loc. cit., n.3).

[7] See, for example, the opinion of William Quartier, a weaver:
. . . quod in scriptura fratris Petri Iohannis sancti patris continebantur, quod in isto tempore debebat esse quidam papa qui esset mysticus Antichristus, qui debebat

If this was one reason for John XXII's various indignities—heretical, illegal, Antichrist—the main one was undoubtedly because he was seen as the author of the Spirituals' and Beguins' sufferings. The indictment against him took two main forms: one was the illegality of his action in trying to dispense the Minors from their vows in *Quorumdam exigit*; the other was that he had caused, or authorized, the burning of the four Spirituals at Marseilles in 1318. Both were widespread; they formed part of the canon of Beguin beliefs. The first was regarded as an attack upon evangelical perfection, an attempt to destroy the rule of St. Francis, and so the life of Christ: 'The vow of poverty is the vow of the evangel,' said Jacoba Sobirana. 'Therefore nothing may be reserved for the morrow or put in a cellar for many years.' To Berangaria Donas John XXII was persecuting 'the poor friends of Christ'.[1] Matthew, rector of Bellodinère, in the diocese of Narbonne, reported having heard Raymond John, one of the prominent Spirituals. He had preached that there had been no true pope in the church since Celestine V, who had protected those pledged to poverty in Sicily.[2]

This belief in the inviolability of the rule, which the pope could not amend, was joined to another that, once a Minor always a Minor: or, more exactly, that the pope could not make a Minor leave his own order and join another. It was asserted frequently.[3] No names or cases were given, but it may well have referred to the pope's pressure upon Angelo (who refused) and Ubertino (who became a Benedictine) to change their order. There was a corresponding conviction in the absolute poverty of Christ and the Apostles, which often went with the rejection of granaries and cellars. They were seen as parts of the same evangelical poverty which the pope was attempting to destroy.[4] Since most of the inquisitional processes took place between 1321 and 1325, the repercussions of *Cum inter nonnullos* had had time to be felt, even if

---

condemnare dictam scripturam quam sanctam et catholicam reputabat, et quod in condemnatione dictae scripturae condemnat vitam Christi, et quod sic perderet potestatem suam papalem. Et credebat tunc ipse loquens quod hoc diceret de domino Johanne papa qui nunc est (Doat 28, 206r-v).

[1] Ibid., f. 219v.

[2] Postea dixit frater (ms fratres) Raimundus Johannis quod in ecclesia Romana non fuit verus papa citra Celestinum, quem ipsi pauperes habebant in Sicilia (ibid., f. 86r).

[3] E.g., Blasius Boerii, sartor. . . . Item quod dominus papa non poterat in ipsa regula fratrum minorum dispensare nec unam religionem in aliam transmutare (ibid., f. 27r.). See also ff. 38r and 246v. Other examples can be found in Limborch, *Liber Sententiarum*, 299, 302, 304, 315, 321, 324, 326.

[4] E.g., Doat 28, ff. 190v, 208, 225r.

they were less direct than the events in Provence. The words of Blasius Boerii, a tailor, can be taken as representative: 'He said that the rule of the Minors was evangelical and the same as the evangel. The pope could not dispense from the rule or from evangelical vows; nor could he concede granaries or cellars to them.'[1]

We have already alluded to the condemnation of the four Spirituals at Marseilles. Here, if anywhere, was the heart of Beguin experience. Hardly a testimony is without it. The four Spirituals themselves were, as Bernard Gui said, regarded as saints and martyrs; the pope, their destroyer, as at least of Antichrist, and often the mystic Antichrist.[2] The repetition becomes monotonous. Here two extracts will suffice. The first, by Berengaria Donas, wife of Peter Donas, said, 'that the lord pope John XXII lost his papal power for having condemned, or caused to be condemned, the four brothers Minor burned at Marseilles. Also that this pope was the mystic Antichrist.'[3] The second, by William Quartier, whom we have already encountered, called them 'men of good and holy life, who were the light of the holy Catholic faith . . . and they were saved and holy martyrs in paradise, and their condemnation was a bad deed'.[4] Both themes, of the martyrs' sanctity and the pope's culpability, were re-echoed; their responsibility was made to rest wholly with John XXII. It provided the main explanation of his being the mystic Antichrist, and was the final proof of his role as the extirpator of evangelical perfection and the life of Christ.

There can be little doubt that the Marseilles condemnations acted as the catalyst to Beguin apocalypticism. As Peter Calveti testified:

from then onwards he and other Beguins used many times and in many places to speak among themselves, of the condemnation of the said brothers and said that they had been condemned wrongly and unjustly by the malice of other Minors and the inquisitor of Marseilles; and that they had died for the sake of the truth of the rule, which was evangelical truth. Both he (Peter) and the other Beguins all called them holy martyrs, which he believed to be true.[5]

With the pope as at least anti-pope, and often Antichrist, it was a short step to seeing the Roman hierarchy as the carnal church. We have

[1] Doat, 27, f. 84v. See also Limborch, *Liber Sententiarum*, 298–330, for repeated statements of the same nature.

[2] Limborch, loc. cit.

[3] Doat 28, f. 221v.   [4] Ibid., ff. 205v–206r.

[5] Limborch, *Liber Sententiarum*, 316–17. This extract is characteristic of the ten other testimonies to be found there, 298–330.

already mentioned some examples, such as William Dominici Verrerrii
and William Quartier. Another was Berengaria Donas, whom we have
seen identify John XXII with the mystic Antichrist; she also referred
to having read in Olivi of two churches, the carnal and the spiritual.
They called the Roman church the carnal church, namely, the pope,
cardinals and prelates, whereas the spiritual church was said to be of
those Friars Minor, and others, who served the poor. One more pope
would be elected in whose time an emperor would humiliate the
Roman church; she also prophesied that a future pope would canonize
Olivi and his writings.[1] The same views were held by Astruga Renund-
aria: John XXII was the mystic Antichrist and there were a carnal and
a spiritual church.[2] Amoda of Limoges had 'read ancient books in which
the Roman church was called Babylon, the great whore'.[3] Germanus
Frettarius of Toulouse actually saw John's successor in Peter of Corbara,
Louis of Bavaria's anti-pope: 'He spoke many blasphemous words
against the lord pope John XXII and in favour of (Louis of)Bavaria . . .
and of the Minor who it was said had been made the new pope'.[4] The
reasons were nearly always the same conjunction of violating the rule
and persecuting its upholders: because of this the pope had forfeited his
authority and was owed no obedience.[5] Peter Gastaudi put it graph-
ically, when he declared that, by persisting in these errors, the pope had
become a heretic and the papal see vacant. Unless he repented, it only
remained for the cardinals to elect a successor.[6] In common with many

[1] Item dixit quod in praedicto libro, quem habuit, fiebat mentio de una ecclesia
carnali et alia spirituali, et de illo mistico Antichristo. Item quod ecclesiam carnalem
dicebant esse ecclesiam Romanam, scilicet dictum dominum papam, cardinales, et
praelatos, et illam ecclesiam spiritualem dicebant esse ipsos pauperes fratres minores
et alios qui servabant paupertatem. Item quod unus alius papa eligeretur cuius tempore
esset unus imperator qui ecclesiam Romanam humiliaret (Doat 28, f. 221v).

[2] Item quod dictus dominus papa . . . erat misticus antichristus . . . Item quod
erant duae ecclesiae, una carnalis et alia spiritualis (ibid., f. 225r).

[3] Ibid., f. 238r.

[4] Doat 27 f. 18v.

[5] E.g., quod dominus papa qui consenserat in condempnacionem dictorum fratrum
et beguinorum et episcopi et inquisitores qui eos condempnaverant essent heretici
(Limborch, *Liber Sententiarum*, 302).

[6] Item credidit quod dominus papa qui nunc est dominus Johannes XXIIus, faciendo
quandam constitucionem seu decretalem in qua dicitur concessisse fratribus minoribus
quod possint habere ad arbitrium prelatorum dicti ordinis bladum et vinum in
communi . . . erravit aliquo modo contra fidem. . . . Item credidit idem quod predictus
dominus papa Johannes XXIIus factus fuit hereticus quando consentiit quod contra
dictos fratres minores qui nolebant dicte constitutioni obedire procederetur tanquam

Beguins he numbered all those who had been implicated in these actions as heretics, prominent among them the Marseilles inquisitor and the archbishop of Narbonne.[1]

Only a minority of Beguins gave much consideration to their vision of the future. There was, as we have said, a widespread belief that John XXII's pontificate would be the last before the advent of Antichrist: for example Maria de Serra, who designated John XXII as the mystic Antichrist, the herald of the great Antichrist. She had heard that another pope would be instituted during his pontificate, which would be followed by general war and suffering. The great Antichrist had already been born and was 20 years of age. She believed that he would be a Franciscan who would feign holiness; he would be attacked by Frederick II of Sicily who would also inflict great harm upon the church. It would also be the time when the Holy Spirit would be given to all those who had held true to God; this would be followed by the conversion of the Jews and an era of happiness and love. Maria believed that the new age would be seen by children then living: an indication of its imminence.[2]

The belief that the great Antichrist would be a Franciscan apostate was widespread; it went with another, that the Fraticelli were among the reprobate who would be destroyed, together with the Franciscan Community and the remainder of the carnal church.[3] The reasons for it are not clear unless they were, as already suggested, a sense that the Italian Spirituals had deserted the common struggle. Certainly the Provençal Beguins saw themselves as a minority of spiritual men, as Peter Moresius put it, from whom the new spiritual church of the third age would be founded.[4] The same person also described John XXII as the snake in the wood, who in destroying the religious life of the church, had done more

---

contra hereticos per inquisitorem Massilensem heretice pravitatis et quod dicti fratres fuerunt martires gloriosi. . . . Item credidit quod idem dominus papa ab illo tempore quo pertinaciter adhesit predicte constitutioni et execucioni perdidit potestatem papalem ligandi et solvendi et absolvendi et excommunicandi et faciendi prelatos . . . et ex tunc vacavit papatus, et nisi predictus papa desisteret a predictis aut revocaret ea canonice requisitus, cardinales poterant ad electionem alterius papae procedere (ibid., 323–4).

[1] Ibid., 324.

[2] Ibid., 318–19.

[3] E.g., Peter Moresius (ibid., 303) and Peter Tort (ibid., 326).

[4] Item credidit et credebat quod, rejecta ecclesia carnali Romana, eligerentur pauci viri spirituales in quibus fundaretur ecclesia tercii status, qui pugnarent contra antichristum super quos equaliter vel in maiori habundancia infunderetur spiritus sanctus (ibid., 306).

harm than all previous heretics; in the past the church had at least remained a church, but now it had become the synagogue of the devil.[1]
Both Peter Moresius and Bernard di na Jacma believed that the coming
age would see the triumph of the Holy Spirit, which, for the persecuted
Spirituals, would flow like flames from a furnace.[2] Few of the Beguins
appeared to doubt that the struggle in which they were engaged was
between the forces of Christ and Antichrist: the composition of the
latter varied from the pope and inquisitors to the entire faithful except
themselves. Matthew Terrenus defined the Beguins' persecutors as the
carnal church, including the prelates and inquisitors who had condemned
the four Spirituals: for this they were excluded from God's church.[3]
The pope himself was the precursor of the great Antichrist, who, as we
saw earlier, would appear at Jerusalem in 1325. Meanwhile he was
present among all the religious.[4] In that sense, then, the change was
already happening; and the Beguins' apocalyptic vision was focused
upon the present, with occasional excursions into the precise course of
events in the foreseeable future. It was the present which commanded
attention, the future being left to unfold what all knew to have been in-
eluctably decreed. Accordingly only a minority of Beguins like Maria
de Serra, Bernard di na Jacma, Peter Tort and William of Dominico
Verrarrio, made the effort to go beyond the present; a few like Stephen
Gramat alluded briefly to what they had heard of Olivi's prophecies, in
the *Postilla* on the Apocalypse, of the wars and trials to come, in which
'the church, kings, nobles and all manner of people would be destroyed'.[5]
Raymond of Antusano was more precise in relating the tribulations
of the present to the coming defeat of Antichrist. By his illegal imposition of granaries and vineyards upon the Franciscan order John XXII
had nullified his authority and forfeited the obedience due to him. He

---

[1] Item credidit et credebat quod dominus papa Johannes XXIIus, qui nunc est, quem
vocat aprum de silva, destruxit clausuram ecclesie, et quod plus fecit de malo ecclesie
dei quam omnes heretici priores, quia tempore priorum hereticorum adhuc ecclesia
dei remansit in statu suo, set nunc non videtur esse dei set dyaboli synagoga (ibid.).

[2] Ibid., 309.   [3] Ibid., 320.

[4] Item quod dominus papa Johannes XXIIus, qui nunc est, esset preparator vie
antichristi maioris . . . pro eo quia persequebatur fratres minores vocatos spirituales,
qui volebant regulam sancti Francisci servare, et quia dabat occasionem fratribus
minoribus quod haberent divicias concedendo eis quod haberent granaria et celaria.
. . . Item quod tempore moderno omnia foramina plena sunt plena antichristo,
intelligens dictum verbum sic quod omnes religiosi temporis moderni erant pleni
antichristo, id est sequebantur viam et faciebant opera antichristi (ibid.).

[5] Doat 27, f. 10r.

was also a heretic as were the prelates and inquisitors involved in the burning of the four Spirituals—glorious martyrs[1]—at Marseilles.[2] Raymond had both heard and read Olivi's *Postilla* on the Apocalypse. From it he had learned of the division of the world into three general states, and the church into seven ages, of which the present was the sixth; it would be followed, thirteen hundred years after Christ's passion, by the coming of Antichrist and the persecution of the followers of evangelical truth. At the end of the sixth age, the carnal church, Babylon, would be judged 'because it has persecuted and will persecute the truth of Christ and so will be attacked and defeated by the ten horns [kings] of the beast of the Apocalypse. Only the elect will remain and they will form the spiritual church and exalt and preach Christ's truth.'[3]

Peter Tort gave an even more exact view, which he presented as the received ideas of the Beguins rather than his own. It went thus: Christ and the Apostles had observed absolute poverty in their lives; so had St. Francis who had in his rule renewed Christ's evangel. It was therefore inviolate; and the pope in imposing granaries and cellars upon its adherents had not only impugned the rule but also Christ.[4] Accordingly he had sinned. Tort did not believe that for this he was a heretic; but he would have been had he been implicated in the executions of the four glorious martyrs at Marseilles, from which again Tort absolved him.[5] He summarized correctly Olivi's identification of the carnal church with the reprobate. This was Babylon, the whore, drunk with the blood of martyrs. John XXII would not have a successor but would be followed by an apostate from the Franciscan order, who many said would be Philip of Majorca or Angelo of Clareno. Tort himself used to believe that John XXII was the mystic Antichrist, an opinion which he based upon Olivi's writings.[6] Frederick II of Sicily, it was also said, would be the emperor who would war against the church.[7] Tort gave the general computation of the great Antichrist's coming as between three and thirteen years[8]—thus once again putting it in the immediate future.

There is a bleakness about these prophecies which contrasts with the earlier examples of Franciscan Joachism. Not only was struggle in the

---

[1] Limborch, 310.   [2] Ibid., 311.   [3] Ibid., 312.
[4] Ibid., 325–6.   [5] Ibid., 328.
[6] Item dixit dictus P. Tort quod ipse credebat dominum papam Johannem XXII qui nunc est misticism antichristum, informatus per scripturas dicti fratris P. Joh[annis] (ibid., 330).
[7] Ibid.   [8] Ibid.

forefront, but there was little awareness of perspective. The fullness of time and place and person had given place to a focus confined to potential Antichrists and world emperors; and here, too, a sense of desertion is to be found in the frequent choice of Spirituals like Angelo of Clareno and Henry of Ceva, and allies like Philip of Majorca,[1] for the role of the great Antichrist, as well as in the hostility towards the Fraticelli. On the whole, the historical framework had vanished leaving only an apocalyptic belief in the wickedness of John XXII and his accomplices, and their impending punishment. Joachism had been whittled away, or—if preferred—distilled into the sufferings of the moment. This, then, was where the line of poverty and prophecy ended in Provence. Its poignancy needs no stressing; nor is that our task. Its manifold details of executions and martyrdoms, the saving of burned relics and the accumulation of memories, have been chronicled elsewhere.[2] For us it has shown how heterodoxy, invariably orthodox in intent, developed into dissent; and how the heresy which was the outcome was as much the product of ecclesiastical action as of the deeds of those condemned. It has shown, above all, how heresy itself, far from being present from the outset, was not even recognized for such by those who were ultimately arraigned for it; not only was it a gradual—often imperceptible—process; it was reached only under duress. To the end the Beguins believed themselves to be true and Catholic, just as they believed their doctrines to be those of the sacred authorities they revered. The ideas of Olivi, Arnold of Villanova, and others, which had inspired them, had —unknown to them—become transformed or at least debased. The pressure of events had helped to make of them what their authors had never intended.

But Provence is important in other ways as well. It was there that we can see most clearly the anatomy of heresy. It was not a revolt of a dispossessed class, nor of laymen against the church, nor of unbelievers against believers. It came from within the heart of the church, originally on an issue—poverty—which was a fundamental tenet of Christian belief. It was pursued in the name of Christian truth on both sides.

---

[1] E.g. Ibid., 330: quem antichristum dicunt esse aliquem apostatam ordinis minorum, quia est alcior status ecclesie, ut dicunt, dicentes quod erit frater Angelus qui est apostata ordinis fratrum minorum. Alii dicunt dominum Phillippum de Majoricis esse Antichristum. Dicunt etiam plures ex eis quod Fredericus rex Sicilie erit imperator et persequetur ecclesiam Romanam, et facit quod dictus antichristus ab omnibus adoretur.

[2] Especially Manselli, *Spirituali*, 143 ff.

Ultimately it became a matter of obedience, in which what for the Spirituals and Beguins was one principle—poverty—became for the pope another and more immediately overriding one—discipline. Thus conflict arose. It spread because of pressure by the church to make the dissidents conform, in due time becoming outright subversion against ecclesiastical authority. Ultimately, then, the issue was one of conformity, and heresy was the outcome of not conforming. For that reason it must be seen first and foremost for what it was: a religious dispute. It was the setting of Provence which made it distinctive. Like any organized grouping it was based upon towns—those primarily of Narbonne, Béziers, Lodève, Carcassonne, Agde. It was drawn from all sections of the community except the higher clergy and the nobility; and was made notable by the alliance of Spirituals and townsmen. One of the contributory factors was undoubtedly the long tradition of hostility towards the inquisition dating back to the Albigensian crusade and the subsequent hatred of the Dominican inquisitors. This made the region peculiarly susceptible to anti-ecclesiastical feeling. Yet the Beguins were far more under the Spirituals' influence than any other, living as pious laymen and reading and discussing the works of Olivi in their conventicles.[1] That they so readily and staunchly followed the Spirituals, treating them first as their masters and then their martyrs, is the best evidence that the Spirituals answered a need which the secular church could not fill. That they became their followers rather than an independent movement, unlike their namesakes in the Rhineland, shows their desire not to revolt against the church but to follow their own path. If this ultimately did become revolt such was not their intention, any more than it had been the Spirituals'. Both were caught up in events which, once started, they could not control. Their heresy was as unwitting as their faith was genuine.

The Fraticelli

We come now to our final topic, the Fraticelli. The term is misleading; it suggests one group, or at least a cohesive number of groups, where in fact there was neither. Through looseness of terminology, which began with the bull *Sancta Romana*, it has come to stand for bands of dissident

---

[1] Olivi called the simple laymen the foot soldiers under the command of the cavalry. Pedites vero sunt quique simpliciores in obsequiis active viriles, ad obediendum prompti et ad exigendum equititibus fideles et animosi (Manselli, op. cit., appendix I, 290).

Franciscans, some derived from the fugitive Anconan and Tuscan Spirituals, under Henry of Ceva, others descended from the followers of Michael of Cesena. The first, who after being expelled from Sicily settled in Southern Italy and the region of the Romagna, are sometimes known as the *Fraticelli de paupere vita*; the second as the *Fraticelli de opinione*. They had nothing in common save a common hostility to John XXII and his successors; nor did they stand for much more in themselves.

Let us begin by considering them in turn. In 1316, when John XXII became pope, he had to deal with three insurgent groups of Spirituals within the Franciscan order: in Provence, Ancona, Tuscany (and Sicily). Against the first he issued the bull *Quorumdam exigit*, in October 1317, after he had summoned them to the papal court; and against the third *Gloriosam ecclesiam* in January 1318.[1] In between, in December 1317, came *Sancta Romana* directed at all three groups indifferently.[2] It was this last bull which was in some ways the most momentous; for it treated the Spirituals, generally, as part of the same tendency without distinguishing their separate groupings. This was not unwarranted. If organizationally there was nothing which joined the Tuscan Spirituals to those of Provence, they shared much of the same inspiration. Olivi had owed much to Conrad of Offida, generally accepted as the doyen of the Italian Spirituals; Angelo of Clareno revered Olivi, as did Ubertino, an Italian whose main struggles were fought in defence of his confrères in Provence; while Olivi himself had doubtless inspired those in Tuscany during his years as lector at St. Croce, Florence. Accordingly, despite the modern tendency to look askance at John XXII's blanket condemnation of 'those commonly called Fraticelli, or brothers of the poor life, Bizochi or Beguins or by other names' it was not unjustified.[3] Nor was it unreasonable that it applied to Provence as well as Italy and Sicily.[4] By the Fraticelli the pope understood the Italian Spirituals, many of whom, he said, pretended that they had been approved by Celestine V as a separate order of penitents, when in reality Boniface VIII had revoked it. In his bull John XXII declared them all dissolved.[5] *Sancta Romana* was thus an attack upon the Franciscan irregulars as a whole; in this sense it was only the latest of a

---

[1] BF v no. 297, 134–5.

[2] Ibid., no. 302, 137–42.

[3] Ibid., 135: nonnulli tamen profanae multitudinis viri, qui vulgariter 'fraticelli' seu 'fratres de paupere vita', aut 'bizzochi' sive 'beghini' vel aliis nominibus nuncupantur.

[4] Ibid.   [5] Ibid.

number of such bans over the preceding decade. Its immediate effect
was moral rather than practical, apart from finally ending Angelo of
Clareno's hopes of separate recognition for his followers.

Gloriosam ecclesiam was, on the contrary, a specific measure designed
to eliminate Henry of Ceva's group of Tuscan Spirituals. Its interest lies
in the charges brought against them (and the Provençal Spirituals),
which for the first time constituted an indictment of Franciscan
Joachism. They were accused of asserting the existence of both a carnal
and a spiritual church: the former was the Roman church under the
pope and its prelates; the latter was constituted by themselves, practising
the highest poverty in contrast to the decadence of the carnal church.[1]
This led to their second and third errors of denying the Roman church
all spiritual power and jurisdiction, stigmatized by the bull as Donatist
and Waldensian and condemned as mortal sin.[2] The fourth was their
view that a priest in mortal sin could not administer the sacraments;[3]
and the fifth that only the Spirituals were the true observers of evangelical perfection, castigated as Manichaean.[4] The bull also referred
to the Fraticelli's other aberrations, such as their rejection of the sacrament of marriage (an opinion also held by Bernard Gui but not apparent from the records) and their prophecies of the end of the world
and the coming of Antichrist. The pope castigated these all as heretical,
insane, and mere lies, which should be damned outright rather than
receive written refutation.[5] Frederick II of Sicily and the authorities
were bidden to take all necessary measures against them.[6] Here, then,

---

[1] Primus itaque error, qui de istorum officina tenebrosa prorumpit, duas fingit
ecclesias: unam carnalem, divitiis pressam, effluentem deliciis, sceleribus maculatam,
cui Romanum praesulem aliosque inferiores praelatos dominari asserunt; aliam
spirtualem, frugalitate mundam, virtute decoram, paupertate succinctam, in qua ipsi
soli eorumque complices continentur, cui etiam ipsi spiritualis vitae merito, si qua
fides est adhibenda mendaciis, principantur (ibid., 139a).

[2] Ibid., 140.

[3] Ibid., 140-1.

[4] Quintus error sic istorum hominum mentes obcaecat, ut evangelium Christi
in se solos hoc in tempore asserant esse completum, quod hactenus, ut ipsi somniant,
obtectum fuerat, immo prorsus extinctum. Quae impietas sic [per] tenebrosos
Manichaeorum calles oberrat (ibid., 141a).

[5] Multa sunt alia quae isti praesumptuosi homines contra coniugii venerabile
sacramentum garrire dicuntur, multaque de cursu temporum et fine saeculi somniant,
multaque de antichristi adventu . . . Quae omnia, quia partim haeretica partim
insana partim fabulosa cognoscimus, damnanda potius cum suis auctoritatibus quam
stilo prosequenda aut repellenda censemus (ibid.).

[6] Ibid., 141-2.

was more than a list of errors; it was a confrontation between two opposed outlooks. *Gloriosam ecclesiam* comes as near to any official declaration did to explaining how poverty and preaching had by the pontificate of John XXII come to represent a challenge to the very *raison d'être* of the church. No wonder that its exponents were treated as heretics and their extirpation a matter of supreme importance.

We have already seen the concerted destruction of the Provençal Spirituals. It was the fate of their counterparts in Sicily and Italy, on the other hand, to linger on for the rest of the fourteenth century, dwindling and losing any definable identity long before the end. The immediate consequence of *Gloriosam ecclesiam* was their expulsion from Sicily. Frederick II, the king, despite his long-standing Spiritual sympathies and his association with Arnold of Villanova, this time complied with the papal decree. Most of the Spirituals migrated either to Tunisia or to Naples, which became their main stronghold through the protection afforded them by the king of Naples, Robert the Wise.[1] From that time onward, we lose trace of them as a coherent body, as they probably joined up with the remnants of the earlier Spirituals from Ancona.

It will be recalled that when Angelo of Clareno went northwards to Perugia and then to Avignon in 1311, he left behind a body of companions in the area around Rome with whom he remained in contact during his seven years' absence. He had succeeded Liberato in 1305 as their leader; and he resumed active command in 1319 on leaving Avignon after the death of cardinal Jacob Colonna, his protector at the papal court. With the suppression of his order, along with all independent forms of organization, in *Sancta Romana*, he finally became a Celestinian hermit.[2] He now established himself near Rome and, protected by the abbot of Subiaco, proceeded to organize his new order along lines very similar to those of his old order.[3] The chief settlements were in the March of Ancona, the Romagna, and Naples, each divided into provinces under a provincial; the Franciscan offices of guardian and custodian were also utilized.[4] Inquisition records suggest that they gained considerable support among the local populace in some areas, the bishops and priests taking them under their protection.[5] As Angelo grew increasingly infirm his control over his members lessened and no doubt accounts for the deterioration of the order. Nor, as the

---

[1] Douie, *Fraticelli*, 211.
[2] *Epistola excusatoria*, ALKG II, 144.
[3] See Douie, *Fraticelli*, 64–7, whose account has largely been followed here.
[4] ALKG IV, 10; Douie, op. cit., 64.   [5] Douie, ibid.

inquisitorial proceedings against Paul Zoppo show, were they all of equal sanctity.[1]

After Angelo's death, the order degenerated, probably for want of proper leadership and the change in the character of its members. The original companions were replaced by men of a different calibre, less spiritually withdrawn and more militantly anti-papal. At about the same time they become lost from sight; and for the rest of the fourteenth century we are confronted with a number of amorphous groups, concentrated in the kingdom of Naples and, to a lesser extent, around Rome and Perugia. A contributory factor to this confusion was that Naples, under Robert the Wise, became the asylum for Fraticelli of every sort, including the remnants of Henry of Ceva's band, and escaped Provençal Spirituals, and even a group of fugitive followers of Michael of Cesena (Michaelists).[2] All these except the last were loosely known as the *Fraticelli de paupere vita*, designated such by the inquisition to distinguish them from the Michaelists—*Fraticelli de opinione*. Even this does not permit any clear identification. The protection of king Robert of Anjou enabled them to remain free, out of reach of the inquisition, and so added to the assortment of refugees within the kingdom of Naples. Knowledge of them is confined to a few inquisitorial proceedings, and treatises by both the Fraticelli and their opponents.

The first of these was the process in 1362 of Cardinal Albornoz, papal representative in Italy, against Louis of Durazzo, patron of the Fraticelli in Naples.[3] It is interesting for the testimony of one of the accused, Novellus of Roccabantre, that the Fraticelli comprised three different sects, including Angelo of Clareno's followers, who, he declared, were not in accord with the others.[4] Attempts at mediation between the three groups, by the bishop of Trevento and Louis of Durazzo, had failed.[5] Perugia and Rome were the Fraticelli's other strongholds, being in the latter city under the protection of the prefect Giovanni di Vico.[6] The outlook of these different groups was fundamentally the same, and may be described as apocalyptic anti-papalism. John XXII was invariably Antichrist; the Roman church was guilty of fornication and simony, and its priesthood in mortal sin; only the Fraticelli were true to the teachings of Christ and poverty. These, with variations, were the themes, worn thin by repetition. Occasionally there were echoes of an

[1] ALKG IV, 78–82.   [2] Douie, op. cit., 211.   [3] ALKG IV, 95–104.
[4] Ibid., 97. Douie, op. cit., 212.
[5] ALKG IV, 100; Douie, ibid.   [6] Douie, op. cit., 220.

earlier Spiritual tradition, as in a fourteenth-century treatise, written in Italian, eulogizing Jacopone of Todi, Conrad of Offida and Olivi as well as naming Arnold of Villanova, Ubertino of Casale and Angelo of Clareno.[1] John XXII was the mystic Antichrist whose errors the writer cited from the writings of Michael of Cesena, Ockham and Francis of Ascoli.[2] A second treatise also attacked John XXII and the luxury of the church, which was the synagogue of Satan;[3] it was Joachist, quoting from the *Liber de concordia* of Joachim of Fiore and treating the present age as the sixth age in which the Franciscan rule would be the principal object of attack.[4] Another Joachite work was the *Revelations of Joachim*, mentioned earlier in connexion with the *Vaticinia Anselmi*, to which they became joined in the sixteenth century. Written before 1350,[5] they were a series of fifteen portraits of popes. Like the *Vaticinia*, they began with Nicholas III, but they differed in their tone of despair: there were no angelic pastors and the last pope was portrayed as Antichrist with the words: 'Haec est ultima fera aspectu terribilis': clearly a reflexion of the disillusionment at their own position and that of the papacy.

It was shared by John of Rupescissa (Roquetaillade), a French Franciscan. While imprisoned at Avignon he wrote in c. 1350 his *Vade mecum in tribulatione*, one of his many prophetic writings.[6] It foretold the coming doom of the papacy. Rupescissa prophesied that within six years the papal curia would flee from Avignon, 'the city of sin'.[7] He accompanied it with dire warnings of the advent of Antichrist in both east and west; much of eastern and central Europe would be conquered and an evil emperor would rule as a second Nero.[8] There would be famine, plague and perdition. But for Rupescissa salvation lay in the coming of an angel pope, a holy Franciscan. Together with a king of France, elected as emperor, the pope would finally overthrow Antichrist. A thousand years of peace and evangelical poverty would follow until the coming of Gog and Magog brought about the world's end.[9]

---

[1] F. Tocco, *Studii Francescani* (Naples 1909), 512–24. Douie, op. cit., 213–14.

[2] *Studii Francescani*, ibid., 513; Douie, op. cit., 214, who gives a summary of the rest of its contents.   [3] *Studii Francescani*, ibid., 502–12.

[4] *Studii Francescani*, ibid., 503; Douie op. cit., 215–16.   [5] See pp. 186 ff. above.

[6] Published in E. Brown, *Fasciculus rerum expetendarum et fugiendarum*, vol. II (London 1690), 499–508. On Rupescissa, or Roquetaillade, see J. Bignami-Odier, *Etudes sur Jean de Roquetaillade* (Paris 1952). She shows that he drew upon most of the Sibylline and other prophesies which we encountered among the Spirituals.

[7] Ibid., 494.   [8] Ibid., 500.

[9] Ibid., 494, 500–1, 507. For a summary see M. Reeves, 'Last World Emperor' 328 ff.

The sequence, by now familiar, is noteworthy for its combination of present despair and future promise. The luxury and depravity of the papal court would be the direct cause of its downfall and Antichrist's advent, inciting men to rise in protest in the name of poverty.[1] But righteousness would finally triumph through an angel pope and a last world emperor. Hope still lay with the regeneration of this world, not simply its supersession by the next one, and it remained vested in the existing institutions.

A similar outlook is also to be found in Telesphorus of Cosenza, the so-called hermit of Calabria. His prophecies, probably written about 1386,[2] shared Rupescissa's belief in a French emperor as the world's saviour from Antichrist—who would be a German ruler, Frederick III, in alliance with a pseudo-pope. Once again victory of the righteous would be achieved through the agency of an angel pope who would release the king of France from imprisonment and the world from its afflictions; once again it was from France that salvation finally would come, after the ravages of Antichrist as punishment for the church's sins. Once again there was to be a millenium on earth where in the wake of untold sufferings all schism and depravity would be banished. The prospect of such tribulations was thus offset by the joy that would follow. It gave a resilience to Joachist prophecy that carried it into the sixteenth century. It does not, however, seem to have had much part in the later history of the Fraticelli *de paupere vita*.

The few surviving documents from among them all follow the same lines of indictment. A letter from Perugia, written during the Great Schism, defended the Fraticelli from the charge of rejecting the sacraments and the priests who recognized John XXII; it accused the latter of heresy and simony. It also attacked the Franciscan order for betraying its founder's ideals, of which the Fraticelli were the only true defenders. The present schism was the result of John XXII's denial of poverty.[3] Despite the unbridled hostility of the writer towards those whom he regarded as the false priests, he remained loyal to the church

[1] Et si praedictae ruinae veniant, hoc proveniet ex culpa sacerdotum qui non curant vigilare super gregem suum, sed absentant se ab ecclesiis suis et dantur in ruinam . . . et quod vita praesidentium et status et praecipue clericorum revocaretur per humilitates, amovendo status, carnalitates et cupiditates, quibus mundus maculatur (ibid., 495).

[2] On Telesphorus see especially E. Donckel, 'Die Prophezeiung des Fr. Telesforus' AFH 26 (1933) 29–104, 282–314. Also Reeves, art. cit., 329 ff.

[3] L. Oliger, 'Documenta inedita ad historiam Fraticellorum,' AFH 4 (1911) 697–712.

and its sacraments; it was the common case of defending an institution by condemning those who had abused it. A similar attitude was expressed in another letter, addressed to the whole of Christendom, denouncing the church for heresy, simony and fornication, and denying the powers of those priests who adhered to John XXII.[1] Much the same sentiments are to be found in the one letter extant from the Fraticelli at Rome in the latter part of the fourteenth century. Written, like the other two above, in the vernacular, it professed loyalty to the church and its teaching. John XXII was a heretic; and any pope guilty of heresy lost his powers, as did any priest.[2] Perhaps the one point of interest in all these declarations was the conviction that the pope could err.

The one other record of the Fraticelli (*de paupere vita*) is from Narni: it consists of a letter written in 1354 attacking John XXII and the church hierarchy for the usual errors. During the next century the community there divided into two groups of hermits—the Clarenists—belonging to the congregation originally founded by Angelo of Clareno; in 1446 Eugenius IV issued a bull granting them the rights of use over the hospital of St. Croce.[3] They were not alone in this tendency towards becoming accepted. A striking example is to be found among a number of groups in the region of Perugio and Città di Castello.[4] Although their leader, Francis Nicolay, had been in contact with the Fraticelli in Sicily[5] and shared their conviction in evangelical poverty, they observed the rule of St. Augustine. They were also unusual in not regarding John XXII and his successors as heretics; only Innocent VI came within this category for having imprisoned John of Rupescissa.[6] At the same time, however, their leader administered the sacraments and refused to recognize the church's power to do so. He was also called their 'pope' and took the novices' professions.[7] Nicolay himself believed in a future angelic pope who would be Jacob of Colonna because of his baldness.[8] The groups were not disbanded but were instructed to join some recognized order.

For the most part, however, the Fraticelli *de paupere vita* remained true both to their idea of poverty and their abhorrence of the memory

---

[1] Douie, op. cit., 219.   [2] Ibid., 220-1; AFH v, 74-84.

[3] Douie, op. cit., 223-5.

[4] L. Oliger, 'Acta Inquisitoris Umbriae Fr. Angeli de Assisio' in AFH 24 (1931) 63-90.

[5] Ibid., 79.   [6] Ibid., 81.   [7] Ibid., 79.

[8] Ibid. Cola di Rienzo reported the same belief from his contact with Fraticelli. P. Puir, *Briefwechsel des Cola di Rienzo. Vom Mittelalter zur Reformation*, II, pt. 2, 309. St. Peter was traditionally bald.

of John XXII. This acted as a brake upon them, riveting them to the past and keeping them in a state of permanent opposition to the church. Their natural tendency to the eremetical life was accentuated by the pressure of the inquisition. Heretics though they were, in their own eyes they remained the true defenders of the faith.

The Michaelists

The history of the Michaelists—the other so-called branch of the Fraticelli (*de opinione*)—followed a parallel progression from heterodoxy to dissent but in an even more marked degree. Men like Michael of Cesena and Bonagratia of Bergamo, who, until their clash with John XXII, had been the personification of inflexible orthodoxy, became heretics; a doctrine, officially canonized by successive popes, that Christ and the Apostles had possessed nothing, became uncanonical; recognized leaders of one of the two main mendicant orders became fugitives. Such was the sequence between 1323 and a decade later. If the ultimate consequences were no more far-reaching than those of the Fraticelli *de paupere vita*, the path to them was more conspicuous, and the effects never entirely lost. To their end, in the mid-fifteenth century, the Michaelists remained more influential than their namesakes with whom they had little in common beyond their repugnance against John XXII and all his works. Their predominantly doctrinal approach constituted a greater challenge; and long after the original antagonists had vanished into the shades, the Michaelists continued to engage—albeit at a not very exalted level—apologists like Andreas Ricchi and James of Marcia. Thus we are confronted with two distinct facets: the original disputes over the absolute poverty of Christ; and their aftermath in the history of the Michaelists.

It will be recalled that the bull *Cum inter nonnullos*, in November 1323, declared anathema the doctrine that Christ and the Apostles had held nothing in common or in private.[1] Far from putting an end to the dispute which had dominated the Franciscan order, and at times the papacy, for over two generations, it opened a new, and in some ways more bitter, conflict. If, as we have stressed already, the participants and the principles involved were different from the previous ones, the ultimate consequences were not dissimilar: the creation of another heretical sect, ironically bracketed with those whom they had persecuted.

The response to *Cum inter nonnullos* among the Franciscan order was

---

[1] BF v, no. 518, 256-9; see pp. 165 f. above.

long in coming. While the Franciscan Cardinals led by Vital du Four submitted to the decree under pressure, and the emperor, Louis of Bavaria, made it the occasion, in his Sachsenhausen declaration,[1] to condemn John XXII as a heretic and a heresiarch, the order made no public response, even at its chapter-general at Lyons in 1324. Already, however, it seems likely that some members of the order had entered into opposition, since the Sachsenhausen declaration was strongly Franciscan in tone, including verbatim the whole of one question (no. 8) from Olivi on poverty.[2] Bonagratia of Bergamo's influence cannot be excluded, despite the apparent improbability that he would draw upon his lifelong adversary. He had, as we have seen, been the first to protest against *Ad conditorem canonum*, for which he had been imprisoned for one year.[3] His protest had followed the line of his treatise *De paupertate Christi et apostolorum*,[4] written in response to John XXII's bull *Quia nonnunquam*, which, it will be remembered, opened the attack on the doctrine of poverty.[5] Since these were the foundation of the Franciscan case it will be as well to resume them briefly. There was nothing strikingly original in what Bonagratia said; he based himself largely upon St. Bonaventure and *Exiit* for the most part. But he also attempted to give a greater legal precision to it. This centred upon the distinction between simple use, founded upon natural law, and the legal right to use which derived from human law. The first, in so far as it was necessary for the sustenance of life, was an obligation common to all men; there could be no dispensation from it.[6] It included the use of food and clothing without therefore involving any title to legal possession.[7] From this it followed that *simplex usus facti* could be separated from dominion and proprietorship, usufruct and *ius utendi*.[8] This was the heart of the Franciscan case, the point to which their arguments constantly returned. In this sense the discussion became essentially legalistic;

---

[1] Baluze, *Misc.* III, 224-32.   [2] Compared by Ehrle, ALKG III, 540-4.

[3] BF v, 237n.-46n.; Baluze, *Misc.* III, 213-21.

[4] Edited by L. Oliger in AFH 22 (1929), 332-5, 487-511.

[5] BF v, 237n.-46n.

[6] Praeterea usus facti rerum necessariarum ad substentationem nature est de iure naturali . . . Nullus qui legis naturalis precepto ad esse nature conservandum indispensabiliter obligatus est, hiis sine quibus non servatur esse nature, renuntiare potest (AFH 22, 503).

[7] Quod autem usus rerum, alimentorum cadat sub precepto legis nature patet . . . ibid., 504).

[8] Falsum est ergo dicere quod simplex usus facti non possit a dominio et proprietate et usu fructu sive iure utendi separari (ibid., 502).

even Ockham, as we shall shortly have cause to remark, did not, in essentials, introduce any new element, despite the much greater range of his dialectical skill. Not that Bonagratia confined himself solely to it. He sought in particular to show that the consumption of goods in use did not entail their ownership, on three main grounds. The first was the distinction already mentioned between *ius utendi* and natural law. This in turn led to Bonagratia rejecting the charge—raised again in *Ad conditorem canonum*—that the profit (usufruct) from the goods used by the order accrued to the order, even while the substance remained with the pope. This could not apply to goods consumed in use; here, he invoked the concept of 'quasi-usufruct', by which the pope could receive back at any time the equivalent of the goods consumed:[1] an instance of the limitations of Bonagratia's predominantly legalistic approach, since, in principle, it conceded his opponents' case. More telling was the resuscitation of Bonaventure's analogy of the relationship of father to son, to support the distinction between use and possession of consumables;[2] he also added his own of master and slave,[3] and a horse eating oats, which, he said, represented the order's relation to the objects it enjoyed.[4] In addition to these arguments from law, Bonagratia also turned to theology for two of his main contentions. One, going back to St. Augustine, was that private property was the result of the fall;[5] therefore, said Bonagratia, Christ and the Apostles in returning to a state of innocence, through their pursuit of evangelical perfection, possessed nothing.[6] It was an ingenious adaptation of a time-honoured theme, and in many ways Bonagratia's most effective riposte. The other argument defended Judas's bag with St. Bonaventure's notion of Christ's occasional condescension to the imperfect, in ministering to

---

[1] Ususfructus autem in rebus que usu consumuntur proprie non consistit, ergo nec transire potest cum dominio, nec ab eo separari potest quod nusquam est . . . utilitatis tamen causa ex interpretatione benigna lex statuit quod quasi ususfructus in hiis rebus constitui possit. . . . Et ab eo cautio desideranda est, ut quandoque hiis mortuus aut capite minutus sit, eiusdem qualitatis restituatur (509–10).

[2] Ibid., 502.   [3] Ibid.   [4] Ibid., 511.

[5] Set nullus ante peccatum habuisset dominium earum rerum, que usu consumuntur, nec aliquarum aliarum rerum. Quia non fuisset meum et tuum, sed fuisset ita communis omnium rerum hominibus sicut communis usus omnibus hominibus in aere, et solis splendore . . . (ibid., 506–7).

[6] Et ipse Christus venerit ad docendum perfectissime omnium terrenorum contemptum, et vitam quietissimam et ad omnem materiam sollicitudinis temporalium perfecte eum sequi volentibus amputandam et ad statum innocentie renovandum (ibid., 489).

the needs of the infirm; he also added the same moral that Judas, who carried the bag, had betrayed Christ,[1] and used the fact of Christ's nightly return to Bethany as evidence that he had no home of his own, or money for lodgings.[2]

With Bonagratia of Bergamo's tractate, and its repetition in more violent terms to oppose *Ad conditorem canonum*, the Franciscan case was effectively stated. It consisted in the dual defence of *simplex usus facti* as a self-subsisting, non-legal state, and the absolute possessionlessness of Christ and the Apostles as an historical fact. These formed the main threads of all subsequent Franciscan arguments, the second in particular leading to seemingly endless scriptural exegesis indulged in by both sides. The search for wider principles was lost in the welter of legal and biblical debate.

It was John XXII who first resumed it after *Cum inter nonnullos*, in the bull *Quia quorumdam mentes*, dated 10 November 1324.[3] It came close to being a declaration of faith, which in its coherent, if limited, vision is more impressive than the glaring inconsistencies between the theory and practice of his opponents. It was the reply of a canonist who believed in the sanctity of law as canonically defined and promulgated; there was no place for vague aspirations which were at variance with the facts. For John XXII these were clear. First, he affirmed that his previous declarations in *Ad conditorem* and *Cum inter nonnullos* conformed to those of his predecessors, which, from Honorius III to Nicholas III, he examined individually.[4] This was the weakest part of the pope's case since it is hard to believe that many could have been convinced that *Cum inter nonnullos* contained nothing which was not in *Exiit qui seminat*. It is true that the point at issue, of whether Christ and the Apostles had enjoyed only *usus simplex facti*, had not been discussed in *Exiit*; in that sense it could be argued that John's view, that they had not, did not violate Nicholas III's bull. But such an argument *ex silentio* was to say the least tenuous. Secondly, John asserted the pope's authority to decide matters of doctrine. There could, he said, be no separation of the key of learning from the keys of binding and loosing. Knowledge was the province of spiritual authority; therefore the pope in possessing the one in the highest degree also enjoyed a corresponding prerogative over the other.[5]

But it was in the attack upon the evangelical basis of the rule that the main blows against the order were struck. The pope denied flatly that

[1] Ibid., 498.   [2] Ibid., 499.   [3] BF v, no. 554, 271–80.
[4] Ibid., 272.   [5] Ibid., 272–3.

his predecessors had interpreted the rule literally as Christ's gospel. 'It is clear,' he said, 'that many things are contained in the rule which Christ neither taught nor confirmed by his example.'[1] This attempt to drive a wedge between the life of Christ and the order went beyond the earlier rejection of the doctrine of Christ's absolute poverty in *Cum inter nonnullos*. Taken in conjunction with the latter it destroyed not only the basis of Franciscan poverty but the order's special claim to sanctity. It was to the twin objects of refuting the claims for poverty in general and Christ's practice of it in particular that John XXII's arguments were principally directed, both here and later in the bull *Quia vir reprobus*. The effect can be seen in the predominantly legal and exegetical form which the discussion took. Even Michael of Cesena's moral indignation and Ockham's dialectical skill could not lift the discussion out of the pope's maze of technicalities. The contrast with the disputes of a decade earlier is striking.

By far the most damaging part of the bull for its opponents was the contention that there was neither merit nor historical truth in pretending that Christ and the Apostles had been without legal rights. In itself this was not new. Both *Ad conditorem* and *Cum inter* had between them said the same. The novelty was in its elaboration into a counter-claim for the intrinsic merits of legality and property. It was to turn the weapons of the pope's opponents against themselves; for it made the possession of rights and dominion superior to the lack of them. It was, he declared, absurd and erroneous to believe that it was more perfect to have no rights than to have them, since it implied that what was unjust was more just and more acceptable to God than what was just.[2] Simple use, denuded of all right, far from being just, meant lack of justice, and therefore could not pertain to perfection.[3] Accordingly, the claim that the greater the act of renunciation, the more exalted the state was false.[4] One must admire the pope's audaciousness. He had not hesitated to confute the one universally acknowledged—and unexamined—premise of the Franciscan order, held equally by simple

---

[1] BF v, no. 274b.

[2] Item est absurdum et erroneum quod actus aliquis non habentis ius actum huiusmodi faciendi sit iustior et deo acceptior quam habentis, cum includat actum iustiorem et acceptiorem deo existere, quam sit iustus (ibid., 277b–78a).

[3] Praeterea si simplex usus denudatus omni iure posset ab aliquo haberi, constat quod actus huiusmodi esset reputandus non iustus cum ille usus fuerit, cui ius non competebat utendi: usus autem non iustus ad perfectionem non pertinet nec aliquid perfectioni adiicit sed sibi repugnare potius noscitur manifeste (ibid., 276b).

[4] Ibid., 277a.

Beguin and worldly prelate, that, in principle, less was better than more. Admittedly the pope did not go very deep in pursuing his argument; it remained within the accepted legal framework. Nevertheless, it was, as it stood, hard to answer: if justice belonged to perfection, and legal right was part of justice (although the pope never attempted to examine the relation of right to supernatural justice), to have legal rights was better than to be without them. An extrinsic human act could not be perfect if it lacked the right to be performed: it would then not even be just.[1]

Theory was confirmed by the fact of Christ's example. It was untrue, said the bull, that Christ had preached or practised the abdication of all rights or had imposed the obligation to do so as an evangelical vow upon the Apostles.[2] The old argument of Judas's bag was resurrected to show that Christ and the Apostles had carried money,[3] while *Exiit qui seminat* was interpreted as implying that they had held property in common.[4] Moreover, they had held it in more than simple *usus facti*; otherwise they would not have been able to dispense money to the poor.[5]

For the Pope the truth of his position lay in the legal fact that use entailed the right of use. This applied equally to Christ and the Minors.[6] Hence the untenability of their claim to absolute poverty both for themselves and for Christ and the Apostles.

Quia quorumdam, although it was followed five years later by *Quia vir reprobus*, effectively completed the formulation of John XXII's position. Together with *Ad conditorem* and *Cum inter* it took him from

---

[1] Impossibile enim est actum humanum extrinsecum esse iustum, si exercens actum ipsum nullum ius habeat exercendi; imo non iustus, sed iniustus necessario convincitur talis usus (ibid., 277b).

[2] Ibid.   [3] Ibid., 275b.

[4] Adhuc non apparet ipsam dixisse sustentationem Christi et apostolorum eius in solo et nudo et simplici consistere usu facti, cum de usu facti simplici quoad Christum et apostolos nullam praefatus Nicolaus praedecessor noster in sua declaratione fecerit mentionem, imo sensisse satis videtur expresse quod ius aliud a proprietate habuisse poterunt. . . . Adhuc idem Nicolaus praedecessor noster videtur sensisse quod Christus et apostoli etiam quoad proprietatem habuerint aliquid in communi . . . (ibid., 275a).

[5] Praeterea si diceretur Christum in loculis tantummodo habuisse simplicem usum facti, frustra diceretur quod in persona infirmorum ipsos Christus habuerit loculos . . . (ibid., 275b).

[6] Adhuc dicimus quod hoc est impossibile, scilicet usum facti simplicem absque iure aliquo, quod nihil aliud quam ipsum uti proprie potest dici, posse in re aliqua etiam usu non consumptibili ab aliquo obtinere (ibid., 276b).

a denial of the distinction between use and possession, and the doctrine of absolute poverty, to the affirmation of the sanctity of property. In its less spectacular way *Quia quorumdam* was perhaps the most theoretically sweeping of the three, as it made general what had previously been mainly arguments *ad hominem*. More important, the three bulls together constituted a challenge to the entire Franciscan concept of perfection; poverty was not merely demoted: it was virtually deposed. For such an affront his opponents never forgave him. The full weight of their attack was slow in coming. Despite signs of hostility at the chapter-general at Lyons in the following year (1325)[1] there was no immediate breach between the leaders of the order and the pope. It was only in 1327, after a number of delays, that Michael of Cesena finally arrived at Avignon in response to John XXII's summons.[2] The Franciscan general had already been secretly negotiating with the emperor, Louis of Bavaria, a fact of which the pope was aware. But for some months he maintained an outward show of cordiality while seeking to prevent Michael from joining the emperor and becoming anti-pope.[3] Finally, in April 1328 at a consistory, the pope publicly denounced Michael of Cesena for his part in declarations of the Perugia chapter (of 1322) on the poverty of Christ.[4] The highly dramatized accounts given by Michael of Cesena depicted the pope's fury culminating in a ban upon his leaving Avignon.[5] Whatever the pope intended, six weeks later Michael of Cesena, together with William of Ockham—who had been at Avignon four years awaiting judgement on certain of his views[6]— Francis Ascoli, and Bonagratia of Bergamo, fled to the emperor at Pisa.[7] From that moment their cause was lost. They were excommunicated[8] and became fugitives from papal authority; their desertion to the anti-papal side and their association with the anti-pope, set up

---

[1] Douie, *Fraticelli*, 166.

[2] BF v, no. 667, 325; Douie, loc. cit.

[3] Douie, op. cit., 167.   [4] See p. 163 above.

[5] The main sources for these happenings are Michael of Cesena's appeals: Baluze *Misc.* III, 237–40, 246–310, and BF v, 341–43, 497–500.

[6] Published by A. Pelzer, 'Les 51 articles de Guillaume d'Occam', RHE, 18 (1922) 240–70. They contain no reference to the question of poverty, with which at this time Ockham was not concerned. See pp. 294 ff. below. See also L. Baudry, 'La lettre de Guillaume d' Occam au Chapitre d'Assise', *Revue d'Histoire Franciscaine* III (1926) ff. 185–215.

[7] BF v, nos. 711–13, 345–6.

[8] Ibid. Michael of Cesena was deposed in the bull *Dudum ad nostri*, 6 June 1328. Ibid., no. 714, 346–9.

by the emperor, Louis of Bavaria,[1] undermined their moral standing. Within a short while they declined into a band of emigrés, out of touch with the majority of their order and obsessed by their own problems to the exclusion of all others; while Michael of Cesena's unending series of letters and declarations, with their repetitious appeals to the iniquities of the pope, blunted their effect. Once again the doctrine of poverty became enmeshed in anti-papalism, the latter ultimately predominating.

For our purposes it is unnecessary to recount the full, and often tedious, recital of the Michaelist charges against John XXII, which were re-echoed down the fourteenth century. Their substance is all to be found in Michael of Cesena's writings with some additions by Ockham. The next generation of Michaelists added virtually nothing. Accordingly we shall consider the exchanges between Michael of Cesena, Ockham and John XXII and then briefly review the subsequent course of events.

Michael of Cesena's two main statements are his longer and shorter appeals issued from Pisa in September 1328.[2] Addressed to Christendom at large they consisted in detailed replies to John XXII's three bulls, *Ad conditorem canonum*, *Cum inter nonnullos* and *Quia quorumdam mentes*, together with partisan accounts of John XXII's behaviour towards the general and his confrères. They sought both to defend Franciscan poverty and to arraign the pope as a heretic: he was referred to as 'the Lord John who calls himself XXII pope'.[3] The appeals both took the form of an enumeration of the pope's errors and said much the same. Little of it was new. They leaned heavily on Bonagratia of Bergamo in particular. Their main contention was that there could be use without possession, even of consumables, and that this had been the case with Christ and the Apostles. Each of the pope's three bulls was examined in turn for its errors in denying these truths. Like Bonagratia of Bergamo, Michael of Cesena held that property had been the result of the fall; in the state of innocence nothing had been owned, but only used.[4] This was supported by the letter of St. Clement, St. Peter's successor.[5] Similarly, the ex-general followed the ex-proctor in comparing the status of the order with that of a slave who has no possessions of his own in civil law, but only by natural law.[6] To the pope's

---

[1] He was an obscure Franciscan, Peter of Corbara, elected in May 1327 after the emperor's entry into Rome. See Douie, op. cit., 167.

[2] Published in Baluze, *Misc.* III, ff. 246–303, and 303–10. The shorter appeal is also to be found in BF v, 410n–25n.   [3] *Misc.* III, 246a.

[4] Ibid., 249b.   [5] Ibid., 249b–250a.   [6] Ibid., 250a.

argument that the Apostles had carried money, Michael of Cesena offered two replies. The first was the standard one that they held it not as property but for dispensing to the needy.[1] The second was the less happy distinction—applied to the use of money by monasteries and the Minors—between the licence and the right to use. To receive a licence from a superior was to enjoy the use of something without possessing it. The line between licence and right was, to say the least, a fine one and it was not accepted—with some reason—by the pope in his reply to Michael of Cesena in *Quia vir reprobus*.[2] Michael of Cesena had put it forward to answer the charge of *Ad conditorem* that use without the right of use was abuse. If, said the bull, use was to be distinguished from possession, the substance of what was used must remain intact with the owner, leaving the user with the benefit of its use—usufruct; otherwise it would be abuse not use. Such a division between possession and use entailed the granting of the right of use by the possessor to the user. Accordingly, all use, which was not abuse, was usufruct and carried with it the *ius utendi*.[3] The pope restated the argument in *Quia vir reprobus*,[4] after Michael of Cesena had attempted to show that simple use, without the right of use, was legitimate use.[5] He also sought to show that Christ had possessed no legal rights in being above the law.[6] The other main point which Michael introduced was that in *Quia quorumdam* John XXII had illicitly made himself the guardian of the key of wisdom, when such a thing did not exist, and had used it as the pretext for pronouncing upon matters of knowledge and overturning the

---

[1] *Misc.* III, 308b and BF v, 419n–20n.

[2] quod tamen evidenter est falsum; si enim aliquis licentiam concedat alicui utendi re sua usibili, ita quod licentia teneat, constat quod iste habet ius utendi re illa cui licentia est concessa (BF v, 433b).

[3] Cum enim uti re aliqua nihil aliud sit proprie quam fructus rei seu utilitatem aliquam in solidum vel pro parte recipere qui ex ea possunt salva rei substantia provenire, restat quod re illa uti quis nequeat, ex qua (eius salva substantia) nulla potest sibi provenire utilitas, quales res usu consumptibiles esse constat. Ex quibus patet quod nec usus, qui est servitus personalis, nec ius utendi, quod non est servitus sed mere ius personalis, nec actus ipse utendi sine iure aliquo possunt in rebus usu consumptibilibus constitui vel haberi. . . . Licet autem in rebus usu consumptibilibus nec ius utendi nec ipsum uti possit constitui vel haberi ipsis tamen poterit quis abuti (*Ad conditorem canonum*, BF v, no. 486, 239–40).

[4] BF v, 410a.

[5] Ibid., 413–14. Shorter appeal.

[6] Constat autem quod qui est supra aliquod ius, non peccat nec iniuste agit agendo sive faciendo sine illo iure. Ergo Christus potuit libere et iuste uti temporalibus . . . (*Misc.* III, 283b).

decrees of his predecessors.[1] On these, and other, grounds that he had undermined the doctrine of the church, Michael of Cesena declared the pope a heretic who was deposed and automatically disqualified from exercising his jurisdiction over any matter concerning the faithful.[2]

John XXII's reply in *Quia vir reprobus* was the culmination of his doctrine of property.[3] It was less a public declaration than a treatise carefully reasoned and copiously documented with biblical and canonical citations. If, as with all of John's writing, it remained fixed within the prevailing canonical concepts it is none the less impressive. Its even tenor—each mention of Michael of Cesena's name was prefixed by 'iste hereticus' as if the sobriquet were self-evident—contrasts with the high-strung tone of the ex-general's appeals; and there was virtually nothing of the personal, self-exculpatory element to be found in the latter. The pope's work, in addition to rebutting his opponents' arguments on use and abuse, consumption and possession, as already mentioned, laid down his own conception of dominion, the diametrical opposite of the Franciscans. The virtues of material poverty were brushed aside as irrelevant to evangelical perfection, which resided in spiritual abnegation, not renunciation of possessions.[4] More important, however, was the pope's direct attribution of dominion to God. Even before the fall, as St. Clement's letter had shown, man in the person of Adam had received lordship over the whole earth. Nor had this been confined simply to the use of its fruits but to all things upon it.[5] Thus from the beginning of time, before the creation of Eve or the laws of kings, property had existed as a divine dispensation.[6] With the fall came private possessions; but they too had been instituted by God in recompense for Adam's sin, as Genesis clearly showed, when God said

[1] BF v, 321.   [2] Ibid., 322–5.

[3] Ibid., no. 820, 408–49, dated 16 November 1329.

[4] Perfectio siquidem evangelicae paupertatis magis consistit in animo, ut scilicet animus amore istis temporalibus non adhaereat, quam in carentia temporalium rerum. . . . Ad illud autem quod dicit quod paupertas evangelica rerum usu consumptibilium dominium et proprietatem excludit, dicimus quod falsum est (ibid., 421a–b).

[5] Procul dubio ista scriptura supponit quod, si primi parentes non peccassent, omnia communia fuissent quoad dominium seu proprietatem. . . . Haec autem divisio facta fuit eius rei cuius prius erat communio; divisio autem facta est rerum et non usus simplici facti (ibid., 417–18).

[6] In scripturis autem divinis habemus quod antequam leges regum, immo etiam antequam reges essent, res aliquae alicuius erant: ergo iure divino aliquis dicere poterat aliquid suum esse . . . videtur enim quod Adam in statu innocentiae, antequam Eva formaretur, solus habuerit dominium rerum temporalium (ibid., 440a).

R

to Adam, 'You shall eat your bread in the sweat of your brow' (3: 19).[1]
Accordingly, property was of divine origin and owed nothing to
human legislation.[2] Having withdrawn material poverty from any part
in evangelical perfection, and transferred its divinity to property, the
pope then proceeded to associate possessions with Christ and the
Apostles. From the outset they had had temporal dominion.[3] Moreover,
except when on missions, it had been private, as could be seen from
Christ's prohibitions upon certain goods; this implied their possession
in normal circumstances and their reversion to private ownership on
their return from preaching.[4] Above all, the pope went so far as to interpret references in *Acts* to the distribution of consumables among the
Apostles and believers, to mean that they had enjoyed private property;
for, once divided up among them, what they received remained theirs.[5]
With full rights of property now conferred upon Christ, the Apostles
and the early Christians, it only remained for the pope to grant them
the right of litigation, which he duly did, although confining it to goods
held in common.[6] With *Quia vir reprobus* the pope's *volte face* from his
predecessors' sanctification of poverty to his own glorification of property was complete. However plausible it might have been to attempt
to reconcile *Cum inter nonnullos* with *Exiit*, as much for what the former
omitted as for what it said,[7] the same could not be done for *Quia vir
reprobus*. This had comprehensively supplanted poverty by dominion

[1] Item quod post lapsum primorum parentum, ante diluvium, et antequam essent
reges, potuerit aliquis dicere: 'hoc est meum', probatur Genesis, cap, 3, ubi Dominus
ad Adam dixit: 'In sudore vultis tui vesceris pane tuo'. Ergo patet quod Adam tunc
potuit dicere panem 'suum'; et tamen tunc non erant reges nec homines alii nisi soli
primi parentes (ibid.).

[2] Unde patet quod nec iure naturali primaevo . . . nec iure gentium nec iure regum
seu imperatorum fuit dominium rerum temporalium introductum, sed per deum,
qui est et erat earum rerum dominus, fuit collatum primis parentibus (ibid., 441a).

[3] Secundo quaeritur utrum Christus alicuius rei temporalis dominium habuerit et
quale. Quod autem dominium rerum temporalium habuerit, sacra scriptura tam in
testamento veteri quam in novo in multis locis testatur (ibid.).

[4] Ibid., 443a–b and 444b.

[5] . . . si detur eis de bonis illis communibus quoad sustentationem vitae suae possint
licite recipere et ut propria retinere, immo hoc scriptura praedicta satis supponit
aperte, cum dicit: 'Dividebatur autem cuique prout opus erat' (ibid., 415b).

[6] Ex quibus satis liquet quod non fuit intentio salvatoris nostri prohibere fideles se
defendere in iudicio et res suas, nisi quando hoc charitas suaderet (ibid., 447b) . . .
illis autem qui habebant communia, pro illis ut pro communibus . . . licuit litigare
(ibid., 448a).

[7] The pope reminded Michael of Cesena that the word dominion had not been
used in *Cum inter nonnullos* (ibid., 439a).

not only in the life of Christ but in the designs of God. Lordship not renunciation was the badge of apostolic life. The pope himself did not admit to any break with the decrees of the past; technically he could be justified, since *Exiit*, the criterion of papal tradition in these matters, had not been concerned with the wider issues of property as such; and Nicholas III's distinction between the different kinds of ownership concerned only goods not consumed in use.[1] The pope also reaffirmed his power to pronounce upon doctrine, taking a passage in Luke 11: 52 as the source of his claim to the key of knowledge.[2]

Quia vir reprobus far outweighed the other replies from the papal side just as Ockham's *Opus nonaginta dierum* (written between 1332 and 1334) did so from that of the Michaelists. The various other exchanges between the contending parties were more in the nature of skirmishes. From the curia at Avignon an anonymous reply to Michael of Cesena's appeals[3] seems to have been concerned mainly to score debating points by showing that Michael of Cesena had supported John XXII and was therefore implicated in his own accusations against the pope. There was also the opportunity which the dispute gave to seculars, such as John of Anneux, to attack the friars.[4] For the Michaelists, the ex-general was tireless in the advocacy of his cause; he protested against the appointment of his successor, Gerald Odo, at the Paris chapter-general of 1329,[5] as did his confrères Ockham, Bonagratia of Bergamo, Francis of Ascoli and Henry of Kelheim, who alleged that only a minority of the provincials had been present.[6] Michael of Cesena also wrote again in vain to the chapter at Perpignan, held in 1331, enumerating twelve errors in *Quia vir reprobus*[7] and once more recounting the events which led to his deposition.[8] Another reply to John XXII[9] (written in 1331) displayed a heightened personal animosity towards the pope and his supporters whom he accused of preparing the way for the sect of Antichrist.[10] He also entered into a fruitless and abusive correspondence with his successor, Gerald Odo.[11]

By far the most considerable Michaelist work was Ockham's *Opus*

---

[1] Ibid., 424–5.

[2] 'Vae vobis legisperitis, qui tulistis clavem scientiae, et ipsi non introistis et illis qui introibant, prohibuistis' (ibid., 448b). This differs from the Vulgate wording.

[3] Summary in BF 425n.–27n.   [4] Douie, *Fraticelli*, 170–3.

[5] *Misc.* III, 314; BF V, 388–96.

[6] Published in *Misc.* III, 315–23; BF V, 388–96.

[7] BF V, 426n.–7n.   [8] BF V, 497n.–500n.

[9] BF V, 527n.–38n.; extract in *Misc.* III, 356–8.

[10] BF V, 435n.   [11] AFH 9 (1916) 134–83.

nonaginta dierum.[1] Running to over 500 printed pages, it was virtually a word for word reply to the pope. Perhaps that is the reason for its flatness. Ockham was fighting on the pope's ground; and although he contested every position he was still accepting the pope's doctrine and the pope's arguments as the basis for his own replies. In these circumstances Ockham could not hope to fashion an alternative system or even to establish a new basis for Franciscan poverty. His were essentially negative spoiling tactics designed to bring down an opponent. How far he was successful must remain a matter of opinion. Frequently Ockham wins the day by sheer power of dialectic; but on the whole it was a war of attrition with the reader as the main victim. It is hard to believe that the *Opus* could have had any great effect upon the contemporary issues: while for us the work is chiefly remarkable for the pertinacity which Ockham brought to his task. On the doctrine of poverty he advanced no argument that Michael of Cesena had not already employed. He stood firmly upon the distinction between possession and use, in consumables, and the poverty of Christ and the Apostles as an integral part of their evangelical perfection. He reaffirmed the validity of a licence to use; without it all religious life would be undermined since it would mean that everything used would also be owned. Thus if an individual monk did not have a licence to ride a horse, he and the monastery would be its proprietors.[2] The same applied to the pope's assertion that Christ and the Apostles had had possessions in private: this would be to render null and void all religious pledges to renounce goods. Moreover, and it was one of Ockham's repeated contentions, if the monks had abdicated private property, so must the Apostles since their poverty was not less perfect.[3] He also denied the pope's claim that solicitude for things temporal was increased by the separation of use from possession: on the contrary the total abdication of ownership sprang from a love of God.[4] Withdrawal of solicitude went with renunciation of possessions.[5] Much of Ockham's attention was taken up with scriptural exegesis to refute John XXII's defence of property as divinely ordained—particularly the claim that Adam and Eve, and subsequently Christ, had owned property.[6] He effectively exposed the pope's often cavalier treatment of his sources and employed the different connotations of words like 'dominion' and 'possess' with telling

---

[1] *Opera politica*, vol. I, chs. 1–6 (Manchester 1940); vol. II, chs. 7–124 (Manchester 1963).

[2] Ibid., vol. II, 377–8.   [3] Ibid., 390.

[4] Ibid., 412–13.   [5] Ibid., 425–6.   [6] Ibid., chs. 14–17.

effect.[1] Thus he disputed that the power of dominion granted to Adam and Eve should be interpreted as owning everything; it was rather to be understood as that of 'governing and ruling with reason'.[2] Their subsequent power to appropriate temporal things was the result of the fall and not an eternal gift conferred by God.[3] From this it followed that the first parents had use without possession;[4] and their initial dominion was not the same as proprietorship.[5] The case was the same for Christ and the Apostles, in their return to a state of innocence.[6] Ockham also took the pope to task for implying that 'to divide' must mean to endow with possessions; money, for example, could be divided among the members of a monastery and yet remain common property.[7] Like St. Bonaventure before him, Ockham distinguished between perfect charity which required no external counterpart, and quasi-perfection, such as absolute poverty or chastity, which demanded complete observance in practice: in this sense to possess goods derogated from perfection.[8] The Apostles, who had enjoyed perfect charity, also observed perfect poverty;[9] as its exemplars their poverty was absolutely devoid of possessions.

In his discussion of simple use and the right to use, Ockham acknowledged that all use entailed a right, but that this could be a natural right —as it was for the Minors—founded in natural law and owing nothing to positive law or human legislation. Hence the natural right to simple use could be enjoyed without entailing ownership of what was used.[10] This was perhaps Ockham's most novel point; it did not alter the substance of the Franciscan case but it did introduce a much needed

[1] Ibid., 440–1.

[2] Ad cuius evidentiam dicunt esse sciendum quod dominium omnium temporalium datum primis parentibus fuit potestas rationabiliter regendi et gubernandi temporalia absque eorum resistentia violentia (ibid., 432). Ockham throughout used the third person plural in order to give the treatise a tone of impersonality as he did in the *Dialogus*.

[3] Et si quaeretur unde ergo habuerunt primi parentes talem potestatem appropriandi res temporales, quam non habuerunt ante peccatum, dicunt isti quod habuerunt illam potestatem ex natura corrupta. (ibid., 435).   [4] Ibid., 435.

[5] Et ex isto sequiter quod, licet dominium ex iure positivo introductum sit idem quod proprietas, dominium tamen si debet vocari dominium, quod competit absque omni iure positivo, divino et humano, non est idem quod proprietas (ibid.).

[6] Ibid.   [7] Ibid., 437–8. See also 401.

[8] Ibid., 455.   [9] Ibid., 456.

[10] Ad hoc dicunt isti quod licet fratres minores in rebus quibus utuntur, non habeant aliquod ius positivum, habent tamen aliquod ius in eis, scilicet ius naturale, licet non semper pro illo tempore quo utuntur (ibid., 561).

flexibility into the rigid separation of use from rights, upon which the pope had played with so much effect in *Ad conditorem* and *Quia quorumdam*. From this Ockham was able to substantiate Michael of Cesena's claim that a licence to use was distinguished from the right of use: the former was granted to the order in cases other than of extreme necessity, whereas the right of use was a natural right only in cases of extremity.[1] It was to such needs that Nicholas III in *Exiit* had applied the term simple *usus facti*: namely the food, drink and clothing upon which sustenance depended; it met these independently of any *ius utendi*.[2] For this reason a licence to use was not a right of use, since it could be revoked, whereas the obligation to meet natural needs could never be renounced. In that sense, all men had some rights, as Nicholas III had recognized.[3] But these—unlike the right of use conferred with usufruct —did not allow the Minors to litigate.[4] One of Ockham's few excursions into philosophy was his employment of the theory of successives to establish the independent existence of the act of use (*actus utendi*) separately from the *ius utendi*:[5] it makes a refreshing, if somewhat extraneous, break from canonical and scriptural exegesis, and probably passed the legalistically-minded pope by. He also admonished the pope for discounting the spiritual—as opposed to temporal—benefits of dominion. To say, as the pope had, that the church's ownership of Franciscan goods was merely verbal and a pretence, was heretical; not only had the arrangement been approved by the church, but, if true, it would mean that future blessedness, which was spiritual, would be equally fruitless.[6]

---

[1] Et ex istis patet quod licentia utendi non est ius utendi. Quia fratres habent licentiam utendi rebus pro alio tempore quam pro tempore necessitatis extremae; sed non habent quodcumque ius utendi nisi pro tempore necessitatis extremae; ergo licentia utendi non est ius utendi (ibid.).

[2] Et ita constat quod Nicholaus vocat simplicem facti usum necessarium usum; et dicitur necessarius, quia requiritur ad sustentandum naturam vel ad aliquid aliud faciendum, quod necesse est fieri. Simplicem autem facti usum vocat actum, qui non habet necessario annexum ius quodcunque, quo aliquis valeat in iudicio litigare. Huiusmodi est actus comedendi, bibendi et huiusmodi . . . (ibid., 508).

[3] [Nicholas III] nunquam dicit eos omnium omne ius abdicare. Quia proprietati et potestati appropriandi licet renuntiare, sed iuri utendi naturali nulli renuntiare licet, quia quilibet omni tempore habet illud ius utendi ex iure naturali sed non quilibet habet illud ius pro omni tempore . . . (ibid., 562).

[4] Sed ordo fratrum minorum non habet usum nudum iuris in rebus nec usumfructum; quia omnis habens talem usum potest pro usu rei in iudicio litigare (ibid., 568).

[5] Ibid., 538.   [6] Ibid., 630.

For the most part, however, Ockham employed the, by then, stock arguments of St. Bonaventure, Bonagratia of Bergamo and Michael of Cesena, barbed with his own dialectic, to answer the pope. He clearly considered property to be an evil in itself, as St. Bonaventure had done; and here, as in his discussion—already mentioned—of charity, we gain a glimpse of a wider outlook within the limits set by *Quia vir reprobus*. Property was the occasion for sin, and as such a danger to the spirit.[1] There could be no point of contact between this view and the sanctification of possessions by the pope. Perhaps because of the completeness of the chasm between them John XXII did not attempt to reply to Ockham as he had done to Michael of Cesena and Bonagratia of Bergamo who, like the pope, kept to the palpable ways of the temporal world.[2]

From Munich the three rebels, together with Francis of Ascoli,[3] maintained a barrage of pamphlets against the ageing pope; they received further ammunition from his pronouncement upon the beatific vision, the errors in which became a regular theme among his opponents.[4] John XXII's obduracy was gradually too much for even the conservative Michael of Cesena who, by the end of the first decade of opposition, had joined his confrères in calling for a general council to depose the heretical pope.[5] Opposition first to John XXII and then to his successor, Benedict XII, increasingly preponderated; the original issue of evangelical poverty ended as it was bound to in becoming more and more an adjunct of imperial policy. This was the weakness of the Michaelists' position. Theirs was a revolt of generals without an army, artificially sustained by a general with an army—the emperor—who was fighting the same enemy but in a different cause. Their position was therefore an artificial one, depending not upon support for their struggle but upon continued opposition against a common opponent. Peace between the pope and the emperor, which more than once

---

[1] Sed possessio quarumcunque rerum temporalium quoad proprietatem et dominium est peccandi occasio, spirituale periculum habens annexum (ibid., 779).

[2] For a list of Bonagratia of Bergamo's polemical treatises see Oliger, 'Bonagratia de Bergamo' AFH 22 (1929) 307-13.

[3] E.g., a treatise against *Quia vir reprobus* in the Laurenziana Library Florence MS. Crucis Plut. 31 sin. con. 3 ff. 23-85. See AFH 11 (1918) 254-5. For an account of his writings see also AFH 20 (1927), 260-304.

[4] First preached in a sermon in 1331. E.g. Ockham *De dogmatibus Johannis* XXII (Goldast, *Monarchia* II, 740-70), and *Contra Johannem* XXII (*Opera Politica* III, 60 ff.). For Bonagratia of Bergamo see Oliger, AFH 22, loc. cit.

[5] Douie, *Fraticelli* 195.

threatened to materialize, would have been the Michaelists' undoing. As it did not come, they gradually faded away, Ockham, the last of the original group, ending his days more as an imperial publicist than as the defender of Franciscan poverty.[1]

The successors—known as the *Fraticelli de opinione*—did little to revivify it. Nothing was said that Michael of Cesena had not already said, as can be seen from the well-known *Appellatio* written some time before the Great Schism, which merely restated the errors with which the ex-general had charged John XXII.[2] Nevertheless, where Michael of Cesena and his supporters had gained little support beyond the adherence for a time of the king of Naples,[3] the Michaelists gained a new impetus in the later fourteenth century. Like the Fraticelli *de paupere vita*, of predominantly artisan composition,[4] they differed in being organized on ecclesiastical lines, with their priests pledged to poverty.[5] Florence was one of the sect's strongholds, and to combat it, the city renewed the emperor Frederick II's anti-heretical legislation in 1382.[6] That the issues had not changed since the time of the original dispute can be seen from the trial of Michael of Calci, who was burned there in 1389: it centred on the poverty of Christ and the heresy of John XXII.[7] There was also an apocalyptic strain in the expectation of the coming of a holy pope.[8] The same views are to be found in the Michaelist pamphlets of the time,[9] of which the *Appellatio* mentioned above was the best known. It elicited numerous refutations from ecclesiastical writers, including James of Marcia's famous *Dialogus*

---

[1] See L. Baudry, *Guillaume d'Occam* (Paris 1950) esp. 126–8. Michael of Cesena and Bonagratia of Bergamo probably died in 1340; Ockham in 1349. They were buried in the Franciscan church at Munich. Francis of Ascoli was captured by the inquisition in Italy in 1341 and recanted (*Misc.* II, 283b–84a).

[2] *Misc.* III, 341–55. Previously attributed to Ockham. See Oliger, AFH 6 (1913) 742–7.

[3] Oliger, ibid., 730–33. The bull is printed on pp. 735–6.

[4] See James of Marcia, *Dialogus contra Fraticellos* (*Misc.* II, 595–610).

[5] E.g., *Catholicus*, Ploro super caecitatem vestram, quia dicitis vos esse ecclesiam, et obeditis vobismetipsis. Quomodo observatis praeceptum beati Francisci, et regulas praecipientes vos obedire, non vobismetipsis, sed papae Romano, catholico, et sanctae ecclesiae, ubi intelligitur beatissimus pater, quod debet esse alia ecclesia, cui obedire teneantur et non sibimet, quia hoc esset quoddam monstrum (ibid., 597a).

[6] Douie, op. cit., 226.

[7] Ibid., 227.

[8] Ibid.

[9] E.g., L. Oliger, 'Documenta inedita ad historiam Fraticellorum' in AFH 3 (1910) 263–6.

contra Fraticellos.[1] The exchanges between the two sides were for the most part a repetition, at a lower level, of the earlier polemics; and apart from identifying the Michaelists are of little intrinsic interest. The foundation of a new reforming group within the Franciscan order, the Observantines, in the early fifteenth century,[2] gave the Michaelists the *coup de grâce*; the Observantines' personal rigour, and their enthusiasm for reform and the extirpation of heresy, gradually overcame the Fraticelli despite the latter's violent resistance. By the time of the trial at Rome in 1456,[3] they were a spent force. Like the Free Spirit, north of the Alps, they had vanished before the end of the fifteenth century into the mists and the hills.

[1] The ecclesiastical party was undoubtedly the better equipped. In addition to James of Marcia there were Andreas Ricchi, the Florentine inquisitor, who wrote a treatise in 1381 (Oliger, 'Documenta inedita', AFH 3 (1910) 267–79, 505–29, 680–99); John of Celle (see Douie, *Fraticelli*, 232–40); St. John of Capistrano (Oliger, art. cit., AFH 6 (1910) 716–720).

[2] Inspired by St. Bernadino of Siena and seconded by James of Marcia and St. John of Capistrano, who, in addition to writing against the Fraticelli, were made inquisitors (BF VII, no. 1710, 653).

[3] ALKG IV, 110–34.

PART TWO

Union with God

III

The Spiritual Climate

The spiritual life of the later middle ages was largely dominated by mysticism in a variety of forms.[1] Much of it was spurious, and some of it heretical; but whatever the quality, they shared in the common striving—or the claim to it—to reach God through an inner movement of the soul. If achieved it resulted in an immediate awareness of him, not as a beatific vision but as an ineffable experience of his presence. This desire for union with God went together with the need to withdraw from contact with the outer world, in order to devote oneself solely to the search for God within. It led to the proliferation of spiritual communities and individuals concerned to detach themselves from the accepted norms of life. Such an attitude, if unregulated, was a threat of the first magnitude to the authority of the church. Not only was it outside its sacramental life; but it could—and in the case of the heresy of the Free Spirit did—challenge its very *raison d'être*. To seek direct contact with God in the soul was to tend to look away from the mediation of the church; it could also mean denying its truths in the name of truths found within. At the very least it was implicitly to introduce two sources of divine sanction; and in the case of the avowed heretics of the Free Spirit, it led to the direct confrontation between their claim to divinity and the demands of the church, which they rejected.

Parallel with the growth of personal piety was the theological development of the doctrine of divine omnipotence. God, it was argued, was so free and all-powerful that his actions were entirely beyond human calculation and hence unknowable. Accordingly, among William of Ockham and his followers, in particular, the emphasis upon God's will led them to an attitude of fideism in which all that concerned God was a matter of belief not accessible to rational demonstration or natural experience.

In both cases, the emphasis was upon God's indefinability in terms of external wisdom—ineffability for the mystic; unpredictability for the

[1] For an account of later medieval spirituality see J. Leclercq, F. Vandenbroucke, F. Bouyer, *La spiritualité du moyen âge* (Paris 1961) 448 ff.

Ockhamist. In both cases it made for an individual acceptance of God: through inner search for the mystic; through faith unembellished for the Ockhamist. If the one tended to militate against an ecclesiastical régime of worship, the other did so against a natural theology. In both cases belief in God was better satisfied without intermediaries, whether ecclesiastical or intellectual. Such were the tendencies implicit in much of the spiritual and intellectual life of the time. They led to the growth of new values and attitudes, which at their most extreme issued in heresy. They were an important part of the spiritual climate of the later middle ages; and for that reason we must examine their non-heretical antecedents as well as their heretical forms.

Eckhart: mysticism

The significance of Meister Eckhart (c. 1260–1327) goes beyond the strict limits of mysticism. A German Dominican, who became vicar-general of his order for his native province of Thuringia, he brought to a new level the combination of scholasticism and Neoplatonism which his confrères Albert the Great and Dietrich of Freiburg had already begun. He thus straddled the paths of speculative theology and mysticism. It is this fact that makes Eckhart's thinking so complex. Even more than most great subjects of academic enquiry, Eckhart studies have provided a particularly fruitful field for learned dispute. He has by turns been made pantheist, Thomist, Neoplatonist; orthodox, heterodox, consistent, muddled, original, derivative. The only point of general agreement is that he cannot be meaningfully approached exclusively as a theologian or as a mystic. But even this has too often led to an unreal division between his scholastic, Latin writings and his vernacular sermons and treatises. It is true that the first, in being designed for an academic audience, were more rigorous and precise than his German works, which besides tending to oversimplify, tend also to misrepresent him through being the reports of his hearers: a fact of which Eckhart complained at his trial at Cologne in 1326.[1] Yet they are a unity; and to break it, effectively destroys Eckhart's system and often his meaning. His metaphysics formed the basis of his mysticism; his mysticism was the response to his metaphysics. The one posits the nature of God and creation; the other the means by which men must act in order to grasp the truth and so attain unity with God. If this

[1] G. Théry, 'Edition critique des pièces relatives au procès d'Eckart', *Archives* I (129–268) 188, 196.

makes Eckhart's mysticism speculative, it also makes it metaphysical, as opposed to affective. The soul remains for him the object rather than the subject; he treats it as one essence in a world of essences rather than the focus of individual experience. In this he was much closer to the Neoplatonist tradition of Plotinus and Proclus than of the western mystics. If he also drew upon his German forerunners, like Mathilde of Magdeburg and Hadewiich for his particular doctrine of the poverty of the soul,[1] the outcome was a distinctive mysticism. It was not simply an attempt to combine accepted elements; Eckhart's significance is that he put mysticism upon a new metaphysical basis. To do so he turned away from the traditional western stream while remaining largely within its theological tradition. For that reason it is unprofitable, and largely impossible, to see Eckhart as either Thomist or Neoplatonist; he was both; and therefore both more and less than either. Nor can he be regarded as mainly a return to St. Augustine.[2] On the one hand, he went beyond theology, unlike St. Thomas and even Augustine: on the other, his mysticism was set firmly within a Christian framework, unlike the Neoplatonists.

Yet it is not simply because of this that Eckhart is important here. It is rather because of his almost incalculable influence upon subsequent religious life. Paradoxically, Eckhart, the most complex of mystics, became one of the main sources for the diffusion of mysticism. Not only did his outlook permeate the German Dominicans, directly inspiring a new school of Rhineland mystics of whom Suso and Tauler were the most prominent; he also indirectly helped to swell the wave of popular and unofficial piety which spread over the greater part of the Rhineland, the Low Countries and Central Europe during the fourteenth century. In particular there was a strong affinity between some of the doctrines attributed to him in the twenty-eight propositions condemned in 1329[3] and the heresy of the Free Spirit.[4] That Eckhart had heretical leanings can be rejected out of hand. As I shall hope to show, the whole tendency of his beliefs was to a profound spirituality; any errors, if such they were, came from the way he expressed his frequently difficult notions as opposed to the almost calculated profanities of the Free Spirit. Yet the seeming *rapport* was not entirely

---

[1] For these see Leclercq, Vandenbroucke, Bouyer, op. cit., especially 433–8, 450–2, 460.

[2] A tendency in J. Ancelet-Hustache, *Master Eckhart* (New York and London 1957) e.g. 60 and 67.

[3] See pp. 293 ff. below.   [4] See ch. IV.

fortuitous. Whatever his intentions, the stress of Eckhart's mystical teaching was upon the individual: upon his ability to disengage himself from the world of things, and to empty the soul of all created images, depended the coming of God's word within him. If this needed the supernatural gift of grace, Eckhart was so concerned to lay down the prerequisites for it that he gave the gift itself little explicit mention. Similarly this emphasis upon the soul's strivings led him frequently to compare external works unfavourably with the soul's inner movement: another of the Free Spirit's characteristics. Above all, his insistence upon the return to God, through the birth of the word (or the Son) in the soul, led him to speak as if the individual himself became part of God as Christ was: *words* which sounded perilously pantheistic, and which the Free Spirit expressed in *deeds*. In these ways Eckhart was a portent; he gave voice to the growing desire, orthodox as well as heterodox, for personal ascesis; he preached the accessibility of God to the individual soul at a time when there was a growing tendency to look away from hierarchy both within the church and thought. Eckhart's mysticism was at once the high point of medieval mysticism and the beginning of its descent to the increasingly affective and subjective forms which it took in the fourteenth and fifteenth centuries. Although he began from the opposite point to Ockham, they each, in their emphasis upon God's inherent unknowability, made faith in God and individual experience their two poles, with no meeting place in the external world. Both accordingly adopted a not dissimilar fideistic attitude to God, on the one hand, and to the limitations of individual knowledge, on the other, as can be seen in some of their condemned propositions.[1] But whereas Eckhart, as a mystic, rejected the external world, Ockham, as an empiricist, took it in its own natural terms: for Eckhart the individual *soul* became the object of experience; for Ockham the individual *thing* given to the senses. Ultimately both made for that same *impasse* between the world of nature and the world of faith which is the dominant fact in the religious life of the later middle ages.

The starting point in any discussion of Eckhart's outlook must be his view of God.[2] It was not only the source from which everything else

[1] See pp. 295 ff. below.
[2] Of the library of books on Eckhart, the late Vladimir Lossky's *Théologie négative et connaissance de Dieu chez Maître Eckhart* stands in a class of its own. For what follows I am indebted to its remarkable insight into Eckhart's thought which makes most of

flowed but it demonstrates his characteristic combination of traditional and Neoplatonic concepts which, taken singly, appear to conflict. God could be conceived in two aspects: in his own nature, and as creator. In his own nature he is simply being without definition or elaboration.[1] To use God's own words, he is the being that is (*sum qui sum*): being in its plentitude, purity and indistinctness;[2] for if he is infinite he cannot be defined, since all definition entails negation;[3] and if he is indefinable he cannot be known beyond saying that he is the One, the name above all names.[4] As such he is the hidden God in the

---

the previous controversies over his pedigree seem irrelevant. Its concern, however, is principally with Eckhart's theology rather than his mysticism. For the latter a useful account can be found in J. Ancelet-Hustache's *Master Eckhart* (London 1957) which, however, tends to make Eckhart more traditional than he was in his teaching on grace. Among the numerous other Eckhart works mention may be made of H. Denifle, 'Meister Eckeharts lateinische Schriften und die Grundanschauung seiner Lehre' in ALKG II (1886) 417-615; H. Hof, *Scintilla Animae* (Lund-Bonn 1952); O. Karrer, *Meister Eckehart: Das System seiner religiösen Lehre und Lebensweisheit* (Munich 1926); M. A. Lücker, *Meister Eckhart und die Devotio Moderna* (Leiden 1950); M. Muller-Thym, *On the universality of being in Meister Eckhart of Hocheim* (St. Michael's Mediaeval Studies, 1939); *Ekhartiana* in ZKG 56-8 (1937-9) by E. Seeberg, M. Pahnke, E. Reffke and others.

[1] Esse est deus per essentiam (Prologue *in Opus propositionum* i L.W. I, 41, see also 156-8, 161-2). And: Deus autem est ipsum suum esse (*Expositio libri Exodi*, L.W. II, 27).

[2] Primum inter 4or, scilicet quod solus deus proprie est ens patet Exodi 3: ego sum qui sum (ibid., 42 and 157-8). And: Dicens ergo deum esse unum, vult dicere quod deum esse indistinctum ab omnibus, quod est proprietas summi esse et primi (*Commentary on Book of Wisdom*, in *Archives* IV, 1929, 247). Again: Adhuc autem quarto, distinctio omnis infinito repugnat (*Expositio libri Exodi*, L.W. II, 66).

[3] in deo autem nec cadit numerus nec multitudo nec negatio, sed mera affirmatio et plenitudo esse secundum illud: 'Ego sum qui sum'... propter quod in ipso nec est numerus, nec multitudo, propter quod tres persone non sunt multi, sed unus deus... (*Commentary on Wisdom*, *Archives* III, 1928, 431).

[4] Sic in divinis personis una essentia est, quia nullus numerus essentiarum est in divina essentia.... Sic in deo omnis perfectio una est, quia in ipso nullus numerus perfectionum est. Hinc est quod qui ipsum deum videret per se ipsum, per essentiam dei scilicet, non ex aliis nec per alia media, videret unicam perfectionem, et per ipsam et in ipsa videret omnes perfectiones, non ipsam per illas. Hec tamen perfectio non esset hec vel illa, sed quid unum super omnes.... Hoc tamen unum non esset nomen sapientie nec potentie, et sic de singulis, sed esset unum omnia super omnia in quo omnia, secundum illud Phil 2, 'donavit illi nomen quod est super omne nomen'. 'Nomen', inquit, in singulari, quia est unum 'quod est super omne nomen' (*Expositio libri Exodi*, L.W. II, 62-3).

S

very nature of his being,[1] not, as with the Neoplatonists and the pseudo-Dionysius, because he is above being. In that sense he is beyond all description and all names: strictly speaking he cannot be called good or true, and so on, because these terms bring number and distinction to the One, which by definition is utterly without all number and distinction in its own nature.[2] But just as that which is superior contains in a higher degree all the perfections in that which is inferior, so that 'name which is above all names' (the One) is not *innominabile*, but *omninominabile*.[3] As Augustine said, 'All things can at once be said of him and are unworthy of him. . . . Seek a fitting name and you will not find it; seek a way of speaking of him and you will find all.'[4] To do so entails the way of negation, in which everything predicated of God has to be denied in terms of created being. Thus to call God being must mean being without relation or negation as these violate God's simplicity; to call him substance must be understood as without a subject, because God can have no division; to call him first can only apply to what is outside him.[5] In himself he is the One in which there is no number and every mode and reason.[6] The only negation which can be posited of him is the negation of the negation; for as the One he alone is first and full being, the source of all other being, and so without negation.[7] Accordingly the negation of the negation is the term alone reserved for the

---

[1] Et subdit (Avicebron) quod scire essentiam primi, dei scilicet, est impossibile, tum 'quia ipsa est super omnia', tum quia 'infinita', tum quia 'non est similis' intellectui, . . . (ibid., 225, also 266). And: Absconditur primo magnitudo et multitudo, quia non videtur, nec magnum nec multum nec longum pre amoris et dulcedinis immensitate . . . secundo absconditur magnitudo in simplicitate, multitudo in uno (*Sermones*, L.W. IV, 84). See Lossky, op. cit., 16, 30, 34, 36 ff. Also *Expositio in Johannem*, L.W. III, 163 ff.

[2] Iuxta quod nota duo: primo quod li bonus, verus, veritas, et similia non proprie de deo dicuntur, quia addunt sive numerum faciunt in cogitatione sive conceptione, aut ratione venire (*Sermons*, L.W. IV, 31). And: Tertio, quia sicut deus est in se indistinctissimus secundum naturam ipsius, utpote vere unus et propriissime . . . (ibid., 28). See also *Expositio libri Exodi*, L.W. II, 51.

[3] 'Nomen' ergo, 'quod es super omne nomen' non est innominabile, sed omninominabile (*Expositio libri Exodi*, L.W. II, 41–2).

[4] Ibid., 42.

[5] Ibid., 42–3.

[6] Ibid., 64–5.

[7] Preterea li unum est negatio negationis. Propter quod soli primo et pleno esse, quale est deus, competit, de quo nihil negari potest, eo quod omne esse simul prehabeat et includat (*Prologus in Opus propositionum*, LW I, 169). Also, ibid., 175; and *Expositio libri Exodi*, L.W. II, 21.

One; it is the height of affirmation, denoting being in its highest and purest and fullest from which nothing can detract.[1]

God then in his own essence is being in itself (*ipsum esse*), the denial and exclusion of all that is not.[2] If he is in his own nature indistinct and indefinable, he is by the same token—as full being—distinct from everything else.[3] Moreover, as pure being and the source of all being, being is the formal principle of God's actions;[4] hence it is in the One, as pure being, that we must seek God;[5] and this entails reducing everything to unity by way of negation, i.e. denying all division and multiplicity until we arrive at the negation of the negation.[6] Hence, as we have said, anything we say about God, other than that he is One, cannot be strictly true. This does not, however, mean that the perfections which we attribute to him are false; it is that they derive from our created concepts, and describe God in terms of our experience rather than his nature. From this aspect they refer to his operations: his goodness, mercy, wisdom, and so on, as they are manifested to us.[7] Here Eckhart parted company with St. Thomas in making the names of God's attributes derive exclusively from us,[8] without any correspondence

[1] Sciendum igitur . . . quod li 'unum' primo est voce quidem negativum, sed re ipsa affirmativum. Item est negationis, que est purissima affirmatio et plenitudo termini affirmati (*Commentary on Wisdom, Archives* IV, 249–50).

[2] Significat li 'unum' ipsum esse in se ipso, cum negatione et exclusione omnis nichili (ibid., 251). Also ibid., 239 and 307; *Expositio libri Exodi*, L.W. II, 142.

[3] Ubi notandum quod cum dicimus omnia esse in deo, sicut ipse est indistinctus in sui natura et tamen distinctissimus ab omnibus, sic in ipso sunt omnia distinctissime simul et indistincta (*Sermones*, L.W. IV, 27–8).

[4] Minor autem, scilicet quod esse sit principium omnis actionis divine, scilicet principium formale, patet, tum quia ipse se toto est esse, tum quia in ipso nihil est aliud quam esse aut preter esse (*Expositio libri Exodi*, L.W. II, 34).

[5] Ad litteram est notandum quod sic est in naturalibus quod esse semper est unum et in uno; esse autem deus est, vel ipso immediate est; et sub pallio unius unitur deus et esse in omnibus; et sub pallio et proprietate unius res omnis capit deum (*Commentary on Wisdom, Archives* III, 426).

[6] Qui enim duo vel distinctionem videt, deum non videt. Deus enim unus est, extra numerum et super numerum . . . (*Expositio libri Exodi*, L.W. II, 65).

[7] 'Impossibile' autem est 'scire essentiam prime essentie absque his facturis que ab ea sunt; possible autem est scire exsuis operibus' (ibid., 225). And: Nota primo quod deus, cum sitinnominabilis pro immensitate sui, ex operibus suis solet nobis innotescere. Que tamen opera exteriora quam sint 'longe in regione dissimilitudinis', patet primo ex operatione omnis creature, que distat ut accidens a substantia (*Sermones*, L.W. IV, 92).

[8] Constat autem quod distinctio attributorum divinorum, potentie scilicet, sapientie, bonitatis et huiusmodi, totaliter est ex parte intellectus accipientis et colligentis cognitionem talium ex creaturis et per creaturas, ubi necessario hoc ipso quod

in God's nature, as opposed to his actions. It takes him much closer to the Neoplatonic tradition of refusing to consider God strictly as other than the One. Yet this similarity is more apparent than real. The Neoplatonists, in putting the One above being, also put him beyond the hypostatic process. The word—or the Son—and the world soul—or Holy Spirit—were both engendered outside the One. For Eckhart, as for all Christian thinkers, the process was internal to God's nature. The divine persons belonged to a single essence; they were inseparable from God's nature as the One.

This brings us to the other facet from which God can be considered, namely, as creator. Here he is no longer undifferentiated essence but a trinity of persons through whose movement he confers being on his creatures, and they in turn—or at least those endowed with reason—can seek to be reunited with him. In this context Eckhart's thought changes perspective. He now approaches God no longer as being but as intelligence, since it is through the Son, or the word (corresponding to the Neoplatonic logos), that he engenders all archetypes or *rationes*—man, lion, stone—from which creation derives. But, unlike the Neoplatonists, this takes place through the direct action of God and within God; the Son, as belonging to the divine nature, is the direct means of conferring being upon that which is outside God and of itself nothing. For that reason we see God no longer as simply being, but as being in relation to itself and to creatures. In that light he is also intellect, of which being is the principle.[1] If, as Eckhart never tires of saying, the two are inseparable as part of the same nature, they nevertheless constitute different aspects of God; in that of creator, intellect is uppermost, since it is the origin of creation and the means of return to God. Accordingly, as we shall see, Eckhart often stresses the primacy of intellect over being; so that he seems both to contradict what we have previously seen him to say[2] and to retreat from Christian tradition to

---

ab uno quidem, sed sub uno sunt, incidunt in numerum, multitudinem et distinctionem . . . (*Expositio libri Exodi*, L.W. II, 64). And: Patet ergo radix et ratio premissorum, et quomodo dicuntur affirmationes omnes sive nomina positiva nullo modo deo competere, nec in ipso esse aliquam dispositionum universaliter sive substantalium sive accidentalium, quantumcumque in nobis sint perfectiones, puta potentia, sapientia, vita et huiusmodi (ibid., 57).

[1] E.g., Ideo solus deus per intellectum producit res in esse, quia in ipso solo esse est intelligere (*Sermones*, L.W. IV, 268); also: Sed natura dei est intellectus, et sibi esse est intelligere (*Expositio libri Genesis*, L.W. I, 194–5).

[2] E.g., M. Grabmann, 'Neuaufgefundene Pariser Questionen Meister Eckharts' in ABAW, Philos-Hist. Klasse XXII, 7, 1927. See Lossky, op. cit., 210 ff.

Neoplatonism.[1] If, however, this is taken in the context of creation, there seems no inherent conflict, as may be seen from what follows.

The emanation of the divine persons is the starting point of creation. As St. John said, 'In the beginning was the word' and at the end 'all things were made by him'.[2] This was taken by Eckhart to mean that the word was also the means of engendering the essences of creatures; in that sense, as Lossky has pointed out,[3] there were two words: the first internal, the second external, but both simultaneous. Now it is precisely this extension of the word to everything created which was the core of Eckhart's system; for it determined not only his conception of being but his mysticism.

To begin with, since in God, being and understanding are one, for God to be is to understand; hence he produces immediately through his intellect.[4] In it reside the forms of all beings.[5] But, in contrast to the Neoplatonists, with Eckhart the intellect is part of God's essence; therefore its archetypes (rationes) inhere in God's essence. The intellect is thus the means by which God in his simplicity can understand a multiplicity without one contradicting the other;[6] for, again, unlike Neoplatonism, God's causality and understanding are not confined to producing the word—or Son—outside himself, which then becomes the source of created forms: God's intellect is part of God and the word is produced in him. Accordingly we may say that the intellect is the immediate cause of creation, as being is its formal principle. If God's being is the source of all being, without which there would be no being,[7] his intellect is, so to say, God's being in action, as it is manifested both to itself and outside it; as such it becomes the means by which God transmits his being to his creatures. In Eckhart's words, 'the intellect is the principle of the whole of nature'.[8] Accordingly, the

---

[1] E.g., E. Bréhier, *La philosophie du moyen âge*, 425. As so often, however, there is much that is illuminating in what Bréhier says.

[2] *Expositio libri Exodi*, L.W. II, 22.   [3] Lossky, op. cit., 54.

[4] Sed natura dei est intellectus, et sibi esse est intelligere (*Expositio libri Genesis*, L.W. I, 194-5).

[5] Sed deus naturaliter prehabet omnes formas et omnium (ibid., 195).

[6] Et per consequens: sic ut sue simplicitate non repugnat intelligere plura, ita nec producere plura immediate (ibid.).

[7] Questio prima est, Utrum deus sit. Dicendum quod sit. Ex propositione iam declarata primo sic: si deus non est, nihil est (*Prologus generalis in Opus tripartitum*, L.W. I, 158; also ibid., 39).

[8] Adhuc autem secundo sciendum quod principium in quo deus creavit celum et terram est natura intellectus. . . . Intellectus enim principium est totius nature (*Expositio libri Genesis*, L.W. I, 189).

generation of the word—or the Son—must not be regarded as a distinct movement within God; it belongs to the same eternal procession of the divine persons in which the Father generated the Son.[1] In that sense the beginning in which God created heaven and earth was simply eternity; it took place within the timelessness of God's existence at the same instant in which the Son was engendered.[2] That does not, however, make the world eternal or creation divine. Here again, Eckhart's insistence upon God's being as the foundation of all his operations enables him to avoid both of these dangers inherent in Neoplatonism. In the first place, they are distinct as being. As we have seen, God alone is being in the strict sense; everything else is thus by definition less than being, at once being and non-being.[3] It is being in that it derives from God; non-being in that of itself it is nothing.[4] In absolute terms, God—or the One—is distinguished from everything else (omnia) as being is to nothing; in terms of creation, it is the difference between the simplicity, fullness and indistinction of the One and the multiplicity, negation, and instability of all things else.[5] They be-

---

[1] Secundo notandum quod in deo, ut pote primo, uno et simplicissimo, necessario ipse intellectus est ipsum esse sive ens reale et realiter. Ex quo patet quod operationes intellectus sive intellectuales in deo sunt reales processus sive productiones et emanationes et producta sunt quid reale, puta fillius et spiritus sanctus. . . . Et propter hoc procedens manet in producente et cum producente in unitate essentie, nature, esse vivere et intelligere et huiusmodi, nequaquam cadens vel recedens ab uno nec sub uno, sed sic procedens reali processione et ipsa essentia producentis intra unum in uno et ipsum unum (Liber Parabolarum Genesis, L.W. I, 690–1).

[2] Rursus tertio principium, in quo deus creavit celum et terram, est primum nunc simplex eternitatis, ipsum, inquam, idem nunc penitus in quo deus est ab eterno in quo etiam est, fuit et erit eternaliter personarum divinarum emanatio. Ait ergo Moyses deum celum et terram creasse in principio absolute primo, in quo deus ipse est, sine quolibet medio aut intervallo. Unde cum quereretur a me aliquando quare deus prius mundum non creasset respondi quod non potuit eo quod non esset. Non fuerat prius antequam esset mundus. Preterea: quomodo poterat creasse prius, cum in eodem nunc mox mundum creaverit in quo deus fuerit? Non enim imaginandum est falso, quasi deus steterit expectans nunc aliquod temporis futurum in quo crearet mundum. Simul enim et semel quo deus fuit, quo sibi filium sibi coeternum per omnia coequalem deum genuit, etiam mundum creavit (Expositio libri Genesis, L.W. I, 190). See also Expositio in Johannem, L.W. III, 181 ff.

[3] Omne citra deum, utpote citra esse, est ens et non ens (Expositio libri Exodi, L.W. II, 77).

[4] Omne autem ens creatum acceptum vel conceptum seorsum per se distinctum a deo non est ens, sed est nihil. Separatum enim et distinctum a deo, separatum et distinctum ab esse (Expositio libri Exodi, L.W. II, 45).

[5] E.g. Expositio libri Sapientie, L.W. II, 347 ff.

come something in virtue of participating in being, without becoming being as such. In the second place God and his creatures are equally distinct as essence. God's essence is the perfect being of the One to which nothing can be added; the forms of things which inhere in his word are not formally in God but only in the things to which they give their name and species—man, lion and so on. So far as God is concerned they are merely in his intellect virtually, as the causes of that which comes into being outside him; in him they possess no being, just as they do not in themselves.[1]

This distinction between God's essence and the forms in his word has its counterpart in creation. Every creature, says Eckhart, is a compound of an uncreated essence or quiddity or form (*essentia et non ab alio*)—man, lion, stone—and created being (*esse ab alio*). Thus, unlike God, whose being is his essence, it is not enough to know that a creature exists to know what it is:[2] being and essence, other than in God, are not being, nor do they confer being:[3] justice or whiteness remain independent of the individuals in which they inhere.[4] They are both prior (*ante rem*) and posterior (*post rem*) to just men or white things.[5] They

---

[1] Preterea tertio, in deo non sunt res ipse aut forme rerum, sed rerum et formarum rationes. Deus enim est verbum, id est logos, quod est ratio, Ioh. I: 'deus erat verbum'. Nihil autem tam simile pariter et dissimile sicut ratio rei et res ipsa. . . . Forme autem rerum que dant rebus speciem et nomen, sunt in rebus ipsis formaliter et nullo modo in deo. E converso nullo modo forme rerum sunt in deo formaliter, rationes autem rerum et formarum sunt in deo causaliter et virtualiter. Et iste nullo modo rem denominant nec dant speciem nec nomen. . . . Sic igitur res creata et eius forma, per quam habet nomen, est in re ipsa, nequaquam in deo. E converso ratio forme est in deo ubi nec dat speciem nec nomen (*Expositio libri Exodi*, L.W. II, 113-14).

[2] Quia igitur in omni creato aliud est esse et ab alio, aliud essentia et non ab alio, propter hoc alia est questio an est, querens de anitate sive de esse rei, alia est questio quid est querens, ut dictum est, de quiditate sive essentia istius rei (ibid., 23-4). Accordingly where God is *anitas* (Avicenna's term) as self-sufficient being, created being is *quiditas*. To affirm that God existed was to affirm that his nature was being; but to say that a creature existed was not to say what his nature was. See Lossky, op. cit., 99-104.

[3] Rursus tertio notandum quod res in sua causa essenciali sive originali non habet esse, similiter nec in arte sua, nec in intellectu (*Commentary on Wisdom*, Archives III, 342. See also *Prologus in Opus propositionum*, L.W. I, 171-2).

[4] Rursus ad evidentiam premissorum notandum quod non est ymaginandum sicut plerique tardiores estimant quod iustitia sit alia in pluribus, iustitia divisa et numerata, fixa et radicem habens in ipsis iustis, sicut se habet et iam dictum de accidentibus corporalibus; sed potius omnes iusti sunt et una numero iustitia, numero tamen sine numero et una sine unitate . . . (*Archives* III, 368. Also 365-7).

[5] Ratio siquidem **rei** prior est et prestantior ipsa re utpote principium et causa illius

are also uncreated, as the forms engendered in God's word.¹ As such
they remain independent essences, indifferent to the created beings
which they inform and to which they are superior.² They therefore
remain whole and undivided in creatures, since the inferior is always
subject to the superior.³ We can thus discern the quiddities of things in
themselves; and it is to these rather than to things that all true knowledge and truth pertain.⁴

Created being, on the other hand, is the sole concern of God. As
being in itself, God is the principle of all being, as he is of unity, truth
and goodness, which are inseparable from being.⁵ Now, since being is
the foundation of all creation, it is the first and most universal state,
coming before all genera and species.⁶ In that sense the first creation
was universal being (*esse commune*)⁷ as the foundation of everything
else. The result was a very different concept of being from St. Thomas's.
For the latter it was synonymous with existence: as that which was
alone actual. Accordingly a creature's essence could only exist when it
was transformed from potential being into actual being. This was the
role of its substantial form—man, lion and so on. God, on the other

---

(*Sermones et Lectiones super Ecclesiastici*, L.W. II, 265); and: Sunt enim ante rem et
post rem . . . (*Archives* III, 343).

¹ Adhuc quarto: rerum creatarum rationes non sunt create, sed nec creabiles, ut sic
(ibid.). Also *Expositio libri Genesis*, L.W. I, 71 and 49–50, 186–8.

² Adhuc autem ipsa rerum ratio sic est principium, ut causam extra non habeat
nec respiciat, sed solam rerum essentiam intra respicit (ibid., 187; 49).

³ *Commentary on Wisdom*, Archives, III, 365–8; *Prologus generalis in Opus tripartitum*,
L.W. I, 37: 152–3.

⁴ *Expositio libri Exodi*, L.W. II, 60; and: Uniuscuiusque enim rei universaliter principium et radix est ratio ipsius rei. Hinc est quod Plato ponebat ideas sive rationes
rerum principia omnium tam essendi quam sciendi (*Expositio libri Genesi*, L.W. I,
187).

⁵ Preterea ens, unum, verum, bonum sunt prima in rebus et omnibus communia.
Propter quod assunt et insunt omnibus ante adventum cuiuslibet cause non prime et
universalis omnium. Et rursus insunt a sola causa prima et universali omnium. . . .
Ex quo manifeste convincitur quod a deo habet omne ens et singulum quod est,
quod unum est, quod verum est et quod bonum est, et quodlibet ens unumquodque
premissorum ab ipso deo non solum habet, sed immediate habet (*Prologus in Opus
propositionum*, L.W. I, 43–4; also 171–2).

⁶ Notandum quod creatum omne, cum sit hoc aut hoc, distinctum quid, proprium
alicui generi, speciei vel singulari. Deus autem non est quid distinctum aut proprium
alicui nature, sed commune omnibus . . . Probat hoc ipsum ens, effectus dei, quod
non est in genere nec proprium alicui generi, sed communi omni generi (*Expositio
in Johannem*, L.W. III, 88–9).

⁷ Lossky, op. cit., 81.

hand, was pure act; in him essence and existence were identical. It was this absence of any potentiality which distinguished him from his creatures. Hence the difference between divine and created being was that between two different kinds of existence: one self-caused, infinite and eternally actual; the other accidental and the result of outside agency. They could only be compared by analogy not through any common nature.

For Eckhart it was the other way round: God, as the source of all being, conferred it upon his creatures; in giving being to what had previously been non-being, he thereby enabled his creatures to partici-pate in his own nature—which was being; and, in so far as a creature was, he shared being in common with God. The difference was not in its actuality but in its completeness: God as the One had being as his essence; everything else was at once being and non-being.[1] In that sense for Eckhart, being came first in the order of creation. It was the con-dition for the forms which gave creatures their quiddities; without being there could be no individual since their natures, as they pre-existed in God, were without being. To become being they had to be created, which meant their production outside God.[2] This could only be done by God; he alone was the universal and immediate cause of all being;[3] in creating he was conferring being upon non-being.[4] As a result no secondary causes or uncreated forms could add to or subtract from being;[5] at most they could make something become what it was.[6]

Superficially this might appear to be the same as St. Thomas's notion of form as the actualization of a being's potentialities. In fact, there was a profound difference. When St. Thomas averred that form gave being to the thing (*forma dat esse rei*) he was taking being to mean existence.

---

[1] Omne citra deum, utpote citra esse, est ens et non ens (*Expositio libri Exodi*, L.W. II, 77).

[2] Omnia autem sunt in deo tamquam in causa prima intellectualiter et in mente artificis. Igitur non habent esse suum aliquod formale, nisi causaliter educantur et producantur extra, ut sint. Et hoc est quod hic dicitur: creavit deus, ut essent omnia (*Expositio libri Sapientie*, L.W. II, 342; *Archives* III, 342-3).

[3] esse autem rerum omnium, sive naturalium sive artificialium, ab ipso deo solo est immediate, utpote primum et perfectum (ibid., L.W. II, 340). Also *Opus tripart-itum*, L.W. I, 38.

[4] Creatio enim est collatio 'esse post non esse' (*Expositio libri Sapientie*, ibid., 340); *Opus tripartitum*, ibid.

[5] Septimum quod nihil creatum addicit vel confert rebus quippiam entitatis, uni-tatis, veritatis, seu bonitatis (*Prologus in Opus tripartitum*, L.W. I, 182, 47).

[6] Hic primo notandum quod rerum fieri est quidem a causis secundariis (*Expositio libri Sapientie*, L.W. II, 340). Also *Sermones et Lectiones super Ecclesiastici*, L.W. II, 276.

With Eckhart, on the other hand, the role of forms had nothing to do with being as such, but only with the nature of a particular being whose existence was already given. As he put it: 'God, however, is total being and operates in creatures through being in itself and under the form of being.'[1] Accordingly the nature or quiddity of creatability is being. It is this which is common to all things produced by God. Whatever they may be in addition—living, understanding, and so on—their sole *ratio* as beings was creatability; living and understanding alone—without being—would be uncreated.[2] Hence the form of, say, fire gave fire not as being or unity, but as the specific quality which made it this or that fire.[3] In that sense form individuated being; for it was the agent which gave it identity, making it recognizable according to its essence as this or that nature—man, stone, and so on—without adding to it as being.[4] Thus a stone was a composition of its being, which was entirely from God, and its form by which it was a stone.[5] The latter in turn engendered all those corporeal qualities, such as matter, form, quantity, by which it was a physical entity; but this physical totality (*corpus mixtum*) remained subject to the overall form of the stone in whose similitude it was fashioned.[6] As we have seen earlier the superior inheres whole and independently in the inferior; hence any essential form—such as man's soul or fire—is immediately and totally present in his being and not successively.[7]

We are thus in world essences, of which, as for Avicenna and Duns

---

[1] *Expositio libri Sapientie*, L.W. II, 343-4.

[2] Rursus sexto notandum quod ratio creabilitatis est esse, secundum illud: 'prima rerum creatarum est esse'. Unde res producta a deo, quamvis sit ens, vivens et intelligens, ratione tamen solius esse est creabilis. Unde si quid esset vivens aut intelligens, non habens esse aliquod preter et extra vivere et intelligere, ipsum esset ut sic increabile (ibid., 344).

[3] Forma enim ignis non dat igni esse, sed hoc esse, nec esse unum, sed esse unum hoc, puta ignem et unum ignem. Similiter de vero et bono. Sed hoc ipsum, puta quod forma ignis dat esse ignem, unum, verum, bonum, habet per fixionem cause prime . . . (*Prologus in Opus tripartitum*, L.W. I, 171-2).

[4] Igitur nihil ens hoc vel hoc dat esse, quamvis forme dent esse hoc aut hoc in quantum hoc aut hoc, non autem in quantum esse (ibid., 178; see also 46).

[5] Sic etiam potius totum compositum, puta lapis, habet esse lapidis a forma lapidis, esse vero absolute a solo deo, utpote a prima causa (ibid., 180, 47).

[6] Adhuc hoc autem non est imaginandum quod cause rei—efficiens puta, finalis, formalis et materialis—singula esse afferant et conferant composito, sed res se tota cum omnibus suis partibus er proprietatibus idem esse a solo fine totaliter finaliter solum, a forma vero formaliter, a materia passive sive receptive (ibid.).

[7] Ibid., 174 and 44.

Scotus, being was the first and most universal. *Esse* and *essentia* were not, as with St. Thomas, two aspects—or states—of the same thing but two separate elements which coalesced in creation. They remained distinct within the very structure of created being. For Eckhart, in contradistinction to St. Thomas, the essential form of a thing remained in itself uncreated; being alone joined it to what was created.

In that sense, being was an accident which neither added to nor subtracted from essence, just as essence did not alter being as such. For that reason a creature was a duality: in its original nature it was firm and stable; but in its created form in the natural world it was infirm and variable.[1] It was both essence (uncreated) and existence (created).

Now this dualism brought Eckhart closer to Plotinus than to Aristotle. The antithesis was less that between God as pure act, the first uncaused cause, and the potentiality of his creatures, than of the One to the many. They differed as beings rather than as being: the One, as pure affirmation, was the negation of all non-being; the other, as multiplicity, was the negation of full being, which was unity. In this situation God's uncreated essences were the middle term between being, which was in God, and nothing, which was outside him. They were the forms by which God conferred being where previously there had been none; through the *rationes* in his intellect what had been non-being became the multiplicity of created being, which in itself remained nothing.[2] Thus uncreated essences were the means by which creatures participated in God's being: their essences were originally indivisible in him, so that they were at once a unity and a multiplicity.[3] This sense of participation was one of the formative elements in Eckhart's outlook; rather than a hierarchy of causes, he conceived the universe as a hierarchy of forms, or essences, in which the superior penetrated the inferior, starting from One as the first principle of creation.[4] The chain of

---

[1] *Expositio libri Genesis*, L.W. I, 238.

[2] Esse autem semper stat in uno, multa enim ut multa non sunt . . . (*Commentary on Wisdom, Archives* III, 430).

[3] Ratio omnium predictorum est quia superius semper afficit secundum se ipsum omne suum inferius et ab ipso in nulla vice versa afficitur. . . . Igitur deus creator afficit omne creatum sua unitate, sua equalitate et sua indistinctione secundum illud Procli: 'omnis multitudo participat aliqualiter uno', et omne divisum ab aliis est indivisum in se (*Expositio libri Sapientie*, L.W. II, 360).

[4] Undecimo, quia deus eo dives profusivus est, quia unus. Primus enim et supremus est ratione qua unus. Propter quod unum descendit in omnia et singula manens semper unum et divisa uniens (*Sermones*, L.W. IV, 266). Also *Expositio libri Sapientie*, L.W. II, 363; *Opus tripartitum*, L.W. I, 38, 41, 153.

being, as it were, reached down from the One through his uncreated forms into creatures. If this was a very different conception from St. Thomas's it also broke off sharply from Plotinus and Proclus in deriving immediately from God's direct actions.

To turn therefore from created being to its uncreated quiddities was a step along the path towards God; they were the only source of stable knowledge in the created world.[1] Even so, they were only the way back to the *rationes* in God's word, not the guide to his own nature; for between the One, by definition unknowable, and the many, who were distinct and defined, there was no analogy, as Eckhart himself conceded.[2] As infinite and indistinct God responded to no created terms like genus and species,[3] which distinguished and circumscribed. As unity he could not be conceived in terms of the multiplicity in creation. As perfect plenitude his was beyond all affirmation other than as One through the negation of the negation: he who sees two, or distinction, said Eckhart, sees not God.[4] Accordingly the path back to him could only be by way of negation through reducing all God's attributes to unity.[5] But this, as we have seen, entailed predicating nothing of God save Oneness; hence his inherent unknowability.

Now it was from this—essentially Plotinian—aspect that Eckhart's perspective changed from that of metaphysics and theology to mysticism. Up to now God has been considered in terms of being, as the state common to him and his creatures, that is, as the One. But if this has meant affirming him as being it meant also denying him as the antithesis of non-being and, with it, all that could be predicated of creatures—goodness, wisdom, mercy, and so on: in Eckhart's words, One is negative as a word but affirmative as thing—being.[6] Hence the negation of the negation was the purest affirmation.[7] It meant in effect divesting the term of all that pertained to created being. The antithesis between the One and the many, which was the core of Eckhart's theology, thus prevented the use of concepts drawn from the world: unlike St. Thomas, Eckhart was unable to take its modes—movement,

---

[1] E.g., *Expositio libri Genesis*, L.W. I, 62, 204, 238.

[2] Deo autem nihil est nec dici potest simile, primo, quia ipse 'nihil commune habet cum aliqua re', sed etiam 'essentia non dicitur de deo et de aliis nisi equivoce pure' (*Expositio libri Exodi*, L.W. II, 44); also, ibid., 44–58.

[3] Deus autem, utpote extra genus, cum nullo convenit nec specie nec genere (ibid., 44–5).

[4] Qui enim duo vel distinctionem videt, deum non videt (ibid., 65).

[5] Lossky, op. cit., 95 ff.

[6] *Commentary on Wisdom, Archives* IV, 249–50.   [7] Ibid., 250.

causality, varying degrees of perfection which were the accompaniment of multiplicity—as an analogy for God's being. The way was barred by his insistence upon the ineffability of God's being. The path of negation thus led away from the world and into the soul; for there alone detachment from created things, the condition of reunion with God, was possible.[1] The ascent to God had to be by an inner movement which entailed the rejection of being for understanding; for this alone—so far as creation was concerned—was uncreated. As we have seen, the essence or *ratio* or *quiditas* represented a being's true nature as conceived in God's word or intellect. It was therefore the principle of both being and understanding, the one outside the soul in *rerum natura*, the other within it as an intellectual concept.[2] Now the first object of man's natural knowledge was being, from which, as the result of the fall, he had to abstract the immaterial essences of things encountered in the senses.[3] Accordingly he could only conceive being as created and temporal—i.e. as multiplicity—and not as eternal.[4] This was a reversal of the true order, which was from the uncreated quiddity to its inherence as the species in corporeal things; being thus added nothing to truth, which was the preserve of the uncreated quiddity, but rather impeded it. Only through the species could a being be known in its true essence, as for example man by his nature of humanity.[5] Truth therefore belonged to the *ratio* in the intellect; what lay outside it were not true essences or perfections.[6] This was not just to separate being from

[1] Quarto, quia volens deo uniri, ipsum invenire, debet esse unus, divisus ab omnibus, in se indivisus abnegatione sui. Ubi nota quod deus non invenitur in multitudine, secundum Augustinum in Soliloquiis, et quantum, bonum facit abnegatio, quantam pacem (*Sermones*, L.W. IV, 321).

[2] ... esse intellectuale in anima quod per *celum* intelligitur ... et iterum ad esse materiale extra animam quod per *terram* significatur. Propter quod Plato ideas ponebat esse principium cognitionis et generationis (*Expositio libri Genesis*, L.W. I, 204).

[3] Secundum est quod intellectus in nobis sterilis est sicut tabula nuda—III De anima —nec concipit nisi prius concipiat sensus (ibid., 374). See also *Expositio libri Exodi*, L.W. II, 35; *Opus tripartitum*, L.W. I, 37, 38.   [4] *Expositio libri Genesis*, L.W. I, 154.

[5] Notandum . . . sicut nullus potest esse iustus sine iustitia, sic nemo potest scire iustitiam nisi per iustitiam et in ipsa iustitia; et sic universaliter unumquodque sicut habet esse per speciem suam solam in natura, puta homo humanitate, sic et cognoscitur unumquodque in sola specie sui ipsius in anima cognoscentis (*Commentary on Wisdom*, *Archives* IV, 305).

[6] Secunda ratio talis est: ratio id quod est ad intellectum pertinet et ad veritatem. Veritas enim in solo intellectu est, non extra. Igitur perfectiones in rebus extra non vere perfectiones sunt (*Expositio libri Exodi*, L.W. II, 152); also *Commentary on Wisdom*, *Archives* IV, 361.

understanding; it was to make non-being the condition of understanding, since it could only come through turning towards immaterial
essences and forms.[1]

Now it is in this context that Eckhart's distinction between being
and intellect in God must be seen. For if God as the One was absolutely
simple being, and synonymous with intelligence,[2] from the standpoint
of creation they could be distinguished and God conceived as both
being and intellect.[3] Moreover, as the principle of all things, God's
intellect was higher than being, since its *rationes* were the cause and end
of all created being.[4] God as the first cause of all things was intelligence;
for otherwise he could not conceive them; and he who was without
understanding could not be God.[5] Thus it was from the aspect of
creation that God was intellect; and where intellect, in turn, as the
principle of being, was higher than being. Far from their separation in
God, just because God's intellect and being were one, he had to be conceived as intellect; to posit his being separately would destroy his simplicity.[6] The distinction was therefore from man. As Eckhart said, God

---

[1] Item: species est principium operationis sensitive vel intellective. Sed species non
est aliquo modo ens. Ergo nec intelligere aut sentire erit aliquo modo ens (*Questiones
Parisienses*, L.W. v, 50–1).

[2] E.g., *Expositio libri Exodi*, L.W. ii. 76; *Expositio libri Parabolarum Genesis*, L.W. i,
658.

[3] Notandum primo quod in deo, principio omnium, est considerare duo, ut sic
dicamus, puta quod ipse est esse verum, reale, primordiale. Adhuc autem est ipsum
considerare sub ratione qua intellectus est. (*Expositio libri Parabolarum Genesis*,
L.W. i, 690), and: Secundo sciendum quod alius est ordo istorum in abstracto, puta
cum dicimus esse vivere, intelligere; alius in concreto, puta cum dicimus ens, vivens,
intelligens. In abstracto enim esse est perfectius inter tria. Ipsi enim esse nullus modus
sive perfectio essendi deesse potest. . . . Pari ratione vivere est nobilius intelligere. In
concreto vero opposito modo se habet: ens enim infimum tenet locum, vivum
secundum, intelligens tertium sive supremum. Et est ratio: nam in concreto sunt
participantia. Omne autem participans ut sic nudum et imperfectum est ex se ipso.
Propter quod primo participat ex sui imperfectione in imperfectiori gradu partici-
pationis, et plus sapit naturam imperfecti. (*Expositio in Johannem*, L.W. iii, 52).

[4] Et huius rationis proprietas altior apparet ex hoc quod omne ens reale in natura
'procedit ad certos fines' er 'per media determinata' tamquam rememoratum per
causam altiorem, ut ait Themistius (*Expositio libri Parabolarum*, ibid.).

[5] Adhuc autem de quocumque quero utrum in ipso sit intellectus sive intelligere
aut non. Si non, constat quod non est deus sive prima causa omnium sic ordinatum
in fines certos quod intellectu caret (*Sermones*, L.W. iv, 267).

[6] Si vero habet aliquod esse aliud quam intelligere, iam est compositum, non
simpliciter unum. . . . Ideo solus deus per intellectum producit res in esse, quia in
ipso solo est intelligere (ibid., 268).

could be variously conceived at the different levels of being, living and understanding; of these, understanding was supreme.[1] The intellect, as the principle of things in their primordial cause, i.e. as reasons before they became being,[2] contained within itself no being; for, unlike our knowledge, which came under being, God's caused being, and so came under his intellect. Accordingly everything in God was, as understanding, above being.[3] Thus when, in the Paris Questions, Eckhart said that God was, because he understood—as opposed to understanding because he existed—this may be taken as referring to him as creator; he not only supported it by St. John 1: 1, 'In the beginning was the word';[4] but he also expressly stated that 'God, who is creator and not creatable, is intellect and understanding and not being'.[5] As being he can only be regarded as efficient cause; but as essence he is exemplary cause.[6] As such he is the principle of created being without being of it: the essence of being (*puritas essendi*) rather than being.[7] For these reasons intelligence comes first in the scale of perfections.[8]

We have thus returned to the same point, via God as creator, as that which we reached from the nature of creation; namely, that being of itself has no form, either in God or creatures, but is the reason of creatability.[9] Intellect, or understanding, is the universal cause of being, and so, on the principle that the cause is not the same as the effect, distinct from it.[10] This applied both to God's intellect and to created

[1] Suprema vero in entibus ipsum audiunt deum non solum per esse et in esse, aut per vivere et in vivere, sed per intelligere et in ipso intelligere (*Liber parabolarum Genesis*, L.W. I, 621).

[2] *Sermones et Lectiones super Ecclesiastici*, L.W. II, 238).

[3] Differt enim nostra scientia a scientia dei, quia scientia dei est causa rerum et scientia nostra est causata a rebus. Et ideo cum scientia nostra cadat sub ente, a quo causatur, et ipsum ens pari ratione cadit sub scientia dei; et ideo quidquid est in deo est super ipsum esse et est totum intelligere (*Questiones Parisienses*, L.W. v, 44).

[4] Tertio ostendo quod non ita videtur mihi modo, ut quia sit, ideo intelligat, sed quia intelligit, ideo est, ita quod deus est intellectus et intelligere et est ipsum intelligere fundamentum ipsius esse. Quia dicitur Ioh 1: 'in principio erat verbum, et verbum erat apud deum, et deus erat verbum'. Non autem dixit evangelista: 'in principio erat ens et deus erat ens' (ibid., 40).

[5] Ibid., 41   [6] Ibid.

[7] Et ideo cum esse conveniat creaturis, non est in deo sicut in causa, et ideo in deo non est esse, sed puritas essendi (ibid., 45).   [8] Ibid., 43.

[9] Cum igitur deus sit universalis causa entis, nihil quod est in deo habet rationem entis, sed habet rationem intellectus et ipsius intelligere (ibid., 46).

[10] Item: ens in causa sua non est ens. Nullum enim univocum habet vere rationem cause. . . . Et ideo in deo, a quo totum ens descendit, ratio entis non invenitur. Cum

intelligences. Consequently they could meet only as intelligences, not as beings.[1] Intellect thus came first among man's faculties; it was superior to the will and so were its virtues of wisdom, understanding, and prudence, compared with the moral virtues acquired through the will's appetites.[2] But above all the intellect had a certain affinity to God (*deiformitas*), since God was himself understanding;[3] its act of intelligence took it to the bare essence of a thing,[4] which ultimately derived from God.

Granted, then, that truth was the property of the intellect and understanding superior to being, in what circumstances could man regain his source in God's word? The short answer was: not by mere intellectual processes; or, more strictly, not by way of intellectual abstraction. The intellect's deiformity lay in its nature as non-being; it therefore had to turn away from being to non-being to realize it; and this meant to the recesses of the soul. For there it entered an incorporeal and eternal region, where understanding was directed to heaven, not to this world. Just as God had created heaven and earth, so he had created corresponding kinds of knowledge, spiritual and corporeal.[5] It was within, as Augustine had said, that God, as truth, dwelt, away from space and time.[6]

Now this region was distinguished from the intellect. In contrast to the latter it had its own innate higher *rationes*, independent of the created world, such as wisdom and truth, which enabled it to know beings not just in their created natures but in their higher natures, as conceived by God.[7] This celestial knowledge—or image as Eckhart

---

igitur nostrum intelligere ab ente causatur, descendit ab ente et per consequens tendit in non-ens nec esse habet (ibid., 54).

[1] Ascendere igitur ad intellectum subdi ipsi, est uniri deo. Uniri, unum esse, est unum cum deo esse (*Sermones*, L.W. IV, 270).

[2] *Questiones Parisienses* (3) L.W. V, 60.

[3] (4) Item: ipsum intelligere quedam deiformitas vel deiformatio, quia ipse deus est ipsum intelligere et non est esse (ibid.).

[4] (3) Ibid.

[5] *Liber parabolarum Genesis*, L.W. I, 692–3.

[6] Tertio nota quod 'in homine interiori habitat veritas', id est deus, cuius natura est semper et solum esse intus et in intimis. . . . Quarto nota quod homo interior nullo modo est in tempore aut loco, sed prorsus in eternitate (*Sermones*, L.W. IV, 79).

[7] Propter quod philosophus dicit quod 'anima est locus specierum', que sunt rationes rerum, 'non tota sed intellectus'. Augustinus etiam ex Platone dicit quod sapientia et veritas non sunt in hoc mundo, sed in mundo alteriori, scilicet intellectuali (*Sermones et Lectiones super Ecclesiastici*, L.W. II, 240.)

called it[1]—was created with the soul, unlike the images of species in the intellect which derived from the external world.[2] It was precisely the need to disengage one from the other, to reject the images of the world, which constituted the prerequisite for attaining this interior awareness.[3] The seed of virtue was in every soul; if allowed to grow it would lead man to eternal life.[4] The habit of knowledge, with which all men were naturally endowed, enabling them to know the difference between true and false and good and bad, was from the light of reason which was a participation in the divine light;[5] this was the source of both understanding and the virtues. Although it could be obscured by evil, it could never be extinguished.[6] Now this light was God's word.[7] Therefore to reach God, it was necessary to follow the light in the soul: the further one penetrated to it the nearer one came to heaven;[8] and the greater the distance from the corporeal world.[9] It was in the incomparable beauty of his interior life that man had originally lived; he had then seen God not through inferiors and exteriors but these through God. His soul had been illuminated by God's immutable truth. Hence man was said to have been made in the image of God, and his paradise was this intellectual realm of the soul.[10]

This was the world of Augustine as adapted from Neoplatonism. The soul had hidden within it knowledge of first principles, impressed there by God. These were the germ of all its knowledge, which could, like a Platonic memory, be recalled to the understanding through application, and the stimulus of the senses.[11] These ideas (*in abdito mentis*) were the means by which the intellect understood. We are far removed here from the *tabula rasa* of Aristotle and St. Thomas: the

[1] After Origen, *Liber parabolarum Genesis*, L.W. I, 665.

[2] Imago enim proprie est quod in anima a deo est concreatum, non superinductum ab extra sive superscriptum et quasi affixum de foris et ab alio (ibid., 666).

[3] Ibid.   [4] Ibid., 671.

[5] Lumen ergo rationis in nobis quod est participatio divine et supremi luminis, semen est tam virtutum quam scientiarum . . . (ibid., 672–3).

[6] Ibid.

[7] Hoc 'semen est verbum dei' Luc. 8 . . . (ibid., 673).

[8] Ratio autem premissorum est quia anima rationalis ex sui perfectione inter omnes formas interiores magis appropinquat et assimilatur perfectioni motoris celi (ibid., 628).

[9] Ibid.   [10] Ibid.

[11] In virtute enim primorum principiorum naturaliter anime impressorum a deo est virtualiter et radicaliter omnis scientia secundum omne sui. Propter quod etiam Plato ponebat scientias anime concreatas, per studium vero et exercitium sensuum ex mentis abdito ad aciem intelligentie revocari . . . (ibid., 694).

T

world of the senses has been relinquished for the inner reaches of the soul; innate ideas and virtues, infused from the 'Giver of Forms',[1] have replaced general concepts drawn from being. The soul was eternally illuminated by God's word; it was for a man to decide whether this light was to remain hidden. If he was capable of God he could be reunited to him through his word.[2] This was the import of Eckhart's theology. It became the theme of his mysticism.

★   ★   ★   ★

It is a commonplace that the centre of Eckhart's mysticism is union with God through the birth of the word in the soul. It is usually termed the mysticism of essence or being (*Wesenmystik*) to distinguish it from subjective or affective mysticism as personal experience. This is undeniable and so far as it goes true. But it cannot alone explain the significance of Eckhart's conception of the birth of the Son in the soul. It went together with his belief in essence as being, and the intellect, in both God and man, as its source. Consequently, Eckhart's mysticism was not just objective and metaphysical; it was intellectual. It centred upon the ability of a man to make himself capable of God by turning inwards to the soul where eternal truth resided. To that degree Eckhart, as we have seen, followed St. Augustine; where he went beyond him was in seeking not simply eternal reasons—truth, wisdom, justice, and so on—but their source in his word through which God was present in the soul; for the soul to be reunited with the word was for it to be restored to its original place in God's intellect. The *ratio* or form or *semen* became not the *terminus ad quem* but the *terminus a quo*: not the destination for knowledge of God; but the point of departure for union with him. Accordingly, intellect—as the spark in the soul—became the operative term; if man were to pass beyond regarding God as an object he had to divest himself not only of the images of created objects, in which God's essences were embodied, but of any awareness of all. He had to empty himself of all signs of himself in order to allow

---

[1] The term was Avicenna's (*Metaphysics* IX, ch 2, 5): dicit iustitiam et virtutem esse a datore formarum (*Expositio libri Sapientie* L.W. II, 367).

[2] lumen quidem sapientie, sub ratione sapientie, non recipitur in corporibus, sed nec in anima rationali ut natura sive ens est in natura, sed in ipso (intellectu) solo, in quantum intellectus est, superius aliquid est et divinius . . . eo enim imago est, quo dei capax est, ut ait Augustinus. . . . Item quod ipse Augustinus docet quod in abdito mentis semper lucet, quamvis lateat lumen divinum (*op. cit.* in *Archives* III, 415-16).

the word to enter. This call to detachment (*Abgeschiedenheit*), or spiritual poverty, was the other aspect of Eckhart's mysticism. It was inseparable from his intellectualism, since, as we shall mention, it sought not an upwelling of love or ecstasy or rapture—all manifestations of the will—but complete renunciation of all feeling and knowing. Only then could the soul be infused with grace and supernaturalized.

Now it was Eckhart's emphasis upon the intellect—as opposed to the will—as the vehicle towards awareness of God which marked him off from St. Augustine and brought him close to Plotinus and Proclus; for like them he conceived the soul's return to God as an ascent through God's traces in the soul; these consisted in the principles and ideas which, as we have seen, were innate to it. Their progressive recognition in the mind gave it a growing awareness of God; to achieve union with him, however, it had to go beyond knowledge and divest itself of all images until it was finally freed from any encumbrances which stood between it and direct awareness of God. With Eckhart, too, orientation was through the intellect; only when the soul had prepared itself to receive God—by casting off all self-identity—did God then join it to him through the word. Supernatural aid came to complete natural effort. For St. Augustine, on the other hand, grace was the initial requisite for a right orientation towards God; right willing came before right-thinking; and so it was the will, reborn through grace, which was the means to awareness of God. As a result, with St. Augustine, the soul's spiritual journey was less a mystical exploration within itself, culminating in union with God, than a careful plotting of the signs by which God could be known: what, with Eckhart, only came at the end was for St. Augustine given at the outset.

The mystical side of Eckhart's doctrine is principally to be found in his vernacular writings. In his sermons, in particular, his endeavours to make himself comprehensible to his hearers—often nuns and invariably without theological training—led him sometimes to simplify to the point of error. Most of the twenty-eight articles, for which he was posthumously censured in 1329, as well as the charges brought against him at Cologne two years earlier,[1] were drawn from this source. To anyone acquainted with Eckhart's outlook as a whole it is inconceivable to regard him as having had pantheistic leanings or the kind of amorality associated with the Free Spirit; but it is undeniable that passages taken out of context could appear to be both, as we shall mention. Eckhart's attempts to express the soul's strivings in terms of his

[1] See p. 293 below.

negative theology were peculiarly prone to misrepresentation; his emphasis upon the need to become nothing tended to blur the distinction between creature and creator and to discount external factors, whether time, place, or works. Furthermore Eckhart's natural love of paradox, which has made his writings a happy hunting-ground for every kind of thinking, from libertinism to German idealism, often betrayed his true meaning. For these reasons alone Eckhart's outlook needs to be considered through the ensemble of his writings. But it is also necessary to do so because they are a totality; Eckhart's mysticism is not only the outgrowth of his metaphysics and theology: it is conceived in terms of them. It was determined by the same antithesis between unity and multiplicity, being and nothing; and to overcome them, man had to rediscover the word, in which all that was not God had originated. The difference was between descent and ascent. His theology and metaphysics described the procession from God to creation and was therefore an externalization of what was within God to what he created outside him; his mysticism was concerned with the ascent to God from creation, and therefore entailed the progressive transcendence of all that was not God in order to return to him. Together they made up the cycle of emanation and return which was eternally enacted.

As we have seen, the soul was the nodal point in this process; and more particularly its inner reaches, variously named by Eckhart ground (*Grund*) or summit (*Haupt*). There resided the inner spark (*Fünklein*) or something (*Etwas*) or power (*Kraft*) which constituted God's immediate presence.[1] Like God it was unnameable and indefinable, above all description as heaven was above the earth; it was so entirely one and simple, free of all forms, that no man could identify it[2]. It came from

---

[1] E.g., *Vom edlen Menschen* (Quint 143, D.W. v, 109 ff., 498 ff.); Predigt 1 (Quint 156, 158, D.W. 1, 14 f., 430–1); Predigt 2 (Quint 161; D.W. 1, 35 f., 435–6); Predigt 6 (Quint 180, D.W. 1, 5*b*, 90, 450); Predigt 8 (Quint 190, D.W. 1, no. 7, 123–4, 457–8); Predigt 11 (Quint 201, D.W. 1, no. 10, 161–3, 467); Predigt 14 (Quint 221, D.W. 1, no. 13, 220, 482); Predigt 20 (Quint 243, D.W. 1, no. 20*a*, 332, 506); Predigt 21 (Quint 247, D.W. 1, no. 20*b*, 344, 511); Predigt 32 (Quint 307); Predigt 34 (Quint 315); Predigt 35 (Quint 318); Predigt 39 (Quint 341); Predigt 42 (Quint 352); Predigt 51 (Quint 392, 3, 4); Predigt 57 (Quint 417). The Stuttgart edition of Eckhart's German works has only reached the first 24 sermons of which the editor, Josef Quint, has only authenticated the first fifteen.

[2] Ich habe bisweilen gesagt, es sei ein Kraft im Geist, die sei allein frei. . . . bisweilen habe ich gesagt, es sei ein Licht des Geistes; bisweilen habe ich gesagt, es sei ein Fünklein. Nun aber sage ich: Es ist weder dies noch das; trotzdem es ist ein Etwas,

the spirit, dwelt in the spirit, and remained wholly of the spirit. Within it was God in all his fullness, sweetness and bliss; beside it all other experience, whether of joy or sadness, paled.[1] There was nothing especially novel in this notion; many mystics before Eckhart, to name only Hugh and Richard of St. Victor, had posited a similar sector of the soul where direct contact with God could be attained. Nor was he alone in making the path to it depend upon withdrawal from all created images. What distinguished Eckhart was the hypostatic nature of the union. The *Fünklein* or *Etwas* was an image of God himself; it was a light or spark, not a faculty.[2] It was accordingly uncreated, belonging not to the soul—whose image it did not contain—but to God.[3] Had it been the same as the soul, the soul would itself have been uncreated; but Eckhart hastened to add that it was not.[4] He compared the *Fünklein* rather to the uncreated light in angels, enabling them to seize God directly.[5] As such it directly radiated God's image as he was himself; it was not therefore part of the soul's being but its life of reason through which a man became God's son.[6] This in effect was to make it part of God's

---

das ist erhabener über dies und das als der Himmel über der Erde. . . . Es ist von allen Namen frei und aller Formen bloss, ganz ledig und frei, wie Gott ledig und frei ist in sich selbst. Es ist so völlig eins und einfaltig, wie Gott eins und einfaltig ist, so dass man mit keinerlei Weise dahinein zu lugen vermag (Predigt 2, Quint 163, D.W. I, 39–40, 437).

[1] Noch eine Kraft gibt es, die ist auch unleiblich; sie fliesst aus dem Geiste und bleibt im Geiste und ist ganz und gar geistig. In dieser Kraft ist Gott ohne Unterlass glimmend und brennend mit all seiner Reichtum, mit all seiner Süssigkeit, mit all seiner Wonne . . . alles, was er leiden könnte und was Gott von ihm erlitten haben wollte, das wäre ihm alles gerinfügig, ja ein Nichts (ibid.; Quint 162; D.W. I, 35–6, 436).

[2] . . . Dieser Knecht das Fünklein der Seele, das da geschaffen ist von Gott und ein Licht ist, von oben her eingedrückt, und es ist ein Bild göttlicher Natur, das allwegs allem dem widerstreitet, das nicht göttlich ist, und es ist nicht eine *Kraft* der Seele, wie etliche Meister meinten . . . (Predigt 20, Quint 243; D.W. I, 20a, 332–3, 506).

[3] Ich habe zuweilen von einem Lichte gesprochen, das in der Seele ist, das ist ungeschaffen und unerschaffbar. Dieses nämliche Licht pflege ich immerzu in meinem Predigten zu berühren. Und dieses selbe Licht nimmt Gott unmittelbar, unbedeckt entblösst auf, so wie er in sich selbst ist (Predigt 34, Quint 315).

[4] Eine Kraft ist in der Seele, von der ich schon öfter gesprochen habe,—wäre die Seele ganz so, so wäre sie ungeschaffen unerschaffbar. Nun ist dem nicht so. (Predigt 14, Quint 221; D.W. I, 13a, 220, 482). Eckhart himself denied saying this at his Cologne trial (Thierry: 'Edition critique', *Archives* I, 187); and in the bull of condemnation it was placed in an appendix (ALKG II, 636–9).

[5] See note 3; also Predigt 32, Quint 306.

[6] Predigt 35, Quint 318.

eternal word, the uncreated essence with which man was endowed. It remained distinct from his created being as whiteness or goodness remained separable from the beings in which they inhered. But whereas to know whiteness or justice was by an act of abstraction which— sensory or intellectual—gave a knowledge of them as archetypal qualities, to find God's image in the soul was to know God. For man as a rational being had been created in his image. We are thus back to the same distinction between the *Fünklein* and the soul as we encountered between any uncreated essence and its created form; namely, between living and understanding, on the one hand, and being, on the other. Just as living and understanding were the properties of the uncreated form so they were of the *Fünklein*; being belonged only to what was created. Accordingly the *Fünklein* was the source of the rational life of the soul, and the way to eternal life. By discovering God's image within him a man became reborn as God's son.[1] It was in that sense, of returning to the word, which was God, that the word was born in him. Such a man was reunited with the eternal image which was at once God and in his soul as God's image.

Here, in true neoplatonist tradition, Eckhart had made the soul's reunion with God come about through the *ratio* or image; it was the assertion of intellect over will; and Eckhart repeatedly stressed the superior nobility of reason.[2] The explanation was that the will took God in the garb of goodness, whereas the intellect took him purely as deity, divested of goodness and being. Blessedness therefore lay in knowing God as understanding.[3] The will signified activity; and activity militated against oneness which was God.[4] The light in the soul was that of understanding which sprang from that whose being was reason.[5]

---

[1] Die Seele hat etwas in sich, ein Fünklein der Erkenntnisfähigkeit, das nimmer erlischt, und in deises Fünklein als in das oberste Teil des Gemütes verlegt man das 'Bild' der Seele. . . . Das innere Erkennen ist jenes, das sich als vernünftartig im Sein unserer Seele fundiert. Indessen *ist* es nicht der Seele Sein, vielmehr *wurzelt* es darin und ist etwas vom Leben der Seele. Wenn wir sagen, dieses Erkennen sei etwas vom Leben der Seele, so meint das *vernünftiges* Leben, und in *diesem* Leben wird der Mensch als Gottes Sohn und zum ewigen Leben geboren (ibid., 318).

[2] Ich aber sage, dass die Vernunft edler ist als der Wille (Predigt 10, Quint 198; D.W. I, no. 9, 153, 464).

[3] Der Wille nimmt Gott unter dem Kleid der Gutheit. Die Vernunft nimmt Gott bloss, wie er entkleidet ist von Gutheit und von Sein. Gutheit ist ein Kleid, darunter Gott verborgen ist. . . . Dadurch allein bin ich selig, dass Gott Vernünftig ist und ich dies erkenne (ibid., 198–9).

[4] Predigt 7, Quint 186, D.W. I, no. 6, 113–14, 455.

[5] Predigt 33, Quint 311.

Not that Eckhart believed that reason as a human faculty could lead to God; the *Fünklein* stood above both reason and will as natural powers; the condition of its awareness was self-oblivion.[1] It was rather that the supreme vision of God was as intelligence by the intelligence which God had implanted in the soul; from the word it came: to the word it must return if it were to be reunited with God.

Eckhart's attitude was thus essentially contemplative. In this he went against the mainstream of Western mysticism, which from St. Augustine to St. Bernard, has stressed the active nature of the ascent to God. The Augustinian tradition had seen the will as the faculty of blessedness; and at the very time when Eckhart was writing and preaching, the claim had been revived by Duns Scotus and his followers. Eckhart shows his awareness of this opposition by his references to the many doctors who held the opposing view to his own.[2]

This difference was not merely formal. The whole of Eckhart's outlook was coloured by the effort to reach this higher awareness. In the first place it meant the rejection of all self-awareness as creature-bound and ego-directed (*Ich-Bindung*). Man could only be perfect when he had become alienated from himself, formed in God's will.[3] Unlike affective mysticism, which became so widespread in the later fourteenth century, for Eckhart feelings of any kind were to be rejected; there was none of the recoil of sadness following the moment of ecstasy described by say Julian of Norwich or St. Catherine of Siena. Sadness was the accompaniment of outer things, in which no consolation could be found;[4] it was a sign of man's involvement with the created and his lack of oneness with God.[5] Secondly, reason was the temple of God. He lived in himself as understanding, eternally knowing himself in complete stillness. It was this same understanding which was the uncreated spark in the

---

[1] Denn du musst wissen, dass sie innen frei und ledig ist von allen Vermittlungen und von allen Bildern, und dies ist (denn) auch der Grund dafür, dass Gott sich (unmittelbar) frei, ohne Bild oder Gleichnis mit ihr vereinigen kann (Predigt 57, Quint 418).

[2] E.g., p. 283 note 2 above.

[3] Nun könnest du fragen, *wann* der Wille ein rechter Wille sei? Dann ist der Wille volkommen und recht, wenn est ohne jede Ich-Bindung ist und wo er sich seiner selbst entäussert hat und in die Willen Gottes hineingebildet und-geformt ist (*Reden der Unterweisung*, Quint 66; D.W. v, 218, 514). See also Predigt 27 (Quint 274); and 7 (Quint 183; D.W. I, 105, 453).

[4] *Das Buch der göttlichen Tröstung* (Quint 106; D.W. v, 474).

[5] Predigt 13 (Quint 215; D.W. I, no. 12, 197, 477).

soul—as a tributary of God's light.[1] It was, therefore, this same reason which united God with man; reason brought him understanding of pure being and with it the birth of the Son in the soul: as St. Matthew said (11: 27), 'No man knows the Father save the Son.'[2] To know God simply as being, as opposed to understanding, was to know him only in his outward aspect.[3] To become one with him could only be through understanding. This was the root of blessedness:[4] it represented the return to man's uncreated essence which was the word and in God.[5] It was what Eckhart meant when he spoke of man's humanity (*Menschheit*): namely his uncreated nature, not as God's creation, but as eternally within God.[6] In the aspect of humanity, as opposed to that of a human being (*Mensch*), a man's nobility gave him likeness to the angels and kinship with God; in his uncreated essence the same oneness which Christ had with the Father was open to him. To achieve it entailed renouncing his individuality, as this or that man, for his quiddity or essence as man.[7] Thus the return to God was through the same medium

---

[1] Wo ist er denn aber in seinem Tempel, in dem er als heilig erglänzt? *Vernunft* ist 'der Tempel Gottes'. Nirgends wohnt Gott eigentlicher als in seinem Tempel, in der Vernunft, wie jener andere Meister sagte: Gott sei eine Vernunft, die da lebt im Erkennen einzig ihrer selbst . . . denn da ist er allein in seiner Stille. Gott erkennt im Erkennen seiner selbst sich selbst in sich selbst (Predigt 10, Quint 197; D.W. I, no. 9, 150, 464).

[2] Ich habe es auch sonst schon gesagt: Erkenntnis und Vernunft vereinigen die Seele mit Gott. Erkenntnis und Vernunft dringt in das lautere Sein, Erkenntnis läuft voran, sie läuft vorauf und bricht durch, auf dass (da) Gottes eingeborener Sohn geboren wird. Unser Herr sagt bei Matthäus, dass niemand den Vater erkennt als nur der Sohn (Matth. 11: 27) (Predigt 3, Quint 165; D.W. I, 48–9, 439).

[3] Wenn wir Gott im Sein nehmen, so nehmen wir ihn in seinem Vorhof, denn das Sein ist sein Vorhof, in dem er wohnt (Predigt 10, Quint 197; D.W. I, no. 9, 150, 464).

[4] Nun hat es etliche Leute bedünkt, und es scheint auch ganz glaubhaft, dass Blume und Kern der Seligkeit in jener Erkenntnis liegen, bei der der Geist erkennt, *dass* er Gott erkennt (*vom edlen Menschen*, Quint 146; D.W. v, 116, 502–3).

[5] Predigt 10, Quint 199; D.W. I, no. 9, 155, 465.

[6] Alle Kreaturen schmecken als Kreaturen (nur) meinem *äusseren* Menschen. . . . Meinem *inneren* Menschen aber schmeckt nicht als Kreatur, sondern als Gabe Gottes. Mein *innerster* Mensch aber schmeckt sie (auch) nicht als Gaben Gottes, sondern als ewig (Predigt 26, Quint 272).

[7] Ich sage nun: 'Menschheit' und 'Mensch' ist zweierlie. Menschheit in sich selbst is so edel, dass das oberste der Menschheit Gleichheit mit den Engeln und Sippschaft mit der Gottheit hat. Die grösste Einheit, die Christus mit dem Vater besessen hat, die ist mir zu gewinnen möglich, wenn ich (nur) ablegen könnte, was da ist von diesem oder jenem, und mich als 'Menschheit' zu fassen vermöchte (Predigt 38, Quint 338).

of the uncreated *ratio* or form as that through which God had engendered him. Where man's creation had meant externalization of his essence from living and intelligence within God to being outside him, his reunion had to come through his internalization: from his being as creature to his uncreated form within the soul. It was this which inhered in him as the divine spark; its presence in the ground of the soul was thereby God's presence. To perceive it was to perceive God, and so to be received once more into God's essence by being reunited with the word from which he had sprung. This was the birth of the word in the soul: the return to its source as an uncreated essence in God's word. It was the eternally unceasing end to which both the soul and God worked.[1] For Eckhart it was the heart of his mysticism; the birth of the word constituted the discovery of man's eternal self—which was in God in the soul—through the renunciation of his temporal self.

In the third place, then, the path to God in the soul was by way of negation, or more strictly by abnegation. Man in entering the ground of the soul entered into an eternal stillness, devoid of time, place or movement.[2] To do so, he had first to cast off these attributes of the world, which meant complete detachment not only from all physical wants but his very awareness as a finite being; if man were to see God he must no longer see or feel as a creature. He had to go beyond the images of both spiritual and corporeal knowledge to an entirely inner awareness, which owed nothing to created things, but came through its union with the eternal uncreated light, or power, in the soul.[3] For

[1] Notwendig *muss* Gott alle seine Werke wirken. Gott wirkt allzeit in einem Nun in der Ewigkeit, und sein Wirken besteht darin, seinen Sohn zu gebären; den gebiert er allzeit (Predigt 52 Quint 396). And: Gott wirkt seine ganze Macht in seiner Geburt aus, und das gehört dazu, auf dass die Seele wieder zu Gott komme (ibid., 397).

[2] aber soweit Gott göttlich and soweit Gott vernünftig ist, ist Gott nirgends so eigentlich wie in der Seele und in der Engeln, wenn der willst: im Innersten der Seele und im Höchsten der Seele. . . . Dort, wo niemals Zeit eindrang, niemals ein Bild hineinleuchtete: im Innersten und in Höchsten der Seele erschafft Gott die ganze Welt. . . . Alles, was vergangen ist, und alles, was gegenwartig ist, alles, was zukünftig ist, das erschafft Gott im Innersten der Seele (Predigt 43, Quint 356).

[3] Diese drei Stücke bedeuten dreierlei Erkenntnis. Die eine ist sinnlich: Das Auge sieht gar weithin die Dinge, die ausserhalb seiner sind. Die zweite ist vernünftig und ist viel höher. Mit der dritten ist eine edle Kraft der Seele gemeint, die so hoch und so edel ist, dass sie Gott in seinem blossen, eigenen Sein erfasst. Diese Kraft hat mit nichts etwas gemein; sie macht aus nichts etwas und alles. Sie weiss nichts von Gestern noch vom Vorgestern, noch vom Morgen noch vom Übermorgen, denn sie in der Ewigkeit gibt es kein Gestern noch Morgen, da gibt es (vielmehr nun) ein gegenwärtiges Nun (Predigt 12, Quint 210; D.W. I, no. 11, 182-3, 473).

this the soul had to lose its very identity.[1] It had both to know nothing and become nothing as a creature.[2] This was Eckhart's sharpest break with St. Augustine and Western tradition. None of the spiritual qualities which were associated with the soul's powers was of any relevance to God: God's nature was that he was without nature.[3] He could not be found through man's wisdom or love; for these were from the operation of the soul's faculties; they referred to man not God.[4] To remain governed by them was to remain bound by creation and separated from God. To be joined to God a man must renounce his separateness and himself as creature.[5]

Such was Eckhart's message. It was a call to empty the soul to let God enter.[6] Only if this had been done could the Son be born within it and man become one with God. The necessity for renunciation, or poverty of the spirit, or detachment—was Eckhart's ceaseless theme. Man as an individual cannot know God as God;[7] he must cease to exist

[1] Denn ein recht vollkommener Mensch soll sich so gewönnt haben, sich selbst abgestorben, seiner selbst in Gott so entbildet und in Gottes Willen so überbildet sein, dass seine ganze Seligkeit darin liegt, von sich selbst und von allem (Sonstigen) nichts zu wissen, vielmehr nur Gott allein zu wissen (*Das Buch der göttlichen Tröstung*, Quint 110; D.W. v, 21, 477).

[2] *So* also ist dein Unwissen kein Mangel, sondern deine oberste Vollkommenheit, und dein Erleiden ist *so* dein höchstes Wirken. Und so, in dieser Weise, musst du dich aller deiner Betägigungen entschlagen und alle deine Kräfte zum Schweigen bringen, wenn du wirklich diese Geburt in dir erfahren willst (Predigt 58, Quint 431), also ibid., 430.

[3] Dies ist *seine* Natur, dass er (Gott) *ohne* Natur ist (Predigt 47, Quint 377).

[4] Die irgend etwas in Gott suchen, sei's Wissen, Erkennen oder Andacht oder was es auch sei, findet es mann, so findet mann dennoch Gott nicht, obzwar einer Wissen, Erkennen, Innerlichkeit findet, was ich (gleichviel) durchaus anerkenne: es *bleibt* ihm aber *nicht*. Sucht er aber *nichts*, so findet er Gott und alle Dinge in ihm ... (Predigt 48, Quint 379). Also ibid., 355: Predigt 42: wie er ein lauteres, reines, klares Eines ist, abgesondert von aller Zweiheit.

[5] Predigt 5 (Quint 175; D.W. I, no. 5*a*, 79, 447).

[6] E.g., Wenn die Seele der Zeit und des Raumes ledig ist, so sendet der Vater seinen Sohn in die Seele (Predigt 4, Quint 173; D.W. I, 74, 445). And: Die Seele, die Gottes Kind sein will, soll nichts in sich gebären, und die, in der Gottes Sohn geboren werden soll, in die soll sich nichts anderes gebären (Predigt 12, Quint 208; D.W. I, no. 11, 177, 472). See also Predigt 38 (Quint 336-7), 39 (Quint 340), 58 (Quint 425-9).

[7] E.g., Ich sage weiterhin: Soll die Seele Gott erkennen, so muss sie auch sich selbst vergessen und muss sich selbst velieren; denn solange sie sich selbst sieht und erkennt, so sieht und erkennt sie Gott nicht (Predigt 36, Quint 325-6). See also *Reden der Unterweisung* (Quint 89; D.W. v, 278-9, 530), Predigt 32 (Quint 306-7).

as a creature by stripping away all that kept him a distinct being;[1] he had thus to turn from his intrinsic nothingness as a finite being to non-existence within God's being.[2] That was the paradox which made Eckhart so liable to misconstruction: a man had to cease to be in order to live fully in God; non-being was the condition of infinite and eternal being.

This helps to explain why Eckhart could appear to lean to pantheism and to disparage traditionally held values; for all impulses and works, however well intended or directed, had to cede to the overriding need of attaining oneness in God. Along the path of negation there was no room for anything that kept man tied to his present condition. Unknowing was the highest state.[3] Eckhart's attitude can be seen very clearly in his treatise on detachment, *Abgeschiedenheit*.[4] As the way to God, detachment came before all the virtues; it released man from created things where they bound him to them: to love meant wanting to give things to God; detachment meant that God loved the soul: it was thus more receptive than any other state.[5] By the same token, in freeing a man from creatures, it freed him from the sadness which accompanied all creation.[6] Moreover, it alone came so close to nothing that only God could enter through it.[7] It was above humility, for it presupposed it; humility, on the other hand, was less than detachment, since its relation was to other creatures.[8] So was mercy, which entailed grief at their infirmities. Detachment remained free of all created beings and so able to receive God's being as its own.[9] It was the means by which man became God's son, living in eternity above all sadness and

[1] Soll ich Sohn sein, so muss ich in demselben Sein Sohn sein, in dem er Sohn ist, und in keinem andern . . . Soll ich aber *dieser* (bestimmte) Mensch sein, so muss ich in *diesem* (bestimmten) Sein dieser Mensch sein (Predigt 43, Quint 356-7).

[2] Wer unmittelbar in der Blossheit dieser Natur stehen will, der muss allem personhaften entgangen sein, so dass er dem Menschen, der jenseits des Meeres ist, den er mit Augen nie gesehen hat, ebensowohl Gutes gönne wie dem Menschen, der bei ihm ist und sein vertrauter Freund ist (Predigt 6, Quint 179; D.W. I, 5*b*, 87-8, 449).

[3] Predigt 58 (Quint 431).

[4] D.W. V, 400-37; modern German rendering 539-47.

[5] so finde ich nicht anderas als, dass lautere Abgeschiedenheit alles übertreffe, denn alle Tugenden haben irgenden Absehen auf die Kreatur, während Abgeschiedenheit losgelöst von allen Kreaturen ist (ibid., 539).

[6] Zum zweiten lobe ich die Abgeschiedenheit vor der Liebe, weil die Liebe mich dazu zwingt, dass ich alle Dinge um Gottes Willen ertrage, während Abgeschiedenheit mich dazu bringt, dass ich für nichts empfänglich bin als für Gott (ibid.).

[7] Ibid., 540.

[8] Ibid.   [9] Ibid., 541.

passion.¹ In being void of creatures the soul was filled with God. Its object therefore, must be nothing.²

What, then, of good works, prayers, fasting and so on? Although, said Eckhart, they were inadequate to bring a man to God, God saw them in all eternity and did not forget them. They would be rewarded according to their deserts.³ At the same time the detached soul cannot pray; to do so is to ask something of God, and he who has renounced all things begs for nothing; he is free from all desire and so from all prayer.⁴ Oblivion is the end of detachment; when it has been reached, God draws the detached soul into himself; in becoming negated it has become one with God.⁵

The same order of priorities between the inner life and outward signs is to be seen throughout Eckhart's other German writings. As he said in the *Reden der Unterweisung*:

There are many people who think that they must perform great works in outward things, like fasting, going barefooted and such other works of penance. But the true and best penance . . . is for man entirely and completely to renounce all that is not fully God and divine and which belongs to creatures. . . .⁶

Only the inner act was divine; were a man to be given a thousand worlds they would not have a hairbreadth of worth compared with knowing God.⁷ A work in itself was neither good nor holy; only man could be that, and his worth could not be reckoned in terms of work or time but only in his nature which was eternal.⁸ Peace in the soul came

¹ Und der Mensch, der so in voller Abgeschiedenheit steht, der wird so in die Ewigkeit entrückt, dass nichts Vergängliches (mehr) bewegen kann, dass er nichts (mehr) empfindet, was leiblich, und er heisst tot für die Welt, denn ihm schmeckt nichts, das irdisch ist (ibid., 541).

² Darauf antworte ich wie folgt und sage, dass weder dies noch das der lauteren Abgeschiedenheit Gegenstand ist. Sie steht auf einem reinen Nichts, und ich sage dir, warum dar so ist: Die lautere Abgeschiedenheit steht auf dem Höchsten (ibid., 544).

³ Ibid., 542.

⁴ Nun frage ich wiederum: Was ist des abgeschiedenen Herzens Gebet? Darauf antworte ich wie folgt und sage: Abgeschiedene Lauterkeit *kann* nicht beten, denn wer betet, der begehret etwas von Gott. . . . Nun begehrt das abschiedene Herz gar nichts, es hat auch gar nichts, dessen es gerne ledig wäre (ibid., 545).

⁵ Ibid.   ⁶ *Reden der Unterweisung* (Quint 75; D.W. v, 244-5, 520).

⁷ *Das Buch der göttlichen Tröstung* (Quint 122; D.W. v, 8-61, 471-97).

⁸ Darum ist es weder gut noch heilig noch selig, sondern der *Mensch* ist selig, in dem die *Frucht* des Werkes bleibt—nicht als Zeit noch als Werk, sondern als eine gute Beschaffenheit, die da ewig ist mit dem Geiste, wie der Geist auch ewig ist in sich selbst . . . (Predigt 44, Quint 363).

before all activity,[1] just as holiness in the ground of the soul was above the love and knowledge in the intellect and will.[2]

Now this emphasis upon inner movement also affected Eckhart's treatment of grace. Here it was not a question of his having demoted it, but rather of its being overshadowed. It is not completely clear at what point Eckhart envisaged grace as entering into the soul's search for God; that is not altogether surprising. Here, if anywhere, Eckhart had chosen the Neoplatonic path of the soul's return to God by way of the divine spark in the soul: and it was precisely in his doctrine of inner union with God, through withdrawal and reason rather than through the will actively inflamed with love of God, that Neoplatonism was farthest removed from the doctrine of grace. With the divine logos within man, what was required was a retracing of the path to the word by turning inwards towards it and divesting the mind of all created images. The boundary between the divine and created tended thereby to become blurred, even if pantheism could be avoided by distinguishing the logos from the forms within it.

Now Eckhart, in taking over this framework, evinced a similar tendency to concentrate upon the soul's renunciation. It was with its journey from the world and its images, in time and space, to the eternal stillness of the ground of the soul that he was principally concerned. The rebirth of the word in the soul through renunciation, as we have seen, was the centre of his mystical teaching. Self-oblivion, not a supernatural access of love, was the means of seeing God. Inevitably, therefore, the role of grace was a subsidiary, or at least a different, one; and Eckhart's infrequent mentions of it were more a formal recognition of its necessity than an attempt to integrate it into his system. These show that far from attempting to discard it he was only too concerned to stress its importance. On the whole he appeared to regard it as the means by which man was able finally to know God, leading to his return to him in the word.[3] Eckhart also suggested on one or two occasions that it was under the influence of grace that man detached himself from creatures.[4] In both of these cases grace was being adapted

---

[1] Predigt 45 (Quint 367).

[2] Predigt 32 (Quint 306).

[3] Am Menschen aber bewirkt es (= das Licht) Seligkeit. Das kommt von der *Gnade* Gottes: die erhebt die Seele auf zu Gott und vereinigt sie mit ihm und macht sie gottförmig (Predigt 54, Quint 406). See also Predigt 8, Quint 190; D.W. I, 122, 457, and Predigt 33, Quint 312; Predigt 27, Quint 274.

[4] E.g., diese Gleichheit aber muss in Gnade erstehen, denn die Gnade zieht den Menschen von aller zeitlichen Dingen weg und laütert ihn von allen vergänglichen

to a somewhat different role from its normal one of enabling a man to perform good acts and resist sin. Nor was there any reference to the grace of final perseverance, as there was not to any doctrine of pre-destination. These may well have been among Eckhart's lost works; but, within the context of his mystical theology as we know it, it is hard to believe that they would have had more than a merely formal place.

The importance of Eckhart needs no arguing. It is attested by the development of *Wesenmystik* throughout the Rhineland during the first part of the fourteenth century.[1] It became the dominant form of mysti-cism north of the Alps, and his disciples, Tauler, Suso and later Ruys-broeck, its leading exponents. They and the association known as the Friends of God sought to further his beliefs and preserve them from contamination with the heretics of the Free Spirit. If none of them ventured as far as Eckhart, or possessed his metaphysical and dialectical daring, it was he who was their mentor; without him Rhineland mysti-cism would no doubt still have flowered, but not with the exoticism which Eckhart imparted to it. Its subsequent history does not enter into this study. Our concern is with the heretical branch of mysticism which is the subject of the next chapter. Here, also, Eckhart was important; but not in the same direct way as with his Rhineland disciples. As a preacher Eckhart was probably even more influential than as a theo-logian; he more than anyone fashioned German into a language of religious expression, whose images could, as we have seen, turn weak heads. It was only too easy to take out of context his sayings on oneness with God—in which man became God's son just like Christ, and the birth of the word in the soul was more important than the virgin birth[2] —or the divinity of the *Fünklein*, or the eternity in the ground of the

---

Dingen (*Von Abgeschiedenheit*, D.W. v, 412–13, 542). He also described it as the soul's indwelling in God (Predigt 52, Quint 398).

Eckhart in his defence against the second list of articles drawn up at Cologne in 1326 gave precision to this: for man's nature to be assumed into the word in Christ demanded the grace of filiation and adoption so that man became God's adopted son (Théry *Edition Critique*, 231 and 265). This of course was in keeping with Eckhart's assertion that man in becoming one with God did not become God: Und unser Herr bat seiner Vater, dass wir mit ihm und in ihm Eins würden, nicht nur vereint. (*Das Buch der göttlichen Tröstung*, Quint 117; D.W. v, 32, 482). But identifying man's oneness with Christ is not the same as identifying it with his mystic body—the church (as Ancelet-Hustache, *Master Eckhart*, p. 67, does). See also Théry, *Edition Critique* 199.

[1] Leclercq, Vandenbroucke, Bouyer, *La spiritualité du moyen âge*, 448 ff.

[2] Predigt 11 (Quint 204; D.W., no. 10, I, 167, 469).

soul, or the subsidiary role of works and prayer, and thereby arrive at a series of pantheistic and quietist notions which were exactly contrary to Eckhart's deeply-rooted spirituality.

The danger was apparent to Eckhart's contemporaries; and in the last year of his life he had to face a series of charges by the Cologne authorities.[1] They were in two groups. The first consisted of 49 propositions, of which fifteen were from his *Buch von göttlichen Tröstung*, twelve from his *Commentary on Genesis*, sixteen from his sermons, and the remainder from his replies to earlier propositions. In his defence Eckhart explained the sense in which each of the statements was meant, besides protesting his orthodoxy and the privilege of his order as a Dominican against the summons.[2] He also complained that he had been misrepresented by the reports of his sermons. Sometime later a second list of fifty-nine articles, all taken from his sermons, was drawn up. Eckhart conceded that they sometimes sounded wrong as they stood and proceeded to give their true meaning. Early in 1327, having appealed to the pope against the illegality of his trial, Eckhart made a public profession of faith in the Dominican church of Cologne. Meanwhile the propositions had been forwarded to Avignon, where they were examined by a papal commission;[3] it seems very probable that Eckhart himself appeared before it.[4] But it was not until 27 March 1329 that twenty-eight articles were condemned in the bull *In agro dominico*.[5] They show, despite Eckhart's repeated explanations, the inflammatory nature of many of his statements and how easily they could be taken over to serve a very different outlook.[6] They included the following statements: that the world was coeternal with God (art. 1); that the Son was coeternal with both (art. 3); that evil redounded to God's glory equally with the good (art. 4); that to revile God and blaspheme against him was also to praise him (5, 6); that God would reward all those who renounced good works and inner devotions (8); that to be in God did not require salvation (eternal life) (art. 9); that men become wholly transformed in

---

[1] G. Théry, *Edition Critique*, 129–268.

[2] Ibid., 185 f.

[3] F. Pelster, 'Ein Gutachten aus dem Eckehart-Prozess in Avignon' in *Aus der Geisteswelt des Mittelalters, Studien und Texte Martin Grabmann* (Münster 1935) 1099–1124.

[4] Ibid.

[5] Printed by Denifle in ALKG II (1886) 636–9.

[6] Eckhart in his replies ridiculed the ignorance of his accusers for imputing, as heretical, opinions taken from St. Thomas, Cicero, Seneca, Origen, St. John the Evangelist, St. Augustine and St. Paul (Théry, *Edition Critique*, 206–7).

God so that there is no distinction between them and him (10); that all God gave to the Son he gives to men, as if they were the Son, and that the Son is synonymous with every good man (11, 12, 13, 20); that the good man can make his will conform to God's will, so that he can will whatever God wills him to will (14); that God can will that a man rightly disposed towards him, and who has never sinned mortally, should sin mortally and that he (God) does not recognize acts or works but only souls (16, 17, 18, 19); that God and nature are one (23, 24); that all creatures are pure nothing (art. 26). Finally there were two articles appended which Eckhart had previously denied: one, on the uncreated something in the soul which, if it inhered in the entire soul, would make the soul uncreated; and, two, an aspect of Eckhart's negative theology in denying God's goodness or perfection. As they stand— as opposed to their meaning for Eckhart—these articles amounted to (i) pantheism in identifying the divine and the created; (ii) amorality in freeing man from the accepted moral obligations of prayer and work; and (iii) uncertainty in the arbitrary conception of God in his conduct towards sin and sinners.[1] It was precisely these aspects which became uppermost among the adherents of the Free Spirit. That Eckhart was not their author either temporally or logically will become apparent in the next chapter. But that he contributed to their dissemination and so the debasement of his own true beliefs cannot be doubted. In that sense his outlook had a very real bearing upon the entire spiritual climate of the later middle ages.

Ockhamism: fideism and doubt[2]

In intellectual matters there was a parallel development to that in spiritual life. From the last decade or so of the thirteenth century there was a movement away from the attempt to furnish a natural theology from the application of natural knowledge to the truths of revelation. It was given fullest expression by William of Ockham (d.1349). He

[1] That Eckhart was associated with such beliefs can be seen in Ockham's reference to Eckhart's trial at Avignon. Eckhart, he said, preached the eternity of the world; that any just man could be converted into the divine essence; and that there was no distinction between God and the divine persons. Contra Benedictum (Opera Politica III, 251–2).

[2] This section is largely based upon my article 'The changing pattern of thought in the earlier fourteenth century' in The Bulletin of the John Rylands Library, vol. 43, no. 2, March 1961, 354–72. I acknowledge with thanks the Librarian's permission to reproduce it here.

denied that knowledge drawn from natural experience could demonstrate or support the tenets of faith. He and his followers, like Robert Holcot (d.1349), Thomas Buckingham (d.1351), Adam of Woodham (d. 1357), John of Mirecourt, and Nicholas of Autrecourt as well as more orthodox contemporaries like Gregory of Rimini (d. 1358) refused to conceive Christian beliefs in created terms: or rather to try to adduce one from the other. Revealed truth was a matter of faith and was beyond the reach of natural understanding. Thus the existence of God, his nature, his actions, creation in time and *ex nihilo*, the requisites of salvation, were the province of faith and should remain such. Conversely, knowledge derived from this world should be treated in natural and physical terms. The effect was to separate theology from the vast corpus of metaphysics and science which had come to the West via the Arabs. It was to abandon the task of assimilating them into a Christian framework, which had been perhaps the dominant theme of thirteenth-century thinking. Indeed, there was an almost obsessive awareness of the chasm between knowledge of God and knowledge of creation. Where God, as supreme being, was both necessary and free, creation was merely contingent, devoid of any inherent *raison d'être* beyond God's willing. On the one hand there was God, eternal and uncaused; on the other his creatures, who could as well have never been. This attitude helped to transform the intellectual attitude of the fourteenth century towards both God and creation.

So far as God was concerned the new element was the emphasis upon his freedom and his consequent unpredictability. It rested upon the time-honoured distinction between his two kinds of power: his absolute power (*potentia absoluta*) and his ordained power (*potentia ordinata*). By God's ordained power it was accepted that there was an inviolable order which he had decreed for this world and to which it was subject. It had been made known through God's word in the bible, the teaching of the *sancti* and the canons of the church. It was enshrined in the sacramental life of the church. By contrast, God's absolute power referred to his omnipotence pure and simple; it represented his own untrammelled nature and owed no obligation to sustain any fixed order. Ultimately, then, God in his absolute power was always able to override his ordinances, for the latter were only a specific application of his infinite power.

Now it would seem that the use of God's *potentia absoluta* was among the most potent forces in earlier fourteenth-century thought, and one which helped to transform traditional conceptions. While not in itself new—Peter Damian had invoked God's omnipotence in the

u

eleventh century—its widespread application was. It reached its height during the decade of the 1340s at Paris, where the university authorities attempted to ban the doctrines to which it gave rise. But already in 1326 Ockham had had fifty-one articles taken from his writings and censured by a papal commission at Avignon, shortly before Eckhart's own articles were examined and condemned. Many of them show a striking similarity. In particular, one of their most important consequences was to dispense with intermediaries so far as God was concerned. God could do directly what he normally did through agents and could do so in his own way. Thus, among the articles for which Ockham was censured, were the statements that God could accept the act of free will of itself as meritorious without the need for prevenient grace (arts. 1–3); that sin can be remitted without grace (art. 4); that God can rightly be hated (arts. 5, 6,); that the will in a state of grace could refuse blessedness (6, 46); that grace and sin do not exclude one another (87 and 8); that sin could be caused without sinning (9); that the vision of something can continue to exist after it has been destroyed (10); that man could only know naturally the proposition that God was the highest good without knowing that he was a Trinity (13) or anything concerning his essence (14, 15, 16, 17, 18); that the divine attributes and divine ideas could not be formally distinguished (25–30, 40, 41, 42, 44, 45); that the principle of something could be believed but the conclusion known (34); that Christ, as a man without grace, could sin (36); that the same body could be in several places at once (47) and several bodies in the same place at once (48).[1] Together, it need hardly be said, these opinions constituted an attitude of uncertainty which made for the dissolution of accepted theological—and sometimes natural—landmarks. How far-reaching its effects were can be seen in the subsequent condemnations at Paris.

By the first, in 1340, the Rector of Paris university, John Buridan, condemned Ockhamism in general terms. It had engendered in the arts faculty an attitude of doubt towards the accepted authorities and towards the correspondence between terms and things, leading to conclusions that 'Socrates and Plato, God and creatures, were nothing'.[2]

---

[1] A. Pelzer, 'Les 51 articles de Guillaume d'Ockham censurés en Avignon en 1326' (RHE 18, 1922, 240–70).

[2] Denifle-Chatelain, *Chartularium Universitatis Parisiensis* (Paris 1891) II, 1042, 506–7. 'Videlicet quod nulli magistri, baccalarii vel scolares in artium facultate legentes Parisius audeant aliquam propositionem famosam illius auctoris cujus librum legunt, dicere simpliciter esse falsam, vel esse falsam de virtute sermonis. . . . Item quod nullus

The climax was reached in 1346 and 1347. In the former year the pope, in a letter to the masters and scholars of the university,[1] attacked the recent tendency in both philosophy and theology to turn away from the accepted authorities to 'new, strange and sophistical doctrines, said to be taught in certain other places of study, together with seemingly unreal and useless opinions which lead nowhere.' The worst feature was disregard of the bible and the *sancti*, the very foundations of faith, in favour of 'philosophical questions and other disputatious matters and suspect views.' This letter, dated 20 May 1346, followed immediately on the condemnation of sixty articles taken from the writing of Nicholas of Autrecourt, on 19 May.[2] When these are considered together with the condemnation of the fifty articles of John of Mirecourt in the following year,[3] they give us some picture of the 'pestiferous and pernicious' doctrines referred to in the pope's letter. Those of Nicholas were mainly concerned with the absence of natural certainty: that knowledge of the existence or non-existence of one thing does not enable us to deduce the existence or non-existence of another (1–8); that there is no certainty of natural substances or of causality (9–19); or of the greater nobility of one thing over another; or that God is 'ens nobilissimum' (22); or that the expressions 'God' and 'creature' signify anything real (32, 54, 55). Finally, God could command a rational creature to hate him (58), and, if the former's will were dependent upon God, he could not sin or err (59). With John of Mirecourt, on the other hand, most of his opinions were concerned with moral theology, above all with God as the cause of sin (10–14, 16, 17, 18, 33, 34), of the soul's hate of him (31–32), and of all acts of the created will (35–38). John also repeated the current notions that Christ could mislead, be misled, and hate God (1–6); that God predestined on account of future good works and the proper use of free will (47–50); and that something higher than God could be envisaged (46).

Without attempting an exhaustive analysis here, it is apparent that each set of propositions expresses what can only be described as an

---

dicat scientiam nullam esse de rebus que non sunt signa. . . . Item quod nullus asserat absque distinctione vel expositione quod Socrates et Plato vel Deus et creatura nichil sunt, quoniam illa verba prima facie male sonant.'

[1] Ibid., no. 1125, 587–90, Litterae Clementis VI ad magistros et scholares Paris., quos de studio et dotrina nonnullorum recentiorum philosophorum et theologorum Paris. objurgat.

[2] Denifle-Chatelain, op. cit., II, no. 1124, 567–87.

[3] Ibid., no. 1147, 610–13.

attitude of philosophical doubt; while most of Nicholas's were over the impossibility of inferring that which was not given in experience, John's emphasized at once the omnicausality of God and his unpredictability: free will was virtually absolved from moral responsibility. The reasons for this attitude are not far to seek. Priority in the consideration of God went to his omnipotence, with his *potentia absoluta* as its vehicle. This in the first place, rendered God unknowable to his creatures, if not in his nature, at least in his ways. Since by his absolute power he could do ever differently from how he had ordained, save of course contradict himself, no constant mode of activity could be ascribed to him. More, he could openly flout what he had decreed by his *potentia ordinata*. Accordingly he could override all the accepted laws of conduct, without in any way impairing his own nature. As Adam of Woodham said: 'Righteousness consists in what he wills and that is wholly rational which he decrees.'[1] If taken to extremes its effects were far-reaching. Thus it was held that God could mislead; that Christ could be misled; that revelation could falsify; that God could love the mortal sinner more than the man in grace; that God could want a man to hate him; that grace and mortal sin could coexist; that free will was more important than grace, and so on.[2] In this aspect, it need hardly be said, God in his *potentia absoluta* was a very different God from that of tradition, and his actions became bereft of any ascertainable principle other than the exercise of his omnipotence. It is true that not every thinker interpreted God's absolute power in so extreme a way. Gregory of Rimini, for example, held strictly to God's traditional attributes of goodness, mercy and wisdom as quite independent of any arbitrary fiat of his will; yet he, too, recognized the indeterminacy of his actions.[3] In this case its purpose was far more the reply of a Christian thinker to the necessitarianism of the Greco-Arab systems; and the overwhelming majority of those in the earlier fourteenth century—Bradwardine excepted—followed Henry of Ghent and Duns Scotus in directing God's absolute power against the assumption of the inviolability of the present dispensation. They exalted God's omnipotence in reply to those who

---

[1] 'Respondeo quod rectitudo est quod vult et rationale est omnino quod fiat sibi' (*Commentary on the Sentences*, Bk. I, d. 17, q. 1, MS. B.N., Paris, Latin 15892). In an even more revealing passage he goes so far as to state as the justification for God's *potentia absoluta* that it enables God to do other than he had decreed by his ordained power (ibid., q. 3).

[2] G. Leff, *Bradwardine and the Pelagians*, (Cambridge 1957), pt. II.

[3] Commentary on the *Sentences*, Bk. I, d. 42–4, q. I, a. 2.

exalted the sovereignty of creation. It was a blow struck not against dogma but its finality; and as such applied to the whole of creation.

Everything depended upon the way in which God himself was regarded. If he was to be viewed solely in terms of his power, the morality of his actions did not arise; and it was here that the division between the radicals, like Ockham and his followers, and the traditionalists, like Gregory of Rimini, Richard FitzRalph and Thomas Bradwardine, arose. For the former, God's omnipotence was its own justification; if he should lie or mislead or ignore his own ordinances, his ability to do so (which by his absolute power was unqualifiedly possible) was sufficient reason. No moral consideration was involved for everything was subordinate to the act of willing. God's *potentia absoluta* lay outside revealed truth; the latter was one, contingent, aspect of his nature, but in no way an exclusive or a necessary one. As such it had no wider relevance to God's ultimate nature than any other dispensation he may have conceived. In order therefore to transcend its inherent limitations the only available light in which to view him was by his absolute will, for this alone was germane to God as God; it enabled recognition of the contingent nature of all that was outside him without attempting to attribute to him qualities which, by virtue of their contingency, were from us, not from him. To reach an understanding of God meant, in effect, cutting through every assumption, other than that he was, as God, necessary, and, as creator, sovereignly free. This was not to deny that God was good or wise or merciful; it meant that we were in no position to define those attributes in any but contingent terms. As with everything known, or revealed, to us they were from the aspect in which we viewed them. There was no reason for concluding that what we saw was the same in God or that it could not be superseded: God was good certainly, but his goodness was not of our devising; he was wise but with a wisdom we could not fathom. He was a law unto himself who could only be believed.

Such were the assumptions, implied rather than stated, behind the theological paradoxes presented by the Ockhamists in the name of God's absolute power. Its relation to an epistemology which refused to give certainty to what lay beyond practical experience is apparent. For the present, however, it is enough to stress that they were not inherent in the conception of God's *potentia absoluta* but represented only one— widespread—interpretation. For Gregory of Rimini, for example, its use was to secure God's freedom from any set course of action, while recognizing the inviolable qualities of his attributes—mercy, justice, goodness and so on. God was by definition good; were he to lie or sin he would not be God.[1]

This brings us to the second aspect of God's *potentia absoluta*: that it served to emphasize the inherent contingency of the created order. This applied equally to its physical and its moral aspects. In each case its role was to point to the possibility of an alternative to the existing laws; it stood as an ever-present *caveat* against taking them as invariable. Thus in the case of the physical world all the accepted evidence of natural experience could be superseded. To begin with, our knowledge could be about nothing; for if God so willed he could create an illusion, thus inducing immediate knowledge of what was non-existent. Similarly, the empirical laws of mechanics and physics could be overridden: two bodies could occupy the same space, or a form could be intensified infinitely; the world could be infinite and eternal; so could creatures; there could be several infinite worlds; something could come into being only for an instance or exist at two separate instances in time, and so on.[2] In all these ways God's *potentia absoluta* expressed the inherent uncertainty of the natural world and the impossibility of a natural theology. Nor were these conceptions confined to a lunatic fringe: they formed part of the discussions of most serious thinkers, often men of impeccable orthodoxy like Gregory of Rimini: and they can be interpreted as much as a testimony to their faith in God's freedom of will as doubt about the world.

In the case of moral laws, the issues were more involved; for whereas the consequences of indeterminacy in the order of nature fell mainly upon Aristotle's cosmology, as undermining his hierarchy of causes, in ethics it was liable to call into question both God's nature and the foundations of scriptural authority. With God ever-liable to supersede what he had ordained, scripture could no longer be regarded as the infallible repository of our knowledge of God's ways or their implication for man. It was God's word, but not necessarily his last word: its prophecies might not come to pass and God's precepts could remain unfulfilled. Once again it was by the extremists that such conclusions were drawn. By doing so they gave rise to two main groups of questions: those connected with grace and free will; and those over God's foreknowledge. Both called into question the very foundations of scriptural authority; and accordingly it was here, as we have mentioned earlier over the

[1] *Sentences*, I, d. 42–4, q. I, a. I.

[2] All of these positions were upheld by Gregory of Rimini. See the writer's *Gregory of Rimini: tradition and innovation in fourteenth century thought* (Manchester 1961).

condemnations at Paris, that the division between tradition and innovation was sharpest.

So far as grace was concerned,[1] Ockham and his disciples employed God's *potentia absoluta* to dispense man from the need for a supernaturally infused habit of charity in order to act meritoriously and resist sin. Instead God, if he so willed, could accept the action of free will in its own right and reward it with merit. By this means the Ockhamists enabled free will to become the main agent in a meritorious act and relegated grace to a secondary cause, which God, in acting directly, could by-pass.

Thus, while dogmatically it was true that all men since the fall were in a state of original sin, incapable of doing good or following God's precepts by their own powers, God could dispense with the intermediary forms of grace, if he so willed. By God's direct intervention a man could reach him unaided, could be born free from original sin, follow his precepts, and win eternal glory. In Ockham's words: 'Nothing is meritorious unless it is voluntary, that is, freely elicited and freely carried out, for nothing is meritorious unless it is in us and in our power. But nothing is in our power of acting or not acting unless this comes from the will, as the principal mover, and not from a habit.'[2]

That some did not stop there we have already seen from the condemned articles of John of Mirecourt and the conclusions of Adam of Woodham. In the process man, no less than God, became transformed. Indeed the unorthodoxy of fourteenth-century thinking is nowhere more apparent than in the swing from straightforward dogma towards the ideal and abstract towards both God and his creatures. Just as God could have created a different world, or have decreed a different order of salvation, so could man have enjoyed a different condition, endowed with powers to accomplish alone that for which a supernatural aid was at present required.

With Gregory of Rimini, on the other hand, God's *potentia absoluta* served merely to emphasize, firstly, God's independence of created habits in deciding whether to reward or punish a man, so that in the last resort it rested with God's will, and not with the presence or absence of grace, to determine a man's destiny; secondly, it stressed the inherent contingency of all created forms, so that if God should so choose he could supersede the habit of grace and do directly that which

---

[1] See *Bradwardine and the Pelagians*, pt. II, passim.
[2] Art. 1 of 51 Articles of William of Ockham condemned at Avignon in 1326.

he did normally through grace. The result was that, with Gregory, we find a full-fledged recapitulation of St. Augustine's doctrine of grace, reinforced, through God's *potentia absoluta*, against any form of natural determinism.[1] It is striking testimony to the changed climate of thought that the traditional concepts needed buttressing by such novel means.

The change is, if anything, more apparent in the discussion over the problem of future contingents: that is, whether God's foreknowledge conflicted with the freedom of free will. As I have suggested elsewhere,[2] it involved nothing less than the certainty of revelation; for if the future was undetermined, how could God foresee it? And how then could revelation be any less contingent than the actions it foretold? The dispute accordingly resolved itself into an issue between either curtailing God's foreknowledge to what alone was determined, or subjecting it to the hazards governing all undetermined knowledge. The first alternative, taken by Holcot,[3] safeguarded the infallibility of God's knowledge at the expense of his omniscience; the second, followed by Buckingham[4] and Woodham,[5] affirmed God's omniscience at the cost of its infallibility: hence the possibility that he could mislead and that Christ and the Apostles could be misled. In both cases the freedom of free will was made the first consideration at the expense of both God's attributes and revealed truth. Small wonder that Bradwardine's *De causa Dei* was virtually a reassertion of dogmatic first principles and directed expressly to vindicating the traditional teachings of both grace and future contingents. Its very extremism was a measure of the extremism of his opponents; and, appearing as it did in 1344,[6] it came virtually in the middle of the counter-attack against Ockhamism. The atmosphere thus engendered was one of condemnation and heterodoxy; the word Pelagian[7] once more became common currency; and it is hard to know what the outcome would have been had not the Black Death of 1348–50 supervened, carrying off the greater part of the participants, Bradwardine included.

When we turn to natural order, we find a similar state of indeter-

---

[1] *Commentary on the Sentences*, Bk. I, d. 17, q. I. Leff, *Gregory of Rimini*, ch. v.
[2] *Bradwardine and the Pelagians*, especially chs. vi, viii, ix.
[3] *Sentences*, Bk. II, q. 3.
[4] *Sentences*, q. 3.
[5] *Sentences*, Bk. III, q. 2 and 3.
[6] For a discussion in favour of this date see *Bradwardine and the Pelagians*, Appendix I.
[7] E.g., *De Causa Dei contra Pelagium*; the first four of the 51 Articles of Ockham, condemned at Avignon, and Gregory of Rimini's *Sentences*, Bk. II d. 26.

minacy. Once again the cause lay in the contingency of all creation. Since this applied equally to man, human knowledge, as that of a contingent being, was correspondingly circumscribed by the contingent; it lacked any transcendental element from which meaningful universal laws could be derived because it was as transient and conditional as the flux from which it sprang. Duns Scotus had been one of the first, if not the first, to urge such an argument against Aquinas's proofs for the existence of God; movement, cause and effect were the categories of this physical, finite world, and as such could have no bearing upon God. But it was above all with Ockham and his contemporaries in the succeeding generation that the scope of reason became firmly bounded by natural experience. The theory of knowledge associated with Ockham, and misleadingly called Nominalism,[1] was essentially a corrective to the luxuriance of concepts which had grown up in the preceding centuries. It was especially directed against the proliferation of categories—genus, species, universal, form, substance, relation, essence —into self-subsisting entities, so that they came to be regarded as the ultimate reality, and the individual physical objects of this world merely their manifestations. Particularly among the Augustinians, attention was diverted away from the validity of everyday sensory experience, and truth was regarded as the property of the extra-sensory idea, or concept, residing in the soul. Even the return, with St. Thomas Aquinas, to the categories taken from this world had not fundamentally shifted the emphasis; for he, no less than his opponents, sought for universal truths in the essences which the mind recognized in and abstracted from the individuals given to the senses; thus Socrates and Plato embodied 'man' the species; and it was this which ultimately enabled us to know that they were human beings. Where St. Thomas differed was in his realization that the universal could only be reached through first encountering the individual. Such a view still equated ultimate reality with the 'cognitio rei universalis', as Gregory of Rimini and others of his contemporaries saw.

The innovation made by Ockham and his confrères lay not so much in their introduction of new categories as their rejection of the old.

[1] I have already in *Bradwardine and the Pelagians*, ch. ix, given my reasons for the inappropriateness of the term, namely, that it suggests an artificial continuity with the disputes of the twelfth century; and that it ignores the wider issues in which Ockham's emphasis upon the mental nature of our concepts was only an element. The wider issues are, in my opinion, to be found among those under discussion here.

Indeed even in his division of simple knowledge into immediate intuitive perception of an object (*cognitio intuitiva*) and abstractive knowledge (*cognitio abstractiva*), and his use of terms (*suppositiones*),[1] Ockham was but following an already established classification. Where, however, he and his contemporaries broke with the past was in their relegation of all categories to the mental order; far from expressing an independent, and indeed ultimate, reality, they were constructions of the mind. They had no correspondence to external being and could not be considered as constituting an independent order of existence. Instead the individual was alone considered real: a man, not man, beings, not being, were the constituents of natural reality; for these alone existed independently of the mind and could be perceived as such.

How widespread such views were can be seen from the Commentaries on the *Sentences* of the time, which, when they do not explicitly reject the independent existence of universals and essences, as with Durandus of St. Pourçain, Pierre Aureole, Ockham, and Gregory of Rimini, became mere skeletons of the classical Commentaries; they frequently comprised no more than six or a dozen questions, as opposed to something like 500 in Peter Lombard's original Book of *Sentences*,[2] just because the area of meaningful discussion has been narrowed. If reason could not operate beyond the terrain of natural experience there could be little point in trying to prove the existence of God or the finite nature of the world. In consequence scholasticism became transformed.

In the first place, what may be called strict empiricism at the natural level, became something akin to scepticism when applied to faith and metaphysics in general; so soon as there was a refusal to take reason beyond the limits of verifiable experience there could be no valid means of discussing let alone demonstrating their truths. The latter at best became the province of faith, to be accepted as a matter of belief; to make them the object of rational consideration was to leave them without tangible support and so at the mercy of uncertainty and speculation. Hence by natural experience there was no more reason for supposing the existence of God than his non-existence, or supposing that there was more than one God; or that the world was finite rather than infinite; or that man always had need of grace.[3] In every case reason

[1] *Commentary on Sentences*, Prologue, q. 4.
[2] As for example with those of Robert Holcot, Robert Halifax, Thomas Buckingham, Adam of Woodham.
[3] Examples from Leff, *Gregory of Rimini*, ch. IV.

was powerless to decide. It could be, and indeed was, argued that the opposite was the case; and so we find the discussion marked by such formulae as *non asserendo sed disputando* and the distinction between speaking *a ratione* and *a fide*. What, therefore, was for the natural world a confession of ignorance became an attitude of uncertainty when applied to matters of faith, for it doubted by reason what was certain by belief. Hence, in spite of strong tendencies to the contrary, it seems undeniable that Ockhamism engendered an atmosphere of uncertainty as we have already observed.

It became common to distinguish not merely universals and essences from individuals, but also verbal expressions as well; that words like God or creature, on analysis, were shown not to refer to anything verifiable but to connote a way of describing a concept—such as, say, 'the supreme being'.[1] This approach was especially associated with Gregory of Rimini, who designated it the *complexum significabile*, to distinguish it from a *simplex* which denoted a real thing. Thus while 'man' denoted an individual (*simplex*), 'rational being' was a statement (*complexum*) about a man which did not directly correspond to any specific being. Yet, as we have already observed, Gregory was perhaps the most traditionalist of all the earlier fourteenth-century thinkers; and in his hands this was in no way designed to undermine belief in God. For men such as he, the most usual course was simply to show that God's existence could not be proved rather than to discuss possible arguments to show that there was no God.

The effect, then, of the sovereignty of individual knowledge was the jettisoning of any attempt at a natural theology; for, in a contingent universe, there could be no bridge between the possible and the necessary. Accordingly the truths of revelation rested on faith alone. Such an attitude infected the orthodox as well as the heterodox, and its prevalence, as we shall mention shortly, meant the virtual rejection of the traditional uses of theology.

The whole notion of proving the existence of God through an order of interacting causes fell to the ground; and similarly, with the concept of goodness. If these were to be regarded as merely mental constructions, offering no correspondence to reality, such time-honoured paths to God as the idea of the 'summum bonum', and the 'primum movens immobile', no longer served to demonstrate him.[2] Once again thinkers

---

[1] This device was one of the targets for the pope's letter mentioned above p. 297 'That Socrates and Plato, God and creatures, were nothing,' loc. cit.

[2] E.g., Gregory of Rimini, *Sentences*, I, d. 3. q. 9, a. 1.

as different as Gregory of Rimini and Ockham were united in rejecting them expressly on the grounds that terms like 'causality' and
'eternity' in no way implied a first cause or a necessary being. Consequently, the fixed and ordered hierarchy of the spheres and intelligences, the constancy in the operation of God's laws, the unchanging
and unchangeable nature of existence, and its relation to God, were
thrown into question.

This brings us, lastly, to the corresponding transformation of theology which such an attitude entailed. At first sight one of the seeming
paradoxes of the earlier fourteenth century is the reversion of theology
from being a *scientia* to its ancient non-scientific status. Most of the
leading thinkers, from Henry of Ghent, Godfrey of Fontaines and
Duns Scotus to Ockham, Bradwardine and Gregory of Rimini, differently though they did so, joined in returning to the older view of
theology as the preserve of scriptural truth, concerned with elucidating
the articles of faith and fortifying its adherents. It was practical rather
than speculative, to glorify God rather than to comprehend him. On
closer consideration, however, we can see how inseparable this view
was from the new outlook generally; far from being an aberrant, the
renewed emphasis upon the exclusive, self-contained nature of theology
was its concomitant. The overriding contingency of creation, with the
consequent unknowability of God and all that was outside practical
experience, cut the ties between theology and knowledge. As deriving
from God's word, theology dealt with truths inaccessible to human
experience. Even where it was held that God's existence was amenable
to proof, as with Henry of Ghent, Duns Scotus and Bradwardine,
theology became increasingly confined to the articles of faith; although
God could be shown to be the first cause or 'ens infinitum', his enactments yet remained the property of revelation, given only to those who
believed. Ultimately, the difference between the age of St. Thomas
Aquinas and that of Duns Scotus and Ockham lay less in the possibility
or otherwise of deducing God's being than in attributing a definable
course of actions to him. For the majority of fourteenth-century
thinkers God's existence was taken for granted, even when the proofs
for it were withheld; yet there still remained no ascertainable relation
between the divine and the created. Indeed, as we have observed, the
entire source of indeterminacy lay with God; it was not that his existence was not to be invoked, but, on the contrary, its very invocation
acted as a solvent of the created order.

In these conditions theology could have no place as an object of independent, rational enquiry: it dealt in eternal truths, where practical knowledge was bounded by contingency; it gave certainty of belief, where knowledge was confronted with unknowability. Where theology enshrined God's decrees, natural knowledge could only express his power to override them. Hence not only God, but the other traditional topics of the Commentary on the *Sentences*—Christ, creation, the sacraments—came no longer within reason's purview. From the days of Henry of Ghent and Duns Scotus, the question, 'Whether theology is knowledge', came to be answered in the negative. Its truths could not be seized directly or by a process of reasoning. Instead there was a common return to the older view of theology as the preserve of the believer; but with an added emphasis upon its exclusiveness. Far from its having a proselytizing role, or even an apologetic one, as was the case with some of the greatest works of St. Augustine and St. Thomas, it acted as a barrier, which reason, and thereby the infidel, could not pass.[1]

The affinities, then, between Eckhart's mysticism and the fideism of the earlier fourteenth-century thought are apparent. Different though the outlooks which produced them were, they each sought faith away from the created world. They each treated the individual as the unit of creation; and they each turned away from natural theology as a meeting point between the divine and the created. The effect in both cases was to make God unknowable in natural terms, and to reject the latter as a yardstick for measuring him. Both morally and metaphysically, God and creatures bore no ascertainable likeness to one another. With Eckhart it took the form of negative theology, with Ockhamism of the uncertainty of God's *potentia absoluta*. For both it led to the paradoxes with which they were charged—apart from pantheism, strikingly similar. They each, thereby, presented to the world an aspect which seemed to doubt some of the most fundamental tenets of Christian faith. As such they helped to form the climate where these doubts, in others, became heresy.

[1] E.g. this was expressly stated by Gregory of Rimini, Commentary on the *Sentences*, Prologue q.1. See my article 'Faith and reason in the thought of Gregory of Rimini' in *Bulletin of John Rylands Library* 42 (September 1959), 88–112.

IV

The Heresy of the Free Spirit

Origins and emergence

The perils to which uncontrolled mysticism could lead are nowhere more apparent than in the heresy of the Free Spirit. In essentials it sprang from the pantheism latent in Neoplatonism; and to this extent it shared, albeit in a distorted and extreme form, the same source as that which helped to inspire Meister Eckhart. Hence, as we shall see, the views attributed to Eckhart by his accusers, exaggerated and out of context as they were, are often echoed in the doctrines ascribed to the Free Spirit. Both made union with God the centre of their outlook; but where for Eckhart this was the end of an arduous journey leading to the renunciation of the world, for the Free Spirit it formed the starting point for participation in the world. Where Eckhart made contact with God the outcome of the soul's detachment from the senses, the Free Spirit made it the pretext for indulgence of the senses; where Eckhart signalized the consummation of the soul's return to God by the birth of the Son within it, through the grace of adoption, to the Free Spirit it meant emancipation from venerating the Son or obeying the church. What for one was spiritual poverty for the other was libertinism.

These divergencies, marked as they were, must not obscure the similarity of their origins. Both arose from emphasizing the directness of the relationship between God and man; the difference was that whereas Eckhart treated it in accepted theological terms, so that man's separation from God could only be overcome by his adoption, the Free Spirit identified divine and created: man as he was could be united with God, and their oneness, far from turning man from the world, brought God into it. Man became God, and in God's name could act with the freedom and self-justification with which God acted. He could thus do anything and whatever he did was right. The extremes to which this led have an unmistakable affinity with a number of the condemned propositions of Ockham, Nicholas of Autrecourt and John of Mirecourt which we examined in the previous chapter, especially those which concerned sin, grace and merit; once again—

308

though for the Free Spirit, not specifically through His *potentia absoluta* —God's power to act directly put into abeyance the normal requirements of the moral order: what was ordinarily sinful or prohibited or necessary was abrogated for those who shared God's divinity.

Now it was this obliteration of the difference between God and man, the infinite and the finite, that marked the Free Spirit off from the outlooks which we examined in the previous chapter. Where Eckhart and the Ockhamists were never in the context of their overall outlook pantheist or Pelagian, the Free Spirit were avowedly both. From their basic tenet that the perfect man is united to God, a series of conclusions followed which absolved such a man from any kind of obligation except his own self-satisfaction. This pantheistic union with God was doubtless inspired, as Eckhart was, by the renewed knowledge of Plotinus, Proclus and the pseudo-Dionysius, which became current during the thirteenth century;[1] and the fact that Amaury of Bène was condemned at Paris in 1210 for pantheism, in openly identifying God with creation,[2] has since the days of the German historians Schmidt, Hahn and Preger,[3] led him and his followers, the Almaricians, to be associated with the founders of the heresy of the Free Spirit. It is true that they were accused of influencing religious women in Northern France from which their ideas may well have spread further north into the Low Countries, one of the great areas of the heresy; but the connexion is too tenuous to be either convincing or fruitful. Nor is it made any more so by transferring it to the followers of another heretic, Ortlieb of Strasbourg and the Ortlibians, with which it has also been connected.[4] From what is known of the latter they were markedly apocalyptic in outlook, which was out of character with the fundamentally quietist individualism of the Free Spirit.[5] Although, as we shall mention, the two traits are found in conjunction during the fourteenth century, this is not generally the case as it would have been had the two originated together. Moreover, continuity in our knowledge of the Free Spirit begins nearly

[1] For the transmission of this knowledge see the writer's *Medieval Thought* (London 1958) 171–6, and especially, G. C. Capelle, *Amaury de Bène* (Paris 1932).

[2] Ibid., 127.

[3] Charles Schmidt, *Histoire et doctrine de la secte des Cathares ou Albigeois* (Paris-Geneva 1849); C. U. Hahn, *Geschichte der Ketzer im Mittelalter*, 2 vols. (Stuttgart 1845–7); Wilhelm Preger, *Geschichte der deutschen Mystik im Mittelalter*, 3 vols. (Leipzig 1874–93).

[4] See Preger, op. cit., I, 213 ff. and H. Grundmann, *Religiöse Bewegungen im Mittelalter* (Hildesheim 1961), 405, 422.

[5] Preger, ibid.

fifty years after the condemnation of Amaury, and then in Swabia—
by any reckoning a different milieu from Northern France. Above all,
what is known of the Free Spirit points to its adherents never having
constituted a sect in the strict sense; its entire orientation was towards
individual perfection, a personal turning away from the church rather
than an organizational alternative to it in the manner of the Waldensians or the Cathars or the Hussites. In this it was true to its mystical
origins; for while, as we shall see, it is to be found principally among
the Beghards and Beguines, it never there took on the form of an independent militant sect.

It would seem more plausible to treat the doctrine of the Free Spirit
as an outcrop of the growing influence of Neoplatonism rather than as
the offspring of a specific heresiarch or group. The condemnations of
John the Scot (Erigena) and David of Dinant as well as Amaury of
Bène at Paris in 1210 and 1215, for among other things, pantheism;[1]
the constant struggle of Christian thinkers against the non-Christian
implications of Neoplatonist notions in the Arabian systems—such as
a world soul or the distinction between the One and the Logos;[2] the
translations of the works of Plotinus and Proclus.[3] All these contributed.[4] By the second half of the thirteenth century, the influence of
Neoplatonism can be seen not only in the widespread diffusion of some
of its leading concepts among even the Aristotelianism of St. Thomas
Aquinas,[5] but also in directly inspiring a new mystical outlook among
the Rhineland Dominicans. It originated with Albert the Great, in
another context the first great Christian exponent of Aristotle, who
with his two disciples, Dietrich of Freiburg and Ulrich of Strasbourg,
represented the precursors of the German speculative mysticism which
was to culminate in Eckhart.[6] Thus in the very region where the first
full traces of the Free Spirit were found, and in the one where it was to
be so pervasive for the next two hundred years, the impact of Neoplatonic ideas was most pronounced. In both their heretical and non-
heretical forms, the emphasis was upon the soul's oneness with God;

---

[1] Leff, *Medieval Thought* 127.   [2] Ibid., 141–62.   [3] Ibid., 171–6.

[4] It is not without interest that among the 219 propositions condemned by Bishop
Tempier at Paris in 1277, several had overtones of the doctrine of the Free Spirit:
e.g. (168), that continence is not a virtue; (169) that perfect abstinence corrupts
virtue; (172) that enjoyment of the sexual act does not impede the use of the intellect.
There were also several anti-sacerdotal opinions common to other sects, like the
Waldensians, that confession need only appear to be made (179), or that there was
no need to pray (180) (Denifle and Chatelain I, no. 473, 553).

[5] Leff, *Medieval Thought* 211–24.   [6] Ibid., 299–301.

it was this identification which formed the keystone of the doctrine of the Free Spirit.

In these circumstances it is not inappropriate that Albert the Great himself should have been the author of the first full comprehensive statement of their heresy, the *Compilatio de novo spiritu*. It consists of 97 propositions, originally found in the chronicle of the Anonymous of Passau[1] and in manuscripts at Munich and Mainz.[2] The statement of John Nider, in his *Formicarius* (Strasbourg 1516), that he had actually seen the same list in one of Albert's own notebooks in his own hand[3] was confirmed by the discovery of a manuscript at Mainz which named Albert as the author;[4] in describing him as the 'sometime bishop of Regensburg' it also enabled it to be dated to between the years 1262, when Albert relinquished the position, and 1280 when he died. Its reference to 'Recia et dyocesis Augustensis' places it in Swabia in the diocese of Augsburg where it is probable that Albert drew up these propositions to help the inquisition in identifying the heresy of the Free Spirit.[5] As such it is more a summary (*determinatio*) of its tenets than the exposition of an outlook; this probably explains its unsystematic presentation, which is full of repetitions. It has also been suggested[6] that occasional contradictory or overlapping statements, such as those which separately deny the need for confession of mortal or venial sins, refer to two different grades of Free Spirit, the novice and the adept.

The *Compilatio* is in the form of a condemnation which in accepted medieval style brands many of the propositions with the name of an existing heresy, such as Pelagian, Donatist or Manichaean; these references tend to be largely formal and do not of themselves offer evidence for the source of the outlook. This is informed by two basic premises:

[1] Published by Gretser (wrongly) as belonging to Rainer Sacconi's *Summa de Catharis et Leonistis* in the *Bibliotheca Maxima Veterum Patrum*, vol 25, Lyon 1677, 266 ff.

[2] I.e., MSS. CLM 311 (where a further 36 propositions are added to it), CLM 9558, and Mainz 331. They are printed in Preger, *Deutschen Mystik*, I, 461–71, Döllinger, *Beiträge* II, 401 ff., both of which are based on CLM 311. H. Haupt in 'Beiträge zur der Sekte vom freien Geiste und das Beghardentums' in ZKG VII (1885) 556–9 has listed the emendations to Preger's reading taken from MS. Mainz Stadtbibliothek 331.

[3] *Formicarius* (Argentina 1516), lib. III, cap. 5; see also Haupt, op. cit., 503–4.

[4] 'Haec est determinatio magistri Alberti, quondam Ratispontensis episcopi, ordinis fratrum predicatorum super articulis invente heresis in Recia dyocesis Augustensis.' (MS. Mainz 331, f. 62) in Haupt, ibid., 506–7.

[5] Ibid.

[6] H. Delacroix, *Essai sur le mysticisme speculatif en Allemagne au XIVe siècle* (Paris 1900), 58 ff.

x

that the soul is of the same substance as God; and hence he who is united with God is, in his perfection, absolved from all the obligations to which the imperfect are subject. This combination of pantheism and amorality distinguished the heresy of the Free Spirit from all others as a kind of divine libertinism. 'Where the spirit of the Lord is, there is liberty' (2 Corinthians, 3: 17): in this case the liberty to do all that was in fact prohibited by the church. It was at this point that the paradoxes of Eckhart and the Ockhamists became heresy; where they in the name of God's absolute freedom (by his *potentia absoluta* or otherwise) allowed him to dispense with intermediaries between God and creation, the Free Spirit abolished the distinction between them entirely, and in the name of divinity made man's passions sacrosanct. What for Eckhart and the Ockhamists referred to God alone was for the Free Spirit transferred to man in God's name: God's freedom became human freedom and God was made in the image of the free man. Thus the attitudes of the Ockhamists and Eckhart towards God were reversed; God, instead of transcending the ways of the world, was confined by the most earthbound of them; and man instead of escaping from their limits, as with Eckhart, brought God down to them. This was the heresy, this the debasement, of the Free Spirit: it did not just reduce God and man to one; it reduced God to man at his lowest. As such it flouted mysticism as much as Christianity.

This can be seen from the propositions of the *Compilatio*. Their single most striking feature is their virtual disavowal of Christ, and his supplanting, together with the Virgin and the saints, by the good, or perfect, man of the Free Spirit. The latter, in neoplatonic style, becomes united with God directly, and thereby himself divine. As a result Christology and, with it, the mediation of the church vanishes; the pattern of man's life is determined solely by the degree of perfection to which he can himself attain. More specifically, it was held that man and every creature are of the same substance as God (propositions 7, 76, 96)[1] and co-eternal with him (95); that man can become God (14, 74); that union with God deifies the soul (25) and makes man God's equal (27), the equal of Christ (23) and entitled to the same veneration (51, 85), since he is truly united to God and not merely God's son by adoption (28, 29, 30); that he can surpass Christ (58) and excel the Virgin in devotion (31, 70, 74); that God acts within him (15, 56) and he does all that God has ordained (66); that he can reach a state of sinlessness (21, 24, 94) in which he is beyond the need of grace (12) or of God, and

[1] Following Preger and Haupt, op. cit.

becomes God in his own body so that, in eating, it is God, not he, who eats (38, 49).

Where, on the one hand, the free man is exalted, Christ, on the other, is diminished, and his incarnation in effect denied. Thus he did not suffer in the passion (59) and was not wounded or lacerated (9, 97); he was not suckled by the Virgin alone (90); his passion is not to be remembered (67) or respect shown to his body (65); his divinity was not present in his humanity (47); he was not resurrected (48) and his precepts need not be obeyed (83). The Virgin and the saints are similarly denied (22, 31, 39, 43, 70, 74). Had it stopped here, the doctrine of the Free Spirit, extreme and blasphemous in Christian terms, would not have gone beyond a neoplatonic reassertion of the return of the soul to God within a timeless christological context. But in combating the claims of Christ the Free Spirit also attacked the entire position of the church and the law which underlay it; man was substituted for Christ, free will for grace, self-indulgence for the sacraments. Resurrection, good angels, fallen angels, demons, the devil's temptations, were all denied; there were only virtues and vices (40, 45, 60, 78, 82). Sin in itself did not exist but only that which was considered such (61); and there could be an act of mortal sin without sinning (!) (6). There was no need to confess venial sins, nor, for the man united with God, mortal sins (41) since he could not conceive of sinning (97). The promptings of the spirit were accessible to all men, and it was these, not external actions, which should be followed (5, 78). The man united with God was absolved from all ecclesiastical obligations, the observance of festivals, fasts, confessions, and prayer, for these were obstacles to perfection (44, 50, 52, 79). Similarly he was freed from all moral constraints, such as lying, breaking promises, theft, fornication (4, 34, 43, 53, 81); and children born to him were free from sin (54). The attack on the priesthood was as explicit: the perfect man did not need a priest (16) and a heretic was on the right path (20). Among the 30 articles appended to these 97 in the Munich Manuscript CLM 311 it is openly stated that 'the man united with God should boldly satisfy the pleasures of the senses in every way and with both sexes' (106); that he has no need to confess his sins, however great, but merely to tell them to another 'good man' (108); nor should he engage in work (111) or dwell on his past sins (119); but he should eat and drink as much as, and of whatever, he likes (114) and recognize that freedom for evil and quietude, together with bodily satisfaction, mean the indwelling of the holy spirit within him (121).

Even if these articles were a distortion of the doctrine of the Free Spirit, its essence was man's withdrawal from moral and sacramental obligations, a turning from the law of Christ to one's own spirit as the true path to God. Hostility or moral indignation towards the church was secondary: the church was simply rejected as at best irrelevant and at worst an obstacle to full perfection: 'It is better to lead one man to such perfection than build a hundred monasteries' expresses the attitude; but where for Eckhart perfection came through spiritual poverty, for the Free Spirit it lay in sensual indulgence. This became its hallmark distinguishing it both from mysticism and from mere anti-sacerdotalism throughout the next century and a half. The degree of interaction between mysticism, fideism and the Free Spirit is too impalpable to be known in any detail and is secondary to the fundamental distinctions between them; but it is at least noteworthy that of the original 97 propositions comprising the *Compilatio*, 35—over one-third—were characterized as Pelagian, and that this was also one of the main charges brought against Ockham and his followers during the period from 1326 to 1350.[1] Again it is not without interest that the two articles in the *Compilatio* denying that Christ was cut or wounded (9 and 97) on the cross are similar to the proposition of Peter John Olivi—that Christ did not receive a spearwound before he died on the cross— condemned at the Council of Vienne, in the bull *Fidei Catholicae funda- mento*, in May 1312.[2] Since most of the propositions were given some such formal designation as Arian or Manichaean (13 times) the incidence of Pelagianism must not be exaggerated but it shows a consonance with other current forms of unorthodoxy.

It is not until the first decade of the fourteenth century that the extent of the heresy of the Free Spirit really becomes apparent. The first full indication of the seriousness with which the church regarded it was Clement V's bull *Ad nostrum*[3] issued from the Council of Vienne in 1311. This condemned as heretical eight propositions; together they resumed the essentials of the outlook contained in the *Compilatio*. They were stated as follows:

1. That a man in this life can attain to such perfection that he is incapable of sinning or surpassing his present degree of grace, since to do so would make him more perfect than Christ.

---

[1] See the writer's *Bradwardine and the Pelagians* and *Gregory of Rimini*, passim.

[2] BF v, 196, 86. See above pp. 155–6.

[3] Fredericq, *Corpus* I, no. 172, 168–9; Hefele-Leclercq, *Histoire des Conciles* VI, 2, 682–4.

2. That he no longer needs to fast or pray for he has gained such control over the senses that he can allow them complete freedom.

3. That he is free from all obedience to the church.

4. That the free in spirit can obtain full blessedness in this life.

5. That every man so blessed does not need the divine light of glory to love God.

6. That the need for virtuous actions belongs to the imperfect man only.

7. That sexual intercourse is not a sin when desired.

8. That there is no obligation to rise before Christ's body in the elevation of the host, or to show him any other signs of respect, since this would entail descending from their heights of contemplation, and so mean imperfection.

Ad nostrum was the doctrinal accompaniment to Clement's other bull against the Beguines, *Cum de quibusdam mulieribus*. Issued at the same time, it was an outright condemnation of the entire Beguine status. On the one hand its adherents owed obedience to no one and no rule and did not renounce property; on the other they presumed to wear a distinctive habit and follow certain religious men. They were also reported to dispute over the Trinity and the divine essence and to denigrate the articles of faith and the sacraments, deceiving many innocent people by their pretence of holiness. Accordingly the pope, in full council, prohibited them and their status for ever, while leaving an escape clause for those honest women who lived continently and obediently in their beguinages.[1] These two bulls together were a landmark in the history of the Beguines and the Free Spirit. In the first place they crystallized the growing tendency to associate the two; from this time onwards the Beguines—and the Beghards—came irrevocably to be treated as the source of the heresy of the Free Spirit. Although this principally affected those in the German Empire, it rendered their status doubly suspect: not only was it in violation of the Fourth Lateran Council's ban on the founding of new religious orders but it was doctrinally subversive. These were the two recurrent themes in the treatises attacking the Beguines over the next century: their mendicancy, by which they usurped the privileges exclusively reserved to the four orders of Friars, and their heresy of the Free Spirit. The natural envy and rivalry excited by the first were given an important lever by the second; in an age where there were enough hungry mouths to feed already, to have the addition of many thousands of able-bodied poor

---

[1] Fredericq, ibid., no. 171 167–8: Hefele-Leclercq, ibid., 681 f. The greater part of the bull has already been translated by E. W. McDonnell, *The Beguines,* 524.

competing for alms on the same ground of apostolic poverty—as was the case in Germany—was in itself insufferable to those who, as it were, possessed the licence to beg; but that they should be heretics as well was an affront to God. Such was the tenor of the opposition to the Beguines and Beghards. Illicit mendicancy and heresy were bracketed together as part of the same evil: one was taken as a sign of the other. Nearly all the official condemnations of the Beguines and Beghards as heretics designated them as such by their mendicant cry of 'Bread for God's sake' ('Brod durch Got').[1] They preponderated, we shall see, in the lands of the Empire—Germany, Switzerland, Austria and to a lesser extent in Bohemia; and it was there, though not exclusively, that the main body of the Free Spirit was located. It was enough to make it a mainly German phenomenon just as the mysticism of the period to which it bore the greatest affinity was mainly German. Hence, since it is with the Free Spirit that we are concerned, the Beguines and Beghards of these regions will be our main consideration, with those of the Low Countries and Northern France of secondary importance.

The second consequence of Clement V's legislation was that it effectively defined the tenets of the Free Spirit for the remaining hundred years or so of its duration as a serious heresy. The eight articles of *Ad nostrum*, subject as they were to variation, formed the basis of most, if not all, inquisitional investigations.

Clement V's bulls marked the beginning of a new era in medieval heresy, which lasted until the Council of Constance. Henceforth the Beguines, Beghards, and the heresy of the Free Spirit became one of the preoccupations of the church and one which exercised it perhaps more consistently than any other heresy until Hus; from time to time they were displaced by other and more immediate sources of trouble, the Franciscan Spirituals during John XXII's pontificate and the outbreaks of Flagellants in 1349–50 and again in the 1370s and at the end of the century. But over the century as a whole the problem of the

---

[1] See, for example, Alvarus Pelagius, *De planctu ecclesiae* (Ulm 1476), II art. 52, I, i, where these were taken as the two main characteristics of the Beghards and the Beguines. Alvarus described their heresy in terms of the eight articles of *Ad nostrum* and its adherents as 'worse than demons' who wandered from place to place begging illicitly with their cry of 'Bread for God's sake' (Brod durch Got). Alvarus Pelagius (c. 1275–1352) entered the Franciscan order in 1304. *De planctu ecclesiae* was written c. 1330 at the papal court at Avignon under the surveillance of John XXII for whose pontificate it was largely an apologia. Among its other targets were John of Jandun, Marsilius of Padua and the pope's other imperialist opponents at the court of the emperor, Louis of Bavaria; it also attacked the Franciscan Spirituals.

Beguines and Beghards and their heresy remained among the most deep-seated in both extent and import; for, and this is where the problem lay, they represented a challenge of another order. Whereas the position of the Waldensians, the Hussites, and, in a different way, the Flagellants, all ultimately turned upon their hostility to the church and its position in society, the Beguines and the Free Spirit were less an alternative from without than rivals from within, postulating, as the Franciscan Spirituals had done, not so much a new religious form as the pursuit of the existing one on their own terms. As with the majority of the reforming movements of the middle ages this was expressed by the twin themes of evangelical poverty and direct communion with God. However incongruous the sanctification of poverty might seem within the context of the debased mysticism of the Free Spirit they were frequently found together; each was an aspect of the state of perfection which they claimed as unique to them alone.[1] They thus made the tenets of the church, or at least of its officially recognized orders, their own. It was here that they diverged from the Waldensians and Hussites, not in annexing to themselves what belonged to the church—this could be said of all heresy in some degree—but in constituting themselves one more religious order. They claimed to be neither a new church nor against the existing church: merely its most perfect member. It was the fact that for, probably, the majority of the Beguines this was a genuine claim—as it was often among those who were also adepts of the Free Spirit[2]—which made the Beguine-Beghard danger so formidable.

They were at once a focus of popular piety and of heterodoxy during the fourteenth century; and they owed each to the inability of the church to make official provision for the needs which they unofficially expressed. In that sense the Beguines and Beghards—heretical and orthodox—were a stifled voice of the church; and the latter in combating them was combating part of itself. Hence the ambiguity of its treatment and its lack of success.

Clement V's condemnation of the Beguines was not out of the blue; nor were its effects immediate. His actions crystallized a growing tendency within the higher reaches of the church to see the Beguines and Beghards as a source of heresy. In particular at the Council of Cologne, in 1307, the archbishop of the province, Henry II of Virnburg

---

[1] E.g., the confessions of John of Brünn and the Sweydnitz Beguines pp. 371 ff. and Appendix I and II below.

[2] Ibid.

(1306–1322),[1] launched an all-out attack against those of both sexes who commonly went under the name of Apostles[2] and who used poverty as a guise for subversion. He charged them on three counts. First their violation of the ban on new religious orders in forming a separate movement with their own habit. Second their mendicancy, instead of living by their own labour, again in contravention of papal authority. Third, of propagating errors which impugned the sanctity of marriage, blasphemed against God, and denied that simple fornication was a sin, which they justified by saying that 'those moved by the spirit of the Lord are free'.[3] The affinity between these propositions and those of the Free Spirit leaves little doubt that Henry of Virnburg already regarded their heresy as the same.

Thus began the first open, if yet somewhat tentative, association of the mendicant Beghards and Beguines with the heresy of the Free Spirit; in making it Henry set the tone for subsequent official ecclesiastical policy against them. He ordered them to renounce their ways and habits within a month, on pain of excommunication as heretics.[4] From the outset this was principally directed against the Beguines and Beghards of the Empire although Henry's edict also included the territories of Liège and Utrecht, his suffragans. The Rhineland, in particular, with its considerable floating numbers, lent itself to their vagrant piety; and much of their history during the following century centred on such towns as Cologne, Strasbourg, Basel and Constance.

Henry of Virnburg's condemnation was the beginning of a chain reaction; he himself renewed it the next year at a diocesan synod. Two years later, in 1310, the synod of Trier prohibited the Beguines and Beghards from being given shelter or alms, and went on to speak of 'false Beguines' who, dressed in the long tunics of their namesakes and despising work, formed conventicles and spread false doctrine among simple souls.[5] In the same year the Council of Mainz proscribed Beguines and Beghards who begged with the cry of 'Bread for God's sake' and prohibited them from preaching both in public and in private, or face excommunication. Unlike Henry of Virnburg the Council did

---

[1] G. Schwamborn, *Heinrich II Erzbischof von Cöln* (1306–22) (diss. Neuss Münster 1904) quoted in McDonnell, *Beguines*, 516.

[2] This designation, a common one for any kind of devout group, has led to a widespread confusion with Segarelli and Dolcino's sect. As we have seen there is not a trace of the Free Spirit among the latter, nor the slightest evidence to associate them with the Rhineland Beghards and Beguines.

[3] Fredericq, *Corpus*, I, no. 161, 151–4.

[4] Ibid., no. 163, 155.   [5] Mansi, *Concilia*, vol. 25, col. 261.

not extend its censure to all Beguines and Beghards; but specifically decreed that among the approved Beguines no one was to be admitted unless 40 or more years of age and of good standing.[1] There was also evidence of Beguine activity of an heretical nature in Northern France and the Low Countries at this period. In 1309 groups of *Gyrovagi* or Lollards[2] were reported in Hainault and Brabant where they deceived women of noble birth. In Flanders a *pseudo-mulier* from Metz, in the guise of a Beguine, falsely claimed revelations with which she deceived not only the nobles but the king and queen.[3] But by far the most prominent individual case of the period concerned Margaret of Porète, a Beguine of Hainault, who was tried for heresy by the bishop of Paris and burned. She had written a book which the bishop of Cambrai had condemned; but she nevertheless continued to propagate her errors among Beghards and other simple folk. This, according to the continuator of the Chronicle of William of Nangis, included the view that the soul consumed with love of God could and should do whatever it desired. For more than a year she remained obdurate in her heresy, refusing to retract what she had written until she was finally handed over to the secular arm and publicly committed to the flames.[4]

How far Clement V was directly influenced by these events, especially the case of Margaret of Porète, cannot be said; but his two bulls against the Beguines had already been preceded by another from the Council of Vienne, *Multorum querela* dated 1311, regulating the procedures against heretics. In this the pope spoke expressly of the growing danger from 'heresy in the guise of piety'.[5]

From the time, then, of the Council of Vienne, if not before, the Beguines, Beghards and the Free Spirit largely became identified, and their association is the nearest that we ever come to encountering the Free Spirit as a sect. For over a century it was the chief source of the suspicion against the Beguines; like many such accusations it probably contained as much prejudice as truth. In the first place we have to remember that the very word Beguine could apply to at least three

[1] Mansi, *Concilia*, vol. 25, col. 325.
[2] By the fourteenth century the terms Lollard, Beghard and Beguine had become synonymous (as had Beguine and Swestrione) as words of abuse. Originally both 'Beghard' and 'Lollard' (together with 'Cellite') denoted pious laymen: 'Lollaerts' were so called because they were said to mutter their prayers (lollen) and 'Cellites' because of their good works of burying the dead associated with monks and monasteries. See McDonnell, *Beguines*, 266–7.   [3] Ibid., 523.
[4] Fredericq, *Corpus* I, 156–60. For her teaching, see pp. 369–71 below.
[5] Ibid., 164–5.

different groups. There were the original (or genuine) Beguines who lived in communities or houses, practising voluntary poverty, or manual labour, such as spinning, and whose strongholds were the Netherlands, where in towns such as Bruges, Ghent and Brussels, they formed autonomous parishes, or beguinages, and the Rhineland cities of which the most prominent were Cologne, Strasbourg and Basel. Next there were, as we have seen, the Beguins of Provence, the lay followers of the Franciscan Spirituals, who bore no relation to their namesakes of the North and who may well have been so called because of the same connotation with the word *Albigenses*, applied to the Cathar heretics of Provence;[1] or alternatively because both groups stood in the same ambiguous relation to members of a third order.[2] Finally the term was used to describe the heretics primarily associated with the doctrines of the Free Spirit as we have seen with Clement V. As so often happens with words there is a Gresham's Law of usage in which the good meaning is debased by the bad, until the term comes primarily to be pejorative. This happened with the 'Beguine' and 'Beghard', which were more frequently terms of opprobrium rather than a true description. In consequence, if the history of the Free Spirit as a whole is inseparable from that of the Beguines and Beghards, it is important to recognize the independent existence of each. There were Free Spirits who were not Beguines or Beghards, notably the *Homines Intelligentiae* and Adamites, both of whom we shall mention in due course; while probably only a minority of Beguines were ever of the Free Spirit. Indeed it was the asymmetry between them, the fact that they were not identical, which provides the motive force of their history during the fourteenth century and beyond. Throughout this period there were successive attempts, at papal, episcopal and imperial level, to stamp out the heresy of the Free Spirit by directly attacking the Beguines and Beghards. But the aftermath on every occasion was not only failure to extirpate the heretics but the indiscriminate harming of the innocent among them. This led in turn to an invariable reaction in favour of the latter, so that although the Beguines as a whole were not recognized as a legally constituted order, provision was made for the genuinely innocent and obedient follower who wished only to lead a

---

[1] See Prologue above, pp. 18 ff.

[2] For the probable etymology of the word from Albigensian see Grundmann, *Religiöse Bewegungen*, 181 f. n.26 and especially McDonnell, *Beguines*, 430–8, who provides a good account of the contentious issues involved. See also Prologue, pp. 18 ff. above.

life of piety and who took no part in subversive activity. Accordingly, official policy towards the Beguines and Beghards went in cycles of persecution followed by phases of amelioration. Although, as we shall see, the latter in particular were far from being uniformly observed in individual dioceses, their regular recurrence is the clearest testimony at once to Beguine-Beghard complicity in the heresy of the Free Spirit and its confinement to a minority. The two facets interacted; fear at the spread of heresy led to wholesale condemnation and the inevitable victimization of the guiltless, which in turn called forth a moderation of the original censures. Then after an interval the supposed or real ill-effects of such laxity, in the continuance or increase of the original heresy, gave rise to renewed persecution and the process was once more repeated. This seeming ambivalence on the church's part reflected the very real contradiction among the Beguines and Beghards, and indeed in Christendom at large, between the convergence of heterodoxy and piety. It was confronted with the problem of how to stamp out one without destroying the other. The task, difficult enough in itself, was made virtually insoluble by the ban of the Fourth Lateran Council upon the founding of new religious orders. Only the mutual waning of both the medieval church and the Beguines in the later fifteenth century brought the conflict to an end.

★   ★   ★   ★

Modern scholarship, certainly in this century, has been noticeably chary of identifying the Free Spirit. Herbert Grundmann, whose *Religiöse Bewegungen im Mittelalter* constitutes the one genuine synthesis of unorthodoxy until the end of the thirteenth century, speaks of its unknown origins as 'the most glaring gap in our knowledge of medieval religious movements and heresies'.[1] It is true that E. Werner and M. Erbstösser in their book *Die Freigeistige Häresie und ihr sozialen Wurzeln* seek, as the title would suggest, the Free Spirit among the Beguines and Beghards, but their desire to establish the class nature of the heresy leads them into unwarrantably confining it to their poorer members as an expression of their hostility to the ruling class. There were no doubt social nuances among the Beguines and Beghards, as we shall have occasion to discuss later; but on the available evidence it is untenable to treat the doctrine of the Free Spirit as the preserve of an oppressed artisan or proletarian class. To take one example only, the references to

[1] Ibid., 534.

rustici and *illiterati*, among hostile chroniclers like John of Wintherthur and Conrad of Megenburg are not only as liable to be terms of abuse as a true description, but they are counterbalanced by constant official condemnation of the lapsed priests among the ranks of the Beguines, Beghards and Free Spirit; while among the women the gentle and aristocratic element was, initially at least, high.

Such distinctions are not necessary to locate the Free Spirit. In the overwhelming majority of recorded cases they were to be found among the Beguines and Beghards, or more strictly they were described as Beguines and Beghards. Virtually all the evidence for the ascription has long been available in the relevant compendia and chronicles;[1] and as long ago as 1790 much of the relevant material was brought together by Mosheim in his *De Beghardis et de Beguinabus*. Even if, as we have just remarked, the Beguines and Beghards are more than the Free Spirit, and the Free Spirit both less and more than the Beguines and Beghards, that the majority of the former belonged to, or at least lived in the guise of, the latter can leave us little room for serious doubt. Not only were chroniclers, popes, bishops, emperors, inquisitors and writers of treatises united in treating them as synonymous, but the individual professions of the doctrine of the Free Spirit were nearly all made by Beguines and Beghards. What is not so precise is the significance which can be attached to the words Beguine and Beghard; quite apart from the looseness which we have already mentioned, they convey little about the manner in which the adepts of the Free Spirit lived: whether as a group within a group, or as an entire community, at once both Beguine or Beghard and of the Free Spirit, or as merely individuals outwardly dressed as and professing to be Beguines or Beghards. All the indications point to the prevalence of the last two modes, but it is impossible to form anything like an exact estimate of their relative importance or how they were realized. Even in confessions of the fullness of John Brünn or the Beguines of Sweydnitz no really clear view emerges of how the activities of the Free Spirit were organized, and how far they extended to the whole community or were merely clandestine. Conrad of Megenburg, one of the most outspokenly hostile of the chroniclers, referred to their secret conventicles where they affirmed the hidden presence of the angel of God's word and discussed the divine attributes and how man could so merit that he became Christ's equal. He claimed that he had discovered these happenings from

[1] E.g., Mansi, Hartzheim, Duplessis-d'Argentré, Martène and Durand, Baluze, Raynaldus, Fredericq.

a Swabian-born member in Regensburg. But there is something very stereotyped about the description, which follows closely Clement V's bull *Ad nostrum* also mentioned by Conrad.[1] This uncertainty probably owes as much to the Beguine-Beghard movement itself as to our lack of firm knowledge; for it was essentially unofficial and extra-regular, without a rule and lacking in the many cases any close oversight from either ecclesiastical or other religious authorities. Accordingly the Beguines and Beghards enjoyed a looseness of structure and autonomy which made them the obvious rallying point not only for the genuine seekers after a life of poverty and piety but those who wished to live in their guise. The donning of a Beguine habit, the entering or the establishment of a Beguine or Beghard house in a crowded Rhineland city, offered probably the best opportunity of flouting the canons of the church without openly inviting reprisals; the very amorphousness of the Beguines and Beghards as a whole diminished the likelihood of individual discovery, a supposition borne out by the comparatively small number of heretics captured even at the height of the offensives against them. Indeed the feature of official policy towards the Beguines and Beghards during the fourteenth century was its emphasis upon mass attack; rather like an irate owner trying to clear his pear tree of wasps by shaking down all the fruit, good as well as bad, the authorities pursued them *en bloc*, hoping to extirpate the heretics among them by banning them as a body. The damage done was greater than the gain, and sooner or later had to be undone. The lack of success of these measures against the Beguines, Beghards, and the Free Spirit is shown by their repetition. Before the advent of the Hussites the prevalence of the heresy of the Free Spirit was one of the central preoccupations of the ecclesiastical authorities as well as of the emperor Charles IV; it equally held a lively place in the attention of chroniclers and other writers, including important scholastics and mystics like d'Ailly, Gerson, Ruysbroeck and Suso. What, then, were its ramifications?

There are four main sources of evidence from which we can attempt

---

[1] asserentes angelum verbi divini adesse occulte, quoadusque conventicula eisdem ypocritis placita congregentur. Quibus secretissimi convenientibus in unum, labia suae malitiae resolvunt, atque de attributis in divinis proprietatibus divine bonitatis differendo. Et sic paullatim descendendo affirmant qualiter ex pietate divina homo ad dei ymaginem creata existat et tantum mereri valeat per exercitium bonorum operum, ut Christo, domino nostro in humana anima sua eque perfectus quis efficiatur. Talium etenim unum de Suevia natum, ego in Ratispona reperi, quia iam predictum, et articulos alios in Clementinis prohibitos (Mosheim, *De Beghardis et Beguinabus*, 315).

an answer: the accounts of the chroniclers; the official condemnations by popes, bishops, church councils and the occasional edicts of emperor and kings; the treatises and polemics by, often anonymous, writers; and the confessions of individual adepts of the Free Spirit. Virtually all these refer to the Free Spirit as found among the Beguines and Beghards. We shall accordingly examine them first in that order; and then consider the few other manifestations of the heresy.

The narrative accounts

The references of the chroniclers to outbreaks of the heresy provide some general indication of its extent and location as well as occasionally throwing light on particular cases. For the most part they confirm what we learn in greater detail from the other sources. In the first place, the principal areas of the Free Spirit were the Netherlands; the Rhineland, including Swabia and what is now the Swiss region of Basel and the diocese of Constance; Saxony, with Erfurt as one of the main centres; the diocese of Passau along the route of the Danube; Northern France; Lombardy and Umbria in Italy; Catalonia in Spain. Of these the Rhineland and the other regions of Germany seem to have been the hard core, centred on the important cities with easy movement along the main trade routes. Thus Berthold of Rorbach, a Beghard heretic of the Free Spirit, was in 1356 finally apprehended by the inquisition at Speier, having previously escaped from its clutches at Würzburg by falsely recanting.[1] Again, in the early years of the fifteenth century, there was the notorious Nicolas of Basel who, as we shall mention later, was responsible for spreading the heresy of the Free Spirit among a considerable following; dressed in a Beghard's habit, his influence extended to Mainz in the North and Vienna in the East.[2]

If we are to go by the reports, the decade following Clement V's decrees saw the widespread outbreaks of heresy not only in Germany and the Rhineland, but also in Northern Italy, Austria, Bohemia, Catalonia and Italy. The chronicler Trithemius writing of the year 1315, reported that one of the Waldensian heretics captured gave their

---

[1] C. Duplessis-d'Argentré, *Collectio* I, p. 377: Trithemius *Annales Hirsaugiensis* II, 231.

[2] Johannes Nider: *Formicarius*, Bk. III, ch. 2: Dicebat paulo antea quidam purus aycus Nicolaus nomine. Hic in linea a Rheni circa Basileam et infra primum velut Beghardus ambulans a multis qui persequebantur hereticos de eorundem hereticorum quasi unus habebatur suspectissimus . . .

number as 8,000 for Bohemia, Austria and Thuringia;[1] although, as ever, no reliance can be put upon the actual figure it suggests that heresy was widespread in the period following the Council of Vienne (1311). Both here, and in the later account by William of Nangis for the Duchy of Milan, there are traces of the Free Spirit: in the first case Trithemius speaks of a girl, named Gisla, who, when asked if she was a virgin, replied that above the world she was, but in this world not,[2] an attitude which conforms closely to the Free Spirit's belief that true virginity went with super-terrestrial perfection and had no bearing upon the present world. In the second case, a certain Manfred, among a group of heretics, was burned for saying that he was the Holy Spirit incarnated.[3] In Catalonia in 1336 Bonanatus, described as the leader of the Beghards, was condemned for the 'heresy of the Beghards' which can only have been that of the Free Spirit, since no other heresy was ever imputed to them.[4] In the same year Otto, the archbishop of Magdeburg, imprisoned a number of Beguines who called themselves 'de alto spiritu', and were found to hold 'blasphemous and detestable opinions'.[5]

Secondly, as these references show, the heresy of the Free Spirit was almost invariably associated with the Beguines and Beghards. From the middle of the fourteenth century the accounts of its persecutions coincide with the successive attacks on the Beguines and Beghards by the authorities, which we shall examine subsequently. In particular, the years immediately following the joint decrees of pope Urban V and the emperor Charles IV, in 1368, and the last few years of the century, seem to have been the peaks of activity. In the earlier of the two, Erfurt especially seems to have come under attack, Beghards being burned there in 1368 and 1369; and one of the extant confessions (which we shall consider) dates from them.[6] The chronicler, who reports it, makes specific reference to the legislation of Urban V and Charles IV, adding that the Beghards were under attack throughout Germany.[7] At the same time the Turlupins, another sect under the influence of the Free Spirit, came under fire in France in 1373.[8] By the end of the fourteenth

---

[1] Duplessis-d'Argentré, I, 284; *Annales Hirsaug* II, 140. See pp. 476 ff. below; this refers to Waldensians.

[2] Trithemius, ibid.   [3] Ibid., 293.

[4] Eymericus: *Directorium*, pt. II, 266.

[5] Duplessis-d'Argentré, ibid., 298.   [6] Mosheim, *De Beghardis*, 341–2.

[7] Ibid. 342: precipiente Urbano papa et cooperante Karolo imperatore secta Beggardorum et Beguinarum ac Swestrionum persecuta est, et damnata, et valide impugnata ubique in Alemannia.

[8] Robertus Gaguin, *Compendium*, Bk. IX, 89.

century, the heresy of the Free Spirit seems to have been as firmly established as before. Hämmerlin in his *Lolhardorum descriptio*, for this time, enumerated a series of heretical groups each under a leader for different parts of Germany and Switzerland: Burkhardt in Thuringia; Charles of Vri in Switzerland; Henry near Constance, John in the lordship of Ulm; and a *magnus hereticus* at Würtemburg.[1] He blamed the Beghards or Lollards for the heresy prevailing in Germany, besides being sodomites and robbers; they were particularly numerous in the diocese of Constance.[2] His view is corroborated by John Nider who regarded Switzerland and Swabia as the two most infested areas.[3] Doubtless this state of affairs contributed to the renewed offensive launched against the Beguines and Beghards by pope Boniface IX in 1393, together with the appointment of Martin of Prague as inquisitor for Germany and the pursuit of the Beguines and Beghards which followed, particularly at Erfurt.[4] With the onset of the Hussites in the second decade of the fifteenth century references to the Beguines tended to vanish.

In the third place, the consensus of opinion on the doctrines of the Beghards and Beguines emphasized their sexual immorality and the blasphemy of their pantheism. The former in addition to the customary tales of orgies also included accusations of perversion with both men and women. Koerner speaks of women wrongly used, and William of Egmont of orgies;[5] while Nider seems to regard the Free Spirit primarily as one great sexual enormity, even though it is more implied than described.[6] Perhaps the most extreme instance of the juxtaposition of immorality and divinity was that given by John of Winterthur in his account of the confession and trial of three Beghards at Constance in 1339.[7] It took place on an eminence in the cathedral cemetery before the assembled clergy and populace, their misdeeds being framed into more than thirty articles. Of the four presented by John, the contrast be-

[1] Mosheim, 452.
[2] Ibid. 'In diebus meis et in dioecesi Constantiensis isti homines infinitos seminaverunt errores.'
[3] *Formicarius*, ch. II, quoted in Mosheim, ibid., 453.
[4] Trithemius, *Annales Hirsaug* II, 296; Duplessis-d'Argentré I, 152.
[5] Körnerus speaks of a Beghard at Erfurt in 1369 who seduced a young girl at Erfurt with the promise of sanctity (Mosheim 341), and William of Egmont of orgies at Cologne in 1325: 'sub terra quoddam mirabile habitaculum fecerant quod paradysam vocabant. Omnibus, divitiis affluebant', ibid., 278.
[6] *Formicarius*, especially Bk. III.
[7] *Chronicon* (MGHS, new series, vol. III) 248-50.

tween one and two seems almost too extreme to be at first sight credible. The first concerned one of the three accused, who to a question by some women on the essence of the Trinity made his reply conditional upon their undressing; when they had done so and were lying down he tied their feet together with cord and proceeded to abuse them, saying 'this is the holy Trinity'. Not content with this he then took his satisfaction of them singly. The second article concerned the accused's claim to have as much divinity in their single foot as there was in an entire man or creature. The other two errors were to do with devaluing the sacraments.[1] Here, then, pantheism was made the justification for libertinism. It was doubtless this blatancy which so enraged critics like Alvarus Pelagius to say nothing of the authorities whose stock epithets were 'hypocrite' and 'wolves in sheep's clothing'.

Were sexual licence the only legacy of the Free Spirit it would not be worth pursuing further; but the fact remains that in the process many of its adherents also seriously challenged basic dogmatic teaching. Thus of the eight errors ascribed by Trithemius to Berthold of Rorbach, the first three threw doubt upon Christ's own faith, and the others upon the sacraments and the accepted church authorities. Berthold is said to have asserted that Christ in his passion felt himself deserted by God (1) and that he cursed the virgin (2) and the world and doubted his own salvation (3).[2] Berthold also put forward the more common Free Spirit tenets that man could attain such perfection that he was absolved from having to fast or pray (4); that mental prayer alone sufficed (5); that an unlettered ignorant layman, illuminated by God, knew more than the most learned priest (6) and was to be believed rather than the Evangelists or all the doctors of the church (7); and that such a man when eating and drinking enjoyed the grace which Christ's body had in the sacrament of the eucharist (8).[3]

---

[1] According to John, when the accused saw that all was lost, they feigned repentance and expressed their readiness to be punished; they were imprisoned in the tower until their death (ibid., 249-50).

[2] Trithemius, *Annales* II, 231; Duplessis-d'Argentré I, 377: Primus, error sive articulus ejus, quem sensit et predicavit fuit. Dixit enim quod Christus Jesus dominus et salvator noster in sua passione usque adeo derelictum se senserit a patre, quod dubitaverit vehementer utrum anima ejus salvanda esset vel damnanda. Secundus error, quod idem dominus Jesus Christus in passione sua pre nimio dolore maledixerit castissime genetrici suae semper intacte virgine Marie. . . . Tertius error, quod Christus in passione sua maledixerit terre, que fusum illius suscepterat pretiosum sanguinem . . .

[3] Ibid.

Y

Sometimes the claim to perfection could take on messianic proportions and become joined to other notions, especially Joachism.
This is most apparent in the case of Nicholas of Calabria, who was
publicly condemned at Barcelona in 1356, the same year as Berthold, on
five counts. These all related to a certain Gondisalvus. The first was that
Gondisalvus was the son of God, born in heaven, even though he
appeared to have parents on earth. Secondly, that the said Gondisalvus
enjoyed eternal life. Thirdly, that in a future incarnation of the Holy
Spirit Gondisalvus would convert the world. Fourthly, that at the day
of judgement Gondisalvus would pray for all those in mortal sin and
eternal damnation, and they would be released from their thraldom
and saved. Fifthly, that man had a threefold origin; his soul was formed
by God the Son and his spirit created by the Holy Spirit, while God
made him from primeval mud.[1] Nicolas is only one example of the
coalescence of what, separately, might seem to be mutually exclusive
doctrines; his example is a warning against making artificial distinctions.
    It is underlined by the striking testimony of Alvarus Pelagius in this
connexion. As we have already mentioned, he reserved his strongest
invective for the Beghards, 'sotis ultimis hypocritalibus'. What makes
his account so singular is that in addition to mentioning Germany and
Italy as the chief areas he also names Provence, and more particularly
members of the Franciscan order there. According to Alvarus they not
only followed Joachim of Fiore in dividing creation into three eras, but
adhered to what he called 'this carnal spirit of liberty', for which many
had been imprisoned in his own time. Among them was one brother
who called himself the Apostle, on account of his perfection and who
was the source of the heresy. He had told Alvarus, when the latter was
a novice, that he could not be made to suffer, which, when he was later
imprisoned for his heresy, Alvarus came to understand as being free to

---

[1] Quoted in Duplessis-d'Argentré, I, 376 from Eymericus, *Directorium* II, 266.
Primus error quem ponit est quod quidam Hispanus heresiarcha magnus vocatus
Gondisalvus de episcopatu oriundus, erat dei filius in coelis eternaliter generatus, licet
videretur patrem et matrem in terris habuisse. Secundus error, quod dictus Gondisalvus numquam moveretur sed viveret in eternum. Tertius error, quod spiritus
sanctus debebat futuris temporibus incarnari. Et tunc ipse Gondisalvus totum mundum
converteret.
    Quartus error, quod in dei judicii Gondisalvus oraret pro omnibus mortuis in
peccato mortali et damnatis inferno, et ejus precibus liberarentur et salvarentur.
Quintus error, quod in homine sunt tria: anima quam formavit deus filius, et spiritus
quem creavit spiritus sanctus (nominative). Adducens illud: formavit deus hominem
de limo terre, et spiravit spiracium vite et factus est in anima viventem.

indulge his desires unconstrained. This Free Spirit died in prison at Florence.[1]

The truth is that the claim to divinity could, and did, lead to endless variations, from being the merest pretext for sexual licence to the highest flights of megalomaniac fancy as with the Beghards reported in Valencia c. 1345. Under their leader, Jacob Justus, they claimed that they were the blessed and Christ's martyrs in heaven.[2] Again, there was Constantinus, a Beghard, who appeared at Erfurt in 1336, claiming to be the son of God and Christ; he denounced Mark and Luke (though accepting Matthew and John!) as story tellers, calling St. Augustine and the doctors of the church frauds and perverters of truth, and denying the worth of the eucharist and the other sacraments except for confession of avarice by priests themselves.[3] This mingling of emphasis and ideas will be equally apparent in the testimonies by members of the Free Spirit; it points unerringly to the fact that the doctrine, so far from being the preserve of an esoteric cult, was common among widely diffused Beguine and Beghard groups; it shows also that the very individuality of its emphasis made it susceptible of different interpretations and at different levels—from the libertine to the superman. According to what these were, it could be added to, subtracted from, or joined with other outlooks, of which Joachism was among the most prominent. As such it was a spectrum, which from the immediate union of the soul with God, embraced quietism and millenarianism, sensuality and divinity, as the case may be.

Finally, what do we learn of the social composition of the Free Spirit from these descriptive accounts? The answer must be very little. Terms

[1] *De Planctu Ecclesiae* II, q. 52; see also Mosheim, 290–2. For traces of the Free Spirit in Italy, see L. Oliger, *De secta spiritus libertatis in Umbria, saec. xiv* (Rome 1943). The originator in Umbria appears to have been Bentivenga of Eugubia, who died in an inquisition prison in 1322 (ibid., 67); he was probably the same person referred to by Alvarus Pelagius in *De planctu ecclesiae* (II, 52). Ubertino of Casale helped to bring him to trial in 1307 (Oliger, op. cit., 76–7); he also attacked the sect in his *Arbor vitae* (Bk. IV, chs. 7, 36, 37). According to Arnold of Villanova there were 240 heretics of the Free Spirit in Umbria (Oliger, op. cit., 88) including seven Friars Minor. One of the questions put to the order by Clement V in 1309 was whether there were any traces of the heresy among the brothers (see pp. 140–1 above). His bull *Dilectus domini* was directed against the Free Spirit in Spoleto in 1311 (Raynaldus, ad annum 1311, no. 66). Oliger's book points to the sparseness of evidence for the heresy in Italy; his account suffers from his failure to recognize its essentially pantheistic nature.

[2] Duplessis-d'Argentré, 341 '. . . erant beati et in coelis martyres Christi'.

[3] From the *Chronica Magdeburgensis* for 1340, quoted in Duplessis-d'Argentré, 299–300.

like *rusticani* and *illiterati* are freely employed by hostile witnesses such as Conrad of Megenburg,[1] but they lack the precision to signify much more than the contempt of clerics for laymen. Moreover, they can be counterbalanced by other references to both clerics and laymen who are Beghards or of the Free Spirit, as with the followers of Jacob Justus.[2] In this connexion Alvarus Pelagius's account of the heresy among the Franciscans is a telling refutation of any attempt to confine it to the lower reaches of urban society. That heresy was an essentially urban phenomenon does not, as we have discussed earlier,[3] thereby make it revolutionary and/or proletarian, certainly not in the case of the Free Spirit which was pre-eminently a withdrawal from society rather than an active attempt to change it. Furthermore we have to remember that, if our sources are to be given normal credence, the Beguines and Beghards were the main source of the heresy. Unless we are to posit a policy of deliberate infiltration, on a continental scale, rather than the infection with heresy of those already inclined to the religious life, the Free Spirit cannot be explained in terms of a class. It was part of the *prise de la conscience* of an entire society for whom the existing forms, social, intellectual, and religious, were no longer adequate. As such it sprang from the very heart of Christendom, not a handful of social outcasts on its margins; its terms of reference were the same as those for Ockham, Eckhart, the Franciscan Spirituals, Dante and Petrarch, the champions of church reform, as well as the Beguines and Beghards themselves. Distorted as the search for new religious forms might become, it lay behind much of the impulse of the Free Spirit, as the confessions of say John of Brünn and Conrad Kannler will show. The quest for perfection took many directions and was not the preserve of any single group. To confine the Free Spirit to the lower orders is tantamount to making lechery, hypocrisy and megalomania their prerogative, which would be to practise class discrimination in reverse.

---

[1] 'Sunt enim huiusmodi viri rusticani, et plerique mechanici, corpore robusti, et litterarum omnino inexperti ac penitus aut idiotae, aut si literas aliqualiter novunt tenuissimum tamen est, quod sciunt.' Mosheim, 314.

[2] ' . . . in Valentia multi Begardi, quorum erat principalis quidam vocatus F. Jacobus Justi qui dogmatizaverunt infra scriptas hereses Beghardorum, et inter alia, quod condemnati religiosi, clerici et laici pro dictis heresibus, tam per dominum Clementem in curia, quam per inquisitores in aliis mundi partibus . . .' Duplessis-d'Argentré, p. 341.

[3] Prologue, pp. 10–11 note above.

Ecclesiastical action

After this preliminary encounter with the general aspect of the Free Spirit we must now approach it more closely from the other points which we have already enumerated. Firstly that of official church action. As we have said this went in waves of repression and (partial) re-habilitation and was directed against the Beguines and Beghards. The first cycle began with Clement V's bulls, *Ad nostrum* and *Cum de quibusdam*. He followed these up with a lengthy communication to the bishop of Cremona, complaining of the presence of the heresy of the Free Spirit in different parts of Italy, and especially the diocese of Spoleto, and denouncing its falsity; such liberty was not from God, in whom sin was banished, not indulged. It was the spirit of the devil in its seven disguises. The pope commanded the bishop to use all his powers to crush it.[1] There followed a hiatus of over five and a half years before Clement's decrees were given effect. This was due primarily to the long interlude between the death of Clement on 20 April 1314, less than one month after they had been finally revised for publication, and the election of his successor, John XXII in 1316; John in turn re-examined them, and it was not until 25 October 1317 that they were at last promulgated at Paris.[2] The effect was to precipi-tate a wave of persecutions against the Beguines and Beghards. As we have already seen, neither grounds nor precedents for doing so were lacking; and it would be wrong to attribute the sufferings which the Beguines and Beghards underwent in the next few years solely to Clementine legislation. Two of the main centres of official hostility towards them, Cologne and Strasbourg, had already taken independent action;[3] while both the Councils of Tarragona (1317) and Mainz (1318) invoked the pope's censures to justify proscription of the Beguines and Beghards for providing a cover for heresy *sub specie sanctitatis*. At Tarragona not only were all Beguine and Beghard conventicles banned but no two individuals could reside together in the same house; they were not allowed to wear a habit or read to or commune with one another. The possession of theological books in the vernacular was for-bidden.[4] The Mainz Council confined itself briefly to prohibiting the status, name or habit of Beguine.[5] Meanwhile, on 30 December 1317

---

[1] Raynaldus, ann. 1311, no. 66.
[2] McDonnell, *Beguines*, 527–8, and K. Müller, *Das Konzil von Vienne* 389–408.
[3] See pp. 334 ff. below.
[4] Mansi, *Concilia*, vol. 25, 627–8.   [5] Ibid., col. 538.

John XXII in his growing enmity towards the Franciscan Spirituals and their Beguin followers in Southern France issued the bull *Sancta Romana*.[1] As we saw earlier[2] he there accused them of heresy in familiar terms; under the pretext of conversing with the angels they were subverting the innocent. After reiterating that it was illegal to form new religious orders, the pope went on to charge them with having ministers and houses from which its members went out to beg and tried to win converts. Some claimed to be the true followers of St. Francis belonging to the separate order of Celestines formed by Celestine V (and afterwards disbanded by Boniface VIII);[3] others that they were members of the Franciscan third order of penitents. But whatever their pretext they were to be perpetually banished under penalty of excommunication.

Now, although throughout the bull John was referring expressly to the Fraticelli, of Italy and Sicily, and their Beguin followers in Provence, his condemnation was subsequently turned against the Beguines and Beghards of the North by popes Urban V, Gregory XI, and Boniface IX. *Sancta Romana* contained the three main gravamina of the case against the Beguines as a whole: their illegality, their mendicancy, and their heresy; and these, as we have seen, were the recurrent themes, either separately or together, on which their accusers drew whenever the Beguines and Beghards came under fire. Hence the use of *Sancta Romana* as ammunition against the latter.

Paradoxically it was John XXII who was above all responsible for rehabilitating the Beguines and Beghards of the North and ending the first campaigns against them; the pope soon showed himself to be increasingly solicitous for the protection of the genuine Beguines, especially in the Low Countries; and early on he began to press the distinction between the heretical and the devout. Thus at the same time as he was driving the Spirituals and the Provençal Beguins into heresy, he was saving the Beguines of the North from a similar fate. In a series of bulls he reiterated the demand that the innocent Beguines should be granted ecclesiastical protection against the indiscriminate persecution to which they had been unjustly subjected. How great this had been can be gauged from the accounts of observers not normally sympathetic to the Beguines. Thus John of Winterthur recounts how the Clementine decrees were made the occasion for the parochial clergy to oppress religious women.[4] The Strasbourg chronicler spoke of the 'many who

---

[1] BF v, no. 297, 134–5; Friedberg II, 1213–14.
[2] Ch. II above.   [3] See pp. 169–70 above.
[4] *Chronica Johannis Vitrodani*, MGHS (new series, III, Berlin 1924) 73–5.

interpreted wrongly and failed to distinguish between good and bad'[1] and of the 'many German prelates who compelled devout women to don bright clothes, forced those vowed to chastity to marry, and evicted them from their habitations'.[2] John XXII's first intervention was on behalf of the Beguines in Germany and the Low Countries. In the bull *Racio recta*, issued in 1318, he distinguished between the heretical Beguines condemned by Clement V in *Cum de quibusdam* and those who pursued stable and honest lives in obedience to the church and their parish, taking no part in disputes on the Trinity, the divine essence or the sacraments, nor preaching dangerous opinions or propagating error. While the former would continue to be pursued, the latter should be allowed to continue their way of life. The authorities were ordered to ensure their protection and act against those who attempted to oppress them.

In the ensuing year the pope turned his attention to the third orders which had suffered the same indiscriminate persecution as the Beguines. Two bulls, *Etsi apostolicae*[3] and *Dilectos filios*,[4] published in February and April 1319 respectively, sought to end the persecution of the third orders. The first was directed primarily to the Empire; and the references to ecclesiastics, who made Clement's ban on the Beguines the pretext for attacking the communities of penitents, confirm the accounts of the chroniclers mentioned above. *Dilectos filios* was designed to give effect to the first bull by placing the third orders under church protection.

John XXII did not let matters rest there. Clearly, once set in train, repression was not easily halted, especially when the ambiguities inherent in the Beguines' position remained unresolved. While some of them were now pronounced free from heresy and were allowed to continue in being, they remained unrecognized as an order within the church. This was firmly stipulated by the pope in *Racio recta*.[5] Small wonder, then, that further papal pressure was necessary, especially in the Low Countries and Germany, for which Clement V's legislation had been principally designed. Accordingly John XXII addressed a number

[1] Fredericq, *Corpus* II, no. 44, 73–4.

[2] Extract from M. Bihl, *Chronica provinciae Argentinensis*, in AHF v (1911) 682–3, quoted in McDonnell, *Beguines*, 529.

[3] *Corpus*, II, no. 46, 77–8, and BF v, no. 354, 163–4.

[4] BF, no. 365, 167–8.

[5] Per hoc tamen statum Beghinarum et observancias huiusmodi, que sic esse permittimus, nisi de ipsis per sedem apostolica aliter ordinatum extiterit, nullatenus ex premissis intendimus approbare (Fredericq, *Corpus* II, 74).

of bulls and letters to these regions reaffirming immunity for the innocent Beguines. Of these the two most important were *Cum de mulieribus*[1] in 1320 and *Romana sacrosancta*[2] in 1324. Both concerned the Beguines of Belgium, the second being mainly to enforce fulfilment of the first by putting the beguinages of Brabant under the pope's guardianship. In the few years following *Cum de mulieribus* its main provisions were extensively repeated, at Louvain,[3] Antwerp,[4] Brussels,[5] Ghent,[6] Cambrai[7] and Cologne.[8] In Utrecht, the bishop, Frederick II, made a series of provisions by which the Beguines not of the Franciscan third order should be protected from unjust persecution, prescribing what they should wear and eat and when they should fast.[9] At about the same time, John XXII wrote to the bishop of Strasbourg directing that genuine Beguines should be allowed to keep their habit.[10]

So far as the greater part of the Belgian Beguines was concerned the cumulative effect of John XXII's activity was something like lasting peace;[11] apart from occasional disturbances they tended to go their own way. The same cannot be said of Germany and the Empire as a whole, which became the main arena of the struggle against the heresy of the Free Spirit.

Nowhere are the Beguines' vicissitudes more clearly to be seen than in the cities of Cologne and Strasbourg, together with Erfurt and Basel the main German Beguine and Beghard centres, and the best documented. The authorities there were from the first particularly sensitive to the dangers inherent in the Beguines' and Beghards' presence in large numbers; they made repeated efforts in both cities to ban them; and showed themselves more than a little unresponsive to periodic papal calls for clemency towards those innocent of heresy. As we have seen, it was Henry of Virnburg's decree as archbishop of Cologne in 1307 which set the official wheels in motion against them; although not the first to have proscribed them he was the first to have openly associated the Beguines and Beghards with subversive ideas, which five years later in *Ad nostrum* Clement V explicitly codified into the eight articles of the Free Spirit. The suspicion which archbishop Henry cast upon the Beguines and Beghards was never really dispelled; and at intervals

---

[1] Fredericq, *Corpus* I, no. 175, 170–2.   [2] Ibid., II, no. 47, 78–9.
[3] Fredericq, *Corpus* II, no. 52, 85–6.   [4] Ibid., I, no. 178, 173–5.
[5] Ibid., II, no. 51, 83.   [6] Ibid., I, no. 179, 176.
[7] Ibid., II, 79–81.   [8] Ibid., I, 185–6.   [9] Ibid., II, 75–7.
[10] Doubtless in response to the bishop's decrees banning them; see p. 318 below.
[11] McDonnell, *Beguines* 539 f.

during the fourteenth century his successors repeated his condemnation. He himself made the need to combat heresy a constant theme of his many diocesan synods.[1] Nor was it groundless. During the period when papal policy under both John XXII and his two successors Benedict XII and Clement VI was seeking to curb activity against the Beguines, at Cologne and elsewhere subversion was at a high level. In 1322 Walter of Holland was condemned and burned for his errors, all efforts at converting him and making him reveal his accomplices having failed.[2] He was described by Trithemius as leader of the Fraticelli and a Lollard, thereby suggesting that he was one of the heretical Beghards with which the two terms were associated.[3] He both preached and wrote in the vernacular, having come, as so often, down the Rhine from Mainz. There is nothing to suggest that he was more than a local heresiarch or exceptional in any way.[4] Although the Cologne synod of 1322 renewed the condemnation of the Beguines and Beghards it did not mention him or frame any new legislation as a result. Over the next few years numbers of heretical Beguines and Beghards were reported to be living in conventicles. Around 1327 a suspicious husband followed his wife to one of them, whither she went on pretext of attending church. Here the members engaged in heretical rites and finally in a sexual orgy.[5] More to the point is the statement of William of Egmont that these heretics called their habitation paradise, where they could enjoy all its benefits.[6] This reversion to the state of sinlessness before the fall, expressed in the permissibility of sexual intercourse, was one of the hallmarks of the Free Spirit; even if the orgies were exaggerated the beliefs which they expressed ring true to its tenets. Members of such conventicles were said to have been either burned or drowned in the Rhine.[7] Moreover, the heresy of the Free Spirit was not confined to

---

[1] Ibid., 516–17, who counts them as seven or eight.

[2] Fredericq, *Corpus* I, no. 177, 172–3.

[3] Ibid. Strictly of course there is a confusion, as the Fraticelli referred to the Spirituals and their followers in Provence, Italy and Sicily, whereas Lollard stood for the northern heretical Beguines and Beghards.

[4] As implied by N. Cohn, *The Pursuit of the Millennium*, 171, when he writes that 'the heretics of Cologne had found a remarkable leader in a certain Walter who came from Holland'.

[5] John of Winterthur *Chronica* 116. Two Munich MSS. CLM 2936 (f. 12rb) and CLM 17541 (f. 49vb) both refer to this event. CLM 2936 explicitly says that Walter was its leader acting in the role of priest and celebrating mass, and also calling himself Christ. They held to a number of Free Spirit tenets.

[6] Duplessis-d'Argentré, I, 278.   [7] Mosheim, 272.

such nocturnal gatherings. From the evidence of John of Brünn there is every reason to suppose that Beguine and Beghard houses of the poor were run by adherents of the Free Spirit[1] at this time; and these may well have formed the location for the majority of its adherents. Accordingly, ecclesiastical hostility towards the Beguines and Beghards seems to have been unaffected by changes in papal policy, and indeed often, as at Strasbourg, went contrary to it. Thus in 1335, the year before Benedict XII renewed John XXII's bull *Racio recta*, confirming immunity for them, Walram, then archbishop of Cologne, had reaffirmed Henry of Virnburg's ban, placing as much emphasis upon the illegality of wearing a distinctive habit as their errors.[2] In the following year at another council he grudgingly recognized the existence of some among them, under certain conditions, but the tenor was still one of hostility rather than acceptance.[3] With the widespread renewal of opposition towards the Beguines and Beghards during the 1350s under pope Innocent VI it was not long before the Cologne authorities did likewise. At a council in 1357 archbishop William repeated with added force the city's now time-honoured proscription of them as a sect without distinction. They were now a 'pestilential sect' whose 'contagion' must be checked; the penalties against those aiding or abetting them were stressed; growing alarm was expressed at their growth which was reaching mass proportions in both diocese and city. The entire sect was accordingly to be pursued without mercy.[4] How successful these measures were cannot be said; persecution continued under the joint stimulus of papal and imperial encouragement in the 1360s and again in the last decade of the century. But by 1423 attention had been turned to the Hussites and the followers of Wyclif.[5]

The case of Strasbourg is not dissimilar. Here, too, episcopal hostility against the Beguines and Beghards was for a time unqualified by distinctions between good and bad; and then it required special interventions to bring about a change. What was perhaps most striking about Strasbourg was the outright identification there of the Beguines with the heresy of the Free Spirit. It was described with a fullness far surpassing the eight articles of *Ad nostrum*. There was also a close parallel

---

[1] See pp. 371 ff. below.   [2] Fredericq, *Corpus* I, no. 188, 184–5.
[3] Hartzheim: *Concilia Germaniae* IV, 436.   [4] Ibid., 482–3.
[5] Ibid., V, 220–1. This is true of the church generally, although references to the Beguines can still be found for Strasbourg in 1435 (Hartzheim, ibid., 248) and Louvain in 1496 (ibid., 336). Whilst the first consists of a somewhat innocuous reference to Clement V the latter is along more habitually hostile lines.

between the policy of the bishop of Strasbourg, John of Dürbheim (1306–28), and papal policy. In both cases the ambiguities towards the Beguines and Beghards led to a series of fluctuations in attitude which were at times openly contradictory. While John XXII began by publishing Clement V's decrees and then sought to modify their effects, John of Dürbheim, at an almost identical period, found himself driven farther and farther along the road of hostility to the Beguines and Beghards until he finally proscribed them in 1319. He was then forced by papal pressure to reverse his actions.

Perhaps the best testimony to the prevalence of the Free Spirit among the Beguines and Beghards in the diocese of Strasbourg is that bishop John's first denunciation of them was independent of papal legislation. On 13 August 1317 he addressed a letter to his diocese in which he accused the Beghards and begging sisters (Schwestriones) of the heresy of the Free Spirit.[1] This, as just stated, was no mere assertion of complicity but a reasoned analysis, under seven heads, of the nature of the heresy. We shall examine its detail later.[2] Here we are concerned with its practical provisions. Since it was published in August, two months before the issue of Clement V's two bulls, John of Dürbheim invoked the Council of Mainz in 1310 for the authority to ban those men and women who begged with the cry of 'Brod durch Gott' and openly called themselves the 'sect of the Free Spirit' and the 'brothers and sisters of voluntary poverty'.[3] They also included many priests and monks as well as married persons. The bishop forthwith prohibited the sect with its ceremonies, conventicles, habits and doctrines, giving its members fifteen days to render up their hymns and books, to be burned, and three days to abandon their habit; their houses were to be taken over by the church. Yet in spite of his severity, John drew the line between expressly the heretical Beguines and Beghards and their orthodox namesakes and members of a third order. The latter were to be allowed to continue as before.[4]

Accordingly, John of Dürbheim's position approximated to that taken by Clement V's two bulls, which appeared in the October following his own legislation. Yet in both cases the taint of heresy, together with no criterion for orthodoxy, exposed the Beguines and Beghards *en masse* to unlimited abuse, as we have earlier mentioned. Both John XXII and John of Dürbheim soon realized this. While the pope started his series of decrees in favour of the innocent, the bishop of Strasbourg

---

[1] Mosheim, 255–61.   [2] See pp. 364 ff. below.
[3] Mosheim, ibid., 256.   [4] Ibid., 260.

is said to have written to the pope for a means of distinguishing them.[1] Whether the pope provided one or not, the bishop's own response to the problem was the opposite of the pope's. He had already followed up his letter of August 1317 by instituting an inquisition in the diocese with the help of doctors learned in theology;[2] in the following year, 26 June 1318, he addressed an appeal to the bishop of Worms to act against those heretics who had taken refuge from the persecution.[3] The climax was reached in January and February 1319 when in two edicts he ordered the Beguines to disband and return to their parishes. There are strong indications, both from events at Strasbourg and the tenor of the first of John of Dürbheim's two letters, that he had been compelled to this step in spite of himself, through pressure from his own clergy. The latter had in the previous August attacked both the Franciscans and the Dominicans for their attitude towards the Clementine decrees; since a number of Beguine houses in the city were under the protection of the two orders it is probable that it was to this that the Strasbourg clergy were referring.[4] John of Dürbheim appears to confirm the likelihood in the opening of his January letter; he speaks of the discrepancy between Strasbourg and the neighbouring dioceses in interpreting the new constitution (*Cum de mulieribus*). Whereas they have taken it for condemnation of the Beguines as a whole, he has not done so because of certain 'probable and special reasons'. In order to combat the scandals and dangers which have resulted from his leniency he now gave the Beguines two weeks in which to renounce their status and their habit.[5]

Bishop John's second decree, a month later, on 17 February, reaffirmed the previous ban and went on to prohibit the Beguines' wearing their former habits or tunics of grey; other colours could be used provided they were not uniform. Only those too poor, and recluses, were exempt.[6]

Thus at Strasbourg the delayed action of John XXII's promulgation of Clement V's bulls was taking effect just when the pope was himself trying to reverse them. John of Dürbheim by his belated ban upon the Beguines had put himself in direct opposition to John XXII; for *Racio recta*, issued in the previous August, had, as we have seen, expressly allowed the Beguines to retain their habits as well as their

[1] Haupt in ZKG 7 (1885), 521.
[2] McDonnell, op. cit., 526.
[3] Mosheim, ibid., 268–9.
[4] McDonnell, op. cit., 532.
[5] Text in Haupt ZKG 7, 560–1.
[6] Ibid., 561–2; also published in M. Bihl, *De tertio ordine S. Francisci in provincia Germaniae superioris sive Argentinensi* in AFH 14 (1921) no. 15, 175.

habitations; and this was reinforced within a week of the bishop's second letter by the bull *Dilectos filios* to be followed in April by *Etsi apostolicae*. Clearly, then, it could only be a matter of time before Strasbourg altered course again. Pressure upon bishop John to do so was not long in coming. Vital du Four, the Franciscan cardinal, wrote to him directly attacking his two decrees and invoking *Etsi apostolicae*.[1] The bishop soon reverted to his earlier position and acknowledged the existence of women of praiseworthy life among the Beguines.[2] In what seems to have been the reply to this letter,[3] the pope enjoined the bishop, in much the same terms as his series of bulls, to make provision for the innocent Beguines while prosecuting those guilty of the heresy of the Free Spirit. Thus the first confusions and fluctuations which arose out of Clementine, and early fourteenth-century episcopal, legislation were for a time resolved.

But only for a time: as at Cologne the latent hostility towards the Beguines and Beghards remained, reinforced by periodic papal offensives against the heretics among them. In the case of Strasbourg it erupted into renewed repression under Lambert von Burne, bishop from 1371 to 1374. Paradoxically, like his predecessor John of Dürbheim, his action came in the wake of a change in papal policy, which together with measures by the emperor Charles IV marked the zenith of their persecution. Gregory XI had already issued his bull *Ex injuncto nobis*, in April 1374, once more discriminating between pious and heretical Beguines and Beghards. Lambert's decree published on 19 August of the same year therefore went against the current.[4] The prefatory note appended to it suggests that it was inspired by the discovery of a number of heretics masquerading as members of the Franciscan third order.[5] The bull itself was in the direct line of descent from earlier condemnations. It began by reproving the Beguines and Beghards for not being an approved order, observing no recognized rule, and obeying no superior authority; and it recalled their prohibition by the Council of Vienne. In spite of this, groups of women continued to

[1] Ibid., 176–8.   [2] McDonnell, *Beguines*, 533 ff.
[3] Printed in S. Baluze, *Vitae Paparum Avenionsium* (ed. G. Mollat) vol. 3, no. LXVI, 353–5. The letter is undated. But it begins with an acknowledgement of Bishop John's letter, and employs the same phrase which the latter had used: 'Preter prescriptam prophanam sectam esse mulieres alias laudabilis status in dyocesi et partibus prelibatis in excessiva copia, quasi ducentarum millium numerum excedentes . . .' (ibid., 354). McDonnell, ibid.
[4] Text in Haupt ZKG 7, 562–4, and Döllinger, *Beiträge* II, 378–80.
[5] Döllinger, ibid., 378.

live as Beguines with their distinctive habit, conventions and conventicles, and their own elected superiors; some formed colleges and
convents; others begged without necessity. On Sundays, in particular,
they confessed to their superiors or one another, which they regarded as
their discipline, and performed all the rites of the church themselves,
refusing to recognize their parish priests or heeding the threat of excommunication. Some under the pretence of sanctity flouted God's
law. To end these abuses the clergy on each of the following three
Sundays were to show these women the error of their ways, and to give
them six days' notice from the publication of the decree in which to
renounce them, and fifteen days to disband.

On this occasion the effects were short-lived; for on 30 December
Gregory XI's bull *Ex injuncto nobis*, published in the previous April[1] and
addressed to the prelates of the Empire, Brabant and Flanders, was submitted to Rainbold von Gemünd for the bishop of Strasbourg.[2] It had,
so Rainbold's preface tells us, been used in response to a deputation to
the pope representing Coblenz, Brussels, Liège, Trier and Strasbourg.
Similar action on behalf of the Cologne Beguines was taken in the following year, February or March 1375, by the magistrates of Cologne;
this time in protest against the excesses of a Dominican inquisitor, who,
they asserted, had bemused 'the poor and unlettered laymen with such
difficult and unanswerable questions' that even a great theologian
would be tried for an answer.[3] Despite these protestations in favour of
the deserving poor Gregory XI still found it necessary once more to
issue a second injunction three years later in 1377[4] to the same authorities in Germany, Brabant and Flanders. In both cases his appeal was
for the poor, both men and women, who were innocent of heresy,
as opposed to the Beguines and Beghards, words which Gregory

---

[1] Fredericq, *Corpus* I, no. 220, 229-31.   [2] Haupt, Döllinger, loc. cit.

[3] McDonnell, *Beguines*, 568-9, quoting from L. Ennen and G. Eckertz *Quellen zur
Geschichte der Stadt Köln* (6 vols.) V, 89-90, n.82; while he here follows Haupt ZKG
7, 553-4, his own account of these events suffers from an inconsistent chronology.
After attributing bishop Lambert's decree to Gregory XI's bull *Ad perpetuam rei
memoriam*, addressed to the archbishop of Mainz and condemning the *Speculum
Saxonum* for which he offers no evidence (567), he then goes on to discuss the Strasbourg and Cologne protests of 1375. His words imply that these led to Gregory XI's
bull *Ex injuncto nobis*, of the previous year, for he says 'In the wake of such testimony
the orthodox extraregulars were to get in Avignon a new lease of life. To the Archbishops of Cologne, Trèves and Mainz . . . the Pope addressed on April 7th, 1374
a bull. . . .'

[4] Fredericq, *Corpus* I, no. 225, 237-8.

avoided.[1] In this respect the second bull of 1377 went further than the first in openly taking the part of the poor brothers and sisters. Yet although this closed the second wave of persecution, a third was to come at the end of the century; and the inquisition continued to be active in the meantime.[2]

The vagaries of fortune among the Beguines at Cologne and Strasbourg underline their inherently precarious position in the fourteenth century. As at once suspect and unauthorized they were doubly vulnerable; as containing both heretics and true believers, the innocent were ever liable to suffer for the guilty. Not surprisingly, then, a state of equilibrium never held for long: for these ambiguities engendered a corresponding ambivalence in the attitude of the ecclesiastical authorities. It could vary not only in time, as the different phases of papal hostility show, but also in level, so that simultaneously the pope, bishops and parishes could all be pursuing a different policy towards them. It was this divergence within the church above all which, as we have seen, largely underlay its fluctuations in policy: where the bishops might see the Beguine problem in terms of heresy, the parish priests saw it in terms of local groups of pious poor, as in the case of their protests in 1374 and 1375, and e contrario as heretics at the time of John of Dürbheim. This in turn frequently meant disparities in emphasis between the pope and the dioceses; and indeed much of the history of the church's relations with the Beguines and Beghards in the fourteenth century revolved round the constant need to direct papal, diocesan and parish actions to the same end.

Accordingly, even at a period when the papacy was treating the Beguines and Beghards with latitude, different conditions might obtain in the dioceses and parishes. Thus while both John XXII's immediate successors adopted the same tenor as he, there were still cases of individual hostility. At Metz in 1334 a number of 'brothers of the highest poverty' were burned by the inquisitor, Garin.[3] In 1338 the Council of Trier renewed its condemnation of the mendicant Beguines and

[1] This was pointed out by Haupt ZKG 7, 526, and repeated by McDonnell, Beguines, 569.
[2] McDonnell, ibid., follows Haupt ZKG 7, 526, in placing the unnamed, undated bull Ad ea que (published by Haupt, op. cit., 565-7, and Döllinger Beiträge II, 381-3) in the period post c. 1400-4. That it belongs to Boniface IX seems clear from the references to his predecessors. But it appears more likely to have come in the early years of his pontificate, before 1396, when he renewed the wholesale condemnation of the Beguines. As late as 1400 he continued to condemn them.
[3] Döllinger, Beiträge II, 403-6.

Beghards, called Apostles, and gave them fifteen days within which to disband and return to a life of gainful labour; it also warned confessors to report any heretical ideas to the authorities.[1]

Nevertheless it was not until in the 1350s that large-scale action was resumed against them. Benedict XII had in 1336 reissued *Racio recta* which, as we have seen, in putting the case for their toleration without granting them recognition, was one of the most formative documents in their history; in its emphasis upon their need to obey the parish priest it sought to regularize their parochial position.[2] Substantially the same outlook was expressed by Clement VI in his bull *Personas vacantes* of 1343, where he laid down their mode of behaviour in religious matters, and added the same disclaimer over their extra-regular state.[3]

The change in papal tone was occasioned by the effects of the Black Death, which raged over Western Europe from 1348 to 1350. It led, among other things, to bands of Flagellants, particularly in the Rhineland, France and the Low Countries.[4] Their processions and public penances created, as we shall consider in chapter six, a ferment from which signs of heresy and unorthodoxy soon appeared. It was not long before the Beguines and Beghards came under official disapprobation. In 1353 Innocent VI gave voice to the renewed threat in a bull addressed to the German church. He specially singled out the Beguines and Beghards and commanded the inquisitor, John Schandelant, to extirpate them.[5] Whether he was successful or not, we hear little more of measures against them for another dozen years until 1365. This was the beginning of nearly a decade of concentrated repression. The climax was from 1369 to 1372 when the pope, Urban V, was actively seconded—or rather preceded—by Charles IV, the German Emperor, who promulgated the most stringent measures of all. These years formed the peak of activity against the Beguines and Beghards before in due course giving rise to another reaction in favour of those who were innocent.

As at the time of Clement V's measures in 1311, those of Urban V were not isolated incidents; they belonged to a series of actions by both pope and emperor which, as we have said, were continued over a number of years. Their sustained nature leaves little doubt of the serious difficulties confronting the church at this time. In addition to the divi-

[1] Fredericq, *Corpus* I, no. 191, 187–8.

[2] Fredericq, *Corpus* II, no. 57, 93.

[3] Ibid., no. 60, 95: Per hoc tamen statum Beghinarum nullatenus ex premissis intendimus approbare.

[4] See pp. 485 ff. below.   [5] Raynaldus, ad annum 1353, no. 26.

sions within the papal curia over the desirability of returning to Rome, religious fervour within the church was at a low ebb. The heretical sects, like the Waldensians and the Fraticelli, and the pervasiveness of mysticism, continued between them to draw most of it away from the church into either anti- or extra-ecclesiastical channels. This was implicitly recognized by Urban himself in his communications to Casimir, king of Poland, and to the archbishop of Rheims. The first, urging the king to renounce his illicit marriage, which came within the prohibited degree of consanguinity, spoke of the many sorrows afflicting him.[1] The second letter lamented the loss of zeal in the church to convoke councils which had in the past preserved its purity and liberty. At the present time evils and lack of piety abounded; liberty was in danger, worship neglected, and faith threatened by love of worldly goods.[2] This was followed by two bulls, one to the French church, the other to both the German church and laity, reopening the attack on the Beguines and Beghards. The bull to the French prelates described the Beguines and Beghards as the sons and daughters of Belial, 'spreading their detestable errors' in diverse cities and localities of France and misleading certain simple believers. He called for immediate action to apprehend them and their followers, and to hand them over to the secular arm. The bull to the German authorities differs in being far more widely directed than the French one, which was addressed simply to the archbishop, bishops and inquisitors. It went beyond the prelates to include ecclesiastics in general and the rulers of all territorial units down to castle and village, itself a pointer to the wider diffusion of the heresy in Germany. It expressed a similar urgency for their extirpation; but added an appeal for help from all in capturing and holding the heretics until they could be taken to proper prisons by the inquisition.[3]

After a pause of four years this was followed in 1369 by a spate of decrees, first by the emperor Charles IV, who issued four separate condemnations of the Beguines and Beghards within ten days; then by Gregory XI, with bulls in 1371 and 1372, to be followed by another edict from the emperor in 1373.[4] These constituted the most intense offensive ever mounted against the Beguines and Beghards and were unique, not only for their number, but for the co-operation between emperor and papacy over almost a decade. That the Beguines and

---

[1] Ibid., ad annum 1365, no. 15.   [2] Ibid., no. 16.
[3] Fredericq, *Corpus* I, no. 209, 206–8.
[4] There was a further bull by Gregory XI in 1376, but already in 1374 he had sought to mitigate their indiscriminate effects.

Beghards were still there to be attacked again at the end of the century is no reflection upon the zeal of their persecutors.

All four of Charles IV's decrees in 1369 were issued between 9 June and 18 June from Lucca. The first was addressed to the full array of spiritual and secular authority in Germany; after acknowledging the actions of the then pope, Urban V, it ordered, under pain of losing all possessions, the extirpation of the Beguines and Beghards. No distinction was made between innocent and guilty—the voluntary poor (Wilge Armen) or sisters of convents (Conventschwestern), with their cry of 'Bread for God's sake' (Brod durch Gott) when begging, and the generality of Beguines and Beghards. They were all 'sheep in wolves' clothing'. Anyone helping them with food or shelter was to be imprisoned by the inquisition under the chief inquisitor, Walter Kerling; he was to be assisted in every way; and prisons put at his disposal for holding the captured heretics.[1]

The second imperial decree announced the appointment of Walter Kerling as chief inquisitor for Germany, and enjoined the protection and co-operation of the princes in helping the inquisition against the heretics; failure to do so or to render up a third of the possessions of Beguines and Beghards or other heretics captured rendered them liable to a fine of 100 marks, while interfering with or impeding the inquisitors would entail the confiscation of all goods.[2]

Charles's third decree was addressed a week later, dated 17 June, to Walter Kerling and the inquisitors for Germany; it authorized them to obtain the help of specially sworn notaries in hunting out and burning heretical treatises in the vernacular, which were circulating in large numbers among laymen and propagating the errors of the Beguines and Beghards. All the authorities in Germany were ordered to help in their detection under pain of loss of liberties and a fine of 100 golden marks.[3] Finally, in the fourth edict Charles, characterizing, in the manner of papal bulls, the Beguines and Beghards as outwardly feigning a poverty which was heretical, spoke of their widespread existence especially in the archbishoprics of Magdeburg and Bremen, and the lands of Thuringia, Saxony and Hesse as well as other parts of Germany. In order to bring about their speedy suppression, their houses and conventicles where they practised poverty, which they claimed to be the most perfect state in the world, were to be handed over to the inquisition as gaols for imprisoning their occupants where no others already existed. Elsewhere their houses were to be sold, and of the proceeds one-third was to go

[1] Fredericq, Corpus I, no. 210, 208-10.   [2] Ibid., 211, 211-14.   [3] Ibid., 212, 215-17.

on alms, distributed by one pious layman and one devout cleric to causes which they considered most deserving, including help to heretics converted from their errors. Another third was for the inquisitor of the locality concerned or his representative. The last part was to be spent on the walls or the roads of the city or town concerned as damages for the harm done to the community from the inmates of the house or houses. This procedure was to take place within three days of expulsion from a house.[1]

As we have said, these measures were unsurpassed in their comprehensiveness and attention to detail. With them, as Lea has said, the inquisition was fully established in Germany.[2] For each imperial decree the authority of the pope, Urban V, was invoked, to form a united front between emperor and papacy. The scale on which Charles IV acted, the sweeping nature of his condemnation, and the extent of Beguine and Beghard influence in the areas mentioned, show how seriously he treated the heresy of the Free Spirit. That this was more than just an obsession on his part is strongly suggested by the equally emphatic series of attacks from Gregory XI which, as we have stated, followed closely on those of Charles IV. The first, the bull *Sedes apostolica* of 1371, expressly commended the emperor as 'a magnificent fighter for the faith and a ready persecutor of the heretics', and ratified his measures for dividing the proceeds from the sale of Beguine and Beghard houses, in response to a request by Walter Kerling.[3]

In the following year Gregory XI issued the bull *Ab exordio nascentis*. Directed to the master and prior provincial of the German Dominicans, it requested them to appoint five suitable members of the order to act as inquisitors in the archbishoprics and bishoprics of Mainz, Cologne, Utrecht, Salzburg and Magdeburg in addition to the two existing Dominican inquisitors, Walter Kerling and Louis of Caluga, whose powers were confirmed.[4] That the measure was aimed primarily at the Beguines and Beghards is supported by an entry for the same year in the *Annales Ecclesiastici* of Odoricus Raynaldus which specifically mentioned the appointment of new judges in the provinces of Magdeburg and Bremen to deal with them.[5] The following year Charles IV

---

[1] Ibid., 213, 219–21.   [2] H. C. Lea, *Inquisition* II, 392.
[3] Fredericq, *Corpus* I, no. 214, 222.   [4] Ibid, no. 215, 223–4.
[5] Raynaldus, ad annum 1372, no. 34, and Fredericq, *Corpus* I, no. 217, 225. A similar statement is also to be found in Bzovius, *Annales Ecclesiastici*, quoted in Fredericq, *Corpus* I, no. 216, 225:
Inter hos Italiae tumultus in Germania plurimi Begardorum et Fraticellorum e

returned to the attack in a letter to the archbishop of Trier and a number of lay rulers, including those of Luxemburg, Limburg, Brabant and Jülich. It informed them that Gregory XI had recently appointed the Dominican John of Boland as inquisitor for the dioceses of Trier, Cologne and Louvain to deal with the heretics, and especially the Beguines and Beghards, who were infesting so many parts of Germany; he was to be invested with all the customary powers and privileges in the exercise of his office. For this purpose Charles IV charged them to act as John's protector and to make the customary concessions to him, including a third of all possessions of Beguines and Beghards thus apprehended.[1]

The presence of the Beguines and Beghards was also being felt at this time in France, where they were often known as Turlupins;[2] it was, together with Lollard, a term of derogation rather than the name for a specific sect. A bull from Gregory XI to the king of France in 1373 spoke of the many Beghards, 'otherwise called Turlupins', infesting his kingdom and spreading heresy, as well as Waldensians in the region of Vienne and elsewhere. He urged the king to facilitate action against them by removing obstacles to the inquisition from secular jurisdiction, and enabling it to proceed independently and without interference.[3] Charles V, king of France, responded by burning a number of Turlupins at Paris, together with their books and clothes. The views attributed to them were certainly those of the Free Spirit—namely, that there should be no shame in anything from God, including sexual promiscuity.[4]

Already, however, Gregory XI was showing himself to be concerned about the indiscriminate persecution of the Beguines and Beghards which recent legislation had stimulated. He wrote to the king of France at this very time to enjoin him to temper severity with mercy, and instructed that those who repented should be taken back into the church.[5] In 1374 he went further. A bull to the archbishops of Cologne, Trier and

Joanno Wiclefo recens exorto magis ecclesiasticam potestatem contemnere docti pullulabant, jamque Magdeburgensi et Bremensi provinciis infectis, partes Rhenanas, Hollandiae et Brabantiae irruperant. Monuit pontifex (Gregorius XI) imperatorem (Carolum IV) et principes Germaniae, ut ad extirpationem haeresum eius criminis inquisitoribus opem ferrent.

From this time they are associated with Wyclif's followers, but they only shared the name in common.   [1] Fredericq, *Corpus* I, no. 218, 226–8.

[2] According to Raynaldus, op. cit., ad annum 1373, no. 19.

[3] Ibid., 240–1.   [4] Ibid., 241.   [5] Ibid., 240.

Mainz virtually trod the same path of withdrawal as John XXII's bulls of fifty years earlier. There were many poor people of both sexes, it said, genuinely living in poverty and chastity, obeying their priests and uninvolved in any errors, who had been unjustly molested by the inquisitors. While the guilty should be punished, the innocent should be left in peace.[1] In spite of an almost concurrent warning to the inquisition in Germany against the circulation of books of vernacular sermons with heretical tendencies,[2] the pope repeated his demand for care in the treatment of Beguines and Beghards two years later in 1376. He particularly emphasized that their clothing, which had been the cause of their unjust maltreatment, was not to be made an occasion for persecution. Those who had been wrongly excommunicated were to be readmitted into the church.[3]

Thus, while it would be untrue to say that within a decade the wheel had once again turned full circle and that the Beguines and Beghards had been restored to the fold, the extreme measures of the late 1360s and early 1370s, especially on the part of the emperor Charles IV, had to some extent recoiled against their sponsors. Gregory XI's distinction between the legitimate and the spurious poor, although not explicitly naming the Beguines and Beghards as such, was tantamount to recognition. Twice within sixty years the attempt to stamp them out had failed, or had at least been reconsidered. The Beguines and Beghards now entered a second period of comparative peace. Not that it was one generally of tranquillity. There were bands of ecstatics called the Dancers as well as the recrudescence in various places of the Flagellants. In 1377 Gregory XI made the first official condemnation of Wyclif's teachings. This was followed by a second made in 1382 at the Council of London, presided over by the archbishop of Canterbury, William Courtenay.[4] The growing association of the Lollards with the Beguines and Beghards probably helped to give a new impetus to latent suspicions. Action, too, against the Beguines and Beghards locally continued, as we shall observe later; but for another twenty years they were free from any centrally directed offensive.

It was renewed by pope Boniface IX who, over a period of some six years from 1394 to 1400, revived all the more oppressive measures of the time of Charles IV. Once more his action was not an isolated one; at about the same time—1393 and 1394—we hear of the activities of the inquisitor of Utrecht, Eylard Schoenveld. He 'greatly molested the

---

[1] Fredericq, *Corpus* I, no. 220, 229-31.　　[2] Ibid., no. 224, 237.
[3] Ibid., no. 225, 238.　　[4] Mansi, vol. 26, 695-715. See ch. VII below.

sisters [of the house of Gerard de Groot] in Utrecht', who were defended by de Groot's followers and successors Werimbold van Buscop
and Florens Radewijns.[1] No doubt it was this tendency to treat non-
heretical groups, like those of Gerard de Groot's Brethren of the Common Life, as Beguines and Beghards, and heretical ones at that,[2] which
led Boniface IX, in his first bull of 7 January 1394, to repeat Gregory
XI's injunction to distinguish between the innocent and guilty ones.[3]
It was dated the same day as a petition asking him to intercede with the
inquisition in order to prevent innocent Beguines from being maltreated.[4] This attitude, however, did not last for long. Within two
years Boniface was repeating the recent legislation of his predecessors,
Urban V and Gregory XI, to whose authority he frequently appealed,
as well as that of Charles IV. His three subsequent bulls of 1396 and 1400
in effect recapitulated the main provisions of these earlier papal and
imperial decrees. That of 1396[5] was a lament for the failure of tolerance
(albeit qualified). The Beguines and Beghards, it stated, in defiance of
ecclesiastical prohibitions against new orders, had formed their own
congregations and conventicles, assumed a common habit, and had
elected their own superiors under whom they publicly begged. For a
hundred years until the present time they had been a source of heresy,
and for that reason the pope's predecessors, Urban V and Gregory XI,
together with the emperor, Charles IV, had promulgated edicts against
them. The concessions made to them had only strengthened them to
the detriment of the church and the faith. Accordingly these were all
revoked without exception. The inquisitors were to act against these
groups and their errors in the way laid down by Charles IV. Over and
above the sweeping nature of the condemnation, it is significant that the
two criteria specifically mentioned in evidence for the Beguines' and
Beghards' heresy and illegality were Clement V's *Ad nostrum* and John
XXII's *Sancta Romana*. The first shows clearly that the heresy with
which they continued to be associated was that of the Free Spirit; the
second, that in addition to their subversion they were not to be toler-
ated because they were not legally constituted. While the reference to
Ad nostrum came in the bull of 1394 (as one of the means of distinguish-

---

[1] Fredericq, *Corpus* I, no. 236, 251.

[2] Ibid., no. 237, 252. In fact de Groot was tireless in combating the heresy of the
Free Spirit, as his prosecution of the heretics Bartholomew and Gerbrand shows. See
the series of letters to the ecclesiastical authorities at Utrecht and Zwolle, c. 1380,
in Fredericq, *Corpus* I, 239–50.

[3] Ibid., no. 239, 254–6.   [4] Ibid., no. 238, 253–4.   [5] Ibid., no. 241, 256–7.

ing the bad from the guiltless) *Sancta Romana* was mentioned then and again in 1396.

The pope's two other bulls, both in 1400, were riders to his general condemnation. The first, to the prior-provincial of the Dominicans of Saxony,[1] repeated Gregory XI's measures for the appointment of six members of the order as inquisitors in the areas served by Mainz, Cologne, Magdeburg, Bremen and other cities; it conferred upon them the customary privileges and exemptions. The second bull, to the ecclesiastical and lay authorities of Germany,[2] commanded their assistance to the inquisition under the direction of Eylard Schoenveld, the chief inquisitor. In particular, heretics and suspects were to be apprehended and held until they could be handed over to the inquisitors or taken to other prisons.

Boniface IX's legislation was in effect a reissue of what had gone before. Thus by the end of the fourteenth century something like a working machinery has been created to deal with the Beguines and Beghards as the result of over a century of official activity. This time their illegality was not subsequently qualified: indeed, there were no further papal declarations on them. This was due in large part to the growing intensity of the efforts to heal the Great Schism and also to the outbreak of the Hussite rebellion: the former dominated the first two General Councils of Pisa (1409) and Constance (1414–18), while Hus was himself condemned and burned at Constance in 1415. The one reference to the Beguines and Beghards occurs at Constance, and suggests that the time-honoured distinction between the genuine and the false continued to hold in spite of their periodic reprobation *in toto*. It came in the censure by the Council of 17 propositions by one Matthew Grabon, a Dominican who had asserted that only those in state of perfection could follow a life of evangelical poverty. Anyone else attempting to abjure possessions sinned mortally; this included the Beguines, who in other respects were free from error or the taint of heresy.[3] These notions were opposed by Pierre d'Ailly, cardinal and bishop of Cambrai, and John Gerson, chancellor of Paris university, two of the main pillars of orthodoxy, who took a leading part in the exposure of heresy within the Council and outside it, and led the prosecution against Hus. In 1317 both denounced Grabon's views as erroneous, scandalous and heretical, and he duly abjured them.[4] Although

---

[1] Fredericq, *Corpus*, no. 243, 258–9.   [2] Ibid., no. 244, 259–61.
[3] Fredericq, *Corpus* II, no. 133 (254³), 261–19.
[4] Ibid., nos. 134 (254⁴) and 135 (254⁵), 220–5, and Mansi, vol. 28, 386–94.

the article on the Beguines was not mentioned, reference was made to propositions 7 and 10, both of which held that poverty was sinful. By implication at least the true Beguine and Beghard were not denied the right to follow it.[1] If this does not in any way come near to recognition, neither does it attempt to single them out for condemnation. Henceforth they tend to disappear from papal and conciliar sight. Pope Eugenius IV in 1431 issued a stereotyped bull to the German and Flemish ecclesiastics, both enjoining rigour for the heretics and leniency for the pious.[2]

But at the more local level they remained prominent and treatises and references to individual heretics of the Free Spirit continued beyond the middle of the fifteenth century. Here, in the actual prosecution of known heretics, there was none of the ambivalence which the papacy had displayed for over a hundred years. The difference is understandable. From an ecumenical point of view the Beguines and Beghards constituted a body of devout women and a lesser number of men, the majority of whom were pledged to a life of prayer and simplicity in obedience to their ecclesiastical superiors, at a time when the officially recognized orders could no longer offer such an existence. On the other hand, their presence was a continuing affront to the decision of the Fourth Lateran Council, frequently repeated, that there should be no new orders. Even more important, their very piety made them an easy prey to infiltration, rendering them at once a source of subversion, as well as a violation of the authority of the church. Hence the fluctuations in the official attitude towards them: to take action on a large scale was to inflict injustice; to remain inactive was to permit heresy. In the main, however, the balance was against them throughout the fourteenth century, and remained so in spite of Eugenius IV's ambiguities in 1431. They were suspect on the very grounds of upholding poverty, as can be seen from the account of the hostility towards Gerard de Groot and his community. Although they supported themselves by manual labour, not begging, the fact that they practised poverty was enough to brand them as Beguines and heretics, neither of which they were. It makes somewhat poignant reading to see the chronicler of Windersheim painstakingly examining the legislation of Clement V and John XXII to show that poverty was not a cause for condemning the Beguines and Beghards, and that it had never been branded heretical.[3] From the 1390s onwards the opposition to the

---

[1] Mansi, ibid., 394.   [2] Fredericq, Corpus I, no. 281, 320-2.
[3] Ibid., vol. II, no. 105 (235 bis), 150-2, for the year 1384. Again, John Brinckerinck

Beguines and Beghards tended to increase. Boniface IX's legislation does not seem to have been followed by any reaction in their favour; both before and after it provincial councils were enjoining severity towards them. In addition, the early fifteenth century saw at least two powerful treatises written against them. Above all, it also witnessed the appearance of the heresy of the Free Spirit, with which their heretical wing was identified, in two other groups—the *Homines Intelligentiae*[1] and the Adamites in Bohemia.[2] Thus even if at the highest level there was little reference to the Beguines and Beghards, opposition to them or those with whom they were associated, increased in other directions.

In 1393-4, for example, Jacob Soest, inquisitor for Utrecht, carried out an investigation of the community of Werimbold van Buscop, the friend and follower of de Groot, in order to try to uncover Beguines and Beghards there. Among the questions asked were those characteristic of the doctrine of the Free Spirit: whether marriage was permissible, whether to live in a married state entailed sin, whether the good man needed the sacrament of penance and confession, and whether it sufficed for the remission of sins to confess among themselves.[3] In the following year the brotherhood made a formal profession of orthodoxy, expressly disavowing the errors condemned by Clement V or any pretensions to being a new order with its own habit or priesthood. The inmates wished only to follow a life in common of manual labour and honest poverty.[4]

Hostility to the Beguines and Beghards came also from the clergy. One example was the series of questions drawn up by Everard Foec, the dean of St. Salvator's church, Utrecht, in which he opposed their independent existence outside the church. He also inveighed against them in sermons.[5] Similar signs of inquisitorial activity in Cologne can be seen at the same time, directed, as we have already mentioned,

---

stated that de Groot during his lifetime sustained many insults and injuries 'qui eum vocabant Baggardum sive Lollardum aut simile opprobriosum vocabulum imponebant . . .' Ibid., III, no. 37 (235³) 46.

[1] See pp. 395 ff. below.

[2] See pp. 399 ff. below.

[3] 'Utrum liceat in matrimonium assumere, et an in matrimonio quis vivere possit sine peccato. . . . De sacramento penitentie, an bonus homo teneatur confiteri. An culpas eorum possint inter se dicere et an per hoc purgentur.' (Ibid., II no. 106 (236 bis) 153-6).

[4] Ibid., no. 107 (239bis).

[5] Ibid., nos. 109 and 110, 160-8, and 113, 176-7.

by Eylard Schoenveld. An anonymous statement speaks of the mal-treatment of devout men and women by the inquisitors there.[1] In Utrecht the bishop in 1401 announced that a number of Beguines within the diocese had agreed to submit themselves to oversight, and where suitable would receive a licence to live communal lives provided they did not beg.[2]

Even increasing preoccupation over the Hussites and the Great Schism did not eliminate the Beguines and Beghards as a live issue in many Rhineland cities. At Strasbourg in 1404 their status was debated by the jurists and declared illegal, as it was at Heidelberg in the follow-ing year.[3] At Basel they were expelled in 1405 in the struggle between the mendicant orders and the secular clergy.[4] Yet these were matters which concerned primarily their standing as a movement and not as the harbourers of heresy. By the turn of the fifteenth century this was no longer an issue of ecumenical importance; henceforth the existence of the Free Spirit became increasingly local and individual.

The treatises

A similar tone of hostility is to be found in the treatises against the Beguines and Beghards. We have already mentioned Alvarus Pelagius who excoriated them on the two counts of heresy and mendicancy. The same two charges re-echo through the discussions on them. For the most part they are found together, the claim of evangelical poverty being treated in conjunction with the heresy—it need hardly be said— of the Free Spirit. In a number of instances, however, the latter received no mention, or was clearly subordinate to the former. These include firstly an anonymous treatise *De Beghardis sive Lollardis* in a Munich manuscript, CLM 6603, addressed to Henry, bishop of Constance, and dated 1438.[5] It was a direct attack upon their mendicancy and idleness. Alms should be given only to those unable to work,[6] and Beguine-Beghard begging cannot be compared with Christ's, which belonged to the evangelical life.[7] Next there is another anonymous tractate which is also concerned wholly with mendicancy and, as Haupt (by whom it

---

[1] Fredericq *Corpus*, no. 111 (242[5]) 169–73.
[2] Ibid., no. 119 (244[4]) 191.
[3] Haupt, ZKG VII, 527.   [4] Lea, *Inquisition* II, 403.
[5] MS. CLM 6603, Munich, ff. 277r–290r.
Incipit: Reverendo in Christo patri et domine Heinrico dei . . . episcopo Con-stantiensis.
[6] Ibid., f. 279r   [7] Ibid., f. 286v.

was published) has said,[1] it bears a strong affinity to John of Mülberg's *Materia contra Beghardos*, the other treatise of this group: voluntary renunciation of worldly goods was only permitted to the recognized orders, a view which was also taken by Matthew Grabon who, as we have seen, was condemned for it at the Council of Constance. John of Mülberg's *Materia* was a collection of twenty folios of material on the Beguines and Beghards.[2] John himself was a Dominican, and one of the strongest opponents of the Beguines and Beghards in Basel at the beginning of the fifteenth century. For its first decade a prolonged struggle between the Dominicans and the Franciscans over the status of the Beguines and Beghards was waged there, leading to the latter's disbandment in 1411.[3] Mülberg's compilation was designed to confute the claims of the Beguines and Beghards and the third orders—all at that time under the protection of the Franciscans in Basel—that they had the right to beg. In his support he produced a series of authorities; they included St. Augustine's *De opere monachorum*; Clement V's bull *Cum de quibusdam*, with the words, 'since they [the Beguines and Beghards] promise obedience to no-one nor acknowledge any approved rule, they do not exist as a religious order';[4] the decision of the second Council of Lyons in 1274; the two bulls of John XXII *Cum de mulieribus* (hardly the most appropriate) and *Sancta Romana*, together with Boniface IX's bull *Sedis apostolicae* of 1396; the condemnation by Lambert, bishop of Strasbourg in 1374; and a series of biblical and patristic citations. It is of interest that, despite John of Mülberg's hostility to the Beguines and Beghards, he kept to the question of mendicancy and was not concerned to introduce heretical imputations.

This was not, however, true of the majority who, with Alvarus Pelagius, put the main stress upon their heretical nature and their errors. The most prominent among these writers was John Gerson, chancellor of Paris University and a leading figure at the Council of Constance (1415-18).[5] Gerson is distinguished from the other polemicists against

[1] H. Haupt, 'Zwei Traktate gegen Beginen und Begharden' in ZKG 12 (1891) 85-8. The treatise in question belongs to a manuscript in the library of the church of Michelstadt in Odenwald, ff. 238-42.

[2] Resumed in H. Haupt, 'Beiträge zur Geschichte der Sekte vom freien Geiste und das Beghardentums' in ZKG 7 (1885) 511-31. It was found in the Colmar manuscript 29, dating from the fifteenth century. Haupt, op. cit., 514.

[3] Ibid., 511-14. [4] Ibid., 516.

[5] For the particulars of Gerson's life see the 'Essai Biographique' in *Œuvres Complètes* (ed. P. Glorieux) I, Paris, 1960.
See also J. B. Morrall, *Gerson and the Great Schism* and pp. 436 ff. below.

the Beguines and Beghards in treating them from the wider standpoint of theological error as a whole; he did not devote any one treatise to them, but included them in a number of writings in which he examined religious doctrine and practice. Moreover, while he did not spare the Beguines and Beghards his lash, he was never led away beyond his terms of reference. From the number of occasions on which Gerson treated the Beguines it is clear that he regarded them as a serious threat; they appear in at least eight different works as well as his attack upon Ruysbroeck for his seemingly heretical leanings.[1] In every case the charge against them was their inculpation in the heresy of the Free Spirit. Thus Gerson added his voice to the unanimous contemporary verdict that the adherents of the Free Spirit were Beguines and Beghards.

Most of Gerson's attack concerned their pretence to love God in the name of their own self-love 'under which Beghards, men and women, perpetrate wicked and abominable crimes'. In particular, they held that the perfect soul, in being merged with God, loses its own volition and becomes part of God's will. Such a being can then do anything to which his senses incline him, and remain free from sin, for he is without a will of his own.[2] Gerson here follows the common view that those who aspire to this state are divided into the adepts and those subject to them. In his opinion the difference was merely a ruse on the part of the clever ones to control the more simple, by arrogating to themselves complete freedom from sin. And they committed numerous sins.[3] In the *Tractatus de distinctione verarum revelationum a falsis* Gerson cited as an example of the heresy of the Free Spirit, Mary of Valencienne's 'incredible book', in which it was asserted that he who succeeded in gaining God's love was released from all his laws, a belief based upon the words of St. Paul: 'Receive my charity and do what you will.'

---

[1] *De examinatione doctrinae*; *De distinctione verarum revelationum a falsis*; *De libris caute legendis*; *Considérations sur St. Joseph*; *De theologica mystica*; *Sermo in die Sancti Ludovici Francorum regis*; *Sermo de spiritu sancto*; *Epistolae* (2) *ad Fratrem Bartholomeum super tertiam partem libri Ruysbroeck De ornatu spiritualium nuptiarum*; *Tractatus contra Romantium de Rosa*. References to those works quoted are either to the Glorieux edition, 4 vols. (G) or the 1489 Nuremberg edition, 3 vols (N).

[2] 'Fuit alter error de lege vel spiritu libertatis sub qua Begardi et Begarde nefanda et abominabilia perpetrarunt facinora. Ponit error iste, quod anima perfecta, reducta in deum, perdit suum velle, ita quod nihil habet velle vel nolle nisi velle divinum, quale habuit ab eterno in esse ideale divino. Quo adiecto dicunt se consequenter posse agere quicquid carnalis affectio deposcit sine peccato vel crimine, cum non habeant velle et nolle', *De libris caute legendis* (N, vol. I, 19 K).   [3] Ibid.

Gerson went on to relate this error to the false claim that mortal sin did not destroy charity or impair love of God above all things else. In each case it confounded divine love with human libidinous passion, with which it had nothing in common.[1] Who Mary of Valenciennes was and when she lived is not clear. Margaret of Porète came originally from Valenciennes and, as we have seen, wrote a book which expressed similar sentiments; it seems highly plausible that Gerson was referring to her. To begin with it is unlikely that another Beguine of comparable notoriety should have left no trace. But secondly, and much more immediately compelling, Margaret of Porète's teaching centred round the image of the saved soul as a seraph, its six wings, as we shall see, denoting its different states. Now the seraph dominated the ideas of the Men of Intelligence at about this very time, as we shall mention. They were prosecuted by Gerson's confrère, d'Ailly. Hence it is more than probable that Gerson knew of them. Certainly he was preoccupied with the heresy in that region.

He invariably included the Turlupins, who were then infesting his native France,[2] in his condemnations of the Beguines and Beghards: they showed how the dangers inherent in mystical aspirations, untutored by knowledge and unregulated by the laws of Christ, could lead to greater error than among unbelievers. This led them to say that, once having reached tranquillity of spirit, a man became freed from God's laws.[3] Elsewhere Gerson denounced the evils of their ways: in

---

[1] Amplius hanc ob causam inter caeteras videntur errasse Begardi et Beghardae ob indiscretam scilicet dilectionem nomine devotionis palliatam. Argumentum hujus rei est in quodam libello incredibili pene subtilitate ab una foemina composito, quae Maria de Valenciennes dicebatur; haec agit de praerogativa et eminentia dilectionis divinae, ad quam si quis devenerit fit secundum eam ab omni lege praeceptorum solutus, adducens pro se illud ab Apostolo suptum: Caritate habe, et fac quod vis. . . . Errabat utique delirus ille qui sic phantasiabatur, dum motum omnem amoris passionalem vel ex consuetudine aut aliunde genitum circa deum, vocabat caritatem, quae tamen non gaudet super iniquitate, et quae deo per inobedientiam praecepti cujusvis nequaquam inimicatur (G, III, 51-2).

[2] In his De examinatione doctrinae he said 'non desunt usque hodie' (N, I, 18 M).

[3] Deinde compertum est multos habere devotionem sed non secundum scientiam, quales proculdubio pronissimi sunt ad errores etiam supra indevotos si non regulaverint affectus suos ad normam legis Christi; si praeterea capiti proprio, propriae scilicet prudentiae inhaeserint, spreto aliorum consilio. Hoc in Beghardis et Turelupinis manifestum fecit experientia. Dum itaque sequebantur affectus suos sine regula et ordine, postposita lege Christi, praesumptio necquissima praecipitavit eos ut dicerent hominem postquam ad pacem tranquillam spiritus pervenisset, absolutum esse legibus divinorum praeceptorum (G III, 255-6).

their lack of natural shame they lived like dogs, naked and physically unconstrained.[1]

Perhaps the strongest testimony to Gerson's preoccupation with the danger of the Free Spirit was his attack on Ruysbroeck's *De ornatu spiritualium nuptiarum* in two letters to Bartholomew Clantier, the Carthusian.[2] Once again his two major concerns were with the perils of uncontrolled mysticism and the confusion between human and divine love. The first letter, written in 1402, was directed to statements made by Ruysbroeck, who had been dead over twenty years (in 1381), in his third book, on the beatific vision. According to Gerson, Ruysbroeck claimed that the soul in a state of perfect contemplation of God not only saw in the light of God but became that light: that is, instead of regarding God as an object, it became merged with him.[3] This suggested pantheism, in making the divine essence the formal means of the soul's existence, so that it could only exist by God's agency and externally.[4] It was the affinity of this error with that of the Beguines and Beghards—for whose exposure by Ruysbroeck Gerson praises him—at which Gerson took alarm. He reiterated his frequent conclusion[5] that the grace of contemplation does not of itself suffice for truth but needs theological understanding.[6]

---

[1] Contra illos qui ignominiosas partes corporis et actus nefandos non solum aperta impudentia nominare audent, sed . . . defendunt, non considerantes quod hec dicendo corruunt in errorem Begardorum et Turelupinorum, qui de nulla re naturaliter data erubescendum esse dicebant. Quemadmodum et cinici philosophi more canum dicebant esse veniendum palam in nuditate et exercitio membrorum pudendorum (*Sermo diei in Sancti Ludovici*, N II 48u). For a full treatment of Gerson's critique of Ruysbroeck see A. Combes, *Essai sur la critique de Ruysbroeck par Gerson*, 3 vols. (Paris 1945–59).

[2] Nos. 13 and 26 in G II, 55–62 and 97–103.

[3] Ponit autem tertia pars libri praefati quod anima perfecte contemplans Deum, non solum videt eum per claritatem quae est divina essentia, sed est ipsamet claritas divina. Imaginatur enim, sicut scripta sonant, quod anima tunc desinit esse in illa existentia quam prius habuit in proprio genere, et convertitur seu transformatur et absorbetur in esse divinum (ibid., 57).

[4] si corpus Christi vel aliud corpus beatificum hoc modo perderet animam suam in sua contemplatione et beatificatione, pro illa haberet essentiam divinam ipsum formaliter vivificantem, alioquin esset absque vita (ibid., 59).

[5] Ibid., 60, where Gerson says that Ruysbroeck was not knowingly a heretic, but was probably influenced by the Beghards' doctrines.

[6] Ad talium itaque quaestionum determinationem aut ad eas plene intelligendas vel explicandas, non sufficit quod homo sit devotus et sit adeptus illam contemplationis speciem, sanctissimam prorsus et optimam, quae versatur in affectione et fervore caritatis, quando scilicet transit homo in affectum cordis ad virtutes. . . . Haec autem

Gerson did not remain unanswered. John of Schoenhaven came to Ruysbroeck's defence; and in 1408 Gerson replied in a further letter to Bartholomew. Once more he showed his concern for the dangers of false and uncontrolled devotion which, he lamented, daily experience showed to be so great. He reaffirmed the need to keep the identity of a creature separate to its own species, and then went on to refer, in what was clearly an allusion to Bloemardine of Brussels,[1] to the case of a woman in the recent past who was reported to be a prophetess and worker of miracles, and with whom he had spoken. She had declared that, in contemplating God, her spirit had been annihilated and then recreated. He had come across innumerable such inanities among the Beguines and the Beghards when preparing his treatise *De distinctione verarum revelationum a falsis*.[2]

Thus for Gerson the danger and depravity of the Beguines and Beghards (and Turlupins) sprang directly from their false mysticism, which in turn resulted from a devotional impulse unregulated by theological understanding. This led to their heresy of the Free Spirit.

Ruysbroeck, despite Gerson's attacks upon him for his tendencies towards the heresy of the Free Spirit, had been quite as outspoken and searching an opponent of it as the chancellor of Paris university. Indeed, his analysis of its sources was more penetrating and his treatment more sustained. He described its adherents as

wicked and diabolic men who call themselves Christ or God, saying that they had created heaven and earth with their own hands and sustained all that existed. They claimed that they were beyond need or desire of the sacraments, and derided the ordinances and usages of the church and the writings of the saints. Only their own detestable heresy did they regard as perfect, and the savage ways which they followed ... In their folly they held that all rational creatures, good as well as bad, angels as well as demons, finally

---

species altera contemplationis versari ponitur in perscrutatione divinarum veritatum ... (ibid., 61).

[1] See pp. 395–7 below.

[2] Addo nunc quod evenit tempore nostro de quadam quae prophetissa et miraculorum operatrix reputata est a multis, quam et vidi et allocutus sum. Haec tandem dixit et scribi jussit quod spiritus suus contemplando deum fuerat annihilatus vera annihilatione, dehinc recreatus. ... Dies me deficeret si numerare vellem innumeras tales insanias amantium, immo et amentium, quia non secundum scientiam quales videntur fuisse Begardi et Begardae, quemadmodum in quodam tractatulo 'De distinctione verarum revelationum a falsis', memini pridem annotasse (G II, 102).

merged into a single undifferentiated essence, without nature or will, which they called God.[1]

For Ruysbroeck these doctrines were 'the most impious and foolish heard since the world began'.[2] They seduced many seemingly spiritual people who, as a result, 'become worse than demons'.[3]

Ruysbroeck saw the source of their iniquity in what he called a certain emptiness in the soul, an inner void in which there were no images or awareness. It caused those in whom it occurred to believe that they had found a new life liberated from all constraints. But uninformed by love of God and in a state of formlessness and nescience, when they imagined themselves to be God they were in fact without virtue. This led them to devalue the entire sacramental life of the church, its scriptures and traditions, and to regard God in the same indeterminate way as themselves, holding that all life would ultimately become merged with him in one eternal being.[4] 'No more senseless and perverse impiety was to be found among pagans, Jews or Christians.'[5]

Ruysbroeck returned repeatedly to this theme of inner emptiness, which was mistakenly identified with God. Founded upon self-oblivion, it meant treating as divine what were in fact natural impulses; freedom of the spirit was merely freedom of the senses. It operated at the instinctual, not the supernatural, level, causing those who adhered to it to live without conscience and in violation of the canons of the church. Having lost God and the path to him they lived in physical and moral depravity. Making the gratification of desires their end, they ultimately suffered the most terrible torments and visions, until they died like 'mad dogs' to be consumed in eternal flames.[6] True union with God could only come about through God's love, as a supernatural gift of charity. It had nothing in common with the sloth of inner emptiness which could be felt by all men; the latter was passive where grace is active; it was blind and sterile where supernatural love brought clarity beyond understanding; it was without justice where grace justified.[7] Its addicts believed they were the poor in spirit because they had abandoned everything, including individual choice; in this

---

[1] *The Mirror of Eternal Salvation*, ch. 16, in vol. I of *Œuvres de Ruysbroeck l'Admirable*, translated by the Benedictines of St. Paul de Wisques, Paris 1921–38, 116.
[2] Ibid., 117.   [3] Ibid.
[4] *Book of the Seven Enclosures* (ibid., 180).
[5] Ibid., ch. 16, 181.
[6] *The Book of the Highest Truth* (ibid., vol. II, ch. 4, 204–6).
[7] *The Adornment of Spiritual Marriage* (ibid., vol. III, ch. 74, 195–6).

state they claimed to have surpassed all needs and virtues and to be beholden to nothing. Free from sin they could yield to their desires with impunity; only those who were still imperfect must still seek to gain merit and guard against sin.[1] For holding these views Ruysbroeck regarded them as the worst and most dangerous of all men.[2]

Much the same denunciation of the Free Spirit is to be found in Henry Suso's *Little Book of Truth*.[3] It takes the form of a dialogue between the disciple (Suso) seeking the way to true self-abandonment and a 'wild man' who personifies the heresy of the Free Spirit. Although it is also an attempt to clarify Eckhart's teaching, which, as we saw, had been condemned and appeared to have superficial affinities with the heresy of the Free Spirit, at the same time it exposed what Suso regarded as the false mysticism of the Free Spirit. This was, firstly, its view of liberty which, for the wild man, consisted in living 'according to his (a man's) own choice, without opposition, without any look before or after'.[4] Unconstrained liberty, he said, should be heedless.[5] Secondly, there was the claim 'that the man who has been annihilated in his eternal nothing knows nothing of distinctions',[6] so that God and man are identical. Suso replied that 'man is never so completely annihilated' that he forgets that he is created and of a different essence from God.[7] Even when rapt in ecstasy the distinction remains[8] as does that between Christ and man, since the latter 'is not a natural son of God'.[9] Hence man cannot do everything that Christ does.[10] Thirdly, the Free Spirit was without true understanding of the divine light,[11] and so lacked 'the proper distinctions of rational truth'.[12] In essence, then, Suso's strictures on the errors of the Free Spirit were very much of a kind with Gerson's and Ruysbroeck's locating their source in a misguided conception of the union with God, of the nature of which they were ignorant.

Gerson, Ruysbroeck and Suso were all first and foremost thinkers and mystics (as opposed to mere polemicists) who viewed the heresy of the Free Spirit within the context of true religious experience. For the majority of writers on the Beguines and Beghards, however, the latter were either immediate opponents to be defeated, or defaulters to be

---

[1] Ibid., ch. 76, 200–1. [2] Ibid., 202.
[3] Chapter 6, translated, together with the *Little Book of Eternal Wisdom* by J. M. Clark (London 1953), 201–5.

[4] Ibid., 201. [5] Ibid., 202. [6] Ibid.
[7] Ibid. [8] Ibid., 203. [9] Ibid.
[10] Ibid., 204. [11] Ibid., 205. [12] Ibid.

A A

apprehended. They therefore operated on a narrower and more practical front. We have already mentioned Alvarus Pelagius. Of the remaining ones by far the most important was the treatise written, probably at the end of the fourteenth century, by an anonymous inquisitor
for the Bavarian province of Cham.[1] It depicts the full sequence from
initiation into a life of apostolic poverty to spiritual perfection. Each
was complementary to the other, since it was from the claim to have
attained the most perfect state among all the religious and mendicant
orders, in pursuit of apostolic poverty, that the path to individual
freedom of the spirit was opened. Its adherents thus modelled themselves on Christ's life of mendicant vagrancy, suffering untold persecutions on its account, especially from the priesthood who, rather than
emulate Christ, indulged themselves in pleasures. Those admitted to
the sect pledged themselves to chastity, obedience, voluntary poverty
and mendicancy, and handed over their goods for common possession.
They were then tonsured, given a habit and underwent initiation; they
were instructed how to master their wills by thwarting their desires,
whether for food, drink, sleep, attending church or anything else, and
by submitting to nauseating food, such as putrid meat. The writer went
on to describe their peculiar method of murmuring their prayers, which
in the case of the adepts (*perfecti*) were not said verbally at all. This
silent communing with God led many of them to be ignorant of the
Lord's Prayer, as the author saw for himself when, in the presence of the
lord of Cham, he presided over a trial. For the same reason they were
easily distinguishable at church for not speaking the words. In their life
they aspired to the state of equality with Adam and Eve before the fall,
their passions controlled by reason. This once achieved, and the senses
vanquished, they gratified themselves without fear, even though this
meant indulging the flesh. They justified their wrongdoing with the
saying of St Paul: 'Where the spirit is free there is liberty.' In this state
they refused to rise at the elevation of Christ's body, saying that they
were better able to contemplate God with spiritual than material eyes.
They confessed only to the perfect among them. Two men superiors
were called father, and the women superiors Martha, which was also
the title designating all those who held offices as, for example, towel
Martha or shoe Martha.[2]

   This short treatise, a mere two pages, is of the utmost significance in
confirming the independent testimonies of two other sources on the life
of the heretical Beguines and Beghards. In the first place its authenticity

[1] Haupt, ZKG 12, 88–90.   [2] Ibid., 89–90.

seems unquestioned; for unlike the assertions of John Wasmod of Homburg, to be discussed shortly, the author clearly knew his subject at first hand, and all that he says is corroborated by what we know from elsewhere. In the second place, and above all, it depicts the life of the Free Spirit within a Beguine-Beghard framework. While many of the Free Spirit were probably individual vagrants, all the evidence points to the Beguines' and Beghards' houses as their main base. Here, to all appearances, they lived as any others, in unofficial piety, without private possessions and dependent upon alms. They regarded poverty as a way of life, and made the austerities of Christ and his disciples the starting point for their ultimate libertinism. How far such a combination of the two extremes of self-mortification and self-indulgence was a matter of genuine belief, and how far a ruse to gain control over innocent followers who could be trained in their ways, cannot, and probably never will, be said; but clearly poverty was an essential element in their life, as we shall have cause to mention again. At the very lowest it shows that it was by following the Beguine way of life, at least outwardly, and not for the most part as clandestine groups, or groups within a group, that the Free Spirit was to be found.

The testimony of another inquisitor makes up the next text. It was from Garin who, as we saw earlier, was responsible for the examination and burning of the Metz Beghards in 1334.[1] What he says has much in common with Wasmod of Homburg's treatise, both of which confuse the Beguines and Beghards with the Waldensians. Garin begins with the Beguines' and Beghards' claim to be in the highest state of poverty, following the example of the Apostles in having not even their tunics for their own. They lived in houses regulated by a head who was called neither master nor doctor, but servant; he distributed their wherewithal gathered from begging. Each year, under the pretext of making a pilgrimage, they would hold a congregation, in the belief that where they were the spirit of God dwelt. They differed from the life and habits of other men; they regarded themselves as superior to the priesthood; they swore not to trespass against their conscience; they refused to acknowledge sentences of excommunication or obey the decrees of the Church, whose powers of binding and loosing they treated with contempt. They also treated disclosing what had been said in confession as a mortal sin. They were against the taking of oaths or life in any circumstances; and they did not accept the official interpretation of the bible by the doctors and *sancti*. Even when under sentence of death at

[1] Döllinger, *Beiträge* II, 403-6.

Metz they would neither swear nor pray to the Virgin or the saints, which to the writer merely proved their obduracy in evil. Apart from the opening statement this description has no real bearing upon the Beguines and Beghards. It belongs to the Waldensians.

The fifth piece, entitled *De Beguinabus*,[1] has as its main burden the non-conformity of the Beguines to the authority and practices of the church, and their claim to follow the rules of a third order by which they were alone bound. They also called themselves hermits while indulging the body in ways prohibited by the church, such as eating meat (on fast days), lying in feather beds, as well as being superstitious and holding wrong opinions. Their religion was in fact nothing more than damnable hypocrisy and worship of worldliness, with their own ceremonies, rites and ornaments. On the one hand they claimed to be sisters of the Franciscan third order and disavowed the name of Beguine; on the other, they wanted to be subject to their parish priests, which they were not entitled to be; while to the Franciscans, under whose jurisdiction they were, they did not confess or show any obedience.

The next treatise, a fragment of eight pages,[2] is framed as a series of questions on the Beguines. The first, on the legality of their status, says that any Beguine or person who aids them is excommunicate, although this does not apply to those who belong to an order of penitence. The second denied them the right to any participation in religious life on the grounds of their excommunication. Their heresy also included among its adherents the Fraticelli and Franciscan tertiaries in Toulouse—an indication of this work's French provenance.[3]

Sixth, comes the most intrinsically worthless but most prominent of all the writings against the Beguines and Beghards: John Wasmod of Homburg's *Contra hereticos Bekardos, Lulhardos et Swestriones*,[4] written in the last years of the fourteenth century. Wasmod of Homburg was inquisitor for Mainz and later professor of theology at Heidelberg university. He was particularly harsh towards the Waldensians. His treatise followed Boniface IX's bull *Sedis apostolicae* of 1396, to which, with

---

[1] Döllinger *Beiträge* II, 703–5.

[2] Haupt, ZKG 7, 531–2, with extracts from Colmar MS. 29.

[3] This question and answer is also to be found in Eymeric, *Directorium Inquisitorum* (II, 15), and contains 55 articles taken from the Provençal Spirituals.

[4] Printed in Haupt, ZKG 7, 567–76, and Döllinger, *Beiträge* II, 406–16. Haupt's version is based upon two texts, Mainz, Stadtbibliothek MS 218, and Frankfurt-a-M, Stadtbibliothek, MS. 141, and gives foliation. Döllinger, on the other hand, provides the more balanced rendering, particularly in the later part, and on grounds of comprehensibility is to be preferred.

other of the pope's decrees, he frequently referred. As an insight into
either the heresy of the Free Spirit or the Beguines and Beghards, whom
he describes as infesting the cities of the Rhine, the treatise is valueless.
Apart from invoking the eight articles of *Ad nostrum*, nearly every
feature of their so-called heresy, as Haupt long ago pointed out,[1] belonged to the Waldensians, not the Free Spirit: the disqualification of
sinful priests, the denial of transubstantiation, their rites of communion
and absolution, their particular forms of venerating Christ, their anti-
sacerdotalism, their hostility towards indulgences. Few of these, as
described by Wasmod, had any affinity with the practices of the Free
Spirit as described by the inquisitor for Cham; nor was their connexion
made any more apparent by Wasmod's attempts at the end of the
treatise to prove how their belief in sinlessness gave rise to their
licentiousness. The contradictions in Wasmod's assertions are glaring:
why should believers in individual perfection need an elaborate hierarchy of ministers (notably absent from the organization of the Free
Spirit)? If they were directly united with God what purpose would an
alternative church serve (of which the Free Spirit had none)? If they
dismissed damnation and salvation as fables why should those not of
their number be, as Wasmod said, damned (which the Free Spirit did
not assert)? If they were predominantly quietist why should they be so
militant in their anti-sacerdotalism? Apart from his invocation of *Ad
nostrum* and his repetition of the austerities and trials undergone by the
initiates, there is little in his account to show that he was conversant
with the heresy of the Free Spirit, still less that he knew it at first hand.
Perhaps he too was a victim of the duplicity with which he charged
them.[2]

Finally, there are a number of texts in which the main tenets of the
heresy of the Free Spirit are ascribed to the Beguines and Beghards
and condemned. These differ from the others in being concerned with
doctrine; they do not purport to be accounts of the Beguines and Beghards as a sect. Among them are two which were the result of John of
Dürbheim's actions against 'those belonging to the sect of Beguines'[3]
at Strasbourg in 1317. As they are representative of a number of other
compilations of the fourteenth century they are worth considering in

[1] Haupt, ibid., 548 ff. [2] Ibid., 568.
[3] The others are 1. a list of 36 articles entitled: 'Haec sunt novae hereses de novo
spiritu' found in the same manuscript as that of bishop John's (Döllinger, *Beiträge* II,
391-3). 2. 29 articles 'de heresi novi spiritus' (ibid., 393-4). 3. Errores . . . de secta
spiritus libertatis (ibid., 416-17). 4. Articuli haereticorum Beghardorum (ibid., 702-3).

full. The first, and more significant, was John's episcopal letter of August 1317 already discussed.[1] It is noteworthy in two respects: it goes beyond the customary vague allusions to Beguine-Beghard subversion, and attributed outright the heresy of the Free Spirit to some among them; moreover, its account of their errors is analytical rather than compilatory. It begins by expressing concern at the danger of heresy from those who in the guise of Beguines and Beghards, with their cry of 'Bread for God's sake', are of the sect of the Free Spirit. They called themselves poor brothers and sisters, followed a life of voluntary poverty and numbered among their followers priests and married men (*coniugati*), in a diversity of conditions; they were distinguished from others by their own confessions and rites.[2] Here, then, is open testimony to the amorphousness of the Beguines and Beghards as a movement, which provided an umbrella for divergent elements. The document then goes on to enumerate the errors of the Free Spirit under seven headings. The first is 'Against God';[3] it included the propositions that God is formally everything; that man can be so united with God that he can do and will whatever God does and wills; that those of the Free Spirit are God by nature and without distinction; that they contain all God's perfections, including infinity and eternity; that they have created all that God has created, and more; that they need nothing, not even God and the Godhead; that they are without sin and so is whatever they do.

The second heading is 'Against Christ',[4] where they asserted that any perfect man is Christ by nature; that Christ suffered for himself, not for mankind; that Christ's humanity is external to him, and is assumed and discarded as the devil's body is. They showed no reverence for Christ, saying that any man can surpass him in merit; and that a perfect man should be free from all virtue and activity, including meditation on Christ's passion and on God. The third error is 'Against the church',[5] in which they treated the church and Christianity as foolish, and absolved the perfect man, in his freedom, from any need to fulfil Christian precepts, such as honouring his parents. Likewise he is free from the obligation of manual work and can live on alms; he can also steal, since all things are held in common. The fourth count is 'Against the sacraments of the church'.[6] Here they hold that any layman is as entitled to carry out the sacrament of the eucharist as a sinful priest;[7]

---

[1] Printed in Mosheim *De Beghardis*, 255–60. See pp. 337 ff. above.   [2] Ibid., 256.
[3] Ibid.   [4] Ibid.   [5] Ibid., 257.   [6] Ibid.
[7] This is quite out of character with Free Spirit tenets and much more characteristic of the Waldensians.

that Christ's body is equally to be found in any bread as in the sacramental bread; that confession to a priest is not necessary for salvation; that all marital association other than that which leads to offspring is a sin, a distinctly Waldensian view.

Fifth comes 'Against heaven and hell'.[1] They do not believe in a last judgement; each man is judged as he dies. There is no hell or purgatory, again like the Waldensians; on death the spirit returns to the source whence it came, leaving nothing but what was eternally God. A man should follow his inner promptings rather than the truth of the gospel preached daily. The sixth is 'Against the gospel',[2] which they say is more poetic than true and should be subordinated to human beliefs, derived from within. Were all the books of the Catholic faith to be destroyed, those among the sect could replace them with better ones.

The seventh and last error was 'Against the holy men',[3] whom they claim they can surpass. They also said that they are more perfect than the Virgin; that some among them are so perfect that they can neither increase nor diminish in holiness; and that the perfect man has no need of the theological virtues of faith, hope and charity.

The letter ends by condemning all the above, on the authority of the Council of Mainz (1317).[4] The archbishop, at this stage (1317), had not yet gone to the extreme of banning all Beguines and Beghards; he merely gave them three days' notice, from the publication of the letter, to discard their habit and to cease living on alms with their cry of 'Brod durch Gott', and to conform to the other mendicants.[5] Religious, like the Franciscan tertiaries and the genuine Beguines, were expressly exempted from this sentence.[6]

The demarcation here between the heretical Beguines and Beghards and the mendicants and the genuine ones, is a further pointer to the danger from the Free Spirit among them; their presence there was taken as an established fact without at the same time making all Beguines and Beghards heretics of the Free Spirit. It was the blurring of the distinction between orthodox and heterodox which accounted for

[1] Ibid., 257–8. This again in its denial of hell and purgatory is Waldensian.
[2] Ibid., 258.   [3] Ibid.
[4] Ibid.   [5] Ibid., 259–60.
[6] Per hanc autem nostram sententiam et prescriptum damnationis nostrae processum, religiosis qui sunt de tertia regula Fratrum Franciscanorum Minorum, aut Beguinis honestis secularibus, vel etiam quibuslibet aliis familiaribus fratrum approbatorum ordinum, et secundum eorum concilium se regentibus, nullatenus volumus praeiudicium generari, sed ex eis iuxta modum servatum in aliis provinciis perdurare (ibid., 260).

the oscillation in official policy towards them, as bishop John's own subsequent actions have abundantly illustrated.

The second of his indictments against them was the result of the inquisition which he directed in his diocese.[1] It presents fundamentally the same doctrine, but in the form of a straight list, without any attempt at systematization. It begins with their claim that they are perfect, united to God, truly God and of one being which is God himself. This pantheism is taken as the source of the heresy of the Free Spirit. 'From this article follow many other articles . . .': that they are eternal; that they created everything with God, and more than God; that they have no need of God as a deity and are as perfect as he in all things; that both God and they are of the kingdom of heaven; that they are immutable, remaining unaffected by everything; that were they to be hanged or suffer in any way bodily, they would refuse to do so in the name of one word—freedom; that after death nothing remains of a man save that he was a man from eternity, and so they deny true resurrection as the faithful understand it; that since God is in all things and all things are God, what is not God does not exist; that therefore there is no evil, or demons, or inferno, or purgatory; that those united with God are impeccable, because they are so free in spirit that whatever they do with their bodies is not sinful, even if they are incontinent or indulge in other vices; that their perfection frees them for acting to gain God's reward, even that of eternal life, beyond praising him; that this same freedom absolves them from obeying God's precepts, especially the obligation to honour one's parents, and similarly priests can flout the decrees of the church, such as the need to observe fasts or to abstain from eating meat, which could be infringed; that this same freedom releases a woman from obedience to her husband; that the able-bodied have no need to work, even though by begging they were defrauding the genuine poor; that confession was at no time necessary; that such freedom extended to all those in servitude, even if previously they had belonged to a king or some other master. 'They are also in error over Christ': some say that they themselves are really Christ; that they can surpass his merits and those of the Virgin or any of the saints; that Christ did not suffer for mankind but for himself, in the same way as any natural man; that any good layman can carry out the ceremony of Christ's body as well as, if not better than, any sinful priest; that some of them need not revere the sacrament (of the eucharist) in church; that Christianity is foolish; that prayers are unnecessary, and some of the

---

[1] Döllinger, *Beiträge* II, 389–91.

heretics do not say them aloud. 'They also hold conventicles and have distinctive ways of speaking, living and conversing, which holy mother church prohibits, both in Rome generally and at the Council of Mainz in particular, as signifying this sect.'

These propositions correspond to the main tenets of the Free Spirit: certain more specific statements are omitted, such as reference to excelling St. Paul or John the Baptist as well as the more disparaging remarks about Christ, which we have encountered in the other version, or the assertion that a perfect man should not grieve over his sins, and need only confess them to another good man. But in substance the condemnation contains all that is germane to the outlook of the Free Spirit as found in the other compilations and as summarized in *Ad nostrum*. The two versions together show indisputably that the location of the heresy of the Free Spirit was among the Beguines and Beghards, even if only a minority of them.

A similar outright identification is to be found in an anonymous polemic, *Reprobatio secte Beghardorum et Beginarum Alemanie et errorum eorundem*.[1] It is based upon Clement V's bull *Ad nostrum*, the eight propositions of which it glosses in the manner of Alvarus Pelagius. Each article is made the theme of a scholastic discussion and shown to be untenable and heretical. In particular it stresses the indispensability of grace to any form of supernatural attainment as opposed to the claim of the Free Spirit to be naturally perfect.

Finally, there is another list of *Articuli hereticorum Beghardorum* from a German manuscript (undated). They number fourteen (before they break into a series of statements[2] by the Ortlibiens); and include a belief in the eternity of the world and the non-existence of the Trinity before Christ's birth. Before then, Jesus was merely the earthly son of Joseph. The propositions attributed to the Beghards seem to have been abstracted from the *Compilatio* of Albert the Great or a similar collection; beyond identifying these with the Beguines and Beghards, they are not in themselves noteworthy.

Between them these treatises provide a considerable body of evidence for the prevailing opposition towards the Beguines and Beghards. They illustrate, as we have said, firstly, that their very existence was an affront to the authority of the church, and an imposition upon the other orders, in not conforming to a recognized rule. Secondly to this was added the far more serious charge that they were the source of

[1] Manuscript CLM 15177, 275r–282v.
[2] Döllinger, *Beiträge* II, 702–3.

the heresy of the Free Spirit; the indictment varied from the unsupported assertions of Wasmod of Homburg and the Metz inquisitor that they constituted an illegal hierarchy to the flat ascriptions of the articles of the Free spirit to them. However inaccurate these accusations were—and in the first two cases they rest on nothing but conjecture—they testify to the climate of opinion towards them in the fourteenth and fifteenth centuries. More than anything else, they show the permanent damage which the Clementine decrees did to their standing: even though official attempts at mitigation were, as we have seen, periodically set in train, the overall effect of the condemnations in *Ad nostrum* and *Cum de quibusdam* was to make Beguines and Beghards a standing object of reprobation for the twin offences of heresy and illegality.

The inquisitorial records

The same widespread association of the Beguines and Beghards with the Free Spirit is confirmed by the final group of evidence—the records of the inquisition. Hitherto we have been concerned with what may be termed the official and the public viewpoints on the heresy of the Free Spirit; both the papal and ecclesiastical decrees, and the treatises, were designed, in their different ways, to call attention to the danger and to point to its sources and forms. The proceedings of the inquisition, however, were concerned with the heretics themselves; the opinions they professed and the lives which they led are revealed more palpably here than anywhere else. Unfortunately the record is far from a full one; it totals in all a mere dozen or so documents, varying from Margaret of Porète's confession in 1311 to that at Mainz in 1458 by a Lollard called John. Also, they were work of officials, recording the answers to set questions framed by the inquisitor or his representative. Yet between them they present a fairly consistent picture of the configuration of the heresy of the Free Spirit, above all its essentially individual character: the inquisitorial confessions rarely concern more than one or two persons, as opposed to the Waldensians, for example, which frequently concerned groups. Similarly, their beliefs were closely bound up with personal experience. The accounts of John of Brünn, John Hartmann, Conrad Kannler or Martin of Mainz are all in greater or lesser degree (depending primarily on the length of the testimony which has survived) part of their own case histories. The emphasis is as much upon their own psychic state as upon a body of doctrine taken in itself; their statements are inner testimonies rather than impersonal formulations in the manner of the Waldensians or Cathars or Hussites. This is in keeping with the outlook of the Free Spirit which, as we have observed, was a debased form of mysticism making the soul's union with God the centre of existence. Accordingly, as with all such attitudes, its practice was a matter for the individual or the small group of initiates; it could not be easily recited or performed *en masse*. All the evidence suggests that such was the case, and that the Free Spirit was never more than a diversity of local adherents. It is the implicit refrain in all the examples we have so far cited, whether papal and ecclesiastical decrees or polemical treatises; they united in seeing the Free Spirit as something clandestine, surreptitious and hidden, masquerading in other clothes, the wolves among the sheep. This did not detract from their importance: just as mysticism in the fourteenth and fifteenth centuries was all-pervasive, while continuing to be the preserve of the individual or small community, so the same seems to have been the case with the Free Spirit. As a mystic could be a member of a united group, like the Brethren of the Common Life, or just one among many with whom he shared merely the externals of life, such as Suso and Tauler in their Dominican convents, or indeed a lone figure like Julian of Norwich or Catharine of Siena, so could the followers of the Free Spirit; indeed only this would explain both their pervasiveness and elusiveness. Ideas and attitudes, once established, become largely independent of physical limitations; short of exterminating every adherent or burning every book which contains them, they can remain proof against the most draconian measures. When they do die it is more likely to be of inanition than by repression. They do not need large numbers to make them dangerous; it is enough for them to be disseminated sufficiently well to survive indefinitely as a challenge to orthodoxy and an incitement to heresy. They then become an ever-present source of disruption, which like an impure tributary pollutes the main stream, and leads to periodic attempts at elimination. This seems to have been the position of the Free Spirit during the later middle ages. The attack upon it, as we have seen, was in the form of intermittent outbursts against the Beguines and Beghards, and the victories gained were over a few individuals. We must now examine more closely those whose records survive.

The earliest and perhaps most prominent individual to be accused and condemned of the heresy of the Free Spirit was Margaret of Porète. She, it will be recalled, was a Beguine whose trial took place immediately before Clement V's two bulls against that sect; it may be, though at present it cannot be proved, that she was the catalyst which caused

Clement to act as he did. According to the record of the case, which was heard at Paris in 1311, Margaret had held that the soul consumed with love of God was freed from all sense of remorse and could act as the senses desired. She had propagated this view in a book which had been burned, as she was for refusing to recant.

It is not unqualifiedly supported by the book—*The Mirror of Simple Souls*, which has been recently edited.[1] It is true that Margaret of Porète did allow that the soul in perfect charity could do as it desired; but this was far from making her the advocate of pure libertinism. She was concerned with the soul's seven-fold ascent to God along a path not dissimilar from that of the orthodox mystics. It began with the 'soul touched by grace and emptied of sin' and culminated in the seventh grace where the soul had attained perfection in fruition of God.[2] In this state it received the gift of the whole Trinity.[3] To achieve this end the soul had to be divested of its identity and devoted entirely to God. It thereby ceased to work or want or give, but lived simply in love of and faith in God, by which it would alone be saved.[4] It was here that Margaret became unorthodox. Through the supernatural infusion of grace the soul now became supernatural, joined immediately to God like the seraphim. This image was one of the most characteristic features of Margaret's teaching: it recurred, as we shall see, among the Men of Intelligence a century later. As conceived by her it represented the perfect soul's immediate conjunction with God, so that it had a multiple awareness of him through Christ, comparable to the six wings of the seraphim.[5] Such a soul could dispense with all intermediaries between its love and God's love,[6] for it knew God more perfectly than anything else.[7] It now willed with God's will who willed within it.[8] Accordingly whatever it willed was God's will. It had no need of the supernatural virtues; it was entirely its own master.[9] In this state it neither desired nor rejected poverty, tribulations, masses, fasts, or prayers, but gave to nature all that it needed without remorse.[10] In receiving God's love it

[1] R. Guarnieri, *Marguerite de Porète: Le Mirourer des simples ames anienties et qui seulement demourent en vouloir et desir d'amour* (Rome 1961). This has been taken from the single manuscript, Chantilly Condé F. XIV, 26, and represents a provisional edition in only 100 copies. The final version is due to be published in the *Archivio Italiano per la Storia della Pietà* IV, which has not yet become available at the time of writing.

[2] Ibid., 10.   [3] Ibid., 14.   [4] Ibid., 15.
[5] Ibid., 16.   [6] Ibid., 15.
[7] Ibid., 16.   [8] Ibid., 17.   [9] Ibid.
[10] Ibid., 17–18, 24.

had become God.[1] The ascent to God thus ended in pantheism and with it freedom from all constraint. For Margaret it was concentrated upon liberating it from works and sacramental obligations. Beyond the vague allusion to 'giving nature what it demands',[2] the emphasis was upon the soul's preoccupation with inner knowledge of God through the exclusion of all works and fasts and prayers.[3] It could easily lead to the full-fledged libertinism of the Free Spirit; but with Margaret of Porète it did not go beyond a mystical pantheism which despised the distractions of the created world, when paradise had already been attained through union with God.[4]

The second case, together with that of the Beguines at Sweydnitz, is in many ways the most illuminating of all. It was a confession by two Beghards, John and Albert of Brünn, on their years as members of the Free Spirit.[5] John was later a Dominican and member of the inquisition under Gallus Neuhaus, appointed inquisitor of Prague in 1330. His confession is undated, but since it was made to Gallus, when he was already Bohemian inquisitor, it must have taken place after 1330. As we have said, it is among other things a case history; but it was also more since, after that of the Beguines of Sweydnitz, it comes closest to giving us an insight into a Beghard house under the aegis of the adepts of the Free Spirit. That it was an entire community controlled by the latter and not a mere group within a group seems clear from his account of his progress from a novice, undergoing the rigours of initiation and instruction in how to beg and comport himself, to his attainment of a state of perfection and subsequent freedom. Such an evolution is inconceivable in terms of a clandestine underground cell, where the need to remain unidentified would have prevented any overt exercise of the discipline which John underwent. Moreover, it would have been virtually impossible to keep separate two different ways of life—piety and libertinism—under the same roof, as Haupt pointed out.[6] But whereas Haupt based their incompatibility upon the assumption that it was a genuine Beguine house in which John lived, so treating his testimony as implausible,[7] the opposite would seem to be the case: namely, that from the outset John was inducted into a Beghard house of the Free Spirit, and that what followed was the normal practice for those seeking to become one of them.

[1] Ibid., 30.　　[2] Ibid., 24.　　[3] Ibid., 20.　　[4] Ibid., 77–8.
[5] The text is printed in Appendix 1 below.
[6] ZKG, 12, 86 n.1.
[7] He suggests it may have been extracted by torture.

John's confession was made at Cologne.[1] In it he recounted that for twenty years he had lived as a Beghard, eight of them in Freedom of the Spirit. He came originally to join the sect when, living in Brünn and legitimately married, he asked an acquaintance how he could attain to a life of perfection. In reply he was told that the life of poverty practised by the Beghards was more perfect than any other, because it was nearer to evangelical truth than clergy, religious orders or laymen were. Upon asking how he could enter upon this life, John was told to sell everything he had and give the money to the poor; but he was warned not to tell the priests, who would try to dissuade him—'for they hate our perfect life'.[2]

He then sold his possessions, giving half of the proceeds to his wife, and with the rest travelled to Cologne, where he was received into a (Beghard) house of the poor under the guidance of his aforesaid mentor, master Nicholas. He agreed to submit to the brothers, and to make over all his money to them. He was then instructed in the austerities of their life, being told that 'the true follower of poverty has nothing for his own but, like Christ on the cross, should be devoid of all things temporal'.[3] Standing naked before them he received a tunic of a hundred pieces to remind him of the derision and contempt suffered by Christ, and to sustain him in the indignities which he would suffer; the more he was able to bear them with patience, the more holy he would be.[4] They told him that if on the morrow he were to be called a heretic or molested in any other way he was to say nothing, and continue to beg with eyes cast down beside the brother who would accompany him. The burden of his régime was upon the need for submission to his superiors rather than the church. Thus, on the one hand, even at this initiatory stage he was to satisfy his natural wants such as, for example, eating surreptitiously from his tunic when he felt hungry, whatever the day or season: as one of Christ's poor it was no sin to do so. All that was required was that on his return to the house he should bend down and kiss the knees of his companion and ask forgiveness for any offence he might have committed. When in church he was to meditate on Christ's passion in one corner: it was enough to have seen the body of Christ elevated once, for to make a practice of it was only for those who cultivated the outer appearance of sanctity, neglecting the inner realm. The

---

[1] W. Wattenbach, 'Über die Secte der Brüder vom freien Geiste', in *Sitzungsberichte der königlichen preussischen Akademie der Wissenschaften* (Berlin 1887) 526–37. Printed in Appendix 1 below.

[2] Ibid., 529.   [3] Ibid., 530.   [4] Ibid.

same applied to many of the other sacramental requirements; confession was explicitly disavowed as unfitting for Christ's poor, even if it concerned fornication. The priests could not understand the depths which moved them.[1] On the other hand, he was to undergo actions which were against his own nature in order to destroy his own spirit, which was worthless, and submit to that of God. While on his own account he could not beg alms, he could if moved by God.[2]

Once proficient, however, his spirit became free; he could indulge his natural desires as he wished, because he was no longer responding to an external prompting of his own nature, which had been annihilated in the service of Christ: he was now acting from the spirit within. He could thus eat and drink what he wanted and when he wanted, including in Lent and at Easter, without needing to confess to a priest or suffering the pangs of conscience. He could lie and deceive, keep money he had been loaned, and, if pressed for its return, kill rather than give it back, or else lose his freedom of spirit. In doing so he need have no remorse, for he whose life he took merely returned to his origin in eternal life; likewise, if he robbed a beggar and caused his death by hunger, he had to fear neither the devil nor purgatory, which were but figments created by priests to instil fear into men.[3] As a Free Spirit he had divine truth and freedom from all constraint, a state which he described as follows: 'I am of the Free Spirit, and all that I desire I satisfy and gratify. Should I seek a woman in the still of the night I satisfy my craving without any feelings of conscience or sin; for the spirit is free, and I am also a natural man. Therefore I must freely satisfy my nature by deeds.'[4] Perfect freedom consisted in giving effect to 'all that the eye sees and desires'.[5] If anything should come between him and that he may justly destroy it, for he was thereby only asserting his freedom. To strike and kill another who struck him need not lead to remorse or confession to a priest, since the victim was merely being returned to the principle from which he sprang.[6] Those of the freedom of the spirit had become so transformed and were so part of God, and God of them, body and soul, that an angel could not distinguish between God and those united to him.[7] Moreover, the brothers and sisters (the terms John used) of the Free Spirit may deservedly kill any child conceived by them or throw it into the water, as they might any worm, without remorse or confession to a priest; for here, too, the child was

[1] Ibid., 531.
[2] Ibid., 532.
[3] Ibid., 532.
[4] Ibid., 533.
[5] Ibid.
[6] Ibid.
[7] Ibid., 533-4.

only being returned to its source. They could even declare that the child belonged to the priest because the poor in spirit (i.e. themselves) may have no means of supporting the child; nor should this cause them any remorse.[1] Their freedom of the spirit, which conferred the highest degree of perfection, also allowed them to lie and deceive and insult with impunity. The brothers and sisters had a series of signs by which they conversed for the purpose of coming together and indulging their natures; at whatever hour they did so it was by the freedom of the spirit and without sin. They said that when they died they would go direct to the heavenly empyrean, even if they were without extreme unction and communion which, like hell and the devil, were only priestly inventions.[2] They also denied transubstantiation of the bread and the wine, since only a priest in grace and charity could accomplish this, and he had never been seen. The truth belonged to them, the poor in spirit, and not to the priests in their vanity, who did not have God or the truth, and to whom, therefore, the free in spirit had no cause to confess, or obey, just as they had no need to fast or perform good works or, because of their divine nature, honour the saints.[3] A brother could also satisfy his hunger and eat before communion, just as he could gratify himself with one or more women, for he has every right to fortify his too feeble nature whether by cunning or force. It was also incumbent upon him to indulge the desires of a sister even if he had just been to communion, and likewise, if sought, to participate in sodomy with a brother. Nor should he ever confess any but his minor sins to a priest, reserving his graver ones for his own home. No one could command or excommunicate those in true freedom—not even popes or archbishops.[4]

Such was John of Brünn's account of the ways of the Free Spirit. In his confession subjoined to it, he stated that for eight years he had held them to be true, and had practised them in the belief that in the freedom of the spirit he was without sins or the need to confess. This conviction

---

[1] Wattenbach, ibid., 534.

[2] Ibid.

[3] Ibid., 534. Wattenbach inserts 'sacerdotes' into the sentence: 'Jejunia et alia bona non agnoscunt', but neither the antecedent nor the context warrants it. The previous sentence has the Free Spirit as the subject: ' . . . nec debent clericis obedire'; it would therefore seem that, unless otherwise stated, they would remain the subject of the following sentence. Nor would it make sense to understand it differently; it is the Free Spirit—not the priests—who do not recognize fasts and good works, just as they do not recognize the authority of the church generally.

[4] Ibid.

was shared by the great majority of the two hundred inmates[1]—further testimony to the heretical nature of the entire house.

There followed the statement of Albert, also a Beghard, who regarded himself as being as well able to say mass as a priest. He also held that frequent communion or celebrations of mass did not make a man more holy, as the example of the priesthood, who daily did so and were worse than those who rarely attended, showed. Similarly, the man who was free in spirit more truly loved God than he who nightly bowed and prayed to him, just as bowing at the elevation of Christ's body at the altar did not take a man to heaven. Albert went on to recount how he knew one man who in his presence in Brünn lay all night with a Beguine and then went to communion. He also repeated the stock positions of the Free Spirit on fasting, good works, the eucharist, hell, sins (or the absence of them), and the priesthood, and made a special declaration on the permissibility of sodomy.[2] He ended with a profession of faith for all Beghards, that a man can become so unconstrained that he is free in spirit and mortal sins become venial sins.[3]

Now there are several things to be noticed about these two confessions. The first, since it bears on the validity of their evidence, is a discrepancy in their attitudes to Christ. John does not make one disparaging remark about him; there are no references to Christ not having been truly God or having suffered only for himself, or advocacy against contemplating his passion. John even goes so far as to call the Free Spirit *Pauperes Christi*.[4] Albert, on the contrary, devotes a considerable part of his testimony to denigrating Christ; he describes how those who occupy themselves with Christ's passion are derided with the word *Blochwerg*.[5] He declared that the perfect should not look upon Christ's body, and that it served nothing to follow the elevation of the host.[6] The difference is enough to be itself of account; but to it must be added the two other references by John to the 'poor in spirit' (*pauperes spiritu*)[7] and 'the poor in whom alone the truth is found'.[8] The conclusion must be that John was both a Beghard, who believed in the

---

[1] Ibid., 235–6.

[2] Ibid., 536: 'Item Albertus interrogatus fuit a fratro Gallo [the inquisitor] ordinis Predicatorum quid (ms. quod) ipsi beghardi habent pro fundamento, quod peccatum sodomiticum non habent pro peccato, nec reputant etiam peccatum.'

[3] Ibid., 536–7. Wattenbach describes Albert and John as brothers (526) but the term is ambiguous and should probably be taken as referring to their status as Beghards and members of the Free Spirit.

[4] Ibid., 534: 'ergo pauperes Christi non debent narrare sacerdotibus veritatem ...'

[5] Ibid., 536.   [6] Ibid.   [7] Ibid., 534.   [8] Ibid.

B B

sanctity of poverty, as well as an adept of the Free Spirit. Like the Beguines of Sweydnitz he never lost his earlier belief even when he became free in spirit. Thus he continued to revere Christ, calling himself a *pauper Christi* whose pattern of life was based upon emulation of the evangelical poverty of Christ and the Apostles. Nor, on closer examination, was such an attitude contradictory. While, as we have mentioned, in formal terms of doctrine, it was incompatible with the notions of the Free Spirit, for John, as for the Beguines at Sweydnitz, communal poverty and individual freedom were two facets of perfection. As John himself said, he entered on a life of poverty in order to attain perfection; one was the concomitant of the other. Moreover, even when a man had become free in spirit he continued to live as a Beghard, dependent upon alms and, in John's case, in the same house. Now mendicancy, as we know only too well from the ecclesiastical censures of the cry 'Bread for God's sake', was so integral a part of the life of the heretical Beguines and Beghards as to be almost their badge, whether of vagrant individuals like Nicholas of Basel or settled groups. In the circumstances, therefore, nothing is more comprehensible than that the saving virtues of poverty should be embraced by some at least of the Free Spirit.

We are thus forced to conclude from John's testimony that the Free Spirit was practised not only by individuals and possibly clandestine conventicles, but by entire Beguine houses in which there was a *cursus honorum* from the austerities of initiation to final acceptance as an adept. Such a conclusion, as well as being substantiated by the evidence of Sweydnitz (to be examined later) is implicit in the history of the church's attitude towards the Beguines and Beghards during the fourteenth century; even the most patent calumnies can hardly retain their force for over a century, involving successive popes, ecclesiastical councils, kings, inquisitors, publicists and self-confessed adherents, without some real ground for doing so. The most convincing sign of it is precisely the phases in which their hostility went: the fact that, although the Beguines and Beghards were its continuing object, it had every so often to be mitigated for harming the innocent. That it was as regularly resumed, suggests more forcibly than anything else that the Free Spirit did exist among the Beguines and Beghards, and that the practices described by John and Albert did take place there. To deny this even after allowing for the greatest possible exaggeration, would be tantamount to rejecting the very sources of historical evidence. This is not to say that there was an invariable sequence from Beguine-Beghard austerity to spiritual libertinism, any more than that the two were in-separable. There could be other and more individual ways of achieving freedom of the spirit, as references to the disciples of masters like Bonanatus and Nicholas of Basel show. This may well have been the case with Albert, whose confessions contain none of the preliminaries to be found in John's.

Albert confronts us as an adept of the Free Spirit, with all its features in place. There is none of the exculpatory tone we find in John, who feels obliged to excuse every sin: some of them, as we have seen, like the killing of a child or disobedience to priests, on the distinctly non-libertarian grounds that they are committed by the poor. This could be interpreted as showing that John had a more tender conscience than Albert; but taking their antecedents into account it points more strongly to different origins: that whereas John began as a genuine Beghard Albert gives no suggestion of having done so; Christ is a term of derision and poverty unmentioned.

These two declarations, especially that by John, for all the uncer-tainties which accompany them, are together with those made at Sweydnitz, by far the most illuminating that we have. The others tend to be more stereotyped. Of these the first took place in 1367 at Erfurt; it consisted of the testimony of John Hartmann given before the chief inquisitor for Germany, Walter Kerling.[1] John, who was described as a Beghard, was also known by the name of Spinner. His interrogation was on the doctrine of the Free Spirit: 'When asked in what spiritual liberty consisted he replied that it meant the complete cessation of remorse and the attainment of a state of sinlessness'.[2] He was then questioned on the eight articles of Clement V's bull *Ad nostrum*. To the first he replied that in such a state of perfection there was no difference between the Free Spirit and God; and that having reached this state he could go no further in being perfect or free from sin. To the second, he said that the perfect man had no need to fast or pray, and since his senses were completely subject to the true spirit and reason, he could indulge his body as he pleased. Thirdly, that he was likewise not bound by any human authority or the statutes and precepts of the church; that he was master of all creation, and if anyone tried to impede him he could rightly kill the offender and take his goods, since he

---

[1] Printed by both Wattenbach, op. cit., 538–44 (Appendix I, below), and Döllinger, *Beiträge* II, 384–91. I have followed Döllinger.

[2] '. . . respondit quod in hoc quod totaliter cessat remorsus conscientie et quod homo redditur penitus impeccabilis' (ibid., 384).

would only be returning him to the first principle from which he derived. Moreover, he could do all things that gave him pleasure; and rather than not realize his desires it was better to destroy the entire world: this held for all members of the Free Spirit; and in reply to questioning, Hartmann said that it could include stealing a golden chalice or killing the emperor himself if he tried to interfere with him and were not of the Free Spirit. Fourthly, he asserted that his perfection enabled him to enjoy the same beatitude as he would have in the beatific life (were his body also immortal) and he was as blessed as the Virgin or St. Peter. Since his union with God was immediate, neither Mary nor the angels could distinguish between him and God; in his contemplation he was transformed into God, and he could choose between which of the persons of the Trinity he wished to be.[1] Fifthly, his own nobility of spirit represented an outflow of divinity and its return to the Godhead;[2] they were one, obviating the need for a special illumination (reserved for the blessed) in order to see God and love him. Sixthly, the free man could do as he wished, including fornicate with his sister or his mother, and anywhere he wished, including at the altar. He added that it was more natural with his sister than any other woman because of their consanguinity. His justification lay in being perfectly free and bound by no law or ecclesiastical statutes and precepts; such a man was a Free Spirit in contradistinction to the gross men who were subject to the existing authority of the church. His sister, far from losing her chastity, increased it as a result of their intercourse. The same applied to any young girl; indeed, if she had already been violated by others she regained her virginity through contact with him as a Free Spirit. Just as calves and bulls were for men to eat, women were for the use of those who were free in spirit; they went first to those in order of seniority, or, where there was no difference between two Free Spirits, by lot. Hartmann also affirmed that Christ was not a Free Spirit, as could be shown from the gospel where he had submitted to his father, saying, 'not as I wish but as you will'; only after he had died on the cross on Good Friday did he gain true liberty—hence the name Friday (*Frytag*) = Free day.[3] Similarly Mary was not of the Free Spirit, for otherwise she would not have so often sighed over the loss of her son.

On the seventh article Hartmann stated that the carnal act was not a sin for the Free Spirit; those treating women amorously for their

---

[1] Döllinger, *Beiträge* II, 386.
[2] Ibid. The affinity with Eckhart's terminology will be noticed.
[3] Ibid., 387.

conversation were idolaters (*Götzen*) and did not know how to converse with men. To the eighth article he said that the Free Spirit could override all the church's statutes; if he were in a state of inner contemplation he should not rise before Christ's body in order not to disturb the purity and elevation of his meditation; nor should he receive any sacrament at all unless he wished to lose himself. He could as well find God in playing chess as in the eucharist, if playing chess was more pleasing to him.[1] The same applied to baptism, which he would only need in order to lose himself; similarly, if a pagan were of the Free Spirit he would not require baptizing. Those of the Free Spirit were also exempt from confession, since they were impeccable; none but they could know the truth and the illumination to be found within which was worth more than all the money in Erfurt tower. It was not occasioned by any physical or mental weaknesses but came from within himself. He alone could express what he had himself undergone, whereas preachers spoke and taught from books, unaware of the truths given to those who had plumbed the divine abyss of the soul. For nine years following his freedom of the spirit Hartmann said that he had never suffered illness or received medicine, although he would not disclose the reasons for his present pallor. As a Free Spirit, he had the right to such refusal in preserving himself without sinning: thus he could rightly deny that he had fornicated with his own sister even if he had done so, because he was referring to eternity, not temporal matters.

Such was Hartmann's testimony which, from the nature of the inquisition, was somewhat repetitive. It contains most of the attitudes associated with the Free Spirit, especially the customary stress upon sexual license which, rather than anti-sacerdotalism, was among its most singular traits. It also displays an abnormal personality.

The next confession of which we have record was that of Conrad Kannler at Eichstädt in 1381, before the inquisitor Eberhard of Freyenhausen.[2] It differs from Hartmann's testimony in showing strong signs of Joachist influence or, as has been suggested, paranoia[3] (they are not mutually exclusive). Kannler regarded himself not only as perfect and absolutely free, but also as a second Adam whose coming would liberate the world from Antichrist; he also showed great truculence in asserting his beliefs which within the space of a few days turned as fully to abject renunciation and submission to authority.

[1] Ibid., 388.
[2] See H. Haupt, ZKG 5 (1882) 487–98: text 494–8.
[3] Ibid.

Like Hartmann, Kannler defined freedom of the spirit as a state without remorse or sin.[1] He was then questioned in the same way on the eight articles from *Ad nostrum*. To the first, he said that he had reached such a degree of perfection that he could go no further, since he was now beyond sin and united with God: neither the Virgin nor the saints could tell the difference between them. To the second, he affirmed that he need not fast or pray, but if his spirit so prompted him he could eat without sin and indulge his body in whatever it desired. His perfection was from God's grace, not his own merits; it was too great for either the angels or the saints to reach. On the third article, he held that he was therefore free of all obligation to human authority and the precepts of the church, citing St. Paul in support; he added that he had the right to kill anyone, even a thousand men, who impeded him and thereby dishonoured God.

Fourthly, his state of perfection allowed him to know final beatitude now as it would be enjoyed in heaven, although its vision could only be indistinct.[2] As free in spirit he was one with God, calling himself Christ's brother by grace and God by nature. Fifth, a rational soul having beatitude received it from God, not from itself, and needed the light of glory to raise it to God.[3] Sixth, he, Kannler, in his perfection had no need to perform virtuous actions, unlike imperfect men. Seventh, he could fornicate without sinning, and where a virgin was involved she remained chaste: he was similarly at liberty to have sexual intercourse with his mother and sister, although he did not believe God would permit it for the imperfect. To the eighth article he replied that a Free Spirit in a state of contemplating the divine essence should not be disturbed, even at the elevation of the host. He was not obliged to show it any reverence, nor was he bound to receive the eucharist or any of the other sacraments; the same held for a pagan who became a Free Spirit.

Kannler declared that all the above statements were made after due deliberation, and not from an infirmity of body or mind; that they came from his own depths which he found within himself; and that

---

[1] 'interrogatus in quo consistit libertas spiritus, respondit: cum penitus cesset omnis remorsus conscientie et redditur homo penitus impeccabilis' (ibid., 494).

[2] This qualification does not accord with the usual exalted claims of the Free Spirit, and suggests faulty transcription or an error in the text.

[3] The same applies here as well: article 5 of *Ad nostrum* states explicitly that 'any intellectual nature is blessed in itself, and does not need the light of glory to lift it to God'.

only that was of worth which was experienced in the freedom of the spirit and a state of perfection. He could not evade what he said even on pain of death.

He then went on, in reply to questions, to tell how he had become a Free Spirit nine years earlier, having fallen into an ecstasy in the choir of the church of St. Willibald in Eichstädt. Then not knowing whether he was in or out of his body he received God's reply: 'Friend, all your sins have been forgiven you because of your condition; henceforth you are absolved from confession and the need to receive the eucharist and the other sacraments. You are free in spirit and free from sin.'[1]

He had received no instruction on the aforementioned articles of the Free Spirit, since knowledge of them could come only from the Holy Spirit. When asked if he believed in other testaments than the Old and the New, he replied that he did; he was the second Adam, sent by God; after the thirty-three years from the time of his perfection, nine of which had passed, he would then be sent into the world by God as Antichrist, endowed with all the powers Christ had possessed. He would not be ill-received, in spite of the hostility with which Antichrist was wont to be regarded; but as the second Adam his advent would mark the beginning of the third age in which men would live in a terrestrial paradise according to Christ's will. Then God would carry them off to heaven, where they would become the progenitors of new generations.[2]

When pressed to renounce his errors Kannler displayed great vehemence in defending them; if he were a heretic, then so were the Father, the Son and the Holy Spirit, together with all the priesthood. He averred that his sanctity was as great as Christ's; that Christ's spirit and that of St. Paul were as drops in the ocean compared with his; that he excelled the Virgin in holiness; and that St. Paul had been converted to save himself from the charge of heresy.[3] Later, however, Kannler retracted, saying that even if threatened with no peril, the promptings of the Holy Spirit would have caused him to change his beliefs, which had been from mental derangement and an evil spirit. He then submitted himself to the judgement of the church.

What is most singular about Kannler's case is his inconsistency and clear emotional unbalance: not only does he make the most grandiose personal claims of any, only to recant (whereas we have no evidence of similar action in the other known trials); he also qualifies the doctrines

[1] Ibid., 496.   [2] Ibid., 497.   [3] Ibid.

of the Free Spirit in a number of ways, which show the mingling of other influences and the extreme unlikelihood of this or any other outlook existing in a pure state; other examples of such permeation will be noticed later, and we shall also encounter it among the Waldensians. As we have already mentioned,[1] he shows a tendency to modify the more extreme statements of the Free Spirit on three occasions: the first is over the lack of a clear vision of God for one still on earth. This contradicts the fundamental tenet of the Free Spirit, and one which elsewhere Kannler asserts—namely, that the adept is already divine and indistinguishable from God; the reason for Kannler's qualification is inexplicable, as is also the second one: that no rational being can attain to glory of itself or dispense with the illumination of glory. This goes completely against article five of *Ad nostrum*, which says just the opposite. It may well be that in both cases there had, as suggested, been a mistranscription in the report of the trial or by the scribe of the manuscript. The changes, however, are too wayward in the context of the rest of Kannler's statement to make any difference; at most, they underline his own confused state. The second discrepancy is in the more traditional Christian form of reference to God and Christ; it is true that Kannler affirms most of the claims made for the superiority of the Free Spirit over Christ, the Virgin and the saints; but he also calls Christ his brother, and refers to his inner contemplation of the divine essence. He also treats the spirit within him as that of the Holy Spirit, in marked contrast to the preceding confessions. At the end of his first deposition he stated that all his declarations had been made under the inspiration of the Holy Spirit.[2] Finally, there is his Joachist outlook: the conviction that the end of the present era is imminent and that he is its herald. Here the belief of the Free Spirit in individual perfectibility is given an historical setting: the adept becomes transformed into the saviour of humanity, the second Adam. Kannler's is not the only example of this coalescence of the Free Spirit and Joachism, as we shall see with the *Homines Intelligentiae*; nor is he alone in modifying those aspects which for one reason or another do not fit his own case, as the case of John of Brünn so clearly shows. Indeed, different though they were from one another, both he and John illustrate the artificiality of seeking any hard and fast barriers between different outlooks; they bear witness to the fact that within the framework of one viewpoint it was possible for seemingly incompatible doctrines to be merged and adjusted to individual inclinations.

[1] p. 380 above, notes 2 and 3.   [2] Ibid.

Next we come to the cases of Martin of Mainz and Nicholas of Basel. Martin, according to a Münich manuscript CLM 14959,[1] was a disciple of Nicholas of Basel and was burned at Cologne in 1393 after having been condemned by the inquisition for sixteen errors.[2] These all related to Martin's acceptance of Nicholas as his mentor who, in much the same way as happened to John of Brünn, substituted his authority for that of the church. Article five described Nicholas as 'a certain layman to whom he [Martin] submitted, and who claimed to understand the gospel more perfectly than the saints or St. Paul had'. He, Nicholas, took upon himself the powers of the church in administering the sacraments and supervising any good works (art. 6). He also held 'that if no one in the world were in a state of charity, then no priest could hear confession' (art. 7); that he, Nicholas, from his perfect submission (to God) could justly resist all precepts without sinning (art. 8); that he could rightly command fornication or homicide (9); and that he could remit freedom from sin and obedience to the church, engendering a state of primal innocence (10). He further taught that the perfect man had no need to pray to God for liberation from his infirmities or help from heaven (15); nor in the Lord's Prayer to beseech God not to lead us into temptation (16).[3] It is of added interest that Nicholas of Basel is described as having 'walked about in a Beghard's habit'.[4] Later, according to the same source, Nicholas and two of his disciples went to Vienna, where despite the efforts of Henry of Hassia,[5] the well-known scholastic, they reverted to their heresy and were burned.[6]

Finally, evidence that well into the fifteenth century the ideas of the Free Spirit were still current and regarded as the work of the Beguines and Beghards can be seen from an attack by an anonymous master of Heidelberg University on the Beguines and Lollards; in addition to extracts from Wasmod of Homburg's treatise and Felix Hämmerlin's *Lolhardorum descriptio*, it includes an account of a certain Lollard, John of Melchilinia, who gained a wide following in Upper Germany, and the confession of a Lollard, 'Johannes Becker', who was tried at Mainz

[1] CLM 14959, 230rb–231rb. The case is discussed in Haupt ZKG 7, 508–11, who based it upon Mainz Stadtbibliothek, MS. 247.

[2] Hec est sententia lata contra Martinum hereticum in Colonia combustum . . . Anno domini M⁰CCCXCIII . . . (CLM 14959, f. 231rb).

[3] CLM 14959, 230rb–231rb.

[4] Haupt, ZKG VII, 510, quoting from Mainz MS. 247.

[5] Also known as Henry of Langenstein; see chapter V below.

[6] This, as Haupt says, op. cit., 510–11, must have taken place before 1397, the year of Henry of Hassia's death.

in 1458 and burned on 20 October.[1] The latter begins characteristically with a description of how in 1442 while in the church of St. Paul, Mainz, he heard a sound from the top of the edifice; it signalized the coming of the Holy Spirit, which caused him to feel a great sadness and subsequently often to be rapt within. The Holy Spirit told him that he could only cry out and rise up under its inspiration. No one, John believed, had ever before or since been so filled with the Holy Spirit as he was. Before its coming he had obeyed holy mother church, and acted according to human agency; but afterwards he could do so no longer, since he could not follow two masters; nor was he any longer his own master, but ruled by the Holy Spirit.[2] Thus he refused to revere the sacrament of the eucharist, going so far as to utter silent abuse during its performance in church: actions which were from the Holy Spirit, not him. Again for thirteen years he had not made confession or communion nor undergone any fasts; these were for those yet imperfect and subject to the church. In the same way he was not bound to observe God's decrees, or to believe either his or the preachers' sermons. The mandates in the bible were those of death; those which he obeyed were of life and within him. The outer man was subject to the inner man.[3] He was not obliged to honour his parents, for what was written in the New Testament or by the Apostles was no more binding than what God had decreed.[4] As St. Paul said: 'The letter kills, but the spirit gives life' (2 Corinthians 3: 6). Only the spirit within, not the New Testament, was eternal.[5] In this way he was absolved from all ecclesiastical obligations.

On Christ he reiterated the contention of the Free Spirit that Christ's humanity was not an object of reverence for those emancipated from the laws of the church; for such, only God's immediate divinity sufficed.[6] Over the past thirteen years, in keeping with his state of per-

---

[1] In G. Ritter, 'Zur Geschichte des häretischen Pantheismus in Deutschland im 15 Jahrhundert' in ZKG 43 (1924) 150–9. The account is taken from the Vatican manuscript Cod. Pal. Lat. 870, 144v–154r. The confession is to be found on 153–8. The condemned 16 articles at Egram in 1467 which follow are not pantheistic or of the Free Spirit but mainly Waldensian and Taborite. See pp. 472 ff. below.

[2] Ibid., 153–4.   [3] Ibid., 154.

[4] Et non solum mandatis dei dicit se non esse obligatum, sed etiam nec scripturis novi testamenti, quos nos vocamus evangelium Christi, et epistolas sanctorum apostolorum (ibid.).

[5] Ibid.; the same sentiments are repeated almost verbatim in the third section on the New Testament, (materia tertia: de novo testamento) 155.

[6] Ibid., under 'quarta materia: de Christo'.

fection he, John, had not venerated Christ as a man or observed his passion as a sacrament. On the contrary, as united to God, he was more perfect than Christ in his humanity, since he was God by nature, whereas Christ was God only by grace and less than the Father. Nor was Christ's death the means to eternal life; that would come about in this world. Even though the crucifixion should lead to salvation it was not in itself regeneration.[1]

On the Holy Spirit,[2] John held that it was Christ's mother; its entry into him meant that Christ lived within him. It differed from what St. Paul had experienced in being not of fear but of truth. As St. John said: 'When he, the spirit of truth, comes he will guide you into all truth' (John 16: 13). His union with God[3] was within him, so that he was to be adored with the Trinity, not separately but as one being; he could do all that God did, and it was not for priests to remit sins or grant indulgences.

So far as the Virgin was concerned,[4] any man could merit enough grace to excel her in sanctity; this was supported not only by scripture but by man's feeling within him, which, as we have seen, was the source of his whole being.[5] It was where the Holy Spirit resided, making him in whom it inhered of Christ and the saints, to be adored with them; he was also one of the blessed for, like them, he saw God within.

Finally there was the church,[6] which was divided into a higher and a lower. The first did not belong to this world; the second was what was called the church or Christian faith: it bore no relation to the one above, but was a place for the damned and heretical. Those whom its priests called heretics were not such, nor were they, or pagans and Jews, unbelievers; for they were all baptized by the Holy Spirit. Different though it was from what the church regarded as baptism, it sufficed for salvation.

John Becker's doctrines were thoroughgoing in the extreme, and without qualification. They went beyond most of the declarations we have encountered, not only in discounting the authority of the church but in denying its divine origin and, more striking, that of scripture as

[1] Ibid., 155–6.
[2] Ibid., 156 under 'quinta materia'. He went on to recall the occasion sixteen years earlier when he first received the Holy Spirit.
[3] Ibid., under 'sexta materia: de deo absolute'.
[4] Ibid., 156–7 under 'septima materia: de beatissima virgine Maria'.
[5] Ibid., 157 discussed under: 'octavia materia: de exteriore et interiore homine'.
[6] Ibid., under 'nona materia: de ecclesia'.

well. At the same time little stress was given to sexual and moral licence, usually so prominent; and although Christ's humanity was duly despatched without regard, the Holy Spirit was exalted to be *fons et origo* of all divine perfection. Fundamentally, however, all the main elements of the Free Spirit were there; John's assertions provide one more example at once of their pertinacity and of the varying emphasis that could be put upon them while remaining true to their essentials.

We have reserved until last the one mass testimony—namely, by the Beguine women of the community of Sweydnitz, in the diocese of Warsaw. It was the result of an enquiry into their life and morals made by the inquisition in 1332 under Henry Schammonis.[1] There were sixteen witnesses; together their evidence depicts the Free Spirit at work within a Beguine community. For the first time we are enabled to form some firm answer to the two vital questions, of who were the Free Spirit and how it operated. The reply to the first is provided by the very existence of a community whose inmates, on the confession of the majority of the witnesses, adhered to the main tenets of the Free Spirit: pantheism and a belief in perfection through union with God; freedom from the authority, laws, prayers, fasts, vigils and sacraments of the church; the absence of outer constraint or inner remorse; sexual licence, both fornication and sodomy, in the name of impeccability, as well as a number of extraneous elements which we shall discuss shortly. These were the daily stock-in-trade of, so far as we can gather, most of the community; they were transmitted to newcomers and they were believed and/or practised by the Beguines themselves. Their reported statements and explanations suggest forcibly that they were a cross-section of any such body of female religious—a mingling of the gullible, devout, naïve and the more coarse-grained. Their descriptions of the state of perfection are anything but the revelations of an esoteric sect, appearing almost uncouth in their matter-of-factness; nor, with one exception of mass ecstasy, did it ever seem to go beyond the more mundane forms of self-indulgence and contempt of the church. Nothing points to the community's composition being in any way exceptional; from the evidence given at the enquiry, new members joined it as they would any such community of poor women,[2] only later

---

[1] The full account is in *Scriptores rerum Polonicarum* XIII (1889) edited by B. Ulanowski, 233–55 (printed in Appendix II below).

[2] The first two witnesses at least were only members of short standing, an impression given by many of the others from the surprise expressed at what they found, and their occasional attempts to remonstrate: e.g., Adelheid 241–2.

coming upon strange views and unwonted practices. Novices entered and were subject to the authority of their seniors.[1] As a community it was certainly not clandestine, as may be surmised from a public enquiry by the inquisition. No doubt, like many other Beguine houses, its very existence as a centre of voluntary poverty and unregulated piety made its inmates vulnerable to heresy and often its unwitting accomplices, as we have mentioned before. But, unless we are to postulate more than the evidence warrants, we may accept as a fact that certainly one ordinary Beguine house, and probably many more, was a source of the heresy of the Free Spirit.

The answer to the second question is of necessity more devious. To begin with, there seem to have been at least three levels at which the heresy operated. The highest was that of the Mistress (*magistra*) who is alluded to on three occasions,[2] and seems to have been called Helbig. From where her authority sprang, how she lived, or in what, if any, official capacity she was connected with the community cannot be said. It may well have been a clandestine one, as a member of the neighbouring male Beghard community to which we shall have occasion to refer again. There is little doubt that she was the supreme authority; when she came among them she was the centre of a special ceremony at which one of the sisters, blind Anna, cut her hair, kneeling while she did so. To her also belonged the power to grant permission to leave the house and attend church without which, said the fourth witness, Margaret the painter, 'they went nowhere, nor dared to go'.[3] Whether Helbig had any part in receiving confessions, or acted in *locum clerici* we do not know; but what has been said leaves no doubt about her great power. Her own reported reference to herself, as fit only to be a carrier of garbage, is uncomplimentary.[4]

Next there were the women Beguines themselves, with a superior at their head; they were to have no possessions and were supplied with habits by a sister on entry.[5] It is among the women themselves that the principles and practices of the Free Spirit are to be found. While, as we have seen, in broad outline these conformed to the canon, the specific forms that they took are illuminating. In the first place, the

---

[1] See below.

[2] Adelheid, 243, 246, 247.

[3] Item iurata et interrogata dicit quod ipsarum magistra vocatur Helbig, sine cuius licentia nusquam vadunt, nec audent ire. Item veniens ad eas Anna ceca precidit sibi crines, coram qua et aliis genuflexit dum sibi hoc fieret (ibid., 246).

[4] Ibid., 243.   [5] Ibid., 253.

neighbouring Beghards had an intimate part in their life; not only did they indulge their passions, safe in the assurance that they could not sin;[1] they influenced their whole outlook and behaviour. This included the full range of Free Spirit doctrine, from direct attempts at theologically-justified seduction to the claims of divinity and freedom from human authority. This tutelage exercised by the men must have been a primary cause of heresy in the women, since it was strongly, if not predominantly, self-interested. Thus Katherina of Lypcz, third witness in the enquiry, described how, while alone in church, a Beghard tried to convince her that fear for her chastity was a sign that she was still possessed by the spirit of grossness; only when the higher virtues had conquered the lower ones would she know that she was safe in God's love and nothing could harm her.[2] She also reported that similar arguments were employed on women who protested against the Beghards' indecent advances.[3] The Beghards, who seem to have been everywhere, instructing them in the doctrine as well as the practice of perfect freedom,[4] were clearly treated by the more gullible with great authority, some going so far as to believe that they individually resembled God.[5] Not least noteworthy are the references to happenings beyond the neighbourhood of the Beguinage, as far away as Aachen and Cologne:

[1] The whole enquiry abounds in descriptions of immoral behaviour. E.g., dixit, se scire de certa scientia quod cum alique que dicuntur perfecte inter eas et ad plenum exercitate exeunt ab earum congregatione ad libertatem, ut dicunt, spiritus veniendo, tunc luxuriantur omni tempore, nullam differentiam temporis opportunitate habita faciendo cum Beghardis commeduntque carnes in vigilis apostolorum et sextis feriis, ubi hoc commode possunt perficere, nec de hoc conteruntur, nec confitentur conscientiam de hoc penitus non habendo, eademque iurata dixit, quod inter tales Beghardos et huiusmodi mulieres portantes ymaginem sanctitatis maxime et artissime paupertatis committuntur opportunitate nacta quasi omnia genera peccatorum sodomiticorum et immundiciarum, hec dicit de certa scientia, quia audivit ab illa cui talia acciderunt, et etiam de certo ab aliis est experta, quod abutuntur se mutuo lateraliter et in anum tangentes se mutuo impudice et linguas suas in ora sua ad invicem . . . (ibid., 242–3).

[2] Item . . . Beghardus de tali secta in Glogovia in ecclesia fratrum dixit ad eam cum esset ibi sola: si vicisti te et superiores virtutes vite vicerunt inferiores, tunc primo perfecta tu es et de subtili spiritu; adhuc enim es de grosso spiritu, tunc quidquid accideret tibi in caritate dei non noceret tibi in castitate, non haberes peccatum . . . (ibid., 246).

[3] Ibid.

[4] Item dicit quod ubicumque congregantur Beghardi semper . . . concurrunt ad eos pro doctrina . . . (ibid., 248).

[5] et post redditum earum solent dicere de eis subditis suis: talis homo . . . habet cum deo magnam familiaritatem et similitudinem et bene scit loqui de eo . . . et deus potest opus suum perfici in eo et consequi (ibid., 248).

a pointer to their extensiveness. We hear of the Beghards at Aachen discussing the Trinity in blasphemous terms, each identifying himself with a different aspect of its divinity.[1] Another witness, when questioned on the eighth article of *Ad nostrum*, abjuring the reverence of Christ in the mass, said she had heard the same opinion in Cologne.[2] Less plausible was the story of the Cologne Beghard who, when cold, would enter churches and burn the images for warmth.[3]

In the second place, however, within this framework of divinity and perfection, impeccability and amorality, there was a medley of variations which, taken apart, might often appear to contradict basic Free Spirit tenets, but which, on consideration, all sprang from the Beguine background to the heresy. Even if the men were mere libertines, using the freedom of the spirit as their justification—and what we have seen of men like John of Brünn and Conrad Kannler suggests that this was not always the case—the women in Sweydnitz show all the traces of being genuine Beguines, at least in the beginning: that is, believers in a life of piety based on voluntary poverty and manual labour. The first element may have become distorted in the course of conversion to the Free Spirit, but a conviction in the supreme importance of poverty, and seemingly of work, survived. Moreover, it remained within the context of the apostolic poverty of Christ and his disciples, so that three of the strongest features of the Sweydnitz Beguines were their devotion to Christ, poverty and work (at least on Sundays in preference to time spent at church). Now, none of these belonged to the canon of the Free Spirit; although we find occasional remarks about freedom from work and indulgence in food and drink, these seem to have played no real part in the lives of the majority of the Sweydnitz Beguines. Thus we can seen how heresy merged with piety, so that the same impulse and many of the same tenets coexisted, even if they were given a new direction. In particular we can see how heresy quite as much as orthodoxy became adulterated and adapted to a more popular and palpable level, bringing it down from an esoteric cult to the embellishment of sexual laxity and anti-sacerdotalism, but not destroying a genuine belief in the religious life.

To take poverty first. This, as we have repeatedly said, was one of the strongest threads in all medieval religious reform, running through all the main movements, orthodox and heterodox. Its strength was equally manifest here. Witness after witness recounts the store set upon its efficacy, indeed divinity. Thus, Adelheid, the second witness, and a

[1] Ibid., 244-5.   [2] Ibid., 248.   [3] Ibid., 245.

former nun, was told by the inmates that they preferred their order to all others because of its perfect state of poverty;[1] in another case, they were reported to have claimed equality with Christ and the Apostles in heaven, just because of their life of poverty.[2] Poverty's divine quality was again stressed even more directly in the testimony of Margaret the Painter, where the Beguines were said to believe that, just as a man united with God could surpass the Virgin, so could they if they followed Christ and held fast to the state of voluntary poverty.[3] Another witness, Elisabeth of Stregovia, reported that a life of poverty would save her from purgatory.[4] The saving power of poverty, then, supernatural in its efficacy, was clearly one of the most deeply held convictions among the Sweydnitz Beguines. In origin it owed nothing to the freedom of the spirit; but it easily became fused with a belief in perfection, thereby putting the entire outlook on a different and more recognizable plane.

The image of Christ was very largely formed by this notion of apostolic poverty; as we have just seen, perfection was conceived as following his example. At the same time the personal sufferings of Christ made a universal appeal to any form of contemplation, from which even adepts of the Free Spirit, like Kannler, were not immune, and certainly not the Beguine women of Sweydnitz and probably elsewhere. They showed the same ambivalence which we have more than once encountered between Christ as divinity, to be emulated and possibly united with, and Christ as a sacramental figure; it was in the latter role that reverence changed to contempt and anti-sacerdotalism became uppermost. The difference in attitude is the difference between regarding Christ for himself and as a symbol of the church's authority. This, too, can be seen at Sweydnitz. Thus one novice from Glacz refused to eat and drink as she lay ill, on the grounds that she had attained to such perfection that she had no need to do so, and that Christ would nurture her.[5] To honour Christ in church, on the other hand, was a very

---

[1] . . . et se ipsas preferunt omnibus aliis ordinibus dicentes in sua secta perfectum esse statum paupertatis (ibid., 242).

[2] respondit quod opinantur et dicunt propter vitam suam pauperem apostolis in celo equabuntur, nec aliquo modo eis erunt inferiores (ibid., 248).

[3] et addit quod affirmat quod homo in congregatione divina possit beatam virginem precellere et opinatur se ipsos eam precellere, si tenent paupertatem voluntariam sicut Christus, quem dicunt se tenere (ibid., 249).   [4] Ibid., 251.

[5] et hec cognominatur de Glacz, et interrogata quare non commederet quid ibi in afflictione iaceret, respondit: Quia ad tantam perfectionem devenisset quod non indigeret commedere nec bibere, quia Christus eam pasceret (ibid., 242).

different matter, as is shown in the very pronounced hostility towards the church in general. It ranged from flat declarations that there was no salvation through the sacraments[1] to confirmation of the eighth article of *Ad nostrum*, that there was no need to show Christ respect.[2] It went together with the flouting of fast days and vigils, one of the most common reports throughout the enquiry,[3] and denigration of the church. This could take various forms: staying away from services;[4] immoral conduct during services;[5] refusal to confess (the most universal of all);[6] and occasional attempts to hold their own confessions.[7] Nothing is more striking than their lack of conviction in the authority of the church and its sacraments; there can be little doubt that it was the root cause of their heresy, prompting them not only to reject its canons but also to put their faith in more personal means of salvation. High among these was work. We nearly always hear of its taking place on Sundays, when its importance was contraposed to time wasted in attending church; there was undoubtedly a strong anti-ecclesiastical element in performing it then, but it also had its own justification, as the statements show. Adelheid reported how, on Sundays and holidays, it was customary for the seniors to work at sewing and other tasks, posting a guard to tell anyone enquiring for them that they were at

---

[1] Ibid., 250.

[2] Item dicunt . . . quod ab intus tantum habent de divinitate et arce contemplationis sue quod non opportet assurgere, nec aliquam reverentiam exhibere corpori Christi, quod dicunt figuram esse, nec occupari de passioni domini et alia misteria incarnationis (ibid., 244).

[3] See, for example, 240, 242, 244, 245, 248, 251.

[4] E.g., Adelheidis, secunda testis, quondam inclusa, iurata et interrogata de vita et moribus capuciatarum . . . dixit quod est communis modus inter seniores earum quod diebus domincis et festivis operantur opera similia nerendo . . . (ibid., 241). See also 245, 246, 250.

[5] . . . pre delectatione mittentes opportunitate habita etiam in ecclesia sive infra sermonem sive missam sive alia divina officia celebrata (ibid., 243).

[6] Nearly every assertion of freedom to do or not to do something was accompanied by its corollary of freedom from confessing it. One example may suffice [Hedwigis] Audivit etiam ab ipsis quod dixerunt: homo hic tantum posset profici quod esset perfectus, et illi qui sunt in tali statu perfectionis et spiritu libertatis non tenentur alicui obedire. Item Hedwigis . . . quod cum diceret ad eas: opportet me confiteri, quod nerebam in ebdomada Pentecostes, ipse responderunt non opportet te hoc confiteri, quia sunt bona opera, et dicit quod earum sit opinio, quod quidquid contra earum voluntatem fit, hoc reputant peccatum (ibid., 240).

[7] Item dicit quod dicunt quod nunquam potest una ipsarum in vita perfici nisi si etiam innocens inculpatur, reddat se ream confiteatur que nocuisse (ibid., 247).

c c

church.[1] When Adelheid remonstrated with them, they expressed great surprise that the church should be her idol.[2] They would also forbid their subordinates to go to church unless accompanied by an approved teacher.[3] They told Katherina of Lypcz that it was not a sin to work on Sundays and holidays, for they were working for the poor and there was no need to confess or feel remorse at having done so.[4] According to Margaret the Painter they said that perfection could come only if they were prepared to work for their sisters rather than to go to church.[5] In all these cases, work was seen as both of value in its own right and as a means of disobeying the church. There can be little doubt that it was regarded with poverty as enjoying a divine sanction, sharing the perfection which belonged to all works done on account of God.[6] Here the Beguine tradition was uppermost over the Free Spirit.

The influence of the latter, however, is easily apparent in the uses of subterfuge to deceive the church. These not only took the more obvious forms of hiding and lying, but also of giving the appearance of sanctity, one of the most repeated charges made against members of the Free Spirit. It included advice to remain pale in order to appear to have undergone fasts and vigils,[7] and a general injunction to observe the statutes and ordinances of the church for their own benefit.[8]

It is with the third level, the novices and new entrants—the latter make up the majority of the witnesses—that the Free Spirit is most clearly in evidence, for it was among these that the doctrine had to be inculcated. There seems little doubt from the testimonies that Sweydnitz as a whole was under the influence of the Free Spirit, and not that a clandestine group operated there. Its activities, and conversions to it,

[1] . . . incluse tamen et custodem ponendo, ut si quis venerit et pro eis scisitatus fuerit, respondeant eas esse in ecclesia vel alibi (ibid., 241).   [2] Ibid.

[3] et prohibent subdites suis ire ad parrochiam et ad alias ecclesias nisi habeant secum per ipsas destinatas pedagogas (ibid., 242).

[4] respondit quod laborabant diebus dominicis et festivis dicentes, hoc non est peccatum ut pro pauperibus laborarent . . . quod sic talibus diebus non esset confitendum, nec de hoc habenda esset conscientia (ibid., 245).

[5] Nulla inter ipsas perfici potest nisi plus prona sit ad faciendum opera pro ipsis sororibus quam ire ad ecclesiam (ibid., 246).

[6] . . . quod dicunt, et est earum opinio, quod cum sint in statu perfectionis, sompnus vigilia, cibus et potus, ieiunium, quantum ad meritum sunt equalia, et omnia opera propter deum per eas facta sint equala (ibid., 240).

[7] Item . . . quod cum ieiuniis, vigilis, et aliis modis se extenuaverint . . . dicentes et docentes hoc, quod semper pallor in facie maneat et appareat, et facies exterminata videatur, quod est pro earum intentione conveniens ut hominibus sancte videantur et religiose (ibid., 245).   [8] Ibid., 247–8.

appear to have been engaged in by the majority, while control over leaving the house suggests that it was firmly in the hands of the adepts. Of the novices, we are not told their numbers or ages, nor their régime, but enough was recounted of their treatment to leave no doubt that it was a rigorous one, as a preparation, or novitiate, for the full-fledged status of the adept. This can be seen from Hedwig's evidence, in which she said that the young were taught never to assert their need for food until they were perfect; once they were, however, they could and should recover what they had previously lost. The same applied to clothing.[1] They were also enjoined to shun all that they desired and to seek all that was abhorrent to them in food, drink, fasting, prayer, clothing and all things else.[2] In one house at Mencz, Adelheid reported, this had been taken to the extremity of compelling them to collect and clean the litters of the dead and eat and drink from their skulls.[3] She also told how they were enjoined to occupy their minds with some grave topic; this could lead to insanity, as in the case of the young Beguine who would not eat or drink.[4] A similar attempt to control the new entrants is to be found in the case of Margaret the Painter who could, they were told, not attain to perfection unless they confessed to their superiors any loss of innocence.[5]

The weight of evidence, then, points to the house having been under the control of the adepts of the Free Spirit, whose doctrine contained a strong admixture of Beguine beliefs. To those must also be added one declaration of apocalyptic belief in the advent of Antichrist and the consummation of their own perfection on the day when they should be risen against.[6]

As to their other practices, beyond those of the Free Spirit and work,

---

[1] dicit de certa scientia quod docent iuvenculas in receptione earum nunquam sumere necessitatem cibi, potus etc., donec perficiantur; perfecte enim effecte, ut dicunt, possunt et debent recuperare que et quantum prius caruerunt, et nec in vestibus habere dicunt necessitatem (ibid., 240).

[2] Item Katherina . . . dicit ut alie due, Hedwigis et Adelheidis quod docent iuvenculas quas ad earum sectam induxerunt: totum ad quod inclinamini non debetis facere et quod abhominabile vobis videtur et contrarium, et hoc tam in cibo quam in potu, quam ieiunio, oratione et vestibus et in ceteris omnibus (ibid., 245).

[3] Ibid., 244–5. [4] Ibid., 242.

[5] Item dicit quod dicunt quod nunquam potest una ipsarum invita perfici nisi sic etiam innocens inculpatur, reddat se ream confiteaturque nocuisse . . . (ibid., 247).

[6] dicuntque quando aliquis incipiet insurgere contra ipsarum sectam, hoc esse signum novissimi diei certissimum et adventus Antichristi et perfectionis earum consumationis (ibid., 244).

we have only one reference. By the first witness, Hedwig, it describes how not infrequently some of them prostrated themselves by the exit to the bathhouse, one falling over another, where they lay inflaming themselves until they were exhausted.[1] In what their ecstasy consisted we are not told; it seems far removed from contemplation. Nor is it mentioned by other witnesses, so that we have little idea of how large a part it played or what it signified. It would seem the kind of mutual excitation that was not uncommon among many religious groups like the Flagellants as well as individuals in a state of mystical ecstasy, and there is nothing to suggest that it was a specifically Free Spirit rite.

The value of the Sweydnitz evidence is that it makes the presence of the Free Spirit among the Beguines a reality, depicting their interaction and the forms it took. More than anything else it shows that at the level of popular piety, which was the mainspring of the Beguine movement, it was not an esoteric cult, nor merely a cloak for immorality, although the latter was certainly present. Rather it fostered at once a latent anti-sacerdotalism and a conviction in their own sanctity based upon apostolic poverty. It thus accentuated subversive tendencies already present in Beghardism, turning its adherents further away from the church and more into a world of their own: a world that was a strange compound of pantheism, libertinism and genuine religiosity. The element of pure fraud, certainly among the Beghards, was no doubt considerable; but it was a fraudulence that could only succeed by playing upon the desire for perfection, which in turn seemed to have the effect of intensifying emulation of Christ and the Apostles. Thus, if Beguine beliefs became more extreme, they also refashioned much of the Free Spirit to their own pattern. What resulted was an amalgam of the two. On the one hand, the striving for poverty and piety in the image of Christ and the Apostles took on anti-ecclesiastical, pantheistic and amoral overtones; on the other, these were conceived in terms of that image. Anti-sacerdotalism, pantheism and amorality sprang from the perfection of their state as Beguines: they were marked off from the church because they were directly joined to God and free of all human authority; and they were joined to God because they followed Christ and the pattern of his life on earth. Such was the reasoning, or more strictly the teaching, behind much of the testimony we have

---

[1] dixit se vidisse quod [non]nunquam plures earum existentes in stuba in exitu prima prostravit se circa limen hostii, quam conculcans secunda in exitu prostravit se iuxta eam, quam conculcans in primam tertia in exitu et sic deinceps concalcaverunt se et prostraverunt donec omnes consumerentur (ibid., 240).

examined. It was not consciously formulated, nor was it entirely consistent: the glorification of Christ's poverty went often with the denigration of his person; the exalting of work was accompanied by the
claim to exemption from it. But time and again the accounts recur to
these basic themes of Beguine beliefs, enabling us to accept the plausibility of their association with the heresy of the Free Spirit.

There only remain to consider the few cases where the heresy of the
Free Spirit was found independently of the Beguines and Beghards.[1]
They do not seem to have been numerous, being confined to the Men
of Intelligence (*Homines Intelligentiae*) and the Adamites. Both were
essentially local and lacked the wider impact of the Beguines and Beghards, although perhaps the first, and certainly the second were influenced by them.

The Men of Intelligence belonged to Brussels, and were said to have
held conventicles outside the city walls.[2] They came into prominence
in 1411, when the teachings of their two leaders, Giles Cantor and
William Hilderniss, were condemned by Pierre d'Ailly as bishop of
Cambrai. No more was subsequently heard of them, but it seems highly
probable that their origins go back at least to the 1330s, in the time of
sister Hadewich, or Bloemardine, as she was commonly called. Her
activities are known only indirectly, mainly in the account by Henry
Pomerius in his *De origine monasterii Viridvallis*[3] of Ruysbroeck's opposition to her. From this two things are apparent. One was that she was
an adept of the Free Spirit 'who wrote much of the spirit of liberty and
impious sexual love, which she called seraphic'.[4] The second was that
she was at the head of a cult whose members honoured her as 'the
founder of a new doctrine'.[5] She wrote and taught seated in a silver
chair, which after her death was presented to the duchess of Brabant;[6]

---

[1] We have already seen above that the Turlupins in France were the same as the
Beguines and Beghards, and were proscribed by Gregory XI in a letter to Charles V,
king of France, in 1373, where he wrote: 'praesertim de secta Beghardorum, quis alias
Turlupini dicuntur, sparsit semen pestiferum multiplicis heretice pravitatis' (Raynaldus, ann. 1373, 19). They were subsequently mentioned by Robert Gauguin for the
year 1376 in his *Compendium de Francorum gestis* (Paris 1500) describing the burning
of two women (ibid., 98v).

[2] To be found in Fredericq, I, no. 249, 269–79.

[3] In *Analecta Bollandiana* IV (1886) 286. Also printed in Fredericq, *Corpus* I, no. 189,
186. See also no. 190, ibid.

[4] Haec multa scribens de spiritu libertatis et nefandissimo amore venereo, quem
etiam seraphim apellabat (ibid.).

[5] tanquam inventrix novae doctrinae a multis suae opinionis discipulis venerabatur
(ibid.).   [6] Ibid.

when she approached the altar during holy communion she was said to have walked between two rows of seraphim.[1] When she died, healing powers were attributed to her remains.[2]

There can be little doubt that there was a direct connexion between Bloemardine and the Men of Intelligence. In the first place, the name seraph occurs twice in Pierre d'Ailly's condemnation, and refers each time to an ancient woman[3] advocate of carnal love. Both the name seraph and her venerability, to say nothing of her doctrine, point to her lineage among Bloemardine's followers. In the second place, the link was affirmed in the account of Henry Selle's activities as inquisitor for Brussels. He was appointed by d'Ailly to investigate the existence of the Free Spirit there, 'in order to extirpate the remains of the nefarious heresy which in the time of John Ruysbroeck a certain woman named Bloemardine had spread'.[4] It was probably due to Henry Selle's investigations that d'Ailly issued his condemnation of 1411.

As to the doctrines of the Men of Intelligence, they are notable for being strongly tinged with Joachism. Giles proclaimed himself saviour of the world; in him Christ could be seen, as the Father could be seen in Christ.[5] It was also asserted that the devil would be saved, and his overweening pride transformed into humility; this would happen finally to all men.[6] They upheld the three ages of the Father, Son and Holy Spirit; the last would be that of Elias, a time when all that had previously been accepted as true would be rejected, such as the Catholic doctrines of poverty, continence and obedience: their opposites would then be preached.[7] They claimed all their inspiration from the Holy Spirit, on

[1] Ibid.   [2] Ibid.

[3] Fredericq Corpus I, 272, article 11: Item est quedam antiqua, quam dictus laicus vocavit Seraphin. Also 276, where the statement is virtually repeated.

[4] ex iniuncto Petri de Aliaco, Camaracensis episcopi et postea cardinales S.R.E., constitutus est Bruxellis inquisitor haereticae pravitatis, pro extirpandis reliquis nefandae illius haeresis quam Bruxellis tempore Joannis Ruysbrochii seminasse quandam feminam, cui nomen Blommardin scribit merhout (extract from J. Latomus and J. Hoybergius Corsendonica (1644) given in Fredericq, ibid., 266–7).

[5] Article one: Item dictus laicus seductor dixit pluries repetendo pluriebus autentibus: Ego sum salvator hominum; et per me videbunt Christum, sicut per Christum patrem (ibid., 271).

[6] Article two: Item dixit quod diabolus finaliter salvabitur, sed tunc non erit diabolus, et superbissimus Lucifer erit humillimus, et quod finaliter omnes homines salvabuntur (ibid.).

[7] Item dicunt tempus veteris legis fuisse tempus patris et tempus novae legis tempus filii, et pro nunc esse tempus spiritus sancti, quod dicunt esse tempus Heliae, quo reconciliabuntur scripturae, ut quae prius tamquam vera habebantur, iam refutentur,

account of which they would often appear totally naked. Giles himself declared that he had been visited by the Holy Spirit, who told him that he was to be as a child of three years, not to fast, and to drink milk during Lent. The same held for his followers, who with him ate meat on all six week days and in Lent.[1] In the same way they did not respect the precepts and statutes of the church or its prayers, saying that what God did he could undo.[2] They confessed to avoid trouble, and then only revealed their venial sins;[3] they also denied the need for penance.[4] Women among the sect who refused sexual intercourse suffered abuse from the others.[5] There follow the usual accounts of sexual irregularity: Giles's own distinctive method of copulation, attributed to Adam in paradise;[6] the view of intercourse as an act of paradise;[7] its comparison with eating and drinking as natural and devoid of sin;[8] promiscuity among the women;[9] William of Hilderniss's demand for sexual gratification as an earnest of truth, and his caution not to mention their sexual activities, which the church condemned.[10] The Men of Intelligence ascribed all their action to God's active willing, not merely his permission.[11] They also derided anyone making the sign of the cross, and denounced chastity, continence and virginity, which they said did not exist.[12] In the event of being questioned on the above articles they were instructed to deny them.[13]

A second group of eighteen articles, which William personally abjured,[14] betray his more theological background and in particular a

---

etiam et catholica doctrina, sicut catholicae virtutes, que consueverant praedicare de paupertate, continentia, obedientia. Quarum veritatum oppositum, ut asserunt, est praedicandum hoc tempore spiritus sancti (art. 18, 272).

[1] Item dixit dictus Egidius quod, ipso quadam vice eunte per viam, spiritus sanctus inspiravit sibi hec verba: Tu es constitutus in statu pueri trium annorum. Non jejunabis, immo comedes lacticinia in quadragesima. Quod idem cum aliis suis sectatoribus et sectatricibus continuat. Nec curant ipsi jejunare quando sine exteriora nota commedere possunt carnes feriis sextis et in quadragesima (art. 4, ibid., 271).

[2] Art. 5, ibid.   [3] Art. 6, ibid.   [4] Art. 7, ibid.
[5] Art. 8, ibid., 262.   [6] Art. 9, ibid.   [7] Art. 10, ibid.
[8] Art. 11, ibid.   [9] Art. 12, ibid.   [10] Arts. 13 and 14, ibid.

[11] Item omnes actus suos, immo et nefarios, referunt ad divinam voluntatem, dicentes deum talia velle, non quidem tantam permissiva ejus voluntate, sed beneplacita et efficaci (art. 16, ibid.).

[12] Art. 20, ibid., 272-3.

[13] Item ad questionem quando ab eis queritur quid responderent si eis imponerentur credulitates supradictorum articulorum, respondent quod negarent (ibid., art. 21, 273).

[14] Sequuntur propositiones falsae, erroneae et haeretiae per me fratrem Wilhelmum in forma quae sequitur revocandae (ibid., 273).

reverence for Christ in whom, he said, all men, including Jews, pagans and devils, would be saved (art. 1); Christ's merits on the cross alone would gain eternal life in this world and would answer for all men, whose merits and demerits counted for nothing (arts. 4 and 5). Christ alone could remit sin, unlike the hearing of confessions which could not, and in his own resurrection all men were associated, so that there would be no future resurrection (art. 11). Other views of a more individual nature were that elaborate vestments were not a sin (art. 8); that those who judge and condemn sinners are more sinful than the judged (art. 9); and that preaching does not mean the salvation of others. These, too, were of a pronounced theological bias, and chime somewhat incongruously with the more customary Free Spirit notions. Thus from the pantheistic position that God is in every stone and every man, William goes on to add the eucharist, concluding that a man has God in him perfectly before he makes communion (art. 13). Again his view of perfection was far more in dogmatic terms of eternal life in the next world than as unbridled libertinism in this one. This can be seen in two respects. Firstly, when he says that God's illumination means a man's eternal security and enables him to understand scripture more clearly than before (art. 12): it may be 'a dangerous and presumptuous assertion', but it is more an exaggeration of an orthodox viewpoint than the heresy of the Free Spirit. Secondly, he introduced the Holy Spirit as the *sine qua non* of individual attainment: without its presence no one could perfectly understand the scriptures (art. 14); its illumination replaced the teachings of the saints and the fathers with the coming of its reign (art. 10). In keeping with this emphasis he dismissed hell (art. 2) and made inner man immune from the faults of outer man and from damnation (arts. 6 and 7).

Finally, there was a group of eight propositions[1] which were more avowedly of the Free Spirit. These included: that the sexual act was of as much worth as prayers (art. 2); that fasting, prayer and abstinence were not necessary for salvation, and he was most perfect who felt no care or remorse (art. 3); that following God's illumination he (Giles) said he was totally changed and could understand the scriptures without any effort; that he could not be deceived, and that his preaching was beyond human understanding (art. 4); that man could be so united with God in this life that he could not sin (art. 5).

The total effect of these different statements is to confirm what has already been abundantly shown, namely, the amalgam of emphases

[1] Fredericq *Corpus* I, 277–8.

which made up the Free Spirit: it lent itself not only to licence and quietism but also to prophecy and varying degrees of megalomania; it was pantheist, but it could also be trinitarian. There was nothing in the doctrines of the Men of Intelligence which, William of Hilderniss's theological niceties apart, was not to be found in one form or another among the other cases we have examined. Joachism was undoubtedly their strongest addition to the established tenets of the Free Spirit, with, perhaps, for that reason, the Holy Spirit exalted as the source of revelation. Above all, the mystic sense of union with God underlay, as ever, all the claims of its adepts, constituting their ultimate and irrefutable sanction. This document apart, we hear no more of the activities of Giles Cantor and his followers. From what we have seen there is little doubt that their importance was merely local. Whether or not they owed anything to the proximity of Beguines and Beghards, they did not share their views on poverty, as the reference to article 18 above shows. More than anything the Men of Intelligence illustrate how the Free Spirit, in identifying man with God, offered a platform for any individual or group to proclaim its own perfection and to justify whatever it willed in virtue of it, whether sexual licence or power over others, as the case may be. As such it was a means to the most divergent claims.

This can be seen with the second of the two sects—the Adamites. They are distinguished in being the product of war: the extreme, and disavowed, wing of the Taborite movement in Bohemia; they were crushed by its leader John Žižka.[1] They came to the fore in 1421 when, having been banned from Tabor and imprisoned in the fortress of Příbenice, fifty of them were burned by Žižka for refusing to recant their heresy.[2] Many, however, numbering some hundreds, escaped further south towards the Moravian border at the towns of Stráz and Jindřichuv Hradec where, pillaging and killing, they practised their beliefs.[3] They were subsequently annihilated, with all but one prisoner burned, by Žižka at the end of 1421, after having put up fanatical resistance on an island fortress.[4] The Adamites, as so often with groups

---

[1] See F. J. Heymann, *John Žižka and the Hussite Revolution* (Princeton University Press 1955) upon which the following account is mainly based. His view of the Adamites as an anarchical sect is challenged by E. Werner and T. Büttner in *Circumcellionen und Adamiten* (Berlin 1959) 129.

[2] Heymann, op. cit., 213. The event is mentioned in Raynaldus, ann. 1421, no. v, and is based upon the account given by Aeneas Silvius in his *Historia Bohemica*, ch. 41.

[3] Heymann, op. cit., 261–2.   [4] Ibid., 263.

cc*

born of upheaval, carried to the ultimate degree beliefs already radical enough in themselves. That these almost certainly derived from the Beguines and Beghards is to be seen from the use of the term *Picardi* to describe them. The name 'Picard' was a corruption of Beghard, and was similarly used to describe heretics associated with the beliefs and practices of the Free Spirit.[1] Their presence in Bohemia should occasion no surprise in view of the almost fanatical attempts by Charles IV to extirpate them there, as elsewhere, in his lands. On the whole, too little account seems to have been taken of these antecedents.[2]

The Adamites themselves were not Beguines or Beghards but, from all accounts, flotsam and jetsam thrown up in the wake of revolution.[3] They believed themselves to have regained the primal innocence of Adam and Eve (whence the name: a parallel to be found in Kannler's claim to be the second Adam) upon whose life in paradise they modelled their own existence. They went naked, and treated all their impulses as good in themselves and divine in origin, giving free reign to their sexual desires and denying the reality of sin and the devil. In basing their way of life upon an outright rejection of the accepted moral—and indeed social—order they employed the doctrine of the Free Spirit for revolt rather than mysticism, making God's inner presence their sanction.

Conclusion

The heresy of the Free Spirit, then, was a state of mind as much as a settled body of doctrine. It held to the conviction in individual divinity as a natural state accessible to men in this life. In doing so it made the pantheism latent in Neoplatonism avowed; where the latter conceived being as the result of an eternal outflow from God, the Free Spirit identified it with God; the Neoplatonic view of the ultimate return of all things spiritual to their source in God became for the Free Spirit a universal law superseding the Christian belief in angels and demons and a heaven and hell; the Neoplatonic quest in the soul for God was realized by the Free Spirit's location of God in the whole man; the Neoplatonic path to God through the soul's disengagement from the senses was for the Free Spirit the sign of the divinity of the senses and

[1] Heymann, op. cit., 263.

[2] This is also emphasized by Heymann, op. cit., 210 n.19.

[3] See Aeneas Silvius, loc. cit. The articles headed Picard in Döllinger, *Beiträge* II, 688–700, are straight Taborite beliefs and are discussed in ch. IX, pp. 701 ff. below.

their freedom from all moral constraint. The eternal cycle from God
to the soul and the soul back to God was thus short-circuited by the Free
Spirit and transferred to this world; the Neoplatonic emphasis upon
inner contemplation, rather than a supernatural grace, as the agent of
man's ascent to God, became in the hands of the Free Spirit the complete reversal of the Christian order: instead of man becoming supernaturalized, God was naturalized. He was conceived in human terms,
and human frailty deified.

Nowhere is this transition to open heresy to be seen more clearly
than in the partly heretical treatise known as *Schwester Katrei*.[1] Written
in the fourteenth century in Middle High German, it appears to be one
of the many such tractates which were constantly being sought and
condemned by the ecclesiastical authorities in their struggle against the
Free Spirit. That it is effectively the sole surviving work from an
heretical source makes it of especial interest. It is in the form of a
dialogue between a confessor and sister Katherine, much of it inter-
polated with stretches of orthodox mysticism in the tradition of
Eckhart, to whom it was for long ascribed.[2] It is distinguished from the
other extant sources[3] on the Free Spirit in being exclusively conceived
in mystical terms of the soul's ascent to God; it contains no reference to
other circumstances or to the heretical consequences of freedom of
the spirit; indeed, the words 'Free Spirit' are not mentioned. It is concerned principally with sister Katherine's attempts to reach God until
they culminate in her apotheosis into God. Hers was an essentially
individual quest: all that she attained came from her alone.[4] At first she
was unable to gain more than transitory glimpses of him: although her

---

[1] Printed in F. Pfeiffer, *Deutsche Mystiker des vierzehnten Jahrhunderts* II (Leipzig
1857), 448–75.

[2] E.g., Pfeiffer, op. cit., where the treatise is headed: 'Daz ist swester Katrei meister
Ekehartes Tohter von Strâzburc'; see also W. Preger, *Deutsche Mystik* I, 311 ff.

[3] A not dissimilar sequence from mysticism to pantheism can be seen in the deter-
minations of Master Eymeric de Campo against the errors contained in two books
written by a Beghard Rhineland hermit (W. Preger, ABAW 21, 1894, 62–3). These
all concern a man's natural divinity in which his essence was identical with God's.
There are echoes of Eckhart's more unguarded statements: e.g., Deus nec est lumen,
vita nec natura; deus est nihil et deus est aliquid, et tamen deus nec est aliquid nec
nihil. But here the distinction between God and creation was lost, so that 'the perfect
man is God' (62) and has been from eternity (63). The whole was conceived in terms
of a union with the Holy Spirit and the Son, which was through nature, not grace.

[4] Ich han in nur funden, daz ich daz alles übergangen hân, des mîn sêle begert hêt,
ânalleine (Pfeiffer, 464).

soul could transcend all obstacles between her and God, it could not remain thus elevated.[1] This was because her will was not strong enough to sustain her in such a condition eternally.[2] Her confessor tells her that she has not yet achieved sufficient self-abnegation; she tries once more, and for a time gains contact with him; but still she remained earth-bound.[3] Finally she withdraws into herself, and this time brings herself to God, crying, 'rejoice with me, I have become God'. After praising God, the confessor tells her to return to her solitude within, away from all people; for that way she would remain God.[4] Over the next three days she was in a state of total oblivion of the outer world so that she was taken for dead, and would certainly have been buried had it not been for the confessor.[5] On regaining consciousness she gave him an account of herself. She was now joined to pure divinity, of which there was no image or form. 'Where I am there is no creature in the likeness of a creature . . . but God alone; neither angels, nor saints, nor heaven with its nine choirs.'[6] The way to God was not by representations of him: 'No soul can come to God unless he is God, as she was and as she had been created.'[7]

It was this claim to divinity, to being God here and now, which went beyond mystical union with God to outright pantheism; *Schwester Katrei* gives the clearest possible illustration of the way in which it could occur. As to the circumstantial value of the treatise, we cannot know how representative it was of the vernacular literature of the Free Spirit, or even be certain that this was its provenance. That it was throughout interlarded with straight accounts of conventional Rhenish mysticism, with its emphasis upon spiritual poverty and renunciation in God,

---

[1] mîn sêle hât einen ûfganc an allez hindernisse; si hât aber niht ein stête blîben (ibid.).

[2] Wizzet, der wille benüeget mir niht, weste ich, waz ich tuon solte dar umbe, daz ich bestêtet wurde in der stêten êwikeit (ibid.).

[3] Si sprichet 'ez gêt mir übel, mir ist himel und ertrîche ze enge' (ibid.).

[4] Er sprichet 'des sî got gelobet. Ganc wider von allen luiten in dein einôte: blîbest dû got, ich gan dir sîn wol' (ibid., 465).

[5] Ibid.

[6] 'Ich bin bewêret in der blôzen gotheit, dâ nie bilde noch forme inne wart. . . . ich bin dâ, dâ ich was, ê ich geschaffen wurde, daz ist blôz got und got. Dâ is weder engel noch heilige noch koere noch himel. Manige liute sagent von aht himeln unde von niun koeren; der enist dâ niht, dâ ich bin' (ibid., 468–9).

[7] 'Ir sult wizzen, allez daz man alsus wortiget unde den liuten für leit mit bilde, daz ist niht dan ein reizen ze gote. Wizzet, daz in got niht ist dan got; wizzet, daz kein sêle in got komen mac, si werde ê got alsô, als si got was . . .' (ibid., 469).

tempers its unorthodoxy; this, together with its ascription to Eckhart, no doubt accounts for its survival. But it is not to say that it was avowedly heterodox in intent; indeed, it could be argued that its pantheism grew out of its mysticism. If so, it had the example to follow of some of Eckhart's more unguarded statements. Moreover, it is free from the more obvious and outrageous Free Spirit propaganda. To begin with, the status of the confessor hardly seems to have been that of an adept of the Free Spirit: he calls himself a priest;[1] refers to his daily celebration of mass;[2] and compares his own appearance of holiness with the true sanctity of Sister Katherine, saying, 'Ah me, poor man, how I am shamed before the eyes of God, that I have so long had the appearance of spirituality and yet I have discovered so little of God.'[3] This is reciprocated by Katherine, who is not only reluctant at first to reveal her communings with God to him, but when he asks her, after her apotheosis, to tell him of her inner state, she replies: 'God well knows that you would not understand.'[4] On the other hand, it is true that she looks to him for guidance both before and after her culminating ecstasy. It is in the advice he gives her after her transfiguration that the strongest traces of the Free Spirit are to be found. She is to eat and drink what she desires, wear soft dresses, and live only for herself; she is to be beholden to nothing created and to bestow no 'Hail Maries'. All things are there to serve her to the glory of God; and in taking her use of them she is but raising them towards their source in God.[5] But this, too, is qualified by Katherine's response; far from treating her new state as the signal for her complete liberation from all constraint, customary in most of the cases we have examined, she at once qualifies it by swearing her undying devotion to a life of poverty. When the confessor tells her that she is wrong, she retorts: 'then shall I live in wrong

---

[1] E.g., 'unde wêre ich niht ein solich pfaffe . . .' (464).

[2] 'als ich weiz daz ich hiute messe sprach' (ibid.).

[3] Er sprichet 'ach mich armen man, wie mac ich mich sô wol schamen vor den ougen gotes, daz ich sô lange geistlîchen schîn hân gehabt und ich so wenic bevunden hân gôttlicher heimlichkeit' (ibid., 463).

[4] Si sprach, 'got weiz wol, ich führte, daz irs niht verstânt' (ibid., 468).

[5] 'Dû solt ezzen als dich hungert unde solt trinken als dich turstet, dû solt senfte hemde an tragen, dû solt slâfen unde senfte besten und allez, daz dû herze begert von spîse und von kurzewîle, soltû an dich nemen und solt niemanne leben denne dir selber. Sêhestû vor dînen ougen allez daz versinken, daz got ie geschuof, daz soltestû niht wenden mit einem âve Marîâ, unde solt dir heizen dienen alle crêateren nâch dînem willen, got ze êren . . . wan wehle crêatûre dû niuzest, die treistû ûf in iren ursprinc' (ibid., 473–4).

... I shall not desert the path of our lord Jesus Christ'.[1] Her soul will remain for ever united with him in the Father as one being,[2] doing as he did.

The purely devotional element in *Schwester Katrei* is too strong to be denied. Whether the work was directly of the Free Spirit or not, is secondary to its expression of the impulse which could only too easily lead there. In leaping the gulf between God and man it opened the way to all the excesses which were made to follow from the claim to divinity. How far they were taken was a matter of temperament and circumstance. But with the barriers once down between the divine and the created, the foundations of Christian authority were swept away. For the free in spirit, perfection and sinlessness were his lot; he lived in a state of paradise without need for laws or sacraments or scriptures; death and punishment, like heaven and hell, were unknown. Sooner or later these blessings would be the property of all men, when here, or in the next world, they should have become God, too, and the divinity within them finally realized. Until such time it sufficed for them to heed authority, knowing that it had no ultimate sanction. It was for this reason that there could be no compromise between the outlook of the Free Spirit and orthodox Christian belief.

From this examination of the Free Spirit we can suggest the following conclusions. Firstly, its incidence was inseparable from the Beguines and Beghards, both in the overwhelming majority of known cases and in the consensus of contemporary opinion. The occasions when the two did not converge were exceptional enough to prove the rule. Secondly, this association applied principally to Germany rather than the Low Countries and France. In the Low Countries the Beguines lived in large stable communities, Beguinages or *curtes* which approximated to small townships. They were almost always under the jurisdiction of the church or religious orders and liberally endowed; by the later fourteenth century most of them had adopted the rule of a third order, normally that of St. Augustine. They were therefore an integral part of the religious life of the region.[3] In France the Beguines were likewise protected, particularly by the Dominicans.[4] In Germany and the Rhineland, on the other hand, the Beguines and Beghards lived either in

---

[1] Si sprach 'an dem unrehte wil ich blîben. Ich wil ellende und arm sîn, daz mac mir nieman benemen' . . . Ir sult wizzen, daz ich der linien unsers herren Jêsû Kristî niht wil abe gân' (474).

[2] Ibid.

[3] McDonnell, *Beguines*, 478–80.   [4] Ibid., 547.

houses, often numbering a mere handful, or wandered from city to city; in no case did their communities approach the size and stability of the Beguines of Belgium and Holland. It was against the essentially unregulated, informal, and frequently errant life of the German Beguines and Beghards that papal and ecclesiastical censure was directed, offering as they did the opportunity for untold subversion. Unlike their namesakes in the Low Countries and France, they more rarely adopted the rule of a third order.

Thirdly, however, the Beguines and Beghards were never identical with the Free Spirit; on the contrary, there were certainly far more Beguines and probably more Beghards who were not of the Free Spirit than were adepts or disciples. This can be seen from the ambivalence in ecclesiastical policy towards them, which throughout the fourteenth century went in a series of cycles or waves of excessive severity, involving the persecution of innocent Beguines, followed by periods of amelioration and relaxation. Fourthly, and perhaps most striking, the doctrines of the Free Spirit were as susceptible to the influence of their milieux as conversely; far from being a series of rigid tenets the outlook was an amalgam of often conflicting notions. Beyond a pantheistic belief in individual union with God, and its accompaniments of perfection and impeccability, the variations, as we have seen, were considerable. Christ could be revered or despised; poverty could be sanctified or ignored; work could be treated as indispensable to the apostolic life and salvation, or shunned as an impediment to perfection; anti-sacerdotalism was not invariable; on occasions the Holy Spirit rather than the Free Spirit could be invoked; and Joachism could prevail rather than quietism. Beguine and Beghard influence was particularly marked, as we saw with John of Brünn and at Sweydnitz, where doctrines of the Free Spirit were assimilated to a belief in piety and poverty. Here may well lie the key to success of the Free Spirit among the German Beguines and Beghards; for, beyond their vulnerability to permeation in being unofficial and loosely constituted, their desire for individual sanctity was met by the claims of the Free Spirit while they continued to follow a life of poverty. At one and the same time they were joined to God and emulating Christ; there was a fusion of individual and communal perfection. This was the outlook which both John of Brünn and the Sweydnitz Beguines seemed to express; it should not be obscured by the licence which accompanied it.

Fifth and last, two problems remain unsolved: How far were the adepts of the Free Spirit sincere? And how were they constituted within the Beguine-Beghard movement? To the first there can never be any firm answer; if the Free Spirit was not simply sex, the latter played a major part in it. A psycho-analyst might be tempted to identify it as a gigantic sexual neurosis, a European-wide revolt against centuries of sexual repression and imposed celibacy. There may well be truth in such a diagnosis: but that it was not the whole truth can be seen from the ramifications of the Free Spirit. It was not solely concerned with sex; it was above all a *Weltanschauung* in which sex played an important but not exclusive part. Whereas some of its adherents made it the centre-piece, others relegated it to the margins. For the Beguines at Sweydnitz, at least, it justified promiscuity without impairing what seems to have been a genuine religiosity. As we suggested earlier, if its tenets attracted the libertine, they also appealed to the devout. After all, of the eight articles of *Ad nostrum*, six were concerned with fundamental matters of Christian belief, as were the confessions of the majority of its adherents which we have examined. It is hard to conceive that, had the Free Spirit been little but a cloak for self-gratification, it would have exercised the church to the extent that it did. After all, there were less con-spicuous ways of obtaining it.

On the second question, again, we are largely reduced to conjecture. From our evidence it would seem that there were entire Beguine and Beghard houses under the control of the Free Spirit, and those who entered them were made to undergo a period of initiation before they could become adepts. Our three main sources in this connexion, the testimony of the inquisitor of Cham, of John of Brünn and the Beguines of Sweydnitz, as well as the less reliable remarks of Wasmod of Hom-burg, suggest it. Moreover, it is difficult to see how within the confines of a Beguine or Beghard house a small clandestine group would have been viable: to maintain any cohesion and to recruit and control novices could hardly have been done for long without revealing their identity. The discipline which was imposed upon the inmates at Cham, Cologne and Sweydnitz would in such circumstances have been im-possible, as would the directives given to John of Brünn on how to beg and conduct himself. We can only surmise that Beguine and Beghard communities (as opposed to isolated individuals like Nicholas of Basel), which practised the ways of the Free Spirit, did so on a communal basis.

The strength of the Beguines and Beghards lay in their being the focal point of extra-ecclesiastical piety in the later middle ages. This gave them a universality, keeping them at the centre of religious life for over a century. Their very lack of ecclesiastical recognition preserved their simplicity and flexibility; for it prevented the accumulation of wealth and the growth of an organization. They remained un-institutionalized, and so an ever-present attraction to the seeker after a life of simplicity and poverty, freed from the sacramental demands of the official religious orders. This amorphousness in turn made them an easy prey to the heresy of the Free Spirit, often actuated by genuine beliefs, often by pretence, and so the main target for its persecution. That the German Beguines and Beghards survived both the successive attacks upon them and the heresy among them is the strongest testimony to the appeal which they exercised in an age of ecclesiastical decline.